Sport & Competition Law

Governance, Markets and Regulation

Alexandre Durand, Ronan David,
Nicolas Charbit

Concurrences
Paris – New York – London

106 West 32nd Street, Suite 144 New York, NY, 10001, USA
www.concurrences.com
book@concurrences.com

First Printing, July 2026
978-1-954750-17-3 (Paperback)
Library of Congress Control Number: 2026944216
Cover Design: Yves Buliard, www.yvesbuliard.fr
Book Design and Layout implementation: Nord Compo

Concurrences Books

The e-book version of these works is available on the website concurrences.com.

Tributes

Huang Yong – Leading and Riding the Tide of China's Competition Law, *Yong Bai (ed.), 2025*

Harry First – A Global Vision for Competition Law, *S. Waller, A. Gavil, D. Bush (eds.), 2025*

James F. Rill – A Life in Antitrust, *2024*

Eleanor M. Fox – Antitrust Ambassador to the World, *2021*

Herbert Hovenkamp – The Dean of American Antitrust Law, *2021*

Frédéric Jenny – Standing Up for Convergence and Relevance in Antitrust, (Vol. I & II), *2019 & 2021*

Albert Foer – A Consumer Voice in the Antitrust Arena, *2020*

Richard Whish – Taking Competition Law Outside the Box, *2020*

Douglas H. Ginsburg – An Antitrust Professor on the Bench (Vol. I & II), *2018 & 2020*

Wang Xiaoye – The Pioneer of Competition Law in China, *A. Emch, W. Ng (eds.), 2019*

Ian S. Forrester – A Scot without Borders (Vol. I & II), *A. Komninos (eds.), 2015*

William E. Kovacic – An Antitrust Tribute (Vol. I & II), *2013 & 2014*

Practical Books

Competition Law in Small and Insular Economies, *J. Peyre, V. Terrien, E. Kross, Y. Lecornu (eds.), 2026*

Guide du droit polynésien de la concurrence, *W. Chaiehloudj, Y. Lecornu, J. Peyre, V. Terrien, (eds.), 2026*

Competition Law and the Challenges of Insular Economies – A Focus on French Polynesia and the Pacific Region, *J. Peyre, E. Silvestro, V. Terrien, T. Emen, Y. Lecornu (eds.), 2025*

Competition Inspections under EU Law, 2nd Edition, *N. Jalabert-Doury, 2025*

Navigating the DMA: Application Across National Jurisdictions, *G. Muscolo & A. Massolo (eds.), 2025*

Artificial Intelligence and Competition Policy, *A. Abbott, T. Schrepel (eds.), 2024*

State Aid & National Enforcement, *J. Derenne, D. Jouve, C. Lemaire, F. Martucci (eds.), 2024*

The 2023 U.S. Merger Guidelines: *A Review, Sean Sullivan (ed.), 2024*

Competition Inspections in 25 Jurisdictions 2nd Edition – A Practitioner's Guide, *N. Jalabert-Doury (ed.), 2024*

EU Antitrust Enforcement – Law, Economics, History, *Policy & Practice, Wouter P. J. Wils, 2024*

The EU Foreign Subsidies Regulation, *Andreas Reindl, Isabelle Van Damme, 2024*

Compendium of Antitrust Damages Actions – ICC – 2nd edition, *J.W.H. Denton AO, F. Brunet, S. Williams, C. Inthavisay (eds.), 2023*

Pharmaceutical Antitrust: An Analysis of US and EU Law, *M. Thill-Tayara, G. Gordon (eds.), 2023*

Innovation Paradox in Merger Control, *G. Gurkaynak, 2023*

Antitrust and the Digital Economy, *Y. Katsoulacos (ed.), 2023 (in collaboration with CRESSE)*

Judicial Review of Competition Cases, *D. Ginsburg, T. Eicke (eds.), 2023*

Competition Law Treatment of Joint Ventures, *B. Bleicher, N. Campbell, A. Hamilton, N. Hukkinen, A. Khan, A. Mordaunt (eds.), 2022 (in collaboration with the IBA)*

Information Exchange & Related Risks, *Z. Marosi, M. Soares (eds.), 2022 (in collaboration with the IBA)*

Rulemaking Authority of the US Federal Trade Commission, *D. Crane (ed.), 2022*

The International Competition Network at Twenty, *D. Anderson & P. Lugard (eds.), 2022*

Competition Case Law Digest – 5th Edition, *F. Jenny, N. Charbit (eds.), 2022*

Competition Inspections in 21 Jurisdictions – A Practitioner's Guide, *N. Jalabert-Doury (ed.), 2022*

Perspectives on Antitrust Compliance, *A. Riley, A. Stephan, A. Tubbs (eds.), 2022 (in collaboration with the ICC)*

Turkish Competition Law, *G. Gürkaynak, 2021*

Competition Law – Climate Change & Environmental Sustainability, *S. Holmes, D. Middelschulte, M. Snoep (eds.), 2021*

Merger Control in Latin America – A Jurisdictional Guide, *P. Burnier da Silveira, P. Sittenfeld (eds.), 2020*

Competition Inspections under EU Law – A Practitioner's Guide, *N. Jalabert-Doury, 2020*

Gun Jumping in Merger Control – A Jurisdictional Guide, *C. Hatton, Y. Comtois, A. Hamilton (eds.), 2019 (in collaboration with the IBA)*

Choice – A New Standard for Competition Analysis? *P. Nihoul (ed.), 2016*

PhD Theses

Three Essays in Law and Economics: Digital Markets and Abuse of Dominance, *J. Mouton, 2026*

Intent in Competition Law, *M.S. Garnier, 2025*

The Economics of Digital Markets – Essays in Theoretical and Empirical Industrial Organization, *E. Arnaud-Joufray, 2024*

Abuse of Platform Power, *F. Bostoen, 2023*

Reform of Chinese State-Owned Enterprises, *X. Bai, 2023*

Competition & Regulation in Network Industries – Essays in Industrial Organization, *J-M. Zogheib, 2021*

The Role of Media Pluralism in the Enforcement of EU Competition Law, *K. Bania, 2019*

Buyer Power, *I. Herrera Anchustegui, 2017*

General Interest

Why Competition? Voices from the Antitrust Community and Beyond, *D. Crane, D. Gerard, R. Tritell (eds.), 2024*

Competition Law Dictionary, *D. Healey, R. Whish, W. E. Kovacic, P. Trevisán (eds.), 2024*

The 5 Labours of Europe, *P.-E. Partsch, 2024*

Great Antitrust Enforcers, *W. E. Kovacic, 2023*

Competition – How to Speak Like an Expert, *E. Combe, 2023*

Women and Antitrust – Voices from the Field (Vol I & II), *E. Kurgonaite & K. Nordlander, 2020*

Sport & Competition Law

Governance, Markets and Regulation

Foreword by
Stephen Weatherill

Editors
Alexandre Durand
Ronan David
Nicolas Charbit

Concurrences
2026
Paris – New York – London

CONTRIBUTORS

Reiko Aoki

Maria Luiza Bittar Khouri

Andrea Bozza

Antoine Burgensis

Vitor Butruce

Olivier Cavezian

Alexandre Cordeiro Macedo

Emilio Cucchiara

Sven Demeulemeester

Benoît Durand

Mohamed El Far

Romain Ferla

Ian S. Forrester KC

Stéphane Gervasoni

Fernando Veiga Gomes

Deborah Healey

Peter W Heermann

Benoît Keane

Lukas Kretschmann

Mathieu Le Bescond de Coatpont

Ryan Lipes

Petros C Mavroidis

Ricardo Medeiros de Castro

Maria João Melícias

Colin Miege

Nina Methens

Mahmoud A Momtaz

Damien Neven

Pieter Paepe

Mathias Pigeat

Fabrice Rizzo

Arthur Roquebert

Vanja Smokvina

Romain Soiron

Jacques Steenbergen

George Tucker

Quentin van Outryve d'Ydewalle

Carmen Verdonck

Stephen Weatherill

SUMMARY OF CONTENTS

Contributors VII

Summary of contents IX

Foreword XIII

Introduction XV

CHAPTER I
SPORTS UNDER COMPETITION LAW

Competition Law and Sports Governance: Is the *ESL* Judgment a Real "Game Changer"? 3
Romain Ferla

How Does Antitrust Law Apply to Sports Governing Bodies? Which Sporting Rules Fall Under the Scope of EU Antitrust Law? 15
Peter W. Heermann

EU Competition Law Scope vs National Competition Law 31
Jacques Steenbergen

CHAPTER II
RESTRICTIONS ON COMPETITION IN SPORTS MARKETS

***ESL* and *ISU* Cases: What Consequences for Sports Federations?** 41
Mathieu Le Bescond de Coatpont

Exclusivity in Sports – Beneficial or Harmful to Competition? 65
Benoît Durand and George Tucker

What is a Public Interest in Sport? What Are the Legitimate Sporting Objectives? 89
Benoît Keane

Specific Characteristics of Sport and EU Law 107
Pieter Paepe

CHAPTER III
PROCEEDINGS

Is the CAS Arbitration System Anticompetitive? ... 129
Jean-Michel Marmayou

CHAPTER IV
STATE AID AND FOREIGN SUBSIDIES DISTORTING THE MARKET

European State Aid Law Applied to Professional Sport ... 143
Colin Miege

CHAPTER V
NATIONAL COMPETITION LAW ISSUES

National Competition Law Issues Europe: Belgium Recent Belgian Decisions Delivered in the Sports Markets ... 161
Carmen Verdonck and Nina Methens

Competition Law and Sport: An Overview of the French Competition Authority's Decision-Making Practice ... 185
Mathias Pigeat

Panorama of the French Competition Authority Decision-Making Practice in the Field of Sport ... 201
Romain Soiron, Olivier Cavezian and Arthur Roquebert

Sport and Competition Law in Italy: Overview of Decisional Practice ... 215
Andrea Bozza and Emilio Cucchiara

Germany: National Competition Law Issues ... 229
Lukas Kretschmann

Collective Sale of Football Media Rights in Portugal: Competition Law, Market Transformation and Investment Dynamics ... 247
Fernando Veiga Gomes and Maria João Melícias

Sports and U.S. Antitrust Law ... 263
Ryan Lipes

Sports and Competition Law in Brazil ... 281
Alexandre Cordeiro Macedo, Ricardo Medeiros de Castro and Maria Luiza Bittar Khouri

The Egyptian Competition Authority's Enforcement Policy in Sports 297
Mohamed El Far and Mahmoud A Momtaz

Sport and Competition Law in Australia: A Fertile Environment for Players and Lawyers? 307
Deborah Healey

Sports and the Japanese Antimonopoly Act 327
Reiko Aoki

CHAPTER VI
TRANSNATIONAL FOOTBALL LAW ISSUES

***Bosman*, Thirty Years Later** 337
Ian S. Forrester KC

The FIFA Regulations on the Status and Transfer of Players in Light of European Union Competition Law 341
Fabrice Rizzo

The Home-Grown Player Rules 359
Vanja Smokvina

Legitimate Objectives in Antitrust Analysis: FIFA Regulation of Agents and the Right to Regulate Football in Europe 373
Petros C. Mavroidis and Damien Neven

Multi-Club Ownership – Multi-Club Investment 397
Romain Soiron, Olivier Cavezian and Antoine Burgensis

Multi-Club Ownership (MCO) and Multi-Club Investment (MCI) in South America: Corporate Structures, Regulatory Fragmentation and Competition Law across CONMEBOL 415
Vitor Butruce

The Organisation of Football Competitions and Calendar Management – A European Competition Law Perspective 437
Sven Demeulemeester and Quentin van Outryve d'Ydewalle

The Court of Justice, UEFA and the Super League: The European Sports Model Put to the Test 461
Stéphane Gervasoni

Table of contents XVII

FOREWORD

STEPHEN WEATHERILL
Faculty of Law, Somerville College
University of Oxford

I am delighted to welcome the publication of this collection of essays which address sports and competition law.

There is an enduring intellectual fascination in exploring how competition law applies (and should apply) to sport. We can probably all agree that in some respects sport is "special' – that is, it is distinct from other sectors of economic activity. There is a relationship of interdependence among participants in a sports league which we don't find elsewhere. Clubs cannot exist in isolation, they need other clubs to play against, whereas car manufacturers or suppliers of financial services are able to operate as monopolies (and would love the economic opportunities on offer were this to occur). Participants in sporting competition must co-operate – on planning fixtures, on agreeing standards, on defining the "rules of the game' – in a way that we do not find in other industries. And governing bodies, which have historically been created for the very purpose of setting a sport's foundational rules, typically enjoy a monopoly power as a regulator. There is in most sports just one governing body charged with a supervisory role covering one jurisdiction. This not how the market for making cars or providing financial services is structured.

These features have important implications for the application of competition law to sport. The characteristic relationship of interdependence among participants urges a higher degree of tolerance for co-operative sporting practices than might be found elsewhere. What might appear anti-competitive when pursued by carmakers or suppliers of financial services might in sport be no more than a process of choosing and enforcing the "rules of the game" with which all competitors must comply in order to protect the integrity of the sport. Moreover, the structural point that most sport is regulated by a single governing body means that legal rules controlling dominant economic power are much more commonly in play than is true in most sectors of the economy.

So, we can probably all agree that in some respects sport is "special", but plenty of disagreement attaches to the determination of just *how* special really is. Sometimes there are compelling reasons for accepting that practices which would be condemned outside sport should be permitted because of the peculiar economics and culture found in sport. Sometimes, and by contrast, one should reflect sceptically on whether governing bodies are making spurious claims to "sporting specificity' as a means to disguise self-serving, pernicious anti-competitive practices. Look hard at the context, look hard at the motivations!

And that is the beauty of *Sports and Competition Law*, it provides a wealth of material and information on just how far the law does go (and should go) in accepting that the orthodox assumptions of competition law should be modified in application to sport. I warmly congratulate the editors and the authors.

INTRODUCTION

NICOLAS CHARBIT, ALEXANDRE DURAND, RONAN DAVID
CEO of Concurrences, Co-founders of Football Legal

As sport has developed into a global economic activity governed by powerful regulatory actors, competition law has emerged as a key tool for assessing the legitimacy of sporting rules, market structures, and governance models. This book provides a coherent and authoritative framework for understanding these issues, combining European Union law with a broader international perspective.

The book first addresses the long-debated concept of the specificity of sport, focusing on the scope and limits of the regulatory autonomy enjoyed by sports governing bodies. It examines how EU competition law applies to sports governance, identifying which sporting rules fall within its scope and how this framework interacts with national competition law regimes. Particular attention is given to the organisation of sports competitions, including the monopoly of organisation, the emergence of alternative competitions, and the territorial dimension of sporting activities in an increasingly globalised context.

Drawing on landmark case law such as *Wouters* and *Meca-Medina*, the contributions analyse the legal tests used to assess restrictive sporting rules, including the economic and proportionality tests and the distinction between restrictions by object and by effect. The book also explores the growing role of arbitration in sport, as well as the conditions under which legitimate objectives may justify restrictions on competition, provided that a rational and proportionate link exists between the measure adopted and the objective pursued.

The analysis is further strengthened by a comparative approach, with insights drawn from a wide range of jurisdictions, including Belgium, France, Italy, the United Kingdom, Germany, Portugal, the United States, Brazil, Egypt, Australia, and Japan. This comparative dimension highlights both common trends and national specificities in the application of competition law to sport, reflecting the transnational nature of sports markets and the regulatory challenges they generate.

A substantial part of the book is devoted to football, which continues to sit at the heart of competition law scrutiny. The contributions examine the legacy of the *Bosman* judgment thirty years on, player transfer systems, home-grown player rules, the regulation of football agents, and the development of multi-club ownership and investment models from both European and South American perspectives. The organisation of football competitions and calendar management, the Super League project, the judgments of the Court of Justice of the European Union concerning

UEFA and the Super League, and the sensitive issue of State aid in sport are also analysed in depth.

By bringing together contributions from leading academics and practitioners, Sport & Competition Law offers a rigorous and practice-oriented analysis of the regulatory challenges facing contemporary sport. Addressed to legal scholars, practitioners, regulators, and stakeholders in the sports industry, this book provides an essential reference for anyone seeking to understand how competition law shapes, constrains, and legitimises sports governance in a globalised environment.

CHAPTER I

Sports under Competition Law

Competition Law and Sports Governance: Is the *ESL* Judgment a Real "Game Changer"?

Romain Ferla*
Bridgestone (Brussels)

1. For many years, non-governmental sporting bodies, especially in the world of football, have been widely criticised for their lack of good contemporary governance standards. The relative disregard of too many sporting bodies for good governance standards is all the more censorious now that these bodies handle huge amounts of money.

2. Whereas, for many years, governments, governmental bodies and corporate organisations have already been involved in a quest for "good governance", it is only recently that the call for good governance has reached the traditionally closed sporting world. A good example of this recent trend is the Recommendation of the Council of Europe of 12 December 2018 on the promotion of good governance in sports, in which the Council of Europe encourages sport governing bodies to adopt more transparent and objective decision-making processes: "By improving their governance, organisations become more inclusive and efficient. Transparent, accountable and democratic governance includes stakeholders in strategic decision-making processes. Moreover, a system of checks and balances encourages trust".[1]

---

* Formerly Avocat au Barreau de Paris

[1] See Council Recommendation (EC) CM/Rec 2018/12 of the 12 December 2018 by the Committee of Ministers to Member States on the Promotion of Good Governance in Sport <https://rm.coe.int/recommendation-of-the-committee-of-ministers-to-member-states-on-the-p/168093fb61> accessed 31 July 2025.

3. Well, it appears that, in its efforts to promote the adoption of good governance standards by sporting bodies, the Council of Europe has just been joined by the European Court of Justice (ECJ) which has stepped into the debate with a remarkable contribution.

I. "Into the Game": When the ECJ Steps into the Debate on Sports Governance

4. On 21 December 2023, the ECJ delivered three highly important judgments that may substantially constrain the latitude of sports federations when they adopt decisions likely to have economic effects. These judgments concern the *European Super League (ESL)*, the *International Skating Union (ISU)* and the *Royal Antwerp FC*.[2]

5. These judgments come exactly one year after the publication of Advocate General (AG) Rantos' Opinion on the former two cases, and nine months after AG Szpunar's Opinion on the latter case.

6. These judgments could have tremendous impact on the governance of sports within the European Union and beyond.

7. The judgments had to deal with an awkward question: can a sport federation restrict or even prohibit the participation of its members in other competitions set up by alternative sport organisations. The recent ECJ judgments confirm that sports governing bodies can in principle adopt decisions authorising (or on the contrary, prohibiting) sporting events of third parties and can regulate participation by their members in these events. However, when a sports governing body is not only the regulator of its own sport but also exploits its own competition(s), it cannot adopt decisions setting the conditions in which potentially competing undertakings may access the market and launch alternative competitions, unless such decisions are based on transparent, objective and precise substantive criteria, and unless the decision-making process leading to such decisions is itself subject to procedural safeguards (ie is transparent and non-discriminatory).

8. In the *Super League* case as well as in the *ISU* case, the ECJ found that neither UEFA/FIFA nor ISU had complied with the above-mentioned standards: the criteria for authorising (or prohibiting) new third-party competitions were not sufficiently clear nor objective and the decision-making process lacked the appropriate procedural safeguards.

9. For some observers and commentators, the *Super League* and *ISU* judgments rendered by the ECJ on 21 December 2023 came as surprise.

10. In particular, when the Court released its judgement in the case involving FIFA and UEFA (against the so-called Super League), many commentators did not expect such a decision from the ECJ. In fact, since 15 December 2022, when AG Rantos issued his Opinion in the *Super League* case, a large majority of observers expected that the ECJ would decide in favour of FIFA and UEFA. It is true that

---

[2] Case C-333/21 *European Super League (ESL)* ECLI:EU:C:2023:1011; Case C-124/21 P *International Skating Union (ISU)* ECLI:EU:C:2023:1012; Case C-680/21 *Royal Antwerp FC* ECLI:EU:C:2023:1010.

AG Rantos' Opinion was very well written, well-argued and seemed to leave little chance that an infringement of Article 101 and 102 TFEU could ultimately be found by the ECJ.

11. Also, in this procedure (a request for a preliminary ruling initiated by the Commercial Court of Madrid), a large majority of EU Member States submitted written observations in favour of UEFA and FIFA[3] and argued that UEFA and FIFA's rules on the prior approval or rival competitions were not anticompetitive. Few cases in the history of the ECJ have seen such a level of mobilisation of the Member States in support of a private party. By supporting UEFA and FIFA, most of these EU Member States wanted to defend the so-called "European Sports Model" which was allegedly jeopardised by the Super League.

12. In this context and given the important support given to UEFA and FIFA by a majority of Member States and by AG Rantos, whose track record in competition law cases before the ECJ is impressive, very few would have bet on a judgement in favour of the Super League. And yet this is what happened.

13. However, if we take a step back, it appears that the surprise is perhaps not as important as it may seem. Indeed, in ruling that FIFA and UEFA rules on prior approval or rival competitions are anticompetitive, the ECJ appears to be in line with several previous decisions rendered by its predecessors, by the General Court, and by the European Commission.

14. In ruling that FIFA and UEFA's power to approve rival competitions, if not made subject to restrictions, obligations, and review, gives rise to an infringement of Article 102 TFUE, the ECJ was undoubtedly inspired by the Commission's decision in the Fédération Internationale d'Automobile (FIA) cases (COMP/35.165), (COMP/36.638) and (COMP/36.776),[4] by the Court's judgement in the *MOTOE* case and by the General Court's judgement in the *ISU* case.[5]

15. In light of these precedents, it appears that the reasoning of the ECJ in the *Super League* case is not fundamentally new. It is essentially based on the idea that FIFA and UEFA are in a "conflict of interest" situation as they are simultaneously in charge of regulating their sport and in managing significant commercial interests (through the organisation of their own competitions) and that, in order to avoid the anticompetitive conduct that may necessarily derive from this conflict of interest, FIFA and UEFA have to submit their power to approve (or disapprove) rival competitions to appropriate restrictions, obligations and review. This idea was already at the core of the above-mentioned precedents.

16. Retrospectively, it appears that the real surprise in this *Super League* case is not so much the judgment of the ECJ, but rather AG Rantos' Opinion submitted in December 2022, in which he was very much in favour of FIFA and UEFA on the

---

[3] Perhaps upon solicitation by UEFA and FIFA.

[4] Notice published pursuant to Article 19(3) of Council Regulation No 17 concerning Cases COMP/35.163 – Notification of FIA Regulations, COMP/36.638 – Notification by FIA/FOA of agreements relating to the FIA Formula One World Championship, COMP/36.776 – GTR/FIA and others [2001] OJ C169/3.

[5] Case C-49/07 *MOTOE* ECLI:EU:C:2008:376; Case T-93/18 *International Skating Union (ISU)* ECLI:EU:T:2020:610.

basis of an innovative argument. This argument was mainly based on Article 165 TFEU relating to the European sports policy in which AG Rantos had detected the basis for a "constitutionalisation" of the so-called "European Sports Model". He then concluded that the defence of this "constitutionalised" European sports model justified the behaviour and governance rules of FIFA and UEFA. Advocate General Rantos considered that Article 165 constituted a "specific" treaty provision, on the basis of which it would be possible to derogate from competition law. In order to validate the competitive restrictions implemented by FIFA and UEFA, AG Rantos applied the so-called "ancillary restraints" doctrine (also called the "Wouters" doctrine). Pursuant to this doctrine, restrictions of competition can escape the application of Article 101 TFEU when they are necessary to achieve an otherwise legitimate objective (here the preservation of the "European Sports Model" as enshrined in Article 165 TFEU). This "ancillary restraints" doctrine was notably used in the well-known *Meca-Medina* case. In the *Meca-Medina* case, the restriction of competition consisting of banning doped athletes and their clubs had been considered necessary in order to meet the legitimate objective of the fight against doping.[6] Advocate General Rantos thought that he could deploy the same reasoning regarding the requirement of a prior approval of FIFA and UEFA for the setting up of a rival competition. The ECJ concluded in completely the opposite direction.

17. The ECJ first explains, through a long and well-written demonstration, that Article 165 TFEU "is not a cross-cutting provision having general application" and that it does not have to be "taken into account in a binding manner" in the application of the competition rules TFEU points 100 and 101 of the *Super League* judgment). In other words, it puts Article 165 TFEU back to where it belongs – a treaty provision with a secondary "supporting" role and makes it clear that the preservation of the "European Sports Model" cannot serve as a basis to justify any competition restrictions. But the real "value added" of the ECJ's judgment in the *Super League* case is that it also clarifies the limits of the "ancillary restraints"(ie the "Wouters" – "Meca-Medina") doctrine. For the ECJ, the Wouters and Meca Medina doctrine (ie the idea that a restraint may escape Article 101(1) TFEU when it is justified by the "pursuit of one or more legitimate objectives in the public interest"), may only apply where the practice is not a "by object" infringement. Some commentators have presented this as a small revolution, but it is probably not, in fact, it was more likely implicit in previous European judgments. Indeed, it is arguable that, where a restraint is justified by the "pursuit of one or more legitimate objectives in the public interest", it means the restraint is "genuinely necessary" to attain a set of public interest regulatory goals. The object of such a restraint cannot be anticompetitive. In any event, the clarification made by the ECJ is very welcome and will make it difficult (if not impossible) for sports federations to rely on the "Wouters" – "Meca-Medina" doctrine when they adopt restrictive decisions in a situation of "conflict of interest".

---

6 Case C-519/04 P *David Meca-Medina and Igor Majcen v Commission of the European Communities* ECLI:EU:C:2006:492, para 42.

18. For the rest, after it rightly dismissed the application of the "ancillary restraints"("Wouters" – "Meca-Medina") doctrine to the case at hand, the ECJ comes back to fairly classic solutions.

19. Indeed, the idea that, when a federation is in a situation of conflict of interest as defined above, the exercise by this sports federation of its regulatory function should be made subject to restrictions, obligations and review, so that it may not distort competition by favouring events which it organises over other events is not new at all. In fact, it is as old as the ECJ's *MOTOE* judgment and was reaffirmed more recently by the General Court in the *ISU* case in 2020.[7]

20. What do these important judgments mean for the future of sports governance? Well, the ECJ certainly did not authorise the Super League project or eliminate the power of sports federations to govern their respective sports. It is however very clear now that federations are also required to handle this power very carefully, by setting up clear, non-discriminatory and proportionate rules.

21. Sports federations cannot straight away prevent the launching of alternative sports competitions or the participation of their members in such competitions. However, federations are not obliged to allow alternative competitions under all circumstances.

22. Following the recent ECJ judgments, sports federations will have to reassess their regimes dealing with the approval of alternative competitions in order to ensure that they are transparent, objective, non-discriminatory and proportionate.

23. The other judgment rendered on 23 December 2023, the *ISU* judgment,[8] may also have another impact, although more indirectly, on the governance of sports federations. Indeed, in this judgment, the ECJ held that sports federations can no longer seek to protect their decision-making powers against legal challenges by providing in their statutes that all their decisions are subject to the exclusive jurisdiction of the Court of Arbitration for Sport (CAS). The ECJ ruled that such exclusive jurisdiction of CAS does not comply with EU competition law as it reinforces the restrictions on competition already found by the ECJ. The governance rules of sports federations and the decisions made on the basis of these rules may now be challenged before national courts within the European Union. This can be a real game changer.

II. "After the Game": What Will Come Next?

24. Many commentators in Europe now wonder about the very concrete consequences of this ECJ judgment for the governance of FIFA, UEFA and also for the Super League. Shortly after the judgment was published, A22 Management, the entity in charge of organising and promoting the Super League, issued a press release announcing that "European club football is free" and that "the near-70-year UEFA monopoly is finally over".[9] Things are probably not that simple.

---

7 *MOTOE* (n 5), paras 51 and 52; *ISU* (n 5), para 70.

8 *ISU* (n 2).

9 A22 Management, Press Release, "A22 Proposes New Open European Competition" (21 December 2023) <https://a22sports.com/en/media/press-release-21-december-2023/> accessed 31 July 2025.

25. First, the ECJ judgment in the *Super League* case was simply a preliminary ruling. The Commercial Court of Madrid, which had initially made the referral to the ECJ for a preliminary ruling, had to take this European judgment into account in its final decision, rendered on 24 May 2024. Despite UEFA's efforts to convince the Spanish court that its former rules on prior approval of rival competitions were not anticompetitive, the court condemned them for abuse of dominance.

26. In any event, as stressed by UEFA in a press release,[10] the Spanish court only condemned it for its past rules. Therefore, this does not mean that the Super League will be revived. First, most clubs initially belonging to the Super League have left. Second, UEFA implemented in 2022 a new prior approval system that seeks to subject UEFA's decisions to appropriate restrictions, obligations and review. In its press release issued after the ECJ judgment, UEFA makes it clear that it considers that its new system is now antitrust compliant and that it still allows it to disapprove the setting up of the Super League:

> We became aware that our authorisation system was imperfect, we started to work on that in 2021 and concluded in 2022 with the decision of the UEFA Executive Committee. We are confident that our rules are fully in line with the ECJ judgement. That said we will of course review further after reading the decision in detail and see if we need to implement further changes." UEFA adds: "So any competition must fit within the system and comply with our new authorisation rules, and among other requirements must respect sporting merit, the international calendar, and solidarity. Those rules also protect UEFA's club competitions. Football remains united as you see today, well protected from breakaway leagues.[11].

27. On the other hand, A22 Management stressed that they also made substantial efforts to adapt their own organisation of the Super League to make it more compatible with the so-called European Sports Model. It recently indicated that the organisation of the Super League will now be based on certain UEFA-like principles: "participation based on sporting merit with no permanent members" and "annual promotion and relegation between leagues".

28. The new modernised rules of UEFA on prior approval provide inter alia that clubs playing in the UEFA Champions League shall only play in this competition for its whole duration and until its completion, which makes it impossible in practice for prestigious clubs to launch a new competition whose duration would overlap with the UEFA Champions League.

29. This means that a new international interclub competition (ie a potential rival of the UEFA Champions League) may only take place, according to the new UEFA rules, during the off-season period, ie at a time when the new FIFA Club World

---

10 UEFA, Press Release, "UEFA Statement on Today's Judgment of the Madrid Commercial Court No.17 in the *European Super League* Case" (27 May 2024) <www.uefa.com/news-media/news/028d-1afd49655461-f39aac5241e7-1000--uefa-statement-on-today-s-judgment-of-the-madrid-commercial-/> accessed 31 July 2025.

11 UEFA, Press Release, "European Football Community Stands Firm against So-Called Super League" (21 December 2023) <www.uefa.com/news-media/news/0288-19bfb0b4fa04-8711d4be5f38-1000--european-football-community-stands-firm-against-so-called-su/> accessed 31 July 2025.

Cup is already scheduled. In light of the recent ECJ judgment, it is not certain that the European Commission will accept that.

30. In addition, the new UEFA rules require that any dispute between the organiser of a competing international interclub competition and the UEFA shall be resolved before the CAS. This provision could also perhaps be held incompatible with EU competition law as, in the *ISU* judgment (published on the same day as the *Super League* judgment), the ECJ ruled that the submission to the exclusive jurisdiction of the CAS of disputes arising from decisions adopted by the ISU by virtue of its discretionary powers of prior authorisation and eligibility reinforced the abuse of a dominant position committed by the ISU.

31. A22 Management may have won the first half of the game, but the other half is still to be played, with the entry into force of the new modernised rules of UEFA on prior approval. Some of these rules could perhaps be disputed on the basis of EU competition law and may perhaps give rise to a new leg of the dispute between A22 Management and FIFA/UEFA.

32. Finally, and perhaps more importantly, the principles set out by the ECJ in the *Super League* case according to which sports governing bodies in a situation of conflict of interest shall be subject to restrictions, obligations and review, may not only apply to the prior approval of rival competitions, but perhaps also to decisions of sports governing bodies affecting internal relationships (ie relationships between an international federation and its members).

33. In this respect, it can be noted that in 2020 the *Ligue Nationale de Rugby* (LNR) filed a complaint with the European Commission against the players' release obligation set out by World Rugby arguing that the latter was infringing EU competition law as it had decided to extend international windows allegedly to favour its own competitions to the detriment of club competitions that are played at the same time (but without players called by national rugby associations.[12] In this respect, it is worth noting that, as early as 2005, Stephen Weatherill was already wondering whether the players' release obligation was compatible with EU competition law.[13]

34. The LNR finally withdrew its complaint as an amicable solution was found with World Rugby. It is nevertheless a good example showing that the principles of the *Super League* case could apply perhaps not only to the behaviour of sports federations vis-à-vis external rivals and new emerging championships but also regarding its own members and therefore to "intra-pyramid" competition.

35. A recent announcement made by European Leagues and FIFPRO confirms that the judgments of 21 December 2023 may have very far-reaching consequences on the governance of international sports federations, well beyond the rules and decisions concerning the launch of new third-party competitions. European Leagues and FIFPRO, which respectively represent the European professional football

---

12 See Rugby Union, "Disgruntled French Clubs Mount Legal Challenge to World Rugby's Authority" *The Times* (London, 11 September 2020) <www.thetimes.com/sport/rugby-union/article/disgruntled-french-clubs-mount-legal-challenge-to-world-rugbys-authority-tm50856g6> accessed 31 July 2025.

13 (Stephen Weatherill, Is the Pyramid Compatible with EC Law?' in *European Sports Law* (ASSER Press, 2014) 3–4 ISLJ 3, 7.

leagues and professional football players, are not promoting a new competition like the Super League, rather they are trying to preserve the interests of national leagues and players against the recent decisions of FIFA to extend its nations' World Cup and to launch a New Clubs World Cup. On 13 June 2024, European Leagues and FIFPRO announced that they submitted a legal claim against FIFA, challenging the legality of FIFA's decisions to unilaterally set the International Match Calendar and, in particular, the decision to create and schedule the FIFA Club World Cup 2025.[14] They claim that FIFA's recent decisions jeopardise both the mental and physical health of international players and the attractiveness and value of national championships.

36. The claim filed with the Brussels Court of Commerce asks the Belgian court to refer several questions to the European Court of Justice for a preliminary ruling. While some questions relate to the alleged violation by FIFA of the EU Charter of Rights and in particular of its provisions guaranteeing healthy working conditions for all workers (including football players), the most important question is probably whether or not FIFA's unilateral decisions with regard to the International Match Calendar and the Club World Cup 2025 give rise to "restrictions of competition" pursuant to Article 101 TFEU.

37. More recently, European Leagues and FIFPRO announced that they were also about to file an antitrust complaint with the EU Commission denouncing FIFA's recent decisions to extend its competitions as constituting violations of Articles 101 and/or 102 TFEU.[15] This complaint was filed in October 2024. FIFPRO's press release about the forthcoming complaint is quite clear about their intention to invoke the *ESL* case against FIFA:[16]

> The complaint will explain that FIFA's conduct infringes EU competition law and notably constitutes an abuse of dominance: FIFA holds a dual role as both the global regulator of football and a competition organiser. This creates a conflict of interest, which, consistent with recent case law of the EU courts, requires FIFA to exercise its regulatory functions in a way that is transparent, objective, non-discriminatory and proportionate. FIFA's conduct in respect of the international match calendar falls well short of these requirements.

38. It seems clear that European Leagues and FIFPRO intend to develop a strong argument essentially based on the ECJ's line of reasoning in the *ESL* case (and also used in the *ISU* case), ie that FIFA is in a conflict of interest situation that forces it to put in place an objective, non-discriminatory and proportionate

---

14 FIFPRO, Press Release, "Europe Statement: Legal Claim against FIFA" (13 June 2024) <https://fifpro.org/en/supporting-players/health-and-performance/player-workload/fifpro-europe-statement-legal-claim-against-fifa> accessed 31 July 2025.

15 It seems that the Spanish Football League (La Liga) may also complain against FIFA, jointly with European Leagues and FIFPRO.

16 FIFPRO, Press Release, "European Leagues, FIFPRO Europe to File Joint Complaint to European Commission against FIFA Regarding International Match Calendar" (23 July 2024) <www.fifpro.org/en/who-we-are/fifpro-members/fifpro-europe/european-leagues-and-fifpro-europe-to-file-joint-complaint-to-european-commission-against-fifa-regarding-international-match-calendar> accessed 31 July 2025.

decision-making process for the adoption of the International Match Calendar and that this implies involving all concerned stakeholders in the process, including leagues, clubs and players' unions. Although the precise contents of the complaint to be filed by European Leagues and FIFPRO still remain to be seen, some commentators agree that it is very likely to be building on the ESL precedent:

> It's the first legal action that comes after the December 21 decision in the European Court of Justice. It's clearly building on that. The landscape has shifted since December 21. The Court of Justice has shown it is expecting much more from the quality of governance of sport's governing bodies. And in this case, they feel through such a complaint they could push further their political power inside FIFA. That might well be true.[17]

39. FIFA quickly and strongly reacted to the announcement of the complaint and legal action of European Leagues and FIFPRO by stressing that its decision-making process was sufficiently open and inclusive and that European Leagues and FIFPRO are being hypocritical when they criticise FIFA.[18] At the end of the day, it will be for the European Commission and for the Belgian court (with perhaps the help and guidance of the ECJ) to decide whether or not FIFA's governance and decision-making process is sufficiently objective, inclusive and transparent. One important aspect of the forthcoming litigation that the EU Commission, the Brussels court and perhaps the ECJ will have to decide upon is whether or not FIFA's conduct when it unilaterally decided to set the International Match Calendar and to extend its own competitions is anticompetitive by object.

III. The "Object of the Game': Is FIFA's Way of Setting the International Match Calendar Anticompetitive "*Per Se*"?

40. In its *ESL* judgment of 21 December 2023, the ECJ found that

> where there is no framework providing for substantive criteria and detailed procedural rules suitable for ensuring that they are transparent, objective, precise, non-discriminatory and proportionate, (…) rules on prior approval,

---

17 Antoine Duval of the Asser International Sports Law Centre, an international and EU law research institute quoted by the *New York Times*, "Explained: Why Players" Unions are Taking FIFA to Court over the Club World Cup" *New York Times* (NY, 14 June 2024) <www.nytimes.com/athletic/5564281/2024/06/14/fifa-fifpro-europe-calendar-congestion/> accessed 31 July 2025.

18 See FIFA's reaction as posted on X (formerly Twitter), FIFA Media, "The current calendar was unanimously approved by the FIFA Council, which is composed of representatives from all continents, including Europe, following a comprehensive and inclusive consultation, which included FIFPRO and league bodies. FIFA's calendar is the only instrument ensuring that international football can continue to survive, co-exist, and prosper alongside domestic and continental club football. Some leagues in Europe – themselves competition organisers and regulators – are acting with commercial self-interest, hypocrisy, and without consideration to everyone else in the world. Those leagues apparently prefer a calendar filled with friendlies and summer tours, often involving extensive global travel. By contrast, FIFA must protect the overall interests of world football, including the protection of players, everywhere and at all levels of the game." (23 July 2024) <*https://x.com/fifamedia/status/1815691543111414126*> accessed 31 July 2025.

participation and sanctions such as those at issue in the main proceedings reveal, by their very nature, a sufficient degree of harm to competition and *thus have as their object the prevention thereof.*[19]

41. It is clear from the ECJ *ESL* judgment that where the organisation of a rival sport competition is subject to a prior approval regime that is not sufficiently transparent and objective, such a prior approval regime is inherently anticompetitive. According to the ECJ, there is an "anticompetitive object inherent in any prior approval mechanism that is not subject to restrictions, obligations and review suitable for ensuring that it is transparent, objective, precise and non-discriminatory".[20]

42. The question which arises here is: what about a regime which enables an international sports federation to arbitrarily levy and exploit for its own benefit some of the most important resources of its member leagues (ie international players): could that also potentially be viewed as anticompetitive by object?

43. One may observe that such a regime may appear *prima facie* to be less restrictive of competition than a prior approval regime for any rival competition which directly affects entry of new players in the market. As ruled by the ECJ, the prior approval regime put in place by UEFA and FIFA is particularly restrictive as it makes subject to the power of prior approval and the power to impose sanctions held by the entities that adopted them, in their capacity as associations of undertakings, the organisation and marketing of any international football competition other than those organised in parallel by those two entities.[21]

44. On the other hand, it could also be argued that while a non-objective, non-transparent, prior-approval regime inherently creates artificial, anticompetitive "barriers to entry", the recent decisions taken by FIFA on the International Match Calendar, which according to FIFPRO and European Leagues were adopted pursuant to a non-objective, non-transparent, decision-making process, could also be seen as inherently creating "barriers to expansion" for national leagues. This is because the way the International Match Calendar is organised and the resulting availability of their international players is absolutely essential for national leagues and their development.

45. Would it not be a bit hypocritical to consider as anticompetitive by object, a practice which creates barriers to entry while refusing this qualification to a practice which only creates barriers to expansion? In the first situation a new entrant is prevented from entering the market, but in the second situation, an actual competitor is prevented from developing and gaining market shares. It is very difficult to determine what is more detrimental to competition. In fact, the kind of practices that FIFPRO and European Leagues seem to be complaining about probably goes further than just establishing barriers to "expansion". By unilaterally setting the International Match Calendar in a way that may advantage its own competitions to the detriment of national leagues and by extending the periods during which it

---

19 *ESL* (n 2), para 178.

20 Ibid para 177.

21 Ibid para 176.

can levy international players from their leagues of origin, FIFA actually has the power to degrade the quality of the product offered by national leagues (ie their national championships).

46. One might also argue that the competition represented by the European Super League for UEFA Champions' League is obvious whereas the rivalry between FIFA and national leagues is less manifest. FIFA itself indicates that it sees national championships more as complementary offers co-existing with its own competitions rather than real rivals: "FIFA's calendar is the only instrument ensuring that international football can continue to survive, co-exist, and prosper alongside domestic and continental club football".[22]

47. It nevertheless remains that FIFA and national leagues are all selling their TV rights to more or less the same broadcasters and that, given that the financial resources of broadcasters are not infinite, they must sometimes arbitrage between purchasing the TV rights of national leagues and those of FIFA.[23] So there is, after all, probably some degree of competition between FIFA and national leagues. As Professor Weatherill elegantly put it, as early as 2005: "there is an element of market competition at stake in these situations".[24] And because there is probably a competitive relationship between FIFA and national leagues, there is probably a competition law issue arising if FIFA unilaterally sets the International Match Calendar in its own interest and to the detriment of national leagues and international players without properly consulting them or taking their views into account. It will now be for the EU Commission, the Brussels court and ultimately perhaps the ECJ to decide if FIFA's rules on the setting of the International Match Calendar are anticompetitive, and if so, whether they are anticompetitive by object or by effect.

IV. Towards a "Fair Game"?: Can We Expect Fair Sports Governance in the Near Future?

48. It is of course too early to try to predict what the outcome could be of the litigation cases initiated by some national leagues and by certain unions of players against FIFA, using the momentum created by the recent *ESL* judgment. In particular, it is hard to anticipate how the complaint with the EU Commission (to be filed by European Leagues and FIFPRO) will evolve. For law practitioners, it would be

---

22 FIFA Media (n 18), statement published on social media in reaction to the news that FIFPRo and European Leagues were initiating legal action against it.

23 Apple, which already purchased the worldwide broadcasting right of the US soccer championship (Major League Soccer, MLS) for USD 2.5 billion (for 10 years), recently announced that it gave up on the acquisition of the worldwide broadcasting rights of the new Club World Cup to be organised by FIFA. Reportedly, FIFA expected Apple to pay USD 4 billion for these rights.

24 See Weatherill (n 13), "[r]emember too that there is an element of market competition at stake in these situations. International football tournaments are to some extent in the same market as club competitions when one considers potential interest from broadcasters and sponsors. So clubs are required to provide a free resource, the players, to an undertaking that is at least in part seeking to make profits from exactly the same sources on which the clubs would wish to draw. One would certainly not find this in a normal industry. Sport truly is special".

great to see how the EU Commission and/or the EU courts assess FIFA's setting of the International Match Calendar in light of Articles 101 and 102 TFEU. This would surely provide fantastic substance for comments from EU competition law specialists. However, in the interest of sports and sport amateurs, one may wish that a negotiated solution will rapidly be found, perhaps through the use of Article 9 Regulation 1/2003, which enables the Commission to end antitrust proceedings by accepting commitments from the defending party which satisfactorily meet the competition concerns raised by the denounced conduct. In the case opposing FIFA to national leagues and football players, such commitments would likely involve changes to the governance of FIFA and to the way concerned stakeholders participate to the setting of the International Match Calendar. Alternatively, commitments similar to those submitted by the Fédération Internationale d'Automobile (FIA) and accepted by the Commission in 2001, could perhaps be an option. In this case, to prevent conflicts of interest, FIA committed to selling all its rights in the FIA Formula One World Championship, thereby losing any influence over the commercial exploitation of the Formula One Championship in order to limit its role to that of sports regulator.[25]

[25] European Commission, Press Release, "Commission Closes its Investigation into Formula One and Other Four-Wheel Motor Sports" (30 October 2001) <https://ec.europa.eu/commission/presscorner/detail/en/ip_01_1523> accessed 31 July 2025.

How Does Antitrust Law Apply to Sports Governing Bodies? Which Sporting Rules Fall Under the Scope of EU Antitrust Law?

Peter W. Heermann*
University of Bayreuth, Germany

I. Introduction

1. There are two possible answers to the questions raised in the title of this chapter, the first approach, favoured by the Court of Justice of the European Union (ECJ), assumes that certain specific, but overall, very few, provisions in the statutes of (inter)national sports federations do not *per se* fall within the scope of application of EU antitrust law. Even though the Court has formed two groups of cases in this regard (see Section II), this approach offers very limited legal certainty at best (Section III.). This is because the distinction from the group of association regulations that definitely fall within the scope of application of EU antitrust law remains unclear. It is to be expected that in antitrust proceedings, sports federations will regularly argue that an analogy should be drawn to the groups of cases already recognised by the ECJ. The central arguments in favour of these exceptions were first stated by the Court in connection with the EU fundamental

* University professor, Dr iur, LLM. (University of Wisconsin), holder of the Chair of Civil Law, Commercial and Business Law, Comparative Law and Sports Law at the University of Bayreuth as well as academic director of the part-time continuing education programme "LLM Sports Law (University of Bayreuth)".

freedoms around fifty years ago and then again in 2000. This approach has been repeated apodictically ever since, and in 2006 it was transferred to the application of EU antitrust law. However, as a result of the ever-increasing commercialisation of sport in the (semi-)professional sports sector, this reasoning is no longer free from considerable doubt, – if it ever was.

2. The second – here favoured – approach (Section V) does not allow for any exceptions and is therefore extremely simple in its basic structure. To a greater or lesser extend though, it requires a complex examination under antitrust law of all association regulations that restrict competition. However, apart from the narrow exceptions, this also applies to the first approach. Therefore, the differences in this respect are negligible. The second approach, which will only be outlined below, offers a coherent concept of dogmatic scrutiny. Moreover, it does not ultimately lead to any different results for the few sports association regulations, recognised by the ECJ to date, which are not supposed to fall within the scope of application of the EU fundamental freedoms and EU antitrust law. In other words, the regulations in question would not be in breach of antitrust law under the alternative approach either.

3. In the following, key passages from various ECJ judgments will be quoted verbatim rather than summarised. This makes it easier to understand the hidden lines of development in the case law of the ECJ, which have sometimes been neglected in previous discussions.

II. Judgments of the ECJ

1. *Walrave and Koch*[1] and *Doná*[2]

4. Walrave and Koch were professional Dutch pacemakers who also formed teams with cyclists from other countries. Following a change to the international regulations by the *Union Cycliste Internationale* (UCI), the international cycling federation, a pacemaker and the respective cyclist had to be of the same nationality at world championships. Because of this, Walrave and Koch felt that their right to freely exercise their activities within the then European Economic Community (EEC) – which at the time was a union of various European states and thus a predecessor of the European Union – was restricted. Even back then, Article 7 of the EEC Treaty, a predecessor provision of today's Article 18 TFEU, prohibited discrimination on grounds of nationality.

5. In a first important step, in its *Walrave and Koch* judgment the Court set out the conditions under which sport falls within the scope of EU law: "[h]aving regard to the objectives of the Community, the practice of sport is subject to Community law only in so far as it constitutes an economic activity within the meaning of Article 2 of the Treaty".[3]

6. This approach remains fully valid to this day – only insofar as sport is part of economic activity, can it fall within the scope of EU law – unlike pure leisure

---

1 Case 36/74 *Walrave and Koch v Association Union Cycliste Internationale and others* ECLI:EU:C:1974:140.

2 Case 13/76 *Gaetano Donà v Mario Mantero* ECLI:EU:C:1976:115.

3 *Walrave and Koch* (n 1), para 4.

activities, for example. This initially opened up access to the prohibition of discrimination. However, it is widely recognised that sport differs from other industries in various respects due to its specific characteristics. In addition, there is another circumstance that the ECJ was of course also aware of: sport functions according to globally standardised rules, whereas to this day EU law does not even apply to all countries in Europe. The relevant association statutes still stipulate that members of a national team in sport must be citizens of the same country for reasons that cannot be disputed. Corresponding questions simply do not arise in economic sectors other than national teams. Against this background, the Court decided not to apply the prohibition of discrimination to national teams in sport: "This prohibition however does not affect the composition of sport teams, in particular national teams, the formation of which is a question of purely sporting interest and as such has nothing to do with economic activity. This restriction on the scope of the provisions in question must however remain limited to its proper objective".[4]

7. This approach was repeated and confirmed by the ECJ some 19 months after *Walrave and Koch* in its *Donà* judgment:

> However, those provisions do not prevent the adoption of rules or of a practice excluding foreign players from participation in certain matches for reasons which are not of an economic nature, which relate to the particular nature and context of such matches and are thus of sporting interest only, such as, for example, matches between national teams from different countries.
> This restriction on the scope of the provisions in question must however remain limited to its proper objective.[5]

2. *Bosman*[6]

8. Subsequently, it took almost two decades before the ECJ revisited the approach in its famous *Bosman* judgment, adding two interesting aspects:

> As regards the difficulty of severing the economic aspects from the sporting aspects of football, the Court has held (in *Donà* […] paragraphs 14 and 15) that the provisions of Community law concerning freedom of movement of persons and of provision of services do not preclude rules or practices justified on non-economic grounds which relate to the particular nature and context of certain matches. It stressed, however, that such a restriction on the scope of the provisions in question must remain limited to its proper objective. It cannot, therefore, be relied upon to exclude the whole of a sporting activity from the scope of the Treaty.[7]

9. First, it is noteworthy that the Court itself recognised that it can be difficult to clearly and unambiguously separate economic aspects from sporting aspects.

---

4 Ibid para 8.

5 *Donà* (n 2), paras 14 et seq.

6 Case C-415/93 *Union Royale Belge Sociale de Football Association, RCL and UEFA v JM Bosman* ECLI:EU:C:1995:463.

7 Ibid para 76.

No less significant and groundbreaking is the finding that not all activities of sports organisations or even the latter themselves can be excluded from the application of the EU fundamental freedoms in general and the free movement of workers in the specific case. Instead, in the opinion of the ECJ, only the association regulations identified in *Walrave and Koch* can claim such an exemption.

3. *Deliège*[8]

10. The *Deliège* judgment concerned a successful Belgian judoka who had repeatedly not been nominated for international competitions by the Belgian Judo Federation for various reasons that can be neglected here. As a result, she had not only been deprived of the attention of a larger international specialised audience, but also of additional opportunities to generate income. The judoka had asserted a restriction of the freedom to provide services in accordance with Article 49 EC, now Article 56 TFEU, but also Articles 81 and 82 EC, now Articles 101 and 102 TFEU, before Belgian courts. In the referral proceedings, the ECJ limited its legal considerations to the alleged restriction of the freedom to provide services.

11. After confirming its previously developed approach, which has already been outlined here, the Court elaborated on the special case scenario now to be assessed:

> The selection rules at issue in the main proceedings do not relate to events between teams or selected competitors from different countries comprising only nationals of the State of which the Federation which selected them is a member, such as the Olympic Games or certain world or European championships, but reserve participation, by the national federation, in certain other international events of a high level to athletes who are affiliated to the federation in question, regardless of their nationality. The mere circumstance that the placings achieved by athletes in those competitions are taken into account in determining which countries may enter representatives for the Olympic Games cannot justify treating those competitions as events between national teams which might fall outside the scope of Community law.[9]

12. Following on from this, the ECJ then adopted an approach that already contained central elements of EU sports antitrust law, which it would develop later:

> In that context, it need only be observed that, although selection rules like those at issue in the main proceedings inevitably have the effect of limiting the number of participants in a tournament, such a limitation is inherent in the conduct of an international high-level sports event, which necessarily involves certain selection rules or criteria being adopted. Such rules may not therefore in themselves be regarded as constituting a restriction on the freedom to provide services prohibited by Article 59 of the Treaty.

---

8 Case C-191/97 *Christelle Deliège v ASBL and François Pacquée* ECLI:EU:C:2000:199.

9 Ibid para 44.

> The answer to the questions submitted must therefore be that a rule requiring professional or semi-professional athletes or persons aspiring to take part in a professional or semi-professional activity to have been authorised or selected by their federation in order to be able to participate in a high-level international sports competition, which does not involve national teams competing against each other, does not in itself, as long as it derives from a need inherent in the organisation of such a competition, constitute a restriction on the freedom to provide services prohibited by Article 59 of the Treaty.[10]

13. In this section, the following aspects are worth mentioning, particularly with regard to the subsequent development of case law on EU sports antitrust law. First, nomination rules for (semi-)professional individual athletes do not in general constitute a restriction on the freedom to provide services. Second, nomination regulations of sports federations inevitably go hand in hand with restrictions (in this case on the freedom to provide services) for athletes due to predetermined participant quotas and capacity limits for sports events. Third, the justification of such restrictions on athletes' freedom to provide services is based on two legal aspects: the inherence criterion and the principle of proportionality, which the ECJ subsequently adopted into sports antitrust law in case *Meca-Medina* and implemented in the so-called *Meca-Medina* test (see Chapter XXX)

4. *Meca-Medina*[11]

14. As in the *Walrave and Koch* and *Delìège* proceedings, the facts of the case *Meca-Medina* concern a peripheral sport: long-distance swimming. Just as in the aforementioned lawsuits, the plaintiff athletes ultimately lost the legal battle. The professional long-distance swimmers, David Meca-Medina from Spain and Igor Majcen from Slovenia, had taken first and second place at the World Championships in 1999. After positive doping tests, both were banned for four years by the Doping Committee of the International Swimming Federation (FINA). Meca-Medina could no longer pursue their sporting careers and make a living from it.

15. This was followed by a legal marathon. An appeal by the long-distance swimmers against this ban before the Court of Arbitration for Sport (CAS) in 2000 was unsuccessful. Three years later, after another hearing before the CAS, the ban was reduced to two years. The plaintiffs did not appeal against this arbitration award to the Swiss Federal Court but instead lodged a complaint with the EU Commission in 2001, alleging a violation of Articles 81 and 82 EC (now Articles 101 and 102 TFEU), but also of the freedom to provide services. In 2002, the EU Commission rejected the complaint because the doping regulation did not fall under the prohibition of Articles 81 and 82 EC.

---

10 Ibid paras 64, 69.

11 Case C-519/04 P *David Meca-Medina and Igor Majcen v Commission of the European Communities* ECLI:EU:C:2006:492.

16. In the same year, the swimmers then brought an action before the European General Court (EGC) for annulment of the EU Commission's decision. After setting out the approach developed by the ECJ to the fundamental EU freedoms,[12] the EGC came to the following conclusion:[13] The anti-doping rules were based on purely sporting considerations and therefore had nothing to do with economic considerations. It followed from this finding that the anti-doping rules, like the rules analysed by the ECJ in the *Walrave and Koch*, *Donà* and *Deliège* judgments, did not fall within the scope of the provisions of the Treaty on economic freedoms, in particular Articles 49, 81 and 82 EC. This would be due to the fact that the anti-doping rules were closely linked to sport as such, the EGC argued.

17. After the EGC essentially confirmed the EU Commission's decision, the swimmers appealed to the ECJ. Advocate General Léger subsequently concurred with the EGC's legal assessment in his Opinion.[14] In its *Meca-Medina* judgment the ECJ initially summarised its previous case law on sports rules that exceptionally do not fall within the scope of the EU fundamental freedoms.[15] However, it then drew a diametrically opposing legal conclusion compared to the EGC with regard to the scope of application of the EU antitrust law:

> In holding that rules could thus be excluded straightaway from the scope of those articles solely on the ground that they were regarded as purely sporting with regard to the application of Articles 39 EC and 49 EC, without any need to determine first whether the rules fulfilled the specific requirements of Articles 81 EC and 82 EC, as set out in paragraph 30 of the present judgment, the Court of First Instance made an error of law.[16]

18. In the following, the Court reviewed the case solely on the basis of Article 81 EC (now Article 101 TFEU).

5. *MOTOE*[17]

19. Two years after the *Meca-Medina* judgment, the ECJ had to decide on a case in which only the allegation of abuse of a dominant market position pursuant to Article 82 EC (now Article 102 TFEU) had to be examined. In its *MOTOE* judgment, the Court adopted the approach it had previously developed in the *Meca-Medina* judgment:

> It should be borne in mind in this regard that any activity consisting in offering goods or services on a given market is an economic activity (see, in particular, Case C-35/96 *Commission v Italy* [1998] ECR I-3851, paragraph 36, and Joined Cases C-180/98 to C-184/98 *Pavlov and Others* [2000]

---

12 Case T-313/02 *David Meca-Medina and Igor Majcen v Commission of the European Communities* ECLI:EU:T:2004:282, para 41.

13 Ibid para 47.

14 Case C-519/04 P *David Meca-Medina and Igor Majcen v Commission of the European Communities* ECLI:EU:C:2006:201, Opinion of AG Léger, para 44.

15 *Meca-Medina* (n 11), paras 25 et seq, para 41.

16 Ibid para 33.

17 Case C-49/07 *MOTOE* ECLI:EU:C:2008:376.

> ECR I-6451, paragraph 75). Provided that that condition is satisfied, the fact that an activity has a connection with sport does not hinder the application of the rules of the Treaty (Case 36/74 *Walrave and Koch* [1974] ECR 1405, paragraph 4, and Case C-415/93 *Bosman* [1995] ECR I-4921, paragraph 73) including those governing competition law (see, to that effect, Case C-519/04 P*Meca-Medina and Majcen v Commission* [2006] ECR I-6991, paragraphs 22 and 28).[18]

20. This established that the approach – as described above – which the Court had developed for decades applies not only to the EU fundamental freedoms, but also to Articles 101 and 102 TFEU, ie the central standards of EU antitrust law.

6. *European Super League (ESL)*[19] *International Skating Union (ISU)*[20]and *Royal Antwerp FC*[21]

21. In three judgments of 21 December 2023, the ECJ fully confirmed its previously developed approach to the question of which rules of sports associations fall within the scope of the EU fundamental freedoms and EU antitrust law, although the wording was partly new. The *ESL* judgment is used here as the starting point:

> Only certain specific rules which were adopted solely on non-economic grounds and which relate to questions of interest solely to sport per se must be regarded as being extraneous to any economic activity. That is the case, in particular, of those on the exclusion of foreign players from the composition of teams participating in competitions between teams representing their country or the determination of ranking criteria used to select the athletes participating individually in competitions (see, to that effect, judgments of 12 December 1974, *Walrave and Koch*, 36/74, EU:C:1974:140, paragraph 8; of 15 December 1995, *Bosman*, C-415/93, EU:C:1995:463, paragraphs 76 and 127; and of 11 April 2000, *Deliège*, C-51/96 and C-191/97, EU:C:2000:199, paragraphs 43, 44, 63, 64 and 69).[22]

22. The ECJ continues to uphold that association regulations, according to which only athletes of the same nationality may compete in national teams – as the name already suggests – as well as nomination criteria of sports associations for participation in sports competitions are not to be related to economic activities. The Court substantiates this finding in *ESL*:

> Apart from those specific rules, the rules adopted by sporting associations in order to govern paid work or the performance of services by professional or semi-professional players and, more broadly, those rules which, whilst not formally governing that work or that performance of services, have an indirect impact thereon, may come within the scope of Articles 45 and 56 TFEU

---

18 *Meca-Medina* (n 11), paras 22.

19 Case C-333/21 *European Super League (ESL)* ECLI:EU:C:2023:1011.

20 Case C-124/21 P *International Skating Union (ISU)* ECLI:EU:C:2023:1012.

21 Case C-680/21 *Royal Antwerp FC* ECLI:EU:C:2023:1010.

22 *ESL* (n 19); *ISU* (n 20), para 92; *Royal Antwerp* (n 21), para 54.

> (see, to that effect, judgments of 12 December 1974, *Walrave and Koch*, 36/74, EU:C:1974:140, paragraphs 5, 17 to 19 and 25; of 15 December 1995, *Bosman*, C-415/93, EU:C:1995:463, paragraphs 75, 82 to 84 and 87; of 12 April 2005, *Simutenkov*, C-265/03, EU:C:2005:213, paragraph 32; and of 16 March 2010, *Olympique Lyonnais*, C-325/08, EU:C:2010:143, paragraphs 28 and 30).[23]
> Similarly, the rules adopted by such associations may come within the scope of Article 49 TFEU (see, to that effect, judgment of 18 July 2006, *Meca-Medina v Commission*, C-519/04 P, EU:C:2006:492, paragraph 28), and even Article 63 TFEU.[24]

23. Here, the ECJ points out that association regulations that only indirectly affect athletes as employees or providers of services can also fall within the scope of the EU fundamental freedoms, although they do not necessarily have to. This will encourage sports federations to argue that further association regulations should also be excluded from the scope of application of the EU fundamental freedoms by way of analogy. The ECJ then transfers this approach to Articles 101 and 102 TFEU:[25]

> Lastly, those rules and, more broadly, the conduct of associations which have adopted them come within the scope of the FEU Treaty provisions on competition law where the conditions of application of those provisions are met (see, to that effect, judgment of 18 July 2006, *Meca-Medina v Commission*, C-519/04 P, EU:C:2006:492, paragraphs 30 to 33), which means that those associations may be categorised as "undertakings" within the meaning of Articles 101 and 102 TFEU or that the rules at issue may be categorised as "decisions by associations of undertakings" within the meaning of Article 101 TFEU.

24. In a next step, the ECJ emphasises the particular importance of the principles of non-discrimination and proportionality in this context:

> Thus, more generally, since such rules come within the scope of the aforementioned provisions of the FEU Treaty, where they set out edicts applicable to individuals, they must be drafted and implemented in compliance with the general principles of EU law, in particular the principles of non-discrimination and proportionality (see, to that effect, judgment of 13 June 2019, *TopFit and Biffi*, C-22/18, EU:C:2019:497, paragraphs 60, 65 and 66 and the case-law cited).[26]
> The rules at issue in the main proceedings, however, irrespective of whether they originate from FIFA or UEFA, do not form part of those rules to which the exception referred to in paragraph 84 of the present judgment might be applied, which exception the Court has stated repeatedly must be limited

---

23 *Royal Antwerp* (n 21), para 55.
24 *ESL* paras 85, 86.
25 Ibid para 87; *ISU* (n 20), para 93; *Royal Antwerp* (n 21), para 55.
26 *ESL* paras 88, 89; *Royal Antwerp* (n 21), para 57.

to its proper objective and may not be relied upon to exclude the whole of a sporting activity from the scope of the FEU Treaty provisions on EU economic law (see, to that effect, judgments of 14 July 1976, *Donà*, 13/76, EU:C:1976:115, paragraphs 14 and 15, and of 18 July 2006, *Meca-Medina v Commission*, C-519/04 P, EU:C:2006:492, paragraph 26).

25. Based on the assumption that the scope of application of EU antitrust law is opened, the Court finally sets out the conditions under which certain specific conduct of sports associations does not come within the scope of Article 101(1) TFEU (in particular due to the *Meca-Medina* test) and Article 102 TFEU, or can be justified.[27] With regard to the initial question of this chapter no further discussion is necessary on this point.

III. Position of the EU Commission and Opinion in the Academic Discourse

26. The EU Commission expressed its legal position in a document accompanying its White Paper on Sport 2007.[28] As far as can be seen, the EU Commission has not deviated from this position to date.

27. The EU Commission's opinion emphasises that some had argued that so-called "purely sporting rules" did not automatically fall within the scope of the EU antitrust rules and could not, by definition, infringe these rules.[29] The ECJ clearly had rejected this approach in the *Meca-Medina* case and ruled that the categorisation of a rule as "purely sporting" was not sufficient to exclude a sportsperson or sports federation adopting the rule in question from the scope of the EC competition rules. On the contrary, the Court had emphasised that whenever the sporting activity in question constituted an economic activity and thus fell within the scope of the EC Treaty, the conditions for its exercise were subject to the obligations arising from the various provisions of the Treaty, including the competition rules. The Court had pointed out that it was necessary to examine, on a case-by-case basis, irrespective of the nature of the provision, whether the specific conditions laid down in Articles 81 or 82 of the EC Treaty (now Articles 101 and 102 TFEU) were fulfilled.

28. In light of the Court's judgment in *Meca-Medina*, the EU Commission was convinced that a considerable number of organisational sports rules, namely all rules that defined the conditions for the exercise of the economic activity of professional athletes, teams or clubs, had to be examined under the antitrust provisions of the EC Treaty. Finally, the EU Commission stated that the

---

27 *ESL* paras 183–188, 189–209.

28 European Commission, Staff Working Document, "The EU and Sport: Background and Context" – Accompanying document to the *White Paper on Sport* COM (2007) 391 final, s 3.4(a) <https://eur-lex.europa.eu/legal-content/EN/TXT/HTML/?uri=CELEX:52007SC0935&from=EN> accessed 24 August 2025.

29 For this discussion cf. Peter W Heermann, *Association Autonomy in Sport – Determination of Legal Limits with Particular Consideration of European Antitrust Law* (Nomos 2022) ch VI, para 75 with further references (also available as an open access publication <www.nomos-elibrary.de/de/10.5771/9783748933298/verbandsautonomie-im-sport?search-click=> accessed 24 August 2025).

groundbreaking judgment in *Meca-Medina* had therefore significantly improved legal certainty by clearly stating that there was no category of "purely sporting rules" that were excluded from the scope of EC competition law from the outset.

IV. Critical Review

1. Approaches of the ECJ and the EU Commission in General[30]

29. In its document accompanying the White Paper on Sport 2007, the EU Commission concluded that the ECJ's *Meca-Medina* judgment had increased legal certainty. Representatives of the sports federations will probably consider this as a mockery or irony. Up until 2006, and most recently also based on the legal opinion of the EGC in *Meca-Medina*,[31] the sports federations had been led to believe that the ECJ would permanently recognise an antitrust exemption in favour of "purely sporting rules". Compared to this long-awaited legal situation, the now-required individual review on the basis of the *Meca-Medina* test (see Chapter XXX), which is appropriate but admittedly complex, doubtlessly entails a slight loss of legal certainty from the perspective of the sports federations. However, it must be taken into account that the category of association regulations of a purely sporting nature could not be determined and defined with legal certainty despite decades of discussion. In addition, such a partial exemption from antitrust law would amount to an unjustified reduction in legal protection. It would not be compatible with the protective objective of Articles 101 and 102 TFEU if, in the case of an available and legally required application of Articles 101 and 102 TFEU, the application of the law were instead ultimately made dependent on the intentions of the association rule-makers.

2. Certain Specific Rules Being Extraneous to Any Economic Activity

30. Based on its previous case law, the Court[32] considers that certain specific rules of federations, which have been adopted solely for non-economic reasons, and which concern matters of interest only to sport as such, must be regarded as being extraneous to any economic activity. This applies in particular to the exclusion of foreign players from the composition of teams participating in competitions between teams, representing their country or the determination of ranking criteria used to select the athletes participating individually in competitions. The ECJ distinguishes from this those federation statutes that regulate work in return for payment or the provision of services by professional or semi-professional athletes and, in a broader sense, those federation regulations that do not formally regulate this work or provision of services but have an indirect effect on it.

---

30 Ibid n, ch VI, para 77 with further references.

31 *Meca-Medina* (n 12), paras 41–47.

32 *ESL* (n 19), paras 84, 89; *ISU* (n 20), para 92; *Royal Antwerp* (n 21), para 54.

31. The finding by the ECJ in the *Walrave and Koch* judgment in 1974 that certain sports rules – allegedly – have nothing to do with commercial activities was hardly convincing even then. These doubts are all the more valid today after decades of ever-increasing commercialisation of sport. This applies both to the national sports federations, which have always generated a large part of their revenue in connection with national teams that are as successful as possible in sport,[33] and to the athletes, whose individual marketing potential, at least in (semi-)professional sport, is still on the rise. As a result, it is not appropriate to completely ignore or neglect any connection between the regularly sport-motivated composition of a national team on the one hand and the economic activities of the sports association and the (non-)nominated athletes on the other hand.

3. Some Criticism of the ECJ's Approach

32. This distinction, which has been practised by the ECJ for fifty years now, is all the less convincing the more extensively the athletes selected for the national teams are remunerated directly or indirectly by the federation for the services provided there. This occurs, for example, through the payment of prize money for achieving a certain sport ranking or through participation in the sponsorship revenue that sports federations generate through their involvement. It should also be taken into account that successful athletes, in particular, increasingly want and are allowed to market themselves individually, even when acting in national teams.[34] In many professionally organised sports, it now seems unrealistic to continue to assume that the motto "taking part is what counts" is the sole motive for sport involvement in national teams.

33. A further circumstance casts considerable doubt on the fact that nomination decisions have no connection whatsoever with economic ones and are based solely on sporting factors. For many years now, non-nominated athletes have not only challenged the decisions of the relevant national sports federations in court but have even sued them for damages after a wrong decision was recognised by the courts. For example, Charles Friedek, a German triple jumper, had wrongly not been nominated by the German Olympic Sports Confederation (*Deutscher Olympischer Sportbund*, DOSB) to take part in the 2008 Summer Olympics in Beijing, as it later turned out. Eight years later he received financial compensation after a veritable marathon of litigation. In 2009, in the main arbitration proceedings, in which antitrust law played no role, it was legally confirmed that the non-nomination was unlawful. In the following six years, the triple jumper pursued a claim for damages through three instances before state courts, which was ultimately awarded to him by the German Federal Court of Justice (*Bundesgerichtshof*, BGH)

---

33 Exceptions prove the rule, cf. Don Riddell, "Ronaldo: The Mystery of the 1998 World Cup Final, and why Brazil's Star Striker Barely Turned Up" (*CNN*, 12 July 2020) <https://edition.cnn.com/2020/07/12/football/ronaldo-brazil-world-cup-final-1998-cmd-spt-intl/index.html> accessed 24 August 2025.

34 cf. in this context, Case B2-26/17 Bundeskartellamt Decision *German Olympic Sports Confederation and IOC* (25 February 2019), paras 103–105 (for an English translation, cf. <www.bundeskartellamt.de/SharedDocs/Entscheidung/EN/Entscheidungen/Missbrauchsaufsicht/2019/B2-26-17.pdf?__blob=publicationFile&v=2> accessed 24 August 2025); cf. also on this problem see Peter W Heermann, "Financial Participation of Athletes in the Revenues of Sports Associations?" (2023) 6 JSL 434–443 with further references.

in a final judgment on 13 October 2015[35] – at that time, Friedek had long since ended his sporting career. Before the Frankfurt/Main Regional Court, to which the BGH had referred the legal dispute, could rule, Friedek and the DOSB reached a settlement in 2016. In the same year, Friedek became national triple jump coach at the German Athletics Association (Deutscher Leichtathletik-Verband, DLV).

34. It is striking that nomination proceedings conducted before sports arbitration tribunals and state courts regularly concern professionally active individual athletes or sports teams consisting of two athletes (eg track and field athletes, beach volleyball players, pacemaker/cyclist), who are in the public spotlight, especially at major international competitions, but not team athletes in the classic sense (such as football players). The reason is to be seen in the fact that at least those team players who are not considered by their clubs in the team line-up have alternatives that can be realised in particular by changing clubs in a timely manner. Additionally, team players who are not considered for nomination to a national team are usually offered above-average income opportunities at club level, at least in popular sports.

35. This is why it is still being questioned here – as elsewhere[36] – whether there are any non-economic federation regulations of a purely sporting nature at all, at least in (semi-)professionally organised sport. Accordingly, it is argued here that the allegedly purely sporting nature of an association regulation is generally a fiction. In professional sport in particular, but also in the economic activities of sports federations, especially through the organisation and staging of sports competitions and their marketing, it is hard to imagine federation rules that cannot be associated with the pursuit of the economic interests.[37] The links between economic and non-economic aspects in the organisational activities of sports federations are usually too close for this to be the case. Even regulations that are issued primarily for sporting reasons usually have a considerable impact on the markets.[38] This also applies, for example, to federation rules that at first glance appear to relate solely to sporting aspects:

- Even the offside rule in football, for example, raises doubts. If the rule were to be changed at some point, this would probably be linked to the expectation that the game would become more attractive, which would then have a positive effect on the development of marketing revenues.
- Amending the rules for match fouls would not only protect the players concerned but would presumably also increase the flow of the game and thus its attractiveness, which would pay off in terms of marketing the event. This motivational pattern can be applied to many so-called rules of the game.
- The size of the pitch or goal is also a decisive factor for the number of high-tension match situations. The duration of the match and in particular,

35 For an overview of the proceedings, cf. Case II ZR 23/14 Bundesgerichtshof Decision in *Charles Friedek* (13 October 2015), paras 7 et seq.

36 Heermann (n 29), ch VI, paras 79–86 with further references.

37 Stephen Weatherill, *Principles and Practice in EU Sports Law* (OUP 2017) 116 "fictional or at least extremely rare creature that is the 'purely sporting' rule".

38 Case AT.40208 European Commission Decision *International Skating Union's Eligibility* (8 December 2017), paras 147 et seq.

the number of regular breaks have a direct influence on the total amount of time that can be used for advertising or other marketing activities, thereby increasing the marketing potential of the respective sporting event.

- Lastly, a current non-fictional example: The international athletics federation World Athletics is considering revising the long jump by testing a new "take-off zone" from which athletes can jump instead of the usual fixed board.[39] Amending the rules in this way could result in fewer misses (currently around a third of all jumps), making the competition more attractive to spectators and, of course, increasing its marketing potential.

V. Alternative Approach

36. Finally, it should be assumed – contrary to the legal interpretation favoured by the ECJ and the EU Commission to date – that association regulations, according to which only athletes of the same nationality may compete in national teams, as well as selection criteria of sports associations for participation in sports competitions, fall within the scope of application of EU antitrust law. How would an antitrust review then be structured? Under what conditions could one conclude that the selection criteria and/or the selection decisions based on them violate antitrust law?

37. Provided that the determination of selection criteria in the sports federation's statutes is based on the decision of an association of undertakings and that the broadly interpreted criterion of affectation of trade between Member States is fulfilled, the scope of application of Article 101(1) TFEU would be opened. From the perspective of the non-nominated athletes, the disputed association regulation would represent a restriction of competition. But is it a restriction of competition by object or only by effect? Since the ECJ's judgments dated 21 December 2023 in *ESL*,[40] *ISU*[41]and *Royal Antwerp FC*[42] the answer to this question is decisive as to whether the *Meca-Medina* test (see Chapter XXX) can be used to justify the restriction of competition or only the much stricter justification in accordance with Article 101(3) TFEU. The *Meca-Medina* test has so far been applied in decision-making practice on sports antitrust law as an inherent justification developed by the ECJ, in particular in the case of a previously established restriction of competition by object *or* effect pursuant to Article 101(1) TFEU. In the opinion of the Court in the above-mentioned judgments, however, the *Meca-Medina* test should in future only be applicable to restrictions of competition by effect under Article 101(1) TFEU. In the case of restrictions of competition by object pursuant to Article 101(1) TFEU, only Article 101(3) TFEU is to be applied as a legal justification, while application of the *Meca-Medina* test to Article 102 TFEU is to be ruled out from the outset.

---

39 Jeremy Wilson, "Carl Lewis: New Long Jump Proposal an April Fools Joke" *The Telegraph* (London, 20 February 2024) <www.telegraph.co.uk/athletics/2024/02/19/long-jump-revolution-take-off-zone-world-athletics/> accessed 24 August 2025.

40 *ESL* (n 19), paras 185–187.

41 *ISU* (n 20), paras 111–114.

42 *Royal Antwerp* (n 21), paras 113–116.

38. As the ECJ has already convincingly stated in its *Deliège* judgment,[43] selection rules inevitably have the effect of limiting the number of participants in a tournament. Such a limitation would be inherent in the conduct of a high-level international sporting event, which necessarily involves certain selection rules or criteria being adopted. Thus, such selection criteria merely constitute a restriction of competition by effect (and not by object) pursuant to Article 101(1) TFEU, so that the *Meca-Medina* test can be applied as justification. However, the selection criteria must be drafted and implemented in compliance with the general principles of EU law, in particular the principles of non-discrimination and proportionality.[44] If these conditions are met, there is a high degree of probability that any restrictions of competition resulting from the selection criteria can be justified by means of the *Meca-Medina* test.[45] When applying it, adequate account must also be taken of the fact that selection criteria, despite their indirect impact on the economic activities of the sports federations and athletes as their members, primarily concern the organisation of the exercise of sport. As a result, sports federations have a considerable margin of appreciation when defining and applying the selection criteria, which can be reviewed by sports arbitration tribunals and state courts only to a very limited extent.[46]

39. Sports federations regularly have a dominant position in the relevant markets for the organisation and conduct of sports competitions and for admission to these. As a result, it cannot be ruled out that a sports association may face accusations of abuse of a dominant position under Article 102 TFEU when defining and applying selection criteria. In such a situation the sports federation may show that conduct liable to come within the scope of the prohibition laid down in that article may yet be justified. In particular, the sports federation may demonstrate, to that end, either that its conduct is objectively necessary, or that the exclusionary effect produced may be counterbalanced or even outweighed by advantages in terms of efficiency which also benefit the consumer.[47] It can be assumed that sports federations will generally succeed in providing such evidence if the principles of non-discrimination and proportionality are observed.

VI. Conclusion

40. According to the established ECJ case law, only certain specific rules which were adopted solely on non-economic grounds, and which relate to questions of interest solely to sport *per se*, must be regarded as being extraneous to any economic activity and thus do not fall under the scope of EU antitrust law. This should apply in particular to provisions on the exclusion of foreign players from the composition of teams participating in competitions between teams representing their country or the determination of ranking criteria used to select the athletes participating individually in competitions (Sections II and III).

---

43 *Deliège* (n 8), para 64.

44 *ESL* (n 19), para 88; *Royal Antwerp* (n 21), para 57.

45 cf. for a comprehensive antitrust assessment see, Heermann (n 29) ch XIII, paras 132–153.

46 Ibid ch VI, paras 316–336 with further references.

47 *ESL* (n 19), para 202.

41. It is argued here that the allegedly purely sporting nature even of the above-mentioned specific association regulations is generally a fiction. In professional sport, in particular, but also in the economic activities of sports federations, especially through the organisation and conduct of sports competitions and their marketing, it is hard to imagine federation rules that cannot be associated with the pursuit of the economic interests (Section IV).

42. It is therefore assumed here that all association regulations fall within the scope of application of EU antitrust law without exception (Section V). This approach does not ultimately lead to any different results for the few sports association regulations recognised by the ECJ to date, which are not supposed to fall within the scope of application of the EU fundamental freedoms and EU antitrust law.

EU Competition Law Scope vs National Competition Law

Jacques Steenbergen*
Belgian Competition Authority

1. The scope of competition law enforcement can be assessed from different angles: eg the sports that have been the object of competition law decisions, sport governance bodies, human relations aspects, media coverage, the type of competition enforcement decisions, etc.

2. This contribution cannot cover every possible angle. It will eg not cover decisions concerning state aid, sports clothing, sports merchandise and the betting and gambling industry. It is based on EU case law and decisions by national competition authorities in the EU jurisdictions dealt with in the chapter by "National Competition Law Issues Europe" where a more exhaustive catalogue of national decisions can be found[1]. It refers also to documents for the OECD Competition Committee Working Party No. 2 Roundtable on Competition and Professional Sports of 4 December 2023.[2] The focus here is on competition law, although national judges may in some jurisdictions also use powers to give cease and desist orders under unfair trade practices law.

I. Sports

3. Please refer for the decisions of national competition authorities and courts to the relevant contributions in the chapter "National Competition Law Issues Europe".

---

* Professor Emeritus, Dr Steenbergen is former President of the Belgian Competition Authority.

1 The tables are based on the national reports available at the time the draft was finalised.

2 OECD, "Competition and Professional Sports" (4 December 2023) Roundtable on Competition Policy Papers, No 300 <https://one.oecd.org/document/DAF/COMP/WP2/M(2023)2/ANN1/FINAL/en/pdf> accessed 1 August 2025.

Sport	EU Institutions	EU national competition authorities and courts
Basketball		*Poland*: decision in respect of wages related to the Covid crisis.[3] *Spain*: the ACB case law.[4]
Bumper pool		*Belgium*: Belgian Competition Authority (BCA) decisions concerning the bumper pool balls that may be used in competition.
Car and motorcycling racing	The *MOTOE* case;[5] and the *FIA* case closed after modifications to Fédération Internationale de l'Automobile (FIA) rules.[6]	*Italy*: case on exclusive powers of the Automobile Club d'Italia (ACI).[7]
Cyclocross		*Belgium*: BCA and Market Court §Brussels Court of Appeal) (Court) *Proximus/Telenet* decisions concerning television rights.[8]
Football	The *Bosman* case,[9] the *Royal Antwerp Football Club*[10] case, the *Royal Football Club Seraing SA v FIFA and others (FIFA)* case concerning CAS arbitral awards;[11] and in particular the *European Super League Company (ESL)* case.[12]	*Belgium*: BCA and Court decisions concerning financial fair play rules, the licensing of teams, the reorganisation of competition because of Covid, the reorganisation of competition[13] and third-party ownership rules. *Denmark*: Superliga joint selling of media rights decision. *Germany*: *German Olympic Sports Confederation and IOC* decision,[14] the 50+1 commitments decisions.[15] *Italy*: case on the organisation of amateur football[16] and also *Juventus* private enforcement case on ticket sales.[17] *The Netherlands*: *Portugal*: decision on non-poaching[18] and media coverage decisions.[19]

---

3 OCCP/UOKiK, Decision referred to at p.35 of the Secretariat paper to the OECD, "Competition and Professional Sports" (4 December 2023) Note by Poland <https://one.oecd.org/document/DAF/COMP/WP2/WD(2023)42/en/pdf> accessed 1 August 2025.

4 OECD Latin American Competition Forum, see contribution by Spain on the competition in Latin America and the Caribes (2005) <https://www.oecd.org/content/dam/oecd/en/networks/latin-american-and-caribbean-competition-forum/LatinAmericanCompForum2005.pdf> accessed 1 August 2025.

5 Case C-49/07 *MOTOE* ECLI:EU:C:2008:376.

6 European Commission, Press Release, "Commission Closes its Investigation into Formula One and Other Four-Wheel Motor Sports" (30 October 2001) <https://ec.europa.eu/commission/presscorner/detail/en/ip_01_1523> accessed 1 August 2025.

7 Case A570 *AGCM v Automobile Club d'Italia (ACI)* (2023) AGCM Bulletin No 40/2023 (pending) <https://www.agcm.it/dotcmsCustom/getDominoAttach?urlStr=192.168.14.10:8080/41256297003874BD/0/B6E35E29C-C3B758AC1258A51004D699B/$File/p30807.pdf> accessed 1 August 2025.

8 XXX

9 Case C-415/93 *Union Royale Belge Sociale de Football Association, RCL and UEFA v JM Bosman* ECLI:EU:C:1995:463. See the contribution on the *Bosman* case in the chapter on "Transnational football law issues".

10 Case C-680/21 *Royal Antwerp FC* ECLI:EU:C:2023:1010.

11 Case C-600/23 *Royal Football Club Seraing SA v FIFA and others* ECLI:EU:C:2025:617.

12 Case C-333/21 *European Super League (ESL)* ECLI:EU:C:2023:1011.

13 BCA press release of 1 August 2025 on the refusal of interim measures.

14 Case B2-26/17 Bundeskartellamt Decision *German Olympic Sports Confederation and IOC* (25 February 2019).

15 Bundeskartellamt, Press Release "Bundeskartellamt Provides Preliminary Assessment of DFL's 50+1 Ownership Rule" (31 May 2021) and (8 March 2023) <https://www.bundeskartellamt.de/SharedDocs/Meldung/EN/Pressemitteilungen/2021/31_05_2021_50plus1.html> accessed 1 August 2025.

16 Case A562 *AGCM v Italian Football Federation (FIGC).*

17 Contribution on Italian cases par. 5.

18 OCCP/UOKiK, Decision (n 2).

19 AdC, Decisions referred to at 35 of the Secretariat paper to the OECD, "Competition and Professional Sports" (4 December 2023) Note by Portugal <https://one.oecd.org/document/DAF/COMP/WP2/WD(2023)43/en/pdf> accessed 1 August 2025.

Sport	EU Institutions	EU national competition authorities and courts
Gymnastics		*France*: *Ineos/Gymnaste Club de Nice* merger law decision.[20]
Ice hockey		*Belgium:RBIHF* case on online activities[21]. *Finland: Jokerit* agreement case.[22]
Jumping		*Belgium*: BCA and Court decisions concerning barriers to entry for third-party organisers including rules on the eligibility of athletes. *Italy*: case concerning barriers to entry including rules on eligibility of athletes.[23]
Pigeon racing		*Belgium*: BCA decisions concerning timing equipment that may be used in competition and the digital transformation.
Rugby		*France*: decision concerning pay television.[24]
Skating	Barriers to entry for third-party organisers: the *International Skating Union (ISU)* decisions.[25]	
Tennis	*Danish Tennis Federation* case on sponsoring.[26]	
Volley ball		*Italy: FIP/VS* decision[27]

Table 1

II. Governance and Governance Bodies

4. Please refer for the decisions of national competition authorities and courts to the relevant contributions in the chapter "National Competition Law Issues Europe". See also the contributions on the *Bosman* case, the player transfer system, the homegrown player rule, the football agent regulation and on multi club ownership/multi-club investment in the chapter on "Transnational Football Law Issues".

---

20 Case 19-DCC-160 Autorité de la concurrence Decision *Ineos/Gymnaste Club de Nice* (21 August 2019).

21 BCA press release 14 August 2025 on the refusal of interim measures.

22 KKV, Press Release, "'Jokerit Agreement' between Finnish Ice Hockey League and League Teams in Violation of Competition Law" (31 October 2019) <https://www.kkv.fi/en/current/press-releases/jokerit-agreement-between-finnish-ice-hockey-league-and-league-teams-in-violation-of-competition-law/> accessed 1 August 2025.

23 Case A378E *ICA v Italian Federation of Equestrian Sports (FISE)* (8 October 2019).

24 Case 14-MC-01 Autorité de la concurrence Decision *BeIN Sports France* (30 July 2014).

25 Case AT.40208 European Commission Decision *International Skating Union's Eligibility* (8 December 2017) and Case C-124/21 P *International Skating Union (ISU)* ECLI:EU:C:2023:1012.

26 European Commission, Notice pursuant to Article 19(3) of Council Regulation No 17 Case IV/F-1/33.055 - *Danish Tennis Federation* [1996] OJ C138/6.

27 AGCA decision of 19 June 2023, case 1861.

Governance	EU Institutions	EU national competition authorities and courts
Applicability of competition law	The *Meca-Medina*[28] case and later case law, and in particular the *Super League* case.	*Belgium*: as from the 2015 FEI decision concerning jumping.[29] *Italy: FIP/VS* decision and the amateur football decision.
Barriers to entry for third-party organisers	See above-mentioned *International ISU* decisions.[30]	*Belgium*: the above-mentioned cases concerning jumping. *Italy*: case on exclusive powers of the Automobile Club d'Italia (ACI).
Appeal procedures	The *ISU* case, the *FIFA* case concerning CAS arbitral awards; and in particular the *Super League* case.	*Belgium*: the above-mentioned case concerning the reorganisation of competition because of Covid.
Doping rules	The *Meca-Medina* case.	
Financial fair play		*Belgium*: the *Lommel SK* decision of the Belgian Arbitration Court for the Sport (BACS).[31]
Organisation of competitions	The *MOTOE and Super League* cases.	*Belgium*: the *Waasland-Beveren* case concerning the impact of Covid and the refusal of interim measures case .[32]
Mergers		*France*: *Ineos/Gymnaste Club de Nice* merger decision.
Nationality requirements	The *Royal Antwerp* case.	
Sponsorship	Negative clearance in *Danish Tennis Federation* case following modifications to the agreement.[33]	
Transfer rules	The *Bosman* and the *FIFA* cases.	
Non-poaching agreements		*Finland*: *Jokerit* agreement case. *Portugal*: decision on non-poaching.
Football agents	The pending case *FT, RRC Sports Gmb v FIFA*.[34]	
Third-party ownership		*Belgium*: the *Royal Football Club de Seraing/Doyen Sports* court cases.[35] *Germany*: the 50+1 commitments decision.

Table 2

28 Case C-519/04 P *David Meca-Medina and Igor Majcen v Commission of the European Communities* ECLI:EU:C:2006:492.

29 Case 2015-V/M-23 ABC Decision *Global Champions League and Tops Trading Belgium v Fédération Equestre Internationale (FEI)* (27 July 2015), confirmed by the Brussels Court of Appeal (3 May 2016) <https://www.abc-bma.be/fr/decisions/2015mr1-fei-ad> accessed 2 August 2025.

30 *ISU* (n 25).

31 XXX

32 XXX

33 *Danish Tennis Federation* (n 22).

34 Case C-209/23 *RRC Sports Gmb v FIFA* (pending).

35 *Royal Football Club Seraing SA* (n 10).

III. Other Issues

5. Please refer for the decisions of national competition authorities and courts to the relevant contributions in the chapter "National Competition Law Issues Europe".

	EU institutions	EU national competition authorities and courts
Athletes' advertising opportunities		*Germany*: *German Olympic Sports Confederation and IOC* decision.[36]
Media coverage		*Belgium*: the *Proximus/Telenet* cyclo-cross case. *Denmark*: Superliga joint media rights selling decision.[37] *France*: See the contribution on Mediaprocases by R.Soiron, O.Cavesian and A. Roquebert. *Portugal*: see above-mentioned media coverage decisions concerning football.
Ticket sales		*Italy*: *Juventus* private enforcement case.
Use of infrastructure		*Denmark*: advisory notice closing case.[38]

Table 3

IV. Type of Decision

6. Please refer for the decisions of national competition authorities and courts to the relevant contributions in the chapter "National Competition Law Issues Europe".

Type of enforcement decision	EU institutions	EU national competition authorities and courts
Infringement cases	The *Meca-Medina* case, the *FIA* case closed after modifications to FIA rules.	*Belgium*: the main case decisions concerning cyclo-cross and jumping. *France*: see the reference to Mediapro cases. *Germany*: *German Olympic Sports Confederation* and *IOC* decision; the 50+1 commitments decision. *Italy*: cases amateur football clubs, jumping and on exclusive powers of the Automobile Club d'Italia. *Portugal*: see media coverage decisions.
Interim measures		*Belgium*: all the BCA and court cases referred to in Tables 1–3 involved interim measures except the *Royal Football Club de Seraing/Doyen Sports* and *Lommel SK* court cases.
Preliminary rulings	The *Bosman, MOTOE, ISU, Royal Antwerp FC, Super League* and *FIFA* cases.	
Notifications	*Danish Tennis Federation* case on sponsoring.	*France*: *Ineos/Gymnaste Club de Nice* decision.

Table 4

36 *German Olympic Sports Confederation and IOC* (n 12).

37 OECD, "Competition and Professional Sports" (4 December 2023) Note by Denmark.

38 DCCA, Press Release, "38 Venues Receive an Advisory Notice on Competition Rules" (28 June 2024) <https://en.kfst.dk/nyheder/kfst/english/decisions/20240628-38-venues-receive-an-advisory-notice-on-competition-rules> accessed 2 August 2025.

V. Assessment

1. EU and National Competition Law

7. The first conclusion on the basis of the decisions referred to in this contribution is that we can assess the impact of decisions by EU and by national authorities and courts and compare the scope and impact of their respective procedures. But that does not allow us to compare the impact of EU and of national competition law. Most of the national decisions are based on EU competition law, or on a combination of EU and national competition law, or on the interpretation of national competition law in the light of decisions of the EU Courts or the European Commission.

8. This should not come as a surprise given the scope of application of the rules of competition in the TFEU and the obligation of national authorities and courts to apply Articles 101 and 102 TFEU in all cases affecting trade between Member States.[39] Many competitions are transnational and organised by or within the framework of international organisations such as the IOS, ISU, FEI, FIA, FIFA and UEFA. Even decisions in respect of a *prima facie* local sport such as the Belgian case on bumper pool affected trade between Member States because it was concerned with the balls that can be used in competition and the applicant was a subsidiary of a Dutch company.[40]

9. Perhaps more importantly, it illustrates that national competition authorities and courts are guided by EU precedents. The impact of decisions by the EU Courts and the European Commission may be limited to the issues with which they are concerned, but not to the sport or the governing body involved in a case.

2. EU and National Institutions

10. The combined lists of decisions by EU and national authorities and courts show that a wide range of sports and issues have been the object of competition law enforcement procedures. And because of the impact as "precedents" of decisions by the EU Courts and the European Commission, there are probably few sports and competition-related sport law issues that are not indirectly or potentially directly affected by EU competition law.

11. Given their economic significance and degree of commercialisation, it is to be expected that in quantitative terms, the largest number of decisions of both EU and national institutions deal with football and with media coverage.

12. It is perhaps more significant that Table 4 shows that at the EU level most decisions are preliminary rulings given by the CJEU. They therefore found their origin in national court cases.

13. And at the national level, except on media coverage, a significant percentage of cases were taken in interim measures procedures. Combined with the number of cases originating in national courts, this tends to show that parties seek

---

39 Council Regulation (EC) No 1/2003 of 16 December 2002 on the implementation of the rules on competition laid down in Articles 81 and 82 of the Treaty [2003] OJ L1/1, art 3.

40 Case 2020-V/M-04 BMA Decision *VBA Hector Cue Sports Belgium*(23 January 2020) <https://www.bma-abc.be/sites/default/files/content/download/files/bma-2020-vm-04-pub.pd>f accessed 2 August 2025.

a swifter resolution of their disputes than infringement procedures by most competition authorities can promise. Except for the media coverage cases, cases are mostly concerned with the right to participate in an ongoing or upcoming competition. Applicants tend to be athletes and often smaller clubs. It is especially true that national judges and competition authorities that must decide on interim or equivalent measures within strict deadlines,[41] can offer a more effective remedy than most cartel or abuse of dominance infringement procedures.

14. That the conclusion is rather different in respect of media coverage cases, can probably be explained by the fact that these cases are often concerned with medium – to long-term contracts and conflicts between larger established media companies.

VI. Conclusion

15. Most of the national decisions are based on EU competition law, or on a combination of EU and national competition law, or on the interpretation of national competition law in the light of decisions of the EU Courts or the European Commission. We can therefore compare the scope and impact of decisions by EU and national courts and authorities. But that does not allow us to compare the impact of EU and of national competition law.

16. Competition authorities may include sports in their defined priorities.[42] But given the limited resources of competition authorities to open *ex officio* cases, both authorities and courts depend on parties to bring cases. And because there are not that many Commission decisions that can be appealed, the CJEU largely depends on national courts to refer cases in a request for a preliminary ruling.

17. Competition authorities can only expect allegedly injured parties to rely on them if they can offer effective remedies. It seems fair to conclude that, except in respect of media coverage cases, that may require the availability and willingness to use effective interim measures or equivalent procedures. Larger, eg institutional stakeholders may be more inclined to seek to settle more legal issues by infringement case decisions. And it is also in these cases important that authorities seek to bring forward the useful effect of their enforcement actions.

18. Given the reliance of national authorities and courts on EU precedents it is very important that national courts have over the years referred a wide range of significant issues to the CJEU in requests for a preliminary ruling.

---

41 See e.g. the Belgian Code of Economic Law, arts IV.72–73, requiring the BCA to organise a hearing within one month after the application and to take a decision within one month after the hearing <https://www.belgiancompetition.be/sites/default/files/content/download/files/CEL%20Consolidated%20BCA.pdf> accessed 2 August 2025.

42 See e.g. BCA, *Note de priorités* (2022) <https://www.belgiancompetition.be/sites/default/files/content/download/files/2022_politique_priorites_ABC.pdf> accessed 2 August 2025.

19. And that requires in turn that the legal community continues to assist stakeholders in defining relevant issues continuing a track record that goes at least back to the 1995 *Bosman* case.[43]

[43] See further, OECD, "Competition and Professional Sports" (4 December 2023) Roundtable on Competition Policy Papers, No 2 (Bibliography Background Paper) <https://one.oecd.org/document/DAF/COMP/WP2(2019)3/en/pdf#:~:text=Independent%20sector%20regulators%20and%20competition,direct%20co-operation%20a%20challenge> accessed 1 August 2025.

CHAPTER II

Restrictions on Competition in Sports Markets

ESL and *ISU* Cases: What Consequences for Sports Federations?

Mathieu Le Bescond de Coatpont*
University of Lille, France

1. On 21 December 2023, the Court of Justice of the European Union (CJEU) handed down three important rulings on the application of competition law and freedom of movement to the field of sport in three separate cases: *European Super League (ESL)*,[1] *International Skating Union (ISU)*[2] and *Royal Antwerp FC*.[3] These judgments follow in the footsteps of the cases that have marked the field of sport since the *Walrave and Koch* case of 1974.[4] This commentary will be limited to the first two cases, which should be read and analysed together as they deal with a similar issue.

2. The outcome of the *ESL* case had been eagerly awaited, as it had been the subject of extensive media coverage. It follows the public announcement on 18 April 2021 of plans by 12 major European clubs from England, Italy and Spain (Real Madrid CF, FC Barcelona, Atlético Madrid, Juventus FC, AC Milan, Inter Milan, Liverpool FC, Manchester United FC, Manchester City FC, Arsenal FC, Tottenham Hotspurs FC and Chelsea FC) to create their own European competition outside the UEFA system, in competition with the UEFA Champions League. The idea was to create a closed league that would provide economic security for clubs by guaranteeing

---

* Associate Professor University of Lille and Director of the Business Law Master (Sports Law Program), Lille, France.

1 Case C-333/21 *European Super League (ESL)* ECLI:EU:C:2023:1011.

2 Case C-124/21 P *International Skating Union (ISU)* ECLI:EU:C:2023:1012.

3 Case C-680/21 *Royal Antwerp FC* ECLI:EU:C:2023:1010.

4 Case 36/74 *Walrave and Koch v Association Union Cycliste Internationale and others* ECLI:EU:C:1974:140.

their participation every year, regardless of their results in their respective domestic leagues. As soon as it was announced, the project aroused very negative reactions from FIFA, UEFA, national football associations and leagues, fans' representative bodies and governments.[5] In particular, it was criticised for representing an Americanisation of European sport in contradiction with a "European Sports Model" specifically characterised by sporting merit. FIFA and UEFA announced that they would impose sanctions on clubs and players taking part in this new competition. All the clubs, except Real Madrid CF and FC Barcelona, have withdrawn from the project. However, the company organising the competition (the *European Super League*) challenged before the Madrid Commercial Court the FIFA and UEFA regulations allowing these sanctions to be imposed, on the basis of European competition law and freedom of movement. The court referred several questions to the CJEU for a preliminary ruling. Essentially, the Court had to decide whether the regulations of FIFA and UEFA and of the member associations and national leagues, which provide for prior approval, exclusive exploitation rights and associated penalties, were likely to constitute an abuse of a dominant position, an anticompetitive cartel or unjustified barriers to freedom of movement.

3. This case echoed an earlier case involving the *International Skating Union (ISU)*, the international skating federation, which was the subject of a decision by the European Commission in 2017[6] and a ruling by the General Court of the European Union in 2020,[7] which was appealed to the CJEU. In this case, the Korean company Icederby International Co Ltd (Icederby) was planning to organise a speed skating competition. The ISU objected on the basis of its statutes, which provided for prior approval and penalties that could go as far as lifetime exclusion from any competition organised by the ISU for skaters taking part in an unauthorised competition. Two Dutch professional skaters (Mark Tuitert and Niels Kerstholt) lodged a complaint with the European Commission under competition law. The Commission took the view that the eligibility rules in the ISU regulations constituted an anticompetitive cartel and, more specifically, a decision by an association of undertakings with the anticompetitive object of excluding competing skating event organisers from the market. It also considered that the arbitration clause providing for the jurisdiction of the Court of Arbitration for Sport (CAS) in the event of a challenge to a decision on ineligibility reinforced the restrictions on competition. It therefore ordered the federation to amend its regulations.[8] The ISU brought an action for annulment of the decision before the General Court of the European Union, which upheld the Commission's position, with the exception of its assessment of the arbitration clause. The purpose of the appeal to the Court of Justice was to challenge these decisions.

---

5 "Football: la Super Ligue annoncée par douze grands clubs fait l'unanimité contre elle" (*Le Monde*, 18 April 2021) <www.lemonde.fr/sport/article/2021/04/18/l-uefa-presente-sa-reforme-de-la-ligue-des-champions-pour-contrer-le-projet-de-superligue_6077227_3242.html>; Clément Martel and Adrien Pécout, "Plus d'argent mais moins de mérite sportif: le football européen secoué par le projet de Super Ligue" (*Le Monde*, 19 April 2021) <www.lemonde.fr/sport/article/2021/04/19/le-football-europeen-secoue-par-le-projet-de-super-league_6077267_3242.html?search-type=classic&ise_click_rank=1> accessed 20 August 2025.

6 Case AT.40208 European Commission Decision *International Skating Union's Eligibility* (8 December 2017).

7 Case T-93/18 *International Skating Union (ISU)* ECLI:EU:T:2020:610.

8 Decision *ISU* (n 6).

4. The question of the compatibility of a power to authorise competing competitions with competition law was not entirely new. In 2008, in the *MOTOE* case,[9] the Court of Justice had ruled in relation to the Greek motorcycling federation that, as it was also a competition organiser and, under Greek law, had the power to authorise competing competitions, that power had to be subject to limits, obligations and supervision in order not to constitute an abuse of a dominant position.[10]

5. The reference for a preliminary ruling in the *ESL* case and the appeal in the *ISU* case thus gave the Court of Justice the opportunity to assess the compatibility of the power of international and national associations in the organisation of sports with economic freedoms (movement and competition), particularly through the example of a particularly structured sport such as football. The Court could decide to follow the reasoning in the *MOTOE* and *ISU* cases, recognising this power but limiting it. On the contrary, it could go back on this reasoning by following the conclusions of the Advocate General, who recommended holding that the system of prior approval, the exclusivity of the exploitation rights and the associated sanctions on UEFA, FIFA, the member national associations and the national leagues were inherent and proportionate in order to achieve legitimate objectives linked to the specific nature of football, with the exception of the sanctions for excluding players not involved in the competing competition project, in particular with regards to their exclusion from the national teams.[11]

6. The Court chose to confirm the judgment of the General Court of the European Union in the *ISU* case and even went further by admitting that sports arbitration reinforced the harm to competition, as the European Commission had decided. Applying the same reasoning to the *ESL* case, it ruled that

> the adoption and implementation of rules by associations which are responsible for football at world and European levels and which pursue in parallel various economic activities related to the organisation of competitions, making subject to their prior approval the setting up, on European Union territory, of a new interclub football competition by a third-party undertaking, and controlling the participation of professional football clubs and players in such a competition, on pain of sanctions, where there is no framework for those various powers providing for substantive criteria and detailed procedural rules suitable for ensuring that they are transparent, objective, non-discriminatory and proportionate

7. The Court decided this was all at once an abuse of a dominant position, a cartel consisting in a decision of an association of undertakings restricting competition by object and a restriction on the freedom to provide services. With regard to the FIFA and UEFA regulations reserving them exclusive rights to exploit football competitions, the Court found that the rules of competition law

> [do not preclude] rules laid down by associations which are responsible for football at world and European levels and which pursue in parallel various economic

---

9 Case C-49/07 *MOTOE* ECLI:EU:C:2008:376.

10 Ibid 87.

11 Case C-333/21 *European Super League (ESL)* ECLI:EU:C:2022:993, Opinion of AG Rantos, para 187.

activities related to the organisation of competitions, inasmuch as they designate those associations as being the original owners of all of the rights emanating from competitions coming under their "jurisdiction", where those rules apply only to competitions organised by those associations, to the exclusion of those which might be organised by third-party entities or undertakings", but that these competition rules "[preclude] such rules in so far as they confer on those same associations an exclusive power relating to the marketing of the rights at issue.[12]

8. The Court specified that a justification for the abuse of a dominant position or an exemption for the cartel with regard to the power to authorise or the exclusive power to market exploitation rights could only be envisioned by demonstrating the required conditions, ie the conditions laid down by the Treaty or case law and consisting, in essence, of the demonstration of pro-competitive effects capable of offsetting the restriction of competition.

9. As a result, the ISU, FIFA and UEFA are seeing their regulations on the organisation of their sports called into question by European competition law and freedom of movement. On the same day as the decisions were taken, the *European Super League* relaunched its project in a new form.[13] However, although these federations have been formally condemned, their role as regulators of the sports in question has been recognised, since the very principle of prior approval for rival competitions has not been called into question, only the procedures. In other words, these rulings recognise the regulatory power of sports associations but make its compatibility with European Law conditional on a framework that guarantees the possibility for competing operators to organise their own competitions.

I. Recognition of the Regulatory Power of Sports Federations

10. The Court of Justice confirms that the regulatory power of sports federations, which is justified by the specific nature of sports, is not in itself anticompetitive but requires that it be subject to limits to ensure that it does not degenerate into an anticompetitive practice.

1. Acceptance of a Regulatory Power Justified by the Specific Characteristics of Sport

11. Considering competition law and freedoms of movement, the Court of Justice has upheld the structuring of sports around national federations affiliated to an international federation, which it justifies on the basis of the specific nature of the sports in question.

---

12 *ESL* (n 1), para 241.

13 A22 Management, Press Release, "A22 Officially Submits Unify League Proposal to UEFA and FIFA" (17 December 2024) <https://a22sports.com/en/>; Clément Martel, "Super Ligue: l'ouverture d'une nouvelle ère pour le football européen ou une décision qui 'ne change rien'?" (*Le Monde*, 21 December 2023) <www.lemonde.fr/sport/article/2023/12/21/super-ligue-l-ouverture-d-une-nouvelle-ere-ou-une-decision-qui-ne-change-rien_6207162_3242.html> accessed 20 August 2025.

A. *Validation of the Principle of Regulation of a Sport by a Federation*

12. In the traditional organisation of sports in Europe, each sport is structured in a pyramid. At a national level, amateur or professional sportsmen and women are members of a national sports federation, which generally has a *de jure* (in France or Greece, for example) or *de facto* monopoly on the organisation of competitions in the sport in question and may have set up a professional league. Clubs are created in the form of associations affiliated to the national federation or in the form of companies that have an agreement with an affiliated association. The national federation is itself affiliated to an international federation which has a *de facto* monopoly at world level on the organisation of international competitions in the sport in question, resulting in particular from its recognition by the International Olympic Committee (IOC).

13. Most international sports federations have their headquarters in Switzerland for historical reasons and because of the advantages offered by this state and its liberal legislation on associations and arbitration. The affiliation relationships give rise to a hierarchy of norms: international sports federations that obtain recognition from the IOC agree to place themselves under its "*supreme authority*" and to abide by its regulations and decisions, even if the IOC nevertheless undertakes to leave them their independence and autonomy in the governance of their sport.[14] Similarly, national federations, by virtue of their affiliation to the international sports federation, must comply with its regulations and decisions. Finally, clubs and sportsmen and women, through their affiliation to the national sports federation, must comply with its regulations and decisions. In the case of football, the Fédération Internationale de Football Association (FIFA), an association under Swiss Law with its headquarters in Zurich, has governed football since 1904. Football clubs in different countries belong to their national sports federation, which in turn belongs to FIFA, the international federation recognised by the IOC. The national football federations are grouped into continental associations. In Europe, this is the Union of European Football Associations (UEFA), an association under Swiss law with its headquarters in Nyon.

14. The sports federations' statutes also provide for prior approval for third parties wishing to organise a competition involving licence holders and sanctions for those who take part in such a competition without approval. This was the case in the statutes of FIFA, the UEFA and the ISU.

15. Furthermore, these statutes generally provide that the sports federation owns the exploitation rights to the competitions it organises. For example, FIFA's statutes provide that "FIFA, its member associations and the confederations are the original owners of all of the rights emanating from competitions and other events coming under their respective jurisdiction, without any restrictions as to content, time,

---

14 IOC, Olympic Charter, Olympic Fundamental Principle (2023), No 3 and art 25 <https://stillmed.olympics.com/media/Documents/International-Olympic-Committee/IOC-Publications/EN-Olympic-Charter.pdf> accessed 23 August 2025.

place and law"[15] and that they are "exclusively responsible for authorising the distribution of image and sound and other data carriers of football matches and events coming under their respective jurisdiction.[16]

16. Finally, arbitration clauses in the statutes require disputes to be settled not by state courts but by an arbitration body based in Switzerland and set up by the sports movement: CAS.[17] CAS awards can only be appealed to the Swiss Federal Tribunal, which limits its review to procedural issues and, on the merits, to their compatibility with Swiss international public policy, the content of which is relatively limited.[18] The international sports federations themselves are responsible for enforcing the court's rulings, and their regulations, like those of FIFA and UEFA, provide for sanctions against those who fail to comply. This system for resolving disputes ensures compliance with the rules specific to the sporting sector and their hierarchy, which constitute a *lex sportiva* and, to a certain extent, exempts it from the various national laws and international treaties. FIFA's statutes provide for

> the independent Court of Arbitration for Sport (CAS) [...] to resolve disputes between FIFA, member associations, confederations, leagues, clubs, players, officials, football agents and match agents' and specify that "CAS shall primarily apply the various regulations of FIFA and, additionally, Swiss law".[19] The Statutes add that "t confederations, member associations and leagues shall agree to recognise CAS as an independent judicial authority" "to ensure that their members, affiliated players and officials comply with the decisions passed by CAS" and specify that "recourse to ordinary courts of law is prohibited.[20]

17. This structure means that a sport is governed at an international level by a single international sports federation recognised by the IOC and, at a national level, by the national sports federations that depend on it. The Court's aim was to examine this type of organisation from a competition perspective.

18. The *ESL* ruling confirms that competition law applies to sports federations because they are entities engaged in an economic activity and that only rules that have non-economic motives and are solely of interest to sport as such are exempt, such as the exclusion of foreigners from the composition of national teams

---

15 FIFA Statutes (2022), art 66.1 <https://digitalhub.fifa.com/m/3815fa68bd9f4ad8/original/FIFA_Statutes_2022-EN.pdf> accessed 20 August 2025.

16 Ibid art 67.1.

17 On this question see, Mathieu Maisonneuve, *L'arbitrage des litiges sportifs* (LGDJ 2011), 267 Antonio Frigozzi, *L'arbitrage international en matière de sport* (LGDJ 2005).

18 Swiss Federal Tribunal, 4A248/2019 and 4A398/2019 (25 August 2020) holding that "the Federal Court's substantive review of an international arbitral award is limited to the question of the award's compatibility with public policy", which "is a more restrictive concept than that of arbitrariness", so much that a violation of the European Convention on Human Rights or the Swiss Constitution cannot be directly invoked but can only be "taken into account in the context of public policy in order to give concrete expression to this concept' in order to determine whether the result of the award is incompatible with "the essential and widely recognised values which, according to the prevailing views in Switzerland, should form the basis of any legal order." (translated from French); On this question, Clémentine Legendre, *La coordination du mouvement sportif international et des ordres juridiques étatiques et supra-étatiques* (LGDJ 2020).

19 FIFA Statutes (2022), art 56 ff.

20 Ibid art 58.

or the ranking criteria for selecting athletes in individual competitions.[21] The Court also points out that the fact that sports federations are established outside the territory of the European Union does not exempt them from the application of European competition law, since their practices have effects within the territory of the Union.[22]

19. It confirms that FIFA and the UEFA have a *de facto* collective dominant position "on the market for the organisation and marketing of interclub football competitions on European Union territory and also the exploitation of the various rights related to those competition", making it possible to punish an abuse of a dominant position.[23]

20. Finally, the *ESL* and *ISU* judgments confirm that the international sports federation and the continental and national associations together constitute an association of undertakings within the meaning of competition law, whose regulations and decisions can therefore be analysed as decisions by associations of undertakings, one of the forms that anticompetitive cartels can take.[24]

21. However, the existence of a dominant position or a decision to form an association of undertakings is not in itself anticompetitive. An abuse of a dominant position or an anticompetitive object or effect of the decision to form an association of undertakings must be established.

22. The Court could have distinguished between *de jure* regulatory power conferred by a state, as was the case in *MOTOE*, and *de facto* regulatory power. It could have held that the setting up by a state of an organisation delegating to a private entity the power to regulate a market was not in itself anticompetitive, but that the fact that private entities, without any state delegation, set up an organisation reserving the market for themselves, in particular through a system of customer sanctions, was anticompetitive in itself and thus characterised the abuse or the anticompetitive object/effect. In the *ESL* case, the Court found that

> the dominant position held by FIFA and UEFA on the market for the organisation and marketing of international interclub football competitions is such that, in practice, at the current juncture it is impossible to set up viably a competition outside their ecosystem, given the control they exercise, directly or through their member national football associations, over clubs, players and other types of competitions, such as those organised at national level".[25]

23. Similarly, in the *ISU* case, the Court found that, while the international sports federation did not exercise any regulatory function delegated by a public authority, it did, in fact, "as the sole international sports federation recognised by the IOC

---

21 *ISU* (n 2), para 91 ff.

22 Ibid.

23 *ESL* (n 1), para 117; The collective dominant position of FIFA and the clubs on the agents market had been recognised: Case T-193/02 *Laurent Piau v Commission of the European Communities* ECLI:EU:T:2005:22, points 110 ff.

24 *ESL* (n 1), para 118; *ISU* (n 2), para 90.

25 *ESL* (n 1), para 149.

for the disciplines in question, a regulatory activity"[26] and organised and controlled the most important speed skating competitions in which skaters had to participate in order to earn a living. Its approval was, in fact, essential for any third-party organiser because, given the very limited income opportunities for the vast majority of professional skaters, it was not viable for them to take part only in third-party competitions, without taking part in those of the international sports federation.[27]

24. The Court decided to take note of the *de facto* regulatory role of these international sports federations, in addition to their capacity as operators, by validating the principle that they could authorise or refuse third-party operators to enter the market, on pain of sanctions, but at the same time supervising the terms of this regulation so that it did not constitute an unjustified obstacle to competition. This is ultimately an application of the reasoning followed in relation to abuse of a dominant position with regard to essential facilities: when an undertaking holds, *de jure* or *de facto*, a resource that is essential for access to the market by other operators, it must provide access on reasonable terms so as not to hinder all competition.[28] Its power to regulate the market by granting access to the facility is recognised but limited.

25. Finally, the Court accepted the principle that associations are, *de facto* or *de jure*, responsible for a sport at national, European or global level, have "legal autonomy entitling them to adopt rules relating, inter alia to the organisation of competitions, their proper functioning and the participation of athletes in those competitions"[29] and thus adopt and implement a system of prior approval for competitions organised by third parties, control and penalise the participation of clubs or sportsmen in those competitions,[30] require recourse to the Court of Arbitration for Sport in the event of a dispute, with limited judicial review by the state,[31] carry on in parallel economic activities linked to the organisation of competitions, reserve for themselves the exclusive rights to exploit their own competitions[32] and require a solidarity contribution from third-party operators in particular.[33] In the Court's view, this organisation does not in itself infringe the competition rules and does not, as such, constitute an abuse of a dominant position, or the anticompetitive object or effect of a cartel. The pyramid organisation of many sports is thus validated under competition law, and this choice is explained by the specific nature of the sports in question.

B. *The Specific Nature of Sport as a Legal Basis*

26. Since 2009, sport has been added to the European Union's competences and Article 165 TFEU states that the Union "shall contribute to the promotion of European sporting issues, while taking account of the specific nature of

---

26 *ISU* (n 7), para 73.

27 Ibid para 74.

28 On this question see, Marie-Anne Frison-Roche et Jean-Christophe Roda, *Droit de la concurrence* (Dalloz 2022) 612 ff.

29 *ISU* (n 2), para 196.

30 *ESL* (n 1), para 258; *ISU* (n 2), para 125.

31 *ISU* (n 2), para 193.

32 *ESL* (n 1), para 258.

33 *ISU* (n 7), para 113.

sport, its structures based on voluntary activity and its social and educational function." This article could be analysed as founding a specificity of sport justifying exemptions from the rules of the Treaties or, at the very least, as imposing a particular interpretation. In the *ISU* case, for example, the EU General Court referred to it and concluded that "in the context of the analysis of possible justifications for restrictions [of competition] in the field of sport, it is necessary to take into consideration the specific characteristics of sport in general and its social and educational function".[34] In the *ESL* case, the Advocate General argued that this was a "horizontal" provision that had to be taken into account in the implementation of other EU policies, in particular competition policy.[35]

27. However, in its "introductory remarks [...] on Article 165 TFEU", the Court is careful to specify the scope it intends to give to that article.

28. It points out that it merely gives concrete expression to the Union's competence to provide support in the field of sport: it does not enable the Union to conduct a sports policy, but only to provide incentives and recommendations, and "is not a cross-cutting provision having general application".[36] It therefore concludes that the elements and objectives of this article and the incentive measures and recommendations "need not be integrated or taken into account in a binding manner in the application of the rules" concerning freedom of movement and competition rules. Consequently, Article 165 TFEU is not "a special rule exempting sport from all or some of the other provisions of primary EU law liable to be applied to it or requiring special treatment for sport in the context of that application".[37] This interpretation, which is in line with the letter of the Treaty, greatly reduces the scope that the sports sector could have intended to give to this article and to the various recommendations that it had enabled the European authorities to adopt: the Commission's 2007 White Paper on Sport, the 2011 Communication "Developing the European Dimension in Sport", the Council's 2011 and 2020 work plans for sport and the European Parliament's resolution on the European dimension in sport, etc.

29. That being said, the Court nevertheless acknowledges the "considerable social and educational importance" of sporting activity for the Union and its citizens "henceforth reflected in Article 165 TFEU" and emphasises that that "activity also undeniably has specific characteristics which, whilst relating especially to amateur sport, may also be found in the pursuit of sport as an economic activity" and that "such specific characteristics may potentially be taken into account along with other elements and provided they are relevant" when applying the articles relating to freedom of movement and competition, but only "in the context

---

34 Ibid paras 78, 79; see also, Case C-22/18 *TopFit e.V. and Daniele Biffi v Deutscher Leichtathletikverband eV* ECLI:EU:C:2019:497, para 34: "It is [...] clear from Article 21(1) TFEU, read in conjunction with Article 165 TFEU, that practising an amateur sport, in particular as part of a sports club, allows an EU citizen residing in a Member State other than the Member State of which he is a national to create bonds with the society of the State to which he has moved and in which he is residing or to consolidate them".

35 *ESL* (n 11), Opinion of AG Rantos, para 35.

36 *ESL* (n 1), para 95.

37 Ibid para 101.

of and in compliance with the conditions and criteria of application provided for in each of those articles".[38]

30. Finally, sport does not therefore enjoy, as a matter of law, a derogatory or exceptional regime in relation to other economic activities, but its specific features may be taken into account in the application of the economic rules of the European Union.

31. Applying this framework of analysis to football, the Court notes that this sport has considerable social, cultural and media importance[39] in the EU and has two specific features. The first is that it gives rise to numerous competitions at European and national levels involving a large number of clubs and players.[40] The second is that, like other sports, it is characterised by the fact that it "limits participation in those competitions to teams which have achieved certain sporting results [...] with the conduct of those competitions being based on matches between and gradual elimination of those teams", so much that "it is, essentially, based on sporting merit, which can be guaranteed only if all the participating teams face each other in homogeneous regulatory and technical conditions, thereby ensuring a certain level of equal opportunity".[41]

32. The Court concludes that those specific features legitimise a system of prior approval for international professional football competitions and rules of participation which make it possible "to guarantee the homogeneity and coordination of those competitions within an overall match calendar" and "to promote, in a suitable and effective manner, the holding of sporting competitions based on equal opportunities and merit".[42] Consequently, neither the adoption of those rules, nor their implementation, nor the sanctions to ensure that they are effective "may be categorised, in terms of their principle or generally, as an "abuse of a dominant position".[43] The Court applies the same reasoning to the prohibition of cartels[44] and to the justification of an obstacle to freedom of movement.[45]

33. Similar reasoning was followed in the *ISU* case, where the EU General Court noted that "it is legitimate to consider [...] that, given the specific nature of the sports, it is necessary to ensure that sporting competitions comply with common standards, seeking in particular to ensure that competitions take place fairly and the physical and ethical integrity of sportspeople is protected".[46]

---

38 Ibid para 102 ff.

39 Ibid para 143.

40 Ibid.

41 Ibid.

42 Ibid para 144.

43 Ibid para 144 ff.

44 Ibid para 171 and spec. 175.

45 Ibid para 253: "the adoption of rules on prior approval of interclub football competitions and on the participation of professional football clubs and players in those competitions may be justified, in terms of its very principle, by public interest objectives consisting in ensuring, prior to the organisation of such competitions, that they will be organised in observance of the principles, values and rules of the game underpinning professional football, in particular the values of openness, merit and solidarity, but also that those competitions will, in a substantively homogeneous and temporally coordinated manner, integrate into the "organised system" of national, European and international competitions characterising that sport".

46 *ISU* (n 7), para 108.

34. However, while the specific attributes of each sport may justify this power of authorisation and sanction at a national, European or global level, the Court points out that none of those specific attributes make it possible to consider as legitimate, the rules on prior approval and participation and the associated sanctions, if they are not accompanied by restrictions.[47]

2. No Justification for Unrestricted Regulatory Power

35. The *ESL* and *ISU* cases show that, if the sports federations' power to regulate, in principle legitimate, is not subject to limits, it degenerates into serious restrictions on economic freedoms (free competition and freedom of movement), the justifications for which seem illusory.

A. *Serious Restrictions on Economic Freedoms*

36. If a sports federation has the power, *de jure* or *de facto*, to regulate a sport, in particular by authorising or refusing the organisation of competitions by third-party operators and by penalising those who take part in them, it can potentially oppose any organisation of competitions competing with its own. The risk for competition is then that the sports federation and its members reserve for themselves the market for the organisation and operation of competitions by hindering the entry of any competitor, which is likely to constitute anticompetitive practices and an obstacle to freedom of movement, all of which are highly serious.

37. The Court held that, as regards the freedoms of movement, the relevant freedom is the freedom to provide services and that the rules on prior approval and participation, in so far as "there is no framework for those rules providing for substantive criteria and detailed procedural rules suitable for ensuring that they are transparent, objective, non-discriminatory and proportionate", allow sports federations to exercise discretionary control over the possibility for any undertaking to organise and market competitions in the sport in question, for clubs to take part in them, and for any undertaking to provide services connected with that organisation or marketing, thereby constituting an obstacle to the freedom to provide services.[48] The Court emphasised the seriousness of the obstacle, finding that the rules at issue "tend not only to impede or make less attractive the various economic activities concerned, but to prevent them outright, by limiting access for any newcomer".[49]

38. This seriousness is reflected in the abuse of dominant position. Thus, where the sports federation has a *de facto* or *de jure* dominant position, the Court holds that if the rules on prior approval and participation are "not subject to restrictions, obligations and review", they constitute, by their very existence, an abuse of a dominant position.[50] Similarly, the associated sanctions are "by their very nature" an abuse of a dominant position "in the absence of substantive criteria and detailed

---

47 *ESL* (n 1), paras 147 ff. and 175 ff.

48 Ibid para 243 ff.

49 Ibid para 249.

50 [50] Ibid para 147, 126.

procedural rules ensuring that the sanctions introduced as an adjunct to those rules are transparent, objective, precise, non-discriminatory and proportionate".[51]

39. Even in the absence of such a dominant position, they constitute, according to the Court, a decision by an association of undertakings with an anticompetitive object.[52] This nature of restriction by object was particularly disputed in the *ISU* case. It should be remembered that a cartel is prohibited if it has an anticompetitive object or an anticompetitive effect.

40. The distinction between the anticompetitive object and the anticompetitive effect has many implications. First, for certain sports, it is possible that a dominant position on the part of the international sports federation cannot be demonstrated. While the existence of a football market and the dominant position of FIFA and UEFA on that market were not in doubt since they are the only ones on the market for world and European competitions,[53] competing operators exist in certain sports (for example, the Euroleague in basketball). Furthermore, it is not certain that each sport constitutes a distinct market. This is certainly the case for athletes, since it is difficult to reach the top level in several sports simultaneously, but it is less obvious for sponsors, broadcasters and spectators, who may consider sports events to be substitutable. The broader the market, the less likely it is that a dominant position will be found. And in the absence of a dominant position, the only anticompetitive practice likely to be characterised in European law is a cartel.

41. Second, in the presence of a cartel, in this case a decision by an association of undertakings, an anticompetitive object or effect must be demonstrated. If the cartel has an anticompetitive object, there is no need to analyse its effects, and the practice can therefore be sanctioned. The possibilities of justification are limited to satisfying the conditions for individual exemption. On the other hand, if there is no anticompetitive object, sanctioning the practice presupposes the demonstration of an anticompetitive effect on the market and, more specifically, of an appreciable anticompetitive effect. The analysis of the effects will therefore make it possible not to penalise the practice if its anticompetitive effects are non-existent or minor, or if they are inherent and proportionate to the pursuit of a legitimate objective. However, an individual exemption will still be possible.

42. In the *ISU* case, the Commission relied on the decision of an association of undertakings to restrict competition by object, which exempted it from having to demonstrate a dominant position on a market and the anticompetitive effects of the practice. ISU criticised this analysis before the Court. After recalling the concept of restriction of competition by object (restriction presenting such a degree of harmfulness that it obviates the need to search for anticompetitive effects) and its strict interpretation, the Court held that rules of approval and participation not accompanied by limits, obligations and control, constitute a restriction of competition by object since they "confer on those entities the power to authorise, control and set the conditions of access to the market concerned for any potentially

---

51 Ibid para 148.

52 *ISU* (n 2), para 123 ff. *ESL* (n 1), para 171 ff.

53 *ESL* (n 1), para 117 ff.

competing undertaking, and to determine both the degree of competition that may exist on that market and the conditions in which that potential competition may be exercised": they restrict "the creation and marketing of alternative or new competitions in terms of their format or content", deprive athletes of the possibility of taking part in them "even though they could, for example, offer an innovative format whilst observing all the principles, values and rules of the game underpinning the sport" and, lastly, deprive "deprive spectators and television viewers of the opportunity to attend those competitions or to watch the broadcast thereof".[54] The same reasoning was followed in the *ESL* case.[55]

43. The seriousness of the harm to competition, reflected in the qualifications of abuse of a dominant position by nature and of cartel with a restriction of competition by object, makes their justification illusory.

B. *The Illusory Justification for Restrictions on Economic Freedoms*

44. Article 101 TFEU provides that, although in principle anticompetitive cartels are prohibited, they may nevertheless benefit from an exemption because the prohibition may be declared inapplicable if the undertakings demonstrate that the practice is ultimately beneficial to competition by satisfying four cumulative conditions: ie it contributes to improving production, distribution or promotes technical or economic progress, in a way that fairly benefits users, without imposing on the undertakings concerned unnecessary restrictions of competition and without giving them the possibility of eliminating competition in respect of a substantial part of the products in question.

45. Article 102 TFEU does not provide for such an exemption for abuse of a dominant position, but case law has accepted that the conduct may be justified by demonstrating either that it is objectively necessary or that it leads to efficiency gains that neutralise the harm to competition in the consumer's interest, without there being any alternative means that are less restrictive of competition and without completely eliminating actual or potential competition.[56]

46. Similarly, it follows in particular from the *Bosman*[57] and *Biffi*[58] judgments that non-state measures impeding freedom of movement may be permissible if they are justified by a legitimate objective in the general interest which is not purely economic and are proportionate to the attainment of that objective.[59]

47. As regards the justification for the abuse of a dominant position, the Court clearly held that "none of the specific attributes that characterise professional football makes it possible to consider as legitimate the adoption nor, a fortiori,

---

54 *ISU* (n 2), para 145.

55 *ESL* (n 1), para 176.

56 Case C-23/14 *Post Danmark A/S v Konkurrencerådet* ECLI:EU:C:2015:651, points 40 ff.

57 Case C-415/93 *Union Royale Belge Sociale de Football Association, RCL and UEFA v JM Bosman* ECLI:EU:C:1995:463, para 73, point 104.

58 *Biffi* (n 34), para 48.

59 *ESL* (n 1), para 251.

the implementation of rules on prior approval and participation which are, in a general way, not subject to restrictions, obligations and review that are capable of eliminating the risk of abuse of a dominant position".[60] In the Court's view, such rules have no objective justification and give the undertakings concerned the possibility of preventing competition on the market for the organisation and marketing of interclub football competitions within the territory of the European Union.[61]

48. For the latter reason, exemption from the cartel is not possible either,[62] and the argument can be transposed to the market for speed skating competitions.

49. Finally, as regards freedom of movement, the Court held that the objectives linked to the specific characteristics of professional football "are not capable of justifying the adoption of such rules where they do not include substantive criteria and detailed procedural rules suitable for ensuring that they are transparent, objective, precise and non-discriminatory".[63]

50. In addition to these general possibilities of justification. In certain cases, the courts have accepted that restrictions of competition may escape the prohibition on abuses of dominant positions and cartels if it can be justified that they are inherent and proportionate to the pursuit of an objective in the general interest. The *Meca-Medina* judgment inaugurated such reasoning in the field of sport.[64] The Court of Justice took advantage of the *ISU* and *ESL* cases to clarify the scope of this case law by ruling that it applies only to cartels with an anticompetitive effect and is therefore excluded for cartels with an anticompetitive object[65] and conduct which, by its very nature, infringes the prohibition on abuse of a dominant position.[66]

51. Finally, the regulatory powers of the federations will therefore necessarily have to be limited to be compatible with European law.

II. A Framework for the Sports Federations' Regulatory Powers

52. Allowing a sports federation to organise its own competitions and to hold, *de jure* or *de facto*, the power to authorise competing competitions and to lay down the conditions governing them places it in a situation of conflict of interests, since it might be tempted to use that power to oppose all competition or to favour its own competitions,[67] and enables it to impede freedom of movement, in particular by limiting the possibility for clubs or athletes to take part in such competitions.[68]

---

60 Ibid para 147.

61 Ibid paras 203 and 207.

62 Ibid para 199.

63 Ibid para 254.

64 Case C-519/04 P *David Meca-Medina and Igor Majcen v Commission of the European Communities* ECLI:EU:C:2006:492, para 31.

65 *ISU* (n 2), para 113; *ESL* (n 1), para 186. In the *ISU* case, the Court had finally applied the *Meca-Medina* jurisprudence to a competition restriction by object (para 77 ff.).

66 *ESL* (n 1), para 185.

67 *ISU* (n 2), paras 125, 131.

68 *ESL* (n 1), para 248.

The Court has thus made the compatibility of sports federations' regulatory powers with the competition rules and the freedoms of movement conditional on their being governed by "substantive criteria and detailed procedural rules suitable for ensuring that they are transparent, objective, non-discriminatory and proportionate".[69] In the *ISU* case, the Court added that the criteria must be verifiable so that the sports federation does not enjoy discretionary power[70] and required effective judicial review.

1. The Substantive and Procedural Limits of the Power

53. The Court requires the sports federation to limit its power of approval and sanction in terms of substantive criteria and procedural rules.[71]

A. *The Substantive Limits on Power*

54. The Court requires that the powers of prior approval of competitions and of control and sanction of the participation of athletes or clubs be limited by substantive criteria in order to avoid arbitrary use.[72] Since the justification for the rules on approval and participation and the associated sanctions lies in the specific features of the sport concerned,[73] it is these specific features that must logically make it possible to determine the material criteria. The Court's reasoning also calls for these criteria to be assessed on a sport-by-sport basis and not for sport in general,[74] even though, in reality, many specific features will be common to many sports.

55. The *Meca-Medina, ISU* and *ESL* cases provide an initial list of legitimate objectives that may be reflected in the criteria for approval and participation: fairness of competitions,[75] equal opportunities for participants,[76] objectivity of competitions,[77] athletes' health,[78] solidarity,[79] sporting merit,[80] openness[81] and coordination of competitions.[82]

56. Guaranteeing fair competitions and equal opportunities will justify requiring compliance with anti-doping rules and mechanisms[83] and "rules seeking to prevent sports betting from creating risks of manipulation of competitions and athletes".[84]

---

69 Ibid para 258.

70 *ISU* (n 2), para 137.

71 On the framework of a private law power see, Emmanuel Gaillard, *Le pouvoir en droit privé* (Economica 1985); Pascal Lokiec, *Contrat et pouvoir* (LGDJ 2004).

72 *ESL* (n 1), paras 135, 255; *ISU* (n 2), paras 131, 136.

73 cf. supra.

74 In this respect, *ESL* (n 1), para 143.

75 *ISU* (n 2), para 112; *ESL* (n 1), para 184.

76 *Meca-Medina* (n 64), para 43; *ESL* (n 1), para 254; *ISU* (n 2), para 132.

77 *Meca-Medina* (n 64), para 43.

78 Ibid.

79 *ESL* (n 1), para 253.

80 Ibid.

81 Ibid.

82 Ibid para 244; see also, *ISU* (n 7), para 97.

83 *Meca-Medina* (n 64), para 43.

84 *ISU* (n 7), para 102.

57. The guarantee of sporting merit will justify that "all the participating teams face each other in homogeneous regulatory and technical conditions, thereby ensuring a certain level of equal opportunity".[85]

58. The guarantee of fairness in the conduct of competitions and the protection of the physical and moral integrity of sportsmen and women will justify the requirement of compliance with "common standards".[86]

59. Solidarity will justify "ensuring a form of redistribution based on solidarity within [the sport in question]".[87] In the *ISU* case, the EU General Court accepted that third-party organisers could be required to pay a solidarity contribution, provided it not be used exclusively to finance the sports federation's competitions but also benefits competitions organised by third parties.[88]

60. The coordination of competitions will justify integration "in a substantively homogeneous and temporally coordinated manner, integrate into the 'organised system' of national, European and international competitions characterising" a sport,[89] in other words, compliance with rules designed "to guarantee the homogeneity and coordination of those competitions within an overall match calendar".[90]

61. To this list should certainly also be added possible criteria recognised as legitimate in other cases, such as, for example, the objective of "encouraging the recruitment and training of young players"[91] or the "dual objective of raising professional and ethical standards for the occupation of players" agent in order to protect players, who have a short career".[92]

62. In addition, the criteria must have certain characteristics: they must be "objective",[93] "proportionate",[94] "clearly defined",[95] "clear and precise",[96] "exhaustive",[97] "set out in an accessible form, prior to any implementation of the powers"[98] and "known in advance",[99] "transparent", "non-discriminatory"[100] and "verifiable".[101]

63. Generally speaking, they must be such as "to circumscribe the exercise of the discretion conferred thereby on the body empowered to grant or refuse that prior approval, so that that power is not used arbitrarily to circumscribe the exercise of the discretion conferred thereby on the body empowered to grant or refuse that

---

85 *ESL* (n 1), para 143.
86 *ISU* (n 7), para 108.
87 *ESL* (n 1), para 196.
88 *ISU* (n 7), para 114.
89 *ESL* (n 1), para 253.
90 Ibid para 144; see also, *ISU* (n 7), para 97.
91 Case C-325/08 *Olympique Lyonnais SASP v Olivier Bernard and Newcastle UFC* ECLI:EU:C:2010:143, point 39; see also, *Bosman* (n 57), para 106.
92 *Laurent Piau* (n 23), para 102 ff.
93 *ESL* (n 1), para 255.
94 Ibid para 257.
95 *ISU* (n 7), para 88.
96 *ISU* (n 2), para 131.
97 *ISU* (n 7), para 87.
98 *ISU* (n 2), para 131.
99 *ESL* (n 1), para 255.
100 Ibid.
101 *ISU* (n 2), para 137.

prior approval, so that that power is not used arbitrarily"[102] or "discretionary"[103] manner and "capable of ensuring the organisers of events effective access to the relevant market".[104]

64. The exhaustive and prior nature of the criteria is important. The Court has thus found that the rules on prior approval and eligibility may be anticompetitive by object independently of their application on a case-by-case basis.[105] In other words, the correctness of the decision cannot be established *a posteriori*. A refusal cannot therefore be based, *a posteriori*, on criteria that had not been defined and communicated before the application was submitted, even if they are legitimate. The Court criticised the ISU for having listed "a certain number of requirements of a general, technical, sporting and ethical nature", but indicated that it would make its decision "in particular" by taking these requirements into account and therefore not exclusively based on these requirements.[106]

65. For the criteria not to be discriminatory, the Court held that

> they must not subject the organisation and marketing of third-party competitions and the participation of athletes in those competitions to requirements that either differ from those applicable to competitions organised and marketed by the decision-making entity, or are identical or similar but impossible or excessively difficult to fulfil in practice by an undertaking that does not have the same status as an association or does not have the same powers at its disposal as that entity and which is therefore in a different situation to it.[107]

66. Focusing particularly on the criteria for determining penalties, the Court ruled that they must ensure that penalties are "objective" and that "they are determined, in each specific case, in accordance with the principle of proportionality taking into account, in particular, the nature, duration and severity of the infringement found".[108]

67. The EU General Court criticised the ISU for having laid down rules that "do not precisely set out the conditions that allow the dividing line between different categories of infringements to be determined" and particularly for "not clearly distinguish infringements deemed to be "very serious" from those which are not".[109] The penalty system must be predictable and exclude the risk of arbitrariness.[110]

68. To ensure that penalties are proportionate, the Court also specified that they must take account of whether the offence is "a first or repeated infringement".[111] It also requires the impact of sanctions to be considered. In the *ISU* case, for

---

102 *ESL* (n 1), para 255.
103 Ibid para 151.
104 *ISU* (n 7), para 88.
105 *ISU* (n 2), para 156.
106 *ISU* (n 7), para 87.
107 *ISU* (n 2), para 133.
108 Ibid.
109 *ISU* (n 7), para 94.
110 Ibid.
111 Ibid para 92.

example, it ruled that a permanent exclusion due to participation in an unauthorised competition was disproportionate, as were temporary exclusions of five or ten years, given that "the average length of a skater"s career is eight years".[112] Substantial supervision of the sports federations" powers must also be backed up by procedural supervision.

B. *The Procedural Framework of the Power*

69. The Court held that

> the powers [...] must be subject to transparent and non-discriminatory detailed procedural rules, such as those relating to the applicable time limits for submitting a prior authorisation request and the adoption of a decision on that request, which are not likely to be to the detriment of potentially competing undertakings by preventing them from effectively accessing the market.[113]

70. Transparency should lead to the requirement for a clear and accessible authorisation procedure with identification of the body of the sports federation competent to make the decision and all the procedures for submitting the application, clearly: to whom it should be sent, in what form, what documents to provide, etc.

71. The authorisation procedure should not require the communication of unnecessary or disproportionate information in order to assess whether the authorisation criteria have been met. For example, the EU General Court ruled that it was legitimate to request information to ensure that the organiser had the means to organise the competition and meet its various obligations (fairness, integrity, etc.), but that the requirement for a "business plan as a whole" was disproportionate, as a simple "planned budget" was sufficient to assess the organiser's financial capacity.[114]

72. The procedure will also have to include a precise deadline for examination, without which the sports federation could never make a decision and thus, *de facto*, hinder the organisation of competitions by third-party operators.

73. Finally, the procedure must be non-discriminatory. This was not the case in the *ISU* case, where the sports federation required its members to submit an application three months before the event, whereas the deadline for third-party operators was twice as long (six months before the competition).[115] In order to ensure that the procedural and substantive limits of the power are respected, judicial review must be possible.

2. Judicial Review of the Power

74. In order not to constitute anticompetitive practices, the Court ruled in *ISU* that the authorisation and eligibility criteria must be "capable of being subject to effective review"[116] and assessed whether the arbitration clause in favour of CAS led

112 Ibid para 93.

113 *ISU* (n 2), para 135.

114 *ISU* (n 7), para 110.

115 Ibid paras 93, 110.

116 *ISU* (n 2), paras 127, 134, 137.

to effective judicial review.[117] Although not mentioned in the *ESL* judgment, the reasoning is transposable, as the FIFA and UEFA statutes also require recourse to CAS.[118] This leads the Court to accept the possibility of review by an arbitral tribunal, provided that an appeal is possible before a court of a European Union Member State.

A. *The Possible Review by an Arbitral Tribunal*

75. In the *ISU* case, the European Commission took the view that, although the conclusion of an arbitration clause did not in itself constitute a restriction of competition, in this case it reinforced the restrictions of competition because the athletes were obliged to accept the clause in favour of CAS in order to take part in ISU competitions and thus to exercise their profession, which made it more difficult for them to obtain effective judicial protection against any ineligibility decisions that were contrary to competition law.[119]

76. This analysis was challenged by the EU General Court, which found that exclusive recourse to CAS could be "justified by legitimate interests linked to the specific nature of the sport"[120] and that the full effectiveness of European competition law was ensured by the possibility of bringing an action before a Member State court for compensation for the damage caused by the anticompetitive practice and by lodging a complaint before a competition authority, whose decision could then be appealed before the courts of the European Union.[121]

77. The Court pointed out that sports federations have "legal autonomy entitling them to adopt rules relating, inter alia to the organisation of competitions, their proper functioning and the participation of athletes in those competitions"[122] and recognises

> that an individual may enter into an agreement that subjects, in clear and precise wording, all or part of any disputes relating to it to an arbitration body in place of the national court that would have had jurisdiction to rule on those disputes under the applicable national law, and that the requirements relating to the effectiveness of the arbitration proceedings may justify the judicial review of arbitral awards being limited.[123]

78. In so doing, it endorsed the position of the European Court of Human Rights, which had ruled that "it is certainly of interest for the settlement of disputes arising in a professional sports context, especially those with an international dimension, to refer them to a specialised body which is able to give a ruling swiftly and inexpensively" and that, in the context of international sporting competitions organised in different countries, by organisations headquartered in different States and open

---

117 Ibid para 188 ff.

118 cf. supra.

119 Decision *ISU* (n 6), para 268; *ISU* (n 7), para 35 ff.

120 *ISU* (n 7), para 156.

121 Ibid para 157.

122 *ISU* (n 2), para 196.

123 Ibid para 193.

to athletes from all over the world, "recourse to a single specialised international arbitral tribunal facilitates a certain procedural uniformity and strengthens legal certainty", this being "all the more so where the awards of that tribunal may be appealed against before the supreme court of a single country, in this case the Swiss Federal Court, whose ruling is final".[124]

79. The CJEU does not in any way call into question the possibility of submitting sports disputes to a specialised arbitration court, even "forcibly", as the European Court of Human Rights puts it.[125] On the other hand, it sets limits, relating to the location of this arbitration court in a third state and to the extent of the judicial review of awards that this entails. It ruled that by imposing recourse to CAS, sports associations "cannot […] limit the exercise of rights and freedoms conferred on individuals by EU law […] which include the rights that underlie [competition rules]"[126] and specified that "judicial review must, in any event, be able to cover the question whether those awards comply with the fundamental provisions that are a matter of EU public policy […] particularly […] when such an arbitration mechanism must be regarded as being, in practice, imposed by a person governed by private law, such as an international sports association, on another, such as an athlete".[127] The Court"s position leads it to require the possibility of an action before a court in a Member State of the European Union if the Union's rules of public policy are affected.

B. *The Need for a Review by a European Union Member State Court*

80. Since the competition rules form part of the public policy of the Union and may be relied on by European citizens by reason of the direct effect of European law, the Court held that "requirement of effective judicial review means that, in the event that such rules contain provisions conferring mandatory and exclusive jurisdiction on an arbitration body, the court having jurisdiction to review the awards made by that body may confirm that those awards comply with [European competition rules]" and

> that court's satisfying all the requirements under Article 267 TFEU, so that it is entitled, or, as the case may be, required, to refer a question to the Court of Justice where it considers that a decision of the Court is necessary concerning a matter of EU law raised in a case pending before it."[128] However, the Court found that the ISU rules "subject the review of the arbitral awards made by the CAS and the last-instance review of decisions of the ISU to the Tribunal fédéral (Federal Supreme Court), that is to say, a court of a third State.[129]

81. Indeed, recourse to CAS leads to the exclusion of any judicial review of the violation of European competition rules, which are nonetheless part of European public policy.

---

124 Case 40575/10 *Mutu and Pechstein v Switzerland* (2 October 2018), points 95 ff, point 98.

125 Ibid para 95 ff.

126 *ISU* (n 2), para 196.

127 Ibid para 193.

128 Ibid para 198.

129 Ibid para 191.

82. First of all, CAS is under no obligation to include European competition rules in its review standards, even if they are European public policy rules.[130] This is particularly true when the law chosen by the parties is not that of a Member State of the European Union, following the example of the arbitration clause in FIFA's statutes, which provides that "CAS shall primarily apply the various regulations of FIFA and, additionally, Swiss law".[131] More generally, CAS seeks to establish a *lex sportiva*,[132] detached as far as possible from state law, and has thus ruled that "internal State rules that are contrary to the principles and legal framework of the rules that FIFA aims to establish should be disregarded. In the specific field of sports law, it is important to be able to have recourse to rules that transcend any particular State system" and that "this possibility of developing rules that are as free as possible from any reference to a particular system of State rules meets a specific need arising from the organisation of sport".[133]

83. Second, as the Court points out, adopting the Commission's reasoning, CAS awards are subject to review by the Swiss Federal Tribunal, its supporting court, which is not required to rule on the question of "whether they comply with the public policy provisions of Articles 101 and 102 TFEU" and, being outside the EU's judicial system, is not entitled to refer a question on that subject for a preliminary ruling.[134] However, as regards the substance of the award, the examination is limited to the compatibility of the solution with Swiss public policy,[135] which therefore does not include European competition rules.

84. Furthermore, as the Court points out, repeating the European Commission's findings, because of the arbitration clause, organisers of competitions who receive a decision refusing prior authorisation and athletes who are the subject of an ineligibility decision cannot seek protective measures before CAS (because it is not obliged to enforce European competition law) or before a national court that would have to deal with the enforcement of the award considering that, in any event, enforcement can be carried out by the international sports federation and its member national associations, without the need for intervention by a national court.[136] The analysis can be transposed to FIFA, since the arbitration rules of its statutes provide that "recourse to ordinary courts of law for all types of provisional measures is also prohibited"[137] and impose disciplinary sanctions on parties who fail to comply with a CAS award,[138] thus making it unnecessary to resort to an exequatur procedure, which would nevertheless lead

---

130 But it sometimes still does so: Case 2016/A/4490 CAS Decision *Royal Football Club Seraing SA v FIFA* (9 March 2017).

131 FIFA Statutes (2022), art 56.1.

132 On this question see, Franck Latty, *La lex sportiva. Recherche sur le droit transnational* (Brill Nijhoff 2007); Legendre (n 18).

133 Case 2012/A/2862 CAS Decision *Girondins de Bordeaux FC v FIFA* (11 January 2013).

134 *ISU* (n 2), para 223.

135 cf. supra.

136 *ISU* (n 2), para 224.

137 FIFA Statutes (2022), art 58.2.

138 Ibid art 14.1(a) stipulates that: "Member associations have the following obligations: (a) to comply fully with the Statutes, regulations, directives and decisions of FIFA bodies at any time as well as the decisions of the Court of Arbitration for Sport (CAS) passed on appeal on the basis of art 56, para 1 of the FIFA Statutes

to an assessment of the award's manifest conflict with the international public policy of a Member State.[139]

85. Finally, the Court, replying to the EU General Court, held that an action for damages before a national court does not ensure the full effectiveness of European competition law because it "cannot compensate for the lack of a remedy entitling that person to bring an action before the relevant national court seeking, as appropriate following the grant of protective measures, to have that conduct brought to an end, or where it constitutes a measure, the review and annulment of that measure, if necessary following a prior arbitration procedure carried out under an agreement that provides for such a procedure" and that "the same applies to persons practising professional sport, whose career may be especially short, in particular where they practise that sport at a high level".[140] It adds that the same applies to the possibility of lodging a complaint with a European competition authority, and in particular with the Commission, because the person lodging the complaint cannot require the Commission to make a final decision on the existence or non-existence of an infringement.[141]

86. Consequently, the arbitration clause in favour of CAS does not meet the requirement of effective judicial review of decisions refusing prior authorisation to organise a competition or imposing sanctions for participation in an unauthorised competition. The CAS arbitration system thus appears insufficient to comply with the requirements of competition law and exposes the sports federations to condemnation for abuse of dominant position or anticompetitive cartel. In this respect, the *ISU* ruling risks causing a major upheaval in the jurisdictional organisation put in place by the international sports movement.

87. Solutions will therefore need to be found by the sports federations and, in particular, in the short term, by the ISU since, following the partial annulment of the decision of the Court of the European Union, the injunction under penalty payment that the European Commission had made to the ISU to amend the arbitration rules in such a way as to ensure effective control of the decisions taken at the end of the prior authorisation and sanction procedures is no longer annulled.[142]

88. The solution of incorporating European competition rules into the Swiss Federal Tribunal's rules of review is difficult to envisage. This is because, unless Switzerland joins the European Union, the Federal Tribunal is not required to apply these rules, it is not one of the European courts that can apply European competition law, and it cannot refer a question to the Court of Justice for a preliminary ruling.

89. If sports federations wish to retain the benefits of recourse to an arbitration institution specialising in sport, they will have to locate the arbitrations in a

---

[…]". In addition, it is stipulated (art 58) that: "The associations shall impose sanctions on any party that fails to respect this obligation and ensure that any appeal against such sanctions shall likewise be strictly submitted to arbitration, and not to ordinary courts of law."

139 French Code of Civil Procedure, art 1488, para 1: "Exequatur cannot be granted if the award is manifestly contrary to public policy" (translated from French).

140 *ISU* (n 2), para 201.

141 Ibid para 203.

142 Ibid paras 33, 237.

Member State of the European Union. Appeals against awards will no longer be lodged with the Swiss Federal Tribunal, but with an EU court. However, the law governing the arbitration (and not the merits of the dispute) will no longer be Swiss law but the law of that state, and the merits of the awards will no longer be subject to Swiss international public policy but to the international public policy of that state, and the rules of EU public policy could no longer be disregarded. This could put off the sports federations, as Switzerland was chosen as the seat of CAS because of the particularly liberal nature of its international arbitration law and, more generally, of its laws on associations.

90. Transferring the seat of CAS to a Member State would obviously be one solution. The creation of a delocalised chamber in a Member State could also be envisaged only for arbitrations involving European competition rules and, more generally, rules of European public policy. However, relocation could be very important because the scope of European competition law is very broad since, as the Court of Justice points out, "only certain specific rules which were adopted solely on non-economic grounds and which relate to questions of interest solely to sport per se must be regarded as being extraneous to any economic activity".[143] These rules include "those on the exclusion of foreign players from the composition of teams participating in competitions between teams representing their country or the determination of ranking criteria used to select the athletes participating individually in competitions",[144] but many others do not meet these criteria. For example, in the *Meca-Medina* case, the anti-doping rules were analysed as falling within the scope of an economic activity because they raised barriers to entry to the sports competition market.[145] However, the territorial scope of European competition law goes beyond that of the European Union.[146] In the *ISU* case, the UE General Court recalled that the European Commission was competent to establish and sanction a behaviour adopted outside the European Union on the basis of the criterion of implementation (place where the conduct complained of was implemented) or the criterion of qualified effects (the behaviour is likely to produce immediate, substantial and foreseeable effects on the territory of the European Union).[147] The latter criterion makes it relatively easy to apply European competition law, since the regulations of international sports federations are intended to apply to all competitions and all participants in the sports in question. As a result, it will very often be possible to characterise an effect on the territory of the European Union either because a competition is being held there or cannot be held there because of these regulations, or because European sporting entities or sportsmen and women are taking part or are likely to take part. In the *ISU* case, it was applied to the rules of a Swiss association, which opposed

143 *ESL* (n 1), para 84; *ISU* (n 2), para 189.

144 Ibid para 84; Ibid para 92.

145 *Meca-Medina* (n 64), para 22 ff.

146 On this question see, Evelyne Friedel-Souchu, *Extraterritorialité du droit de la concurrence aux États-Unis et dans la Communauté européenne* (LGDJ 1994).

147 *ISU* (n 7), para 124 ff.

the participation of European skaters in a competition taking place in Dubai. In addition, the criterion of appreciable effect on trade between Member States, which is a condition for the applicability of European competition law,[148] is widely[149] and fairly easily considered to be met in the case of the practices of international sports federations.[150]

148 Articles 101 and 102 TFEU and European Commission, Guidelines on the effect on trade concept contained in Articles 81 and 82 of the Treaty [2004] OJ C101/81.

149 Frison-Roche and Roda (n 28).

150 Legendre (n 18); Antoine Duval, "La lex sportiva face au Droit de l'Union européenne: Guerre et Paix dans l'Espace Juridique Transnational" (DPhil thesis, European University Institute 2015), 98 ff.

Exclusivity in Sports – Beneficial or Harmful to Competition?

Benoît Durand and George Tucker*
RBB Economics, London

I. Introduction

1. Exclusive dealing arrangements have long attracted suspicion under competition law. Where a dominant firm conditions access to its platform, product, or ecosystem on a buyer or supplier foregoing dealings with rivals, competition authorities and courts have frequently treated such conduct as an abuse of dominance – a mechanism by which market power is entrenched rather than earned. The underlying concern is straightforward: exclusivity imposed by a firm with significant market power can deny rivals the critical mass they need to survive, foreclosing competition not on the merits but through structural lock-in.

2. Yet the application of this framework to professional sport is considerably more complex than in conventional markets. Exclusivity in sport does not operate at a single level. It arises in the relationship between agents and their clients, between academies and the young players they develop, and – most contentiously – between league organisers and the clubs, athletes and tournaments that constitute the competitive ecosystem. At each of these layers, the economic rationale for exclusivity differs, and the risk of competitive harm varies accordingly.

---

* Both authors are economists at RBB Economics. The views expressed in this article are those of the authors in their personal capacity and do not represent the views of RBB Economics, its partners, or any of its clients. Nothing in this article should be taken to reflect the position of RBB Economics on any matter of competition law or policy.

3. Arguably the most controversial layer is also the most economically significant: the exclusivity enforced by sports leagues and governing bodies over participation in their competitions. Sports leagues occupy a structurally unusual position. They are, almost by definition, monopolists. In most jurisdictions and most disciplines, there is only one credible organiser of elite competition – one league that controls access to the fixtures, rankings, broadcast rights and prize structures that define a professional career. When such an organiser conditions participation in its competitions on a commitment not to compete in rival events, it is deploying the tools of exclusive dealing from a position of considerable, often unchallengeable, market power. It is therefore unsurprising that this layer of sports exclusivity has become the primary battleground of modern competition enforcement, attracting challenges across football, tennis, golf, ice-skating, basketball, cricket and padel, among others.

4. This chapter examines the economics of sports exclusivity with the aim of providing practitioners with a rigorous framework for assessing when such arrangements cross the line from legitimate governance into anticompetitive foreclosure. We argue that the analysis cannot be reduced to a simple presumption in either direction. On one hand, the post-Chicago economic literature demonstrates that dominant incumbents can and do use exclusivity strategically to deny rivals the minimum efficient scale required to compete, exploiting coordination failures among participants and imposing switching costs that have nothing to do with merit. On the other hand, the "peculiar economics" of professional sport mean that a degree of exclusivity may be indispensable to the very existence of a coherent, high-quality competitive product – protecting title integrity, concentrating elite talent, sustaining financial solidarity and preserving the meritocratic pyramid that underpins the "European sports model".

5. The challenge for competition practitioners is therefore not to ask whether exclusivity exists, but to assess whether a specific arrangement is proportionate to a legitimate sporting objective or whether it serves primarily to insulate a dominant incumbent from the competitive pressure of a more innovative or efficient rival. That assessment requires a careful, case-by-case analysis grounded in the economic realities of each sport. Critically, however, such an analysis must not treat efficiency justifications as merely theoretical counterweights to be mechanically balanced against theories of harm. In many sporting contexts, proponents argue that exclusivity is not simply one way of delivering a high-quality product – it may be the only way. Where the value of a competition depends on the concentration of elite talent, the integrity of a single undisputed title and the preservation of a solidarity-based ecosystem, exclusivity is not incidental to the product. It is constitutive of it.

II. The Multiple Layers of Exclusivity in Sports

6. To understand the nuances of exclusivity in sports, one must first distinguish between restrictions that seek only to stifle competition and those designed to address specific market failures. Not all exclusivity arrangements in sport are created equal, and, importantly, the effect can be different depending on the layer at which a given restriction operates.

7. A first example – which would seem relatively unlikely to raise serious competition concerns – is found in the FIFA Football Agent Regulations. Specifically, the regulations prohibit "multiple representation", ie they prevent an agent from representing both the selling club and the buying club, or both the player and the club, in a single transaction transferring a player between clubs. Thus, the regulations restrict the scope of an agent's activities.

8. From an economic perspective, this can be seen as a targeted response to a classic principal–agent problem which is exacerbated by asymmetric information between the parties involved in a transfer negotiation (players, clubs and agents). An agent attempting to serve two (or more) principals in the same negotiation with essentially opposing interests faces an inherent conflict of interest, given that they cannot act in the best interests of both such parties at the same time. This, coupled with the additional information available to the agent compared to the player and/or club(s), can lead to opportunistic behaviour on the part of the agent, who can maximise their own gains from the transfer at the expense of the best interests of those they purport to represent.

9. While the restriction on multiple representation limits the agent's freedom to contract, it nevertheless reduces the scope for agents to take advantage of their principals. In doing so, it reduces transaction costs associated with distrust and information leakage, thereby protecting the users of agents' services. Therefore, this restraint likely enhances, rather than hinders, the efficiency of the transfer system.

10. A second, perhaps more complex, layer of exclusivity concerns the development of human capital in the form of training future professional footballers. Youth players typically must be nurtured in professional football academies in order to reach their full potential as professional players. This activity represents a significant sunk cost for clubs, given that it is a high-risk investment in future talent that may not bear fruit for many years, if at all. From an economic perspective, this creates a classic hold-up problem. Because the skills acquired by a young player are highly portable, rival clubs have an incentive to free ride on the training investments of other clubs by poaching talent at the moment of peak development, ie after significant investment has been made in developing the player, but before it has begun to bear fruit for the investing club.

11. To mitigate the negative effects of such opportunistic behaviour, regulatory frameworks often permit a degree of exclusivity, such as the requirement for players to sign their initial professional contracts with their home academy.[1] While this restricts a player's immediate mobility, it serves an essential efficiency purpose: it ensures that clubs can reap the returns on their investment in developing players. Without such protections, the incentive to invest in youth development would diminish, leading to a sub-optimal supply of footballing talent and harming the long-term competitiveness of the sport.

12. These two examples share a common analytical structure: in each case, exclusivity is a targeted response to a clearly identified market failure. In each case,

---

1 See for example, FIFA, Regulations on the Status and Transfer of Players, clause 18.2, (February 2024), <https://digitalhub.fifa.com/m/6a0797ec77cbc02c/original/Regulations-on-the-Status-and-Transfer-of-Players-February-2024-edition.pdf> accessed 13 May 2026.

a proportionate restriction, with readily identifiable benefits and beneficiaries, gives rise to an obvious efficiency rationale.

13. Perhaps the most complex and contentious application of exclusivity in sport operates at an altogether different level: the conditions imposed by league organisers and governing bodies on participation in their competitions. Here, the stakes are higher, the market failures less clearly defined, and the potential for strategic foreclosure considerably greater. On the one hand, such constraints may be seen as anticompetitive, given that they neutralise the threat of a rival league, which may be a powerful driver of innovation by forcing incumbents to evolve their formats and improve the quality of the product for fans. On the other hand, such restraints may seek to resolve market failures, given that a sports league is a joint-venture product that may require not only coordination but exclusivity to generate the highest-quality product – for instance by sustaining a "pyramid" style of competition that seeks to optimise both commercial value and a solidarity-based redistribution model on which the wider sporting ecosystem depends. It is this layer of exclusivity that has become a central battleground of competition enforcement in sport, and to which the remainder of this chapter is principally addressed.

III. Challenging the Incumbent: The Growing Antitrust Assault on Sports League Exclusivity

14. The debate over the exclusivity of professional sports competitions has become a widespread battleground of modern sports. For decades, incumbent league organisers and governing bodies operated with a degree of autonomy that has largely shielded their exclusivity arrangements from scrutiny. However, we are now witnessing a widespread challenge to these structures, as new entrants have increasingly relied on European competition law to challenge exclusivity arrangements imposed by incumbent organisers.[2] These challenges test a fundamental economic question: under what conditions can an incumbent "lock in" its participants to the benefit, rather than detriment, of consumers?

15. Recent examples of such exclusivity are widespread, and include the following:
    - *Football*: the CJEU ruled on the FIFA and UEFA prior-authorisation rules, which prevented clubs and players from participating in the European Super League (ESL), a potential new entrant tournament.[3] While the project was eventually abandoned in February 2026 following a landmark agreement between the parties, the case established that governing bodies cannot exercise unfettered discretion to block rival tournaments without transparent and objective criteria.[4]

---

2 See for example "Competition Law and Sports – A New Era for Sports Regulation?" (11 September 2024) Hausfeld Competition Bulletin <https://www.hausfeld.com/en-gb/what-we-think/competition-bulletin/competition-law-and-sports-a-new-era-for-sports-regulation> accessed 13 May 2026.

3 Including those either organised by UEFA directly (eg the Champions League) or indirectly by UEFA's sister organisations (including domestic European leagues and the FIFA World Cup). See Case C-333/21 *European Super League (ESL)* ECLI:EU:C:2023:1011, para 30.

4 Ibid para 151.

- *Ice-skating*: in a seminal decision of the CJEU, the International Skating Union (ISU), the governing body of speed and figure ice-skating, and incumbent organiser of speed ice-skating tournaments, was found to have breached competition law by threatening lifetime bans for athletes participating in unauthorised events like Icederby.[5] The ISU justified this on the basis of protecting the sport's integrity (eg against illegal betting), athlete health and safety, the pyramid structure of the sport, the good functioning of the sporting calendar and solidarity with grassroots sport, among others, although these arguments were rejected in this case by the EC (a finding which went unchallenged by ISU in appeals to the CJEU).[6,7] This case is cited in subsequent disputes as establishing that eligibility rules imposed by governing bodies must satisfy objective justification criteria and cannot be based solely on the protection of commercial interests.[8]
- *Horse riding*: the Fédération Equestre Internationale (FEI), the international governing body for Olympic horse riding, faced similar scrutiny for its "six-month" and "12-month" clauses, which restricted riders from participating in non-FEI events (notably the Global Champions League). That was justified on the basis of, inter alia, protecting horse welfare. The Belgian Competition Authority investigated following a complaint by a rival tournament but closed the investigation without finding on the merits of the restrictions, following the complaint being withdrawn once the rival and the FEI reached a settlement. This resulted in a settlement that loosened the exclusivity requirements.[9]
- *Golf*: the PGA Tour and DP World Tour (PGA Europe) have faced a series of challenges regarding their treatment of players joining LIV Golf. While high-profile mergers and settlements have shifted the landscape, the core economic question remains whether a tour can legally penalise "contractual disloyalty" when a player seeks to participate in a rival, innovative format.[10]
- *Tennis*: the Professional Tennis Players Association (PTPA) – which secured an early-stage settlement with Tennis Australia in January 2026 – continues to challenge the allegedly cartel-like structure of the ATP, WTA,

---

5 Case AT.40208 European Commission Decision *International Skating Union's Eligibility* (8 December 2017) (*ISU* Decision). Also, Case C-124/21 P *International Skating Union (ISU)* ECLI:EU:C:2023:1012, para 15.

6 *ISU* Decision, paras 213–216.

7 Ibid para 90.

8 See for example *ESL* (n 3), para 38.

9 Lauran Donellan, "Equestrianism: FEI and the Global Champions League Settle Long-Standing Legal Action over Unsanctioned Events" (30 January 2017) Sports Law & Taxation <https://sportslawandtaxation.com/news/650-equestrianism-fei-and-the-global-champions-league-settle-long-standing-legal-action-over-unsanctioned-events> accessed 13 May 2026.

10 See the arbitration case Sport Resolutions, SR/165/2022. This also resulted in lawsuits by LIV Golf alleging anticompetitive conduct on the part of PGA Tour. These were settled when the two announced a potential merger. The US Department of Justice opened a competition investigation into this conduct and is reported to be investigating the merger. See Case SR/165/2022 SR Decision *Golfers v PGA European Tour* (3 April 2023) <https://sportslitigationalert.com/from-enemies-to-partners-liv-golf-and-pga-tour-resolve-antitrust-lawsuit-through-merger/#:~:text=In%20response%2C%20a%20group%20of,the%20market%20for%20professional%20golf> accessed 13 May 2026.

and Grand Slams.[11] The central allegation is that the calendar and ranking system create a de facto exclusivity that forecloses new entrants. This is allegedly because tennis players do not have time to play in rivals' tournaments and may be fined for doing so.[12]

- *Snooker*: the NST Worldwide claim currently before the UK Competition Appeal Tribunal (CAT) alleges that the World Snooker Association has used its dominant position to prevent top players from appearing in rival tournaments.[13]
- *Basketball*: in the UK, Super League Basketball (SLB) has taken the British Basketball Federation (BBF) to the High Court. This case is particularly notable for its focus on "non-price" barriers to entry: SLB alleges the BBF used its role as the national visa-endorsing body to block foreign players from joining the new league, effectively using regulatory power to favour a preferred incumbent.[14]
- *Padel*: the governing body for padel, the Federación Internacional de Pádel (FIP) complained to the EC that it could not start a new tournament because the top players are locked in to playing in rival events run by the World Padel Tour. The latter threatened to fine players playing in tournaments organised by other entities, including the governing body.[15]
- *Swimming*: the Federation Internationale de Natation (FINA), swimming's global governing body, allegedly urged its member national federations (and their affiliated swimmers) to boycott tournaments organised by a new entrant, the International Swimming League (ISL). This, it is claimed, hampered ISL's ability to compete. A US court judgement found, however, that this did not constitute a significant enough barrier to prevent ISL from competing effectively.[16]
- *Cricket*: the England and Wales Cricket Board (ECB) has faced questions over its refusal to grant: "no objection certificates" for players seeking

11 Dhwanil Shah, "Tennis Australia Breaks Free from the Pack by Settling in Pro Tennis Antitrust Litigation" (*Sports Litigation Alert*, 6 March 2026) <https://sportslitigationalert.com/tennis-australia-breaks-free-from-the-pack-by-settling-in-pro-tennis-antitrust-litigation/> accessed 13 May 2026.

12 PTPA, Antitrust Complaint s III.D (18 March 2025) <https://ptpaplayers.com/wp-content/uploads/2025/03/PTPA-UK-Complaint-18-March-2025.pdf> accessed 13 May 2026. A similar lawsuit has been launched in the US (see Rachel Reed, "Is an Antitrust Suit against Top Tennis Organizations a Grand Slam – or an Unforced Error?" *Harvard Law Today* (18 June 2025) <https://hls.harvard.edu/today/is-an-antitrust-suit-against-top-tennis-organizations-a-grand-slam-or-an-unforced-error/> accessed 13 May 2026).

13 See a summary of the claim here: Case CAT 1701/5/7/25 *NST Worldwide Limited v World Snooker Limited and others* (8 January 2025) <https://www.catribunal.org.uk/cases/17015725-nst-worldwide-limited> accessed 13 May 2026.

14 SLB, "Superleague Basketball Statement" *SLB* (1 August 2025) <https://www.superleaguebasketballm.co.uk/super-league-basketball-statement-3/> accessed 13 May 2026.

15 As reported here, MLex <https://content.mlex.com/#/content/1361412/boom-in-padel-racket-sport-triggers-eu-antitrust-complaint-over-rival-tour?referrer=portfolio_openrelatedcontent>. The complaint and related lawsuits were dropped in favour of a merger between the two entities, as reported here, MLex <https://content.mlex.com/#/content/1495126/padel-s-eu-antitrust-fight-ends-as-sport-organizers-merge?referrer=portfolio_openrelatedcontent>.

16 Cases (Case No. 18-cv-07393-JSC, Dkt. No. 100.) and (Case No. 18-cv-07394-JSC, Dkt. No. 100.), notably at 11–15 <https://www.govinfo.gov/content/pkg/USCOURTS-cand-3_18-cv-07393/pdf/USCOURTS-cand-3_18-cv-07393-22.pdf> accessed 13 May 2026.

to play in overseas leagues (like the PSL) that overlap with the domestic calendar – justified by "integrity" and "player welfare" but arguably serving as a temporal exclusivity restraint.[17]

– *Rugby Union*: nine of Rugby Union's ten top-tier nations announced that players who play in a mooted new entrant rugby tournament, Rugby 360, would find themselves ineligible for selection for international matches. This was justified on the basis that the new tournament would hollow out solidarity payments and the need to manage the calendar.[18]

IV. The Economic Framework: Balancing Efficiency and Harm

16. To assess whether exclusivity in sports is pro- or anticompetitive, one must first locate the conduct within the broader economic theory of vertical restraints.

17. Importantly, it is well established that exclusivity can improve economic welfare. For example, as explained by Motta, situations can arise where an upstream producer can invest in a downstream retailer in order to improve the retail experience, and thereby increase sales of the product.[19] For example, a product may be complex, and retail sales staff may need training in order to sell the product effectively. This gives rise to a risk, however, that the producer will invest in the retailer, but the retailer will use the resulting improvement in its service quality to sell other producers' products. Faced with this risk, the producer will invest less than is optimal.

18. An exclusivity clause ensuring that the retailer sells only the investing producer's products would ensure that any investment made by the producer is directed toward selling their products alone. Therefore, this would ensure that the producer reaps the full benefit of its investment. In turn, this ensures that investments are at optimal levels, improving the retail experience and ultimately benefitting consumers.

19. Indeed, the example given in Section II above of exclusivity clauses ensuring that players play for the teams of their home academies addresses the same underlying economic issue. Namely, that exclusivity is designed to ensure that the returns on investments in developing players are reaped by those clubs that make the investment, which in turn improves the level of investment in player development.

---

17 As far as we are aware this has not been officially reported by the ECB, but is widely reported in news outlets, where the ECB's Chief Executive has been quoted. For example, "England to Ban Players from PSL, Other Non-IPL Leagues over Domestic Season Clash – Report" (*Wisden*, 29 November 2024) <https://www.wisden.com/series/hbl-pakistan-super-league/cricket-news/england-to-ban-players-from-psl-other-non-ipl-leagues-over-domestic-clash-report#:~:text=%E2%80%9CWe%20need%20to%20protect%20the,to%20issuing%20No%20Objection%20Certificates> accessed 13 May 2026.

18 Eight nations signed a joint press release IRFU, Press Release, "Statement on Proposed R360 Competition" (7 October 2025) <https://www.irishrugby.ie/2025/10/07/statement-on-proposed-r360-competition/> accessed 13 May 2026. Wales, not included in the eight signing the joint press release, made a separate announcement to the same effect. See "Rugby's Rebel League Explained: Everything You Need to Know About R360" (*ESPN*, 15 October 2025) <https://www.espn.co.uk/rugby/story/_/id/45759462/rugby-rebel-league-explained-everything-need-know-r360> accessed 13 May 2026.

19 Massimo Motta, *Competition Policy: Theory and Practice* (2004) ch 6.

20. Consequently, any economic assessment of an exclusivity clause must consider the potential for, and indeed likelihood of, improving economic efficiency.

21. The prospect of improved efficiency must, however, be weighed against the potential for exclusivity to harm consumers. Classically, that is posited to come about through the mechanism illustrated by the following example. Imagine a market with one dominant brewer – BrewCo – supplying 80% of all beer sold in a country. A new entrant, CraftBrew, wants to enter with a better and cheaper product. To reach consumers, both brewers need access to the same network of pubs and bars.

22. Suppose that CraftBrew needs access to at least 40% of the pub network to cover its fixed costs – brewing equipment, distribution and marketing – and to build a credible brand presence. Call this its minimum efficient scale. Suppose that BrewCo approaches the major pub chains and offers them an attractive discount on kegs, on the condition that they stock BrewCo products exclusively. If BrewCo locks up 70% of pubs, CraftBrew has access to only 30% of the network – below its minimum efficient scale. It cannot cover its fixed costs nor build a viable business and is foreclosed from the market. In this example, consumers are likely to be harmed through the exclusivity agreements because they are denied a better beer.

23. There are however several important limitations to this theory of harm which need to be addressed in order to make it robust. First, and most obviously, the market coverage of the exclusivity clauses is a pivotal variable. If instead BrewCo were only to lock up 10% of pubs, CraftBrew would retain access to 90% of the network. This would be well above its minimum efficient scale of 40%. In this scenario no foreclosure concern arises, and the exclusive deals cause no material harm.

24. Second, the market power and market presence of the firm imposing exclusivity is critically important. If BrewCo supplied a much smaller proportion of beer sold in the country, say 10%, then the prospect of BrewCo locking up sufficient pubs to deny CraftBrew efficient scale is effectively negligible.

25. Indeed, following this logic, the consensus in modern industrial organisation is that when the firm imposing exclusivity does not have market power, it can be assumed that the exclusivity clause has no prospect of causing harm, and thus is likely to improve economic efficiency.[20] Therefore, the economist's first inquiry in any assessment of an exclusivity provision is the degree of market power of the firm imposing such exclusivity arrangements.

26. Third, and importantly, the Chicago School (led by figures like Robert Bork and Richard Posner) famously challenged the hostility toward exclusivity even when imposed by a monopoly firm – ie one with, by definition, significant market power. According to them, a dominant firm – even a monopolist – can only extract a single "monopoly rent" from its customers. Therefore, it has no rational incentive to impose an exclusive contract that is *inefficient*.

27. For instance, if a monopoly supplier seeks to "bribe" a buyer into an exclusive deal, it must offer a discount or benefit at least equal to the additional value that buyer would have received from a potential entrant to which the buyer might,

---

20 Ibid.

in the absence of exclusivity, have turned. If a new entrant is substantially more efficient than the incumbent supplier, the value it brings to the buyer (in terms of a higher quality product, or lower costs) will exceed the monopoly profit the incumbent is trying to protect. To block such an entrant, the incumbent would have to offer the buyer a bribe in compensation so high that it would outweigh its own monopoly gains. Consequently, the Chicago School posits that when exclusivity is sought, it is likely driven by efficiencies (like protecting relationship-specific investments or preventing free- riding) rather than a desire to block superior competition.

28. While the Chicago logic is a powerful starting point, post-Chicago economists – most notably Aghion and Bolton and Segal and Whinston – showed that a dominant firm *can* profitably exclude a more efficient rival under specific, realistic conditions.

29. Aghion and Bolton refined the Chicago School analysis by demonstrating that an incumbent need not aim to block entry outright.[21] Rather, a dominant firm can use an exclusive contract to *extract a portion of the efficiency gains* that a more efficient entrant would otherwise capture – a mechanism better described as "taxing" the rival's efficiency advantage, than simply preventing its entry.

30. The mechanism works as follows. An incumbent signs a long-term contract with a buyer that includes a financial penalty – ie a "liquidated damages" clause – for switching to a rival supplier. This contract raises the switching cost for the buyer: to win the buyer's business, an entrant can no longer simply offer a marginally better deal. Instead, it must offer terms sufficiently attractive to compensate the buyer for the cost of breaching the contract with the incumbent.

31. This has two consequences. First, an entrant that is *slightly,* but not *substantially*, more efficient than the incumbent will be unable to offer a price low enough to profitably cover the liquidated damages. It will therefore remain outside the market, even though it could have served the buyer more efficiently. Second, and crucially, even where a highly efficient entrant does enter, the incumbent would successfully extract a portion of the entrant's efficiency gains: the entrant is forced to reduce its price aggressively to induce the buyer to switch, the buyer pays the liquidated damages to the incumbent, and thus rents are transferred indirectly from the entrant to the incumbent through the exclusive contract. As a result, the incumbent profits not by being the most efficient supplier, but by making it artificially costly for the buyer to choose a better alternative.

32. Importantly, Aghion and Bolton show that this strategy typically produces *partial* rather than complete exclusion: the contracts are not fully exclusionary in all cases, and the profitability of the strategy arises precisely from this rent-shifting effect rather than from foreclosure alone. This distinguishes their model from a simple entry-blocking story and has important implications for competition analysis: harm can arise even where entry is not entirely prevented, if the entrant's ability to compete effectively is structurally constrained by the incumbent's contractual arrangements.

---

21 Philippe Aghion and Patrick Bolton, "Contracts as a Barrier to Entry" (1987) 77(3) Am Econ Rev388–401.

33. Another strategy, known as "divide and conquer", has been built on the framework of naked exclusion first introduced by Rasmusen, Ramseyer and Wiley and subsequently refined by Segal and Whinston, who provided a corrected and more general analysis of the conditions under which such exclusion is profitable.[22,23] Together, these contributions demonstrate that a dominant incumbent can prevent a rival from reaching the critical mass it needs to operate viably, by exploiting the fact that individual buyers fail to coordinate their responses to the incumbent's offers.

34. The underlying mechanism turns on a negative externality: when a single buyer signs an exclusive contract with the incumbent, it reduces the profitability of entry for the rival, thereby harming all other buyers by making the rival a less credible alternative. Each buyer, acting individually, does not take into account the collective harm. The incumbent can exploit the buyers' coordination failure to achieve exclusion at a relatively low cost.

35. What follows is a simplified illustration of how this strategy operates in practice. In broad terms, it proceeds in three steps:

1. *Targeting key buyers with discounts*: The incumbent supplier offers attractive, discriminatory deals (such as loyalty bonuses) to a small but strategically important group of buyers, on the condition that they purchase only from the incumbent.
2. *Denying the entrant critical mass*: If enough of those key buyers accept the exclusive deals, the entrant is denied the scale it needs to be commercially viable. It can no longer offer a credible alternative to the remaining buyers.
3. *Eroding the remaining buyers bargaining power*: The remaining buyers, recognising that the entrant is no longer a viable option, are left with no alternative but to contract with the incumbent. This is likely to be on worse terms than those offered to the initial group.

36. In this way, the incumbent need not offer attractive deals to the entire market. By securing commitments from just enough participants to undermine the rival's viability, it can maintain its market position at a relatively low cost to itself – even where the rival would have offered a superior product or format.

V. Strategic Foreclosure in Action

37. In sports where the incumbent is the "only game in town," the strategic use of exclusivity may raise significant competition concerns. The potential for harm arises, on this view, where an incumbent with significant market power uses exclusivity in ways that deny a rival the minimum efficient scale required to operate viably. To evaluate the potential for such foreclosure, one must therefore assess whether a restriction materially weakens a rival's ability to compete effectively.

38. In this context, in professional sports the "product" is not a single team, but an organised competition between several (elite) teams or participants. For a rival

[22] Eric B Rasmusen, J Mark Ramseyer and John S Wiley Jr, "Naked Exclusion" (1991) 81(5) Am Econ Rev 1137–1145.

[23] Ilya R Segal and Michael D Whinston, "Naked Exclusion: Comment" (2000) 90(1) Am Econ Rev 296–309.

to be viable, it must attract a critical mass of elite participants to secure fan attention, broadcasting and advertising contracts. Thus, in professional sports, foreclosure would typically rely on denying a new entrant access to elite participants. A restriction could facilitate this by increasing those participants' switching costs. In particular, it could force participants into an all-or-nothing choice: to join a new entrant, they must forfeit their right to participate in the incumbent's tournament.

39. The effectiveness of this dynamic would be amplified when the incumbent's product is well-established and difficult for an entrant to replicate (at least in the short term). For example, in the European Super League dispute, participants were not merely choosing between two rival European tournaments; they were effectively required to choose between the new entrant and a comprehensive "bundle" of domestic and international competitions offered by UEFA and its affiliates.[24] Notably, such foreclosure need not be direct, but can occur through indirect temporal barriers. For instance, in professional tennis, the requirement to accrue ranking points in incumbent-run tournaments as a prerequisite for participation in the Grand Slams may effectively deplete the time available for players to participate in rival events.[25]

40. By creating these high-stakes switching costs, incumbents may be able to protect their market position notwithstanding an entrant's relative efficiency. This section examines the mechanisms through which this may occur. Drawing on the post-Chicago frameworks discussed in Section IV, it first identifies the two primary economic mechanisms through which exclusive restrictions may harm competition – the rent-extraction dynamic modelled by Aghion and Bolton, and the coordination failure exploited through divide and conquer strategies as analysed by Rasmusen, Ramseyer and Wiley and refined by Segal and Whinston. It then considers the dimensions of consumer harm that may follow from successful foreclosure and concludes by addressing the conditions under which foreclosure of a rival translates into a meaningful loss of competitive constraint on the incumbent.

1. The "Tax" and the Entry Barrier (Aghion and Bolton)

41. As established in the Aghion and Bolton model, exclusivity can be used to "tax" the entrant's efficiency rather than simply blocking its entry. Applying the Aghion and Bolton framework, critics argue that when a governing body conditions participation on exclusivity – through mechanisms such as eligibility restrictions, ranking point requirements or access to flagship competitions – this may function analogously to a financial penalty for switching, increasing the cost a rival must overcome to attract participants.

42. One such example may be a new entrant like LIV Golf, whose participants would face fines from PGA Europe.[26] Given that LIV Golf reportedly paid these fines,

---

[24] The ESL was to be a single European tournament, whereas UEFA and FIFA (with their affiliates) offer a variety of different domestic and international tournaments. *ESL* (n 3), paras 23, 31.

[25] As alleged by the PTPA, Antitrust Complaint (n 12), s III.D.

[26] *PGA European Tour* (n 10).

this may be a mechanism through which PGA Europe "taxed" the new entrant.[27] This, and other examples, so the argument goes, represent a significant additional hurdle that the entrant would have to meet. The entrant cannot simply match the incumbent's terms. The new league must offer a premium high enough to compensate the player or club for the penalty.

43. This can be particularly damaging in sports where the incumbent controls a bundle of rights (eg both domestic play and international eligibility). If a player must forfeit access to a broad set of existing tournaments, or even their entire career's accrued status, to join a rival tournament, this could make it prohibitively expensive for an entrant to compensate the participant. Therefore, this could represent a mechanism through which an incumbent can successfully use an exclusive contract to make entry prohibitively expensive, protecting its monopoly, even if the new entrant offers a superior format.

2. Coordination Failure: The "Divide and Conquer" Strategy (Segal and Whinston)

44. The most potent theory of harm in league exclusivity might be the exploitation of coordination failures, as modelled by Segal and Whinston. This relies on the fact that a potential new entrant, ie a rival competition, is in effect a joint-venture product that needs a specific threshold of elite participants to be viable.

45. An incumbent may be able to foreclose such a rival by targeting a small, key subset of elite participants with exclusive loyalty deals, and/or loyalty points systems (as alleged in the tennis PTPA complaint). By securing the commitment of a sufficient number of key participants, the incumbent may deny the rival the critical mass needed to become commercially viable. The remaining participants, realising the rival is no longer a viable alternative, are left with no bargaining power and must accept the incumbent's terms.

46. As a result, restrictions on the "top tier" of players or teams may be particularly powerful. Such restrictions would strategically deny the entrant the inputs, ie participants, necessary to be viable.

3. The Dimensions of Consumer Harm

47. When these foreclosure mechanisms succeed in insulating an incumbent from competitive pressure, this can typically be expected to harm fans, broadcasters and the broader ecosystem in two primary dimensions.

48. First, an incumbent can exercise market power across all its revenue streams. In the broadcasting market, a high price for exclusive media rights acts as a direct input cost for broadcasters, which, at least in part, is likely to be passed on to sports fans through inflated subscription fees. In the ticketing and sponsorship markets,

---

[27] As reported by Sports Illustrated in September 2024, "LIV Golf to date has paid some £12 million (approximately $15.75 million) in fines for LIV golfers to compete in DP World Tour events (run by PGA Europe) – with another £10 million outstanding". Bob Harig, "DP World Tour Rejected LIV Golf's Attempt to Pay Jon Rahm's Fines" (16 September 2024) <https://www.si.com/golf/dp-world-tour-rejected-liv-golf-attempt-pay-jon-rahm-fines> accessed 13 May 2026.

the harm might be more direct: by restricting the total "output" (ie the number of high-stakes, elite matches), the incumbent creates scarcity, which, in turn, allows it to command higher prices for both stadium entry and brand associations than would be possible in a more contestable market with a greater volume of elite competition.

49. Second, beyond price, the most significant harm in sports is likely to be the stifling of non-price competition. Competitive entry may in many cases be the primary catalyst for format innovation. For example, as seen in the *ISU* case with *Icederby*, rivals often enter with the specific goal of disrupting incumbents' formats. Foreclosure removes the threat of entry that would otherwise force an incumbent to improve. In doing so, it reduces the incumbent's incentive to invest to improve the quality of the sports-fan experience, whether through superior broadcasting technology, more engaging rules or enhanced officiating. Ultimately, this leads to a diminished consumer experience.

4. Closeness of Competition and Consumer Harm

50. It is a fundamental principle of competition economics that the foreclosure of a rival only translates into consumer harm, including that discussed in the previous subsection, if that rival would have exerted a meaningful competitive constraint on the incumbent. Consequently, the mere fact that an exclusivity arrangement blocks an entrant is not a sufficient condition for a finding of harm. Rather, the extent of that harm is typically proportional to the degree of substitutability between the two tournaments.

51. Where an entrant is a "close substitute" – meaning fans, broadcasters, and/or participants view it as a direct and attractive alternative – its presence would exert significant pressure on the incumbent to lower prices and/or improve quality. For example, the European Super League (ESL) was designed to feature the same so-called "blue-chip" clubs as the UEFA Champions League, making it a direct and potent competitor for the same audience and sponsorship revenue. Foreclosing such a rival could, in principle, result in a substantial loss of consumer welfare by insulating the incumbent from the necessity to innovate or price competitively.

52. That said, where a challenger is an exceptionally close substitute, its entry may not result in a situation where both rivals sustain competition *within* the market, but rather the outright replacement of the incumbent. In this context, the successful rival may simply emerge as the new monopoly tournament organiser. In the case of the ESL, for instance, the stated ambition was effectively to supplant the UEFA Champions League.[28] Given the finite pool of top-tier clubs, and the scarcity of calendar slots in which they can play each other, it may well be difficult for two such competitions to continue to coexist in parallel over the long term.

[28] The press release by the ESL at the time of launch stated that they intended to "establish a new midweek competition" while "continuing to compete in their respective national leagues". This suggests that participating clubs would no longer play in the UEFA Champions League, a midweek European, rather than domestic, competition. The press release is available here (and on the websites of other participating clubs). ESL, Press Release, "Leading Football Clubs Announce New Super League Competition" (18 April 2021) <https://www.manutd.com/en/news/detail/leading-football-clubs-announce-new-super-league-competition-18-april-2021> accessed 13 May 2026.

53. Conversely, if the foreclosed rival is a "weak substitute," – meaning fans, broadcasters and/or participants do not view it as an attractive alternative – the potential for harm is diminished or even non-existent. A useful example could be the relationship between the Pakistan Super League (PSL) and the English County Championship. Because these tournaments use different formats (ie matches last a few hours in the case of the former, and multiple days in the case of the latter) and have distinct geographic locations, the PSL may pose a negligible competitive constraint on the English domestic game.[29] To the extent this is the case, even if exclusivity rules prevent certain players from appearing in both, the impact on the "English" consumer or the commercial intensity of the County Championship is likely to be immaterial.

54. Ultimately, therefore, for a competition concern to be robust, one must demonstrate that the foreclosed rival was a credible threat to the incumbent's market power. On that basis, a restriction that excludes a distant or "complementary" competitor may be restrictive in form, but it is benign in effect.

VI. Pro-Competitive Justifications for Exclusivity

55. While exclusivity arrangements can theoretically lead to foreclosure, the "peculiar economics" of professional sports suggests that such restraints may often be essential to the creation and viability of the product itself. Unlike many industries where competition between firms is seen as the primary driver of value, the value of a sports tournament is derived from the joint production of a contest. To evaluate the efficiency of exclusivity, we must therefore move beyond the standard firm-centric model and recognise the elite sports league as a unified platform that requires coordination – and in many cases, the exclusivity that makes such coordination sustainable – to maintain its economic and sporting utility.

56. It is worth noting at the outset that many of the efficiencies discussed in this section are not uniquely attributable to exclusivity as such. Rather, several arise from coordination, and in particular the idea that a single, monopolist organiser has a unique, or at least enhanced, ability to align the behaviour of participants around common rules, schedules and standards. Exclusivity serves to protect that organiser's capacity to provide such coordination: without a binding commitment from participants, the organiser's ability to manage the sporting calendar, preserve competitive balance and sustain the collective product is structurally vulnerable to defection. We discuss these coordination-based efficiencies in sub-section 1 below. On the other hand, certain efficiencies are more distinctly tied to exclusivity itself: in particular, the preservation of title integrity and the prevention of product dilution, which we discussed in sub-section 2, are unlikely to be achieved through coordination alone. They require that the pool of elite participants be committed to a single competitive structure, such that only one undisputed champion can

---

29 For example, matches in the English County Championship last up to four days, whereas in the Pakistan Super League they last only a few hours. See for instance, "James Vince, No-Objection Certificates and the PSL: Why are the ECB and County Cricketers Clashing over T20 Leagues?" (*Sky Sports*, 16 January 2025) <https://www.skysports.com/cricket/news/12123/13289325/james-vince-no-objection-certificates-and-the-psl-why-are-the-ecb-and-county-cricketers-clashing-over-t20-league> accessed 13 May 2026.

be crowned. Finally, at sub-section 3, we turn to the European sports model – a framework that draws on both sets of efficiencies, combining the coordination benefits of a unified structure with the exclusivity-dependent features of a merit-based, solidarity-sustaining pyramid, and which represents perhaps the most comprehensive justification for exclusivity arrangements in the European context.

1. The Necessity of Coordination in Joint Production

A. *Sports Competitions as Jointly Produced Products*

57. As Walter Neale observed, the first peculiarity of sports economics is that "receipts depend upon competition among the teams, not upon business competition among the firms running the contenders."[30] The sports product is inherently joint: no single team or participant can produce a contest unaided, and the competition itself only exists through the coordinated interaction of multiple independent competitors.

58. Flynn and Gilbert developed this insight further, noting that the product of a professional sports league is not any individual game but the season-long competitive narrative – "hundreds of individual games among all member clubs, leading to divisional or conference titles and, ultimately, to an overall league champion".[31] No club can produce even a single match unaided, let alone the cumulative series of contests that constitutes the league product. This joint production therefore requires a degree of coordination – setting rules, scheduling matches, ensuring the right teams meet in high-stakes environments – that would be considered collusive in almost any other sector.

59. This gives rise to an important efficiency implication: because the product is inherently joint, any arrangement that fragments the pool of participants may degrade the product itself. In particular, fragmentation could mean that the best teams no longer play each other, the best players are not always fielded by participating teams, and the sporting calendar becomes too crowded for participants to perform at their best. Such issues are likely to be avoided by effective coordination between participants – and that coordination is most effective when participants are bound by a commitment to a single structure, since the credibility of any collective arrangement depends on the assurance that clubs cannot simply defect when it suits them.

60. While in some cases such coordination may arise absent exclusivity, in others exclusivity could form an important mechanism through which such coordination is supported and sustained. This is particularly apparent in relation to the cartel-like arrangements that leagues routinely deploy to maintain competitive balance – measures such as revenue-sharing schemes, squad and roster limits, and prize-distribution formulas that would be considered anticompetitive coordination in any other industry,

---

30 Walter C Neale, "The Peculiar Economics of Professional Sports" (1964) 78(1) QJ Econ 2.

31 Flynn and Gilbert noted "the product of a professional sports league is season-long competition involving hundreds of individual games among all of the member clubs, leading to divisional or conference titles and, ultimately, to an overall league champion. No single member club can produce even a single contest, much less the season-long series of contests that would amount to a product competitive with the product of the professional sports league". See Michael . Flynn and Richard J Gilbert, "The Analysis of Professional Sports Leagues as Joint Ventures" (2001) 111(469) Econ J F27–F46.

but which serve the specific function of preventing the concentration of talent and resources among the wealthiest clubs. These mechanisms only function as intended if all participants are subject to them: a club that retains the option to defect to a rival structure that imposes no equivalent obligations can arbitrage away the redistributive constraints, undermining competitive balance across the league as a whole. Carlton, Frankel and Landes provide empirical support for this broader logic, demonstrating in the context of the National Hockey Leage (NHL), that restrictions on club behaviour which superficially resemble anticompetitive coordination can in fact correct genuine externalities generated by the joint-venture structure of professional sports.[32]

B. *Internalising Externalities and the Management of Spill-Over Effects*

61. The need for coordination extends beyond the structure of competition itself to the management of the broader sporting ecosystem. Indeed, a central efficiency justification for exclusivity lies in the ability of a single tournament organiser to "internalise" the significant externalities that exist between sporting events. These spill-over effects can be both positive and negative. For example, a successful Roland Garros tournament may increase the general appetite for tennis, benefiting Wimbledon shortly thereafter. Conversely, a player injury at one event directly diminishes the quality of the next.

62. These externalities require some coordination. Clashes in the sporting calendar is a prime example. There has been friction between the ATP Cup and the Davis Cup in tennis. When they were scheduled too close together, player fatigue led to several high-profile withdrawals. This is a typical example of the negative externality caused by lack of coordination, through which fragmentation directly lowers the quality of the "product" for fans.

63. From a competition perspective, these arguments suggest that a unified organiser has a superior incentive to manage the ecosystem optimally. When a single entity oversees the calendar, it reaps the full rewards of investments in player safety, health standards and scheduling. In a fragmented market, a rival organiser might free ride on the health and reputation of athletes managed by the incumbent, leading to sub-optimal investment in player welfare and a cluttered calendar that reduces overall spectator utility.

C. *Protecting Competitive Balance and Uncertainty of Outcome*

64. A further example of the need to coordinate between participants stems from the fact that the economic value of sports contest is intrinsically tied to consumer interest, which the literature identifies as being driven by the "uncertainty of outcome hypothesis". This hypothesises that fans are primarily drawn to sports as

---

32 "Competitive balance may also be important. Past a certain point, further improvements in the quality of a single team relative to other teams may diminish the value of the league as a whole". See Dennis W Carlton, Alan S Frankel and Elisabeth M Landes "The Control of Externalities in Sports Leagues: An Analysis of Restrictions in the National Hockey League" (2004) 112 J P Econ S268-S288.

a form of entertainment because the result is not a foregone conclusion. Fans' interest therefore diminishes when results are easily predictable and is heightened when the outcome is more uncertain.

65. The uncertainty of outcome hypothesis has generated a substantial empirical literature, and while the evidence broadly supports a link between competitive balance and fan demand, the relationship is more nuanced than the conventional account suggests. As Szymanski's survey of contest design in sport demonstrates, demand sometimes peaks at outcomes that are far from evenly matched, with some studies finding that attendance is maximised when the home team is roughly twice as likely to win as the visiting team – a markedly unbalanced contest by most measures.[33] The empirical picture therefore does not straightforwardly confirm that maximising balance maximises consumer welfare, and the theoretical relationship between specific redistribution mechanisms and competitive balance is itself contested. Késenne and Szymanski's formal modelling of gate revenue sharing suggests that under certain conditions – including where the supply of talent is elastic and teams behave non-cooperatively – redistribution mechanisms may in fact worsen competitive balance, because the dampening effect on investment falls disproportionately on the weaker club.[34] The relationship between redistribution and balance thus requires case-by-case assessment rather than a simple presumption in either direction.

66. That said, the broader case for a unified competitive structure does not rest solely on the uncertain empirics of competitive balance. Szymanski's survey also documents the full range of mechanisms that leagues deploy as instruments of collective contest design – revenue redistribution formulas, squad and roster limits, prize-based distribution structures and draft systems – each of which would constitute impermissible coordination in most other industries, but which serve the specific function of managing the externalities inherent in joint production.[35] These mechanisms share a common structural dependency: they presuppose a unified

---

33 Stefan Szymanski, "The Economic Design of Sporting Contests" (2003) XLI J Econ Lit 1137–1187, at 1163–1165. The author notes that the empirical evidence on the uncertainty of outcome hypothesis, while broadly supportive, is far from unambiguous, with several studies finding that demand peaks at considerably unbalanced contest probabilities.

34 Stefan Késenne and Stefan Szymanski, "Competitive Balance and Gate Revenue Sharing in Team Sports" (2004) 52(1) J Ind Econ 165–177. The authors show that, under Nash conjectures and elastic talent supply, increased gate revenue sharing worsens competitive balance. This result contrasts with the earlier "invariance principle" developed by Quirk and El-Hodiri, which held that revenue redistribution would have no effect on the distribution of talent under certain conditions, including profit-maximising behaviour by clubs. See Mohamed El-Hodiri and James Quirk, "An Economic Model of a Professional Sports League" (2004) 79(6) J P Econ 1302–1319, 1971; and James Quirk and Mohamed El-Hodiri, "The Economic Theory of a Professional Sports League" in Roger Noll (ed), *Government and the Sports Business* (Brookings Institution 1974). The relationship between redistribution mechanisms and competitive balance thus remains sensitive to the assumptions made about club objectives and the elasticity of talent supply.

35 Szymanski (n 33), 1176–1184. The survey discusses salary caps, luxury taxes, roster limits, draft systems, and prize-based revenue distribution as design instruments deployed by league organisers to manage competitive balance, noting that each represents a form of collective coordination that would face antitrust scrutiny outside the sporting context. European football provides concrete illustrations of several such mechanisms in operation: prize-based distribution formulas, common across UEFA club competitions, serve to even up the ex-ante incentives to invest among clubs by tying a share of revenues to league or competition performance. Squad limits, such as UEFA's "List A" restriction capping registered squads at 25 players, serve a complementary function

competitive framework to which all participants are subject. A club free to defect to a rival tournament that imposes no equivalent obligations can arbitrage away the redistributive constraints of the incumbent league, undermining whatever competitive balance those mechanisms were designed to protect. In this light, exclusivity may in certain contexts represent not merely a commercial preference of the incumbent organiser, but a governance mechanism whose removal could compromise the collective framework on which the sporting product's value depends – though whether it is a proportionate and necessary response to that risk remains, as always, a matter for case-by-case assessment.

2. Preserving Prestige and Avoiding Product Dilution

67. The most direct efficiency justifications for exclusivity – ones that cannot be replicated by coordination alone – lie in three closely related but analytically distinct effects: the concentration of elite talent, the preservation of title integrity and the prevention of product dilution.

A. *Talent Concentration and Contest Quality*

68. A fundamental, if perhaps underappreciated, virtue of a single unified tournament is that it concentrates the best available talent into one competitive arena. Since elite athletes are a scarce resource, any parallel tournament structure necessarily disperses that talent across competing events. The consequence is straightforward: no individual contest, in either tournament, will be as compelling as it would have been had the full pool of elite participants been available to compete against one another. As explained above at sub-section 1 above, fans do not merely want to watch great players; they want to watch great players compete *against each other*. A fragmented market prevents this. Exclusivity, by contrast, ensures that the finest talent meets in the same competition, maximising the quality and intensity of individual contests. Ultimately, this enhances the core product that fans, broadcasters and sponsors are purchasing.

B. *Title Integrity and the Uniqueness of the Champion*

69. Beyond contest quality, exclusivity also protects something more fundamental: the ability of a competition to crown a single, undisputed champion. This may not be merely a ceremonial outcome; it may instead be the fundamental "product" that fans, broadcasters and sponsors pay for. Where elite participants are dispersed across parallel competing tournaments, each purporting to crown a champion, the result is an inevitable dilution of that product. If two rival tournaments each feature a unique credible subset of elite participants, there is no definitive answer to the question of who is the best.

70. This problem of title dilution can be illustrated by the recent history of European basketball. Since the 2016 introduction of the Basketball Champions League

by preventing the wealthiest clubs from hoarding talent and thereby concentrating competitive advantage. Both mechanisms presuppose the unified structure discussed in the main text: their effectiveness depends on all competing clubs being subject to equivalent obligations.

alongside the pre-existing EuroLeague and EuroCup, the sport has been characterised by multi-polar fragmentation, with multiple parallel entities each claiming to offer a "top-tier" or "second-tier" European title. This, some argue, has risked eroding the symbolic value of being a "champion". As Jorge Garbajosa, President of FIBA Europe, suggested, fans "don't even know what they're watching", such that there is uncertainty among fans about the relative standing of competing titles.[36] Many commentators have observed that this "self-destruction" reflects a failure to protect the scarcity value of the sporting prize.[37,38] That said, whether this has translated into a measurable erosion of commercial value remains debated, as other factors – including market size and broadcaster strategies – may also account for the observed outcomes.

C. *Preserving Long-Term Prestige and Continuity*

71. The arguments above address the immediate, structural consequences of fragmentation. But exclusivity also serves a longer-term function that is equally significant: preserving the prestige and historical continuity upon which the commercial value of major tournaments depends. The value of a major sports tournament is likely to be at least partly derived from its historical legacy. Research into the media coverage of the UEFA Champions League, for instance, demonstrates that the competition's continuous history is an important component of its market identity.[39]

72. A unified, exclusive tournament structure protects this asset through two distinct economic mechanisms. First, by concentrating talent, it ensures a premium product that commands sustained broadcaster and sponsor interest over time. Second, it preserves the integrity of the historical record. Consumers value the determination

---

36 Edvinas Jablonskis, "Jorge Garbajosa Talks Improved Relationship with EuroLeague, Potential BCL-EuroCup Merger" (20 February 2024) <https://basketnews.com/news-202149-jorge-garbajosa-talks-improved-relationship-with-euroleague-potential-bcl-eurocup-merger.html> accessed 13 May 2026.

37 For example:

- The sport Journalist Emmet Ryan noted that "European professional basketball features a complex landscape" and "It's all very confusing". See Emmet Ryan, "A Comprehensive Guide to FIBA and Euro League Action" and <https://www.ballineurope.com/virtus-bologna-tenerife-basketball-champions-league-final-preview-8084/>.
- Aris Barkas, a journalist specialised in basketball, also noted: "The usual question in recent years is which continental competition can be considered second best to the EuroLeague". Aris Barkas, "The BCL and Spanoulis Stealing the Show over EuroCup" (13 July 2022) <https://www.eurohoops.net/en/trademarks/1368235/the-bcl-and-spanoulis-stealing-the-show-over-eurocup/> accessed 13 May 2026.
- Journalist Bruno Ferret also wonders: Bruno Ferret, "Eurocup vs. Basketball Champions League: What is the Best "Second European Cup?"" (22 December 2019) <https://www.basketeurope.com/eurocup-basket-ball-champions-league-quelle-est-la-meilleure-deuxieme-coupe-deurope/> accessed 13 May 2026 (Free translation).
- Similarly, the journalist Dylan de Abreu asks: Dylan de Abreu, "Champions League vs Eurocup: Who are the best teams?" (6 August 2018) <https://www.basketeurope.com/champions-league-vs-eurocup-qui-a-les-meilleures-equipes/> accessed 13 May 2026. (Free translation).

38 Jose Manuel Puertas, sport journalist, commented: "If there is a sport specialized throughout history in trying to self-destruct, it is undoubtedly basketball". Jose Manuel Puertas, "FIBA Windows: A Timeline of the Suicide of European basketball" (22 November 2017) <https://www.libertaddigital.com/deportes/baloncesto/2017-11-22/ventanas-fiba-la-guerra-entre-fiba-y-euroliga-que-amenaza-con-destruir-el-baloncesto-europeo-1276609513/> accessed 13 May 2026. (Free translation).

39 Matthew Holt, "Branding of The UEFA Champions League" (2007) 9(1) IJSM&S 46–56.

of an absolute ranking – the crowning of a single, undisputed champion – and this value may compound over time as the tournament's legacy deepens. Once fragmented, or lost, a legacy build on the basis of longstanding continuous primacy cannot, by definition, easily be reconstructed.

73. These are plausible and potentially significant considerations, though their precise commercial weight will vary by sport and context and is not easily quantified. That said, they are likely to be best understood as reinforcing the case for a unified structure rather than as freestanding justifications for exclusivity in their own right (for the reasons we explain in the next sub-section).

D. *The Single-Tournament Problem: When Exclusivity Reflects Market Reality Rather Than Strategic Foreclosure*

74. Taken together, the considerations above – talent concentration, title integrity and long-term prestige – point toward a broader structural insight. The efficiency case for exclusivity is at its strongest where the market can only sustain a single viable tournament – not because of artificial foreclosure, but because of the structural economics of elite sport itself. Where the pool of elite participants is finite, where title integrity requires a single undisputed champion, and where the commercial value of the competition depends on concentrating scarce talent in one arena, the market may simply not support two parallel tournaments of equivalent standing over the long run.

75. This insight reframes the competition analysis in an important way. Where a rival entrant is a sufficiently close substitute for the incumbent – competing for the same elite participants, the same broadcast audiences and the same sponsorship revenues – the realistic long-run outcomes are not a choice between exclusivity versus parallel competition. They are instead a choice between exclusivity versus resolution through consolidation. The practical experience of recent sports disputes bears this out: in both padel and golf, antitrust challenges that were framed as battles for market access ultimately resolved not through the establishment of parallel competing structures, but through merger or commercial settlement. The market, in effect, confirmed that in these cases there was no room for additional credible organisers at the elite level.

76. This has a significant implication for the competition analysis. If the counterfactual to exclusivity is not sustained parallel competition but eventual consolidation – potentially on terms less favourable to participants and with fewer solidarity obligations than the incumbent structure – then the consumer welfare case against exclusivity is materially weakened. An enforcement outcome that dismantles exclusivity arrangements may, paradoxically, produce a period of damaging fragmentation followed by reconsolidation under a structure that offers fewer of the public-interest features – meritocratic qualification, solidarity redistribution, grassroots investment – that characterised the original. Decision-makers should therefore be cautious about assuming that "opening the market" produces sustained competition; in single-tournament sports, it may merely determine *who* ends up as the monopolist, and on what terms.

3. Protecting the "European Sports Model" and the Solidarity Pyramid

77. The quality and sustainability of a sports tournament cannot be assessed in isolation from the structural ecosystem in which it sits. Across Europe, professional sport is organised according to what is commonly referred to as the "European sports model" – a pyramidal structure linking elite professional competition at the apex to grassroots participation at the base, held together by principles of open promotion and relegation, sporting merit and financial solidarity. This model is not merely a sporting convention; it is an explicit policy objective. The European Council's 2021 Resolution called on the European Commission and Member States to support its key features, including the pyramidal structure, the open system of promotion and relegation, and the grassroots approach to solidarity.[40]

78. Exclusivity plays a protective role in relation to each of these features, in ways that go beyond the efficiencies discussed in earlier sections.

A. *Preserving the Hierarchical Structure and Sporting Merit*

79. A pyramidal structure is, by definition, one in which each tier is unambiguously differentiated from the others by sporting performance. In European football, qualification for UEFA club competitions is determined by year-on-year domestic league performance, meaning that the right to compete at European level must be earned, not acquired. This meritocratic logic underpins the legitimacy of the entire structure in the eyes of fans and participants alike.

80. A parallel closed league directly undermines this logic in two ways. First, where clubs qualify for – or are invited to participate in – a rival tournament outside the pyramid, it becomes impossible to determine the relative ranking of the two competitions. The hierarchical clarity that gives each tier its meaning dissolves. Second, as the experience of European basketball illustrates, parallel tournaments have historically awarded participation rights on the basis of licence agreements or commercial negotiations rather than sporting merit. The EuroLeague's club licensing model, which effectively grants permanent or semi-permanent membership to a select group of clubs, represents a structural departure from the open promotion and relegation system that characterises the European sports model. An exclusivity requirement that prevents clubs from simultaneously participating in such structures preserves the integrity of merit-based qualification.

B. *Protecting Financial Solidarity*

81. Perhaps the most significant – and most frequently underestimated – efficiency of a unified tournament structure is its role in sustaining the financial solidarity mechanisms that fund the wider sporting ecosystem. UEFA operates as a non-profit organisation, redistributing approximately 95% of its club competition revenues

---

40 Resolution of the Council and of the representatives of the Governments of the Member States meeting within the Council on the key features of a European Sport Model [2021] OJ C501/1 <https://eur-lex.europa.eu/legal-content/EN/TXT/?uri=celex%3A42021Y1213%2801%29> accessed 13 May 2026.

back into football.[41] This redistribution takes several forms: solidarity payments to non-participating clubs, distributions to national associations to sustain grassroots development and investment in less commercially attractive competitions such as women's and youth football.

82. The introduction of a parallel closed league would place this solidarity model under strain through three compounding mechanisms. First, as discussed in sub-section 2 above, fragmentation is likely to reduce the aggregate commercial value of elite competition – diminishing the total pool available for redistribution. Second, competition between an incumbent and a rival league to attract and retain top clubs would likely drive up the proportion of revenues distributed to participating clubs, compressing the share available for broader solidarity payments. Third, and most fundamentally, a for-profit parallel organiser has a weaker structural incentive to redistribute revenues to non-participating clubs or grassroots initiatives relative to a single non-profit governing body. The economic literature on solidarity mechanisms supports this structural concern: as the debate around the invariance principle illustrates, redistribution mechanisms that appear robust within a unified league may be substantially undermined when clubs retain the outside option of participating in a parallel structure that does not impose equivalent obligations. Even in a scenario where a parallel league ultimately displaced the incumbent and a single top tournament re-emerged, the solidarity flows that currently sustain the wider pyramid would be materially reduced. In combination, these three mechanisms reveal a structural dynamic that goes beyond any individual efficiency justification – one best understood as a coordination failure operating at the level of the sporting ecosystem as a whole.

83. This is not a theoretical concern. The parallel basketball experience again provides a concrete illustration: EuroLeague revenues are largely reinvested into its shareholder clubs, with no established solidarity mechanism benefiting the wider basketball ecosystem in the way that UEFA's redistribution model benefits football.

C. *The Systemic Risk: A Prisoner's Dilemma at the Pyramid Level*

84. Taken together, these dynamics point to a potential systemic risk operating at the level of the sporting ecosystem as a whole. While it may be individually rational for an elite club to join a higher-paying rival tournament, the collective consequences – the erosion of the merit-based pyramid, the fragmentation of title integrity and the reduction of solidarity flows – could produce outcomes that are suboptimal for the sport as a whole. On this view, exclusivity may function as a mechanism for addressing a coordination failure that market forces alone might not resolve. However, whether exclusivity is the appropriate or proportionate response to that risk, as opposed to less restrictive alternatives, remains a matter for case-by-case assessment

41 UEFA, *Financial Report 2022/23* (2023) <https://editorial.uefa.com/resources/0295-1cee154c3733-a7de-3ba62d06-1000/uefa_financial_report_23-24_.pdf> accessed 13 May 2026.

VII. Conclusion

85. Exclusivity arrangements in professional sport operate at multiple levels and serve multiple functions. At their most benign, they address well-defined market failures – the principal–agent problems that arise in agency relationships, or the hold-up problems that would otherwise deter investment in youth development. At their most consequential, they determine whether a rival organiser can assemble the critical mass of elite participants needed to mount a credible challenge to an incumbent tournament.

86. The conventional competition concern is straightforward: exclusivity imposed by a dominant incumbent can deny rivals the scale they need to compete, harming fans and broadcasters through higher prices, reduced output and diminished innovation. Where a foreclosed rival would have exerted a meaningful competitive constraint, that harm is real.

87. Yet the peculiar economics of professional sport complicate this picture in ways that a simplistic, conventional analysis is ill-equipped to capture. Joint production requires coordination that would be considered collusive in other sectors, and that coordination depends on participants being committed to a single structure. Certain efficiencies – the concentration of elite talent, the preservation of an undisputed title, the prevention of product dilution – cannot be achieved through coordination alone. And in the European context, the solidarity-based pyramid adds a further dimension: exclusivity may function as a structural precondition for a redistribution model that serves broader public interests beyond the commercial.

88. The challenge for competition practitioners is therefore not to ask whether exclusivity exists, but to assess whether a specific arrangement is proportionate to a legitimate sporting objective or whether it serves primarily to insulate a dominant incumbent from competitive pressure it could not otherwise resist. That assessment requires careful, case-by-case analysis grounded in the economic realities of each sport.

What is a Public Interest in Sport? What Are the Legitimate Sporting Objectives?

Benoît Keane*

Keane Legal, Brussels

1. The specific characteristics of sport may justify restrictions of free movement or competition arising from sports regulations. Indeed, in the first ever EU law case concerning sport, *Walrave and Koch*, the CJEU held that EU law is not concerned with a sports rule that is "of purely sporting interest and as such has nothing to do with economic activity".[1]

2. However, sports regulations often have a direct effect upon the economic activities of those active in sport such as clubs, organisers and athletes as well as indirect effects upon other undertakings active in the sports sector such as agents. The fact that EU law applies to sports regulation does not mean that it cannot be justified. In this, sport is not necessarily different to other sectors or indeed Member States (in free movement cases).

3. In the *Bosman* case[2] concerning the player transfer system, the CJEU held that the private or public nature of the rules in question did not affect the justifications that could be provided. As with EU Member States, sports federations could justify a discriminatory restriction to free movement on grounds of public policy, public security or public health.[3] Likewise, non-discriminatory restrictions could be "justified on non-economic grounds which relate to the particular nature and context of certain matches."[4]

---

* Benoît Keane, Solicitor Advocate and Avocat, Keane Legal, Brussels. All views expressed are strictly personal.

1 Case 36/74 *Walrave and Koch v Association Union Cycliste Internationale and others* ECLI:EU:C:1974:140, para 8.

2 Case C-415/93 *Union Royale Belge Sociale de Football Association, RCL and UEFA v JM Bosman* ECLI:EU:C:1995:463.

3 Ibid paras 85–86.

4 Ibid para 76.

4. A similar approach was taken in EU competition law. Again, the fundamental principles are not so different to other sectors. In the seminal *Gøttrup-Klim/DLG* case, the CJEU held that a cooperative could prohibit its members from joining a rival cooperative association as it was ancillary to the purchasing power of the cooperative.[5] This approach to commercial ancillary restraints was applied to so-called "regulatory ancillary restraints".[6]

5. In *Wouters*, the CJEU held that the Dutch legal bar could prohibit partnerships between lawyers and accountants in order to preserve the independence of the legal profession. What makes the ruling particularly striking is that a number of EU Member States permitted such hybrid partnerships. However, the CJEU did not consider this to be determinative; it was considered "*reasonably*" necessary for the Dutch bar to put the ban in place to protect the independence of the profession and client secrecy.[7] As such, there is no regulatory race to the bottom. If a regulation pursues a legitimate objective that is reasonably necessary and proportionate, then it is a permitted restraint on freedom of action of those subject to the rules. Formally speaking, such regulatory restraints do not constitute restrictions prohibited by Article 101(1) TFEU.[8]

6. The same approach is applied to sports regulations that affect economic activities in sport. In the *Meca-Medina* case (concerning anti-doping rules), the CJEU stated:

> [T]he compatibility of rules with the Community rules on competition cannot be assessed in the abstract. Not every agreement between undertakings or every decision of an association of undertakings which restricts the freedom of action of the parties or of one of them necessarily falls within the prohibition laid down in Article [101(1) TFEU]. For the purposes of application of that provision to a particular case, account must first of all be taken of the overall context in which the decision of the association of undertakings was taken or produces its effects and, more specifically, of its objectives. It has then to be considered whether the consequential effects restrictive of competition are inherent in the pursuit of those objectives and are proportionate to them.[9]

7. The test is one that applies to any regulatory body. The CJEU confirmed the importance of analysing EU competition law "not in the abstract" but in the "overall context" in which it operates. As such, the sporting context is critical, with the specific characteristics of sport distinguishing the application of the test from other regulatory sectors. For example, as set out below, the CJEU recognises competitive balance to be a legitimate objective in sport. It is doubtful that it would be an acceptable legitimate objective in other professional sectors, but it is essential to the interest of sporting competitions. "Nobody wants boring football", as Advocate General (AG) Szpunar wryly put it.[10]

---

5 Case C-250/92 *Gottrup-Klim Grovvareforeninger v Dansk Landsbrugs Grovvareselskab AmbA* ECLI:EU:C:1994:413.

6 Richard Whish and David Bailey, *Competition Law* (11th edn, OUP Oxford 2024).

7 Case C-309/99 *Wouters* ECLI:EU:C:2002:98, paras 106–110.

8 It is also often referred to as a form of "rule of reason" approach to EU law.

9 Case C-519/04 P *David Meca-Medina and Igor Majcen v Commission of the European Communities* ECLI:EU:C:2006:492, para 32 which illustrates the origin of the CJEU's approach by referencing *Gøttrup-Klim* (n 5), para 31 and *Wouters* (n 7), para 97.

10 Case C-680/21 *Royal Antwerp FC* ECLI:EU:C:2023:188, Opinion of AG Szpunar, para 3.

8. With pure sporting rules and regulatory restraints, it may reasonably be asked why little attention was paid to the provision set out specifically in the Treaty to exempt a restriction of competition: Article 101(3) TFEU. In the *Wouters* case, AG Léger saw no need for a regulatory ancillary restraints doctrine; he considered that Article 101(3) TFEU was sufficiently flexible to exempt "social concerns" and "considerations in the public interest."[11] The approach of the CJEU may have been simply pragmatic: at the time the European Commission alone had the right to grant an exemption pursuant to Article 101(3) TFEU – a legal position that no longer applies since Regulation 1/2003 decentralised its application.[12]

9. In any event, Article 101(3) TFEU was seen to relate to economic justifications (such as the collective selling of media rights[13]) rather than public interest justifications of a non-economic nature.[14] The position dramatically changed in the *Super League* judgment.[15] The CJEU limited the application of the public interest objectives applied in *Meca-Medina* to restrictions of competition by effect; restrictions by object could no longer be justified by public interest objectives.[16] However, such by object restrictions may still be permitted by Article 101(3) TFEU which exempts restrictions by object or by effect[17] provided the economic efficiencies outweigh the negative effects to competition in accordance with four cumulative conditions.[18]

---

[11] Case C-309/99 *Wouters* ECLI:EU:C:2001:390, Opinion of AG Léger, para 113: "I would point out that in Community competition law there are no infringements which are inherently incapable of qualifying for an exemption under Article [101(3) TFEU]. According to the case-law, the wording of Article [101(3) TFEU] makes it possible to take account of the particular nature of different branches of the economy, social concerns and, to a certain extent, considerations connected with the pursuit of the public interest. Professional rules which, in the light of those criteria, produce economic effects which are positive, taken as a whole, should therefore be eligible for exemption under Article [101(3) TFEU]."

[12] In his Opinion in *Wouters* (n 11), para 106, AG Léger noted that the finding of an infringement would have required professional associations to notify their rules to the European Commission for exemption. Whether intentional or not, the approach of the CJEU avoided this administrative dilemma.

[13] Case AT.37398 European Commission Decision *UEFA Champions League – Joint selling of the commercial rights* (23 July 2003).

[14] The exception being a case concerning FIFA Football Agents Regulations which predated the *Meca-Medina* (n 9) ruling. See Case T-193/02 *Laurent Piau v Commission of the European Communities* ECLI:EU:T:2005:22.

[15] Case C-333/21 *European Super League* ECLI:EU:C:2023.

[16] Ibid para 186: "Given that the absence of a subjective intention to prevent, restrict or distort competition and the pursuit of potentially legitimate objectives are not decisive either for the purposes of application of Article 101(1) TFEU and that, moreover, Articles 101 and 102 TFEU must be interpreted consistently, the Court finds that the [Meca Medina] case-law … does not apply either in situations involving conduct which, far from merely having the inherent "effect" of restricting competition, at least potentially, by limiting the freedom of action of certain undertakings, reveals a degree of harm in relation to that competition that justifies a finding that it has as its very "object" the prevention, restriction or distortion of competition. Thus, it is only if, following an examination of the conduct at issue in a given case, that conduct proves not to have as its object the prevention, restriction or distortion of competition, that it must then be determined whether it may come within the scope of that case-law."

[17] *Super League* (n 15), para 189: "It follows from the very wording of Article 101(3) TFEU that any agreement, decision by associations of undertakings or concerted practice which proves to be contrary to Article 101(1) TFEU, whether by reason of its anticompetitive object or effect, may be exempted if it satisfies all of the conditions laid down for that purpose."

[18] The conditions for the application of an exemption pursuant to Article 101(3) TFEU are: First, it must be demonstrated with a sufficient degree of probability that the agreement, decision by an association of undertakings or concerted practice in question makes it possible to achieve efficiency gains, by contributing either to improving the production or distribution of the products or services concerned, or to promoting technical or economic progress. Second, it must be demonstrated, to the same degree of probability, that an equitable part of the profit resulting from those efficiency gains is reserved for the users. Third, the agreement, decision or practice in question must

10. The question is whether public interest objectives can also be economic efficiencies. According to the CJEU, they can. The CJEU held "the existence of such objectives, however laudable they may be, do not release the associations that have adopted those rules from their obligation to establish ... that the pursuit of those objectives translates into genuine, quantifiable efficiency gains, on the one hand, and that they compensate for the disadvantages caused in competition terms by the rules at issue in the main proceedings, on the other."[19]

11. In other words, a legitimate objective, for example to protect health and safety, should be translated into an economic efficiency to fall under Article 101(3) TFEU. However, this formalistic approach with its emphasis on "efficiency gains" sits uncomfortably with the underlying public interest ethos of many professional bodies. Advocate General Emiliou proposed instead in *RRC Sports* that the CJEU apply a pragmatic approach and simply recognise non-economic justifications as falling within the scope of Article 101(3) TFEU:[20]

> The term "economic progress" in Article 101(3) TFEU cannot be read as a synonym of "economic growth" or of "wealth". Article 3(3) TEU refers to the European Union's aim to "establish an internal market [which] shall work for the sustainable development of Europe based on balanced economic growth and price stability, a highly competitive social market economy, aiming at full employment and social progress, and a high level of protection and improvement of the quality of the environment. It shall promote scientific and technological advance". Using a basic metaphor, I would say that "progress" – from an internal market and competition perspective – means that not only is the size of the cake increasing, but the quality of the cake is also improving, the cake is being shared more equitably, or it is ensured that an equally tasty cake can also be baked in the foreseeable future.

12. Certainly, this proposed approach would remove some of the more tortious attempts to convey social objectives into economic efficiencies. Indeed, it is essentially a dusting off of the proposal by AG Léger in *Wouters* (which can now be practically applied in the post-modernisation era). It would recognise that EU competition law is a part of society, not apart from society.[21]

13. In summary, there are three different categories of justifications that may either result in a restriction not being prohibited or alternatively being exempted:
    - First, there is the pure sporting rule exception;

---

not impose on the participating undertakings restrictions which are not indispensable for achieving such efficiency gains. Fourth, that agreement, decision or practice must not give the participating undertakings the opportunity to eliminate all effective competition for a substantial part of the products or services concerned.

19 *Super League* (n 15), para 196.

20 Case C-209/23 *RRC Sports* ECLI:EU:C:2025:362, Opinion of AG Emiliou.

21 See for example the section on environmental objectives in the European Commission's Horizontal Guidelines which attempt to translate a public interest objective of the European Union into an economic efficiency. See, European Commission Horizontal Guidelines on the applicability of Article 101 of the Treaty on the Functioning of the European Union to horizontal co-operation agreements [2023] OJ C259/1.

- Second, there are legitimate objectives in the public interest that fall outside the prohibition on restrictions of competition (*Meca-Medina* test);
- Third, there are economic efficiencies falling under Article 101(3) TFEU that exempt any restrictions by object or effect of competition.

14. There is no exhaustive list of such exceptions. In *Super League*, the CJEU observed that the objectives set out in Article 165 TFEU relating to sport have a bearing upon such a determination even if there is no exemption or special treatment for sport.[22] The following items have been recognised as either pure sporting rules, legitimate objectives in the public interest or economic efficiencies relating to the regulation of sport:

1. Pure Sporting Rules: Rules of the Game and Organisational Rules
2. Recruitment and development of young players and athletes
3. Competitive Balance, Sporting Merit, and Regularity of Sporting Competition
4. Health and safety of athletes and spectators
5. Integrity of sporting competitions
6. Financial Sustainability
7. Good functioning of the international calendar
8. Uniform interpretation of rules
9. Ethical rules
10. Future justifications

I. Pure Sporting Rules: Rules of the Game and Organisational Rules

15. Pure sporting rules relate to rules adopted solely on non-economic grounds and which relate to questions of interest solely to sport per se.

16. Clearly, they relate to rules of the game. To date, there has been no attempt to claim that the offside rule or a limitation on the number of players that can be fielded over the course of the game is a restriction of competition (or free movement). In the *Murphy* case (concerning broadcasting rights), the CJEU held that a football match is not in itself subject to EU copyright law (unlike for example a dramatical work) because it is "subject to rules of the game, leaving no room for creative freedom for the purposes of copyright."[23] Similarly, EU law is not concerned with the minutiae of sports, such as the offside rule in football or the scoring system in tennis. Although often dismissed as an irrelevant rule, it is actually an important borderline between the application of EU law and sport.

17. The pure sporting rule is not just limited to the rules of the game; it also relates to some organisational features of sport. In *Walrave and Koch*, pure sporting rules were associated with rules relating to the nationality of athletes or participants for the

---

22 *Super League* (n 15), paras 95–107.

23 Joined Cases C-403/08 and C-429/08 *Football Association Premier League Ltd v QC Leisure* ECLI:EU:C:2011:631, para 98.

organisation of international sports competitions (but not to club competitions as held in *Bosman*). Likewise, in *Deliège,* the determination of ranking criteria used to select the judoka athletes participating individually in competitions was considered to be a pure sporting matter that fell within the proper competence of sports federation.[24]

18. However, there is not a bright line with respect to such organisational rules. In *Meca-Medina*, the Advocate General considered anti-doping rules to be pure sporting rules even if they had some secondary economic effects.[25] The CJEU, however, took a different approach noting that the anti-doping rules affected the economic activities of those subject to the rules.[26] This may be because such rules have a direct impact upon the ability of athletes to conduct their profession. Nonetheless the case highlights the difficulty sometimes in clearly establishing what constitutes a pure sporting rule. In his recent Opinion, AG Emiliou provided a useful rule of thumb in *RRC Sports*:

> In my view, the "sporting exception" encompasses, by and large, the basic "rules of the game" and some organisational aspects of a non-economic nature: for example, how matches take place (number of players, length of the match, the forms of conduct allowed or disallowed on the pitch, clothing requirements of athletes, and so forth) and how tournaments are structured (number of teams participating, number of matches per tournament, schedule of the matches, and so forth).[27]

19. Ultimately, the litmus test should be whether the sports regulation affects directly an economic activity (or EU citizenship rights[28]). If the impact is incidental then common sense should prevail and EU law should be declared inapplicable to the organisation of the sport.[29] After all, it is not the purpose of EU law to become a Code du Sport.

---

24 Joined Cases C-51/96 and C-191/97 *Deliege v Ligue Francophone de Judo et Disciplines Associees ASBL* ECLI:EU:C:2000:199.

25 Case C-519/04 P *David Meca-Medina and Igor Majcen v Commission of the European Communities* ECLI:EU:C:2006:201, Opinion of AG Léger.

26 This finding led the European Commission to state that "The ECJ has unequivocally rejected this approach in Meca Medina and held that the qualification of a rule as "purely sporting" is not sufficient to remove the athlete or the sport association adopting the rule in question from the scope of EC competition rules." However, this interpretation did not take into account that EU competition law is only concerned with undertakings when engaged in economic activities. In *Super League* (n 15), the CJEU clarified that pure sporting rules also fall outside the scope of EU competition. See European Commission SWD, "White Paper on Sport" COM (2007) 391 final.

27 *RRC Sports* (n 20), Opinion of AG Emiliou.

28 See Case C-22/18 *TopFit eV v Deutscher Leichtathletikverband eV* ECLI:EU:C:2019:497 in which EU citizenship rights were applied to amateur sport.

29 Advocate General Emiliou stated at paras 24–26: "Just to give some, obviously extreme, examples: the fact that football teams are only allowed to play matches with 11 players per side (and not, for example, 12 or 15) cannot be said to have no influence whatsoever on the free movement of workers. More players on the pitch would – one can presume – increase the intra-EU mobility of football players. […] By the same token, the decision to limit the number of teams that participate in a football league to a given and predetermined number (for example, 18 teams in the Bundesliga), and that only a few new teams can join the first division, at the end of the season, on the basis of a system of promotion from and relegation to lower divisions, de facto raises extremely high barriers to entry into the markets in which those teams are active. […] However, those are not the kind of restraints that the EU free movement and competition provisions are concerned with."

II. Recruitment and Development of Young Players and Athletes

20. In *Bosman*, the CJEU held that the aim of "of encouraging the recruitment and training of young players must be accepted as legitimate" in view of "the considerable social importance of sporting activities and in particular football in the Community."[30]

21. In that case, the CJEU held that the actual rules in place at the time, enabling the payment of a fee after a player's contract had ended, did not meet this objective due to its ad hoc nature which was not related to the actual costs of training a player. However, the recognition of the legitimate objective opened up the door to a new regime which culminated in the 2001 FIFA Regulations on the Status and Transfer of Players (RSTP) agreed by FIFA (and UEFA) with the European Commission. These rules included:

    - A system of training compensation in the case of players aged under 23, to encourage and reward the training effort of clubs, in particular small clubs;
    - Creation of solidarity mechanisms to redistribute a proportion of income from transfer fees to clubs involved in the training and education of a player.[31]

22. In the *Olympique Lyonnais* case,[32] concerning compensation for a player who refused to join his training club Olympique Lyonnais for a contract at Newcastle United, the CJEU reiterated that "the prospect of receiving training fees is likely to encourage football clubs to seek new talent and train young players".[33] By contrast, the CJEU considered that "clubs could be discouraged from investing in the training of young players if they could not obtain reimbursement of the amounts spent for that purpose where, at the end of his training, a player enters into a professional contract with another club."[34] As such, the CJEU recognised the legitimacy of training compensation. Moreover, the CJEU considered that such a training compensation scheme could take "due account of the costs borne by the clubs in training both future professional players and those who will never play professionally."

23. In so finding, the CJEU recognised the specific characteristics of sport may justify compensation for training costs. The CJEU observed that "the returns on the investments in training made by the clubs providing it are uncertain by their very nature since the clubs bear the expenditure incurred in respect of all the young players they recruit and train, sometimes over several years, whereas only some of those players undertake a professional career at the end of their training, whether with the club which provided the training or another club."[35] In other

---

30 *Bosman* (n 2), para 106.

31 FIFA 2001 Regulations on the Status and Transfer of Players (RSTP).

32 Case C-325/08 *Olympique Lyonnais SASP v Olivier Bernard and Newcastle UFC* ECLI:EU:C:2010:143.

33 Ibid para 41.

34 Ibid para 42.

35 Ibid para 43. Advocate General Sharpston referred to a training contact with a football club as a "magic key opening the door to a professional career". See Case C-325/08 *Olympique Lyonnais SASP v Olivier Bernard and Newcastle UFC* ECLI:EU:C:2009:481, Opinion of AG Sharpston, para 1.

words, the investment risks in training young persons in other sectors may be far less than in football where even good players do not make it professionally.[36] Although the case did not actually concern FIFA's RSTP (and indeed the French rules at issue did not meet the relevant standards), the post-2002 transfer system is seen as being aligned with its principles with respect to training compensation and solidarity.[37]

24. The training and development of young players is not necessarily limited to compensation. Indeed, the *Bosman* ruling also recognised the importance of encouraging the recruitment of young players.

25. In 2007, UEFA adopted the "locally trained player" (LTP) rules to encourage the training and recruitment of young players by requiring clubs participating in UEFA club competitions to have at least eight locally training players in their squad, at least four of whom should be club-trained players and the remaining four may be association-trained players (ie trained by a club in the same Member Association). Unlike the pre-*Bosman* transfer rules, there is no restriction on nationality so, for example, a Belgian player could become a LTP in France by training with a French club.

26. Following a review, the European Commission determined that the UEFA LTP rule, even if a potential form of indirect discrimination, was justified by the recruitment and training of young players.[38] A number of national football federations and leagues adopted versions of the UEFA locally-trained player rules, including Belgium. In the *Royal Antwerp* case,[39] a reference was made to the CJEU concerning UEFA's LTP rules[40] as well as those of the Royal Belgian Football Association (RBFA) which, unlike UEFA's LTP rule, have no club-trained player element but instead focus upon association-trained players.[41]

27. Having determined that the LTP rules may have an effect upon competition or free movement,[42] the CJEU recalled that the recruitment and training of young players is a legitimate objective in the public interest. As regards suitability, the CJEU held that the rules need only create "real and significant incentives"[43] to increase the prospects of recruitment and training of young players – but it is not necessary

---

36 *Olympique Lyonnais* (n 35), Opinion of AG Sharpston, para 31. For example, most trainee lawyers go on to qualify as lawyers so the investment risk for law firms in training lawyers is considerably less than in sport.

37 Advocate General Sharpston also made a reference to the potential relevance of the ruling for the RSTP regime. Ibid paras 59–62.

38 European Commission, Press Release, "UEFA Rule on "Home-Grown Players": Compatibility with the Principle of Free Movement of Persons" (28 May 2008) <https://ec.europa.eu/commission/presscorner/detail/en/ip_08_807> accessed 19 May 2026.

39 Case C-680/21 *Royal Antwerp FC* ECLI:EU:C:2023:1010.

40 Note UEFA was not originally a party to the case as the case only initially concerned the RBFA's LTP rules. However, UEFA intervened as a party after the reference was made when it transpired that questions had been referred relating to the validity of UEFA's LTP rules and not just those of the RBFA.

41 Ibid.

42 *Royal Antwerp* (n 39), para 107. The CJEU considered that the LTP rules are likely to have an impact "not only in the "upstream or supply market", which, from an economic point of view, is constituted by the recruitment of players, but also in the "downstream market", which, from the same point of view, is constituted by interclub football competition."

43 Ibid para 145.

for this to be demonstrated in a certain and quantifiable manner. Such suitability should be conducted in particular with respect to association-trained players to ensure that clubs still have an incentive to train players. As for proportionality, the number of LTPs required as a proportion of the total players required is the most important factor to be taken into account.

28. In its competition analysis, the CJEU translated the public interest justification into an economic efficiency for the purpose of Article 101(3) TFEU, stating that the UEFA and RBFA's LTP rules "encourage professional football clubs to recruit and train young players, and therefore intensify competition through training."[44] As for a benefit to consumers, the CJEU stated that the rules may benefit clubs and players as well as fans who take a stronger interest in clubs that field locally-trained players. The indispensability of the rules required assessing whether other realistic alternative measures[45] (such as financial incentives for clubs fielding trainee players) would be as effective *and* less restrictive.[46] In order to ensure no elimination of competition, the determining factor is that the minimum number of LTP players as regards the total players are on the match sheet.

29. The case has now returned to the Belgian court for final deliberation. However, the CJEU judgment is seen as largely endorsing the LTP model, in particular where the emphasis is upon club-trained players. It is noteworthy that the CJEU highlighted that the European Commission considered the level of the UEFA LTP rule to be proportionate.[47]

III. Competitive Balance, Sporting Merit and Regularity of Sporting Competitions

30. Competitive balance is the lifeblood of sport. As AG Szpunar observed:

> The specific markets of competitive sport rely on the existence of competitors. No restrictions could potentially lead to a situation where one club, capable of buying all players, would be in a position where de facto it can no longer be beaten by other clubs. It would be a pity if, say, Wisła Kraków were in a position to dominate the entire Polish league. The "beautiful game" would lose some of its attraction.[48]

31. Competitive balance and sporting merit were at the heart of the *Super League* case, which concerned a proposal by leading clubs to form a closed European

---

44 Ibid para 129.

45 Ibid para 124.

46 See also, Ibid para 131: "As regards the third condition, relating to the strict necessity of the rules at issue in the main proceedings, it will be for the referring court to ascertain, in the light of the specific arguments and evidence produced or to be produced by the parties, whether alternative measures such as those raised before the Court, namely the imposition of player training requirements for the purposes of granting licences to professional football clubs, the establishment of financing mechanisms or financial incentives aimed, in particular, at smaller clubs, or a system of direct compensation for the costs borne by training clubs, would be likely to constitute, in compliance with EU law, measures that are less restrictive of competition."

47 *Royal Antwerp* (n 39), para 132.

48 *Royal Antwerp* (n 10), Opinion of AG Szpunar, para 64.

club competition. The CJEU recognised that football is "essentially, based on sporting merit" whereby participation in club competitions is limited to those "which have achieved certain sporting results … with the conduct of those competitions being based on matches between and gradual elimination of those teams."[49] In addition, the CJEU also emphasised that "the proper functioning, sustainability and success of [football] competitions depend on maintaining a balance and on preserving a certain equality of opportunity as between the participating professional football clubs, given the interdependence that binds them together."[50] These specific characteristics of sport, amongst others, justified UEFA and FIFA requiring the prior approval of club competitions in order to ensure there are "common rules… to promote, in a suitable and effective manner, the holding of sporting competitions based on equal opportunities and merit."[51]

32. Competitive balance is also a central objective of the football transfer system. In *Bosman*, the CJEU recognised as a legitimate objective "the aims of maintaining a balance between clubs by preserving a certain degree of equality and uncertainty as to results."[52]

33. With respect to transfer windows, the CJEU held in *Lehtonen* that "late transfers might be liable to change substantially the sporting strength of one or other team in the course of the championship, thus calling into question the comparability of results between the teams taking part in that championship, and consequently the proper functioning of the championship as a whole."[53]

34. Applying this reasoning in the 2002 agreement on principles for the RSTP, the European Commission and FIFA (with UEFA) agreed on the necessity to foster "stability of contracts" to ensure the good functioning of football club competitions.[54]

35. In *Diarra*, despite its finding that the FIFA rules on joint and several liability of clubs for a breach without just cause by a player were disproportionate, the CJEU accepted that "the objective consisting in ensuring the regularity of sporting competitions is a legitimate objective in the public interest."[55] The CJEU recognised that the composition of teams is "one of the essential parameters of the competitions in which clubs compete".[56] Consequently, the CJEU considered it legitimate for rules to maintain "a certain degree of stability in clubs" player rosters, which serve as a pool for the composition of the teams that are likely to be fielded by those clubs in interclub football competitions."[57]

---

49 *Super League* (n 15), para 143.

50 Ibid para 253.

51 Ibid para 144.

52 *Bosman* (n 2), para 106.

53 Case C-176/96 *Lehtonen v FRBSB* ECLI:EU:C:2000:201, para 54.

54 European Commission, Press Release, "Commission Closes Investigations into FIFA Regulations on International Football Transfers" (5 June 2002) <https://ec.europa.eu/commission/presscorner/detail/en/ip_02_824> accessed 19 May 2026

55 Case C-650/22 *Lassana Diarra and FIFPRO v FIFA and URBSFA* ECLI:EU:C:2024:824, para 100.

56 Ibid para 102.

57 Ibid para 102.

36. FIFA is now in the process of putting in place a new regime that protects contractual stability in line with the ruling. The matter has also been considered by the EU Social Dialogue Committee for Professional Football.

IV. Health and Safety of Athletes and Spectators

37. The health and safety of athletes is clearly a legitimate objective in the public interest. In *Meca-Medina*, the CJEU recognised the health of athletes as amongst the legitimate objectives pursued by anti-doping rules.[58] The physical integrity of sportspersons is explicitly recognised by Article 165 TFEU. The protection of health and safety is not limited to athletes but also includes spectators.[59]

38. In the *ISU Eligibility Rules* case, the European Commission recognised that the health and safety of athletes to be a legitimate objective.[60] However, it rejected the relevance to the case at hand. By contrast, the EU General Court recognised a pre-authorisation system to be "a suitable mechanism" to achieve the legitimate objective of ensuring "sporting competitions comply with common standards, seeking in particular to ensure that competitions take place fairly and the physical and ethical integrity of sportspeople is protected."[61] The ISU was subsequently permitted to take into account health and safety when approving proposed skating events and testing novelties to proposed skating formats.[62]

39. Health and safety concerns remain, however, a potential flashpoint between EU competition law and sport in the absence of a clear authorisation regime in place by the sports federation. In the Swedish motorsport case, *Svenska Bilsportförbundet*, the Swedish Market Court recognised in its judgment (pre-dating the *ISU* and *Super League* cases) that a sports federation could protect health and safety even in the absence of an authorisation regime.[63] However, other national competition authorities turned a blind eye to such risks.[64] While, of course, health and safety should not be used as cover for anticompetitive conduct, EU competition law should not prohibit action by a sports federation where such concerns are

---

58 *Meca-Medina* (n 9), para 43.

59 European Commission SWD, The EU and Sport: Background and Context – Accompanying Document to the White Paper on Sport SEC (2007) 935 final, s 2.1.5.

60 Case AT.40208 European Commission Decision *International Skating Union's Eligibility* (8 December 2017) (*ISU* Decision), para 219.

61 Case T-93/18 *International Skating Union (ISU)* ECLI:EU:T:2020:610, para 108.

62 ISU Communication No 2171 Open International Competitions, which established the authorisation procedure for international skating competitions following the decision of the European Commission. See <https://isu-d8g8b4b7ece7aphs.a03.azurefd.net/isudamcontainer/uploads/images/decisionsoftheisucouncil/2171Open_Intl_Competitions.pdf> accessed 20 May 2026.

63 Case A 5/11 *Svenska Bilsportförbundet* MD 2012:16 (20 December 2012) Swedish Market Court.

64 In *Global Champions Tour*, the Belgian Competition Authority imposed interim measures preventing the FEI from applying its authorisation rules to an independent organiser notwithstanding concerns for the welfare of horses at unauthorised events. After the *ISU* Decision (n 60), the BCA accepted some modest modifications to the rules to enable the FEI to reinstate its authorisation regime. See, Case 2015-V/M-23 ABC Decision *Global Champions League and Tops Trading Belgium v Fédération Equestre Internationale (FEI)* (27 July 2015), confirmed by the Brussels Court of Appeal (3 May 2016) <https://www.abc-bma.be/fr/decisions/2015mr1-fei-ad> accessed 20 May 2026.

genuine. The competition risk of a conflict of interest is irrelevant when the risk to the health and safety of athletes (and indeed animals) at such unauthorised sports events is real.

V. Integrity of Sporting Competitions

40. In *Meca-Medina*, the CJEU confirmed the "integrity and objectivity of competitive sport and ethical values in sport" as legitimate objectives, in that case with respect to anti-doping rules.

41. Not only is integrity recognised as a legitimate objective but its public perception in sporting competitions is equally important. In the *ENIC* case (concerning UEFA's rule on multi-club ownership), the European Commission upheld the prohibition on clubs coming under the same ownership from participating in the same UEFA Club Competitions on this basis:

> The ratio of the rule is manifest: if two or more clubs participating in the same contest are under control of or managed by one single entity, there is cause for concern that in a given situation the existence of opposing interests which underlies any sport competition will not be apparent. For instance, should two clubs under joint control or ownership meet at a certain stage of the competition, the public's perception of the authenticity of the result would be jeopardised.[65]

42. As recently confirmed by the Court of Arbitration for Sport (CAS), this position remains valid.[66]

VI. Financial Sustainability

43. A key feature of sport is its interdependent nature. The organiser or a league requires clubs – often fierce rivals – to coordinate in order to create a product. However, there are short-term incentives in sport that drive unsustainable practices. Competitions take place over seasons usually lasting around 10 months; with each season, all clubs start again. In many sports such as football, promotion and relegation create strong pressure for a club to perform.[67] Likewise, qualification for a coveted spot in European club competitions can have a significant impact upon the sporting and commercial success of a club. And that is to say nothing of the social pressure from the clubs' fans to perform.

44. In these circumstances, there is strong financial pressure on clubs to overspend today in the hope that it pays off tomorrow. This incentivises other clubs to also engage in overspending in an arms race for talent. If all clubs engage

---

65 Case AT.37806 UEFA Decision *ENIC* (25 June 2002). The Court of Arbitration for Sport (CAS) came to a similar conclusion in a case concerning the same parties (Case 98/200 CAS Decision *AEK Athens and SK Slavia Praha* (20 August 1999).

66 In 2025, the CAS dismissed competition claims against a revised version of the MCO rule on the basis that the *ENIC* case remained valid. See Case 2025/A/11604 CAS Decision *Crystal Palace FC v EUFA and Others* (21 October 2025), para 162.

67 Indeed, from 1992–1993 (when relegation started) until the 2025–2026 season, only six clubs have never been relegated: Arsenal, Chelsea, Everton, Liverpool, Manchester United and Tottenham Hotspur.

in unsustainable practices this risks not only the collapse of clubs concerned but systemic issues for the league as a whole as costs spiral out of control for all clubs. As the European Commission stated:

> If sport events are to be of interest to the spectator, they must involve uncertainty as to the result. There must therefore be a certain degree of equality in competitions. This sets the sport sector apart from other industry or service sectors, where competition between firms serves the purpose of eliminating inefficient firms from the market. Sport teams, clubs and athletes have a direct interest not only in there being other teams, clubs and athletes, but also in their economic viability as competitors.[68]

45. In the *Saracens* case (concerning the salary cap in Premiership rugby), the distinguished panel summed up the risks as follows:

> Clubs are principally motivated by a desire to win and retain [Premiership] membership, not by a desire to make profits (as evidenced by their continuing loss-making). Absent a restriction on player salaries, there would be a rapid return to player costs spiralling out of control as clubs outbid each other to secure the best players, which would in turn lead to some clubs folding.[69]

46. These factors distinguish sport from other sectors where financial sustainability would not necessarily be a legitimate objective. Following concerns for the financial sustainability of European football in the wake of the financial crisis, UEFA adopted the UEFA Financial Fair Play (FFP) rules which centred around the break-even rule. The Commissioner for Competition, Jaoquin Almunia, welcomed the central objective of the rules to ensure that clubs "live within their means".[70] In so doing, he compared the purpose of the FFP rules as being similar to that in state aid as preventing unsustainable spending in football.

47. In the *Galatasaray* case[71] concerning the FFP rules, the CAS upheld the FFP rules on the basis that they were consistent with EU competition law in requiring clubs to act as any reasonable entity in normal market conditions:

> [The FFP] Regulations do not appear to prevent the clubs from competing among themselves on the pitch or in the acquisition of football players. The Panel agrees with [UEFA] that, on the contrary, they produce the effect that competition is not distorted by "overspending", i.e. by those clubs that, operating at a loss, allow themselves operations that could not be conducted on a sound commercial basis, and gain an advantage over those clubs which respect the constraints of financial balance (i.e., which take a behaviour that should be expected by any reasonable entity in normal market conditions). In other words, their effect is to prevent a distortion of competition.

---

68 White Paper on Sport (n 26), s 3.4.

69 Case *Premier Rugby Ltd v Saracens Rugby Club* (4 November 2019) Disciplinary Panel, para 99.

70 Letter from Commissioner Almunia to UEFA President Michel Platini (21 March 2012) <https://competition-policy.ec.europa.eu/system/files/2022-03/2012_financial_fairplay_and_state_aid_in_professional_football_letter_almunia_en.pdf> accessed 20 May 2026.

71 Case 2016/A/4492 CAS Decision *Galatasaray v UEFA* (3 October 2016), para 76.

48. This link between financial sustainability rules with normal market conditions can be seen in the recent *Manchester City* case.[72] The legitimacy of financial sustainability was accepted by the tribunal as justifying the regulation of associated party transactions (APTs) to prevent overspending above market value by organisations associated with the club. However, the tribunal considered an exception for shareholder loans created a distortion of competition similar to the risk of inflated APTs. The tribunal compared the situation to a state aid[73] stating that a "subsidy via a non-commercial loan is just as damaging to its effectiveness of PSR and to competition between clubs as a subsidy via an inflated sponsorship agreement."[74] In its view, both are "equally injurious to the objective of the PSR."[75] This resulted, according to the tribunal, in a "clear distortion of competition between clubs".[76] Simply put, the APT rules did not go far enough. The upshot was that the Premier League incorporated shareholder loans into the scope of its APT rules.[77]

49. While financial sustainability takes different forms, from the break-even rule to salary caps to ratios between player expenditure and income, the key factor is ensuring the financial sustainability rules are necessary and proportionate in that they leave sufficient scope for competition (in particular for players' services).

VII. Good Functioning of the International Calendar

50. The good functioning of the international calendar is recognised as a legitimate objective in sport.

51. In the Opinion in the *MOTOE* case,[78] AG Kokott stated that "it is in the interests of the sportspersons participating in the event, but also of the spectators and the public in general, that the individual competitions in a particular sport are incorporated into an overarching framework so that, for example, a specific timetable can be followed." In her view, such coordination makes "sense to prevent clashes between competitions so that both sportspersons and spectators can participate in as many such events as possible."

52. In *Super League*, the CJEU held that it is legitimate for sports federations to put in place pre-authorisation rules as the "specific characteristics [of sport] support a finding that it is legitimate to subject the organisation and conduct of international professional football competitions to common rules intended to guarantee the homogeneity and coordination of those competitions within an overall match calendar …"[79] The CJEU further stated that it is justified to ensure that "competitions

---

72 *Manchester City Football Club (MCFC) v Premier League* (25 September 2024).

73 Ibid s 255. The Tribunal stated that "it is instructive to look at the EU state aid regime". Again, it is interesting to see the influence of EU law upon the application of UK competition law post-Brexit.

74 Ibid s 252.

75 Ibid s 254.

76 Ibid s 340–s 350. Applying the *Super League* test, the tribunal held that this by object restriction could only be justified in accordance with c.9 CA but that the relevant conditions were not met.

77 In a second arbitral award, the same tribunal considered that the amended APT rules were void. The Premier League then adopted a new set of rules. Manchester City and the Premier League settled a further dispute concerning these amendments in September 2025.

78 Case C-49/07 *MOTOE* ECLI:EU:C:2008:142, Opinion of AG Kokott, para 94.

79 *Super League* (n 15), para 144.

will, in a substantively homogeneous and temporally coordinated manner, integrate into the "organised system" of national, European and international competitions characterising that sport."[80]

53. As such, it is justified for sports federations to put in place measures to facilitate the good functioning of different levels of the sport as well as coordination between national and international competitions. Likewise, it may be legitimate for sports federations to balance a range of complex issues in determining the scheduling of a major sports event, such as sporting[81] or health and safety[82] considerations.

VIII. Uniform Interpretation of Rules

54. Uniform rules require uniform enforcement. A feature of sports judicial systems is its mandatory nature to ensure a neutral, efficient and – crucially – uniform enforcement of the rules. For example, UEFA had high profile cases concerning its multi-club ownership rules over the 2025 summer that had to be resolved quickly before the commencement of the UEFA club competitions. In the *RFC Seraing* case,[83] the CJEU stated such mandatory arbitration may be justified by legitimate objectives:

> "It is true that that imposed recourse to arbitration may be warranted in principle, in the light of the legal autonomy enjoyed by international sports associations and having regard to their responsibilities by the pursuit of legitimate objectives such as ensuring the uniform handling of disputes relating to the sporting discipline that is within the purview of their jurisdiction or enabling the consistent interpretation and application of the rules applicable to that discipline."[84]

55. The CJEU balanced such considerations with the principle of effective EU judicial review (Article 19 of the Treaty on European Union) for the review of arbitral awards. Where the seat of arbitration is in an EU Member State, there is a direct legal remedy before the EU national courts (with a reference to the CJEU if necessary). However, there is no requirement to have the seat of arbitration in the EU.[85] The CJEU recognised that the seat of arbitration for sports cases (and indeed other arbitral cases) may take place outside the EU. The CJEU accepted that effective judicial review may instead be guaranteed through other mechanisms, in particular the application of the New York Convention[86] which enables a party

---

80 Ibid para 253.

81 For example, the scheduling may take into account the Winter or Summer Olympics or other major sports events taking place the same year may affect scheduling in order to facilitate broadcasting and media coverage.

82 For example, a pandemic or war may require a sudden change to the schedule of a major event or even its relocation. Geographic location may also be of relevance with risks of extreme heat or cold at certain periods of the year affecting the scheduling.

83 Case C-600/23 *Royal Football Club Seraing SA v FIFA and others* ECLI:EU:C:2025:617.

84 Ibid para 94.

85 Ibid para 99.

86 Convention on the Recognition and Enforcement of Foreign Arbitral Awards (10 June 1958) (New York Convention). Although the European Union is not a signatory, it is binding on all 27 Member States, with a total of 172 signatories worldwide as of 2026.

that is the subject of an arbitral award to challenge its recognition or enforcement on grounds of public policy before its national courts,[87] which "as regards the Member States includes EU public policy".[88]

IX. Ethical Values

56. It is legitimate for sports associations to put in place that are aligned with their ethical values. The protection of the moral integrity of sportspersons is also an objective pursued by Article 165 TFEU. Clearly, protecting athletes, in particular minors, from sexual harassment and other forms of unethical conduct is legitimate.

57. However, ethical values also relate to economic activities in sport. While tobacco advertising in sports is now banned in the EU, it seems reasonable for sports organisers to regulate or ban sponsorship relating to strong alcohol or gambling or unhealthy products irrespective of the position in different EU Member States.

58. Ethical values may differ from sport to sport; however, this does not mean it is necessarily unreasonable to regulate or ban such conduct. For example, betting is associated with horse racing, however, in some sports it would be an anathema to the values of the sport to allow on-site betting (as well as being a risk to the integrity of the sport). Indeed, this concern was the origin of the *ISU Eligibility Rules* case – with the ISU being ultimately permitted to prohibit skating events based on betting provided this was clearly stipulated in its authorisation regime.[89]

X. Future Problems, Future Justifications

59. Sport is constantly changing. A glance at the coverage of football, rugby or tennis from the 1990s – just a generation ago – shows just how much modern sport has changed. With new opportunities come new challenges for sports federations. Not every problem can be predicted. Financial sustainability, which developed in the wake of the financial crisis, is a good example of this. Likewise, the Covid-19 pandemic required unprecedented interventions by sports federations and organisers.[90] Who, for example, can foresee what challenges AI will present to the

---

87 *Royal Football Club Seraing* SA (n 83), para 117: "although any State party to it must recognise the existence and the authority of foreign arbitral awards made pursuant to an agreement under which natural or legal persons have undertaken to submit to arbitration all or part of any disputes which may arise between them concerning a particular legal relationship, that obligation goes hand in hand with the obligation, for such a State, to ensure that the persons concerned have the possibility of obtaining from the national court or tribunal having jurisdiction, either at those persons" request or of the court's or tribunal's own motion, a review of those awards for consistency with that State's public policy."

88 Ibid para 117.

89 ISU Communication No 2641 Code of Ethics (2024) <https://isu-d8g8b4b7ece7aphs.a03.azurefd.net/isudamcontainer/CMS/isucommunications/pdf/2641CodeofEthics2024UPDATEDNovember1820241731924557.pdf> accessed 20 May 2026.

90 For example, UEFA adopted special rules to protect sporting merit when a number of national club competitions had to be terminated early following the outbreak of Covid-9 in March 2020. See UEFA Guidelines on eligibility principles for 2020–2021 UEFA Club Competitions – Covid 19 (2021) <https://www.uefa.com/MultimediaFiles/Download/uefaorg/General/02/64/17/45/2641745_DOWNLOAD.pdf> accessed 20 May 2026.

future governance of sport? It may be that new legitimate objectives or economic efficiencies will have to evolve to address such new challenges. Sports federations should, therefore, have the freedom to adapt to the times. Just because it is not in the rulebook today does not mean it should not be there in the future. Sport is timeless but of its time.

Specific Characteristics of Sport and EU Law

Pieter Paepe*
Edson Legal, Brussels (Belgium)

1. This chapter explores the role of the "specific characteristics of sport" in the three judgments issued by the Court of Justice of the European Union (the Court) on 21 December 2023 – *European Super League (ESL)*,[1] *International Skating Union (ISU)*,[2] and *Royal Antwerp FC*[3] – as well as in the judgment of 4 October 2024 in the *Diarra* case.[4] It will be explained that the specific characteristics of sport play in essence a dual role in the Court's case law: on the one hand, justifying the need for common rules to regulate some of the most fundamental aspects of a given sport, and on the other, limiting and overseeing the exercise of regulatory power by sporting associations such as FIFA and UEFA.

2. Throughout the judgments discussed, the Court repeatedly affirms that sport, and professional football in particular, possess "specific characteristics".[5] In *Diarra*, the Court references the "undeniable specific characteristics of sporting activity".[6] This is not surprising, as Article 165 TFEU recognises the "specific nature of sport"

---

* Attorney, Brussels bar. Pieter Paepe represents the football players' unions FIFPro, FIFPro Europe and the UNFP (the French football players' union) in the *Diarra* proceedings.

1 Case C-333/21 *European Super League (ESL)* ECLI:EU:C:2023:1011.

2 Case C-124/21 P *International Skating Union (ISU)* ECLI:EU:C:2023:1012.

3 Case C-680/21 *Royal Antwerp FC* ECLI:EU:C:2023:1010.

4 Case C-650/22 *Lassana Diarra and FIFPRO v FIFA and URBSFA* ECLI:EU:C:2024:824. This judgment is commonly referred to as "*Diarra*" after former French football player Lassana Diarra.

5 See also Aurélie Villanueva, "Accounting for the Specificities of Sport in EU law: Old and New Directions in the 21 December 2023 Judgments" (2023) 23 ISLJ 422–430.

6 *Diarra* (n 4), point 84.

and previous case law has already acknowledged the "particular nature and context of certain sports matches",[7] as well as the "specific characteristics of sport in general, and football in particular, as well as their social and educational functions".[8] The principle that sport has specific characteristics was already well-established in EU law.

I. Specific Characteristics of Sport in the Context of EU Primary Law

3. The specific characteristics of sport can – and if relevant should – be taken into account when applying EU primary law. The judgments discussed clarify and demonstrate that this obligation does not arise from Article 165 TFEU but rather from the standard application of EU primary law.

4. A key development in *ESL* and *Royal Antwerp* is the Court's analysis of Article 165 TFEU. Article 165(1) TFEU mentions "the specific nature of sport, its structures based on voluntary activity and its social and educational function" and Article 165(2) TFEU refers to "fairness and openness in sporting competitions and cooperation between bodies responsible for sports" and "the physical and moral integrity of sportsmen and sportswomen, especially the youngest sportsmen and sportswomen".

5. While Advocate General (AG) Rantos advocated for an expansive interpretation of Article 165 TFEU in *ESL*, AG Szpunar, relying on a literal, systemic, and teleological interpretation, supported a much narrower reading of Article 165 TFEU in *Royal Antwerp*. On Article 165 TFEU, AG Szpunar emphasised, among other points, that it is addressed to the Union, not to Member States or private entities, that its wordings is typically found in soft law, and that its fourth paragraph does not provide a legal basis for the institutions to adopt legally binding acts. He concluded that Article 165 TFEU remained "helpful" for two main reasons: it can provide a basis for justifying a restriction on the freedom of movement for workers (Article 45 TFEU), and it offers "an indication of what is acceptable throughout the Union when applying the proportionality test".[9] Faced with differing opinions,[10] the Court of Justice has adopted a narrow interpretation of Article 165 TFEU, aligning in essence with the perspective of AG Szpunar.

6. The Court observes that Article 165 TFEU is "not a cross-cutting provision with general application".[11] As a result – the Court explains – the various elements and objectives outlined in Article 165 TFEU, as well as any incentive measures

---

7 Case C-22/18 *TopFit e.V. and Daniele Biffi v Deutscher Leichtathletikverband eV* ECLI:EU:C:2019:497, point 49.

8 Case C-325/08 *Olympique Lyonnais SASP v Olivier Bernard and Newcastle UFC* ECLI:EU:C:2010:143, point 40.

9 Case C-680/21 *Royal Antwerp FC* ECLI:EU:C:2023:188, Opinion of AG Spunzar, point 55.

10 Melchior Wathelet, a former judge and Advocate General, observes that there was a "total collision between two interpretations". See Melchior Wathelet, "Il y a bien eu du sport à la Cour de Justice de l'Union européenne… et il y en aura encore" [2024] Journal des Tribunaux 214.

11 Advocate General Rantos had argued, by contrast, that this provision is "by its very nature, a 'horizontal' provision, inasmuch as it must be taken into consideration when implementing other EU policies" (Case C-333/21 *European Super League (ESL)* ECLI:EU:C:2022:993, Opinion of AG Rantos, point 35).

and recommendations adopted by the EU institutions under Article 165(4) TFEU, must "not be integrated or taken into account in a binding manner" when applying EU primary law. This holds true regardless of whether the issues at hand relate to the freedom of movement of persons, services and capital (Articles 45, 49, 56, and 63 TFEU) or to the competition rules (Articles 101 and 102 TFEU).[12] More generally, the Court emphasises that Article 165 TFEU must not "be regarded as being a special rule exempting sport from all or some of the other provision of primary EU law liable to be applied to it or requiring special treatment for sport in the context of that application".[13]

7. The Court states that the specific characteristics of sport can be considered "only in the context of and in compliance with the conditions and criteria provided for in [Articles 45, 49, 56, 63, 101 and 102 TFEU]" and "provided they are relevant" for the application of these provisions.[14] As demonstrated by the judgments discussed, any specific characteristics of sport can – and if relevant should – be taken into account as part of the standard application of EU law. This standard approach provides enough flexibility and, in fact, mandates the consideration of any specific characteristics, provided they are relevant to the application of these rules.

II. Dual Role of the Specific Characteristics of Sport

8. The specific characteristics of sport play a dual role in the Court's case law discussed here: they justify the need for common rules governing a given sport and are central to how EU law limits the exercise by sporting associations of their powers to adopt these rules.

1. Common Rules for the Organisation of Sporting Competitions

9. Stefan Késenne, a leading sports economist, refers to the "inverted joint product" as the most important economic characteristic that makes the industry of professional sports different from other industries. The idea of "inverted joint production" refers to a situation where two production processes by two companies are needed to produce and supply one single product. In team sports, the companies are the sports clubs, and the product is the game. One team cannot play a football match; it needs an opponent team.[15] The organisation of a sporting competition requires a certain degree of cooperation between the participating athletes and/or teams. The organisation of one single game of football requires not only two teams, but also an agreement on the rules of the game, the place and time where the game will be played, rules on integrity, rules on arbitration, etc. The organisation of a

---

12 *ESL* (n 1), points 100–101; *Royal Antwerp* (n 3), points 68–69.

13 Ibid point 101; Ibid point 69.

14 Ibid point 104; Ibid point 72; *ISU* (n 2), point 96. See also *Diarra* (n 4), point 84.

15 Stefan Kesenne, *The Economic Theory of Professional Team Sports. An Analytical Treatment* (2nd edn, Edward Elgar 2014) 2. Also, AG Rantos argued that sporting activities are different from other economic sectors and refers to the fact that sport is characterised by "a high degree of interdependence", since clubs are "dependent on one another in order to be able to organise themselves and to develop in the context of sporting competitions" (*ESL* (n 11), Opinion of AG Rantos, point 41).

sporting competition, with multiple participating athletes or teams, is an even more complex undertaking. Team sporting competitions are organised in leagues, with separate governance structures and bodies. These governance bodies determine the rules of the game, promote the sport and usually collect revenues.[16]

10. The discussed judgments acknowledge the need for common rules in sports and affirm that, in principle, it is legitimate for associations responsible for a sporting discipline to adopt and enforce rules addressing some of the most critical aspects of a given sport.[17] In *ISU*, among the four judgments, the only one not related to football, but to ice speed skating, also reaffirms the principle that a sporting association "may establish, implement, and enforce rules governing the organisation and conduct of international competitions within the relevant sporting discipline, using sanctions to ensure compliance".[18] A combined reading of these judgments yields the following list:[19] rules relating to the organisation and conduct of competitions; rules on prior approval and participation by professional football clubs and players in competitions; rules intended to guarantee the homogeneity and coordination of competition within an overall annual or seasonal calendar; rules to promote the holding of sporting competitions based on equal opportunities and merit; rules concerning the conditions in which professional football clubs can put together teams participating in competitions; rules concerning the conditions in which players or athletes can take part in competitions. Since it is legitimate to subject the organisation and conduct of football to common rules, the Court also acknowledges that it is "legitimate to ensure compliance with those common rules".[20] Sanctions, the Court holds, that have been introduced as "an adjunct" to common rules are "legitimate, in terms of their principle"" since they guarantee the effectiveness of those rules.[21]

11. The conclusion that common rules can, as a matter of principle, be adopted and implemented by sporting associations is precisely based on considerations that concern the "specific characteristics" of sport and professional football in particular.[22] The Court refers to the fact that football gives rise to the organisation of numerous competitions at both the European and national levels, which in turn involves the participation of many clubs and a large number of players. In addition, the Court points out that participation to competitions is limited to teams which have achieved a certain sporting result. Competitions, the Court adds, are based on matches between teams and their gradual elimination. The Court emphasises the importance of "sporting merit" and observes that this can only be guaranteed if all participating teams face each other under homogeneous regulatory and technical

---

16 OECD, "Competition and Professional Sports" (4 December 2023) Roundtable on Competition Policy Papers, No 2 (Background Note) <https://one.oecd.org/document/DAF/COMP/WP2(2019)3/en/pdf#:~:text=Independent%20sector%20regulators%20and%20competition,direct%20co-operation%20a%20challenge> accessed 4 August 2025 6.

17 *ESL* (n 1), points 143–144 and 175–176; *Royal Antwerp* (n 3), points 103–104; *Diarra* (n 4), point 143.

18 *ISU* (n 2), point 144.

19 *ESL* (n 1), points 144–146; *Royal Antwerp* (n 3), points 103–104; *Diarra* (n 4), point 142.

20 *ESL* (n 1), point 144.

21 Ibid point 146; *Royal Antwerp* (n 3), point 104; *Diarra* (n 4), point 143.

22 Ibid points 144 and 175; Ibid point 105; Ibid point 142.

conditions to ensure a minimum level of equal opportunity.[23] In *Royal Antwerp*, the coexistence of interclub competition and competitions between national teams is also mentioned.[24]

12. While the specific characteristics of sports may justify the adoption of "common rules", as the case may be, by a private law sporting association, the question remains whether there are limits to the scope of the regulatory powers that sporting associations possess in the first place. This issue is distinct from the question of how these powers are exercised. The *Diarra* case involved certain provisions of FIFA's Regulations on the Status and Transfer of Players (RSTP), which regulate essential aspects of the employment relationship between clubs and players. In these proceedings, the players' unions argued that FIFA does not have the authority to regulate such employment relationships in the first place, as this is the prerogative of legislators or, alternatively, should be determined through collective bargaining agreements between employers and employees. To support that position, reference was made to the 2005 *Laurent Piau* judgment, in which the General Court held that "[t]he very principle of regulation of an economic activity concerning neither the specific nature of sport nor the freedom of internal organisation of sports associations by a private-law body, like FIFA, which has not been delegated any such power by a public authority, cannot from the outset be regarded as compatible with Community law" and that "such regulation, which constitutes policing of an economic activity and touches on fundamental freedoms, falls [in principle] within the competence of the public authorities".[25] These arguments are echoed in point 99 of the *Diarra* judgment, where the Court notes that FIFA is a private law association that has not been entrusted by public authorities with any particular mission in the area of worker protection. Additionally, the Court notes that the protection of workers is not included among FIFA's objectives as outlined in its statutes. *Diarra* suggests strong doubt as to whether regulating worker protection falls within FIFA's powers at all.

2. EU Law Limits to the Exercise of the Powers to Adopt Common Rules

13. Whereas the Court recognises that it may, in principle, be legitimate to subject a sporting discipline to "common rules" governing several of that sport's most fundamental aspects, and that the existence of such broad powers may be justified by several "specific characteristics" of sport and football, EU law does limit the exercise of those regulatory powers. The judgments discussed highlight and clarify the EU law boundaries, in these cases through competition rules and internal market freedoms, that limit the exercise of the power to establish and implement common rules in sports, and to impose sanctions for their violation. It will later be discussed how the specific characteristics of sport play a role at two stages: first, in identifying an obstacle to an internal market freedom, a restriction of competition, or an abuse of a dominant position; and second, once that is established, in assessing whether it can be justified.

---

23 Ibid point 143; Ibid point 104.

24 *Royal Antwerp* (n 3), point 106.

25 Case T-193/02 *Laurent Piau v Commission of the European Communities* ECLI:EU:T:2005:22, points 77–78.

14. In *Diarra*, it was argued that the FIFA rules in question were not only incompatible with Article 101 TFEU and the freedom of movement of workers – EU law provisions on which the referring court sought the Court's interpretation – but also with the fundamental rights and freedoms protected by the Charter of Fundamental Rights of the European Union (Charter). *Diarra* was ultimately decided by the Court on the basis of the freedom of movement of workers and the competition rules only, without any reference to the implications of the Charter for FIFA's regulatory power. However, the question of whether, and if so how, the Charter may limit the exercise of regulatory powers by a sporting association is a central issue in the Opinion of AG Szpunar.[26] According to Article 51(1) of the Charter, it applies only to Member States when they are implementing Union law.[27] Although FIFA is a private entity and not a Member State, the Advocate General argues that, based on the reasoning applied in *Walrave and Koch*,[28] a sporting association like FIFA should be treated as if it were a Member State when it attempts to justify a restriction on internal market freedoms or competition. In such cases, the Advocate General states, the Charter is applicable, and FIFA is bound by the provisions of the Charter.

III. An Obstacle to the Internal Market Freedoms and a Restriction of Competition

15. *ESL*, *Royal Antwerp*, *ISU* and *Diarra* illustrate that specific characteristics of sport can play a crucial role in identifying restrictions on the freedom to provide services (Article 56 TFEU), the freedom of movement of workers (Article 45 TFEU), or in assessing whether there has been an "abuse of a dominant position" (Article 102 TFEU) or a "restriction" of competition (Article 101 TFEU). The Court explicitly states that the specific characteristics of sport can be relevant at this stage of the analysis, suggesting that, at the most abstract level, these characteristics may concern "the nature, organisation or functioning of the sport concerned and, more specifically, how professionalised it is, the manner in which it is practised, the manner of interaction between the various participating stakeholders and the role played by the structures and bodies responsible for it at all levels".[29]

16. If relevant to the application of competition rules and internal market freedoms, the specific characteristics of sport may not only be considered but actually should be taken into account. The Court explains that the characterisation of a rule adopted by a sporting association as an obstacle or as a restriction of competition "must, at any rate, be based on a specific assessment of the content of that rule in the actual context in which it is to be implemented".[30] If there are any specific characteristics of sport relevant to the application of internal market freedoms and competition rules, they should typically emerge during the analysis of the "actual context" in which a rule governing a specific sport is applied.

---

26 Case C-650/22 *Lassana Diarra and FIFPRO v FIFA and URBSFA* ECLI:EU:C:2024:375, Opinion of AG Spunzar.

27 And to the institutions, bodies, offices and agencies of the Union.

28 Case 36/74 *Walrave and Koch v Association Union Cycliste Internationale and others* ECLI:EU:C:1974:140.

29 *ESL* (n 1), point 105; *Royal Antwerp* (n 3), point 73; *ISU* (n 2), point 96.

30 Ibid; Ibid.

1. Identification of an Anticompetitive "Object"

17. The judgments discussed provide a summary and clarification of the Court's case law regarding the analytical framework for determining whether certain conduct[31] has the "object" of preventing, restricting, or distorting competition within the meaning of Article 101(1) TFEU.[32] These judgments outline that the assessment follows a three-step analysis.[33] First, the "content" of the agreement, decision or practice must be assessed. Second, the "economic and legal context" in which the conduct occurs should be analysed. Third, the "objectives" of the conduct must be examined, that is, the objective aims which the conduct seeks to achieve from a competition standpoint. In a later judgment of 29 July 2024, the Court states that the concept of "objective aims" refers, in its legal sense, to the primary reason for the conduct in question, that is to say, to the immediate and direct aims pursued by the coordination in question which led the undertakings concerned to participate in it.[34]

18. Importantly, it has been established that, to determine whether certain conduct has an anticompetitive "object", it is not necessary to examine or prove its "effects" on competition, whether those effects are actual or potential, or negative or positive.[35]

19. Any specific characteristics of sport that may be relevant to the application of Article 101(1) TFEU should come to the surface as part of this three-step analysis. In particular the second step that involves examining the "economic and legal context" of which the conduct forms a part, provides significant flexibility to consider any specific characteristics of sport.[36] This is particularly true because, as the Court highlights, it is "necessary", and not merely optional, to consider, as part of the analysis of the economic and legal context, "the nature of the products or services concerned" and the "actual conditions of the structure and functioning of the relevant sectors or markets".[37] In a later judgment of 27 June 2024, the Court states again that determining a collusive practice as a restriction of competition by object necessitates the three-step analysis outlined here, and further emphasises the importance of considering "in particular the specific characteristics of the market where the effects will actually occur".[38]

---

31 The Court uses the term "conduct" to refer to agreements between undertakings, decisions by associations of undertakings, and concerted practices.

32 See also Giorgio Monti, "EU Competition Law after the Grand Chamber's December 2023 Sports Trilogy: European Super League, International Skating Union and Royal Antwerp FC" [2024] Concurrences 20 <https://awards.concurrences.com/IMG/pdf/ssrn-4686842_2_.pdf?134209/f76f810a7f9dff0a0e12ee0b4076140f-4c7731814b7e07b982b01a1b8fe3352b> accessed 4 August 2025; Pablo Ibanez Colomo, "Restrictions by Object under Article 101(1) TFEU: From Dark Art to Administrable Framework" (2024) 00 YBEL 1–37; Bernadette Zelger, "Object Restrictions in Sports after the ECJ's Decisions in *ISU* and *Superleague*" (2024) 15(2) JECL&P 90–101.

33 *ESL* (n 1), point 165; *Royal Antwerp* (n 3), point 92; *ISU* (n 2), point 105; *Diarra* (n 4), point 130.

34 Case C-298/22 *Banco BPN v BIC Português SA* ECLI:EU:C:2024:638, point 56.

35 *ESL* (n 1), points 159, 162 and 166; *Royal Antwerp* (n 3), point 93; *ISU* (n 2), point 106; *Diarra* (n 4), point 131.

36 In particular *Royal Antwerp* (n 3), point 110, indicates that as part of the exercise to consider the "economic and legal context" in which the home-grown player rules were adopted, also the "specific characteristics of sports" must be taken into account.

37 *ESL* (n 1), point 166. See also *Royal Antwerp* (n 3), point 93; *ISU* (n 2), point 106; *Diarra* (n 4), point 131.

38 Case C-151/19 P *European Commission v KRKA* ECLI:EU:C:2024:546, point 146.

20. The Court applies the three-step analysis as a framework to assess whether the FIFA and UEFA rules on prior approval of interclub football competition and on the exclusive exploitation of rights related to sporting competitions (in *ESL*), the home-grown player rules (in *Royal Antwerp*), the authorisation and eligibility rules (in *ISU*), and certain FIFA rules on contractual stability (in *Diarra*) reveal a sufficient degree of harm to competition, such that they can be considered to have the "object" of restricting competition.

A. *Rules on Prior Approval of Interclub Football Competition (ESL)*

21. The Court holds that the adoption and implementation of rules by sporting associations such as FIFA and UEFA, considering that they pursue in parallel various economic activities related to the organisation of competitions, which make the setting up of a new interclub football competition by a third-party undertaking subject to their prior approval and which control the participation of professional football clubs and players in such a competition, has as its object to prevent competition if there is no framework with substantive criteria and detailed procedural rules suitable for ensuring that these powers are exercised in a transparent, objective, non-discriminatory and proportionate way.[39]

22. The three-step analysis outlined earlier has allowed the Court to consider and balance various specific characteristics of football that the parties involved had invoked either to justify or to challenge the rules on prior approval. The Court's analysis of the economic and legal context surrounding the rules in question enabled it to affirm that "it is legitimate, in terms of their principle, to have rules on prior approval".[40] The Court further justified this position by referencing the specific nature of international football competitions, along with the principles, values, and rules of the game. Nevertheless, these "contextual elements" are not sufficient to legitimise the absence of the substantive criteria and procedural rules suitable to ensure that the rules on prior approval are transparent, objective, precise and non-discriminatory. Regarding the sanctions applicable to clubs and players, the Court has considered that they constitute the "resources available" in the market necessary to set up a new competition in the first place. It was explicitly observed that players are in a "vulnerable" position.[41]

B. *Homegrown Player Rules (Royal Antwerp)*

23. The judgment in *Royal Antwerp*[42] explains that UEFA and several national football associations, including the Belgian football association, have implemented rules requiring professional football clubs to include a minimum number of "homegrown" players on the match sheet. These homegrown player rules are designed to encourage

---

39 *ESL* (n 1), point 179.

40 Ibid point 175.

41 Ibid point 177.

42 See also Richard Parrish and Luka Zivic, "Royal Antwerp and Home-Grown Players: Re-Shaping Sports Governance and EU Sports Law and Policy" (2023) 23 ISLJ 453–459.

clubs to recruit and train young players and can take two forms. Homegrown players may refer to those trained by the club that employs them, in which case the limitation applies at the level of the individual club. Alternatively, homegrown players can also refer to players who have been trained either by the club employing them or by a club affiliated with the same national football association, in which case the limitation operates at the level of the association (and, by extension, at the national level).

24. The Court applies the three-step analysis and offers guidance to the referring court on each of the criteria that must be assessed – the content of the homegrown player rules, the economic and legal context of these rules, and the objective aims they seek to attain in terms of competition – to conclude that the degree of harm to competition may be sufficient for these rules to be considered as having the "object" of restricting competition.[43] It is expressly indicated that these criteria must be considered "together with the specific characteristics of football".[44]

25. As in *ESL*, as part of the analysis of the economic and legal context, the Court makes various references to the specific characteristics of football and to the specific nature of the "products" which sporting competitions are from an economic point of view, to highlight that it is in principle legitimate for sporting associations to have broad regulatory powers. According to the Court, "it is generally open to associations that are responsible for sporting discipline [...] to adopt rules relating, inter alia, to the organisation of competitions in that discipline, their proper functioning and the participation of athletes in those competitions".[45] In line herewith, the Court also states that the specific characteristics of professional football "suggest" that it is legitimate for sporting associations to regulate the conditions in which professional football clubs can put together teams.[46] At the same time, the Court reiterates that EU law imposes limits on how these powers can be exercised. The guidance provided by the Court on the economic and legal context of the homegrown player rules thus reflects the structure discussed in Chapter II : while there is a need for common rules to organise a sporting discipline, which may in principle justify the broad regulatory powers of sporting associations, these powers must nonetheless be exercised in accordance with EU law standards.

26. The Court makes some important observations on the objective aims which the homegrown player rules seek to achieve from a competition standpoint. Sports economists indicate that players are the most crucial factor of production and labour input in the professional team sports industry.[47] Athletes play a "central role" in sports competitions:[48] without them, there are no games or competitions to organise. In line with these insights, the Court states that "one of the essential parameters of the competition in which professional football clubs may engage" is, in fact, "the recruitment of players".[49] It further clarifies that players are "essential

43 *Royal Antwerp* (n 3), points 101–112.

44 Ibid point 110.

45 Ibid point 103.

46 Ibid point 104.

47 Kesenne (n 15), 48.

48 OECD (n 16), 6.

49 *Royal Antwerp* (n 3), point 107.

resources" for a club's success and that clubs compete for players in the upstream or supply market. The homegrown player rules, therefore, limit or control one of the essential parameters of the competition between clubs.

27. The homegrown player rules aim to incentivise clubs to recruit and train young players. In line with the clarifications provided by the Court,[50] the pursuit of a legitimate objective is not decisive in assessing whether these rules have an anticompetitive object. The Court did not mention the objective to incentivise clubs to recruit and train players at the stage of the analysis of whether these rules have as their object to restrict competition. That objective was only taken into account as part of the Court's assessment of the potential exemption under Article 101(3) TFEU.[51]

C. *Certain FIFA Rules on Contractual Stability (Diarra)*

28. The application of the three-step analysis – considering the content of the FIFA rules at hand, the economic and legal context in which they operate, and the objectives they aim to achieve from a competition point of view – has again enabled the Court to take into account several characteristics specific to football. The Court ultimately concludes that the FIFA rules in question demonstrate a significant degree of harm to competition, finding that they have the object of restricting and even preventing competition among football clubs in their efforts to unilaterally recruit players who are already employed by a club or players whose contracts are allegedly terminated without just cause.[52]

29. As part of the analysis of the "economic and legal context" in which the FIFA rules at issue have been adopted and implemented, the Court reiterates, fully in line with *ESL* and *Royal Antwerp*, that it is, in principle, legitimate for a sporting association such as FIFA to establish certain "common rules", given precisely the specific nature of sporting competitions. One of the common rules explicitly mentioned is the coordination of sporting competitions within an overall annual or seasonal calendar.[53]

30. Stability, whether in terms of contracts or the composition of a team, is central to the discussion in *Diarra*. Chapter IV of the FIFA regulations RSTP is explicitly titled "Maintenance of Contractual Stability Between Professionals and Clubs. According to FIFA", "[t]he principle of contractual stability between professional players and clubs is one of the fundamental pillars underpinning the Regulations and a core objective of the football transfer system".[54] The FIFA rules at hand aimed to contribute, in one way or another, to that stability.

---

50 Ibid point 94. See also *ESL* (n 1), point 186, where it is stated that "the pursuit of potentially legitimate objectives [is] not decisive […] for the purposes of application of Article 101(1) TFEU".

51 *Royal Antwerp* (n 3), point 128.

52 *Diarra* (n 4), point 148.

53 Ibid points 142–143.

54 FIFA, "Commentary on the Regulations on the Status and Transfer of Players" (2023) 122 <https://digitalhub.fifa.com/m/40da0f707efdd011/original/FIFA-Commentary-on-the-FIFA-Regulations-for-the-Status-and-Transfer-of-Players-2023-edition.pdf> accessed 5 August 2025.

31. Before the Court, the players' unions contended that the concepts "contractual" and "team" stability are notably ambiguous and open to multiple interpretations. In the discussions leading to the adoption of the RSTP, it was suggested that the rules on contractual stability were required to ensure the integrity and regularity of competitions, maintain team stability within a single sporting season and across multiple seasons, and provide teams with adequate time to develop and build their squads.[55] While a certain level of stability – during a single sporting season – seemed acceptable, particularly to ensure the proper organisation of sporting competitions and the comparability of results, the players' unions argued that extending this stability beyond one year is unnecessary. This argument addressed a fundamental question regarding the specificity of football compared to other industries: should football clubs, unlike employers in other sectors, receive special protection that guarantees workforce stability for more than one year? It was contended that football is not so unique that clubs should be granted specific protection, through FIFA rules, to allow them to build a team and ensure team stability *over several years*. All employers, across all sectors, must address workforce mobility and the possibility for employees to exercise their freedom to work, which may require offering reasonable compensation. Finally, it has also been argued that it is questionable whether stability was genuinely the underlying purpose of the FIFA rules, and that this objective may have been used as a cosmetic layer for economic goals that were, in addition, unsubstantiated. In that framework, reference was made to the decision of the Court of Arbitration for Sport (CAS) in *Matuzalem*, where it said that "the concept of contractual stability was introduced to move forward and replace the former transfer fee system: accordingly, the pre-Bosman transfer fees due after the expiry of a contract have been replaced by compensations due for the breach or undue termination of an existing agreement".[56]

32. In relation to team stability, the Court adopts a balanced approach. Taking into account the specific characteristic that interclub football competitions occur on an annual or seasonal basis, the Court acknowledges that it may be legitimate for FIFA "to seek to ensure, to a certain extent, the stability in the composition of the player rosters". However, it also clarifies that this stability pertains only to "a given season" or "a given year".[57]

33. Although the "absence of a subjective intention" to restrict competition and the "pursuit of potentially legitimate objectives" are "not decisive" for applying Article 101(1) TFEU, the judgment in *Diarra* shows that intention can still be relevant. The Court has considered the stated objectives, but the strong wording of its judgment implies that it doubts whether the FIFA rules in question genuinely pursue those objectives. The Court notes that "under the guise" of preventing

---

55 Several of these objectives are mentioned in the European Commission's letter of 28 May 2002, which responds to a complaint filed by the Belgian workers' union (SETCA/FGTB) in European Commission, Decision AT.IV36.583 *SETCA/FGTB v FIFA* (28 May 2002) <https://ec.europa.eu/competition/antitrust/cases/dec_docs/36583/36583_54_3.pdf> accessed 6 August 2025.

56 Case CAS 2008/A/1519 *FC Shakhtar Donetsk v Matuzalem Francelino da Silva and Real Zaragoza SAD and Fédération Internationale de Football Association (FIFA)*; Case CAS 2008/A/1520 *Matuzalem Francelino da Silva & Real Zaragoza SAD v FC Shakhtar Donetsk and Fédération Internationale de Football Association (FIFA)*, award (19 May 2009).

57 *Diarra* (n 4), point 144.

aggressive recruitment practices, the rules essentially amount to "no-poaching agreements" between clubs. It further states that, although these rules are "presented" as measures to prevent player-poaching practices by clubs, they are, in reality, "a general, absolute and permanent ban on the unilateral recruitment of players who are already employed".[58] These rules are, the Court adds, a "manifest restriction" of the competition in which those clubs would be able to engage in their absence.[59]

D. *Exclusive Exploitation of Rights Related to Sporting Competitions (ESL)*

34. Applying the three-step analysis outlined earlier, the Court confirms that the FIFA and UEFA rules, which grant exclusive control over all rights arising from inter-club football competitions organised by them,[60] have as their object to restrict competition.[61] In particular the analysis of the "economic and legal context" of the rules in question has allowed the Court to consider several elements that may be considered as characteristic to football: the rights in question constitute the principal source of revenue that can be derived from professional interclub football competitions for both the organisers of those competitions and the professional football clubs; those rights are at the heart of the economic activity to which those competitions give rise and their sale is intrinsically linked to the organisation of those competitions; FIFA and UEFA have absolute control over the organisation and marketing of professional interclub football competitions.[62]

2. Identification of an "Abuse of a Dominant Position"

35. Similar to the issue of a "by object" restriction of competition under Article 101(1) TFEU, the Court has provided a summary and clarification of its case law regarding the conditions under which an "abuse of a dominant position" can be established.[63] An important development is that the case law, which holds that the granting of exclusive or special rights to an undertaking by public authorities cannot result in that undertaking abusing its dominant position – such as by preventing potentially competing undertakings from entering the relevant or a neighbouring market – has now been applied to undertakings in a dominant position due to their own conduct, rather than as a result of exclusive or special rights granted by public authorities.[64] FIFA and UEFA are private law associations and have not been entrusted with any particular tasks by EU Member States.[65]

---

58 Ibid points 145–146.

59 Ibid point 146.

60 This does not only cover intellectual property rights, but also financial rights, audiovisual and radio recording, reproduction and broadcasting rights, marketing and promotion rights. See *ESL* (n 1), point 221.

61 *ESL* (n 1), point 230. Note that the Court concurrently ruled that this constitutes an "abuse" of a dominant position under Article 102 TFEU, with essentially the same reasoning supporting this conclusion. In point 217, the Court observes that FIFA and UEFA hold a dominant position resulting from the exercise of a regulatory power and hence from the exercise of a means which is different to those which govern competition on the merits between undertakings.

62 *ESL* (n 1), points 223–224.

63 Ibid points 129–138.

64 Ibid points 132, 133 and 137.

65 See also the later judgment in *Diarra* (n 4), point 99, where the Court observes that FIFA was not entrusted by public authorities of any particular mission in the area of worker protection.

36. The analytical framework outlined by the Court offers substantial flexibility for parties to present arguments concerning the specific characteristics of sport, and for courts or competition authorities to consider these characteristics in their assessment, especially since the establishment of an “abuse of a dominant position” must be made “in light of all the relevant factual circumstances”“ with the Court noting that these circumstances may concern “the conduct itself, the market(s) in question or the functioning of competition on that or those market(s)”.[66] Under this framework, any specific characteristics of football should come to the forefront. One of the specificities that the Court has taken into account is the market reality that it is currently not feasible to viably set up a competition outside the ecosystem of FIFA and UEFA, particularly considering the control these associations exercise over clubs and players.[67]

37. As noted above, the Court recognises that there are several specific characteristics of football that justify subjecting the organisation and conduct of international professional football competitions to common rules. On that basis, the Court confirms that the rules on prior approval and participation are, in principle, legitimate, clarifying that this applies in the “specific context of professional football” and stating that the adoption of such rules cannot be considered an abuse of a dominant position “in terms of their principle and generally”.[68] Nevertheless, the Court indicates that the specific characteristics of professional football are not such that they can justify adopting rules on prior approval if they are not subject to “transparent, objective and precise substantive criteria and transparent and non-discriminatory detailed procedural rules”.[69] These criteria and rules should be adopted in particular to “eliminate the risk” of an abuse of a dominant position.

3. Identification of an Obstacle to an Internal Market Freedom

38. Considering the detailed analysis of the rules on prior approval from a competition law perspective in *ESL*, the Court simply observes that the flaws identified in its competition analysis prevent any third-party undertaking from organising and marketing an alternative competition, as well as hindering clubs from participating in such competitions, constituting an obstacle to the freedom to provide services.[70] In *Royal Antwerp*, the Court is also brief, noting that the homegrown player rules restrict the freedom of movement of players who wish to pursue an economic activity in Belgium but do not qualify as homegrown players.[71] In *Diarra*, the Court separately examines each provision of the FIFA rules in question and concludes that, taken together, they restrict the freedom of movement of workers.[72] This analysis is confined to the wording of the FIFA rules, while their broader context and practical implementation are considered during the Court’s assessment at the justification stage.

---

66 *ESL* (n 1), point 130.
67 Ibid point 149.
68 Ibid point 145.
69 Ibid points 147, 151 and 152.
70 Ibid points 248–249.
71 *Royal Antwerp* (n 3), points 137–138.
72 *Diarra* (n 4), points 86–94.

IV. Justification of an Obstacle or Restriction of Competition

39. If a rule adopted by a sporting association is found to restrict an internal market freedom or competition, the "specific characteristics of sport" may also be relevant at the justification stage, which is the second step in the standard EU law analysis.

1. Application of Article 101(3) TFEU

40. One of the major novelties resulting from *ESL*, *Royal Antwerp*, and *ISU* is that conduct, which has the "object" of restricting competition, can no longer be justified under the test established in the judgments of *Wouters* and *Meca-Medina*.[73] Such conduct can only be exempted if all four conditions set out in Article 101(3) TFEU are met,[74] with the Court stating that the criteria for applying Article 101(3) TFEU are "more stringent" than those established under the *Wouters* and *Meca-Medina* case law.[75] This important development in the Court's case law aspect has been discussed elsewhere.[76] As far as the four conditions for applying the exemption under Article 101(3) TFEU is concerned, the Court indicates, in general, that it "may require taking into account the particularities and specific characteristics of the sector(s) or market(s) concerned [...] if those particularities and specific characteristics are decisive for the outcome of that examination".[77]

A. *Efficiency Gains – Objective Advantages (First Condition)*

41. Efficiency gains must be understood as "appreciable objective advantages [...] in the different sector(s) or market(s) concerned".[78] Not only their "actual existence and extent" must be established, but also that they "are such as to compensate for the disadvantages caused [...] in the field of competition". The conduct in question must lead to "genuine, quantifiable efficiency gains" and these gains must "compensate for the disadvantages caused in competition terms".[79]

42. Whereas the legitimate objectives in the general interest that can be invoked to justify an obstacle to an internal market freedom cannot have a purely economic nature,[80] the efficiency gains that can be considered under Article 101(3) TFEU

---

[73] *ESL* (n 1), points 183–188; *Royal Antwerp* (n 3), points 113–117; *ISU* (n 2), points 111–113; *Diarra* (n 4), points 149–152. See Case C-519/04 P *David Meca-Medina and Igor Majcen v Commission of the European Communities* ECLI:EU:C:2006:492; and Case C-309/99 *Wouters* ECLI:EU:C:2002:98.

[74] The objective justification under Article 102 TFEU, examined in *ESL* (n 1), will not be discussed separately. The discretionary nature of the prior approval rules out the possibility of an objective justification by technical or commercial necessities. Also, the second justification ground is excluded, notably because the rules allow FIFA and UEFA to prevent all competition on the market concerned.

[75] *ESL* (n 1), point 189; *Royal Antwerp* (n 3), point 118.

[76] See Ben Van Rompuy, "EU Court of Justice Delineates the Scope of the Wouters Exception" (*Kluwer Competition Law Blog*, 15 January 2024) <https://legalblogs.wolterskluwer.com/competition-blog/eu-court-of-justice-delineates-the-scope-of-the-wouters-exception/> accessed 6 August 2025; Stephen Weatherill, "The Impact of the Rulings of 21 December 2023 on the Structure of EU Sports Law" (2023) 23 ISLJ 409–415.

[77] *ESL* (n 1), point 200; *Royal Antwerp* (n 3), point 126.

[78] Ibid point 192.

[79] Ibid point 196.

[80] See, for example, *Royal Antwerp* (n 3), point 141; and *Diarra* (n 4), point 95.

should essentially be economic in nature by contributing either to improving the production or distribution of the products or services concerned, or to promoting technical or economic progress. There is a certain dissonance between the concept "legitimate objectives in the general interest", which cannot be purely economic, and "efficiency gains", which should focus on economic efficiency. This dissonance is also evident in *ESL* and *Royal Antwerp*. Legitimate objectives in the general interest cannot be merely re-used as efficiency gains for the application of Article 101(3) TFEU.

43. Therefore, in *ESL*, the Court indicates that the objectives that were pursued by the rules on prior approval – guaranteeing observance of the principles, values and rules of the game underpinning professional football, in particular the open, meritocratic nature of the competitions concerned, and ensuring a certain form of "solidarity redistribution" within football – should, in the framework of Article 101(3) TFEU, be "translated" into genuinely quantifiable efficiency gains.[81] In *Royal Antwerp*, the Court observes that the homegrown player rules may not only incentivise football clubs to recruit and train young players – this being the non-economic objective in the general interest that could, in principle, justify a restriction of the freedom of movement of workers – but may also, as a result, "intensify competition through training".[82] The intensification of competition through training appears to be an efficiency gain that could be considered under the first condition of Article 101(3) TFEU, provided, as the Court indicates, that not only the reality of that incentive is demonstrated, but also the extent of the efficiency gain resulting from those rules in terms of training, as well as whether these gains are likely to compensate the competitive disadvantages resulting from the homegrown player rules.[83] In connection with the FIFA and UEFA regulations concerning the exploitation of rights related to sporting competitions, the Court highlights several potential efficiency gains that could be utilised. First, it would result for the potential buyers in a significant reduction in transaction costs and a reduction of the uncertainty they would face if a negotiation on a case-by-case basis with the participating clubs had to be undertaken. Second, buyers of these rights would have access to rights which are infinitely more attractive than what would be proposed to them jointly by clubs participating in a match.[84]

B. *Reservation of Efficiency Gains for All Users – Favourable Effect for All Users (Second Condition)*

44. Under the second condition to apply Article 101(3) TFEU, an equitable part of the profit resulting from the efficiency gains must be reserved for the users. The term "users" must be interpreted broadly and refers to "all users, be they traders, intermediate consumers or end consumers, in the different sectors or markets concerned".[85] For the rules on prior approval at stake in *ESL*, the "users" include national football

---

81 *ESL* (n 1), point 196.
82 *Royal Antwerp* (n 3), point 129.
83 Ibid point 129.
84 *ESL* (n 1), point 232.
85 Ibid point 193.

associations, clubs, players (professional and amateur), young players, and consumers (spectators or TV viewers).[86] Regarding the centralised sale of rights concerning sporting competitions, the Court notes that the "users" extend to not only clubs participating in FIFA and UEFA competitions but also to non-participating clubs, amateur clubs, professional players, women's football, young players, supporters, TV viewers and all EU citizens involved in amateur football.[87] Similarly, in *Royal Antwerp*, the users encompass professional football clubs, players, live spectators and television viewers.[88]

45. The existence and extent of the favourable effect on each of these users must be proven to be real and concrete.[89] Specific arguments and evidence must be produced. *Royal Antwerp* illustrates that not only the relevance of factors specific to football, but also that producing the required arguments and evidence will not be a straightforward process. While the interest of spectators and television viewers in a football competition may depend on the presence of local teams and of homegrown players in those teams,[90] the Court suggests that the second condition will only be satisfied if it can be shown that the homegrown player rules "have a genuine favourable effect not only on the players but also on all the clubs and on the spectators and television viewers".

46. In relation to the centralised sale of rights to interclub football competitions, the Court states that the argument based on "solidarity redistribution" can be accepted, provided it can be demonstrated – particularly on the basis of accounting and financial evidence – that the profits generated from such centralised sales benefit all users, including amateur clubs, spectators and television viewers. In this context, the Court highlights characteristics which are specific to interclub football competitions at the global or European level: the "interdependence" of professional clubs participating in these competitions and the necessity of maintaining a balance among these clubs and ensuring equal opportunities for them. Furthermore, and importantly, the Court underscores the "trickle-down effect" that benefits smaller professional and amateur clubs, which invest at the local level in the recruitment and development of young players.[91]

C. *Indispensable for Achieving the Efficiency Gains (Third Condition)*

47. Under the third condition the conduct at issue must be indispensable or necessary for achieving the efficiency gains. This condition is one of "strict necessity".[92] To establish whether this condition is satisfied, the Court indicates that it is required to assess and compare the impact of the anticompetitive conduct and that of "alternative measures which might genuinely be envisaged"" to determine whether the efficiency gains expected from the conduct restricting competition may be attained by measures which are less restrictive of competition.[93] *Royal Antwerp*

86 Ibid point 195.
87 Ibid point 234.
88 *Royal Antwerp* (n 3), point 130.
89 Ibid point 123; *ESL* (n 1), points 194 and 236.
90 *Royal Antwerp* (n 3), point 130.
91 *ESL* (n 1), points 234–237.
92 *Royal Antwerp* (n 3), point 131.
93 Ibid point 124.

demonstrates that the alternative measures that need to be considered will be specific to the industry or market in question. The alternatives cited by the Court include: the imposition of player training requirements as a condition for granting licences to professional football clubs, the establishment of financing mechanisms or financial incentives aimed primarily at smaller clubs, and the establishment of a system for direct compensation for the costs borne by training clubs.[94]

D. *No Elimination of Competition (Fourth Condition)*

48. The conduct at hand cannot give the participating undertakings the opportunity to eliminate all effective competition for a substantial part of the products or services concerned. The Court indicates that this condition implies to examine the quantitative and qualitative aspects that characterise the functioning of competition in the sectors or markets concerned,[95] which again allows to take into account the specific characteristics of a given sport. In addition, the Court observes that in situations involving a decision by an association of undertakings or agreements to which undertakings have adhered to as a group, which will usually be the case for sporting associations such as UEFA and FIFA, their sizeable market share is an "indicator" of the possibility to eliminate all competition.

2. Legitimate Objective in the General Interest

49. With regard to internal market freedoms, such as the freedom to provide services, applied in *ESL* and *Royal Antwerp*, and the freedom of movement of workers, which was at issue in *Diarra*, the specific characteristics of sport are relevant in two key ways: first, in identifying a legitimate objective in the general interest, and second, in applying the principle of proportionality. As discussed, certain specific characteristics of sport can, in principle, justify the adoption of common rules to govern the organisation of a given sport. This perspective is reflected and mirrored in the Court's case law regarding the legitimate objectives that a sporting association may invoke to justify a restriction on an internal market freedom. The reasons that justify the adoption of common rules for a sport may also be used by a sporting association to try to justify any obstacles to the internal market freedoms that these rules create. The Court also indicates that these legitimate objectives "are contingent on the specific characteristics of the sport concerned".[96]

A. *Rules on Prior Approval of Interclub Football Competitions (ESL) and Homegrown Player Rules (Royal Antwerp)*

50. The Court refers to several public interest objectives that may justify, "in terms of its very principle" "the adoption of rules on prior approval of interclub football competitions: ensuring that football competitions are organised in observance of

94 Ibid point 131.

95 *ESL* (n 1), point 198; *Royal Antwerp* (n 3), point 125.

96 Ibid point 106; Ibid point 74.

the principles, values and rules of the game underpinning professional football, in particular the values of openness, merit and solidarity, and that those competitions will take place in a substantively homogeneous and temporally coordinated manner, and be integrated into the organised system of national, European and international competitions characterising that sport.[97] However, these public interest objectives cannot justify these rules since they do not include substantive criteria and detailed procedural rules that would ensure that these rules are transparent, objective, precise and non-discriminatory.[98]

51. In *Royal Antwerp*, the Court indicates that UEFA can rely on the objective of promoting the recruitment and development of young professional football players. In reaching this conclusion, the Court once again references characteristics specific to sport, such as its social and educational functions, as well as the considerable importance of sport.[99] Specific characteristics of football also play a role in the Court's guidance regarding the suitability of the homegrown player rules to encourage the recruitment and development of young football players. The Court is sceptical that rules defining a homegrown player as one trained by any club within a particular association – regardless of which club – will create a meaningful and significant incentive for clubs, especially those with substantial financial resources, to recruit and train young players. If the referring court reaches the same conclusion, these homegrown player regulations are likely to be deemed unsuitable for effectively promoting the recruitment and development of young football talent.

B. *FIFA Rules on Contractual Stability (Diarra)*

52. *Diarra* illustrates the disciplining effect of identifying the legitimate objective a sporting association may invoke to justify restrictions on the freedom of movement of workers. FIFA put forward three objectives to justify the restrictive effects of the RSTP rules in question: maintaining contractual stability and the stability of professional football clubs, preserving the integrity and proper functioning of interclub football competitions, and protecting professional footballers. Regarding the protection of professional footballers, the Court does not take position on whether this can constitute a legitimate objective, as it was clear to the Court that the rules in place could not contribute to achieving that objective.[100]

53. The regularity of sporting competitions was a legitimate objective capable of justifying the restrictive effects of transfer windows.[101] In *Diarra*, the Court holds that the same objective can justify – in principle and without prejudice to their actual content – rules to ensure a "certain degree of stability in the club's player rosters". The Court references various elements that are considered as essential

97 *ESL* (n 1), point 253.

98 Ibid points 254–255.

99 *Royal Antwerp* (n 3), point 144.

100 *Diarra* (n 4), point 99. A separate issue was whether FIFA holds the authority to issue rules on the protection of workers in the first place. FIFPro strongly opposed this before the Court. As discussed, the wording in *Diarra* at least suggests that the Court considers that FIFA cannot adopt rules in this domain.

101 Case C-176/96 *Lehtonen v FRBSB* ECLI:EU:C:2000:201.

for football: the importance of sporting merit in both European and national competitions, the need to maintain a certain level of equal opportunity between teams and the need for homogeneous regulatory and technical conditions for teams when facing each other. Crucially, the Court determines that the third objective cited by FIFA – maintaining contractual stability and the stability of professional football clubs – does not, by itself, qualify as a legitimate objective. Rather, it must be seen as an instrument to ensure the fairness and regularity of interclub football competitions.

54. In light of the specific objective of maintaining "a certain degree of stability in the player rosters"" the Court concludes, as part of its proportionality analysis, that the FIFA rules in question were disproportionate and, therefore, unlawful.[102] The Court's language was particularly strong, emphasising that the FIFA rules not only exceeded what was necessary to achieve this objective, but in some instances, went "far beyond" what was required.[103]

55. The Court's reasoning on the proportionality test, which cannot be discussed in full here,[104] once again is based on and takes into account certain specific characteristics of football. Article 17(1) RSTP lists "the fees and expenses paid or incurred by the former club (amortised over the term of the contract)" as a criterion for calculating the compensation due for terminating a contract without just cause. It is indeed common practice for clubs to book transfer and agent fees as intangible assets and to amortise them linearly over the duration of a player's contract.[105] The Court considers it "particularly excessive" that the compensation owed by the player may include such fees and expenses, observing that these fees are, in principle, negotiated exclusively by other persons in their own interest, in particular the clubs parties to a transfer or third parties involved in those transfers. The Court makes clear that these fees cannot be passed on to players.

56. Importantly, the Court also indicates that these compensation criteria do not genuinely aim to safeguard the integrity of sporting competitions but rather appear to protect the financial interests of clubs in the economic context specific to transfers of players between them. The player unions have drawn the Court's attention to certain CAS decisions, in particular *Matuzalem* and *Suárez.*[106] *Matuzalem* sets out that it is the "economic reality in the world of football, that services provided by a player are traded and sought after on the market, are attributed an economic value and are – according to [Article] 17 FIFA Regulations – worth legal protection" and that "the amount of the transfer fee is likely to represent the value in exchange of which the transferring club was willing to waive its rights as employer

---

[102] *Diarra* (n 4), points 103–113.

[103] Ibid point 104.

[104] See the detailed discussion in Stefano Bastianon and Michele Colucci, "The Evolution of FIFA Transfer Football Regulations: Challenges, Opportunities, and Innovative Approaches in the Wake of the *Diarra* Judgment" (2024) RDES <www.rdes.it/RDES_2024_BASTIANON_COLUCCI_copyright.pdf> accessed 6 August 2025.

[105] Sam Hoey, Thomas Peeters and Francesco Principe, "The Transfer System in European Football: A Pro-competitive No-Poaching Agreement?" (2021) IJSL 3 <https://papers.ssrn.com/sol3/papers.cfm?abstract_id=3631763> accessed 6 August 2025.

[106] Cases CAS 2018/A/5607 *Matías Ezequiel Suárez & CA Belgrano v RSCA 2018/A/5607* and CAS 2018/A/5608 *SA Royal Sporting Club Anderlecht v Matias Ezequiel Suarez* and *Club Atlético Belgrano de Córdoba.*

and to renounce to the services of the player". In *Suárez*, the compensation owed by the player was equal to the replacement costs, that is the cost incurred by the club to acquire the services of a new player to replace the outgoing player.[107] The Court specifically references the interpretation of the FIFA rules in question and, in its proportionality analysis, has therefore considered one of the most specific characteristics of football: the existence of a transfer market.

V. Conclusion

57. *ESL*, *Royal Antwerp*, *ISU* and *Diarra* all acknowledge that sport has certain specific characteristics. These judgments highlight various specific characteristics and illustrate their relevance in the application of EU primary law. This is not mandated by Article 165 TFEU but rather forms part of the standard application of EU primary law. The competition rules and internal market freedoms provide sufficient room and flexibility to take into account any relevant specific characteristics when applying these rules.

58. An advantage of integrating the specific characteristics of sport into the standard application of competition rules and internal market freedoms is that the association responsible for a sport can (and should) explain and justify why certain specific characteristics of sport required to issue rules, such as homegrown player rules, prior approval rules, or rules on contractual stability. This approach enables the Court of Justice, as well as national courts, to assess, *inter alia*, whether these rules genuinely pursue a legitimate objective or efficiency gain and whether they pursue these in a proportional manner. By doing so, the Court has established, through these cases, an important and nuanced set of criteria that fundamentally aim to enhance the accountability and good governance of sport, albeit on an ad hoc basis.

---

107 The replacement cost included the transfer fee for the new player, the remuneration paid to the new player, double holiday pay, allowance for a leasing car and performance bonuses paid to the new player.

CHAPTER III

Proceedings

Is the CAS Arbitration System Anticompetitive?

Jean-Michel Marmayou[*]
Centre for Economic Law, Aix-Marseille University

1. The autonomy of an international private legal system depends in particular on the autonomy of its private international justice system. It needs an internal justice system that acts as a filter to reduce the number of disputes that are likely to arise outside the private legal system. The Court of Arbitration for Sport (CAS) system is a prime example of such internal justice systems. It is designed to keep state law out of sports disputes and thus prevent sports rules from coming into direct conflict with state law.

2. The statements made by its designers when it was created are enough to convince us of this.[1] That said, it is worth describing its organisation in very broad terms.

3. Strictly speaking, the CAS is not an arbitral tribunal. It is an arbitration centre that is part of a genuine "global arbitration system".[2] Awards are made under the CAS Rules, but by panels formed for each case and not by the CAS itself. The system

---

* Professor at Aix-Marseille University. Director, Sports Law Centre; Member of the Centre for Economic Law, Aix-Marseille University.

1 See the comments by Kéba M'Baye, "Sport et arbitrage" (Sport and arbitration) (1990) 2 ASA Bulletin 116: "In reality, another idea may have been behind the creation of this court: the International Olympic Committee had just been involved in a lawsuit brought by one of its members, which had somewhat irritated certain leaders of the Olympic Movement. It was decided that a provision would be added to the oath that all new members of the International Olympic Committee must take, stating that the decisions of the International Olympic Committee are final for its members, but it quickly became apparent that this was not sufficiently effective. It was then thought that perhaps having a court would make it possible to avoid resorting to the ordinary courts and to be able to settle problems arising in the field of sport in a specialised court. But this idea was quickly abandoned. It was realised that this sports court could in fact have much, much broader jurisdiction". (Free translation).

2 Magali Boucaron-Nardetto and Jean-Baptiste Racine, "L'apport du Tribunal arbitral du sport au droit de l'arbitrage international" in *Sport et droit international (aspects choisis)* (PUAM 2016) 289.

actually involves not only the CAS, but also the persons appointed to the lists of arbitrators, the arbitration panels actually constituted are: the International Council of Arbitration for Sport (ICAS), which administers and finances the CAS, the sports institutions that finance it, and, of course, the Swiss Federal Court, which is both the supporting judge and the appeal judge (we can certainly now include the European Court of Human Rights (ECtHR) since its ruling in *Semenya v Switzerland*.[3]

4. This is "forced" arbitration, based in Lausanne, Switzerland, where the *favor arbitrandum sportiva*[4] policy gives the Swiss Federal Court, as the court of appeal, remarkable discretion. Concerned about the attractiveness of the Swiss Confederation as an arbitration venue, and particularly since it cannot refer questions to the Court of Justice of the European Union (CJEU) for a preliminary ruling (an argument it has itself raised), the Swiss Federal Court considers that EU public policy on competition is not included in the Swiss concept of international public policy.[5]

5. And since the panels of the CAS are fully aware that requests for exequatur are exceptional,[6] they do not hesitate to make use of Swiss flexibility without worrying about considerations specific to the foreign legal systems in which their awards will have concrete effects.[7]

6. However, while the CAS takes full advantage of a "combination of favours'[8] granted to arbitration in general to develop its own autonomy and put it at the service of the sports regulatory system, the CAS system is still part of the state legal system. The system is not established outside of it. It does not exist alongside the state legal order. It is fully integrated into it, in a space where normative pressure is certainly less intense, but still present.

7. The *Mutu and Pechstein*[9] and *Semenya*[10] judgments of the ECtHR recalled this, with a certain degree of leniency with regard to the ECHR.[11] The *ISU* and the *RFC Seraing* rulings confirmed this with much greater severity with regard to EU law.

---

3 Jean-Michel Marmayou, "Chronique de jurisprudence arbitrale en matière sportive" (2023) 3 Revue de l'arbitrage 848 (note under Case *Semenya v Switzerland* App no 10934/21 (ECtHR 10 July 2025)).

4 Mathieu Maisonneuve, "Chronique de jurisprudence arbitrale en matière sportive" (2016) 3 Revue de l'arbitrage 921.

5 Case 4P 278/2005 *Tensacciai SpA and Terra Armata Srl* (8 March 2006) ATF 132 III 389.

6 Exceptional but not non-existent. Antoine Duval, "Oberlandesgericht Bremen, Case 2U 67/14 *SV Wilhelmshaven v Norddeutscher Fußball-Verband e.V*" in Antoine Duval and Antonio Rigozzi (eds), *Yearbook of International Sports Arbitration* (TMC Asser Press 2015) 315.

7 The hierarchical structure of the sports movement effectively renders any exequatur procedure unnecessary for the enforcement of awards in the sports legal system. On this point, see: Mathieu Maisonneuve, *L'arbitrage des litiges sportifs* (LGDJ 2011) esp. 403ff. Franck Latty, *La lex sportiva. Recherche sur le droit transnational* (Thesis, University Paris Nanterre 2005) spec. 578ff. This power is even recognised by the Swiss Federal Court, Case 4P 240/2007 *Rayo Vallecano de Madrid SAD c/ FIFA* (5 February 2007) in "Chronique de jurisprudence arbitrale en matière sportive" (2008) 3 Revue de l'arbitrage 37, obs. Antonio Rigozzi. Swiss Federal Court, Case 4P 172/2006 *Guillermo Cañas c/ ATP Tour & TAS* (22 March 2007) in "Chronique de jurisprudence arbitrale en matière sportive" (2008) 3 Revue de l'arbitrage 36.

8 Jean-Michel Marmayou, "L'autonomie vivante de la justice internationale du sport. Les faveurs faites au système TAS" (2022) 52 L'Observateur des Nations Unies 77.

9 Case *Mutu and Pechstein v Switzerland* App nos 40575/10 and 67474/10 (ECtHR 1 October 2018).

10 Case *Semenya v Switzerland* App no 10934/21 (ECtHR 11 July 2023) and Ibid (ECtHR 10 July 2025).

11 The ECtHR does not have the same conception of the relationship between its legal order and others as that held by the ECJ. While the latter is convinced of the primacy of its own legal order, the ECtHR respects the principle of subsidiarity. It is more a court of harmonisation than a court of standardisation, and it only intervenes after the national courts of the Member States, seeking consensus rather than imposing its own

I. *ISU* Ruling

8. The *ISU* ruling deals with an additional issue compared to the *European Super League* and *Royal Antwerp FC* rulings handed down on the same day: ie the question of *judicial review* applicable to rules adopted by sports bodies in their relationship with EU law.[12]

9. In this case, the intervention of the EU courts arose from a complaint lodged with the European Commission by two speed skaters concerning the "eligibility rules" established by the International Skating Union (ISU). It should be noted that these rules provided for a dual system of prior authorisation, first for athletes, who could only participate in competitions authorised by the ISU, and second for competition organisers, who had to obtain authorisation from the ISU through a procedure that greatly favoured ISU member entities over external organisers. These rules were accompanied by arbitration rules under which athletes, who were liable to sanctions, including lifetime exclusion from all competitions organised by the ISU, as well as candidate organisers, had the possibility of appealing against a decision of ineligibility, but only to the CAS. Interested in the case[13] the Commission decided to initiate proceedings against the ISU, at the end of which it adopted a decision finding that the ISU had committed a competition infringement, which the ISU was required to remedy or face financial penalties.[14] In support of its decision, the Commission considered that the ISU could influence competition in the global market for the organisation and commercial exploitation of speed skating, which was established as the relevant market. In its view, the ISU was an association of undertakings, and its eligibility rules constituted a decision by an association of undertakings within the meaning of Article 101(1) TFEU. However, those eligibility rules not only had the object but also the effect of restricting competition in breach of Article 101(1) TFEU. In addition to those findings, the Commission did not hesitate to assert that the arbitration rules accompanying the disputed eligibility rules reinforced the restrictions on competition caused by the latter. For the Commission, which nonetheless expressly recognises the validity in principle of recourse to arbitration in relation to competition law, the arbitration rules made it difficult to obtain effective judicial protection against any decisions of ineligibility of the applicant that would not be in accordance with Article 101 TFEU, especially since athletes were required to accept the arbitration rules and the exclusive jurisdiction of the CAS.

10. This decision obviously did not satisfy the ISU, which lodged an appeal with the European Court of Justice (ECJ) and, in addition to criticising the eligibility rules as contrary to Article 101 TFEU, strongly contested the Commission's conclusion that the arbitration rules reinforced the restriction of competition.

---

views. It thus develops a greater sense of coordination than the CJEU.

12 Case C-333/21 *European Super League* ECLI:EU:C:2023:1011; Case C-680/21 *Royal Antwerp FC* ECLI:EU:C:2023:1010; Case AT.40208 European Commission Decision *International Skating Union's Eligibility* (8 December 2017) (ISU Decision). XXX footnote added to cases XXX

13 When it comes to sport, the Commission is rather sparing in its investigative resources and tends to dismiss complaints against overly large sporting bodies, which it assumes will ardently defend their regulations.

14 *ISU* Decision (n 12). Erika Szyszczak, "Competition and Sport: No Longer So Special?" (2018) 9 JECL&P 188. Andrea Cattaneo, "*International Skating Union v Commission*: Pre-authorisation Rules and Competition Law" (2021) 12 JECL&P 318.

11. The appeal was upheld by the General Court of the European Union (GC), which, despite the Commission's strong arguments, refused to consider that the CAS arbitration clause included in the regulations on prior authorisation for the organisation of skating competitions constituted an aggravating circumstance of a restriction of competition.[15]

12. On appeal, however, the ECJ took the opposite view to the GC and upheld the Commission's reasoning.

13. In its view, the arbitration clause in favour of the CAS does not lead to effective judicial review of the application of EU law.

14. In this regard, the Court's firm stance rejecting the GC's assertion that athletes subject to CAS jurisdiction have other means of benefiting from EU competition law is to be welcomed. This assertion was in fact biased in three ways, and therefore false. First, an action for damages is, by definition, a posteriori in nature, seeking compensation for an unlawful act that has already been committed, and, apart from its hypothetical deterrent effect, contributes only modestly to the prevention or cessation of the unlawful act. Second, national competition authorities, like the Commission itself, have limited resources, which leads them to prioritise complaints by refusing to deal with the majority of them. Finally, it is well known that the rules of international arbitration, followed by almost all countries in the world, give priority, or even exclusive jurisdiction, to arbitration, which makes parallel recourse to the state courts, the guardians of competition rules, completely illusory.

15. To date, unless we are mistaken, we are aware of only one state judge who was not "impressed" by either a CAS clause or the 1988 Lugano Convention and took the initiative to implement provisional measures intended to put an end to conduct denounced as infringing EU competition law.[16]

16. As is well known, the Swiss approach to the arbitrability of disputes is very liberal; substantive review of international awards is virtually non-existent under Article 190 of the Federal Act on Private International Law (PILA);[17] the Swiss Federal Court, as the court of appeal, continues to consider that competition law does not fall within the scope of international public policy within the meaning of Swiss law; the hierarchical structure of the sports movement renders any exequatur procedure for the enforcement of awards in the sports legal system effectively useless.[18] In other words, it is only after the damage has been done that an athlete affected by an anticompetitive rule imposed by a sports authority may be able to obtain compensation or have the rule annulled for the future. And even

15 Case T-93/18 *International Skating Union v European* Commission ECLI:EU:T:2020:610.

16 Case *A22 Sports Management SL European Super League Company SL v UEFA and FIFA* (Commercial Court No 17 of Madrid, 11 May 2021 and Commercial Court No 17 of Madrid, 1 July 2021). In other countries, unless the CAS arbitration clause is set aside on grounds of invalidity (eg Case 2016/AR/2048 Case C-600/23 *Royal Football Club Seraing SA v FIFA and others* ECLI:EU:C:2025:617 (Brussels Commercial Court, 17 November 2016).

17 On the question of the relationship between public policy and arbitration: Clémentine Legendre, *La coordination du mouvement sportif international et des ordres juridiques étatiques et supra-étatiques* (LGDJ 2020) spec. 301ff.

18 *Tensacciai SpA and Terra Armata Srl* (n 5).

then, if the athlete chooses to challenge the arbitral award in only one country, the most they can hope for is a refusal of exequatur in that country. In addition, the athlete in question cannot count on any provisional measures, since the only ones to which he or she could lay claim are those provided for in the CAS rules.[19]

17. Furthermore, national and international sports institutions do not really practice ex-ante self- assessment,[20] since the notification procedure no longer exists; the procedure for requesting informal guidance[21] is not applicable to sports institutions that do not meet the conditions set by the Commission;[22] and insofar as none of the self-assessment tools (communications, block exemption regulations and guidelines) published by the Commission specifically concern the sports sector.[23] Finally, the obligation of loyal cooperation does not apply to arbitration panels[24] and the *amicus curiae* procedure under Article 15(3) Regulation 1/2003 is not used and does not appear to be usable, neither does the information and consultation procedure under Article 15(1) of the same regulation. It could always be argued that the Swiss Federal Court is concerned that the CAS should examine all the arguments raised before it under EU competition law, but that would be to forget that its review is limited to that. It will never verify whether EU law has been correctly applied:[25] it certainly does not wish to do so, as this would imply recognition of the CJEU's hierarchical superiority.[26]

18. If recourse to CAS arbitration, which in many cases is compulsory arbitration,[27] requires the persons subject to it to bring either an action for damages or a complaint before a competition authority in order to have a right recognised that its natural legal order recognises as a matter of public policy[28] but which the arbitration system

---

19 While Article 37 of the CAS Rules of Procedure provides for the possibility of provisional and protective measures, it stipulates that the parties "waive the right to seek such measures from state authorities or courts". It may be argued that it is sufficient not to refer the matter to the CAS in order to open up the possibility of an interim measure being decided by a national state judge, but athletes affected by a problem of access to a competition are faced with a strategic dilemma and many opt to appeal to the CAS, reasoning that if successful, the award will have more effect than the state interim measure.

20 On these measures, see Nicolas Petit, *Droit européen de la concurrence* (3rd edn, Montchrestien 2020) 601ff.

21 Procedure referred to in the preamble to Regulation (EC) No 1/2003 of 16 December 2002 on the implementation of the rules on competition laid down in Articles 81 and 82 of the Treaty [2003] OJ L1/1, para 38.

22 Conditions specified in the Commission Notice on informal guidance relating to novel questions concerning Articles 81 and 82 of the EC Treaty that arise in individual cases [2004] OJ C101/78.

23 European Commission, "White Paper on Sport" COM (2007) 391 final, cannot really be counted as a Commission communication on competition.

24 See Petit (n 20), 1654ff.

25 One award is frequently cited to show how sensitive CAS panels are to EU competition law (Case 2016/A/4490 *RFC Seraing v FIFA* (2017) 3 Revue de l'arbitrage 1046, see, M Peltier), but it is rarely pointed out that the arbitrators, after giving a lengthy overview of the substantive rules of EU competition law, completely ignored its most essential procedural principles, particularly those relating to the burden of proof. The error is obvious, but the Swiss Federal Court found nothing wrong with it in accordance with its view of international public policy (Case 4A_260/2017 *RFC Seraing v FIFA* (Swiss Federal Tribunal, 20 February 2018)).

26 It cannot refer any questions to the CJEU for a preliminary ruling and, unless it is prepared to accept the risk of a divergence of interpretation, it cannot afford to develop case law that runs parallel to that of the CJEU.

27 This is not a major obstacle; in fact, it is very useful in a world such as international sport, but it must be offset by greater guarantees for litigants.

28 On the relationship between public policy in competition law and private arbitration: Laurence Idot and others, "Ordre public, concurrence et arbitrage" (Public policy, competition and arbitration) (2006) e-Competitions Art. No 12028 10–32 www.concurrences.com/. See Petit (n 20), 1649 et s. On the relationship between sports

does not guarantee, then it must be concluded that the arbitration system constitutes a means of reducing the effectiveness of this public policy right. The effectiveness of European competition law is guaranteed by its verticality and horizontality: any national judge in any dispute has jurisdiction to apply it. However, if a person is forced to resort to an arbitration system in which the arbitrators refuse to apply European competition law or apply it in a significantly watered-down form, that person is forced to relinquish part of their rights, which might not be serious if those rights were not of public policy.

19. The Commission was therefore right, after a particularly thorough analysis, to say that "the Appeals Arbitration rules make it difficult to obtain effective judicial protection against ineligibility decisions of the ISU that violate Article 101 of the Treaty".[29]

20. It was right to consider that the arbitration rules "reinforced the infringement" it had identified "by making judicial review more difficult, in terms of EU competition law, arbitration awards by the CAS following decisions adopted by the ISU under the discretionary powers conferred on it by the rules on prior authorisation and eligibility".[30]

21. Once this point has been settled, the CJEU can proceed to lay down the conditions under which judicial review of arbitral awards could be considered effective.

22. The first condition is that judicial review must, in any event, "relate to the question of whether those awards comply with the fundamental provisions of EU public policy, which include Articles 101 and 102 TFEU (CJEU 1June 1999, Eco Swiss, C-126/97, para. 37)".[31] This is all the more essential, according to the Court, when the arbitration in question is "imposed by a private law entity, such as an international sports association, on another, such as an athlete".[32]

23. The second condition is that the appeal must be brought before a "court [which] meets all the requirements of Article 267 TFEU, so that it can or, where appropriate, must refer the matter to the Court when it considers that a decision of the Court is necessary on a question of EU law raised in a case pending before it".[33]

24. The finding is indisputable, but it is a severe blow to the CAS system, since the Federal Court is not a court of a Member State, but a court outside the EU's judicial framework, which is not empowered to refer a question to the CJEU for a preliminary ruling on this matter.

25. The Court's position is both logical and legitimate. It should also be noted that the German competition authority took the same position when, after accusing the Olympic authorities of abusing their dominant position in the application of Rule 40 of the Olympic Charter, it emphasised that proceedings before the CAS

arbitration and EU law: Mathieu Maisonneuve, "Le Tribunal arbitral du sport et le droit de l'Union européenne" (The Court of Arbitration for Sport and European Union law) in *Le sport au carrefour des droits* (Mélanges G Simon, LexisNexis 2021) 383.

29 *ISU* Decision (n 12), para 270.

30 Case C-124/21 P *International Skating Union (ISU)* ECLI:EU:C:2023:1012, para 228.

31 Ibid para 193.

32 Ibid para 193.

33 Ibid para 198.

were considerably more expensive, required more effort than proceedings before a state court and did not allow for effective control of EU competition law.[34]

26. This does not prevent the CJEU from acknowledging the possibility for a litigant to resort to private judicial arbitration and recognising "that the requirements of the effectiveness of the arbitration procedure may justify the judicial review of arbitral awards being limited in nature".

27. However, it could not, on the one hand, reject the idea of a sporting exception and, on the other, allow an arbitration system to flourish that offers immunity from EU law, certain provisions of which, such as "Articles 101 and 102 TFEU are provisions with direct effect that create rights for individuals, which national courts must safeguard (…)".[35]

II. *RFC Seraing* Ruling

28. The *RFC Seraing* ruling confirms the CJEU's position of principle and clarifies certain points which it had not previously had the opportunity to address.[36]

29. This case arose because FIFA had adopted a regulation in 2014 imposing a total ban on third-party ownership (TPO) with effect from 1 May 2015. This ban led Royal Football Club Seraing and its financial partner, Doyen Sports Investment, to initiate two separate sets of proceedings simultaneously.

30. On the one hand, the applicants had brought proceedings before the Belgian courts seeking a declaration that this ban was incompatible with several provisions of the TFEU, in particular the freedoms of movement and the rules on competition. On the other hand, as the club had been subject to disciplinary sanctions imposed by FIFA for failing to comply with the disputed regulations, it had sought to challenge them before the CAS, without success, since the CAS had upheld the sanctions, a decision which the Swiss Federal Supreme Court, acting as the court of appeal, had endorsed.

31. Whilst the Belgian courts of first and second instance had held that the dispute had been definitively settled by the arbitral award, the Belgian Court of Cassation referred questions to the ECJ for a preliminary ruling on the compatibility with EU law of the recognition of the *res judicata* effect and probative value of a CAS award reviewed exclusively by a court of a non-EU Member State.

32. The case raised a key question: can a Member State, without infringing the right to effective judicial protection guaranteed by Article 19 TEU and Article 47 of the Charter of Fundamental Rights, recognise the authority and effects of an arbitral award made in the context of compulsory sports arbitration, when the review of that award was carried out solely by a court not empowered to refer the matter to the ECJ?

---

[34] Case B2-26/17 Bundeskartellamt Decision *DOSB IOC v Athleten Deutschland eV* (27 February 2019), see esp. paras 76 and 124 of the decision.

[35] *ISU* (n 30), para 192.

[36] *Royal Football Club Seraing* SA (n 16). See Phillip Landolt, "The CJEU's Judgment in RFC Seraing v. FIFA: Legal Clarity but Diminished Finality and Independence of Sports Awards" (*Kluwer Law Blog*, 21 August 2025) <https://legalblogs.wolterskluwer.com/arbitration-blog/the-cjeus-judgment-in-rfc-seraing-v-fifa-legal-clarity-but-diminished-finality-and-independence-of-sports-awards/> accessed 29 May 2026.

33. In its judgment, the Court adopts a balanced approach. It points out, first of all, that EU law does not, in principle, preclude the use of arbitration to resolve disputes that may concern the interpretation or application of EU law, including competition rules. Competition disputes are arbitrable, and CAS arbitration is not, in itself, incompatible with EU law, even where it is mandatory. The mandatory nature of the arbitration clause is not sufficient in itself to constitute an abuse of a dominant position or an independent breach of competition law. The mandatory use of arbitration may be justified by legitimate objectives specific to the organisation of sport, such as consistency in disciplinary matters and regulatory coherence.

34. This recognition is, however, subject to strict conditions. The ECJ therefore sets out, second, the conditions under which a private arbitration system may be compatible with the legal and judicial framework of the European Union. The first condition laid down by the Court is that there must be no fraudulent use of arbitration. A CAS arbitration clause may be set aside if it has been imposed or used with the aim of circumventing the application of fundamental rules of EU law. Arbitration may not serve, either directly or indirectly, as a mechanism for circumventing European public policy. The second, key condition concerns the possibility of effective judicial review. Arbitral awards must be subject to a review procedure capable of ensuring compliance with EU public policy. This requirement is particularly stringent where arbitration is imposed on litigants.

35. The ECJ states that such monitoring need not be systematic, but that it must be genuinely accessible. The structural impossibility of such monitoring is sufficient to render the system incompatible with EU law.

36. As regards the nature of this review, and contrary to the Advocate General's proposal, the Court limits the scope of the review to public policy within the Union. It does, however, provide a broad and evolving definition of this concept. In its view, the principles and provisions of primary or secondary law that are essential to the legal order of the Union or of fundamental importance to the fulfilment of its tasks fall within the scope of public policy of the Union.

37. With regard to the level of scrutiny, the Court draws a crucial distinction. Whilst limited scrutiny may suffice for arbitrations that are freely entered into or do not involve EU law, this is not the case for mandatory CAS arbitrations. In such cases, the review required is substantial: it must cover not only the effects of the judgment, but also the interpretation and application of the principles and provisions relating to the public policy of the Union, as well as the legal consequences drawn from them.

38. Finally, whilst the Court does not require the existence of a direct appeal against CAS awards, it does at the very least require the existence of an effective incidental appeal allowing for review in accordance with European requirements.

39. Member States must adapt their procedural rules to ensure that mechanisms such as *res judicata* or the negative effect of the "competence-competence" principle do not deprive litigants of any effective protection.

40. The *RFC Seraing* ruling is a direct follow-up to the *ISU* ruling and clarifies its procedural implications. Without calling into question the existence or even the legitimacy of international sports arbitration, the Court strictly limits its effects

where rights and freedoms falling within the scope of the Union's public policy are at stake.

41. This results in a significant erosion of the authority traditionally accorded to the arbitrator. Where a dispute concerns the public policy of the Union, national courts must be able to intervene, including before an award is made, in order to prevent or put an end to a breach. The decision marks a significant shift away from the traditional approach of favouring arbitration. Where recourse to arbitration is imposed and interferes with fundamental principles of EU law, national courts cannot hide behind the authority of the award or the negative effect of the principle of competence-competence. On the contrary, they must be able to exercise substantive review, which may lead to the setting aside of the award and the redress of the infringements found.

42. The ruling thus highlights the limits of the autonomy of the *lex sportiva*. This autonomy remains recognised, but only by virtue of a concession granted by the EU legal order and subject to effective compliance with its fundamental principles. In this sense, the *RFC Seraing* ruling confirms that sports arbitration cannot constitute an area outside the scope of European law and that it is ultimately for the courts of the Member States, under the supervision of the ECJ, to ensure the preservation of the public policy of the Union.

43. Under the pretext of global standardisation, there can be no question of allowing a situation to arise in which European athletes see their European citizenship diminished, solely on the grounds that they are athletes and must submit to a private justice system.

44. Following the *ISU* and *RFC Seraing* rulings, the CAS system faces an extremely thorny problem. It cannot remain as it is, that much is clear. The CAS system faces a dilemma.

45. Indeed, it is frequently called upon to apply EU law. This is almost imposed on it by the Federal Court, which encourages CAS panels to do so in certain disputes to avoid criticism for not having taken into account a standard considered to be a mandatory rule of foreign law under Swiss arbitration law.[37] Some CAS panels now do so without hesitation. As we know, the arbitral nature of a court does not prohibit or disqualify it from applying a body of state or supra-state law.[38]

46. When called upon to deal with a dispute of a primarily sporting nature and, on that occasion, one or both parties ask it to consider the compliance of the applicable sporting rule with EU law or the compliance of the situation that its application will entail, it may be granted that legitimacy (whether it applies it in an orthodox way or not). Recognising the parties" right to invoke EU law before their arbitrator means recognising that arbitrator's right to apply it.[39]

---

[37] According to the Swiss Federal Court, ignoring the application of EU law would amount to a violation of Article 19 of the Swiss Federal Act on Private International Law: *Tensacciai SpA and Terra Armata Srl* (n 5), consid. 3.3.

[38] *Ex multis*: Case 2016/A/4492 CAS Decision *Galatasaray v UEFA* (9 March 2017); *RFC Seraing v FIFA* (n 25).

[39] When a simple conflict of norms arises before the CAS, it is, as the competent forum, empowered to decide according to its own methods and rules of conflict because its jurisdiction is sufficient to confer on it the legitimacy to choose and, where appropriate, coordinate the competing norms presented to it.

47. The problem is that there is a world of difference between the right to apply it and the legitimacy to apply it. However, the CAS is not the most legitimate jurisdiction to judge the application of EU competition law and freedom of movement. The most legitimate court is the ECJ. All EU legislation recognises not only its jurisdiction but also its supreme jurisdiction, since it is precisely the court established to ensure the harmonised application of primary and secondary EU law.

48. European Union law and ECHR law are supranational public policy laws, and the courts responsible for monitoring their uniform or harmonised application are very concerned about the right to effective remedy for those who benefit from the rights guaranteed by their public policy.

49. As the CAS is not part of a system that guarantees such effective remedy, the rulings it issues are likely to be simply ignored by the state.

50. One could always argue that exequatur is not really necessary to ensure the enforcement of CAS awards. But now that the ECtHR and the ECJ have ruled, they have become avenues of appeal and are firmly established in the CAS system, above the Swiss Federal Court. Indirectly, they place each of the state courts of the member countries of the ECHR and the EU within the CAS system as parallel jurisdictions.

51. The consequences of the *ISU* and *RFC Seraing* rulings for the architecture of the CAS arbitration system are immense, far more serious than those following the *Semenya* ruling by the ECtHR. Indeed, the imperfections pointed out by the Strasbourg Court in relation to the CAS system can easily be corrected: CAS panels can take better account of the guarantees of the ECHR, and the Federal Court can conduct a more thorough (less restricted) examination of issues related to the fundamental rights included in the ECHR. However, as Switzerland is not a member of the EU and the ECJ still refuses to allow arbitral tribunals to refer questions for a preliminary ruling on the grounds that they do not have the status of a court of a Member State,[40] no body within the CAS system is in a position to meet the requirements set by the ECJ.

52. Will the shock be enough to bring down the whole edifice?

53. The question obviously arises, especially as there is little to be expected from the EU.

54. However regrettable the ECJ's distrust of international judicial arbitration may be, it still refuses to recognise that a panel of arbitrators can be regarded as a court within the meaning of the Treaty, even though this would be the means of achieving better coordination of legal systems and would avoid leaving such important arbitral institutions as the CAS, established outside the EU, without any real tools to render awards under EU law in a legitimate and therefore indisputable manner.

55. The legal framework governing sport has made significant efforts to move away from viewing itself as a completely autonomous system. There is certainly still work to be done, but the European legal system must also take some steps forward.

---

40 Case 102/81 *Nordsee Deutsche Hochseefischerei GmbH v Reederei Mond Hochseefischerei Nordstern AG & Co KG* ECLI:EU:C:1982:107.

It needs to acknowledge the existence of the legal framework governing sport in a more practical and less political manner. Indeed, this is very much in its own interest, as it would ensure a wider dissemination of the principles of EU law.

56. This reluctance is all the more regrettable given that, for some time now, a significant section of legal scholarship has been arguing that the CJEU should hear preliminary rulings requested by arbitral tribunals.[41]

57. And the arguments put forward in favour of this development are not merely political. Thus, beyond an amendment to Article 267 TFEU – which is unlikely to be feasible within a reasonable timeframe – certain Member States (France, for example, if it were to host the CAS headquarters) could instruct their courts to cooperate with CAS panels in order to refer preliminary questions raised by arbitrators to the ECJ.[42]

58. Alternatively, the CJEU could interpret Article 267 TFEU differently and consider that the conjunction "where" refers only to specific scenarios (those in which a national court refers a question to the Court) and does not necessarily preclude the possibility of other scenarios (such as where the ECHR or the ICJ, or even an arbitral tribunal, refers a question to the Court).[43]

59. Regrettably, the ECJ is not yet prepared to make the small effort required to incorporate an arbitration system such as that of the CAS into EU law.

60. We must therefore hope that the solution will come from the ICAS, which has already demonstrated in the past that it is capable of thinking outside the box.

61. As international arbitration law has a legal concept of the notion of seat, the ICAS can, while retaining its premises in Lausanne, establish the seat of the CAS in an EU Member State.[44] It can also, in our view, establish a seat for certain CAS panels in an EU Member State and thus an appeal judge authorised to refer questions to the ECJ. This would certainly require amending the institution's arbitration rules and finding appropriate criteria for distributing cases between the two seats, but there is no principle prohibiting this.

62. In any case, the ICAS is responsible for this and not the federations, which cannot decide on their own to waive Article R28 of the CAS Code. In this respect,

---

41 See the text adopted at the IInd International Congress on Arbitration (Rotterdam, the Netherlands 1966) 62 Revue de l'arbitrage (Special). *Contra*: A Mourre, "Faut-il un statut communautaire de l'arbitrage?" (2005) 2 Revue des Affaires Européennes 191.

42 An idea put forward in general terms by Philippe Fouchard [1982] Revue de l'arbitrage 491 et par Catherine Kessedjian, "L'arbitrage comme mode de règlement des différends est-il remis en cause par le droit européen?" in *Le droit européen et l'arbitrage d'investissement* (Panthéon-Assas 2009) 107, spéc. 120). For this proposal to be accepted by the ECJ, the Court would need to relax its position that, in order to be admissible, a reference for a preliminary ruling must come from the court hearing the main proceedings.

43 Interpretation proposed by Xavier de Mello "Arbitrage et droit communautaire' [1982] Revue de l'arbitrage 384.

44 France has all the qualities required to be this host state because, apart from a few difficulties relating to the arbitrability of certain disputes, it has a system that is very favourable to international arbitration, in some respects more favourable than the Swiss system. It should be noted, for example, that appeals for the annulment of arbitral awards must be brought exclusively before the International Chamber of Commerce of the Paris Court of Appeal, which is an additional step before a possible appeal to the ECtHR or the CJEU (Article L. 311-16-1, Code of Judicial Organization).

although UEFA has provided for disputes arising from the application of its new Authorisation Rules governing international club competitions to be dealt with by the CAS, which has its headquarters in Dublin, Ireland, there is no guarantee that the ICAS will accept this arrangement.

63. In a slightly different vein, the ICAS could follow the practice of other arbitration institutions and leave the choice of seat to the parties; or it could include in its rules a specific provision for certain actions for annulment before a court in an EU Member State. Even more radically, the ICAS could amend its regulations to require the federations to renounce self-execution of CAS awards in their favour and systematically initiate exequatur proceedings in the defendant's country. As it stands, on the basis of the *ISU* and *RFC Seraing* rulings (and the *Mutu and Pechstein*, *Semenya 1* and *Semenya 2* rulings of the ECtHR), an athlete who is a national of an EU Member State may obtain, in summary proceedings or on the merits set aside the negative effect of the jurisdictional principle (possibly an anti-suit injunction) by arguing that the CAS arbitration clause applied in a dispute involving EU public policy (and/or the ECHR) does not guarantee effective judicial protection and is therefore manifestly null or inapplicable.[45] Perhaps the best solution, without modifying the CAS arbitration system, would be for the international sports federations to take steps upstream to ensure that they do not enact regulations whose purpose or effect is to violate competition law and, more generally, to undermine public policy in the European Union.

64. In the *Bosman* ruling, the judges noted that "while the practical consequences of any judicial decision must be carefully weighed, one cannot go so far as to compromise the objectivity of the law and its application because of the repercussions that a court decision may have".[46] Given the "*disgust*"[47] that the ECJ feels about arbitration, it was to be expected that the CAS system would not be treated leniently and that the principle would be reiterated that a private justice mechanism can only be accepted if it guarantees the effectiveness of the fundamental rights of the parties concerned.

---

45 *RFC Seraing v FIFA* (n 25), para 82.

46 Case C-415/93 *Union Royale Belge Sociale de Football Association, RCL and UEFA v JM Bosman* ECLI:EU:C:1995:463, para 77.

47 The word is from Thomas Clay, "Droit de l'arbitrage et des modes amiables de règlement des conflits" [2022] Recueil Dalloz 2330.

CHAPTER IV

State Aid and Foreign Subsidies Distorting the Market

European State Aid Law Applied to Professional Sport

Colin Miege*

I. Introduction

1. As an economic activity, sport has been impacted since the 1970s by European law provisions relating to the free movement of workers.[1] However, it was not until the 2000s that European competition law began to be applied to sport, particularly professional football. Although all the competition rules enshrined in the Treaty may be applied to sport, this chapter will focus solely on the prohibition of state aid laid down in Article 107 TFEU.[2]

II. The Framework for National Public Aid Granted to Sports Clubs

2. Both national and local authorities may be tempted to grant public resources to certain professional clubs in order to improve their financial situation, thereby

---

* *See case 36/74 Walrave and Koch v Association Union Cycliste Internationale and others, dec. 1974, and mainly case C-415/93 Union Royale Belge Sociale de Football Association, RCL and UEFA v JM Bosman,, dec. 1975.*

1 Since 1974, the Court of justice has ruled that « *the practice of sport is subject to community law only in so far it constitutes and economic activity"* (Case 36/74 *Walrave and Koch v Association Union Cycliste Internationale and others* EeCLI:EU:C:1974:140). A decade later, the Bosman ruling,has asserted the pre-eminence of the free movement principle in setting up professional football teams 1 (Case C-415/93 *Union Royale Belge Sociale de Football Association, RCL and UEFA v JM Bosman* ECLI:EU:C:1995:463.

2 Provisions prohibiting any agreement between undertakings which may affect trade between Member States (Article 101 TFEU), abuse of a dominant position (Article 102 TFEU) and the improper granting of state aid (Article 107 TFEU).

enabling them to increase their wage bill, recruit high-profile players and enhance their profile. This may also take the form of special tax measures to make up for a financial deficit (debt write-offs, reduction in social security contributions or tax exemptions, payment facilities, etc.). The provision of land or infrastructure on preferential terms is also worth noting. Receiving such aid is likely to give the beneficiary clubs a significant economic advantage and indirectly boost their sporting results. However, once a sports club recruits professional players and regularly participates in official matches on the international calendar, it is considered a business under European law. All the provisions of the Treaty concerning economic entities are therefore applicable to it, in particular those of Article 107 TFEU prohibiting public aid that may affect trade between Member States and distort competition within the internal market.[3]

3. State aid may also take the form of support provided by public authorities for the construction or renovation of sports facilities. Such expenditure from public funds may be subject to notification, examination by the European Commission and appeal.

4. From 2010 onwards, the Commission began to take an interest in reports submitted to it concerning possible infringements of state aid rules, considering that public aid granted to professional clubs could reach high amounts and have a significant effect on inter-club competitions by giving them an unfair competitive advantage over other teams.

5. At the same time, preserving the fairness of competitions was considered an essential part of the vision of sport developed within the European Union, an integral part of the concept of the "European sports model".[4] The reaffirmed objective of ensuring the fairness of sports competitions at European level requires maintaining a certain balance between competitors from Member States. Although not expressly prohibited, public support for sports clubs must therefore remain compatible with the provisions of Article 107 TFEU and must not contribute to upsetting the competitive balance between clubs. Since 2010, the Commission has therefore exercised greater control over state aid granted to professional football, with clubs being asked to "finance their operating costs and investments through sound financial management rather than at the expense of the taxpayer". In a break with its previous more accommodating position, its increased commitment has been reflected in a number of decisions.

6. In order to determine whether public intervention in favour of economic operators is compatible with the internal market, the Commission usually checks that the

---

3 Under European law, an undertaking is defined as "any entity engaged in an economic activity, regardless of the legal status of that activity and the way in which it is financed" (Case C-41/90 *Klaus Höfner and Fritz Elser v Macrotron GmbH* ECLI:EU:C:1991:161).

4 Reference should be made in particular to the declaration annexed to the Treaty of Nice (December 2000, points 2 and 14), the White Paper on Sport (July 2007), and, above all, Article 165 TFEU introduced by the Treaty of Lisbon 2009, which states that "Union action shall aim (…) to develop the European dimension in sport, while promoting fairness and openness in sporting competitions…" (para 2). The White Paper listed certain types of public aid that could be challenged (see European Commission, "White Paper on Sport" COM (2007) 391 final; and European Commission SWD, "The EU and Sport: Background and Context – Accompanying document to the White Paper on Sport" SEC (2007) 935 final, point 3.2.1 <*https://eur-lex.europa.eu/legal-content/EN/TXT/?uri=celex%3A52007SC0935*>).

transaction was carried out on terms that a private operator guided by market criteria would have accepted (the "market economy operator principle"). If this principle is not verified, support granted from public funds may be considered state aid within the meaning of Article 107 TFEU, insofar as it confers on its beneficiary an economic advantage that its competitors do not enjoy. The selective and individualised nature of the aid granted, which distinguishes it from a general aid measure "which would benefit all undertakings located on the national territory", is also taken into account. Other criteria such as the size of the market, the effects on competition or the impact on trade between Member States are also taken into consideration. However, football clubs facing significant deficits are considered to be undertakings in difficulty and, as such, may receive public aid to restore their financial situation, provided that certain conditions laid down by the Commission are met.[5]

III. Implementation of Checks on the Legality of Aid Granted to Professional Clubs

1. A Gradual Start

7. The Commission began examining state aid granted to sport with the law adopted by France in 1999, which allows professional clubs in certain sports, particularly football, to receive subsidies from local authorities when they carry out tasks of general interest[6] in agreement with those authorities. After negotiations, the Commission decided in 2001 not to raise any objections to the scheme, considering both its limited impact on competition between major clubs and its educational and integration objectives.[7] The approved measures were incorporated into the Sports Code and have remained unchanged since then.

8. In 2002, the Italian Parliament adopted a law known as "Salva calcio" concerning the accounting of professional football clubs, which included, in particular, a ten-year depreciation scheme for the acquisition of players, designed to reduce the tax burden on clubs. These measures were found to be contrary to Community rules, as the Commission observed that they gave national clubs tax advantages that favoured them over their competitors in other Member States. In 2005, the Italian Government decided to withdraw the disputed measures and the case was closed.[8]

---

[5] According to the European Commission Guidelines on State Aid for Rescuing and Restructuring Firms in Difficulty [2014] OJ 249/31, which specify in particular that aid must be conditional on the implementation of a restructuring plan to which the beneficiary must contribute.

[6] Such as financial support for training centres for young players or initiatives to improve public safety and prevent violence in stadiums.

[7] See European Commission Decision 118/00 Authorisation for State Aid Pursuant to Articles 87 and 88 of the EC Treaty Cases where the Commission raises no objections [2001] C333/6; see also European Commission, Press Release, "Dialogue with Citizens: Commission Launches New Guide on Data Protection Rights" (15 May 2001) <https://ec.europa.eu/commission/presscorner/detail/en/ip_01_697>.

[8] See European Commission, Press Release, "Commission Probes Measures for Professional Sports Clubs in Italy (Salva calcio)" (11 November 2003) <https://ec.europa.eu/commission/presscorner/detail/en/ip_03_1529> and European Commission, Press Release, "Commission asks Italy to Change its Rules on Accounting by Professional Sports Clubs (Salva calcio)" (7 July 2004); and European Commission, Press Release, "State Aid: Commission Closes State Aid Investigation into Tax Breaks for Sports Clubs in Italy (the "Salva calcio" law)" (22 June 2005).

9. In 2013, the Commission examined the financing of five professional football clubs in the first and second divisions in the Netherlands (Arnhem, Nijmegen, Maastricht, Tilburg, Eindhoven and Hertogenbosch). Various forms of public support had been granted to them in the form of debt buybacks, debt write-offs, retroactive rent reductions and the purchase of land for lease to the club. After investigation, the Commission issued a favourable decision in 2016 concerning the aid granted to the Nijmegen and Maastricht clubs, while noting that the Netherlands had failed to comply with its obligation to notify the Commission in advance of the state aid.[9]

2. In-Depth Scrutiny of Aid Granted to Certain Spanish Football Clubs

10. This complex case marked a turning point in the European authorities" control strategy, both in terms of the number and reputation of the clubs involved and the amounts at stake. It began in 2002 with a written question to the Commission concerning a property transaction benefiting Real Madrid, which had been the subject of an agreement by the city of Madrid to reclassify 150 hectares of land owned by the club in the heart of the Spanish capital, which would have provided the club with a capital gain of more than €470 million and the cancellation of a debt estimated at €270 million.

11. However, it was not until 2013 that the Commission decided to open an investigation into the land transfer between the city of Madrid and Real Madrid. At the same time, it opened two other investigations. One focused on the tax advantages granted to Real Madrid CF, Barcelona CF, Athletic Club Bilbao and Atlético Osasuna. It concerned "the possible granting of privileges in relation to corporation tax (…); these four clubs are exempt from the general obligation imposed on professional football clubs to convert into public limited sports companies. Thanks to this exemption, they benefit from a preferential corporate tax rate of 25%, instead of the 30% applicable to public limited companies".[10] The other investigation concerned loans granted by the public institution Instituto Valenciano de Finanza to three clubs, Valencia FC, Hercules FC and Elche CF. According to the Commission, "all these measures were financed by state resources and confer advantages on specific clubs that carry out economic activities within the EU internal market. They are therefore likely to affect trade between Member States. Consequently, they appear to constitute state aid within the meaning of EU rules." In July 2016, the Commission announced in three decisions that it considered all of this aid to be illegal.[11]

---

9 See European Commission Decision 2016/2078 on State Aid Implemented by the Netherlands in Favour of the Professional Football Club NEC Nijmegen [2016] OJ L320/40 and European Commission Decision 2016/1847 on the State Aid SA.41612 – 2015/C (ex SA.33584 (2013/C) (ex 2011/NN)) Implemented by the Netherlands in Favour of the Professional Football Club MVV in Maastricht (notified under document C(2016) 4053) [2016] OJ L282/53.

10 See European Commission, Press Release, "State Aid: Commission Opens In-Depth Investigation into Public Funding of Certain Spanish Professional Football Clubs" (18 December 2013) <*https://ec.europa.eu/commission/presscorner/api/files/document/print/en/ip_13_1287/IP_13_1287_EN.pdf*>.

11 See European Commission, Press Release, "State Aid: Commission Decides Spanish Professional Football Clubs Have to Pay Back Incompatible Aid" (4 July 2016) <https://ec.europa.eu/commission/presscorner/detail/en/ip_16_2401>.

12. The first ruling states that "a market economy investor in a situation similar to that of the Madrid City Council would not have signed the 2011 agreement" and concludes that the €18.418 million in state aid granted to Real Madrid is incompatible with the internal market. It must therefore be repaid by the beneficiary, with interest accruing from the date of its allocation until its recovery by the Spanish Government.

13. The Commission's second decision notes that by reserving the right to benefit from the preferential tax rate applicable to non-profit organisations to certain professional football clubs, the provision of the Spanish Sports Law constitutes state aid. This aid, granted illegally to Athletic Club Bilbao, Club Atlético Osasuna, FC Barcelona and Real Madrid CF, is incompatible with the internal market. The Spanish Government must therefore recover it from the beneficiaries, including interest.

14. Finally, the third decision states that the state guarantees granted by the Instituto Valenciano de Finanza to the three beneficiary clubs for bank loans constitute state aid granted in breach of the provisions of the Treaty and must therefore be repaid, with interest until the date of their actual recovery.

15. However, the five clubs challenged the sanctions before the European Court of Justice (ECJ) in 2016, initiating a long legal battle that lasted a decade, the main episodes of which are outlined below.

3. The Dispute Over State Aid to Spanish Clubs

16. On 26 February 2019, the ECJ handed down two judgments on the appeals lodged by Athletic Club de Bilbao and FC Barcelona, followed by judgments on 22 May 2019 concerning Real Madrid, and then on 12 March 2020 concerning Valencia CF and Elche CF. Most of these decisions were setbacks for the Commission.

A. *Rejection of Athletic Club de Bilbao's Application*

17. The Court considers that the tax measure contested by the Commission constitutes an aid scheme leading to the application to its beneficiaries of "a preferential rate of corporation tax which was no longer available to other football clubs", which benefited certain clubs and not others. The Commission therefore did not err in its assessment in concluding that it was selective in nature. It does not dispute that the contested measure is liable to affect trade between Member States, on the basis that the beneficiary clubs compete with clubs in their own country but also abroad in order to capture revenue from broadcasting rights, merchandising and sponsorship, which strengthen their ability to attract the best players. It notes that the revenue received by each club depends on its performance, which is itself linked to its ability to recruit the best players and, therefore, to the funding it can raise for that purpose. Consequently, "the conditions of distortion of competition and effect on trade between Member States must be regarded as fulfilled".

18. The club's appeal is therefore dismissed, but the judgment only validates part of the decision.[12]

---

12 The appeal is dismissed insofar as it is directed against Articles 1 and 4(4) of the Commission's decision.

B. *Annulment and Subsequent Validation of the Commission's Decision Against FC Barcelona*

19. The Court first points out that the concept of state aid, which must be established on the basis of objective criteria, includes not only subsidies but also measures likely to reduce the costs of undertakings, such as favourable tax treatment. When examining an aid scheme, the Commission must consider the complex measures implemented as a whole in order to determine whether they confer on the beneficiary undertakings an economic advantage that they would not have obtained under normal market conditions.

20. In this case, the Court is examining whether the Commission has established that the tax regime for non-profit entities was such as to place its beneficiaries in a more advantageous position than if they had had to operate as SAS companies. However, Real Madrid contested the advantage conferred by the exceptional measure, arguing that the tax deduction for reinvestment of exceptional profits was higher for SASs than for non-profit entities.

21. The Court considers that the Commission erred in its assessment of the facts and failed to prove that the contested measure conferred an advantage on its beneficiaries. It was criticised for not taking sufficient account of the specific characteristics of professional football and for not fully examining the advantages and disadvantages resulting from the exceptional tax regime to which the four clubs were subject (lower tax rate and lower tax deduction capacity compared to SASs). This error of assessment was punished by the complete annulment of the decision of 4 July 2016.[13] The Commission has lodged an appeal against this judgment with the CJEU.

22. The Court first notes that the Tribunal erred in law by analysing the contested decision as relating to both a general aid scheme and individual aid. The tax provisions applicable to non-profit entities, such as the reduced tax rate, can benefit each eligible club without any additional implementing measures and therefore constitute a general aid scheme.

23. The Court then observes that the Court of First Instance's error of law led it to erroneous conclusions as to the Commission's obligations to prove the existence of an advantage resulting from the reduced tax rate. In the present case, the aid scheme was likely to favour the four clubs concerned as non-profit-making entities, as compared with clubs operating as public limited sports companies, thereby conferring on them an advantage that could fall within the scope of Article 107(1) TFEU.[14]

24. Consequently, the Commission was not required to establish whether the deduction for reinvestment of exceptional profits or the carry-forward in the form of a tax credit neutralised the advantage resulting from the reduced tax rate. The

---

13 Commission Decision SA.29769 Case T-865/16 *Fútbol Club Barcelona v European Commission* ECLI:EU:T:2019:113.

14 The Court interprets the concept of state aid as any intervention "which is liable to favour certain undertakings directly or indirectly or which must be regarded as an economic advantage which the recipient undertaking would not have obtained under normal market conditions".

Court's judgment annulling the Commission's decision is therefore set aside and the action is dismissed as a final result, with the consequence that the measures taken by the Commission in 2016 are validated.[15]

C. *Annulment of the Commission's Decision Against Real Madrid*

25. In this complex real estate case, the municipality of Madrid had decided that it should compensate Real Madrid for a plot of land that it should have transferred to it, offering compensation of €22.693 million, corresponding to its estimated value. The compensation took the form of a transfer to the club of several other plots of land, the value of which was established by the Madrid city authorities. Following this transfer and the payment of €6.6 million, Real Madrid finally became the owner of a building plot located in front of its stadium.[16]

26. The Commission considered that this transaction was very advantageous for the club, as Spanish law did not oblige the municipality to fulfil its commitment by granting Real Madrid compensation of such an amount. According to the market economy operator principle, the Madrid City Council should have sought external legal advice before concluding such an agreement. The Commission therefore concluded that Real Madrid had received selective state aid from the city that was likely to distort competition, falling under the prohibition laid down in Articles 107 and 108 TFEU, and requested its repayment.[17]

27. In its ruling, the Court found that "the Commission did not err in concluding that a prudent market operator (…) would have sought legal advice before (…) accepting full legal responsibility for the impossibility of transferring the plot of land(…)".[18] Despite significant differences in the value of the plot that was not transferred, the judge considered that the Commission had not made a manifest error of assessment in setting the value at €4,275,000 (ie a quarter of the value estimated by the municipality). However, the judge noted that the plots transferred in place of the non-transferred plot had not been assessed by the Commission, which had merely taken the values stated in the agreement between the municipality and Real Madrid. He concluded that the Commission had not taken into account all the elements of the disputed transaction that demonstrated that the measure conferred an advantage on the club. It could not therefore classify it as state aid within the meaning of Article 107(1) TFEU. Its decision was therefore annulled.

---

15 Case C-362/19 *European Commission v Fútbol Club Barcelona* ECLI:EU:C:2021:169. Annulment of the judgment of the General Court of 26 February 2019 (*Fútbol Club Barcelona* (n 13)).

16 This refers to the Bernabéu Stadium. See Colin Miège, "Illegal Aid Granted to Spanish Professional Football Clubs: Repayment is now Required" (2016) 45 Les Cahiers de Droit du Sport.

17 The amount to be repaid was estimated at €18,418,000. In November 2016, Real Madrid repaid €20.3 million to the city of Madrid, corresponding to the illegal aid plus interest.

18 Commission Decision of 4 July 2016 on aid granted to Real Madrid, SA.33754 (advantageous land transfer).

D. *Annulment of the Commission's Decision Concerning Valencia CF*

28. In November 2009, the Valencian Regional Government's financial institution (Instituto Valenciano de Finanzas) granted two guarantees to a non-profit organisation, Fundacion Valencia, to cover a bank loan of €81 million, enabling it to acquire 70% of the shares in Valencia Football Club, which was then in financial difficulty.

29. In July 2016, the Commission considered that these public guarantees granted by the financial institution for the subscription of shares in Valencia CF as part of a capital increase constituted aid incompatible with the internal market and requested their repayment. It considered that the aid granted exceeded €20 million and that, given the financial situation of the club, which was comparable to that of a company in difficulty, it constituted an undue advantage that could have distorted competition and affected trade between Member States.

30. In its appeal against the Commission's decision, Valencia FC argues that the Commission made a manifest error of assessment in classifying it as a firm in difficulty and claims that it failed to take into account the "specific characteristics of the business model of professional football clubs", with reference to Article 165 TFEU. In this regard, the Court considers that the Commission was not required "to take into account the specific characteristics of the applicant as a professional football club, other than those relevant to the assessment of the concept of a firm in difficulty", as that concept "must be assessed solely on the basis of concrete evidence of the financial and economic situation". It also considers that the Commission's assessments of the market value of the club's players are not manifestly erroneous, as it did not ignore the market value of the club's players, the relatively high amount of which does not imply that Valencia CF is not in financial difficulty. Furthermore, the Commission noted that the forced sale value of the players would be relatively low, as "buyers would take advantage of the club's proven difficulties to drive prices down".

31. The judge then considered that the Commission could describe the club's viability plan as insufficient to enable it to restore its financial situation. However, considering that the bank loan guarantee had not been granted at market price, which would constitute an undue advantage, the Commission did not carry out an in-depth assessment.[19] The judge considered that there could be a market price for guarantees granted to a company in difficulty and that the Commission had therefore committed a manifest error of assessment.[20]

32. Furthermore, the Commission considered that the value of the shares held by the Foundation and offered as collateral to the financial institution had become virtually nil due to the club's losses. However, the judge noted that

---

19 She merely stated that "given the financial situation of the club, which was a company in difficulty, there was no market price that could be used as a reference".

20 Case T-32/16 *Valencia Club de Fútbol v European Commission* ECLI:EU:T:2020:98.

in November 2010, the club's share capital had increased tenfold, and its equity had become largely positive. Therefore, the Commission's assessment of the value of the club's shares on the date the measure was granted was vitiated by a manifest error. The judge therefore annulled the decision on these two grounds.

33. In July 2016, the European Commission ruled that the public guarantee granted for the subscription of shares in the club constituted illegal aid, incompatible with the internal market. It ordered the Spanish Government to recover "immediately and effectively" the aid granted, estimated at €3,688,000.

34. Following an appeal against this decision, the Court verified that the Commission had correctly assessed the financial situation of the club, but also of the Fundacion Elche, in order to determine whether the measure in question conferred an actual advantage. However, it found that the Commission had not taken into account the financial situation of the foundation, thereby committing a manifest error of assessment. On the other hand, it did not err in its assessment that the club was, at the date on which the measure in question was granted, a firm in difficulty. The concept of a firm in difficulty is an objective concept, which must be assessed on the basis of concrete evidence and not on the basis of the alleged specific characteristics of professional football.

35. However, in considering that the value of the club's shares offered as counter-guarantee for the loan was "virtually nil", the Commission failed to take into account neither the effect of the club's recapitalisation, nor the mortgage on six hectares of land given as counter-guarantee to the financial institution by the Fundacion Elche. It therefore made a double error of assessment in this respect, by merely stating that there was no market price for the guarantees granted to a company in difficulty and by failing to establish that a private operator would not have behaved in the same way as the public authorities in question. The Commission's decision of 4 July 2016 is therefore annulled.[21]

36. The Commission also challenged this judgment before the CJEU. The Court confirmed the General Court's initial analysis that, since the Commission had considered that there was no market price for a guarantee granted to Valencia CF due to its deteriorated financial situation, it was required to use a reference rate to assess the scope of the contested aid. It was incumbent on the Commission to prove that the conditions for applying the private operator principle were not met. The judge was therefore right to consider that it had not complied with the requirements it had imposed on itself in its 2008 communication on public guarantees.[22] The Court's judgment annulling the Commission's initial decision is therefore upheld.[23]

---

21 Case T-901/16 *Elche Club de Fútbol SAD v European Commission* ECLI:EU:T:2020:97.

22 European Commission Notice on the application of Articles 87 and 88 of the EC Treaty to State aid in the form of guarantees [2008] OJ C155/10.

23 Case C-211/20 P *Valencia Club de Fútbol v European Commission* ECLI:EU:C:2022:862. Confirmation of the judgment of the General Court of 12 March 2020 (Case T-732/16 R *Valencia Club de Fútbol SAD v European Commission* ECLI:EU:T:2018:17).

IV. The Framework for Public Aid for the Construction or Renovation of Sports Facilities

37. Aid for the construction or renovation of sports facilities is another type of state aid that may be challenged on the grounds that it distorts competition. However, it may be accepted by the Commission under certain conditions, in particular if the facility is likely to benefit the public by not being dedicated exclusively to professional sport.

1. European Commission Decisions

38. In 2011, the Commission examined the aid schemes for sports facilities set up by certain Member States. It considered that the Hungarian public funding scheme for sports infrastructure used by sports clubs constituted state aid, but also found that it included measures to limit distortions of competition between clubs and to ensure that the aid benefited citizens. It therefore authorised the scheme.[24]

39. In 2013, the Commission also authorised the Belgian aid scheme for the construction or renovation of football stadiums in certain regions. The aim was to improve the quality of first and second division club stadiums so that they would meet UEFA standards for European competitions, while encouraging professional clubs to emphasise the social role of football through educational and integration projects. The scheme included various measures to minimise distortions of competition. The professional football clubs using the facilities had to pay an appropriate price. Each stadium receiving state aid had to be multifunctional and meet broader societal objectives. The Commission therefore considered that the proposed scheme would make sport more accessible to citizens without distorting competition in the single market, and that it was compatible with state aid legislation.[25]

40. With a view to Euro 2016 and in order to facilitate the involvement of local authorities, the French legislature adopted provisions in 2009 allowing public or private sports venues intended to host international sporting competitions to be declared of general interest. After reviewing the case, at the end of 2013 the Commission authorised French aid for the construction and renovation of nine stadiums in preparation for UEFA Euro 2016, amounting to approximately one million euros. It considered that the project, which contributed to the achievement of a common objective of the Union, would not have been viable without public support, that the aid was limited to the strict minimum and that it was not likely to distort competition within the internal market.[26]

---

24 European Commission Communication regarding sport infrastructure development scheme case SA.31722 supporting the Hungarian sport sector via tax benefit scheme C(2011)7287 final.

25 See European Commission Communication regarding state aid case SA.37109 Belgium Football stadiums in Flanders C(2013) 7889 final.

26 See European Commission, Press Release, "State aid: Commission approves French aid for construction and renovation of stadiums for UEFA EURO 2016 Championship" (18 December 2013). The Commission had previously authorised state aid for various stadiums in Sweden and Germany, including €200 million for access to the Munich stadium for Euro 2006.

41. Similarly, in April 2014, the Commission approved Northern Ireland's plan to grant aid of £110 million (approximately €133 million) for the reconstruction of three stadiums in Belfast, considering that the operation was part of an overall programme to promote urban renewal and social cohesion. The stated public interest objectives, in particular the accessibility of the renovated stadiums to the general public, contributed to the acceptance of the case. We can also mention the positive decisions taken by the Commission in 2013, 2014, 2016 and 2017.[27]

42. However, the granting of public aid for the Nürburgring complex in Germany, including the construction of a leisure park linked to a motor racing circuit, gave rise to significant litigation. In 2014, the Commission found that certain aid measures in favour of the project promoters were unlawful and ordered Germany[28] to recover them. In 2019, the ECJ, hearing two applications for partial annulment of the Commission's decision, rejected the applications.[29] However, in 2021, the CJEU partially annulled the two judgments of the ECJ, as well as part of the Commission's initial decision, which has been validated in essence.[30]

2. Introduction of a Blanket Exemption for Certain Sports Facilities

43. In view of the increasing number of cases submitted to the Commission, a block exemption measure was introduced by the Council of the EU in 2013. This regulation authorises the Commission to declare that certain categories of state aid are compatible with the internal market and are therefore not subject to the notification requirement laid down in Article 108 TFEU. It thus classifies aid for sport among the categories of aid that can be considered compatible, as it is, a priori, state aid "intended for amateur or small-scale sport, which often has limited effects on trade between Member States and does not significantly distort competition".[31] Public aid for sport is therefore permitted insofar as sporting activities are considered

---

27 Multipurpose complex in Uppsala (Sweden), Commission Decision 2013/452 of 2 May 2013 on state aid case SA.33618 (12/C) which Sweden is planning to implement for Uppsala arena (notified under document C(2013) 2362 final). Commission Decision 2014/297 of 15 May 2013 on state aid case SA.33728(12/C) which Denmark is planning to implement for the financing of a new multi-arena in Copenhagen (notified under document C(2013) 2740 final). European Commission Communication regarding state aid case SA.38045 (2013/N) – Spain – Prolongation until 30 June 2014 of the approved state aid scheme SA.32026(2010/N) – Research and development aid scheme C(2014)578 final. European Commission Communication regarding state aid case SA.44439 Ireland and Sporting Arena Cork C(2016) 4625 final. European Commission Communication regarding state aid case SA.46530 Slovakia National Football Stadium C(2017) 3222 final. European Commission Communication regarding state aid case SA.37900 support for local sports associations in Denmark C(2017) 4175 final.

28 Commission Decision 2016/151 of 1 October 2014 on state aid SA.31550 (2012/C) (ex 2012/NN) implemented by Germany for Nürburgring (notified under document C(2014) 3634 final).

29 Case T-353/15 *eXovation Inc v European Commission* ECLI:EU:T:2019:434, and Case T-373/15 *Ja zum Nürburgring eV v European Commission* ECLI:EU:T:2019:432.

30 Case C-647/19 P *Ja zum Nürburgring eV v European Commission* ECLI:EU:C:2021:666, and Case C-665/19 P *NeXovation, Inc v European Commission* ECLI:EU:C:2021:667.

31 See Council Regulation (EU) No 733/2013 of 22 July 2013 amending Regulation (EC) No 994/98 on the application of Articles 92 and 93 of the Treaty establishing the European Community to certain categories of horizontal state aid [2004] OJ L204/11. These are block exemptions as opposed to individual exemptions. This text has been replaced by Council Regulation (EU) 2015/1588 of 13 July 2015 on the application of Articles 107 and 108 of the Treaty on the Functioning of the European Union to certain categories of horizontal state aid [2015] OJ L248/1, as last amended in November 2018.

to be of essential importance for economic and social development within the European Union.

44. In application of this, in June 2014 the Commission adopted a regulation which preliminarily justifies the exemption: "A block exemption should be provided for investment aid measures in favour of sports infrastructure which fulfil the conditions of this Regulation, in so far as they constitute state aid. In the sports sector, certain measures taken by Member States may not constitute state aid because the beneficiary does not engage in any economic activity or because the measures in question have no effect on trade between Member States. (...). A block exemption should also be provided for aid for sports infrastructure that has multiple recreational purposes and is therefore multifunctional. (...). The compatibility conditions for aid for such facilities must, in particular, ensure open and non-discriminatory access (...) and a fair procedure for awarding concessions to third parties responsible for building, modernising and/or operating the facility (...). Where sports facilities are used by professional sports clubs, the pricing conditions for their use by those clubs must be made public in order to ensure transparency and equal treatment between users". Overcompensation should also be avoided.[32]

45. The Commission Regulation first sets the thresholds below which aid for sports and multifunctional recreational infrastructure may be exempted from the notification requirement. Such aid may relate to both the investment and the operation of the sports infrastructure. For investment aid, the maximum amount is now €30 million, or total costs not exceeding €100 million per project. For operating aid for sports facilities, the maximum amount is €2 million per facility per year, with the maximum aid intensity set at 75%.

46. The regulation lists 12 conditions that must be met for aid to be considered compatible with the internal market and for the exemption to be granted. It also specifies the eligible costs and how they are calculated. In the case of operating aid, eligible costs are broad, as they may include costs related to staff, contracted services, communications, energy, maintenance or administration, but do not include depreciation or financing costs.

47. This calculation applies to investment or operating aid exceeding £2 million. Below this threshold, the maximum amount of aid may reach 80% of eligible costs. Furthermore, it should be noted that state aid must have an "incentive effect", ie it must lead to a significant increase in the scope of the project or activity concerned and accelerate its completion.

48. In all cases, the total amount of public aid granted for the activity or project is taken into account, whether it be subsidies from the state or local authorities.

49. In addition to these threshold and intensity conditions, there are other requirements. First, sports facilities eligible for public support must not be reserved for a single user belonging to the world of professional sport. Other users,

---

[32] Commission Regulation (EU) No 651/2014 of 17 June 2014 declaring certain categories of aid compatible with the internal market in application of Articles 107 and 108 of the Treaty [2014] OJ L187/1, arts 4 and 55, point 74.

whether professional or not, must account for at least 20% of annual occupancy slots.

50. Furthermore, access to multifunctional sports or recreational facilities, while open to multiple users, must be granted on a transparent and non-discriminatory basis. It is specified that companies that have financed at least 30% of the investment costs of the facilities may benefit from privileged access on more favourable terms, provided that these are made public. If the sports facilities are intended for use by professional sports clubs, Member States must ensure that the pricing conditions for their use are also made public.[33]

Conclusion

51. Professional sports stakeholders cannot, in principle, invoke the specificity of sport enshrined in the Treaty to attempt to evade the application of European competition law. However, the application of this law is highly complex, even if certain constants have been established by case law, such as the market economy operator principle. Each dispute therefore requires an in-depth examination of the specific context that gave rise to it, which often leads to an uncertain outcome.

[33] Commission Regulation (EU) No 651/2014, art 2, point 143. The regulation provides a precise definition of professional sport.

Annex

Stages of the dispute brought by the European authorities against state aid granted to Spanish football clubs

1. Initial Decisions of the Commission

Commission Decision of 4 July 2016 on state aid SA.36387(2013/C) granted by Spain to Valencia Club de Fútbol, Hercules Club and Elche Club (guarantees for loans at favourable rates).[34]

Commission Decision of 4 July 2016 on aid granted to Athletic Bilbao, Athletico Osasuna, F.C. Barcelona and Real Madrid (preferential tax treatment).[35]

Commission Decision of 4 July 2016 on aid granted to Real Madrid, SA.33754 (advantageous land transfer).[36]

2. Appeals Lodged by the Clubs Concerned

Action for annulment on 26 September 2016, brought by Athletic Club Bilbao.[37]

Action on 20 October 2016, brought by FC Valencia.[38]

Action on 14 November 2016, brought by Real Madrid.[39]

Action on 7 December 2016, brought by FC Barcelona.[40]

Appeal lodged on 21 December 2016, by Elche Club.[41]

3. Orders Issued by the General Court

Order concerning FC Valencia of 10 November 2016 is set aside. In this case, seven orders dismissing the action were issued by the Court between April 2017 and May 2018.[42]

Order concerning Club Herculès of 11 November 2016 is revoked.[43]

The CFI orders the suspension of the Commission's decision of 4 July 2016 on the recovery of state aid concerning Elche Club SA.36387.[44]

---

34 See Commission Decision (EU) 2017/365 of 4 July 2016 on the state aid SA.36387 (2013/C) (ex 2013/NN) (ex 2013/CP) implemented by Spain for Valencia Club de Fútbol Sociedad Anónima Deportiva, Hércules Club de Fútbol Sociedad Anónima Deportiva and Elche Club de Fútbol Sociedad Anónima Deportiva (notified under document C(2016) 4060 final).

35 See Commission Decision (EU) 2016/2391 of 4 July 2016 on the state aid SA.29769 (2013/C) (ex 2013/NN) implemented by Spain for certain football clubs (notified under document C(2016) 4046 final).

36 See Commission Decision (EU) 2016/2393 of 4 July 2016 on the State aid SA.33754 (2013/C) (ex 2013/NN) implemented by Spain for Real Madrid CF (notified under document C(2016) 4080 final).

37 Case T-679/16 *Athletic Club Bilbao v European Commission* ECLI:EU:T:2019:112.

38 Case T-732/16 *Valencia Club de Fútbol v European Commission.*

39 Case T-791/16 *Real Madrid Club de Fútbol v European Commission* ECLI:EU:T:2019:346.

40 *Fútbol Club Barcelona* (n 13).

41 *Elche Club de Fútbol SAD* (n 21).

42 Case T-732/16 R *Valencia Club de Fútbol SAD* (n 23).

43 Case T-766/16 R *Hércules Club de Fútbol SAD v European Commission* ECLI:EU:T:2018:170.

44 Case T-901/16 R *Elche Club de Fútbol SAD v European Commission* ECLI:EU:T:2018:268.

4. Judgments Handed Down by the CFI

CFI judgment of 26 February 2019 in FC Barcelona annulling the Commission's decision on state aid SA.29769.[45]

Judgment of the General Court of 26 February in Athletic Club Bilbao. Dismissal of the action and order for the Club to pay the costs.[46]

Judgment of the General Court of 22 May 2019 in Real Madrid Club de Fútbol annulling the Commission's decision on state aid SA.33754.[47]

Judgment of the General Court of 12 March 2020 in FC Valencia annulling the Commission's decision on state aid SA.36387.[48]

Judgment of the General Court of 12 March 2020 in Elche Club annulling the Commission's decision on state aid SA.36687.[49]

5. Judgments of the CJEU

Judgment of the Court of 4 March 2021 annulling the judgment of the General Court of 26 February 2019 in FC Barcelona (SA.29769).[50]

The Court confirms on 10 November 2022 the judgment of the General Court of 12 March 2020 in FC Valencia.[51]

---

45 *Fútbol Club Barcelona* (n 13).

46 *Athletic Club Bilbao* (n 37).

47 *Real Madrid Club de Fútbol* (n 39).

48 Case T-732/16 R *Valencia Club de Fútbol SAD* (n 23).

49 *Elche Club de Fútbol SAD* (n 21).

50 *Fútbol Club Barcelona* (n 13).

51 Case C-211/20 P *Valencia Club de Fútbol* (n 23).

CHAPTER V

National Competition Law Issues

National Competition Law Issues Europe: Belgium Recent Belgian Decisions Delivered in the Sports Markets

Carmen Verdonck* and Nina Methens**
ALTIUS, Brussels

I. Introduction

1. The intersection between sports and competition laws has been extensively dealt with by the various bodies are that are competent for issues related to sports in Belgium: the Belgian Competition Authority (BCA), the Belgian Arbitration Court for Sports (BACS) and the various judicial courts. The relatively high number of sports-related cases in Belgium reflects not only the professionalisation and commercialisation

---

* Carmen Verdonck is a partner at the ALTIUS law firm in Brussels and heads its Competition law department. She was admitted to the Brussels Bar in 1996 and advises a wide range of domestic and multinational clients about all aspects of Belgian and EU competition law, including merger control, cartel cases, distribution networks, technology transfer agreements, abuse of dominance, and state aid matters. Carmen also regularly represents clients in antitrust cases before the Belgian and European competition authorities and courts. Carmen has been appointed an Assessor in the Belgian Competition Authority and Maître de Conférences at Liège University, where she teaches in the LLM in European Competition and IP law.

** Nina Methens is an associate in ALTIUS' Commercial and Competition team in Brussels and specialises in all aspects of EU and Belgian competition law and distribution systems in a wide variety of sectors including sports, telecoms and media. Prior to joining the firm, Nina obtained an MA from the Université Catholique of Louvain-la-Neuve and an LLM in international law, international relations and foreign trade at the Instituto Superior de Derecho y Economía in Madrid, Spain. The authors wish to thank Sébastien Willems for his contribution in the research for this publication.

of sports and the consistently higher stakes involved in the sports industry, but Belgium has also been at various times the forum for cases external to Belgium or those giving rise to preliminary rulings of the European Court of Justice (ECJ). The prerogative of the BCA to impose interim measures in short proceedings and the willingness of the BCA to use this prerogative, makes the BCA an attractive competition authority to deal with cases in the sports sector, where time is very often of the essence given the strict sporting competition calendars and short sport careers in some professional sports.

2. In 2022, for the first time, the BCA explicitly named the sports sector as one of its priorities. However, the BCA's focus on sports should not come as a surprise. Indeed, as the BCA itself noted, "in the past, the BCA has investigated several competition law breaches in various sports disciplines". The BCA noted that "for centuries, sports and games have been an important binder in society". While the BCA has acknowledged sports' major social role, it has also explicitly stressed the sports sector's economic characteristics, which bring it within the ambit of competition law: "The sports world is today - at least as far as certain branches are concerned - an important economic sector. Just as fair play can and must be expected of athletes, competition law must also be complied with by sports administrators, sport unions and sports federations". The BCA announced in its 2022 priorities' note that it will "pay attention to the enforcement of competition rules in the sports sector, with a focus on fair access to sports leagues, the organisation of sports competitions and events, no poaching agreements and the rise of e-sports and (online) sports betting".

3. Next to the BCA's recent interest in competition law issues related to sports, it should be noted that competition law arguments have been invoked successfully for a long time in sports litigation[1] and sports arbitration[2] in general in Belgium, various times also giving rise to preliminary rulings of the ECJ. The enforcement bodies' action has moreover focused on various sports and not only on professional football. Also other sports that are economically important and/or popular in Belgium such as show jumping, pigeon racing, pool, karting, inline hockey or cyclocross have got the competition authority's attention.

4. The present contribution will not deal with all competition law cases in the sport sector in Belgium, but only with a selection of the most important recent cases. It will focus also in particular on restrictive measures taken through sports associations' regulatory powers (Chapter II) and an overview of the case law related to media rights in the sports' sector (Chapter III).

II. Restrictive Measures and Abuses through Sports Associations' Regulatory Powers

1. Introduction

5. Following the general European trend in this area, the (BCA)[1] and the BACS[2] have taken various antitrust decisions in the sports sector in recent years concerning

1 BCA official website <www.belgiancompetition.be/en> accessed 23 August 2025.

2 BACS official website <www.bas-cbas.be/nl/rechtspraak.php> accessed 23 August 2025.

restrictive measures taken by sports associations through their regulatory powers and their compliance with the competition law rules.

6. In particular, these decisions concern measures preventing or impeding new players from entering a market or sector, which has the effect of limiting competition in that market. The first set of decisions concern restrictive measures taken by sports associations creating barriers to entry for third-party organisers (see Section 2), while the second set of decisions discussed below tackle the issue of unfair participation conditions for athletes and other stakeholders (Section 3).

2. Barriers to Entry for Third Party Organisers

7. The BCA has made various decisions regarding restrictive measures in Belgium in recent years, which are together referred to as the Fédération Equestre Internationale (FEI) saga.[3] The BCA decision is based on the European Commission's *International Skating Union (ISU)* decisions which resulted recently in a Court of Justice ruling on this topic.[4]

8. To understand the "ins and outs" of the Belgian FEI decisions (Section B), it is first necessary to set out the principles laid out in the European courts' ISU decisions (Section A). Although the latter are not Belgian decisions as such, they have answered and shed light on important and long-standing questions regarding the rules that sports federations may adopt and that limit the ability to organise leagues/championships outside their competence and the BCA's decisions now have to be read in light of this recent ruling of the Court of Justice.

A. *International Skating Union (ISU)*

9. The ISU is an international sports federation recognised by the International Olympic Committee as the international sports federation globally administering figure skating on ice and speed skating on ice. The ISU is the sole regulator of both these sports and is composed of the individual national associations (who are its members), which administer figure and speed skating on ice at the national level.[5]

10. Following a complaint by two professional speed skaters, Mark Tuitert and Niels Kerstholt, the European Commission investigated the existence of potential competition law breaches arising from the ISU's eligibility rules.[6] Under these rules, an athlete would become ineligible to participate in ISU activities and competitions by skating in an event not authorised by an ISU member and/or the

---

3 All the decisions in the *FEI* case can be found on the BCA's website <www.bma-abc.be/nl/beslissingen/18-vm-33-lisa-nooren-et-henk-nooren-handelsstal-sprl-fei-gcl-ttb> accessed 23 August 2025.

4 Case AT.40208 European Commission Decision *International Skating Union's Eligibility* (8 December 2017) (*ISU* Decision); Case T-93/18 *International Skating Union (ISU)* ECLI:EU:T:2020:610 and Case C-124/21 P *International Skating Union (ISU)* ECLI:EU:C:2023:1012.

5 *ISU* Decision (n 4) 6. See also European Commission, "The EU Commission decides that an international sport association has breached European competition rules (International Skating Union)" (8 December 2017) e-Competitions art. No. 85430 and Romano F Subiotto QC, "The EU Commission decides that an international sport association's eligibility rules breached EU competition law (International Skating Union)" (8 December 2017) e-Competitions art. No. 88192.

6 The case concerns the 2014 version of the Eligibility Rules, which have been updated during the investigation (in 2016) and afterwards.

ISU. Moreover, the ISU rules required the ISU's prior approval for the organisation of international competitions. The Commission heavily relied on the example of Icederby International Co Ltd (Icederby), an event and entertainment company that launched a new format of ice racing and ice entertainment events.[7] Given the gravity of the ISU's penalties (ineligibility could take the form of a lifetime ban), ISU in effect was forbidding athletes from participating in non-authorised events.

11. In 2017, the European Commission found that the rules on the authorisation of competitions and athletes' participation infringed EU law. They directed the ISU to prevent the organisation of events in competition with its own and prevented professional skaters from taking part in them. The Commission's decision relied on settled case law concerning competition law's application to the sports sector.[8] It then confirmed that international sports associations could be considered as undertakings[9] or an association of undertakings.[10] In the ISU case, since the ISU's members themselves qualified as undertakings, the ISU constituted an association of undertakings within the meaning of Article 101(1) TFEU, and it was active in the market for the organisation and commercial exploitation of international speed skating events.[11] Hence, the ISU's eligibility rules were deemed to be a decision of an association of undertakings. This qualification under Article 101 TFEU allowed the Commission not to assess the existence of a potential dominant position by the ISU on the relevant market.[12]

12. According to the Court of Justice in the *Meca-Medina* judgment,[13] such rules may fall outside the application of Article 101 TFEU in certain circumstances, taking into account: the overall context in which the rules were taken or produced their effects and their objectives; ie whether the consequential effects that are restrictive of competition are inherent in the pursuit of the objectives; and whether they are proportionate to such objectives.

13. In the present case, the European Commission analysed the various objectives the ISU put forward to justify its eligibility rules. Among them, the following could

---

7 *ISU* Decision (n 4) 20.

8 Ibid 9 and the following Court of Justice cases: Case 36/74 *Walrave and Koch v Association Union Cycliste Internationale and others* ECLI:EU:C:1974:140, para 4; Case 13/76 *Gaetano Donà v Mario Mantero* ECLI:EU:C:1976:115, para 12; Case C-415/93 *Union Royale Belge Sociale de Football Association, RCL and UEFA v JM Bosman* ECLI:EU:C:1995:463, para 73; Case C-176/96 *Lehtonen v FRBSB* ECLI:EU:C:2000:201, para 32, Joined Case C-51/96 *Christelle Deliège v Ligue francophone de judo et disciplines associées ASBL* and Case C-191/97 *Christelle Deliège v ASBL and François Pacquée* ECLI:EU:C:2000:199, para 4; Case C-519/04 P *David Meca-Medina and Igor Majcen v Commission of the European Communities* ECLI:EU:C:2006:492, para 22; Case C-49/07 *MOTOE* ECLI:EU:C:2008:376, para 22; Case C-325/08 *Olympique Lyonnais SASP v Olivier Bernard and Newcastle UFC* ECLI:EU:C:2010:143, para 27.

9 To the extent they themselves carry out activities of an economic nature (such as the organisation and commercial exploitation of sports events), see Cases 33384 and 33378 European Commission Decision *Distribution of package tours during the 1990 World Cup* [1992] OJ L326/31, paras 52–53.

10 If their members carry out activities of an economic nature, regardless of whether the international sports associations themselves carry out such activities, see Case T-193/02 *Laurent Piau v Commission of the European Communities* ECLI:EU:T:2005:22, para 72.

11 *ISU* Decision (n 4), 39.

12 Ibid 131 and following, where the European Commission merely qualifies the position of the ISU as "very strong".

13 *Meca-Medina* (n 8), para 42.

be considered as legitimate objectives: the protection of the sport's integrity, the protection of health and safety, the organisation and proper conduct of competitive sport, some forms of horizontal (for instance, equal distribution of revenues to all the clubs participating in the same competition) or vertical solidarity (for instance, redistribution of revenues from the elite/professional level of a sport to the lower/grassroots level), and the protection of the volunteer model of sport. On the other hand, the protection of economic and/or financial interests and the prevention of free riding could not be considered as legitimate objectives.[14] Then, the Commission examined these restrictions of competition imposed by the ISU and concluded that they were neither inherent in the pursuit of these legitimate objectives, nor proportionate to achieving them.

14. The Commission ordered the ISU "to bring the infringement established in this decision effectively to an end and henceforth refrain from any measure that has the same or an equivalent object or effect" and it imposed a daily periodic penalty payment of 5% of the ISU's average daily turnover in the preceding business year in the event of failure to comply with the order.[15] The Commission did not impose a fine on the ISU because of the novelty of the case, the eligibility rules had been publicly known and available since 1998; and the ISU was a sports federation, that therefore devolved part of its revenue to the development of the sport.[16]

15. The ISU appealed the decision before the General Court of the European Union[17] and, in the meantime, amended its eligibility rules to comply with the European Commission's decision. The amendments to its eligibility rules included:
    1. More precise definitions of the authorisation requirements for third-party event organisers, particularly regarding the legitimate objectives that the requirements pursue, concerning integrity, health and safety;
    2. Lessened potential penalties on athletes for participating in unauthorised third-party events; and
    3. A revised code of ethics applying to private companies organising events.[18]

16. In 2020, the General Court dismissed the ISU's appeal against the European Commission decision and confirmed that the rules governing authorisation and participation were unlawful. The case was then appealed again before the Court of Justice.

17. On 21 December 2023 and following the Commission and the General Court's rulings, the Court of Justice confirmed that the ISU eligibility rules, which empowered it to subject international skating competitions to its approval and to impose severe penalties on athletes who participated in unauthorised competitions, were

---

14 *ISU* Decision (n 4), 54–57. The European Commission also considers that "the principle of having one regulator per sport can be considered as legitimate objective capable of justifying restrictions of competition law, the measures established by the ISU (that is, the pre-authorisation system embodied by the ISU's Eligibility rules and by Communication No 1974 on Open International Competitions) are neither inherent in the pursuit of those objectives nor proportionate to them" (Ibid 56).

15 Ibid 82 and 83.

16 Ibid 83.

17 *ISU* T-93/18 (n 4).

18 Subiotto (n 5).

unlawful. The Court of Justice found that the unlawful character of the rules lay, in particular, in the fact that they were not subject to any guarantee ensuring that they were transparent, objective, non-discriminatory and proportionate; they gave the ISU a clear advantage over its competitors and had unfavourable effects for athletes as well as for consumers and broadcast audiences.[19]

18. First, the Court of Justice observed that the organisation of sporting competitions clearly constitutes an economic activity. Therefore, that activity must comply with the competition rules, even though sport as an economic activity has certain specific features, such as the existence of associations with regulatory control and punishment powers.

19. Second, the Court of Justice stressed that a sports association such as the ISU may adopt and ensure compliance with rules relating to the organisation and holding of competitions, if necessary, by means of penalties. However, those rules must be subject to a framework that ensures they are transparent, objective, non-discriminatory and proportionate. If this is not the case, then those rules may enable the sports federation to exclude any competing undertaking from the market and restrict the organisation and holding of new competitions. Additionally, they may prevent athletes from taking part in those competitions. Lastly, they may deprive spectators and broadcast audiences of any opportunity to watch such competitions.

20. Following these findings, the Court of Justice confirmed that the prior authorisation and eligibility rules constituted a restriction of competition by object that could not be justified.

B. *Belgium's Fédération Equestre Internationale (FEI) Saga*

21. The European Commission's ISU decision, which has now also been confirmed by the ECJ, is echoed by the multiple decisions taken by the BCA and the Belgian courts in two proceedings involving another international sports federation: the Fédération Equestre Internationale (FEI).

22. The first proceedings *Global Champions League and others v FEI*[20] began with a simultaneous complaint[21] and request for interim measures by Global, an organiser of a series of jumping events[22] against the FEI. Global was the organiser

---

[19] *ISU* C-124/21 P (n 4); CJEU, Press Release, "The Rules of the International Skating Union on the Prior Authorisation of Skating Competitions Infringe EU law" (2023) <www.concurrences.com/IMG/pdf/cp230202en.pdf?119390/4cc213f1c968940eb6c950e7b265673ea9f922d597897b33c8048c618637e9c7> accessed 23 August 2025.

[20] The different decisions regarding the request for interim measures are to be found on the BCA website <www.abc-bma.be/fr/decisions/15-vm-23-gcl-ttb-vs-fei> accessed 23 August 2025. The principal decision being, Case 2015-V/M-23 BCA Decision *Global Champions League and Tops Trading Belgium v Fédération Equestre Internationale (FEI)* (27 July 2015), confirmed by the Brussels Court of Appeal (3 May 2016) <www.abc-bma.be/fr/decisions/2015mr1-fei-ad> accessed 11 August 2025.

[21] Originally, a veterinarian (active in horse jumping), two FEI-judges and several companies part of a group active in horse jumping also complained to the BCA, but the latter all withdrew their complaints, which did not preclude the BCA from taking a decision on these complaints.

[22] Or rather the companies behind the organisation of the events concerned. Global later also withdrew its complaint.

of the Global Champions Tour (GCT), a series of jumping events recognised by the FEI. Besides the GCT, Global wanted to organise another series of jumping events, the Global Champions League (GCL). Jumping is, by essence, an individual sport (with the notable exception of competitions between countries) and, according to Global, the attraction and the novelty of the GCL was that it would be a competition between teams.

23. At the heart of the legal proceedings were the FEI rules on participation by athletes, horses and officials in unauthorised events, which were the events not recognised by the FEI. Another major point in the proceedings was the FEI procedures' alleged lack of clarity regarding as an authorised event.

24. The interim measures requested by Global sought to:

    1. Suspend the FEI rules on participation by athletes, horses and officials in unauthorised events;
    2. Prohibit the FEI from suspending or penalising athletes, horses, officials and/or organisers participating in a competition not authorised by the FEI; and
    3. Order the FEI to communicate such a suspension of the rules, in writing, on its website and to all stakeholders.

25. The BCA decided to order the imposition of these interim measures (though in a slightly modified version). Following an appeal by the FEI, the Brussels Court of Appeal[23] confirmed the BCA's decision. Two days after the Court of Appeal's decision, Global initiated proceedings before the BCA against the FEI for failure to implement the third interim measure. The BCA sided with Global.

26. Following the BCA's decision on interim measures, the FEI amended its rules and allowed Global to organise its GCL, following which Global withdrew its complaint.[24] The fact that the complaint had been withdrawn did not preclude the BCA from continuing its investigation. On 20 December 2018, the BCA therefore delivered its decision on the merits. Just as with the European Commission in the *ISU* case, the BCA ultimately decided not to impose a fine on the FEI, given that FEI had amended its rules.

27. The second proceedings (*Lisa Nooren et Henk Nooren Handelsstal SPRLv. FEI-GCL-TTB*) flowed from the first. The FEI's decision to allow Global to organise its GCL tournament prompted an athlete and a stable to file a complaint and a request for interim measures before the BCA, arguing that the system for selecting the athletes participating in the GCL events was discriminatory. They argued that only a fraction of all professional riders could be part of a team, while a place in a team would allow members to take part in the most lucrative events: the GCL events. The rules on the selection of the athletes participating in a GCL event were indeed different from the general FEI rules. According to the claimants, those athletes that were members of a GCL team were given a substantial and unfair

---

23 Appeals against the BCA's decisions are brought before a special section of the Brussels Court of Appeal, the Market Court.

24 Case 2018-I/O-41-AUD BCA Decision in CONCP/K-15/0014 – *GCL v FEI*; CONC-P/K-15/0041 *Stephex v FEI*; CONC-P/K-16/0009 *Docteur De Baker v FEI*; CONC-P/K-16/0022 *Rogier Van Iersel v FEI* and CONC-P/K-16/0023 *Rob Jansen v FEI* (20 December 2018).

advantage by receiving a higher chance of taking part in the most lucrative events (in terms of prize money and points for the individual FEI ranking).

28. In a first decision,[25] the BCA awarded interim measures to the claimants and ordered Global and the FEI to align the rules of invitation for athletes to GCL events to the rules of other similar events recognised by the FEI. This decision shows that the BCA does not shy away from also penalising international sports federations, such as the FEI with its registered offices in Switzerland, whose seat is not in Belgium, if their behaviour or regulations have an effect on the Belgian market.

29. The FEI and Global refused to comply with this first decision, which led the BCA to take a second decision[26] that imposed a periodic penalty payment on the FEI and Global for their failure to implement the first decision. In the meantime, Global had appealed the BCA's first decision before the Brussels Court of Appeal, which annulled the BCA's first decision for procedural reasons. The case was then sent back to the BCA, which led to another appeal by Global before the Brussels Court of Appeal on procedural grounds.[27] Finally, the BCA ruled[28] that there was, *prima facie*, no imminent risk of serious and difficult to repair damage and (in contrast to its first decision) the BCA decided not to impose interim measures on the FEI and Global.

30. This last decision has not been appealed, and no decision has been taken yet by the BCA regarding the complaint on the merits in the second proceedings.

3. Barriers to Entry and Unfair Conditions of Participation for Athletes and Other Stakeholders

A. *Football – Seraing and Doyen Sports*

31. In 2014, the International Federation of Football Association (FIFA) decided to ban the principle of third-party ownership (TPO) for any player or club. Since then, no club or player has been allowed to sign an agreement with a third party enabling the latter to claim compensation payable in connection with the future transfer of a player. In other words, the ban on TPO is the prohibition of economic ownership of players by third parties (ie not a football club).

32. Despite the newly applicable ban on TPO, on 30 January 2015, the football club, Royal Football Club de Seraing, which had just bought a registration number

[25] Case 2017-V/M-38 BCA Decision in CONC-V/M-17/0037 (20 December 2017). See also Belgian Competition Authority, "The Belgian Competition Authority imposes interim measures in the context of competitions of the Global Champions Tour (GCT)" (21 December 2017) e-Competitions art. No. 85513.

[26] Case 2018-V/M-11 BCA Decision in CONC-V/M-17/0037 (13 April 2018). See also Belgian Competition Authority, "The Belgian Competition Authority fines equestrian competition organisers for lack of implementation of provisional measures (Fédération Equestre Internationale / GCT / GCL)" (16 April 2018) e-Competitions art. No. 87067.

[27] The case was sent back to the BCA, which was composed of the same members as for the first decision in these proceedings. Whereas, according to Global, and followed by the Court of Appeal, other members should have composed the BCA. The case was therefore returned a second time to the BCA, which was this time composed of other members; Case 2018-V/M-33 BCA Decision in CONC-V/M-17/0037 (28 September 2018).

[28] Case 2018-V/M-33 BCA Decision in CONC-V/M-17/0037 (28 September 2018).

to move up from the provincial Division 1 to the national Division 2 (which has now been renamed Division 1B or the "Challenger Pro League"), signed an agreement with Doyen Sport Investments Ltd, a private company incorporated under Maltese law and active in the provision of financial assistance to football clubs and in the purchase and sale of players. Under this agreement, Doyen Sports acquired 30% of the rights to three named players for 300,000 euros. A second agreement was signed for a fourth player in July 2015. That same year, Seraing together with Doyen Sports and the former president of FC Twente, a Dutch football club, and ten supporters of this club (the Individuals) initiated proceedings against FIFA, UEFA (the Union of European Football Associations) and the Royal Belgian Football Association (RBFA) regarding FIFA's decision banning TPO. They argued, among other things, that FIFA's decision would infringe competition law.

33. In a first judgment of 27 November 2016, the Brussels French-speaking Commercial Court (largely) sided with FIFA, UEFA and the RBFA. This decision was later appealed, which led to the Brussels Court of Appeal's judgment of 12 December 2019.[29]

34. Between the first and the second judgment, the Court of Arbitration for Sport (CAS), established in Switzerland, made an arbitral award in favour of FIFA on 9 March 2017.[30] The CAS ruled that the new articles challenged by Seraing were legal under European Union law.[31]

35. In its decision of 12 December 2019, the Brussels Court of Appeal rejected the appeal by Doyen Sports, Seraing and the Individuals, partly because of the existence of the arbitral award delivered by the CAS, but also on other procedural grounds. The Court of Appeal dismissed Seraing's appeal particularly on the grounds that the CAS arbitral award, which had considered that European law had not been violated, had the force of *res judicata* (*autorité de la chose jugée*). Seraing and Doyen Sports decided to appeal the Court of Appeal's decision before the Belgian Supreme Court *(Cour de cassation)*. In particular, they argued that in the way it organises football at an international level, FIFA promotes only its own interests, effectively excluding, through its rules and the imposition of forced arbitration, any competition in a market worth billions of euros. Therefore, Seraing and Doyen Sports requested the Belgian Supreme Court to submit a request for a preliminary ruling to the European Court of Justice.

36. On 8 September 2023, the Belgian Supreme Court finally delivered a judgment in which it decided to stay the proceedings and request the Court of Justice for a preliminary ruling.[32] The question asked by the Supreme Court was whether

---

29 Case 2016/AR/2048 *Royal Football Club Seraing SA v FIFA and others* (12 December 2019) Brussels Court of Appeal.

30 CAS is an international body established in 1984 to settle disputes related to sport through arbitration. FIFA's Statutes provide that CAS shall be competent to settle disputes in which FIFA is involved.

31 Case 2016/A/4490 CAS Decision *Royal Football Club Seraing SA v FIFA* (9 March 2017).

32 Case C.20.0429.F/2 *Royal Football Club Seraing v FIFA, UEFA and RBFA* (8 September 2023) Belgian Supreme Court; see also Case C-600/23 *Royal Football Club Seraing SA v FIFA and others* ECLI:EU:C:2025:617. Summary of the request for a preliminary ruling under Article 98(1) of the Rules of Procedure of the Court of Justice (2 October 2023) <https://curia.europa.eu/juris/showPdf.jsf?text=seraing&docid=280548&pageIndex=0&doclang=en&mode=req&dir=&occ=first&part=1&cid=3179797> accessed 23 August 2025.

an arbitral tribunal such as the CAS, established outside the EU (in Switzerland) and imposed by FIFA's statutes, may be given the right to decide with the force of *res judicata* whether or not European law had been violated, and so prevent the claimants from turning to a national court in the European Union to protect their European rights. Through this request for a preliminary ruling, the Supreme Court has asked for guidance on the legitimacy of the private justice mechanism imposed by FIFA and UEFA"s statutes on all clubs and players, who can only challenge a decision made by these federations by means of forced arbitration before the CAS, whereas the CAS can choose to apply or not apply EU law as it sees fit thus protecting these international federations from the genuine application of European law.

37. The initial grounds on which this case was based, concerning recourse against the ban on TPO, therefore evolved to the more substantive question of the force/authority of a CAS arbitral award, regarding the application of European law by such a non-EU court of arbitration.

B. *Football – Waasland-Beveren*[33]

38. Following the Covid-19 pandemic, Belgium's professional football governing body, the Pro League, decided in a decision of 15 May 2020 to end the season for Belgium's two professional leagues (Divisions 1A and 1B) before all the matches had been played. This decision led, amongst other things, to the relegation of professional football club, Waasland-Beveren, from Division 1A to 1B.

39. Waasland-Beveren argued that the Pro League's decision infringed competition law. It asked the BCA to impose interim measures on the Pro League, and in particular:

   1. To order the Pro League and/or the RBFA to maintain Waasland-Beveren in Division 1A for the 2020–2021 season; and
   2. To prohibit the Pro League and/or the RBFA from imposing a penalty on Waasland-Beveren for seeking legal remedies, in particular from the BCA, regarding the decision of 15 May 2020.

40. On 2 July 2020, the BCA decided that given the Covid-19 pandemic, it was not unreasonable for the Pro League to have decided to end the 2019–2020 season on 15 May 2020, which caused the relegation of Waasland-Beveren, and to maintain a competition format in Division 1A of 16 clubs for the 2020–2021 season. The BCA also concluded that this decision was the closest possible to the RBFA football regulations and to sports logic.

41. However, given the change in circumstances and in particular the possibility of resuming sporting competitions from 1 July 2020, the BCA considered that upholding the 15 May 2020 decision could *prima facie* result in discrimination if the Division 1B promotion final were to be played (but not the matches deciding a club's relegation from Division 1A to 1B). The BCA examined the possibility

[33] Case 2020-V/M-26 BCA Decision CONC–VM–20/0017 *Foodinvest/Pro League v Union Royale Belge Sociale de Football Association* (2 July 2020).

of playing the two matches to decide which club would be relegated, or all remaining matches of the final day of the 2019–2020 season. The parties, including Waasland-Beveren, argued against such a measure.

42. The BCA also considered that it could not impose a provisional change on the competition format in an interim measure decision for the 2020–2021 season (ie a 17- or 18-team championship in Division 1A) without imposing a disproportionate burden on the clubs and organisers, while offering Waasland-Beveren the right to remain in Division 1A, without this being the result of the sporting competition.

43. Consequently, the BCA ordered the Pro League to suspend the provision in its 15 May 2020 decision that allowed for penalties on Waasland-Beveren or any other club in the Pro league for seeking legal remedies, eg from the BCA, regarding the decision of 15 May 2020. However, the BCA decided that Waasland-Beveren's relegation to Division 1B was *prima facie* not incompatible with competition law.

C. *Football – CVBA Kortrijk*[34]

44. Also following the Covid-19 pandemic, the Pro League added a new provision to its football regulations obliging players to have certain qualifications (such as Covid testing) to participate in a game. A control strategy was put in place, and it was provided that when seven players of one club tested positive with Covid-19, the club concerned could request postponement of the game. A few months later, this provision was deleted.

45. On 25 December 2021 (ie after the temporary rule on postponing a game due to Covid infection had been removed), the Pro League's calendar manager[35] informed two football clubs, CVBA Kortrijk and NV Royal Antwerp, that he had decided to postpone the game initially planned between the two clubs for 26 December 2021. Indeed, nine players had been identified as being infected with Covid-19 within the Antwerp football team. Although there was no regulatory or legal basis for making this decision, the Pro League's calendar manager invoked the risky situation linked to the new Covid variant and the potential health threat that could result from the game being played; consequently, the game was cancelled.

46. Kortrijk challenged the Pro League calendar manager's decision before the BACS. Kortrijk invoked, among other things, that the calendar manager and the Pro League's conduct and decisions concerning postponing the game against Antwerp lacked any legal or regulatory basis, and infringed both the prohibition of anti-competitive agreements, decisions of association of undertakings and concerted practices contained in Article IV.1 Code of Economic Law (CEL) and Article 101 TFEU, and the prohibition of abuses of a dominant position based on Articles IV.2 CEL and Article 102 TFEU. In its arbitral award of 8 February 2022, the BACS considered that the contested calendar manager's decision was reasonable and justified and there was no evidence that the calendar manager made that decision

---

34 Case 248/22 BACS Decision *CBVA Kortrijk Voetbalt v Pro League and URBFSA* (8 February 2022).

35 The Pro League's calendar manager is proposed by the Pro League and appointed by the board of directors of the RBFA. His responsibilities include preparing and managing the professional football's divisions' calendar of games.

following pressure by Antwerp or the Pro League. Consequently, the BACS found that postponing the game between Kortrijk and Antwerp did not appreciably prevent, restrict or distort competition in the Belgian market concerned, nor did it constitute an abuse of a dominant position.

D. *Bumper Pool*

47. On 23 January 2020, the BCA imposed an interim measure on the Belgian Bumper Pool Association (*Belgische Golfbiljartbond* or BGB) concerning the bumper pool balls that may be used in official competitions and matches.[36]

48. The interim measure followed a request from Hector Cue Sports Belgium BVBA (HCSB), a bumper pool ball producer that had challenged the BGB rules stipulating that only two types of balls produced by Saluc (the world market leader in the production of pool balls) may be used in pool games. The BCA gave the BGB two choices: to either suspend the obligation to use Saluc's bumper pool balls exclusively or to organise a non-discriminatory tender to determine the authorised bumper pool balls. In both situations, the BCA authorised the BGB to stipulate that the balls must have certain objectively determinable characteristics that make them functionally suitable for playing bumper pool and that would not create a statistically significant advantage for players who have practised with a particular brand of ball. These characteristics included ball weight, diameter, material and rotation speed.

49. Following the BCA's decision of 23 January 2020, HCSB introduced a formal request with the BCA to monitor the BGB's compliance with the interim measure imposed on it, at the start of the 2020–2021 season. HCSB argued that the BGB opted for a different form of implementation than the measures imposed in the first BCA decision. The BGB had indeed introduced a revised proposal of its rules and procedures on 19 June 2020, in which it introduced fixed values for ball weight and diameter. According to the BCA and HCSB, these fixed values were nevertheless not in conformity with the BCA decision of 23 January 2020.

50. In its decision of 28 August 2020,[37] the BCA recognised the non-conformity of the BGB's revised rules and procedures with its previous decision regarding the objectively determinable characteristics of the balls. The BCA found that stipulations about a fixed measurement size for balls was disproportionate as there should always be some margin for error. The BCA concluded that the BGB had not sufficiently amended its rules and procedures to allow for competition in the supply of pool balls and had therefore failed to fully comply with the interim measure imposed. The BCA also stressed the urgency of the situation as the previous decisions urged the BGB to modify its rules and procedures before the national competition and competitions organised by clubs or associations that referred to the BGB regulations. Therefore, the BCA obliged the BGB to amend its rules

---

36 Case 2020-V/M-04 BCA Decision in MEDE-C/M-19/0041 *BVBA Hector Cue Sports Belgium v VZW Belgische Biljartond* (23 January 2020); Belgian Competition Authority, "The Belgian Competition Authority imposes interim measures against a sports association because of its anticompetitive rules (Belgian Bumper Pool Association)' (24 January 2020) e-Competitions art. No. 93147.

37 2020-V/M-28 BCA Decision in MEDE-V/M-19/0041 (28 August 2020).

and procedures by 4 September 2020 in accordance with its 23 January 2020 decision and imposed a periodic penalty payment of 125 euros for each day of delay in implementing the measures.

51. The HCSB brought a similar case against the BGB before the Leuven Enterprise Court.[38] The BGB had entered a sponsoring agreement with Saluc in July 2020, which granted Saluc the exclusive right to supply bumper pool balls for certain competitions. The BGB also agreed with Saluc that pool balls of competing brands could not be advertised during those competitions. Advertising for Saluc/Aramith would be visible during the free matches, and Saluc would pay an annual "subsidy" to the BGB. According to HCSB, by signing this sponsoring agreement, the BGB infringed Belgian competition law rules and abused its dominant position in breach of Articles IV.1 and IV.2 CEL and Articles 101 and 102 TFEU. The Enterprise Court requested the BCA to issue an *amicus curiae*, which the latter did on 25 August 2021.[39] Following the BCA's point of view in its *amicus curiae*, the Enterprise Court's President decided that the BGB had indeed infringed competition law, in particular Articles IV.1 and IV.2 CEL (and Articles 101 and 102 TFEU), by continuing to grant exclusive rights to certain suppliers of pool equipment (ie pool balls or pool tables) from an absolute dominant position regarding bumper pool competitions without first organising a tender or a call for tenders for this purpose in a transparent and objective manner. In so doing, the BGB hindered HCSB's commercialisation of its pool balls and tables and deprived it of the opportunity to enter into its own sponsorship agreements with the BGB in an objective, non-discriminatory and transparent manner.

52. Finally, similar cases have also been brought against the BGB before the BACS in 2019 and 2020.[40]

53. BC Mister 100 Lier and BC Couronne, two bumper pool clubs, were penalised by the BGB for not using the required brand of bumper pool cloth for official competition games. Indeed, the BGB rules and procedures stipulated that only a cloth of a certain brand (Simonis), could be installed on the bumper tables for these games. The two bumper pool clubs brought a complaint before the BACS invoking, among other things, that the rule requiring bumper pool clubs to use cloth exclusively from one specific producer violated Articles 101 and 102 TFEU and Articles IV.1 and IV.2 CEL. Although the BACS did not find the existence of a cartel between the BGB and Simonis, it found that BGB abused its dominant position by setting very strict rules forcing the clubs to install bumper pool cloth from Simonis exclusively. The BGB could not provide any objective justification for approving only Simonis brand cloth. The categorical approval of only one type and brand was not found to be objectively justified and was found to be at least a disproportionate measure and thus not permitted.

---

38 Case A/20/01287 *Hector Cue Sports Belgium BV v VZW Konklijke Belgische Biljartbond* (30 November 2021) Leuven Enterprise Court.

39 Ibid. BCA, *amicus curiae* based on art IV.88, s 1 CEL.

40 Cases 139/19 and 140/19 *BC Mister 100 LIER and others v VZW Koninklijke Belgische Biljartbond* (14 May 2019); Case 165/19 BACS Decision *BC Mister 100 LIER and others v VSW Koninklijke Belgische Biljartbond* (17 august 2020); Case 177/20 *BC Couronne and other v VSW Koninklijke Belgische Biljartbond* (17 august 2020).

54. The BACS further clarified that an abuse of a dominant position can occur when the company with a dominant position in one particular market (here, the BGB in the market for the organisation of bumper pool games) takes a decision that distorts competition in a related market (here, the market for the sale of competition bumper pool cloth). The BACS found that the arbitrary nature of the criteria applied by the BGB regarding the approval of cloth and the far-reaching penalties that the BGB sought to attach to non-compliance with that rule, constituted an infringement of the applicants' rights.

55. In its defence, the BGB argued that Simonis sold a very specific bumper pool cloth composed of 75% wool, which had specific attributes for the bumper pool competitions and would allegedly be better than synthetic cloth. Again, the BACS assessed whether there was an objective justification for the decision to compulsorily include in the regulations that only cloth made up of at least 75% wool should be admitted. The BACS concluded there was no legitimate objective to justify that rule nor the distortion of competition resulting from it in the related market of the sale of bumper pool cloth.

56. These cases clearly demonstrate the typical Belgian feature consisting of stakeholders' ability to raise the same issues in the sports sector before different bodies such as the BCA and the BACS, in addition to the regular courts.

E. *Football – RE Virton*[41]

57. In 2020, the Royal Belgian Football Association's Licensing Commission refused to issue a new professional licence to professional football club, Royal Excelsior Virton, because the club did not satisfy the RBFA regulations licence requirements. The RBFA found, in particular, that the club was not financially viable and had failed to demonstrate its financial stability, which was an important criterion to qualify for a professional football licence. This RFBA decision led to RE Virton's relegation from Division 1B to the amateur Division 2.

58. In April 2020, RE Virton brought a complaint to the BCA against the RBFA's decision and requested interim measures be taken, alleging that the RBFA's rules regarding the licensing conditions for football clubs amounted to a restriction of competition and that those rules were being applied to different Belgian football clubs in a discriminatory manner. In this specific case, RE Virton claimed that the RBFA did not consider that a sponsorship agreement with a company that belonged to the same group as the club could guarantee economic continuity. RE Virton also complained that the RBFA's requirements concerning "comfort letters" ensuring a club's financial stability were excessive. RE Virton sought to be reinstated in Division 1B.

59. RE Virton also initiated proceedings before the BACS criticising the RBFA's rules regulating the acquisition of such a licence based on infringements of Belgian and European competition law rules. RE Virton requested the annulment of these

---

41 Case 2020-V/M-36 BCA Decision in CONC-V/M-20/0012 *RE Virton v URBFSA* (19 November 2020); see Sandrine Mathieu and Guillaume Azevedo Mendes, "The Belgian Competition Authority rules that a national football association's conditions to obtain a professional license are prima facie incompatible with competition law and orders interim measures (Virton / RBFA)' (19 November 2020) e-Competitions art. No. 101393.

licensing provisions and the immediate suspension of all procedures for granting licences in this regard. On 10 May 2020, the BACS dismissed RE Virton's request, arguing that the RBFA's provisions relating to the licensing conditions pursued a legitimate objective and were proportionate to that objective.[42]

60. On 19 November 2020, the BCA ordered the imposition of interim measures against the RBFA following RE Virton's request. The decision partly granted the club's request to be reinstated in professional football (Division 1B) as they had been given the opportunity to rejoin Division 1B for the next 2021–2022 season. The BCA ruled that the refusal by the RBFA's Licensing Committee to grant RE Virton a licence in April 2020 (which was subsequently confirmed by the BACS' arbitral award of 10 May 2020), was motivated by certain conditions in the granting of the professional licence that RE Virton had not fulfilled, but which were found to be *prima facie* incompatible with competition law.

61. In particular, the BCA found that RE Virton had been deprived of the opportunities that the RBFA's Licensing Commission or the BACS usually considered relevant for granting a licence. In other words, the BCA, on a preliminary basis, found that the RBFA's refusal to take into account sponsoring contracts with a company linked to the club constituted a barrier to entering the Belgian professional football market.

62. Note that on 29 June 2020,[43] the BCA had taken a first decision rejecting RE Virton's request for interim measures. RE Virton appealed that decision before the Brussels Court of Appeal. On 23 September 2020,[44] the Brussels Court of Appeal annulled the BCA's first decision and referred the case back to the BCA which had at that time a different composition of members. This newly composed BCA adopted the decision of 19 November 2020, which this time granted RE Virton the interim measures. The RBFA appealed the Brussels Court of Appeal's decision of 23 September 2020 before the Supreme Court, who in its decision of 5 January 2023[45] then quashed the Court of Appeal's decision. This meant that, from a legal point of view, the BCA's decision of 19 November 2020 could not be taken, and that the Court of Appeal had to review the case with a different composition of members. From a legal perspective, the Brussels Court of Appeal therefore still had to make its ruling on the BCA's first interim measures judgment, approximately four years after the relevant facts that first led to that case.

63. The RE Virton case reiterates the increasing relevance of competition law for football associations and sports federations in general, which are subject to the scrutiny by the competition authorities.

F. *Football – Lommel SK*[46]

64. In June 2010, UEFA introduced its Financial Fair Play (FFP) regulations to improve European football clubs' economic and financial capacity and to ensure

42 Case 178/20 *RE Virton v URBFSA* (10 May 2020), 22.

43 Case 2020-V/M-24 BCA Decision CONC-V/M-20/0012 *RE Virton v URBFSA* (29 June 2020).

44 Case 2020/MR/1 *RE Virton v BCA* (23 September 2020) Brussels Court of Appeal.

45 Case C.20.0472.F *URBFSA v RE Virton and BCA* (5 January 2023) Belgian Supreme Court.

46 Case 172/20 *VZW Voebtalclub Lommel United and NV Voetbalclub Lommel SK v VZW Koninklijke Belgische Voetbalbond* (1 April 2020).

that European football clubs would be aware of the balance between their income and expenditures. These regulations were necessary, according to UEFA, given the high number of European football club bankruptcies. As a result, the Pro League board amended the Belgian Federal Regulations to extend the FFP principle to professional football clubs with a national licence. The new rules came into force on 1 July 2017 in Belgium.

65. On 31 October 2019, the professional football club, Lommel SK, submitted a file on FFP to the RBFA's Licensing Committee to obtain its licence for the following season. However, the RBFA's Licensing Committee argued that the file and licence request had been submitted too late and were incomplete and imposed a fine of 67,500 euros on Lommel SK in accordance with a specific provision of the Federal regulations.

66. On 13 February 2020, Lommel SK filed a petition before the BACS asking for the annulment of the penalty. The club argued that the slightest non-compliance with the RBFA's rules had far-reaching consequences for football clubs as very high fines were being imposed. If the provisions of the regulations in question, and the penalty mechanism in particular, were to pursue a legitimate objective, Lommel SK argued that the penalty provisions contained in the regulations for the late submission of certain documents and their concrete application by the RBFA's Licensing Committee constituted a practice that restricted competition. Lommel SK further claimed that the penalty imposed in no way served its supposed legitimate purpose and would constitute an abuse of the RBFA's dominant position in the market for the organisation of official football competitions in Belgium.

67. In its decision of 1 April 2020, the BACS ruled that the RBFA had a monopoly position on the Belgian market for the organisation of official football matches and the associated organisational and regulatory interventions and therefore held a dominant position in that market. Accordingly, the RBFA must not abuse its dominant position by, for example, taking certain actions that could create a distortion in related markets, including the market in which Lommel SK was active.

68. To ascertain whether the RBFA, by means of its imposed penalty, had abused its dominant position, the BACS examined whether that penalty:

1. served a legitimate purpose;
2. was objectively justifiable; and
3. was proportionate.

69. While the BACS found that the penalty served a legitimate purpose and was objectively justifiable, it decided that the penalty at issue, or at least its unabated persistence in the then Covid-19 pandemic, was disproportionate. The RBFA's decision would reasonably distort the market in which Lommel SK operated to the extent that the overall magnitude of the penalty was such that it could affect Lommel SK's ability to recruit and retain players. In doing so, the BACS took account of the Covid-19 pandemic and the unexpected financial difficulties faced by football clubs, such as Lommel SK, in that context.

70. Accordingly, the BACS decided that the abusive nature of the penalty imposed had to be remedied by reducing the penalty at issue to an amount that would be proportionate. The BACS decided that a penalty of 30,000 euros would be proportionate given all the circumstances of the case.

G. *The Pigeon Racing Sector*[47]

71. As explained in the introduction above, the BCA has been one of the most active national competition authorities in imposing interim measures in competition-related cases among various sectors. The sectors tackled by the BCA do not only concern the classic football cases, but also lesser-known sectors, such as the pigeon racing sector.

72. On 20 September 2022, the BCA imposed interim measures to remedy the disregard of the competition rules applying to the development of a standard for Cloud applications in the pigeon racing sector. The complaint was brought by four manufacturers of electronic registration systems for pigeon races (ETS) against the Belgian Colombophile Federation. The complainants requested that the BCA impose interim measures together with an investigation on the merits.

73. Regarding the request to impose interim measures, the BCA decided that it was *prima facie* not unreasonable to conclude that the 2022 standard governing the development of ETS had been determined by the Belgian Colombophile Federation in breach of Articles IV.1 and 2 CEL and Articles 101 and 102 TFEU.

74. Such a standard determined the technical requirements that ETS must meet to be used in races and ensured compatibility between the ETS systems of different manufacturers. In particular, the 2022 standard concerned the introduction of Cloud-ETS, which enabled flight times to be calculated and recorded via a cloud application.

75. The BCA imposed interim measures on the Belgian Colombophile Federation to ensure the transparent and non-discriminatory determination of the standard for the 2023 season, mainly through further consultation with all ETS manufacturers and the organisation of tests allowing for the timely homologation of compatible ETS. The BCA also imposed that all registration systems supplied by any and all manufacturers that were homologated for the 2020 season and/or 2021, 2022 seasons could continue to be valid up to one year after the entry into force of any new upcoming standard. The text of the interim measures were to be published on the Belgian Colombophile Federation's website and communicated to its members. The BCA has not yet adopted a formal decision in the proceedings on the merits.

H. *Football – U23 quota*[48]

76. This decision of 1 August 2025 concerns a request for interim measures brought by three professional football clubs - Royal Francs Borains, Koninklijke Sporting Club Lokeren, and Royal Football Club Seraing – against the Royal Belgian Football Association (RBFA). The dispute centred on a set of new regulations introduced by the RBFA for the competitive season 2025-2026, which mandated that at least four U23 teams, affiliated with clubs playing in the Jupiler Pro League

---

[47] Case 2022-RPR-32 BCA Decision MEDE-RPR-22/0004 *KBDB Duivenklokken* (20 September 2022); see also Belgian Competition Authority, "The Belgian Competition Authority imposes interim measures to remedy the disregard of competition rules applicable to the development of a standard for Cloud applications' (21 September 2022) e-Competitions art. No. 109007.

[48] Case 20025-RPR-30 BCA Decision in CONC-RPR-25/0026 (1 August 2025).

D1A top division, must always participate in the second division (D1B). This decision imposing at least four U23 teams in the D1B division formed part of a broader agreement on the championship's format and the allocation of TV rights. The three clubs challenged these new rules, arguing that this system created an uneven playing field, as U23 teams were less likely to be relegated regardless of their sporting performance, and their parent clubs could move U23 players between squads playing in the first and second divisions to gain a competitive advantage. Furthermore, the clubs contended that the new structure distorted the distribution of television revenue and undermined the principle of merit-based competition. The RBFA, joined by the Pro League (representing the Belgian professional football clubs and manager of the TV rights) as an intervener, justified the rules as necessary to promote the development of young talent and to ensure the league's financial stability. They insisted that U23 teams can still be relegated under certain conditions, and the allocation of players between D1A and D1B remained strictly regulated.

77. The BCA found that the new rules imposed by the RBFA established different standards for U23 teams and traditional clubs within the same competition, thereby undermining the principle of equal treatment, equal chances and sporting merit that characterise football competitions. The BCA further recognised that these measures could distort competition by reducing the risk of relegation for U23 teams and altering the incentives and strategies of all participating clubs. Additionally, the difference in treatment was not justified by the objectives put forward, and that less restrictive alternatives might exist. On that basis, the BCA found that it was not manifestly unreasonable to consider that the new rules could constitute a prima facie infringement of competition law. However, the BCA refused to grant immediate interim relief to the complainants. It held that there was no urgent need to prevent a serious, imminent and irreparable harm, reasoning that the potential harm to traditional clubs - such as relegation or financial losses - was neither imminent nor certain at the time the BCA decision was adopted. While the quota would affect the likelihood that traditional D1B clubs may be relegated at the end of the season, this does not result in a relegation with certainty. The effects would only materialise at the end of the season. The risk, the BCA noted, would ultimately depend on the season's outcome and potential future developments, such as further reforms by the RBFA or a new possible decision on interim measures by the BCA. Lastly, the BCA considered that suspending the rules on the eve of the new season would cause significant disruption and uncertainty for all clubs involved, as these rules formed part of a wider agreement between the clubs approved with a two-thirds majority after months of negotiations, and would take significant effort to renegotiate. As a result, the BCA concluded that, although there was a prima facie case of infringement of competition law, the conditions for interim measures were not met and so the request for interim measures was rejected. The proceedings on the merits are still pending. However, by determining the existence of a prima facie infringement and pointing to the fact that during the football season new interim measures could be requested and possibly imposed if the situation would become urgent, the BCA appears to be strongly encouraging the RBFA to change its contested rules proactively to avoid further proceedings and possible sanctions.

I. *Inline hockey*[49]

78. This decision of 13 August 2025 addresses a request for interim measures filed by eight Belgian inline hockey players and the Deutscher Inline Hockey Verband e.V. (DIHV) against the Fédération Royale Belge de Hockey sur Glace/Koninklijke Belgische Ijshockey Federatie (RBIHF). This dispute arose when these eight Belgian inline hockey players, seeking to continue their activities after the RBIHF ceased organising national inline hockey competitions in Belgium, joined a team (the "Panthers") to participate in the Deutsche Inline Hockey Liga (DIHL), a competition organised by the DIHV. RBIHF's internal regulations required prior approval for player participation in non-RBIHF competitions, with sanctions for non-compliance. In early 2025, RBIHF became aware of the Panthers' DIHL participation and responded by prohibiting these players from participating in non-sanctioned competitions, threatening them with disciplinary sanctions, and instructing referees not to officiate their matches. The federation also suspended the players from the national team, effectively limiting their opportunities to compete at both the domestic and international levels. The players and the DIHV complained to the BCA, asking for urgent protection through interim measures. They contended that the RBIHF's actions constituted an unjustified restriction on their freedom to participate in alternative competitions and amounted to an abuse of regulatory power, causing significant harm to their sporting careers and reputations. The RBIHF, for its part, maintained that its actions were in accordance with its established rules, which were designed to preserve the sport's integrity and orderly administration.

79. However, during the proceedings, the RBIHF announced its withdrawal from all inline hockey activities and stated that a new body, the Belgian Inline Hockey Association (BIHA), formed by the clubs, would take over responsibility for the inline hockey sport. RBIHF would further only focus on ice hockey. The RBIHF informed the BCA that it no longer organised or regulated inline hockey and, as a result, had no longer the authority to sanction players for participating in the DIHL and that this would also be publicly communicated. Therefore, the players would not be subject to the RBIHF's rules for inline hockey any longer, could freely participate in the DIHL competition and none of the sanctions imposed would be maintained.

80. The BCA noted that the factual circumstances had changed materially in the course of the proceedings: very shortly after the complaint and application for interim measures had been filed the RBIHF decided to formally cease all involvement in inline hockey activities, relinquished its regulatory authority over the sport, and provided assurances that all sanctions and threats of penalties would be lifted. The BCA concluded that, in light of these developments, there was no longer an urgent or ongoing risk of harm that would justify the imposition of interim measures. As it was already established that this condition for imposing interim measures had not been fulfilled, the BCA refrained from determining whether RBIHF's conduct constituted a prima facie infringement of competition law at the moment of the request for the interim measures.

---

[49] Case 2025-RPR-31 BCA decision in case MEDE.RPR.25/0024 (13 August 2025).

81. The possibility of the BCA imposing interim measures within a very strict time frame is a powerful tool for addressing competition law infringements and for stopping anti-competitive effects within short timeframes. In contrast to the European Commission, the BCA has repeatedly made use of its power to impose interim measures, including in sports matters. As appeared again in this inline hockey decision interim measures procedures before the BCA can have significant effects, even if no interim measures are imposed. The very act of bringing the complaint combined with the application for interim measures prompted the federation to relinquish its role in governing inline hockey, transferring responsibility to a new association. This move effectively and quickly addressed the players' urgent concerns.

III. Sports and Media Rights

1. Introduction

82. Sports media rights constitute one of the main factors that has driven economic growth in the sports sector over time. In its White Paper of 2007, the European Commission stressed the economic impact of modern sport, stating "sport in a broader sense generated added value of 407 billion euros in 2004, accounting for 3.7% of EU GDP, and employment for 15 million people or 5.4% of the labour force.'[50] At present, more than 50% of the funding for sports organisations and teams is financed by the sale of audio-visual rights.[51] The acquisition and sale of broadcasting rights for sporting events is subject to the competition rules, particularly the prohibition of anticompetitive agreements and the abuse of dominant positions.

83. Contracts concluded between league associations and media operators regarding the sale and acquisition of audio-visual content (the upstream market) have a significant effect on the downstream markets in which the media operators, who acquire the broadcasting rights, are active.[52] The application of competition law to sports-related broadcasting rights therefore has a dual dimension. First, horizontally with the once very controversial issue of collective selling by sports leagues of broadcasting the rights to exclusive live coverage of their sports in the upstream market. Team sports, by definition, need to cooperate, which they do through leagues and tournaments. While the individual sale by each club of their rights would allow more broadcasters to obtain rights, it has to date been widely accepted that the collective sale of those rights has pro-competitive effects.[53]

---

50 European Commission, *White Paper on Sport* (11 July 2007), 3.

51 UNCTAD, "Competition Issues in the Sale of Audiovisual Rights for Major Sporting Events" (2 May 2018) <*https://unctad.org/system/files/official-document/ciclpd50_en.pdf*> accessed 23 August 2025; Tom Evens and Petros Iosifidis, "Competition Law and Sports Broadcasting" in *The Political Economy of Television Sports Rights* (Palgrave Macmillan 2013), 85–103.

52 Philip Kienapfel and Andreas Stein, "The Application of Articles 81 and 82 EC in the Sport Sector" (*Competition Policy Newsletter*, 2007) <https://op.europa.eu/en/publication-detail/-/publication/3bd66bd2-5ef2-4f50-ae8b-d7b1ab6df25f> accessed 23 August 2025.

53 Case 2005-I/O-40 BCA Decision MEDE_I/O-05/0025 and MEDE-P/K-05/0036 *Jupiler League - Belgacom Skynet* (29 July 2005); see also Dieter Gillis and Peggy Valcke, "The Belgian Competition Council concludes that the joint selling of media rights is in line with the decision practice of the EC Commission and is not infringing Art. 81(1) EC (Jupiler League - Belgacom Skynet)" (29 July 2005) e-Competitions art. No. 480;

Second, the licensing agreements through which the sports broadcasting rights are distributed in the downstream market have attracted attention to the vertical dimension of sports-related media rights. The Commission and subsequently the Member States have intervened to draw the outlines of the principles to be taken into account when selling and acquiring those rights to avoid competition constraints. Since the principles applying to horizontal and vertical issues in the sale of media rights have long been discussed and clearly outlined, this contribution does not examine the subject further.

84. Rather, more recent discussions have emerged concerning the redistribution of collectively sold media rights and the monies related to that between individual football clubs (see Section 2 below). The BCA and the BACS have recently been confronted with competition complaints regarding the football association and/or Pro League's rules governing the redistribution of monies deriving from the collective sale of media rights between different football clubs from Divisions 1A and 1B. It is expected that these bodies' decisions will provide guidance and clarity for this topic in the near future.

2. Redistribution of Media Rights between Individual Football Clubs

85. Besides the long-standing discussions on horizontal and vertical issues related to the sale and purchase of sports media rights, more recently the issue of the redistribution formula and features of monies deriving from the sale of TV rights among individual football clubs, has been called into question.

86. In Belgium, some football clubs have issued complaints against the Pro League, arguing that certain rules relating to the redistribution of these monies would be in breach of competition law. These cases have been brought both before the BACS (section A) and the BCA.

87. These cases concern, in particular, revenues redistributed to the teams in Division 1B. As a reminder, the Belgian Pro League is the association organising and managing the men's professional football leagues in Belgium in National Division 1A (or Jupiler Pro League), the first-tier football competition, and in National Division 1B (Challenger Pro League) (the second-tier football competition). The Pro League brings together 26 professional football clubs participating in Divisions 1A and 1B, which together form the Belgian Professional Football League.

88. The Pro League is responsible for distributing the share of audio-visual rights to the clubs participating in the Division 1A and 1B football leagues. The Pro League's general assembly decides on the redistribution formula for the media rights in the Challenger Pro League on an annual basis. As a principle, revenues redistributed to the teams in Division 1B come partly from their own audio-visual rights, and partly from revenue that in principle belongs to the teams in Division 1A, but that has been the subject of redistribution agreements with Division 1B teams,

Case 2015-V/M-65 BCA Decision *Telenet* (5 November 2015); see also Tim Kasten, "The Belgian Competition Authority imposes provisional measures in a case involving TV rights for a series of cyclocross competitions (Telenet)" (5 November 2015) e-Competitions art. No. 77176.

as part of negotiations within the Pro League. These agreements, according to the latter, have legitimate objectives (solidarity, merit, investment in infrastructure and youth training). This is the case, among other things, due to a total sum of 3,500,000 euros (500,000 euros per team in Division 1B, excluding the team that dropped down from Division 1A) distributed to clubs in Division 1B provided that the club has infrastructure and facilities meeting the conditions for a level Division 1A licence, ie a "stadium which must have a capacity of at least 8,000, including at least 5,000 seats" (the other criteria concerning facilities being in any case also applicable to holders of a Division 1B licence). In other words, football clubs in Division 1B that comply with the stadium infrastructure conditions required to play in Division 1A, automatically receive 500,000 euros from the sale of media rights. According to the Pro League, this rule is intended to compensate for the investments football clubs make in their infrastructure.

A. *BACS: Virton v Pro League*[54]

89. As discussed above, RE Virton is a Belgian professional football club that was promoted at the end of the 2018–2019 season to Division 1B, in which it played during the 2019–2020 season. Although RE Virton did not receive its licence to play professionally during the 2020–2021 season, it managed to obtain that licence again for the 2021–2022 season and was reinstated in Division 1B, in which it is still playing to date.

90. In 2023, RE Virton initiated proceedings before the BACS, arguing, among other things, that the Pro League's rule described in which football clubs who comply with the Division 1A infrastructure requirements are granted a lump sum of 500,000 EUR, constituted a decision of an association of undertakings containing a condition contrary to Article 101 TFEU and that that should therefore be declared null and void. RE Virton also preliminarily requested the BACS to request an *amicus curiae* from the BCA under Article IV.88 CEL.

91. First, in its arbitral award of 11 February 2023,[55] the BACS first rejected RE Virton's demand to request an *amicus curiae* from the BCA. The BACS argued that only the courts and tribunals of the Belgian judiciary order are competent to request such an *amicus curiae* from the BCA. By contrast, the BACS is a court of arbitration and therefore does not qualify as a "court" in the sense of Article 267 TFEU. Consequently, the BACS found that it could not request the BCA to issue an *amicus curiae*.

92. Second, regarding the compliance with competition law of the Pro League's rule to grant a lump sum of 500,000 euros to the football clubs of Division 1B who comply with the infrastructure requirements of Division 1A clubs, the BACS found that the Pro League's decision qualified as a "decision of an association of undertakings" in the sense of Article 101 TFEU and Article IV.1 CEL. The BACS explained that the fact that a club that had not invested in infrastructure to meet or maintain the Division 1A criteria could not benefit from the 500,000 "grant" did not constitute a competitive disadvantage restricting competition. Moreover, the BACS found that

---

54 Case 273/22 *RE Virton v Pro League* (11 February 2023).

55 Ibid.

the objective pursued by the contested decision, which was to improve sporting infrastructure and, as a corollary, the training of young people, was legitimate, and the means used by the Pro League to achieve it, through the redistribution process in question, was proportionate.

93. As a result, the BACS dismissed RE Virton's complaint. It is noteworthy that other football clubs have in the meantime brought similar complaints against the same Pro League rule before the BACS, based on alleged infringements of competition law. To date, the BACS has rejected these complaints like it did in the RE Virton case discussed in this section.

B. *BCA proceedings: RFC Liège, Francs Borains and Patro Eisden*

94. The BACS is not the only body currently in charge of investigating the Pro League rules relating to the redistribution of football media rights revenues between the various football clubs of Divisions 1A and 1B. The BCA has also been requested to assess the compliance of these decisions with competition law.

95. On 4 October 2023, the football clubs RFC Liège, Francs Borains and Patro Eisden – the three clubs promoted to Division 1B for season 2023–2024 – lodged a complaint with the BCA against a 2023 Pro League decision regarding the redistribution formula of TV media rights among football clubs. At its general meeting on 20 June 2023, the Pro League voted, in their absence, for a distribution formula for TV rights for the 2023–2024 season which, according to the three claimants, penalised the clubs who had just joined Division 1B in that year.

96. Their complaint concerned in particular the Pro League rule providing for the redistribution of 1.8 million euros to the football clubs of Division 1B who comply with the Division 1A infrastructure requirements. According to the complainants, these redistribution principles were designed to favour football clubs that would have been in existence for several seasons, to the detriment of smaller clubs who would have just moved up into Division 1B and a fair distribution among all Division 1B clubs. The complainants further argued that this redistribution rule restricted and distorted competition because regardless of whether a football club received the monies because it had the infrastructure to play in Division 1A, the rule constituted a barrier to entry for new entrants, who inevitably would not have infrastructure meeting the Division 1A criteria. Therefore, "established" football clubs would not have to spend anything and receive a grant, while "new" clubs would have to spend large sums on their infrastructure, without receiving a grant. In the opinion of the three plaintiff clubs the Pro League's rule constituted a breach of European and/or Belgian competition law.

97. To date, the BCA has not yet publicly communicated about this complaint. Contrary to the horizontal and vertical issues related to the sale and purchase of sports media rights, it will likely be very interesting to see how the BCA will assess the Pro League's rules concerning the redistribution of monies deriving from the sale of media rights to individual football clubs. A finding by the BCA that these rules are anticompetitive may trigger various consequential complaints by smaller football clubs and even call into question the general decision-making process within the Pro League.

IV. Conclusion and Outlook

98. Antitrust enforcement has increased over the last decade in the sports sector and, given the ever-increasing importance of the sports sector in the Belgian economy, new enforcement actions and proceedings can be expected. Also, in pending cases, there are further decisions expected, whether or not following a reference for a preliminary ruling from the ECJ (ie the case pending before the Brussels Court of First Instance between SA Royal Antwerp Football Club and URBSFA that gave rise to the judgment of the Court of Justice, *Royal Antwerp FC*[56] and the case pending before the Belgian Supreme Court between Royal Football Club Seraing and FIFA, UEFA and URBSFA that gave rise to the very recent judgment of the Court of Justice, *Royal Football Club Seraing*)[57].

99. Moreover, in the case of acquisitions of or investments in the sports sector not only will the merger control rules now have to be taken into account, but possibly also: (i) the new Foreign Direct Investments regime that entered into force in Belgium on 1 July 2023; and (ii) the new EU Regulation 2022/2560 on foreign subsidies distorting the internal market.[58] It is to be noted in this respect, that on 4 May 2023, Royal Excelsior Virton, a professional football club in Belgium's second division, announced that it had lodged a complaint against a competing club, SK Lommel, with the European Commission under this new Regulation. It seems that this complaint regarding the Belgian football sector was the first public request to the European Commission to open an *ex officio* investigation under this new regulation. It appears that competing sports clubs do not shy away from trying to use the legal tools and procedures available to win their competition, including outside the sports field. It remains to be seen whether the European Commission will act upon the complaint as it is not legally obliged to do so.

100. Finally, it must be noted that in 2023 the BCA was restructured and reinvigorated, and its functioning was further enhanced by the formal appointment of a new president from 1 March 2024 (after more than a year with the role being unoccupied). It is expected that following its significant increase in manpower and budget, the BCA will continue its path of vigorous enforcement using all its formal and informal enforcement tools.

---

56 Case C-680/21 *Royal Antwerp FC* ECLI:EU:C:2023:1010.

57 Case C-600/23 Royal Football Club Seraing ECLI:EU:C:2025:617.

58 Council Regulation (EU) 2022/2560 of the European Parliament and of the Council of 14 December 2022 on foreign subsidies distorting the internal market [2022] OJ L330/1.

Competition Law and Sport: An Overview of the French Competition Authority's Decision-Making Practice

Mathias Pigeat
Autorité de la Concurrence

1. Sport has, for several reasons, come to occupy a prominent place in our contemporary societies. First and foremost, sport is what it originally is: a physical activity practised individually or collectively with a view to maintaining good physical and psychological health. It serves in this respect to respond to the contemporary imperative of a healthy mind in a healthy body, as well as to the values of personal surpassing and self-improvement, which are very much in keeping with the spirit of the times. Sport has also established itself as a spectacle, more or less professionalised, a driver of popular gathering and social cohesion, as the Paris Olympic Games of 2024 once again demonstrated. Sport is therefore a protean subject, and it is unsurprisingly the definition contained in Article L. 100-2 of the French Sports Code that reflects these multiple dimensions: "Physical and sporting activities shall be understood to encompass all forms of participation, at all levels, in physical activities which, whether organised or not, are aimed at the expression or improvement of physical and psychological condition, the development of social relations, or the achievement of competitive results." Sport is so important in our daily lives that it has also become an object of fashion and inspiration. It structures consumption patterns and collective imagination well beyond sporting practice itself, with professional athletes becoming the heroes of modern times.

2. However, whatever angle we adopt on this complex subject, one finding is inescapable: sport has become a lucrative business, each of its components now

monetised, and it has undergone strong economic development in recent years. This economic activity unfolds in multiple ways: sports equipment, organisation of competitions, merchandising, ticket sales, television broadcasting rights, the market for professional athletes and even sports clubs, sports betting, and so on. It accounts for 2.6% of France's GDP in 2022, more than the weight of agriculture.

3. As a thriving sector, sport has naturally become an object of particularly strong interest for competition law and European competition authorities. It is unsurprisingly across each of these areas that the activity of competition authorities – and in particular the *Autorité de la concurrence* – can be found: distribution of sports equipment and the organisation of professions related to sporting activities, the saga of the audiovisual broadcasting rights for football and rugby, sports betting, and the question of how merger control apprehends the acquisition of sports clubs or sports betting sites.

4. Yet the application of competition law in this domain did not seem natural to everyone, given that the tension between the federal and/or associative organisation of sport and the free play of the market could appear, at first sight, difficult to resolve. Sport in Europe rests on a hierarchical architecture, characterised by unified rules and equality – at least in theory – between competitors, whereas competition presupposes a plurality of operators and the confrontation of offers. It is from this tension, between sporting unity and economic pluralism, that the specificity of competition law as applied to sport is born.

5. This tension is all the more productive in that it brings about a singular encounter between two forms of competitiveness: that of the market, where innovation and economic performance determine success, and that of the playing field, where sporting merit consecrates victory. Both rest on a common requirement of fairness and equity, and it is doubtless this conceptual proximity that makes the dialogue between sport and competition as rich as it is complex.

6. There is, somewhat ironically, a form of mirroring between the instrument and its object: competition law, designed to guarantee fair rivalry between undertakings, applies to a domain – sport – whose very essence is competition. The legal system tasked with framing economic competition thus finds itself confronted with an activity that reproduces its mechanisms on a different plane.

7. This parallel between sporting competition and economic competition is not merely an intellectual exercise: it has shaped, from the outset, the manner in which competition law has approached sport. Because rivalry constitutes the very condition of sporting activity, sport has established itself as a privileged analytical terrain for refining the tools of economic qualification and the balance between freedom and regulation.

8. It is within this framework that the *Conseil de la concurrence*, and subsequently the *Autorité de la concurrence* (hereinafter 'the Authority'), have applied the rules on anticompetitive agreements and abuses of dominant position to the world of sport, without any derogation, on the basis that any activity presenting an economic dimension falls fully within the scope of competition law.

9. Thus, whether in relation to ticket sales, the marketing of audiovisual rights, the distribution of equipment, or the setting of conditions for access to a profession, Articles L. 420-1 and L. 420-2 of the French Commercial Code – and their

European equivalents, Articles 101 and 102 of the Treaty on the Functioning of the European Union (TFEU) – have served as a constant basis for analysis.

10. Through its interventions, the Authority has fully aligned itself with the evolution of European case law. At European level, the Court of Justice of the European Union has progressively framed the restrictions specific to sport (*Walrave and Koch, Bosman, Meca-Medina, Royal Antwerp, International Skating Union, European Superleague*). At the national level, the Authority has transposed these principles by adapting its economic analysis to the specific characteristics of the markets concerned.

11. What has changed over the decades is therefore not the scope of competition law, but the economic nature of sport itself.

12. The Authority has accompanied this transformation without any break, through analytical continuity: its early, modest cases laid the foundations of a coherent economic reading, subsequently put to the test in landmark proceedings.

13. From the very first Decision No. 91-D-07, *École du ski français*, the Authority had held that ski instruction constituted an economic activity subject to the freedom of trade and competition.

14. A few years later, Decision No. 00-D-83, *Coupe du monde 1998*, affirmed the competence of competition law to address the ticketing conditions for a world-class event, including where the organisation involved an international federation.

15. Through these foundational decisions, the Authority established a simple principle: sport is not an immune space. It is subject to common law, and the sporting purpose cannot in itself justify a derogation.

16. Cases concerning audiovisual rights, equipment exclusivity arrangements, or merchandising have not only led to the sanctioning of practices; they have made it possible to refine our understanding of the competitive mechanisms specific to an industry often structured around exclusive rights.

17. Thus, whether in football or in rugby, the Authority's successive opinions have helped to establish a methodology of competitive tendering founded on transparency, proportionality, and predictability – notions that transcend the sporting sector itself and today permeate the general doctrine of competition law.

18. Through these interventions, the Authority has exercised a dual function:

    - enforcing competition law to sanction anticompetitive conduct;
    - contributing to the economic regulation of sport, by guiding public authorities and private operators on the structuring of a sector in transformation, through its opinions and its merger control activity.

19. It is this dual intervention – repressive and advisory – that this article proposes to trace, in two parts:

    - first, by analysing the Authority in its role as a repressive authority in the sports sector, applying common competition law without derogation to a sector in transformation (Part I);
    - second, by examining its contribution to the economic structuring of sport, through its opinions, its regulation of transparency, and its periodic control of ownership structures (Part II).

I. The Application of the Law on Anticompetitive Practices to the Sports Sector: An Unconditional Application

20. This Part focuses on the application of common competition law on anticompetitive practices in the world of sport.

21. Historically, the entry point was through the prohibition of anticompetitive agreements, but the Authority very quickly also turned its attention to the alleged or established abuses implemented by federations or associations responsible for managing the exclusive rights to competitions, and by major equipment manufacturers.

1. Sanctioning Concerted Practices in the Organisation of Sporting Professions and the Distribution of Sports Equipment

22. From the earliest cases, the *Conseil de la concurrence* and subsequently the Authority applied Articles L. 420-1 of the French Commercial Code and 101 TFEU to the sports sector without establishing any special regime.

23. The sporting specificity has never constituted an exception to the application of competition law: at most, it has required the contextualisation of the analysis.

24. The *École du ski français* case (Decision 91-D-07) is, in this regard, foundational. The *École du ski français* (ESF), an association of ski instructors that held a majority position in most French ski resorts at the time of the facts, had negotiated with ski-lift operators priority access arrangements reserved for its instructors. At the same time, it imposed on instructors leaving or being excluded from its organisation a clause prohibiting them from practising their profession in the same or neighbouring municipalities.

25. The Authority characterised these agreements as an anticompetitive agreement within the meaning of Article 7 of the 1986 Ordinance (now Article L. 420-1 of the French Commercial Code). In particular, it dismissed the justifications drawn from economic progress advanced by the *Syndicat national des moniteurs du ski français* (SNMSF), which manages the ESF, and reiterated a fundamental point: the regulated nature of a sporting activity does not remove it from the scope of competition law.

26. In this regard, the following passage is particularly instructive on the balance between the organisation of a sporting activity and the competitive process: "*whilst the rational organisation of the profession may justify the existence of agreements between self-employed workers, it in no way justifies ski schools removing themselves from the competitive process by applying a clause that obstructs access to the market, or through concerted actions restricting the free exercise of competition by other professionals*".

27. Following this first milestone, the Authority turned its attention to restrictions on the distribution of sports equipment – whether in the form of imposed resale prices or restrictions on online sales.

28. Decision No. 06-D-37 concerning mid-range and high-end bicycles led the *Conseil* to sanction 22 companies for having implemented a series of anticompetitive agreements and for having inserted anticompetitive clauses into their general terms and conditions of sale and other distribution contracts, aimed at impeding the free setting of prices by distributors of these products.

29. The Authority found that several retailers, operating within retail networks, had established anticompetitive concerted practices with a view to reserving the distribution of bicycles to traditional networks. It considered that the fixing of "recommended" minimum resale prices and predefined margin rates were serious practices, all the more so given that members of these networks had intervened within their respective networks to enforce these guidelines and had exerted pressure on their suppliers to cease supplying competing discount retailers.

30. The Authority also sanctioned certain suppliers for having coordinated their commercial policy with retailers.

31. In Decision 21-D-24 (*Espace Foot*), the Authority had occasion to examine the issue of resale price maintenance in the football sector. By this decision, the Authority sanctioned the company Espace Foot for having imposed on its franchisee stores the prices of sports articles sold in those stores. In its franchise contracts, Espace Foot had introduced contractual clauses requiring franchisees to comply with the pricing policy it defined. One article of the franchise contract provided: "*In the spirit of protecting brand image, the FRANCHISOR shall communicate current sale prices, and the FRANCHISEE shall apply the communicated prices.*" These clauses featured in all franchise contracts between July 2002 and September 2018. In practice, Espace Foot invited its franchisees to comply with the recommended prices of manufacturers, and in particular those of Nike, Adidas, and Puma. The company did not contest the practices complained of and benefited from the settlement procedure.

32. With the rise of online sales, the Authority subsequently turned its attention to restrictions imposed by suppliers on the online distribution of their products.

33. Decision 19-D-14, *Bikeurope/Trek*, thus sanctioned the general prohibition of online sales imposed on authorised distributors in connection with the distribution of high-end bicycles. In its general terms and conditions of sale, Bikeurope had inserted provisions providing, initially, that any online sale of its bicycles had to be accompanied by delivery at the "authorised point of sale" – that is, mandatorily at the distributor's shop – before subsequently explicitly prohibiting all online sales. This prohibition limited the commercial freedom of distributors and prevented consumers from benefiting from competition between resellers in terms of price or product. In light of these elements, the Authority imposed a sanction of €250,000 on Bikeurope.

34. Another interesting case concerning online sales of sports equipment concerns the prohibition imposed by Adidas on its resellers from selling on online marketplaces. At a time when online marketplaces were experiencing significant growth, Adidas prohibited, in its selective distribution contracts, its authorised resellers from trading on such platforms. During the investigation, Adidas decided to remove from its selective distribution contracts the prohibition on its resellers' use of online marketplaces, allowing resellers to use such platforms provided they met certain

qualitative criteria. As a result, and in a quite unprecedented manner, the Authority closed the investigation against Adidas France without issuing a decision.

35. A clear lesson emerges from these cases: ancillary markets in sport (classes, distribution of articles and equipment, visibility at events) are treated like any other market.

36. Another lesson from these decisions is the presence of important operators, often in a position of strength – whether federations and/or associations that hold exclusive rights to competitions, or major equipment manufacturers.

2. Abuses of Dominant Position: Controlling the Economic Power of Organisers and Major Equipment Manufacturers

37. It is therefore unsurprisingly through the analysis of the conduct and relationships of federations and major equipment manufacturers that the Authority has had numerous occasions to lay down the applicable framework for abuses of dominant position in the sports sector. Several cases, at the boundary between anticompetitive agreements and abuses of dominant position, have shed light on the manner in which the Authority intended to address these dangerous liaisons.

38. A first decision shedding light on the relationship between a federation and a dominant equipment manufacturer in its segment is the *Sport-Boules* case (Decision No. 97-D-90 of 9 December 1997). In this decision, the Authority examined exclusivity clauses concluded between the *Fédération de Sport-Boules* (Sport-Boules Federation) and a sports equipment supplier in a dominant position on that market. These clauses reserved privileged access for that equipment manufacturer to official competitions – for the supply of equipment, advertising presence, and promotional operations. This exclusivity, initially limited to national competitions, had progressively extended to local competitions, depriving other manufacturers of access to those events and thereby distorting competition on the *boule lyonnaise* market. The *Conseil* held that these clauses constituted vertical restrictions by object, prohibited under Article L. 420-1 of the French Commercial Code, and ordered the Federation and its partner to remove them.

39. Another case allowed the Authority to go one step further. It concerns the saga of the exclusive supply of equipment to professional football clubs between Adidas and the *Ligue Nationale de Football* (LNF), which unfolded in the course of the 1990s. This decision – or rather this series of decisions – is structuring in that it explicitly set out the manner in which the Authority intended to address abuses of dominant position implemented by an equipment manufacturer.

40. The LNF had put in place, for the benefit of Adidas, a framework agreement providing for the exclusive supply of equipment to first and second division clubs of the men's professional football championship, supported by a set of regulations. This agreement provided for:

- the exclusive supply of equipment to first and second division clubs;
- the right for Adidas to use the title of "Official and Exclusive Supplier of the LNF";

- a financial contribution of 60 million francs;
- a duration of five years with a priority clause.

41. Seised of an application for interim measures by several competing equipment manufacturers – including Asics France, Uhlsport France, Puma, Mizuno, Nike, and Reebok – against the LNF, the Authority considered that competition law could apply to the LNF's conduct on the grounds that the exclusive supply of sports equipment to players in the French championships constituted a distribution or service activity, severable from the exercise of its public authority powers, to which competition rules applied. The *Conseil* accordingly suspended that agreement (Decision No. 95-MC-10).

42. By its decision on the merits No. 97-D-71 of 7 October 1997, the Authority subsequently sanctioned that agreement on account of the absence of any prior competitive tendering, its duration which was deemed excessive, and the dominant position of Adidas (holding more than 40% of the football boots market). The Authority also took into account the accumulation of other sponsorship contracts already held by Adidas (concerning the Coupe de la Ligue and the Coupe de France, two other men's football competitions).

43. The practices were characterised both as an anticompetitive agreement in respect of the framework agreement aspect, and as an abuse of dominant position committed by Adidas by reason of the priority clause contained in the sponsorship contracts. The Authority noted in this regard that that clause had indeed as its object to ensure the renewal of the sponsorship contracts and thereby to limit competitive play on the relevant markets.

44. In a subsequent case, Decision No. 97-D-72, the Authority this time sanctioned the market-sharing agreement between Adidas and Uhlsport which, within the framework of that general agreement, concerned the kits of goalkeepers. This was also characterised as a prohibited anticompetitive agreement in that it aimed to preserve Uhlsport's position for all clubs in which that company sponsored goalkeeper kits. In that same case, the Authority held that the priority clause agreed between Adidas and professional club AJ Auxerre constituted an abuse of dominant position under the same conditions as in Decision No. 97-D-71. The financial sanctions were accompanied by injunctions to remove the relevant clauses and, more generally, by a framework governing the relations between the league, clubs, and equipment manufacturers in order to prevent lasting lock-ins.

45. In another case, the Authority had a further opportunity to examine vertical restriction practices and abuses of dominant position implemented between a federation and a major equipment manufacturer. This time it concerned conduct by the *Fédération française d'escrime* (French Fencing Federation, FFE). In that case, the Authority examined discriminatory refusals of access to commercial stands at competitions and to telematics services (3615 ESCRIME), in a context where the FFE had also concluded a long-duration exclusivity agreement, with tacit renewal, with a single partner.

46. The Authority found that the FFE was the sole supplier on the market for the provision of commercial stands at prestigious fencing competitions that it organised, and that it accordingly held a dominant position on that market.

47. It found an abuse by the FFE – discriminatory refusals of commercial stands at competitions and refusal to list the contact details of the complainant company on its 3615 ESCRIME server – as well as an illegal agreement by reason of the partnership convention providing for an unjustified period of exclusivity with automatic renewal and without competitive tendering.

48. Subsequently, the Authority was able to examine purely exploitative abuses. In the *pétanque* sector, the Authority analysed the conduct of the company Obut in the market for competition-grade *pétanque* boules. By its Decision No. 17-D-02 (*La Boule Obut*), it found an exploitative abuse on the market for approved competition *pétanque* boules – a market distinct from the leisure segment – where the company held very high market shares and also operated downstream (website, shops, stands).

49. The Authority accused the French leader in *pétanque* boules of having abused its dominant position by imposing a pricing policy on certain of its distributors and by threatening or taking action against certain of them in the context of commercial retaliation. Not contesting the facts, Obut benefited from the settlement procedure.

50. The Authority also had occasion to examine sports betting in the context of the opening up of those markets, which had until then been covered by the legal monopoly of the *Française des Jeux* (FDJ) for gambling and the lottery, and of the *Pari Mutuel Urbain* (PMU) for horse-race betting. Betclic referred the matter to the Authority, arguing that the fact that the PMU, holder of the legal monopoly on "physical" horse-race betting in France, pooled the stakes it registered on that basis with those it registered on its online horse-race betting site Pmu.fr considerably enhanced the attractiveness of its online horse-race betting offer, to the point of threatening the entry and development of competitors. In the context of this case, and in response to the competition concerns it had identified – in particular, the fact that the advantages that Pmu.fr derived from this stake-pooling practice did not stem from competition on the merits but from the use, on a market open to competition, of the resources of a legal monopoly – the Authority accepted the commitments proposed by the PMU to separate the stakes it records under its "physical" horse-race betting activities (PMU physical points of sale: bar-tobacconists, press kiosks, etc.) from those it records under its online horse-race betting activities (Pmu.fr).

51. Subsequently, seised by the online gaming companies Betclic and Zeturf, the Authority held that the PMU had failed to comply with its 2014 commitment to separate its online and "physical" betting pools for foreign races that were the subject of a pool-sharing partnership between the PMU and several foreign operators, and imposed a sanction on the PMU. This decision was set aside by the Paris Court of Appeal in a judgment of 2 September 2021, essentially on the ground that no element in the file allowed the conclusion that foreign races were included within the initial commitments, and that, during the commitment-monitoring proceedings, the Authority had not noted that they had to be included on pain of rendering the commitments ineffective or leading to a finding of non-compliance.

52. The Authority's decisional practice demonstrates a continuity: sport, as soon as it operates on economic terrain, is subject without derogation to common competition law on anticompetitive agreements and abuses. There is no "sporting exception" – only a controlled application of common law.

II. The French Competition Authority as Actor in the Economic Structuring of Sport: Opinions, Regulation, and Merger Control

53. But it is truly in the audiovisual rights saga that the Authority has been able to deploy the full breadth of its experience and range of tools in implementing competition law. In this area, it has been able to examine the conduct of the actors concerned – namely, federations and broadcasters – from the perspective of the law on anticompetitive practices, and to issue recommendations to public authorities through its advisory function, in the form of opinions.

54. The exercise of the advisory function, combined with the enforcement function, has enabled the Authority to intervene as an actor in the economic regulation of this sector, contributing to shaping French professional sport regulation, in particular in the marketing of audiovisual rights.

1. Building a Competitive Framework for Audiovisual Rights: From Sanctioning Abuses to Structuring a Key Market in the Sports-Entertainment Sector

55. The marketing of broadcasting rights has progressively concentrated the Authority's attention, given the considerable economic stakes involved. Here again, the Authority applies common competition law (agreements/abuses), paying particular attention to procedural conditions (transparency, non-discrimination, lotting), the duration of exclusivity arrangements, and the tools of an *ex ante* governance approach informed by opinions that also irrigate contentious analysis.

56. Decision 03-MC-01 (*TPS / LFP–Canal+*) constitutes the first step in this domain concerning Ligue 1 – the first division of men's professional football in France. Faced with the award of all lots to a single operator, Groupe Canal Plus (hereinafter "GCP"), the Authority suspended the effects of the award pending a decision on the merits.

57. It implicitly established the logic that would continue to be refined: a premium rights product such as Ligue 1 can, by its ability to attract subscribers, confer upstream market power on its holder (the league) and, correspondingly, decisive competitive advantages downstream for the broadcaster that exploits it; effective competitive tendering must therefore be organised.

58. In rugby, it was Decision 14-MC-01 (*beIN Sport / LNR–Canal+*) that transposed these requirements to the Top 14 – the first division of men's professional rugby in France. It found that the elements on the file showed that the broadcasting of the Top 14 was a subscription driver for pay-television channels. "*As such, the rights to this competition may be characterised as premium rights and their marketing should be conducted, for a limited period, under transparent and non-discriminatory conditions, in accordance with settled case law.*" It accordingly held that the fact that negotiations had taken place directly between the *Ligue nationale de rugby* (LNR) and GCP to extend the latter's exclusivity, then that the invitation to tender had been suspended before its conclusion without waiting

for the submission of offers, and that exclusive negotiations had been resumed to conclude an agreement granting GCP all Top 14 rights for a long period (five years), were elements capable of revealing an anticompetitive agreement. Competing operators of GCP had not been in a position to participate in the award of the Top 14 rights and had no longer any possibility of accessing, in whole or in part, these attractive rights for a period of five years. Noting the risk of a long-term exclusivity in favour of a single operator, the Authority ordered interim measures: an obligation to conduct an open and non-discriminatory procedure, calibration of the duration, vigilance on lotting, and a prohibition on communicating as if the award were a fait accompli.

59. Conversely, in Decision No. 16-D-04 concerning the broadcasting rights for the second division of rugby (the Pro D2), the Authority rejected the complaint: the "semi-premium" market scope proposed by the complainants had not, in the Authority's view, been demonstrated, the competitive process conducted by the *Ligue nationale de rugby* did not appear discriminatory, and no abuse was established.

60. The Authority thus demonstrates that it does not impose a single model: it intervenes when serious indications of foreclosure exist; absent such indications, it refrains from intervening.

61. The Mediapro saga confirms this maturity.

62. This case – or rather this succession of cases – concerns the aftermath of the default by the initial broadcaster, Mediapro, which had won in 2018 a share of the Ligue 1 rights for the 2020–2021 to 2023–2024 seasons.

63. The Ligue 1 rights were divided into seven lots: five of these lots had been awarded to Mediapro (lots 1, 2, 4, 5, and 7), one to beIN Sports (lot 3, which was subsequently sub-licensed to GCP and is therefore exploited by the latter), and one to Free (lot 6, corresponding to near-live match highlights).

64. Following Mediapro's default, recorded by an agreement approved by the Nanterre Commercial Court on 22 December 2020, the *Ligue de Football Professionnel* (LFP) organised a partial reallocation of lots – namely, only the rights previously awarded to Mediapro (excluding from this reallocation the lots previously held by beIN/GCP and Free).

65. This consultation, launched on 19 January 2021, was declared unsuccessful, as the LFP had received offers but the reserve prices set had not been reached.

66. According to GCP, the LFP had abused, during the January 2021 consultation, the dominant position it held by putting back on the market only the rights surrendered by Mediapro. The failure to include in the consultation lot 3 exploited by GCP, in the first place, would impose inequitable transaction conditions on GCP and, in the second place, would constitute abusive discrimination.

67. By its Decision No. 21-D-12, the Authority analysed the conduct complained of and found that GCP had not provided sufficiently probative elements in support of its complaint. It rejected the application for interim measures: lot 3 (initially won by beIN and sub-licensed to Canal+) being, in its view, severable, the LFP was not required to put all lots back up for tender.

68. With regard first to the allegation of imposition of inequitable transaction conditions, the Authority held that the LFP's choice not to include lot 3 in the contested market consultation was both necessary and proportionate. It noted that such a requirement was all the less justified given that the objective pursued by the LFP in the present case – namely, to best preserve its interests and those of the clubs following Mediapro's default, for which it bore no responsibility, in the context of a health crisis that had also contributed to deteriorating their revenue prospects – was consistent with its mission.

69. With regard second to the allegation of abusive discrimination, the Authority found, on the one hand, that the conditions for submission to the LFP's market consultation were, on the basis of the file, both in conformity with its recommendations and identical for all potential candidates. On the other hand, the Authority considered that the circumstance that GCP was, in fact, the only party bearing, at the time of the launch of the market consultation, the financial burden associated with lot 3, was not relevant in the analysis of the existence of discrimination. Indeed, other potential candidates might equally have entered into commitments relating to Ligue 1 or other rights, and might be confronted – particularly in the case of new entrants – with the need to organise in a constrained timeframe the distribution of their commercial offers and a programme schedule. GCP, for its part, could on the contrary benefit from its presence on the downstream pay-television distribution market and its longstanding experience on the Ligue 1 rights acquisition market. The Authority accordingly held that the 2021 market consultation had not established any discrimination between potential candidates in an equivalent situation.

70. This decision was confirmed by the Paris Court of Appeal on 30 June 2022, and then by the Court of Cassation on 25 September 2024.

71. With regard to the abuse of discrimination, the Court of Cassation, applying the relevant European case law, held that the mere finding of a disadvantage affecting one operator is insufficient to characterise an abuse of dominant position by discrimination, and is likewise not sufficient, in itself, to establish the plausibility of such an abuse:

> "22. Fourth, according to the case law of the Court of Justice of the European Union, for the conditions of application of Article 102(c) TFEU to be met, it must be established not only that the conduct of an undertaking in a dominant position on the market is discriminatory, but also that it tends to distort the competitive relationship – that is, to impede the competitive position of certain trading partners of that undertaking relative to others (CJEU, judgment of 19 April 2018, *MEO – Serviços de Comunicações e Multimédia*, C-525/16, paragraph 25). It follows that the mere finding of a disadvantage affecting one operator is insufficient to characterise an abuse of dominant position by discrimination, and is likewise not sufficient, in itself, to establish the plausibility of such an abuse." (emphasis added)

72. Subsequently, the LFP awarded the rights previously held by Mediapro to Amazon. This award took place through a direct negotiation conducted after the failure of the aforementioned invitation for applications.

73. GCP and beIN Sport referred this situation to the Authority. According to them, the grant of Mediapro's former lots for the 2021–2022 to 2023–2024 seasons to Amazon for €250 million per season constituted an abuse of discrimination, in circumstances where, at the same time, they were required to broadcast matches from lot 3 alone for €332 million per season.

74. By its Decision No. 22-D-22, the Authority rejected these complaints. It found that the complainants did not provide sufficiently probative elements to conclude that they had been discriminated against in the procedure that led to the selection of Amazon for the takeover of Mediapro's former lots. It considered that beIN and GCP also failed to provide elements demonstrating that the LFP should have, as they claimed, preferred their offer over that submitted by Amazon.

75. Finally, the LFP being required to put the Ligue 1 broadcasting rights back up for tender at the end of relatively short cycles (currently four years), the Authority also found that the complainants did not provide sufficiently probative elements to indicate that the LFP could have been required to adjust the price of lot 3 to reflect the level of prices – lower than that resulting from the 2018 tender – ultimately agreed for Mediapro's lots after the latter's default. This decision was not appealed.

76. A final conclusion was brought to this saga, at least before the Authority. By its Decision No. 23-D-10, the Authority rejected for lack of priority a new application for interim measures filed this time by Mediapro against GCP, on the grounds that GCP had abused its dominant position on the pay-television distribution market by implementing various practices aimed at excluding it from the market for the publication of pay sports channels (unacceptable financial and commercial conditions for the distribution of its Téléfoot channel, denigrating statements regarding its services, discrimination, loyalty-inducing offers tying consumers for a long period).

77. It should be noted that this case has a judicial dimension: in parallel with the complaint filed with the Authority, GCP and beIN Sport had referred the matter to the Commercial Court against the LFP and Amazon with a view to having the 2021 tender annulled and the direct award of lots set aside.

78. Alongside these enforcement decisions, the Authority has been able to address the question of television broadcasting rights through its advisory function. Several opinions have intervened on this subject, allowing the Authority, step by step, to lay down the framework for audiovisual broadcasting rights.

79. The first is Opinion No. 04-A-09 on a draft decree on the marketing by professional leagues of the audiovisual exploitation rights to sports competitions or events. By this opinion, the *Conseil* issued a favourable opinion on the draft decree, to the extent that the rules laid down did not appear contrary to competition rules and guaranteed calls for tenders in compliance with the principles of transparency and non-discrimination (centralised sale; transparent and non-discriminatory calls for tenders; maximum duration set by regulation).

80. Opinion No. 07-A-07 on the conditions for competition in the marketing of sports rights allowed the Authority to refine this approach. The Authority expressed reservations about excessively long durations for Ligue 1 and advocated for short cycles in order to guarantee contestability. Opinion No. 07-A-15 on the draft

decree amending Decree 2004-699 on the marketing by professional leagues of audiovisual exploitation rights to sports competitions or events was to the same effect (no objection to a move to four years, with an alert on the risks should the duration become excessive).

81. Opinion No. 13-A-19 on an application for an opinion from the Paris Commercial Court concerning the invitation for applications launched by the LFP on 24 February 2010 for the award of the audiovisual exploitation rights to Ligue 2 allowed the Authority to state that Ligue 2 rights are non-premium. The Authority indicated that the circumstance that the LFP might not hold a dominant position on this market, and that centralised selling is provided for by law, did not exempt the LFP from complying with competition law.

82. Finally, Opinion No. 23-A-12 on a draft decree concerning the duration of contracts concluded for the marketing of the audiovisual exploitation rights to professional football allowed the Authority to update its analysis. Noting market developments – in particular the rise in the prices of those rights and the investments necessary for their exploitation – the Authority invited the Government to engage in more general reflection on the framework. It accepted the idea of extending the duration of rights on the basis that this could increase the incentives for new entrants to enter the market, while specifying that the investigation had not established that an extension of the duration from four to five years was a necessary condition for new operators to enter the market. It further found that the broadcasting of Ligue 1 as part of a pay-television offer appears less indispensable today than it was in 2007. In this context, the risk of exclusion of losing bidders in calls for tenders relating to that competition – highlighted by the *Conseil* in its 2007 opinions – appears less acute.

83. The opinion, through its dual pedagogical and structuring function, has thus proved particularly well-suited to a sector such as sport, where the regulation of activities must be articulated with compliance with competition law. Through this activity, the Authority disseminates a culture of transparency and proportionality in the economic relations of professional sport, sometimes anticipating developments in European law.

84. While broadcasting rights occupy a central place, other opinions have addressed the distribution of sports equipment (Opinions No. 09-A-40 of 26 June 2009 and No. 13-A-01 of 17 January 2013 examined derogations from rules on payment terms in the sports goods sector, taking into account the specific characteristics of these activities – seasonality and the existence of special rules); the sale of tickets for sporting events (Opinion No. 03-A-01 of 10 January 2003 on the sale of tickets for the Roland Garros tennis tournament); and sports agents (Opinion No. 99-A-20 of 23 November 1999 on the conditions for exercising the profession of sports intermediary).

85. All these opinions have contributed to establishing the Authority as an indispensable body of economic expertise for public authorities and professional leagues. Its recommendations have often been incorporated verbatim into the regulations, in particular in relation to tender procedures, the duration of exclusivity arrangements, the publication of results, and the framework governing partnership agreements.

86. This advisory role has also served to ensure doctrinal coherence between the national and European levels: market analyses, the segmentation between "premium" and "non-premium" competitions, and the conditions for the assignment of audiovisual rights are in keeping with the same logic as that developed by the European Commission and the Court of Justice.

2. Merger Control: A Limited but Strategic Field

87. The Authority has also been able to make use of another *ex ante* power of intervention to act on the structuring of the sports sector: merger control.

88. While the sports sector remains an area that is still relatively underdeveloped in terms of merger control, several concentration decisions have allowed the Authority to intervene in the development of certain activities – such as sports betting – or to foreshadow what the future examination of professional sports club acquisitions might look like.

89. The liberalisation of the sports betting sector constituted an important source of cases, the Authority accompanying the development of a competition culture and ensuring that the structuring of the market and the acquisitions made by operators holding historical legal monopolies – the FDJ for gambling and the PMU for horse-race betting – did not damage this nascent competition.

90. Most of these decisions concerned acquisitions by the FDJ of operators active in other markets (horse-racing or poker markets) or offering innovative solutions (payment and till solutions). In this regard, one may cite the transactions FDJ/ZEturf (23-DCC-191), FDJ/Aleda (22-DCC-219), and FDJ/Kindred Group (24-DCC-197). It is interesting to note that all these authorisation decisions were accompanied by behavioural commitments from the FDJ: separation between monopoly games and competitive activities; access on objective and non-discriminatory terms to the pool of online horse-race betting stakes; continuation of existing pool-sharing agreements; brand separation; controls on promotional activity; controls on bundled selling. These commitments all aim to prevent the advantages that the FDJ could derive from its status as a historical monopoly operator, which could harm competition.

91. In parallel with sports betting, the Authority has been able to examine acquisitions of football clubs. The financialisation and professionalisation of sport has indeed led to a multiplication of equity stakes in clubs, leagues, or event management companies, sometimes within multi-sport groups, media conglomerates, or by specialised funds.

92. As matters currently stand, notified transactions remain rare and of limited scope, but the Authority ensures that the rules of Book IV of the French Commercial Code apply fully to these transactions.

93. It analyses the definition of the relevant markets – ticketing, merchandising, audiovisual rights, sponsorship, or infrastructure management – and assesses whether the concentration is liable to harm effective competition in any of these segments.

94. By way of illustration, the Authority examined the acquisition, on 22 July 2019, by the INEOS Group of the French professional football club *Olympique Gymnaste Club de Nice Côte d'Azur* (OGC Nice).

95. While the Authority authorised the transaction without any specific conditions, this decision is interesting in that it constitutes the first time the Authority examined a transaction in the football clubs sector.

96. It accordingly set out to determine the relevant markets on which football clubs in France are active. It paid particular attention to the market for professional player transfers, which had not previously been defined by its decisional practice. At the conclusion of the investigation, it held that there exists a market of at least European, if not global, dimension on which the various professional football clubs compete to attract the best players.

97. The Authority also took into account the market for sports marketing, the scope of which is becoming increasingly international.

98. This decision foreshadows what the examination of this type of acquisition of control might look like in the future, as certain operators – such as the BlueCo consortium that holds both the English football club FC Chelsea and the French football club RC Strasbourg – now hold stakes in several clubs simultaneously.

99. The development of this type of operator in professional sport raises a new issue: that of minority shareholdings.

100. Even below merger control thresholds, these equity stakes can create structural links between clubs or between operators active in related markets (broadcasting, sponsorship, equipment).

101. The Authority has recently stressed, in its public communications and in several of its opinions (notably on artificial intelligence), the need for increased vigilance regarding these configurations, which can produce effects of tacit coordination or of privileged access to information.

102. In the sports sector, this vigilance is all the more justified given that the multiplication of multi-club investors (in football, basketball, or rugby) raises, in the long term, a risk for sporting integrity.

103. Sport therefore remains a laboratory for innovation in competition law. The diversity of its business models, the multiplication of actors – federations, leagues, broadcasters, equipment manufacturers, investors – and the growing value of the rights associated with it continue to make it a privileged area of observation for competition authorities.

104. The French Competition Authority, in particular, has undoubtedly not yet completed its work: as sport becomes increasingly financialised and globalised, new questions are emerging, whether with regard to multi-club concentrations, the management of sports data, or the business models of broadcasting platforms – not to mention the rise of new models such as e-sports or short-format competitions (such as the Kings League launched by former footballer Gerard Piqué in Spain) that are meeting with growing success and are distributed on online platforms.

105. Thus, far from being concluded, the encounter between competition law and the world of sport appears destined for new developments.

Panorama of the French Competition Authority Decision-Making Practice in the Field of Sport

Romain Soiron, Olivier Cavezian and Arthur Roquebert
Joffe & Associés, Paris, France

1. In 2023, the French Competition Authority (FCA) issued a decision and an opinion in the field of sport, and more specifically in the football rights sector.

2. On 4 October 2023, the FCA ruled on the dispute between Mediapro Sport France (Mediapro) and Group Canal Plus (GCP) concerning the distribution by GCP of the channel published by Mediapro to broadcast the main matches of the French Ligue 1 football championship for the period 2020–2024 (Section I).[1]

3. A few weeks earlier, the FCA was consulted on a draft decree extending the duration of agreements for the audiovisual exploitation of sports competitions marketed by a professional league. In its opinion of 26 July 2023, the FCA authorised such extension of the contracts to five seasons (Section II).[2]

I. FCA Decision Regarding the Dispute Between Mediapro and GCP

4. On 26 November 2020, Mediapro lodged a complaint with the FCA under Article L 420-2 of the French Commercial Code and Article 102 TFEU, claiming

---

1 Case 23-D-10 FCA Decision *Mediapro Sport France (Mediapro) v Group Canal Plus (GCP)* (4 October 2023).

2 FCA Opinion 23-A-12 on the Duration of Contracts Concluded for the Marketing of Audiovisual Exploitation Rights in French Sports Code, art L 333-2 (26 July 2023) <www.autoritedelaconcurrence.fr/sites/default/files/integral_texts/2023-09/23a12.pdf> accessed 2 September 2025.

that a series of practices implemented by GCP companies constituted an abuse of a dominant position on the pay-tv distribution market.[3]

1. Background

5. The decision of 4 October 2023 was issued in a rather peculiar context regarding the award and subsequent reallocation of audiovisual exploitation rights for the French Ligue 1 and Ligue 2 football championships for the period 2020–2024.

6. In April 2018, the Ligue de Football Professionnel (LFP) launched an invitation to tender to market the audiovisual rights of Ligue 1 and Ligue 2 for the 2020–2021 to 2023–2024 seasons. In accordance with the provisions of the French Sports Code, the LFP marketed the rights in several separate packages.

7. Following the invitation to tender in respect of Ligue 1, Mediapro won most of the packages put up for sale, with the exception of package 3, which was awarded to BeIN Sports, and package 6 to the operator Free.

8. As permitted under the terms and conditions of the invitation to tender, BeIN Sports sub-licensed package 3 to GCP, which at the same time undertook to distribute BeIN Sports's channels on an exclusive basis. GCP is unique in that it operates on the French market both as a publisher of television services (Canal+ and C8 in particular) and as a distributor of television services.

9. Mediapro, the then recent successful bidder of the main Ligue 1 packages, launched its pay-tv channel Téléfoot before the start of the 2020–2021 Ligue 1 season. This channel was distributed by the main internet service providers[4] (ISPs) and was available via the internet on an *over-the-top* basis[5] (OTT). However, no agreement has been reached between Mediapro and GCP regarding the distribution of the Téléfoot channel.

10. Mediapro quickly encountered difficulties in honouring its due dates for payment of rights to the LFP. A conciliation procedure between Mediapro and the LFP was opened by the Nanterre Commercial Court on 19 October 2020, and the court approved an agreement on 22 December 2020, whereby the LFP and Mediapro agreed "to terminate in advance the contract concluded between the LFP and Mediapro". As a result, the LFP recovered full ownership of the packages that had been granted to Mediapro. Following this default by Mediapro, the LFP marketed the packages formerly held by Mediapro in the form of a market consultation, which ultimately proved unsuccessful. The said packages were finally acquired by Amazon as part of a one-to-one negotiation with the LFP, at a much lower value than previously offered by Mediapro.

11. Numerous legal proceedings were then initiated by BeIN Sports and GCP. GCP mainly criticised the LFP for failing to take note of the concomitant caducity of package 3 and for refusing to reduce its value; these legal remedies proved to

---

3 TFEU, art 102 and French Commercial Code, art L 420-2.

4 Orange, SFR, Bouygues Télécom and Free.

5 OTT services may be subscription-based or free.

be groundless since, to date, all the courts and authorities seized with this matter have consistently upheld the LFP's position.

12. It was against this backdrop that in October 2023 the FCA once again ruled on a dispute, in this case between Mediapro and GCP, concerning the failure of negotiations between the two parties regarding the distribution of the Téléfoot channel by GCP. Before examining the content of the FCA decision in this case, it is useful to briefly review the organisation of the French sports audiovisual sector and the relevant markets as defined by the FCA in its decision-making practice.

2. The French Audiovisual Sector and the Relevant Markets, as Analysed in the FCA Decision-Making Practice

A. *Organisation of the Audiovisual Sector*

13. In its opinion 21 February 2 2019[6] and in its decision of 11 June 11 2021[7] the FCA carried out an in-depth analysis of the organisation of the audiovisual sector and its development factors, from which the following outstanding elements emerge:

- *With regard to free-to-air television*: the FCA notes that channel publishers either produce their own programs in-house or acquire broadcasting rights from third parties for selected audiovisual content according to the theme and editorial line of their channels. The resources of free channels mainly derive from the sale of advertising slot surrounding their programs; and
- *With regard to pay-tv*: unlike free-to-air television, publishers of pay-tv channels derive their revenue mainly from subscriptions purchased by subscribers. Channels may be marketed to subscribers either directly (in particular as part of OTT services) or through television channel distributors (eg GCP or ISPs). The latter are responsible for compiling a pay-tv offer in the form of channel packages, accessible by subscription or "à la carte".

14. Regarding the channel distribution methods, the FCA notes that the audiovisual sector has changed significantly in recent years: terrestrial broadcasting has gradually been supplanted by internet broadcasting. This new distribution method has led to an explosion of new non-linear uses on new terminals. Mobile devices are now competing with televisions. Video-on-demand services are competing with traditional linear services. We are now witnessing more interactive and non-linear consumption of sports content, particularly among young people.

15. Given the limitations of terrestrial broadcasting and the gradual improvement in the quality of internet connections, the FCA pointed out the strong development

---

[6] FCA Opinion 19-A-04 on a Request for an Opinion from the French National Assembly Committee on Cultural Affairs and Education in the Audiovisual Sector (21 February 2019).

[7] FCA Decision 21-D-12 Concerning Practices Implemented by the LFP in the Sector of the Sale of Television Broadcasting Rights for Sporting Events (11 June 2021).

of a new method of broadcasting audiovisual content via the internet (IPTV), in particular through ISP "triple play" services combining internet access, fixed telephony access and access to television channels via ISP boxes.[8]

16. In addition, beyond the closed ISP network, internet television has also developed via OTT, offers, which the French Audiovisual and Digital Communication Regulatory Authority (ARCOM, formerly Conseil Supérieur de l'Audiovisuel) defines as a method of distributing content over the internet without the intermediary of distributors or ISPs beyond the routing of data. ARCOM specifies that OTT broadcasting is defined as opposed to traditional television service distribution networks[9] through which television content is broadcast without being subject to intermediation by the ISP.[10] The special feature of OTT is that it can be widely received on any terminal connected to the internet, since content offers using OTT broadcasting are marketed directly online and routed over the general internet. As a result, the supply of content via OTT services is theoretically unlimited insofar as OTT services are characterised by the absence of, (i) technological constraints (it is not necessary to have terrestrial frequencies or to pass through the intermediary of dedicated ISP networks to reach the consumer); (ii) temporal constraints (the non-linear offer remains available to the consumer); and (iii) territorial constraints (the often international content is accessible from any portable terminal connected to the internet).

17. The main advantage of IPTV *triple play* offers from ISPs and OTT over traditional terrestrial broadcasting lies in the provision of a non-linear service – in other words, the offer of an audiovisual program available on demand based on a choice by the user from a catalogue. Such an offer frees the consumer from the constraint of linear time – the program is available at any time, and for the duration chosen by the consumer.[11]

18. In this respect, the FCA notes that the offers of operators using OTT distribution services – via subscription video-on-demand services, for example – are becoming increasingly popular with consumers and could eventually challenge the business model of the pay and free television operators mentioned above.

19. In view of all these factors, the FCA stresses that, at this stage, substitutability between the market for the distribution of subscription-based OTT offers and the market for the distribution of pay-tv services is imperfect, but it nevertheless notes that the phenomenon of convergence already identified by the FCA in 2017[12] between the two types of services is accelerating, suggesting a significant change in the competitive landscape in the future.[13] In this respect,

---

8 The boxes offered by ISPs make it possible to access television via the internet using a layer of bandwidth dedicated exclusively to television use.

9 Networks managed by ISPs, terrestrial networks, cable, etc.

10 *Arcom.fr website <www.arcom.fr/> accessed 2 September 2025.*

11 FCA Opinion 19-A-04 (n 6).

12 FCA Decision 17-DCC-92 (22 June 2017) re-examining the injunctions of Decision 12-DCC-100 Concerning the Acquisition of Exclusive Control of TPS and CanalSatellite by Vivendi SA and Canal Plus Group (23 July 2012).

13 FCA Opinion 19-A-04 (n 6).

the FCA concludes that "an upheaval in the balance of the markets, which is in its early stages, but which augurs major changes in the years to come, is underway".[14]

B. *Definition of Relevant Markets in the Pay-tv Sector*

20. To date, the FCA's decision-making practice indicates that the pay-tv sector is composed of several types of markets:

- The *upstream markets for the acquisition of broadcasting rights*, where the supply of audiovisual programs rights holders and the demand from pay-tv service publishers meet.
- More specifically, the *decision-making practice of the competition authorities distinguishes between rights relating to cinematographic works*, sports rights and rights relating to other audiovisual programs. With regard to sports rights, the FCA distinguishes between broadcasting rights for football competitions and broadcasting rights for other sports because of the unrivalled appeal of football, its ability to generate large audiences and, in particular, to encourage paying subscriptions to television channels. Furthermore, within football competitions, regulatory practice distinguishes between the rights to regular competitions that take place throughout the year (generally from August of year N to May of year N + 1) and the rights to competitions that take place at different intervals (for example, the Euro Football Championships or the Football World Cup, which are held every four years).
- The *intermediary markets for the publishing and marketing of thematic pay-tv channels,* where the supply of publishers and the demand of pay-tv distributors meet.
- The *downstream markets for the distribution and broadcasting of special-interest pay-tv channels*, where distributor offers and subscriber demand for pay-tv services meet. In this respect, the FCA distinguishes between pay-tv and free television.

21. This definition of the relevant markets resulting from the FCA's decision-making practice could, however, change in the near future, particularly with regard to the convergence of the markets for the distribution of OTT services offers via subscription and the distribution of pay-tv services. Even if, as we shall see below, the FCA and the French courts continue to refer to the above-mentioned markets, a significant change in the next few years cannot be ruled out.

3. Mediapro and GCP Proceedings before the Economic Activity Court Paris

22. In parallel with the complaint filed with the FCA, Mediapro and GCP brought claims for compensation before the Economic Activity Court (EAT) as a result of the failure of negotiations concerning the distribution of the Téléfoot channel by GCP.

---

[14] Ibid.

23. The EAT Paris handed down its judgment on 31 January 2023.[15] Mediapro mainly claimed that GCP had abused its dominant position on the market for the distribution of pay-tv channels in order to eliminate it from the market for the publishing of pay-tv sports channels (eg refusal to negotiate a distribution agreement for the Téléfoot channel, proposal of discriminatory and unfair commercial terms, marketing by GCP of loyalty building and abusive retaliation offers). In return, GCP claimed that Mediapro had abused its dominant position by refusing to negotiate (or at least delaying negotiations) a distribution agreement for the Téléfoot channel and by proposing discriminatory commercial conditions for this distribution compared to ISPs and which GCP considered impossible to make profitable.

24. As regards the distribution of Téléfoot, Mediapro had entered into distribution agreements with the main ISPs in France: SFR in July 2020, then Bouygues Télécom, Free and Orange in September 2020. The documents submitted to the court show that the four ISPs had agreed to pay Mediapro a total of 65 million euros (excluding VAT) per year in guaranteed minimum royalties for the distribution of Téléfoot. Under these distribution agreements with the ISPs, we understand that revenue sharing was between 80% and 90% for Mediapro as publisher and between 10% and 20% for the ISPs as distributors. In addition, Mediapro had also decided to distribute its channel directly, without going through an ISP box, *via* the OTT distribution method.

25. One of the main sticking points between the parties during the negotiation of the distribution agreement related to the amount of the minimum guarantee required by Mediapro. Mediapro sought a minimum guarantee calculated on a subscriber base of 1.5 million subscribers from the first year, while GCP considered that the minimum guarantee should be calculated on a subscriber base of between 100,000 and 300,000 viewers.

26. In accordance with the FCA decision-making practice referred to above, the court considered firstly that the relevant market in this case is the intermediate market for the publishing and marketing of pay-tv channels broadcasting live Ligue 1 matches.

27. As regards the assessment of the dominant position alleged by each of the parties, the court mentioned that it is necessary to take account of the dynamic competitive structure of the market when examining a dominant position. In this respect, the EAT noted that on the market for the publishing and marketing of pay-tv channels broadcasting live Ligue 1 matches, only two channel publishers were selling products or services at the time of the contested practices (Téléfoot and BeIN Sports, then only Téléfoot after the sub-licensing of BeIN Sports's rights to GCP). On the buyers" side, the bulk of the demand comprised only five companies (GCP and the four ISPs: Orange, SFR, Bouygues and Free). According to the EAT, regardless of any prohibited practice, competition on the relevant market was therefore structurally imperfect due to the limited number of operators.

28. In the present case, however, the court considered that neither Mediapro nor GCP had demonstrated that the other party would have been able to behave independently of its competitors, suppliers, or customers in such a way as to further

---

15 Case J2021000092 (31 January 2023) Economic Activity Court Paris.

distort competition on the relevant market to its own advantage and to the detriment of television viewers. For example, the revenue sharing proposed by GCP (80% of revenues for Mediapro as publisher and 20% for GCP as distributor) was in line with practices in the downstream pay-tv channel distribution market and comparable to the revenue sharing that Mediapro had agreed with ISPs.

29. After pointing out that the minimum guarantee is the result of, (i) market potential; and (ii) the level of risk that each party agreed to take, the EAT also found that in this case neither party had the ability to impose its will on the other with regard to the minimum guarantee.

30. Accordingly, the court held that Mediapro had failed to establish that GCP held a dominant position and that each of the parties had failed to prove that the other party was able to distort competition on the market for the publishing and marketing of pay-tv channels broadcasting live Ligue 1 matches. In addition, the EAT pointed out that it is not for it to control the negotiations between those two companies, which fall within the scope of freedom of trade, irrespective of their divergent assessments of the size of the potential market.

31. The EAT therefore adopted a cautious stance and did not wish to take a position on whether the negotiation of the distribution agreement between GCP and Mediapro complied with competition law. However, it hardly seemed reasonable to assume that a channel exclusively dedicated to broadcasting the majority of Ligue 1 matches would have attracted only between 100,000 and 300,000 subscribers. In this respect, the court observed that the number of subscribers to Amazon's Ligue 1 Pass is estimated at 1.8 million and that the number of subscribers effectively obtained by Téléfoot solely via ISPs during the channel's first months of existence was estimated between 400,000 and 500,000 subscribers. It would seem that the court is denying competition law one of its main virtues, namely, to encourage the entry of new competitors into markets by ensuring that established operators do not benefit from better conditions than new entrants. It is not surprising to note that the only operator that ultimately remained in competition with GCP from 2021 was Amazon – the only operator that had both a large, established base of subscribers from another market and a technical platform that allowed it to exploit audiovisual rights without having to enter into a distribution agreement with GCP. All the other operators (eg BeIN Sports, RMC, etc), who depended on GCP for their distribution, refrained from doing so in view of Mediapro's experience.

4. The FCA Decision

32. In its claim, Mediapro complained of the same practices as those alleged in the proceedings before the EAT discussed above: GCP held a dominant position on the pay-tv distribution market and implemented various practices aimed at eliminating Mediapro from the pay-tv sports channel publishing market (ie unacceptable financial and commercial conditions for the distribution of its Téléfoot channel, disparaging remarks about its services, discrimination and offers making consumers captive over a long period of time).

33. The FCA decision was eagerly awaited since the court refused to take a position on the dispute between Mediapro and GCP.

34. However, the FCA rejected the claim on the basis of the French Commercial Code,[16] as it did not consider it to be a priority. This is the second case in which the FCA has rejected a claim on the basis of this provision.

35. Relevant factors for considering that a claim should not be considered a priority include the potential seriousness of the alleged practices, the scope of the case, the need to clarify a legal or economic issue in order to provide guidance to the concerned parties, and the strategic nature of the FCA's intervention in a given case.[17] The strategic nature of the FCA's intervention is assessed in particular with regard to the possibility that other authorities, in particular the commercial or administrative courts, may be better qualified to deal with the issue identified.

36. In this case, the FCA rejected Mediapro's claim on the grounds that proceedings had already been brought before the EAT Paris concerning the same facts and the same alleged abuse of a dominant position. The FCA also noted that the Téléfoot channel ceased broadcasting definitively on 7 February 2021, and that Mediapro has filed for bankruptcy. The FCA therefore considered that the abuse of dominant position allegations made by Mediapro against GCP are essentially based on a logic of compensation. This type of compensation dispute is more appropriately dealt with by the EAT Paris and does not fall within the jurisdiction of the FCA. Eventually, it should be noted that the claim concerned practice whose impact on consumers or on the competitive operation of the market appears to be relative. In this respect, the FCA emphasises in particular that Mediapro's failure was not an obstacle to the arrival of a new operator on the market for the exploitation of the Ligue 1 audiovisual rights initially acquired by Mediapro (ie, Amazon). However, in this regard, it seems that the disappearance of Mediapro (as for any new entrant) and its difficulties in penetrating the French pay-tv market necessarily had an impact on the upstream market, to the detriment of the entities responsible for marketing sports audiovisual content. It is therefore regrettable that the FCA did not express an opinion in this case and that it did not wish to examine further and devote internal resources to the issue of negotiating distribution contracts for thematic pay-tv channels. It would have been invaluable to know the FCA position on this issue, which is of crucial importance for sports rights sellers.

37. Another means of controlling and regulating relations between publishers and distributors of audiovisual services lies in the provisions of the Freedom of Communication Act and the powers that the ARCOM derives from this Act.[18] As such, ARCOM is competent to settle disputes that may arise between publishers and distributors of audiovisual services and in this respect benefits from the power to issue injunctions affecting the conclusion, content or performance

---

16 French Commercial Code, art L 462-8, provision resulting from the transposition into French law of Directive (EU) 2019/1 of the European Parliament and of the Council to empower the competition authorities of the Member States to be more effective enforcers and to ensure the proper functioning of the internal market (11 December 2018), known as "ECN+".

17 FCA, Press Release, (on the implementation of rejection for lack of priority) "Resale of Postage Stamps for Franking: The Autorité Rejects the Complaint of Culture Presse against La Poste" (20 October 2022) <www.autoritedelaconcurrence.fr/en/press-release/resale-postage-stamps-franking-autorite-rejects-complaint-culture-presse-against-la> accessed 2 September 2025.

18 Freedom of Communication Act No 86-1067 (30 September 1986), art 17-1.

of agreements between the parties to the dispute, including, if the circumstances so require, an injunction to make the other party an offer of an agreement that complies with certain requirements (eg, an offer that is transparent, objective, fair and non-discriminatory and complies with the principle of quality and diversity of programs). However, in the context of the dispute between them, Mediapro and GCP appear to have disregarded this provision and have relied solely on the principles and provisions of competition law to assert their positions.

II. Opinion on the Duration of Contracts Concluded for the Marketing of Audiovisual Exploitation Rights

38. In 2023, the FCA had to deal with a related issue concerning audiovisual exploitation rights for sports competitions.

39. The Minister for the Economy, Finance and Industrial and Digital Sovereignty requested the FCA's opinion on a draft decree aimed at extending from four to five years, the duration of agreements for the marketing of audiovisual exploitation rights for the sports competitions referred to in the French Sports Code.[19] The proposed extension of the duration of audiovisual rights to sports competitions (currently applicable only to competitions organised by the LFP) had to be assessed in the light of any consequences it might have for fair competition in the market for the broadcasting of *premium* sports content – which is one of the FCA's responsibility.[20]

40. Following the FCA opinion on 26 July 2023, this decree was finally issued on 8 September 2023, just a few days before the marketing of the rights to the Ligue 1 and Ligue 2 championships for the 2024–2029 period.

1. Background and Content of the 2023 Decree

41. The decree of 8 September 2023 supplements the legal provisions applicable to the marketing of the audiovisual exploitation rights to a sporting competition by the professional league (including its commercial subsidiary) marketing the audiovisual belonging to the clubs by providing in particular that the maximum duration of agreements relating to the audiovisual exploitation rights to sporting competitions concluded between the professional league (or its commercial subsidiary) and the purchaser of the said rights is extended from four to five years. Until this date and from 2007,[21] contracts between a professional league and its broadcasters could not last longer than four years.

42. Background and reasons for extending the duration of audiovisual exploitation rights: following the Mediapro bankruptcy, the French National Assembly Committee on Cultural Affairs and Education published an information report[22]

19 French Sports Code (n 2).

20 Ibid.

21 Decree No 2023-864 (8 September 2023). The duration of contracts for the marketing of audiovisual exploitation rights was extended from three to four years in 2007, pursuant to Decree No 2007-1676 (28 November 2007).

22 French National Assembly, *Information Report No 4815* (15 December 2021), submitted by the Committee on Cultural Affairs and Education in conclusion of the work of the mission on the audiovisual broadcasting rights of sporting events, presented by Mr Cédrice Roussel.

in which a number of proposals were put forward to encourage greater competition between the various potential purchasers of audiovisual exploitation rights for French sporting events. To this end, it was suggested to "allow greater flexibility in the duration of the marketing of rights, within the limit of five years and in compliance with competition law provisions".[23]

43. The main advantages mentioned by[24] stakeholders in favour of extending the marketing period for rights lie in the fact that such a measure would constitute:

- On the one hand, a factor of competition stimulation between the potential purchasers of sports audiovisual rights insofar as it would make it possible, (i) to encourage the entry of new operators on the market for broadcasting of *premium* sports content; and (ii) for the so-called traditional broadcasters to secure their products of call on the market over the long term. In particular, such a measure would be a source of incentive for potential new entrants, who would enjoy more time to enter the market and thus amortise over a longer period their investment price for the acquisition of the audiovisual rights concerned and the additional costs they would incur in penetrating this new market (ie, the costs of broadcasting, marketing, production, communication, distribution, etc) – costs which might prove to be very high, especially in the first stage of exploitation of the rights. The incentive for these new operators to enter the market is likely to generate a stronger competitive dynamic in the acquisition of audiovisual rights and thus enable new entrants to challenge the established position of the historical and traditional operators. As a result, increased competition in the acquisition of audiovisual rights would have a direct impact on the acquisition value of these rights and indirectly on the financing of amateur sport.[25]
- On the other hand, a securing factor for the purchaser of the relevant audiovisual rights and a reinforcement of the said purchaser's confidence in his investment. Extending the duration of the exploitation of audiovisual rights enables the purchaser to get a better return on their investment and to implement an innovative and more ambitious commercial strategy by ensuring a return on investment over a longer period. In this respect, it has also been argued that such a measure would help to encourage players to adopt a more balanced and rational approach towards the exploitation of audiovisual rights.[26]

44. The adoption of this new measure is welcome to stimulate competition between broadcasters in a context where competition has been weakened by the failure of Mediapro on the one hand and by the conclusion of the exclusive distribution agreement between GCP and BeIN Sports on the other.

---

23 Ibid 77.

24 Ibid 75 and onwards. Also, FCA Opinion 23-A-12 (n 2).

25 Part of the income earned by professional leagues or commercial companies set up by these leagues is used to fund amateur sport through the Buffet tax mechanism.

26 FCA Opinion 23-A-12 (n 2).

2. FCA Opinion

45. On 26 July 2023, the FCA issued a favourable opinion[27] on the draft decree extending the duration of agreements for the sale of audiovisual rights to sporting events from four to five years. While the FCA has not expressed any significant objections to the provisions of this decree, it has nevertheless indicated that it is unable to confirm the effectiveness of the measure in terms of the objective pursued by its adoption – ie the entry into the market of new operators with a view to stimulating competition and increasing the resources derived from the sale of audiovisual rights of sporting events.

46. On the necessity of limiting the duration of exploitation rights – as a preliminary point, the FCA refers to the European Commission decision-making practice according to which the centralised sale of audiovisual rights[28] – as opposed to the individual sale of rights by each club[29] – may be regarded, under competition law, (i) as an agreement between companies[30] entered into by the LFP and the professional clubs which benefit from the ownership of the rights assigned by the French Football Federation (FFF); and (ii) as a restriction of competition within the meaning of Article 101(1) TFEU, since it hinders the ability of the clubs to determine individually the conditions of sale, including prices.[31] It further adds that the joint selling of audiovisual rights may, however, be exempted on the basis of Article 101(3) TFEU or be deemed to comply with the competition law provisions provided that the joint marketing of audiovisual exploitation rights satisfies certain conditions likely to remedy competition concerns such as the sale of rights divided into separate packages, a transparent and non-discriminatory tender process open to all interested operators and the limitation of the duration of the award of rights[32] – conditions which, in French law, are provided for by French Sports Code.

47. With regard to the condition of limiting the duration of the allocation of rights, the FCA refers to its previous opinion of 25 July 2007, in which it noted that the purpose of limiting the duration of the exploitation rights "is, on the one

---

27 Ibid.

28 One of the special features of the French system is that federations have the option of transferring the audiovisual exploitation rights for competitions organised by the professional league to the clubs free of charge. In this case, the rights are marketed exclusively and centrally by the professional league (or by the commercial company set up by the latter under the conditions set out in the French Sports Code, art L 333-1) on behalf of the clubs. For the time being, this option has only been used in football: in 2004, the FFF granted ownership of the audiovisual exploitation rights to the clubs and the LFP (and now its commercial company LFP Media) is responsible for marketing these rights.

29 While the sale of rights by each club was practised in the Spanish and Italian leagues in particular, it was abandoned in view of the excessively high costs and inequality between clubs that it engendered.

30 (Case COMP/C.2-37.398 – *Joint Selling of the Commercial Rights of the UEFA Champions League*) Commission Decision 23 July 2003 [2003] OJ L291/25,106.

31 FCA Opinion 23-A-12 (n 2), 25.

32 On the risks of cartelisation of the upstream audiovisual rights market in the event of pooling of rights for the benefit of a professional league, see Wladimir Andreff, "Sport et télévision : une dépendance économique" in P Arnaud, M Attali and J Saint-Martin (eds), *Le Sport en France. Une approche politique, économique et sociale* (Documentation française 2008) 16. See also the European Commission decisions in Cases (COMP/C-2/37.214 – *Joint selling of the media rights to the German Bundesliga*), and (COMP/C-2/38.173 – *Joint selling of the media rights to the FA Premier League*). These conditions are set out in the French Sports Code, art R 333-3.

hand, to limit the exclusive power of the seller, and, on the other hand, to limit the risk of eviction of a bidding operator that has not been awarded the rights and has consequently been unable to make available to its subscribers content that the latter consider essential, thereby jeopardising its survival on the pay-tv markets in the medium term".[33] The FCA had also stressed the importance and necessity of guaranteeing exclusivity for a certain period of time to purchasers of audiovisual rights to enable them to effectively amortise the investments made to acquire these rights and those required to enter the market and capture a sufficient subscriber base for new entrants.

48. In the light of these considerations, the FCA sought to determine the theoretical and practical consequences of extending the duration of broadcasting rights on the reduction of barriers to entry into the market for the broadcasting of *premium* sports content. At the time, the FCA took the view that extending the duration of the allocation of broadcasting rights was not a suitable solution for attracting new entrants, particularly insofar as, (i) such an extension could, on the contrary, have a dissuasive effect on a new purchaser by forcing it to make more substantial investments; and (ii) television operators were hostile to such a measure.

49. A few months later in 2007, the FCA was again asked to give its opinion on the proposed extension of the marketing period for audiovisual rights from three to four years. Once again, the FCA reiterated that it was not convinced of the effectiveness of this measure in strengthening competition on the audiovisual rights market.[34] However, it was not opposed to this project insofar as it considered that this measure did not constitute an infringement of competition law provisions.

50. As part of the process of drafting the decree aimed at extending audiovisual rights from four to five years, the FCA was once again asked to give its opinion on this project. On 26 July 2023, the FCA took into account the developments in the sector[35] and successively examined the effect of extending the maximum duration of marketing contracts to five years, (i) on barriers to market entry; and (ii) the risks of such a change for downstream operators and consumers.

51. The FCA has certain reservations on the uncertain effect of extending the term of exploitation rights on barriers to entry – on the question of whether extending the term would actually lead new operators to enter the market. While it cannot be ruled out that such an extension would increase incentives to enter the market, it notes that the investigation has not established that extending the duration from four to five years was a necessary condition for new operators, particularly for platforms, to enter the market. In particular, the FCA notes that there is no evidence to show that the extension in 2007 from three to four years of the duration of the audiovisual exploitation rights for Ligue 1 matches was the reason for the

---

33 FCA Opinion 07-A-07 on the Conditions of Competition in the Marketing of Audiovisual Rights (25 July 2007).

34 FCA Opinion 07-A-15 on the Draft Decree Amending Decree 2004-699 Relating to the Marketing by the Professional Leagues of the Audiovisual Exploitation Rights for Competitions or Events (9 November 2007).

35 Developments in the TV rights acquisition market have been characterised by less concentration, due in particular to the arrival of players from the digital economy, and by a lesser role for Ligue 1 matches in the business model of pay-tv publishers.

entry of new operators into the market (Orange, BeIN, Mediapro), especially as the last two, which entered the market in 2007 and 2018 respectively, exited in 2016 and 2020 respectively. In any event, the FCA considers that it is not certain that the entry of new operators has significantly increased the price of broadcasting rights in view of Mediapro's failure and its disastrous financial consequences for French football. The FCA also notes that the ability of operators to amortise the value of audiovisual exploitation rights to sports competitions in the event of an increase in the duration of contracts must be balanced with the resulting increase in the acquisition price of such rights. This increase in the acquisition price may in fact discourage smaller operators.

52. On the absence of a risk of exclusion downstream operators and the absence of an incentive to increase subscription prices for consumers – as regards the competitive risks that would result from extending the duration of the exploitation rights to five years with regard to downstream operators (ie a broadcaster), the FCA considers that the risk of exclusion and concentration of all the broadcasting rights by a single operator is limited by the other conditions imposed the French Sports Code, namely that the sale of the rights be divided into separate packages by means of a transparent and non-discriminatory tender process open to all interested operators.[36]

53. As regards the competitive risks that such a change would entail for consumers, the FCA notes that the risk of an increase in subscription prices is not serious, since there are, (i) several offers on the downstream markets integrating Ligue 1 content from several operators; and (ii) competitive pressure resulting from the multiplicity of these offers.

54. The FCA has no significant reservations regarding the draft decree and is pragmatic in that it considers that extending the exploitation period for audiovisual rights does not threaten the competitive structure of downstream markets or consumer welfare. However, as it did in its 2007 opinions, the FCA again questions the effective impact of such a measure on reducing barriers to entry and increasing the sale price of audiovisual rights. The FCA has also stressed the need for a more comprehensive review of the framework set out in the French Sports Code (invitation for tender, award procedure, duration of agreements, etc).[37]

---

36 French Sports Code, art 333-3; French Sports Code, art R 333-2 also states that the marketing of audiovisual rights "must comply with the rules of free competition, in particular those relating to advertising and non-discrimination".

37 French Sports Code, art R 333-3.

Sport and Competition Law in Italy: Overview of Decisional Practice

Andrea Bozza and Emilio Cucchiara[*]
Deloitte Legal, Italy

I. Introduction

1. The latest decisions of the European Court of Justice (ECJ) involving football institutions have re-ignited the post-*Super League* saga debate concerning the interplay between sports and competition law.
2. This chapter focuses on the relation between sports and competition law in light of latest and less recent decisional practice and case law from the Italian Competition Authority Autorità Garante della Concorrenza e del Mercato (ICA) and competent national courts.
3. After a brief overview of the Italian sporting regulatory framework from an institutional perspective, the following notions are examined, (i) the notion of "'undertaking'; (ii) whether the notion of 'undertaking" is applicable to sporting entities; and (iii) in the affirmative, the extent to which sporting entities are subject to the antitrust scrutiny, including relevant case law on abuse of dominant position and anticompetitive agreements.[1]

---

* Andrea Bozza is the Head of Football at Deloitte Legal Italy. Emilio Cucchiara is the Head of Antitrust and State Aid at Deloitte Legal Italy. The authors wish to thank their colleagues Arianna Corno and Vincenzo Calandrelli for their contribution in the preparation of this chapter.

1 For ease of reading and for systematic reasons, the present chapter does not aim to cover the analysis of how media rights have been addressed under national competition law.

II. Sports Regulatory Framework in Italy

4. The discipline of the sports sector in Italy is based on a system that sees at its top the Italian National Olympic Committee (CONI), the entity in charge of organisation and promotion of national sports, which is in turn a member of the International Olympic Committee (IOC). For each sports discipline, CONI recognises only one National Sports Federation (NSF) or a so-called Disciplina Sportiva Associata (DSA for the purpose of this chapter).[2] As of today, CONI recognises 48 NSFs and 15 DSAs.[3]

5. NSFs carry out sporting activities in accordance with the resolutions and guidelines of the IOC, the respective international federations and CONI. With regard to CONI, this is also because of "the public value of specific types of activities identified in the CONI's Articles of Association".[4,5]

6. Indeed, the organisational structure of NSFs and DSAs (as reflected in their respective Articles of Association) must comply with the fundamental principles issued by CONI.[6]

7. As specifically concerns NSFs, they are non-profit associations with legal personality and "technical, organisational and management autonomy, under the supervision of CONI".[7] In fact, in furtherance of the indications of the relevant international federations, NSFs adopt rules aimed at regulating the type of sports events/competitions, making a distinction between professional, amateur and recreational activities, such regulations not being subject to control and approval by CONI.

III. Sporting Activities and Notion of Undertaking

8. Also based on ECJ case law, from a competition law perspective the ICA defines an undertaking as "any entity engaged in an economic activity, regardless of its legal status and the way in which it is financed", as well as whether it seeks to obtain a profit.[8]

---

2 According to the Italian sporting regulatory framework, a DSAs can be defined as tier-2 federations, labelled as such due to the fact that they are responsible for organization and government of non-Olympic sports, differently from the NSFs.

3 See the Italian National Olympic Committee (CONI) <www.coni.it/it/coni.html#:~:text=Fondato%20il%209%20e%2010,Sportiva%20Nazionali%2C%2019%20Associazioni%20Benemerite> accessed 24 August 2025.

4 Legislative Decree No 242/1999, art 15 <www.normattiva.it/uri-res/N2Ls?urn:nir:stato:decreto.legislativo:1999-07-23;242> accessed 24 August 2025.

5 In particular, CONI recognises NSFs that manage sports disciplines within the national territory in accordance with the Olympic Charter and the rules of the relevant international federation to which they are affiliated, and identifies the *activities of public value* of the NSFs relating, among others, to: admission and affiliation of clubs, sports associations and individual members; control over the smooth running of professional sports competitions and championships; use of public subsidies; activities relating to Olympic Games; training of technicians and the use and management of public sporting facilities.

6 see CONI's Resolution No 1613 <www.coni.it/images/1-Primo-Piano-2018/Principi_Fondamentali_Statuti_FSN_4-9-2018_approvati.pdf> accessed 24 August 2025.

7 See CONI's Articles of Association, art 20, paras 3 and 4 <www.coni.it/images/coni/Statuto_21-11-2023_delibera_n._1745_pubblicazione.pdf> accessed 24 August 2025.

8 Case I101B *Tariffe amministratori di condominio* (14 December 1994).

9. As a consequence, sporting clubs are normally qualified as "undertakings" under Italian competition law,[9] as well as under European Union law.[10]

10. Accordingly, the management of sports entities normally involves the performance of "economic activity" pursuant to competition law's general principles.[11] It follows that each sports federation, insofar as they act "as an organiser of events and manages the membership of athletes", directly carry out remunerated economic activity.[12]

11. For instance, the ICA considered that the Automobile Club D'Italia (ACI)[13] – the Italian federation for motorsports – in addition to having an associative nature and performing representative, regulatory and/or organisational activities for companies active in the automotive sector, also operates in the direct management of economic activities by carrying out both the promotion of sporting events and their organisation, therefore being qualifiable as an undertaking for the purposes of Italian and EU competition law.

12. In another case, the ICA clarified that NSFs, also in their quality of "representatives of members who carry out economic activities", are themselves entities carrying out economic activities. Therefore, by qualifying as association of undertakings, ICA concluded that NSFs' conducts are also subject to competition law rules.[14]

13. More specifically, such case concerned the Italian Volleyball Federation (FIPAV), the entity representing and regulating the activities of clubs active in the field of volleyball, beach volleyball and sitting volleyball. The ICA held that, since the clubs affiliated to FIPAV carry out economic activity in the world of volleyball, beach volleyball and sitting volleyball, the same FIPAV "*directly carries out economic activity*",[15] insofar as it organises and manages sports events and its athletes" membership.

14. Therefore, NSFs are entities that carry out economic activities and represent entities that, in turn, carry out economic activities. Consequently, NSFs can be qualified both as undertakings and associations of undertakings.[16] In this regard,

---

9 Case I650 *Lega Calcio-Prezzi Biglietti Play Off* (23 November 2005) in which the ICA observed that the notion of "undertaking" under Italian competition law appears to have a "broader scope than that recognised from the national civil law since it includes, in its definition, any body that carries out activities of economic nature, regardless of its legal form and financing methods".

10 Case C-650/22 Fédération internationale de football association (FIFA) v BZ ECLI:EU:C:2024:824, para 118, in which the Court of Justice concluded that national football associations can be categorised as «undertakings» inasmuch as they carry on an economic activity related to the organisation and marketing of interclub football competitions and the exploitation of the rights related thereto.

11 Case A562 *AGCM v Italian Football Federation (FIGC)* (18 June 2024); Case A570 *AGCM v Automobile Club d'Italia (ACI)* (2023) AGCM Bulletin No 40/2023 (17 December 2024) <www.agcm.it/dotcmsCustom/getDominoAttach?urlStr=192.168.14.10:8080/41256297003874BD/0/B6E35E29CC3B758AC1258A51004D-699B/$File/p30807.pdf>.

12 *AGCM* A562 (n 11).

13 The ACI was one of the first founders of the Fédération Internationale de l'Automobile (FIA), which recognises it as the only national authority in Italy for motor sports, as well as being federated with CONI, which in turn recognises it as the Italian federation of reference for motor sports.

14 Case I861 *Federazione Italiana Pallavolo (FIPAV)* (19 June 2023)

15 Ibid (emphasis added)

16 *AGCM* A570 (n 11), Order No 30807 10 October 2023 (start of investigation).

for example, the ICA has clarified that the decision of FIPAV – which, as mentioned, represents and brings together sporting clubs active in the volleyball sector – can be qualified as resolution of an association of undertakings within the meaning of Article 101 of the Treaty on the Functioning of the European Union (TFEU).[17]

15. The above-described approach of the ICA seems to be fully in line with the well-established EU case law, according to which the concept of an association of undertakings is broad and disregards the commercial or non-commercial nature of the pursued activity, as well as the legal status held by a person under national law.[18]

16. For instance, in Decision 27 June 2018, *FIGC – Regolamentazione dell'attività di direttore sportivo, collaboratore della gestione sportiva, osservatore calcistico e match analyst*, the ICA observed that the Italian Football Federation (FIGC) qualifies as an association of undertakings for the purposes of Article 101 TFEU "regardless of the lucrative or non-lucrative nature of the activity pursued, as well as the legal qualification held within the national legal system to which it belongs", in line with EU previous decisions in which sports federations (national or international) are qualified as association of undertakings, if not undertakings themselves.[19]

17. Moreover, for the purposes of determining whether the activities carried out by a sporting federation are "economic in nature" and whether NSFs qualify as association of undertakings within the meaning of Article 101 TFEU, it is also irrelevant that the activity regulated by the sporting federation concerns the *amateur sector* or the professional one. In this regard, the ICA insisted that the functional

---

17 See TFEU, arts 101(1), (2) and (3) <https://eur-lex.europa.eu/LexUriServ/LexUriServ.do?uri=CELEX-%3A12008E101%3AEN%3AHTML> accessed 24 August 2025.

18 See, for example, Case 123/83 *Bureau national interprofessionnel du cognac (BNIC) v Guy Clair* ECLI:EU:C:1985:33, point 17; and Case C-35/96 *Commission of the European Communities v Italian Republic* ECLI:EU:C:1998:303, point 40. See also Case AT.40208 European Commission Decision *International Skating Union's Eligibility* (*ISU* Decision) (8 December 2017), according to which the eligibility rules of the International Skating Union's Eligibility Skating Union actions were intended to restrict competition within the meaning of Article 101(1) TFEU, in that they limited the possibilities for professional speed skaters to freely participate in international events sanctioned by third parties and thus deprived potential organisers of competitive events of the services of athletes which were necessary to organise those competitions, decision confirmed by the General Court on 16 December 2020.

19 Case I812 ICA Decision *FIGC v Regolamentazione dell'attività di direttore sportivo, collaboratore della gestione sportiva, osservatore calcistico e match analyst* (27 June 2018). *Ex pluribus*, see Case C-49/07 *MOTOE* ECLI:EU:C:2008:376; Case T-93/18 *International Skating Union (ISU)* ECLI:EU:T:2020:610, paras 19 et seq. Specifically, the Court reminded that any "activity consisting in offering goods or services on a given market is an economic activity" and that, provided that such condition is satisfied, "the fact that an activity has a connection with sport does not hinder the application of the rules of the Treaty [...] including those governing competition law". Consistent with the above, the Court concluded that the organisation of motorcycling events in Greece by ELPA (Automobile and Touring Club of Greece) "constitutes a source of income" and that the fact that ELPA is (also) engaged in the decision-making process of the public authorities "does not prevent its being considered an undertaking for the purposes of Community competition law so far as concerns its economic activities referred to above". See also Case C-519/04 P *David Meca-Medina and Igor Majcen v Commission of the European Communities* ECLI:EU:C:2006:492, para 28, in which the Court clarified that if a sporting activity falls within the scope of the Treaty, the conditions for engaging in it are then subject to all the obligations which result from the various provisions of the Treaty, including competition law.

concept of undertaking for competition law purposes disregards the purely economic dimension of the activity carried out, requiring instead only that the goods or services concerned are offered on the market.[20]

18. The above approach followed by the ICA reflects the one adopted at European-Union level also on this matter. Particularly in the *Laurent Piau* case, the European General Court – in classifying FIFA as an association of undertakings – noted that "the mere fact that a sports association or federation unilaterally classifies sportsmen or clubs as "amateur" does not in itself mean that they do not engage in economic activities".[21]

19. In conclusion, the activities carried out by sporting federations and clubs can be generally qualified as "economic activity" and, as a result, they qualify as "undertakings" or "association of undertakings", being fully subject to competition law rules.

IV. Sports and Antitrust Scrutiny

20. Against this backdrop, in principle NSFs are subject to antitrust control regardless of the fact that they (also) play a public service role. It is therefore a question of understanding to what extent sporting federations (i.e. their activities) are subject to antitrust scrutiny.

21. As previously pointed out, NSFs play an institutional role in the functioning of the sports sector in Italy. Notwithstanding this, NSFs are subject to antitrust scrutiny, at least insofar as they carry out economic activities. In other words, the fact that NSFs also perform public functions does not limit the ICA's scrutiny of the ways in which they carry out economic activity.[22]

22. In this regard, the ICA has clarified that the regulation of economic activities in the sporting sector is fully subject to antitrust scrutiny.[23] This position, again, does not significantly differ from that followed by the ECJ in its previous judgments.[24]

23. This said, the application of competition law provisions to sporting entities may somehow interfere with "purely sports rules", insofar as the functioning of such rules may sometimes restrict competition on the market. In this case, based on the ICA's approach, a certain discretionary margin should be allowed to sporting bodies when they lay down "purely sporting rules", which "unquestionably fall" within their prerogatives.[25] In such a case, any restrictions arising from the sports regulations must be assessed on the basis of the context in which they were introduced and the objectives pursued and, in any event, may not go beyond what is

---

20 *FIGC* (n 19).

21 Case T-193/02 *Laurent Piau v Commission of the European Communities* ECLI:EU:T:2005:22, para 70.

22 *AGCM* A562 (n 11); *AGCM* A570 (n 11); Case A378E *ICA v Italian Federation of Equestrian Sports (FISE)* (8 October 2019), confirmed by the first instance administrative court of the Italian region named Lazio (TAR Lazio), Section I, Case 8326, later annulled by the Consiglio di Stato (second instance Italian administrative court), judgment No 05054/2024; Fact-finding inquiry IC/27 2007 in the professional football sector.

23 *FISE* (n 21); *FIGC* (n 19); *AGCM* A562 (n 11).

24 *Meca-Medina* (n 19), para 31, in which the Court clarified that even those rules that "concern questions of purely sporting interest" cannot *per se* be excluded from the scope of application of Article 101 TFEU.

25 *FIGC* (n 19).

strictly necessary and proportionate to ensure their coordination with the sporting activities to which they are linked, with the sole aim of preserving the proper functioning of those activities (i.e. in *Meca Medina*:

> … account must first of all be taken of the overall context in which the decision of the association of undertakings was taken or produces its effects and, more specifically, of its objectives. It has then to be considered whether the consequential effects restrictive of competition are inherent in the pursuit of those objectives (Wouters and Others, paragraph 97) and are proportionate to them).[26]

24. In other words, the compatibility of sporting rules with competition law cannot be assessed in the abstract, but in the overall context in which the said rules – and, more generally, conducts of sporting bodies – have been adopted, in order to verify whether any restriction of competition that they cause is necessary for the proper functioning of a given sporting activity and, in any event, whether they constitute the least restrictive means of pursuing that aim.[27]

25. For instance, the ICA has clarified that the provisions concerning the access to sporting professions that do not require "the performance of any sport practice", but are rather an expression of typically economic activities, cannot be qualified as "purely sporting rules" and, therefore, are fully subject to antitrust scrutiny.[28] Specifically, the ICA took the view that the FIGC regulations governing the access to certain sporting professions (i.e. sport director (direttore sportivo), sport manager (collaboratore della gestione sportiva), talent scout (osservatore calcistico) and match analyst) should not be seen as a discipline of "the technical-sporting point of view of the services directly related to football competitions", rather as that of "an economic activity peripheral to sporting activity".

26. In another case concerning the Italian Tennis Federation, the Rome administrative court recognised the restrictive nature of the prohibition imposed by the said Federation on tennis clubs to use technical personnel not registered within the said sports federation. In particular, the court clarified that such a prohibition prevented access to a specific sector by professionals of undisputed ability (i.e. those not registered with the Italian Tennis Federation) and impacted the tennis clubs' freedom to select their coaches "not only based on the technical skills but also on the fees required", without any objective and proportionate justification. As a result, the court concluded that the imposition of such requirement implied a clear restriction of competition.[29]

27. In this vein, the ICA has recently opened a case in order to assess whether the national motorsports federation ACI is hindering the organisation of amateur

---

26 *Meca-Medina* (n 18), para 42.

27 *FIPAV* (n 14).

28 *FIGC* (n 19).

29 TAR Lazio, judgment No 37668/2010. For the sake of completeness, it is worth noting that the TAR Lazio judgment was later annulled by the Consiglio di Stato (second instance Italian administrative court), judgment No 302/2012, on the grounds of lack of jurisdiction. Specifically, the Consiglio di Stato did not go into the merits of the aforementioned assessment of TAR Lazio.

motor events by its competitors through "sending reports to the Prefectures, Police Headquarters and/or Municipal Authorities aimed at highlighting to the aforementioned bodies that the events had not been submitted to the prior approval of ACI and would have taken place in non-compliance with its technical-sporting regulations".[30]

V. Proceedings for Abuse of Dominant Position

28. In 2023, the ICA launched two proceedings for alleged abuse of a dominant position against, respectively, FIGC and ACI. Both proceedings (i.e. the respective starting decisions) identify the prerequisite for a dominant position in the fact that the sports federations are entitled with "special and exclusive powers of regulation and coordination" of their respective sporting activities.

29. In previous cases, the ICA had already qualified sports federations as operators in a dominant position in the organisation of sporting events, due to their exclusive regulatory powers.

30. For instance, in *ICA v FISE*, the ICA had considered that the Italian Federation of Equestrian Sports (FISE) derived its position of dominance in the market for organisation of professional sports events from its "powers of regulation and coordination", as well as from its statutory, technical, organisational and managerial autonomy.[31]

31. In particular, the ICA contested the attempt by FISE to extend its dominant position (already existing on the market for competitive sports activities) to that of *amateur activities*, on which other operators compete with FISE. At first, the ICA closed such proceeding against FISE by accepting the commitments submitted by them (concerning, among others, the limitation of FISE's "reserved area" only to Olympic and other equestrian disciplines "carried out exclusively in competitive form and on the basis of well-identified rules of a technical-sporting nature").

32. Subsequently, however, the ICA contested to FISE its non-compliance with the aforementioned commitments, for having exercised its regulatory power to "*de facto* restrict competition in the amateur field" and prevent its competitors from organising amateur competitions. In addition to this, according to the ICA, FISE has repeatedly intervened against competing sports associations and bodies to prevent or oppose their events and sports competitions.[32]

33. The ICA decision was later annulled by the Consiglio di Stato (second instance Italian administrative court), that considered the evidence submitted by the ICA to be inadequate to substantiate the existence of FISE's dominant position in the market, as well as to assess the proportionality and the effects of the contested regulatory measure on the structure of the relevant market.[33]

---

30 *AGCM* A570 (n 11).

31 *FISE* (n 22).

32 For instance, by initiating disciplinary proceedings against the managers of the clubs hosting events allegedly deemed not compliant with the FISE regulatory provisions.

33 Judgment No 05054/2024 (n 21).

34. Likewise, in *Gargano Corse v ACI*, ACI's dominant position on the market for promoting and organising sports events was inferred "mainly, but not exclusively" from its "institutional role" and the exercise of powers of regulation and coordination. Specifically, the ICA took into consideration the fact that ACI, through "the set of statutory and regulatory provisions", as well as "the methods of their concrete application", attempted to reserve for itself "all motorsports activities, and therefore not only those that can be defined as real "competitive" activities".[34]

35. In *ICA v Automobile Club d'Italia (ACI)*[35], the ICA assessed whether ACI has used its regulatory and coordination power to hinder competitors in the organisation of non-competitive events. In particular, the conduct concerned the sending of cease-and-desist letters to various prefectures located throughout the national territory in which it was claimed the alleged failure by the organisers to obtain ACI's approval on the aforesaid events (approval that, based on the position anticipated by the ICA in the starting decision, would have not been required for this type of event), as well as the application of sanctions by ACI to its members who had taken part in such events. Specifically, the conduct carried out by ACI – based on *theory of harm* identified in the starting decision – might have been aimed at extending its dominant position to the organisation of recreational and amateur events and would have presented two aspects of abusiveness, i.e. (i) the letters sent to the competent authorities did not indicate the elements based on which the contested events would have been competitive; and (ii) the timing of sending the letters, delivered to the authorities a few days before the events took place, might have been aimed at hitting the most important events and with the greatest number of participants.[36]

36. However, in December 2024, the ICA closed the proceedings as the investigation – while highlighting ACI's central role in organizing motor sport events – did not provide sufficient grounds to confirm that the alleged conducts effectively hindered or prevented competitors from organizing non-competitive events[37]. As already mentioned above, in 2023 the ICA initiated a similar case against FIGC, concerning an alleged abuse of dominant position.[38] In brief, the ICA verified whether FIGC, which already holds a "position of absolute importance" in the organisation of competitive and amateur football competitions, tried to hinder or prevent the amateur sporting associations associated with the FIGC (Associazioni Sportive Dilettantistiche, ASD) from participating in amateur youth football competitions organised by other sports promotion bodies.

37. In June 2024, the ICA concluded that FIGC, by virtue of the special and exclusive powers of regulation and coordination of football activities granted to it by CONI with regard to the organization of competitive football competitions – where it holds a dominant position – had implemented a complex exclusionary strategy aimed, on the one hand, at strengthening its position in the market and,

---

[34] Case A396 *Gargano Corse v ACI* (11 June 2009).

[35] AGCM A570 ACI (n 11).

[36] *AGCM* A570 (n 11).

[37] AGCM A570 (n 11).

[38] *AGCM* A562 (n 11).

on the other, at extending it to the market for recreational and amateur activities. This strategy took the form of a series of conducts aimed at discouraging the ASDs associated with the FIGC from participating in youth amateur tournaments organised by FIGC's competitors, through, (i) intimidation actions (consisting of acts by which a significant number of FIGC member clubs were warned for not having requested prior authorisation for participation in tournaments organised by competing bodies); (ii) improper use of its regulatory and coordination powers, such as the introduction of an obligation to enter into agreements with FIGC also for promotional and recreational amateur events; (iii) obstructionist actions (e.g. the federation had introduced a further provision requiring its affiliated clubs to obtain FIGC's pre-approval for participation in tournaments organised by its competitors).

38. However, in February 2025 TAR Lazio upheld the appeal filed by FIGC against the ICA decision and annulled the sanction imposed by the latter, holding that the argumentation provided by the ICA was insufficient to demonstrate that FIGC abused its dominant position[39].

39. A further case relates to the private enforcement claim brought by Indaba – a tourism services and sport events operator in relation to the sale of tickets for the Champions League final match held in Munich on 28 May 1997 - *Indaba v Juventus FC.* In a nutshell, Indaba and Juventus FC had entered into a contract by which the former undertook to sell the said tickets exclusively in a bundle with travel packages (including services not normally needed by football supporters). The travel package proved unsuccessful, and Indaba sued Juventus before the Turin Court of Appeal for antitrust damages (claiming that Juventus abused its dominant position). The Turin Court confirmed, among others, that Juventus had abused its dominant position in the relevant market for the sale of the final tickets by imposing excessive prices and illegally tying the sale of the tickets to that of the other tourism services (however, no damages were awarded to the plaintiff as the Court noted that Indaba had passed on the full amount of the illegal overcharge over its own customers).[40]

40. Finally, albeit not resulted in a ICA's judicial decision, it is worth mentioning a sporting, regulatory development stemmed from a recent moral suasion activity carried out by the ICA towards the FIGC. In short, FIGC had amended Article 33 of one of their main sports regulations (so-called *Norme Organizzative Interne Federali* – NOIF) to reintroduce an ultra-biennial constraint for youth players registered with professional clubs (*giovani di serie*), granting clubs the right to unilaterally impose a (up to) three-year professional apprenticeship contract regardless of the players' will.[41] Following the ICA's remarks during several hearings, FIGC adopted a new version of Article 33 of the NOIF: as from the 1st July 2025 clubs' unilateral right is no longer applicable and the conclusion of the mentioned professional apprenticeship contracts is subject to the express consent of the player.[42]

---

39 Judgment No 3409/2025.

40 Case *Indaba Incentive co v società Juventus FC SpA* (6 July 2000) Turin Court of Appeal.

41 See FIGC Official Release (*Comunicato Ufficiale*) No. 233/A of 31 May 2024 - https://figc.it/media/236970/233-modifiche-noif.pdf.

42 See FIGC Official Release (*Comunicato Ufficiale*) No. 159/A of 30 January 2025 - 159-modifica-artt-33-e-99-noif.pdf.

VI. Anticompetitive Agreements in the Sports Sector

41. As anticipated, the ICA generally qualifies sports federations as associations of undertakings due to their representative, regulatory and/or organisational activity on behalf of undertakings active in the respective sports sector. Consequently, the measures adopted by sport federations are normally classified as "decisions of associations of undertakings" for the purposes of Article 101 TFEU.

42. In this respect, the most significant ICA decision in recent years is probably that adopted in the aforementioned *FIGC* Decision of 27 June 2018, *FIGC* concerning the provisions of FIGC regulating the access to, and the discipline of the sporting professions already indicated in the above section IV.[43]

43. In particular, the ICA scrutinised certain qualitative and quantitative restrictions imposed by FIGC, namely the provisions by which the access to such professions was reserved to professionals who, (i) had the Italian citizenship or their residence in Italy; (ii) had attended courses organised by the FIGC and obtained the related certification; and (iii) were registered within a list held by the FIGC (the only exception to the obligation to be registered in the said list being represented by the possibility granted to sports clubs to appoint for those roles "the members of the statutory bodies who have the power to validly represent the Club towards third parties'[44]).

44. The ICA concluded that the aforesaid requirements introduced "an artificial balance between supply and demand of professional services" and qualified them as competitive restrictions by object. More specifically, by providing such limitations, according to the ICA, the FIGC had reserved an economic activity to a limited group of professionals (those registered on the FIGC's list) with respect to which there was no need of special protection. Similarly, regarding the obligation to follow the training courses defined exclusively by the federation, the ICA noted that such obligation was "not compatible with the competition law, as exclusivity in training goes far beyond what is strictly necessary to ensure the proper conduct of sports competition".

45. The FIGC tried to justify such restrictions by insisting on the fact that the aforesaid professional figures should have been qualified as "sport coaches" and, therefore, the provisions regulating the access to such professions should have been qualified as "purely sporting" rules, as such not subject to full antitrust scrutiny.

46. By its final decision, the ICA rejected such defensive arguments (as well as the commitments submitted by FIGC) and contested the breach of Article 101 TFEU. The ICA decision was substantially confirmed by both the competent first instance administrative court (TAR Lazio) and the second instance administrative court (Consiglio Di Stato).

47. In its judgment of 22 May 2019, the TAR Lazio observed that the ICA had correctly explained the reasons why the aforementioned roles did not imply sporting activities, but rather an economic professional activity required by football clubs.[45]

---

43 *FIGC* (n 19).

44 Ibid.

45 TAR Lazio, judgment No 7177 (22 May 2019).

In fact, these individuals "do not practice sports" and their skills (including the knowledge of the football sector) are functional to the carrying out of an economic activity which is "ancillary" to the sporting one (focusing on the technical management of the team and the sporting performance on the playing field).

48. Specifically, the activities of sport director and sport manager, according to the Tar Lazio, concern the care of the administrative/organisational structure of football clubs, including the football players transfer market.

49. As for talent scout and match analyst, the commented judgment clarifies that such figures carry out activities relating to the monitoring, analysis and scouting of football players and teams (talent scout), as well as technical-tactical analysis and collection of statistical data of players and teams (match analyst).

50. In this regard, the TAR Lazio recalled the judgment of the EU Court of First Instance in *Laurent Piau*, that, in relation to the Players' Agents Regulations, clarified that such rules "do not have a sport-related object, but regulate an economic activity that is peripheral to the sporting activity in question and touch on fundamental freedoms' and that, since such regulations do not concern "neither the specific nature of sport nor the freedom of internal organisation of sports associations", its lawfulness must be verified in light of competition law provisions.[46]

51. Similar considerations, according to TAR Lazio, can be applied to the aforementioned *FIGC* Decision of 27 June 2018, as the four figures analysed in the ICA's proceedings were "peripheral" with respect to the performance of sporting activity. Specifically, the fact that the activities carried out by talent scouts and match analysists require a specific degree of competence and knowledge of the football world does not imply that they can be defined as "sports activities", since the technical management of the team (which instead qualifies as a "sporting activity") is still under the sole responsibility of the football team's coach. The Consiglio di Stato substantially confirmed the first-instance judgment.[47]

52. In particular, it was highlighted that – in line with the principles recalled by the ECJ in *Meca-Medina* – any regulation, even if it consists of "purely sporting rules", may be in contrast with competition law. Therefore, a generalised exemption of some sectors (e.g. the sports markets) from compliance with competition law cannot be invoked; on the contrary, it must be verified, on a case-by-case basis, whether the rules governing any activity may restrict competition, and if such restriction affects trade between Member States. In the affirmative, "such rules must be considered in contrast with competition law, regardless of whether their object is fully or partially the regulation of sporting activity".

53. In *Federazione Italiana Pallavolo (FIPAV)*,[48] the ICA contested the so called "vincolo sportivo", i.e. an obligation by which the FIPAV tied amateur players to their clubs for a certain period of time (five or ten years). In other words, through the "vincolo sportivo", athletes were required to perform their sporting activity only and exclusively in favour of the club with which they had registered,

---

46 *Laurent Piau* (n 21), paras 76, 77.

47 Consiglio di Stato, judgment No 5346 (26 July 2021).

48 *FIPAV* (n 14).

without the possibility of changing club before the end of the aforesaid period. Such restriction (which is no longer in force in Italy) could lead, according to the ICA, to a "general reduction in the incentive for sports clubs to compete, with further negative effects on athletes". Specifically, the ICA noted that the "excessive extension of sports constraints" produces a market-sharing effect. As a result, competition between sports clubs – for example, through lower registration costs and fees or through the provision of better services such as, for instance, sports facilities – would be strongly discouraged.

54. Less recently, in *Associazione Italiana Calciatori-Panini*,[49] the ICA did investigate two agreements between the Italian Footballers Association (AIC) – a professional association of footballers registered with the FIGC – and Panini SpA (Panini), a company active, among others, in the market for production and selling of adhesive stickers. Such agreements governed the transfer by AIC to Panini of the right to use the images of football players for the purpose of manufacturing and marketing sticker albums and related self-adhesive stickers, as well as other products belonging to the editorial collectible.

55. Namely, by the first agreement (1992), AIC and Panini jointly determined the conditions under which other licensees were required to place their football collections on the market, assigning them differentiated dates to initiate marketing of their product and limiting the relaunch period thereof by the end of the year. Such agreement, according to the ICA, caused a restriction of competition for the following reasons:

   1. AIC had not determined the conditions for issuing the licenses assigned to the various operators present in the downstream market independently, though had agreed the same with their main company competitor; therefore, Panini, through the contract with AIC, was able to influence the behaviour of the competitors in such a way as to prevent them from being able to freely choose the most suitable means adequate to attract the consumer; and
   2. AIC did not enable potential licensees to compete on an equal basis for the acquisition of licenses. In fact, it did not prepare standard licenses that each company could purchase to compete, instead regulating them according to the commercial space it intended to reserve to individual operators.

56. The second contract, stipulated on 5 May 1995, provided for a three-years exclusive in favour of Panini of the rights of economic exploitation of the images of the players for the creation and marketing of a large number of products, including stickers to be collected in albums. The ICA – while acknowledging that the assignment of an exclusive license does not in itself constitute a restrictive agreement of competition – noted that, due to the effective market conditions, the agreement was able to prevent Panini's competitors from operating on the market collections on football stickers.

57. In *Lega Calcio-Prezzi Biglietti Play Off*, the ICA clarified that the Professional Football League (at that time named Lega Calcio) – which represents professional Series A football clubs – qualifies as association of undertakings and, as a result,

---

49 Case I195 *Associazione Italiana Calciatori v Panini* (31 October 1996).

its resolutions fall within the definition of decisions of associations of undertakings under Article 2 of the Italian competition law (and Article 101 TFEU). Specifically, the aforesaid case concerned the resolutions by which Lega Calcio set the ticket prices for the Series B play-off and play-out matches for the 2004–2005 season.

58. The ICA, as said, qualified such resolution as an agreement pursuant to Article 2 of the Italian competition law (namely as a decision of an association of undertakings). Moreover, the ICA concluded that, through such resolution, the League, as an association of Series A and B clubs, had *de facto* adopted a price-fixing decision, "removing any degree of decision-making autonomy that characterises competitive market structures". A different solution, according to the ICA, might have been justified in case of matches to be played in a "neutral playing-field" (i.e. a playing-field other than that of the hosting football club) but, since the playoff and play-out matches were played in the hosting clubs' playing fields, "there were no reasons to deviate from the rules in force for the other Championship matches, for which the fixing of the ticket price is left to the individual clubs".

Germany: National Competition Law Issues

Lukas Kretschmann*
University of Münster, Germany

I. Introduction

1. German courts and the Federal Cartel Office (Bundeskartellamt (FCO)) have been applying competition law to the sports sector for many years. In recent years, this intersection has attracted greater attention, particularly through high-profile European cases like *Super League*. This chapter provides an overview of how German courts and the FCO apply competition law in sports, with a focus on recent proceedings.

2. The structure of this chapter is based on the two distinct types of markets typically present in the sports sector.[1] First, there are markets for organising sports competitions, where suppliers are sports associations or league organisations, and the demand comes from athletes, teams or clubs.[2] Second, there are markets for marketing competitions, such as through TV rights or advertising, where suppliers are again usually sports or league associations, but the demand primarily comes from media companies and sponsors. The distinguishing factor between the two

---

* Lukas Kretschmann is a research assistant (Wissenschaftlicher Mitarbeiter) and a PhD candidate at the Institute of International Business Law (Professor Dr Petra Pohlmann), University of Münster.

1 See Peter W Heermann, "Kartellrechtskonforme Ausgestaltung von Zugangsbeschränkungen Im Sport" [2025] Zeitschrift für Wettbewerbsrecht 305, 319, 320, who distinguishes between two different types of access restriction.

2 Daniel Grätz, *Missbrauch der marktbeherrschenden Stellung durch Sportverbände* (Mohr Siebeck 2009) 201–204.

types of markets is that various products are offered to different customer groups. It is therefore questionable that courts[3] and competition authorities[4] sometimes assume that these are a single market.[5]

II. Regulations Regarding Access to Sports Competitions

1. Nomination, Admission and Exclusion

3. Athletes repeatedly take legal action against non-nomination or non-admission to a sports competition or against exclusion from such a competition. German courts review such decisions by sports associations primarily on the basis of the prohibition of abuse of a dominant position under Section 19 of the German Competition Act (GWB), and less frequently on the basis of the prohibition of abuse under Article 102 TFEU. German courts have repeatedly ruled that sports associations have a dominant position in the market for the organisation of certain sports competitions.[6] German courts usually examine whether there has been abuse of a dominant market position on the basis of the typical example of unfair impediment of an undertaking in accordance with Section 19(2) No 1 GWB. The courts assess whether an "unfair impediment" exists on the basis of an overall assessment of all interests involved, taking into account the freedom of competition, the ensuring of competition on the merits, and the openness of market access.[7] In this balancing of interests, German courts have also integrated the requirements of the ECJ's *Meca-Medina* doctrine.[8] Therefore, it must be examined whether the impediment is necessary in order to pursue a legitimate objective and whether it is proportionate to that objective.[9]

4. In balancing interests, according to case law, sports associations have discretion that the courts review only to a limited extent. This includes, for example, the design and specification of nomination rules.[10] However, the nomination rules must be reasonable and free from discrimination.[11] For example, it is legitimate for an association to set a shorter qualification period for a nomination decision in order to give greater weight to an athlete's short-term performance.[12] If, on

---

3 Case C-333/21 *European Super League* ECLI:EU:C:2023:1011, para 199.

4 Case B2-26/17 Bundeskartellamt Decision *German Olympic Sports Confederation and IOC* (25 February 2019), para 43.

5 Heermann (n 1), 318, 319; an alternative approach would be to treat this as a multi-sided platform, see Tim Hülskötter, *Die (Un-)Wirksamkeit von Schiedsvereinbarungen im Berufssport* (Duncker & Humblot 2020) 221–227.

6 Case KZR 6/15 (Kart) Bundeskartellamt Decision *German Olympic Sports Confederation and IOC* (17 June 2016), para 45; Case 11 U 60/21 (Kart) *Motorsport* (2022) Higher Regional Court of Frankfurt a. M., NZKart 2023, 40, para 38; Case VI-6 W 1/22 (Kart) *Admission to the Winter Paralympics 2022* (2022) Higher Regional Court of Düsseldorf, SpuRt 2022, 110, 112.

7 *Admission to the Winter Paralympics 2022* (n 6), 113; *Motorsport* (n 6), para 42; Case VI-W 12/16 (Kart) *Exclusion from the 2016 Paralympics* (2016) Higher Regional Court of Düsseldorf, SpuRt 2017, 69, para 8.

8 *Motorsport* (n 6), para 45; Case 3 U 894/19 *Wrestling Association* (2021) Higher Regional Court of Nürnberg, WuW 2022, 54, para 69.

9 *Wrestling Association* (n 8), para 69.

10 Case 11 U 169/20 (Kart) *Beach Volleyball* (2022) Higher Regional Court of Frankfurt a. M., BeckRS 2022, 10368, para 100; Case 11 W 22/16 *Nomination Criteria for the Olympics* (2016) Higher Regional Court of Frankfurt a.M., BeckRS 2016, 13014, para 25.

11 *Beach Volleyball* (n 10), para 101.

12 *Nomination Criteria for the Olympics* (n 10), para 25.

the other hand, a sports association does not make a nomination even though its own nomination requirements are met, this may constitute an abuse of a dominant market position because it treats the non-nominated athletes differently from the nominated athletes without any objectively justified reason.[13] However, if several athletes meet the nomination requirements, the selection is at the association's discretion.[14] The discretionary decision not to include a particular sport in a competition has also been found to comply with competition law.[15]

5. Despite the discretion of sports associations, there are still cases in which athletes' interests are not sufficiently taken into account, resulting in an abuse of a dominant market position. The non-admission of a para-athlete who belonged to a class in which no competition took place due to too few participants to a class that was not actually suitable, did not sufficiently take into account the athlete's interest.[16] The decisive factor was that the para-athlete did not want to switch to a class that was advantageous for her, but rather to one that was disadvantageous for her, but which was in line with the nature of her impairment.[17] In the case of changes to classification rules that resulted in athletes no longer being able to participate, the changes were not unlawful per se.[18] However, the interests of athletes were not sufficiently taken into account, as no transition period was provided for professional reorientation.[19] The exclusion of Russian athletes from the 2016 Paralympic Games was not an unfair impediment because the fundamental interest in ensuring fair competition conditions and "clean games" outweighed the interests of athletes suspected of doping.[20] On the other hand, the exclusion of athletes who participated in rival competitions was an unfair impediment, because in both cases there was a lack of clear and transparent rules within the meaning of *Meca-Medina*.[21]

6. Pursuant to Section 33(1) GWB, the rectification of conduct that infringes competition law can be demanded, meaning that athletes or teams who have been wrongfully excluded can be entitled to admission. Pursuant to Section 33a(1) GWB, they may also be entitled to collect damages. However, for both claims, it is not sufficient that a decision was unlawful. The entitlement to rectification only exists if the claimant is also "affected" (Section 33(3) GWB). This requires the claimant to provide evidence of the real risk of (at least indirect) damage caused by the anticompetitive behaviour. This is not the case if the claimant has not attempted, and is not prevented from attempting, to challenge unlawful admission decisions within the association or before state courts.[22] In order to be entitled

---

13 *Beach Volleyball* (n 10), para 91.

14 Case VI-W 3/24 (Kart) *Karate World Championships* (2024) Higher Regional Court of Düsseldorf, BeckRS 2024, 12291, para 25.

15 Case U 13/21 (Kart) *CP Football* (2022) Higher Regional Court of Düsseldorf, BeckRS 2022, 55914, para 94.

16 *Admission to the Winter Paralympics 2022* (n 6), 112.

17 Ibid 114.

18 Case VI U 7/21(Kart) *Change to Paralympic admission rules* (2023) Higher Regional Court of Düsseldorf, SpuRt 2023, 138, 143.

19 Ibid 145, 146.

20 *Exclusion from the 2016 Paralympics* (n 7), para 17.

21 *Motorsport* (n 6), para 65; *Wrestling Association* (n 8), para 75.

22 Case VI-U 6/24 (Kart) *Legal protection against Classification Decisions* (2025) Higher Regional Court of Düsseldorf, SpuRt 2025, 578, 580.

to claim damages under Section 33a(1) GWB, athletes must demonstrate that they must have been nominated; otherwise, there is no causation.[23]

2. DFL's 50+1-Rule

7. Perhaps the best-known restriction of access to a sports competition is the 50+1 rule of the German Football League Association (Deutsche Fußball Liga (DFL)). In the context of sports and competition law, it is one of the most discussed cases in Germany. Members of the DFL are all licensed participants of the Bundesliga and 2. Bundesliga. Not only clubs, but also corporate entities can participate in the Bundesliga and become members of the DFL. It is important that a *club*, in this sense, be understood as a non-profit, membership-based association in which individuals can become members (eingetragener Verein). The 50+1 rule is laid down in Section 8 No 3 of the DFL's statutes and is a specific precondition for a *corporate entity* to obtain a licence to participate in the Bundesliga. It requires that the original football club holds a majority of the voting rights in the corporate entity that wants to participate in the Bundesliga. *De lege lata,* there is also an exemption rule: the majority of votes may be held by another legal entity if that entity has continuously and significantly promoted the original football club's football activities for more than 20 years and will continue to do so in the future with regard to amateur football. This exemption is currently being used by Bayer 04 Leverkusen and VfL Wolfsburg.[24]

8. There have been doubts about the legality of the 50+1 rule under competition law for some time. The DFL therefore proactively initiated proceedings with the FCO to clarify compliance with competition law. In 2021, the FCO decided that the basic rule could be justified but was concerned about the exemption rule.[25] The DFL proposed commitments to remove the exemption rule, while protecting existing exemptions under certain conditions. Initially, the FCO declared its intention to accept this offer.[26] Following the ECJ's *Super League* Ruling, the FCO did not change its position, but wanted to review the DFL's application practice more closely.[27] In 2025, the FCO then came to a different assessment and identified a considerable need for improvement.[28]

---

23 *Beach Volleyball* (n 10), paras 108, 130.

24 TSG 1899 Hoffenheim also used the exemption rule in the past but is now back in compliance with the basic rule.

25 Bundeskartellamt Press Release, "Bundeskartellamt Provides Preliminary Assessment of DFL's 50+1 Ownership Rule" (31 May 2021) <https://www.bundeskartellamt.de/SharedDocs/Meldung/EN/Pressemitteilungen/2021/31_05_2021_50plus1.html?nn=55030> accessed 29 May 2026.

26 Bundeskartellamt Press Release, "50+1 Proceeding – Commitments Offered by DFL to be Declared Binding" (12 July 2023) <https://www.bundeskartellamt.de/SharedDocs/Meldung/EN/Pressemitteilungen/2023/13_07_2023_DFL.html?nn=55030> accessed 29 May 2026.

27 Bundeskartellamt Press Release, "50+1 Rule – Effects of the ECJ's Case Law and Next Steps in the Proceeding" (29 May 2024) <https://www.bundeskartellamt.de/SharedDocs/Meldung/EN/Pressemitteilungen/2024/29_05_2024_50plus1.html?nn=55030> accessed 29 May 2026.

28 Bundeskartellamt Press Release, "Bundeskartellamt Sees Need for Improvement in 50+1 Rule" (16 June 2025) <https://www.bundeskartellamt.de/SharedDocs/Meldung/EN/Pressemitteilungen/2025/06_16_2025_50plus1.html?nn=55030> accessed 29 May 2026.

9. In the following sections, some crucial aspects of the 50+1 procedure will be analysed more closely. It should be noted that the FCO has so far only examined the 50+1 rule under Article 101 TFEU and Section 1 GWB. This is reasonable because the DFL's statutes are both an agreement between undertakings and a decision by an association of undertakings.

A. *Relevant Markets and Restrictions of Competition*

10. One notable characteristic of the 50+1 rule is that it leads to restrictions of competition in different markets. The FCO also assumes that competition is restricted but has not yet publicly stated which specific markets are affected.

11. First, the 50+1 rule affects the market for the organisation of the Bundesliga. On the supply side of this market, the DFL offers participation in the Bundesliga to football undertakings. Compliance with the 50+1 rule is a precondition for the award of a licence and participation. It therefore restricts access to this offer.[29] As the DFL holds a monopoly in this market, it would also be possible to examine the 50+1 rule under Article 102 TFEU and Section 19 GWB.[30]

12. The 50+1 rule also affects another market, as the FCO points out: it restricts investment opportunities in Bundesliga clubs.[31] However, the FCO does not define the relevant market. Upon closer examination, the relevant market must be defined as a market for equity investments in professional football undertakings.[32] Demand in this market comes from potential investors;[33] the previous owners – predominantly the football clubs – act as suppliers. There is some debate about whether a distinction should be made between minority and majority shareholdings[34] and whether the market is purely national[35] or EU-wide.[36] In any case, under the 50+1 rule, suppliers no longer have the freedom to decide the extent to which they offer equity investments. If the relevant market is limited to majority shareholdings in Germany, that market is foreclosed, save for the exemption rule.[37]

13. The FCO considers the entire 50+1 rule to be a restriction of competition. Others, however, assume that the exemption rule constitutes a separate restriction of

---

29 See Heermann (n 1), 321, 322; Jan-Frederick Göhsl and Alexander Scheuch, "50+1? Wenn schon, denn schon!" [2025] Zeitschrift für Sport und Recht 328, 331; Konstantin Richard Putzier, *Kartellrechtliche Anforderungen an Private Rechtssysteme Im Sport* (Duncker & Humblot 2021) 234.

30 See Putzier (n 29), 234; Grätz (n 2), 390–395; Philipp Schaefer, *Die Vereinbarkeit der '50+1'-Regel mit dem Europarecht* (Nomos 2012) 219–233; Vito Esposito, *Private Sportordnung und EU-Kartellrecht* (Nomos 2014) 365–372; Johannes Scherzinger, *Die Beschränkung von Mehrheitsbeteiligungen an Kapitalgesellschaften im Deutschen Ligasport* (Nomos 2012) 183–194.

31 Bundeskartellamt Press Release, "FAQ on the Press Release of 16 June 2025" no 2 <https://www.bundeskartellamt.de/SharedDocs/Publikation/DE/Pressemitteilungen/50plus1_FAQ.html?nn=55030> accessed 29 May 2026.

32 Scherzinger (n 30), 160–165; Esposito (n 30), 286.

33 Scherzinger (n 30), 171–174.

34 Ibid 164, 165; Matthias Rothammer, *Die "50+1"-Klausel des DFB und des Ligaverbandes aus verfassungs- und europarechtlicher Sicht* (Dr. Kovac Publisher 2013) 156.

35 Scherzinger (n 30), 166–168; Esposito (n 30), 287–289.

36 Simon Weiler, *Mehrfachbeteiligungen an Sportkapitalgesellschaften* (Duncker & Humblot 2006) 164–165; Grätz (n 2), 242, 243.

37 Peter W Heermann, *Verbandsautonomie im Sport* (Nomos 2022) 683.

competition, because it privileges undertakings in competition with others.[38] They argue that, in accordance with *Super League*, the DFL must regulate access to the market for sports competitions in a transparent, objective, proportionate and non-discriminatory manner.[39] However, the European Court of Justice (ECJ) has used these criteria to classify restrictions imposed by sports associations as by object or by effect. The sole fact that a restriction of competition meets or does not meet these requirements should not be interpreted as an additional restriction of competition. Therefore, the 50+1 basic rule and the exemption rule constitute a uniform restriction of competition in the relevant markets.

B. *Restriction by Object or by Effect?*

14. The question remains whether the restrictions on competition resulting from the 50+1 rule are by object or by effect. The predominant opinion in the literature has been that the restriction of competition is by object,[40] without attaching great importance to this question in the past. Following the ECJ's decision in *Super League*, according to which the *Meca-Medina* doctrine only applies to restrictions of competition by effect, this is now a crucial question. In *Super League*, the ECJ classified the rules of FIFA and UEFA as a restriction of competition by object because they were not "transparent, objective, precise and non-discriminatory".[41] In the 50+1 proceedings, the FCO appears to assume that the restriction of competition could be, maybe only under certain circumstances, just by effect, because it considers a justification based on the *Meca-Medina* doctrine to be possible.[42]

15. When it comes to football undertakings' access to the Bundesliga, there is, in contrast to *Super League*, a precise regulation with specific requirements. It is also essentially non-discriminatory because it applies equally to all competitors. The exemption rule is also open to all competitors *de lege lata*. Thus, there are no unequal conditions of competition per se. However, if the exemption rule were removed, while individual undertakings would still enjoy the protection of their exemption, as provided in the DFL's commitment offer, this would create unequal conditions for access to the Bundesliga. This would already constitute discrimination against competitors in the regulation itself, rendering the 50+1 rule a restriction of competition by object. The FCO has also changed its legal assessment and no longer considers this proposal suitable. An alternative solution would be to abolish all exemptions. The FCO generally seems to favour this solution. However, the rule could also be non-discriminatory if it continues to allow an exemption for all competitors.

16. Given that the 50+1 rule also affects the market for equity investments in professional football undertakings, there is no doubt that the aim of the 50+1 rule is to prevent offers

---

38 Göhsl and Scheuch (n 29), 328.

39 Ibid 328.

40 Heermann (n 37), 683; Scherzinger (n 30), 174; Schaefer (n 30), 130; Esposito (n 30), 293, 294; Rothammer (n 34), 168.

41 *Super League* (n 3), para 177.

42 Bundeskartellamt Press Release (n 31), nos 4, 5.

of majority shareholdings.[43] Depending on the market definition, it could thereby foreclose this market. In *Super League*, the ECJ cited "limitations on production capacity" as an example of particularly harmful conduct.[44] On the other hand, "it is necessary to examine, first, the content of the agreement, decision or practice in question; second, the economic and legal context of which it forms a part; and, third, its objectives".[45] It therefore appears appropriate to classify the restrictions on competition imposed by the 50+1 rule, which are mutually dependent, uniformly as by object or by effect. The 50+1 rule is not intended to prevent potential competitors because the DFL does not operate in the market for equity investments in professional football enterprises. Unlike FIFA and UEFA in *Super League*, the DFL is therefore not concerned with defending its own monopoly. The primary objective appears to lie in sports policy (see below), rather than being anticompetitive per se. It can also be argued that the 50+1 rule primarily serves internal regulation within the association and only indirectly restricts investors.[46] If the DFL ensures non-discriminatory access restrictions in any way, this should result in a restriction by effect for both the Bundesliga organisation market and the professional football equity investment market.

C. *Meca-Medina Doctrine*

17. Provided that the 50+1 rule is only a restriction by effect, the competition law assessment of the 50+1 rule depends on the *Meca-Medina* doctrine. The FCO does not even mention an exemption under Article 101(3) TFEU.

a) Legitimate Objective

18. First, the rule must pursue one or more legitimate objectives in the public interest which are not, per se, anticompetitive.[47] Identifying the legitimate objective pursued by the 50+1 rule appears to be difficult and has a significant impact on the legal assessment.

19. In 1999, the German Football Association (Deutscher Fußball-Bund (DFB)) amended its statutes to allow clubs to outsource their professional football business to a corporate entity, enabling investors to buy into these entities. In an accompanying policy paper, the DFB explained that the 50+1 rule served to organise the connection between professional and amateur sport and was intended to ensure the club's active influence on the corporate entity.[48] In the current proceedings, the FCO has defined a similar objective: the 50+ rule pursues the goal of maintaining the "club character of the sport" and the associated opportunity for broad sections of the population to participate in decision-making. In 2024, the FCO described this as a "social and ethical" reason.[49] However, the FCO does not mention the organisational link between professional and amateur sport, which

---

43 Esposito (n 30), 293.
44 *Super League* (n 3), para 163.
45 Ibid 165.
46 Alexander Seyb, *Autonomie der Sportverbände* (Mohr Siebeck 2020) 139, 140.
47 *Super League* (n 3), para 183.
48 As cited in SpuRt 2011 259 (DFL Arbitration Court).
49 Bundeskartellamt Press Release (n 27).

the DFB cited as a partial objective in 1999. At least, the FCO has not repeated its assessment that the 50+1 rule ensures competitive balance.[50] This seems reasonable, as the 50+1 rule is not suitable for ensuring competitive balance.[51] At best, it could only indirectly limit competitors' financial possibilities that would result from the entry of majority shareholders. However, it cannot prevent financial inequalities through other financing options (eg sponsorship or minority investors).

b) Genuinely Necessary

20. Second, the specific means used to pursue the legitimate objectives must be genuinely necessary for that purpose.[52]

21. The 50+1 rule can essentially achieve the goal of maintaining the club character of German football. If a club has at least 50% plus one vote, it has, at least formally, far-reaching – if not always sole – decision-making power over the corporate entity that participates in the Bundesliga. However, it is doubtful that this formal position of a club is always sufficient to guarantee its influence and the "club character". From an economic perspective, influence can also be gained in other ways, eg by the investor owning the infrastructure on which the football entity depends.[53] The FCO has also taken this divergence between formal and factual reality into account and recognised problematic cases. It takes the view that the DFL does not apply the 50+1 rule systematically and consistently.[54] The FCO is obviously applying the criterion of coherence, which had already been developed in German literature. According to this criterion, a legitimate goal must be pursued systematically, stringently, consistently and without inconsistencies.[55]

22. In doing so, the FCO appears to be referring to RasenBallsport Leipzig without explicitly naming it publicly. Formally, a club holds the majority of votes in the football entity. However, outsiders cannot become voting members of this parent club.[56] In doing so, RasenBallsport Leipzig circumvents the participation by broad sections of the population without having to comply with the strict conditions of the exemption rule. On the other hand, the FCO explicitly refers to the *Hannover 96* case, in which the DFL tolerated the managing director of the football association to ignore an instruction from the parent club.[57] The FCO is to be agreed with on this point: if the DFL tolerates the 50+1 rule and the conditions for exemptions being circumvented, the 50+1 rule cannot be suitable for achieving its legitimate objectives.[58]

---

50 Bundeskartellamt Press Release, "DFL Offers Commitments in the 50+1 Proceeding" (*Bundeskartellamt*, 8 March 2023) <https://www.bundeskartellamt.de/SharedDocs/Meldung/EN/Pressemitteilungen/2023/08_03_2023_DFL.html?nn=55030> accessed 29 May 2026.

51 Esposito (n 30), 332–336.

52 *Super League* (n 3), para 183.

53 Esposito (n 30), 317, 318.

54 Bundeskartellamt Press Release (n 31), no 6.

55 Tassilo Mürtz, *Meca-Medina-Test des EuGH* (Nomos 2023) 331–333; Heermann (n 37), 399.

56 See Deutscher Bundestag, "Kartellrechtliche Aspekte der 50+1-Regel der Deutschen Fußball Liga" 9 <https://www.bundestag.de/resource/blob/928506/ef229d7d8a31d24e02493fa8fb5e67da/WD-10-037-22-pdf.pdf> accessed 29 May 2026.

57 Bundeskartellamt Press Release (n 31), no 6.

58 See also Göhsl and Scheuch (n 29), 332.

c) The Restriction Does Not Go Beyond What Is Necessary

23. Finally, it is required that the restrictive effect on competition does not go beyond what is necessary, in particular by eliminating all competition.[59] The question is therefore whether the DFL can achieve its goal of maintaining the club character of German football in a more competition-friendly way.

24. In the FCO's view, the 50+1 basic rule is not particularly harmful to competition and pursues the goal of maintaining the club character in a proportionate manner. It opens up the possibility of (minority) investments in corporate entities and serves to balance the idealistic and economic interests.[60] However, this assessment does not appear to be inevitable. It may be sufficient to require clubs to hold blocking minorities with veto rights to maintain the club character while allowing greater economic freedom.[61] In German handball, for example, there is only a "25+1 rule" if the club remains the original owner of the licence at the same time.[62]

25. Since the FCO only refers to the basic rule, it appears to consider the exemption rule to be disproportionate. For the market for equity investments, the exemptions could be positive, as they reduce the anticompetitive effects of the basic rule by allowing at least a limited supply of majority shareholdings. However, when considering the restriction of access to the Bundesliga, the exemption has the opposite effect, leading to unequal treatment of competitors in this market, as the FCO also notes.[63] Nevertheless, it is important to differentiate in this case. An exemption does not necessarily constitute unequal treatment if it is available to all competitors on equal terms. However, unequal treatment arises *de lege lata* from the requirement that the exemption can be granted only after 20 of continuous promotion. New competitors are thus effectively excluded from the exemption and are therefore disadvantaged. The DFL's current proposal would only further increase this unequal treatment. Therefore, alternatives must be sought to eliminate the unequal treatment. The most obvious solution would be to abolish the exemption rule. It would also be possible to design the conditions for the exemption in such a way that all competitors are eligible and new competitors are not disadvantaged, eg by removing the 20-year promotion period.[64] This would give all competitors the same level of freedom of action. It would be up to each football undertaking and its owners to decide how to structure their ownership.

D. *Outlook*

26. Based on the FCO's statements, the DFL's approach to circumventions of the 50+1 rule and to the exemption rule appears to be crucial for the competition

---

59 *Super League* (n 3), para 183.

60 Bundeskartellamt Press Release (n 31), no 5.

61 Scherzinger (n 30), 324, 325.

62 Ibid 89.

63 Bundeskartellamt Press Release (n 31), no 8.

64 Johannes Scherzinger, "Bundeskartellamt setzt DFL unter Druck: Quo Vadis 50+1?" [2021] Sportrecht und E-Sportrecht in der Praxis 178, 183.

law assessment. The DFL will have little choice but to put an end to the de facto forms of circumvention. The same may also apply to the exemption rule, which the FCO is generally in favour of abolishing. However, abolition does not need to be the only solution. Legal uncertainty is nevertheless likely to persist, as the FCO intends to close the proceedings despite its concerns. It argues that prohibiting the 50+1 rule altogether would ultimately undermine its objective of ensuring broad population participation.[65] Greater legal certainty could be achieved if individual DFL members or (potential) investors were to challenge the 50+1 rule before the courts. Assuming that the 50+1 rule constitutes an infringement of competition law, the affected parties would be entitled, pursuant to Section 33(1) GWB, to have the infringement remedied. It would then fall to the DFL to determine how to end the infringement. As matters currently stand, the 50+1 rule as a whole is void due to its incompatibility with competition law.[66] Accordingly, the DFL should no longer take the rule into account when licensing corporate entities.[67]

III. Regulations Regarding the Marketing of Sports Competitions

1. Advertising during the Olympic Games

27. In 2019, the FCO extended the advertising opportunities for German athletes during the Olympic Games. According to Rule 40 No 3 of the Olympic Charter, athletes are prohibited from using themselves or their sporting achievements for advertising purposes during the so-called frozen period unless prior authorisation has been granted. The Deutscher Olympischer Sportbund (DOSB) and the International Olympic Committee (IOC) have specified the conditions for obtaining permission with guidelines. The FCO came to the preliminary assessment that the DOSB and IOC had infringed Article 102 TFEU and Section 19(1) and (2) No 1 GWB in their application of these rules.[68] The FCO assumed that there was a single market for the organisation and marketing of the Olympic Games.[69] Even if these activities constituted separate markets, the FCO considered that the Olympic movement, a collective entity[70] of which the DOSB and the IOC are members, would in any event hold a dominant position on those markets.[71] Inter alia, the FCO objected to the short registration deadlines and excessive restrictions on athletes' advertising opportunities. Furthermore, there were far-reaching and non-transparent sanctions regulations.[72] In addition, undertakings in the sports sponsorship market would be impeded by the strict rules, which would prevent them from switching to sponsoring individual athletes; instead, they would have

65 Bundeskartellamt Press Release (n 31), no 8.
66 See Göhsl and Scheuch (n 29), 332.
67 Ibid 332.
68 Case B2-26/17 Bundeskartellamt Decision (n 4), para 41.
69 Ibid 43.
70 Ibid 59–60.
71 Ibid 43.
72 Ibid 75, 76.

to become official sponsors of the Olympic Games.[73] However, the FCO also concluded that, within the context of the *Meca-Medina* doctrine, the prevention of so-called ambush marketing, aimed at ensuring the financing and organisation of the Olympic Games, constituted a legitimate objective.[74]

28. In the end, DOSB and IOC made commitments that expanded the advertising opportunities for German athletes. For example, advertising measures no longer have to be registered and approved. Restrictions on the use of certain images and terms have also been eased. Furthermore, sporting sanctions can no longer be imposed for non-compliant conduct. In addition, these matters will no longer be decided by arbitration tribunals, but by state courts.[75] Even after the conclusion of these proceedings, the FCO continues to monitor the DOSB guidelines on an ongoing basis.[76]

2. FIS's Centralisation of Media and Broadcast Rights

29. In 2024, the Fédération Internationale de Ski (FIS) tried to establish a centralised marketing model for FIS World Cup events. The new regulation provided that national ski associations could only market their competitions if they had previously concluded a Media Rights Centralisation Agreement (MRCA) with the FIS. If they failed to do so, the FIS would have exclusive marketing rights. The German Ski Association filed for preliminary injunctive relief against this before the Regional Court of Munich – and won the case.

30. First, the court ruled that there had been an infringement of Article 101 TFEU. The FIS decision was a decision by an association of undertakings with the object of restricting competition. The new rules effectively forced the national associations to enter into an agreement with the FIS.[77] According to national law, the national ski associations are at least co-owners of the rights to the competitions they organise, as they have organisational and financial responsibility.[78] Originally, the FIS rules also provided that national ski associations were authorised to market the competitions they organised on their own. Under the centralised marketing model, FIS would have complete control over the marketing rights and eliminate horizontal competition.[79] Since the restriction of competition was found to be by object, justification under the *Meca-Medina* doctrine was ruled out.[80] The court also rejected an exemption under Article 101(3) TFEU. The FIS was unable to prove that the planned

---

73 Ibid 77ff.

74 Ibid 96.

75 See as summary: Bundeskartellamt Press Release, "German Athletes and Their Sponsors Obtain Further Advertising Opportunities during the Olympic Games Following Bundeskartellamt Action - IOC and DOSB Undertake to Change The Advertising Guidelines" (*Bundeskartellamt*, 27 February 2019) <https://www.bundeskartellamt.de/SharedDocs/Meldung/EN/Pressemitteilungen/2019/27_02_2019_DOSB_IOC.html?nn=55030> accessed 29 May 2026.

76 Bundeskartellamt Press Release, "Olympics 2024: Bundeskartellamt Secures Self-Marketing Options for Team Germany Athletes" (*Bundeskartellamt*, 20 March 2024) <https://www.bundeskartellamt.de/SharedDocs/Meldung/EN/Pressemitteilungen/2024/20_03_2024_Olympia.html?nn=55030> accessed 29 May 2026.

77 Case 37 O 7091/24 *Deutscher Skiverband/FIS* (2024) Regional Court of München I, SpuRt 2024, 518, para 521.

78 Ibid 521ff.

79 Ibid 523.

80 Ibid 523, 524.

centralised marketing model would increase efficiency or even compensate for the disadvantages. Furthermore, competition in the relevant media rights market would be eliminated to a significant extent.[81]

31. The court also found an infringement of Article 102 TFEU. The FIS has a dominant position in the market for the organisation of international skiing competitions that are linked by means of a cross-event sporting ranking.[82] Since the national ski associations would effectively be forced to conclude the MRCA, the FIS was abusing its market power.[83]

3. DFL's Centralised Selling of TV Broadcasting Rights

32. The DFL sells the TV broadcasting rights for Bundesliga competitions exclusively and in its own name.[84] This centralised selling model has been a focus of the FCO since 2008. Since then, it has been preliminarily reviewing the DFL's planned selling model for compliance with Article 101 TFEU, although not with Article 102 TFEU.[85] In response to preliminary concerns raised by the FCO, the DFL has in the past offered commitments that the FCO subsequently declared binding.[86] In 2024, the FCO simply closed the proceedings. DFL's central selling model is a controversial issue that is also being addressed by the German Monopolies Commission (Monopolkommission), an independent expert committee appointed by the German Government. The application of German and European competition law to the selling model is undisputed today.[87]

A. *Relevant Markets*

33. The DFL's centralised selling model affects different market levels.[88] On the one hand, it affects the upstream market for TV rights. The demand here comes from media companies, while the supply comes from rights holders. On the other hand, it also affects the downstream market for football broadcasts. The demand here comes from end customers, predominantly football fans, while the supply comes from media companies.[89] However, the markets are linked because the demand in the upstream market depends on the anticipated exploitation opportunities in the downstream market.[90]

---

81 Ibid 524.

82 Ibid.

83 Ibid.

84 S 6 No 2a. DFL Statutes and ss 1 and 9 of the „Ordnung für die Verwertung kommerzieller Rechte".

85 With criticism of this, Monopolkommission, *Main Report XXIII: Competition 2020* (2020) paras 472, 473 <https://www.monopolkommission.de/de/gutachten/hauptgutachten/330-xxiii-gesamt.html> accessed 29 May 2026; Peter W Heermann, "Zentralvermarktung von Fußball-Medienrechten" [2024] Gewerblicher Rechtsschutz und Urheberrecht 1571, 1575.

86 S 32b para 1 GWB.

87 Until 2005, s 31 GWB contained a sectoral exemption for the centralised selling of TV rights to sporting events.

88 See C-Philipp Heller, Slobodan Sudaric and Ann-Christin Winkler, "The Centralised Sale of Football Media Rights in Europe" (2023) 19 ECJ 449, 460, 461.

89 Heermann (n 85), 1572.

90 Monopolkommission, *Main Report XXI: Competition 2016* (2016) paras 374–377 <https://www.monopolkommission.de/de/gutachten/hauptgutachten/88-xxi-gesamt.html> accessed 29 May 2026.

a) Upstream Market

34. The FCO assumes that, at the upstream level, there is a national market for TV rights to men's football competitions held throughout the year with the participation of teams from the Bundesliga.[91] This includes football matches in the Bundesliga and 2. Bundesliga, the DFB Cup and international UEFA competitions.[92] This does not include the UEFA EURO and FIFA World Cup.[93] The FCO does not make any further subdivisions of the market.[94] According to the FCO, the DFL had a market share of 80–85% in the relevant market.[95]

35. However, this market definition has faced criticism: cup and league competitions, as well as international competitions, shouldn't be part of a single market, because the competitions take place at different times and vary in their attractiveness to media companies, eg due to the level of play and sporting interest.[96] This criticism is at least partially justified. It does not seem plausible to assign the matches of the 2. Bundesliga or the UEFA Conference League, which have a much lower sporting significance and attractiveness, to the same market as the highly attractive matches of the Bundesliga or UEFA Champions League.

b) Downstream Market

36. At the downstream level, the FCO defines the market in much the same way as it does at the upstream level. It considers a national end-user market for live audiovisual broadcasts of men's football competitions held throughout the year with the participation of teams from the Bundesliga and 2. Bundesliga.[97] Highlight coverage does not belong to this market because it only contributes part of the coverage; however, it does exert "substitute competition" as a neighbouring market.[98] The Monopolies Commission also assumes that "at least some viewers would be willing to replace live broadcasts with highlight coverage once a certain price is reached."[99]

37. This market definition by the FCO is subject to criticism for a reason. It implies that, from the end consumer's perspective, all matches are substitutable. However, this does not correspond to the interests of a large number of end consumers. The majority of end consumers are supporters of a specific football team.[100] They are primarily interested in this team's match; it cannot be replaced by another team's

---

91 Case B6-28/19 Bundeskartellamt Decision *Joint selling of media rights to matches of the German Bundesliga from the season 2021/22 onwards* (20 March 2020); Case B6-32/15 Bundeskartellamt Decision *Joint selling of media rights to matches of the German Bundesliga from the season 2017/18 onwards* (11 April 2016) para 86.

92 Case B6-28/19 Bundeskartellamt Decision (n 91), para 108.

93 Ibid 113; Case B6-32/15 Bundeskartellamt Decision (n 91), para 89.

94 Case B6-28/19 Bundeskartellamt Decision (n 91), para 115.

95 Ibid 123.

96 Christian Dohmen, *Rolle und Rechte der Fans bei Sportübertragungen* (Nomos 2024) 191, 192; Monopolkommission (n 90), para 383.

97 Case B6-28/19 Bundeskartellamt Decision (n 91), para 154.

98 Ibid 170–172; previously, the FCO had assumed a partial competitive relationship: Case B6-32/15 Bundeskartellamt Decision (n 91), para 90.

99 Monopolkommission (n 90), para 89.

100 Ralf Dewenter and Gordon J Klein, "Entscheidungspraxis des Bundeskartellamts im Bereich der Bundesliga-Übertragungsrechte" (2020) 71 ORDO 275, 284.

match.[101] The matches of the favoured team, eg on the first and last match days, are also not exchangeable, but complementary.[102] Therefore, from the perspective of such end consumers, each match must be a separate market. Only for consumers who are not committed to a particular team, all matches could be substitutable.[103] However, it can be argued that even these consumers care whether they are watching a match between two top teams competing for the championship or a match between two average teams.[104]

B. *Restriction of Competition*

38. When it comes to restrictions on competition, a distinction must be made between different provisions of the marketing model. On the one hand, there is the centralised selling model, through which media rights are bundled and exclusivity sold by the DFL. On the other hand, there is the granting of exclusive rights to media providers.

a) Centralised Selling

39. To determine whether there is a restriction of competition, the hypothetical situation in which there would be no exclusive centralised selling must be considered. However, there is legal uncertainty as to whether the individual DFL members and/or the DFL itself are the original (sole or joint) rights holders under German law. The FCO has not yet provided a definitive answer to this question, but – similar to the Munich Regional Court in the *FIS* case – assumes that at least the DFL members in whose stadiums the match takes place could market the games as co-owners of the rights.[105] At the same time, the FCO assumes that they are only partial competitors. With regard to the (hypothetical) selling of a club-related offer, the offers are not substitutable; only the offers of certain DFL members – eg the "top clubs" – could be in competition with each other.[106] When considering the selling of an individual match as part of the complete league product, the clubs would be competitors because a buyer seeking a complete league product would need to acquire all rights.[107] However, it is not a "classic horizontal competitive relationship" because the offerings are complementary.[108] Even if the FCO mitigates the severity of the restriction of competition, the centralised selling prevents competing offers by original rights holders.[109]

---

101 Ralf Dewenter, "Das Ende der No-Single-Buyer-Rule im Fußball" [2024] Wirtschaft und Wettbewerb 121; Monopolkommission (n 90), para 391; Heermann (n 85), 1578, 1579; Heermann (n 37), 885; Johannes Rottmann and Alexander Sand, "Die exklusive Zentralvermarktung der Bundesliga-Übertragungsrechte" (2024) 79 JuristenZeitung 11, 493; Fabian Ziermann, "Aligning Sports Market Definitions with Consumption Realities" (2025) SpuRt 552, 554; Heller, Sudaric and Winkler (n 88), 462, 463.

102 Dohmen (n 96), 206, 207.

103 Monopolkommission (n 90), para 391.

104 Dohmen, (n 96) 208.

105 Case B6-114/10 Bundeskartellamt Decision *Joint selling of media rights to matches of the German Bundesliga from the 2013/14 season onwards* (30 March 2012) paras 39, 40.

106 Ibid para 41.

107 Ibid paras 41, 42.

108 Ibid para 42.

109 Ibid para 43.

40. There are some contradictions in the FCO's arguments, as has already been pointed out in the literature. When defining the upstream market, the FCO assumes a single market comprising all games. This would mean that the original rights holders of individual games would also be competitors in this market.[110]

b) Exclusivity

41. The DFL's current selling model has exclusive effects in various ways. On the one hand, centralised selling, as such, is exclusive because it does not allow DFL members to make their own offers. However, in the FCO's view, this is not the main focus of the restrictive effect.[111] Instead, the FCO is increasingly focusing on the foreclosure of the downstream market. The DFL's dominant market position creates an incentive to offer media companies as much exclusivity as possible to achieve the highest possible fee, particularly to remain financially competitive with other leagues internationally.[112] For this reason, in 2016, the FCO considered it necessary to impose a *no-single-buyer rule*, according to which a purchaser was not allowed to acquire all live rights packages.[113] This assessment remained unchanged in 2020.[114] In 2024, the FCO abandoned this assessment because market conditions had changed.[115]

42. If all Bundesliga matches are part of a single market and are interchangeable, a no-single-buyer rule may prevent foreclosure and ensure competition. However, the FCO fails to recognise that, from the perspective of many end customers, each match is a separate market, meaning that the DFL continues to give media companies a monopoly position in these markets. The FCO's no-single-buyer rule was never able to change this because it did not apply to individual matches.[116] A specific Bundesliga match was and still is only available from one provider, meaning that end customers have no alternative.[117] This leads to a double monopoly mark-up, first at the upstream market and then at the downstream market – at the expense of the end consumer.[118]

c) Restriction by Object

43. The restrictions on competition imposed by the centralised selling model are by object, because the exclusive joint selling and exclusive granting of rights are designed to prevent competition.[119] In *Super League*, the ECJ found that the exclusive exploitation of all rights by UEFA and FIFA constituted a restriction

---

110 Dohmen (n 96), 218, 219.

111 Case B6-32/15 Bundeskartellamt Decision (n 91), para 108.

112 Case B6-28/19 Bundeskartellamt Decision (n 91), para 203; Case B6–32/15 Bundeskartellamt Decision (n 91), para 111.

113 Case B6-32/15 Bundeskartellamt Decision (n 91), paras 120, 121.

114 Case B6-28/19 Bundeskartellamt Decision (n 91), paras 201ff.

115 Case V/B 6 – 21/22 Bundeskartellamt Chairman letter *Joint selling of media rights to matches of the German Bundesliga from the season 2025/26 onwards* [26 February 2024] 5 <https://www.bundeskartellamt.de/SharedDocs/Publikation/DE/Pressemitteilungen/DFL_Medienrechte_Vorstitzendenschreiben.pdf?__blob=publicationFile&v=4> accessed 8 June 2026>.

116 See regarding the unsuitability of such rules, Heller, Sudaric and Winkler (n 88), 475.

117 Dohmen (n 96), 225.

118 Dewenter and Klein (n 100), 285; Dohmen (n 96), 226; Heermann (n 85), 1574; Rottmann and Sand (n 101), 495.

119 Dohmen (n 96), 241, 242; Rottmann and Sand (n 101), 297.

of competition by object.[120] According to the ECJ, this also rules out justification under the *Meca-Medina* doctrine.[121] Nevertheless, the FCO has so far assumed only restrictions of competitions by effect.[122]

C. *Exemption under Article 101(3) TFEU*

44. The possibility of an exemption under Article 101(3) TFEU is crucial for the competition law compliance of DFL's selling model. The FCO has so far assumed that it improves products as an efficiency advantage. This includes the offering of league-related rights packages, league-related products such as conference or highlight coverage, the predictability of league-related coverage and comprehensive exploitation and granting of all rights. No DFL member could offer these products on its own.[123] Furthermore, the FCO considers the competition restrictions to be essential for achieving these objectives: without centralised selling, the exploitation of league-related rights packages and comprehensive reporting on all matches would be made considerably more difficult.[124] It also assumes that the efficiencies would offset the disadvantages in the downstream market.[125] Thus, the minimum requirement for consumer participation is timely highlight coverage of the matches taking place on a match day on free-to-air television.[126] In the FCO's view, there is also no reason to assume that competition will be eliminated, as freely available highlight coverage limits the scope of purchasers of live rights through substitution-based competitive pressure. In addition, there is a transparent, non-discriminatory award procedure which does not create any significant barriers to market entry.[127]

45. This assessment by the FCO deserves criticism. Consumers may benefit from a centralised selling model, as it enables a league-wide product with comprehensive highlight coverage and live conferencing.[128] However, these efficiency gains do not require the rights of a single match to be granted exclusively to a single media company.[129] It only allows charging end consumers a higher price. Consumers are not compensated for this disadvantage.[130] Product quality would not suffer either and league-related offers would still be possible if a match could be viewed live on at least two providers.[131]

46. The FCO has only issued an unsatisfactory statement on this matter. It could "still tolerate" the games being awarded exclusively because this "currently seems to

---

120 *Super League* (n 3), para 230.

121 Dohmen (n 96), 247; Rottmann and Sand (n 101), 297.

122 Case B6-114/10 Bundeskartellamt Decision (n 105), para 36; with reference to *Super League*: Case V/B 6 – 21/22 Bundeskartellamt Chairman letter (n 115), 3. X

123 Case B6-32/15 Bundeskartellamt Decision (n 91), paras 139, 140.

124 Ibid 147–149; Case V/B 6 – 21/22 Bundeskartellamt Chairman letter (n 115), 5.

125 Case B6-28/19 Bundeskartellamt Decision (n 91), para 276.

126 Case V/B 6 – 21/22 Bundeskartellamt Chairman letter (n 115), 6.

127 Ibid 7.

128 Monopolkommission (n 90), para 444.

129 Heermann (n 85), 1578, 1579.

130 Dohmen (n 96), 298.

131 Heermann (n 85), 1578.

be the international standard".[132] It seems to fear that the DFL would otherwise generate too little revenue to remain competitive internationally. The Monopolies Commission considered it conceivable that higher revenues could at least improve the quality of sport.[133] However, there is no evidence that non-exclusive granting reduced sporting quality and competitiveness.[134] In view of the purposes of competition law, such an argument would also be doubtful. In other sectors of the economy, undertakings are also not allowed to form cartels simply to earn more money. In addition, exclusivity in the downstream market completely eliminates competition.[135] At least the FCO has announced that it will conduct a more detailed review in the event of negative market developments. It also refers to the ECJ's *Super League* ruling, according to which the extent of exclusivity is the decisive factor. So, there is still hope that the FCO could change its assessment. After all, the argument of international competitiveness could also be countered if the selling of media rights by football leagues were assessed equally under competition law across Europe.[136]

47. Regardless of this, the FCO considers horizontal and vertical revenue distribution to be a potential efficiency advantage – and explicitly links this to the *Super League* ruling. Horizontal revenue distribution among DFL clubs could be an efficiency advantage because the proper functioning of a competition depends on competitive balance and the promotion of young talent.[137] The vertical distribution of revenue to the DFB, in turn, serves to strengthen youth development and voluntary work in lower leagues, for example.[138] Unfortunately, the FCO leaves open the question of whether the objectives achieved could compensate for the competitive damage. At least, in the FCO's view, the 50+1 rule could ensure that stakeholder interests are considered.[139] However, it can be argued that club members are not equivalent to end consumers.[140]

48. As a result, a centralised selling model may qualify for an exemption under Article 101(3) TFEU insofar as it enables the creation of a league-related product. However, the exclusive granting of rights in the downstream market raises substantial doubts about whether it can genuinely satisfy the conditions for an exemption. The legal uncertainty surrounding the DFL's selling model – similar to the 50+1 rule – is due to the fact that the FCO has so far circumvented extensive investigations and market analyses by issuing only preliminary assessments and closing proceedings against commitments.[141]

---

132 Case V/B 6 – 21/22 Bundeskartellamt Chairman letter (n 115), 9.

133 Monopolkommission (n 90), para 492.

134 Dohmen (n 96), 296–298; Heermann (n 37), 936.

135 Dohmen (n 96), 329.

136 Monopolkommission (n 85), para 485.

137 Case V/B 6 – 21/22 Bundeskartellamt Chairman letter (n 115), 10.

138 Ibid 11.

139 Ibid 12.

140 Heermann (n 85), 1577.

141 With criticism: Monopolkommission (n 90), paras 471, 475.

IV. Conclusion

49. Even though German courts have already established case law, significant challenges persist at the interface between sport and competition law. This is particularly evident in proceedings such as those concerning the 50+1 rule, in which sports policy objectives encounter the realities of competition law. While the *Meca-Medina* doctrine may, in principle, ensure compliance with competition law, the 50+1 proceedings illustrate the difficulties inherent in specifying and applying its requirements to individual cases. The proceedings relating to the DFL's centralised selling of TV rights, as well as those concerning the advertising opportunities for Olympic athletes, further demonstrate how the economic interests of sports federations may conflict with those of fans and athletes.

Collective Sale of Football Media Rights in Portugal: Competition Law, Market Transformation and Investment Dynamics

Fernando Veiga Gomes and Maria João Melícias[*]
Abreu Advogados

I. Introduction and Scope

1. The football industry in Portugal has become a fertile ground for competition advocacy and enforcement initiatives in recent years. From the first antitrust investigation into a no-poach agreement between football clubs – thereby pioneering the current trend in Europe of applying competition rules to labour markets[1] – to sev-

---

* Fernando Veiga Gomes is Partner and Head of the Sports Law Practice at Abreu Advogados. Maria João Melícias is Partner and Co-Head of the Competition, Regulation and EU Practice at Abreu Advogados, former Commissioner of Portugal's Competition Authority and *référendaire* of the ECJ. The authors would like to acknowledge the excellent research work conducted for this article by Francisco da Cunha Moreira, trainee-lawyer at Abreu Advogados

1 In 2022, the AdC sanctioned an agreement among football clubs competing in the first and second professional leagues which, following unsuccessful negotiations between the clubs and the players' union, precluded the hiring of players who might seek to unilaterally terminate their employment contracts during the Covid-19 pandemic. Having regard to the relevant economic and legal context, the AdC classified the arrangement as a restriction of competition by object, on the grounds that it reduced player mobility, curtailed clubs' recruitment autonomy, and was liable to negatively affect both wage levels and competitive dynamics in the labour market. The Court of Justice of the European Union ruled on the case following a reference for a preliminary ruling. The Court of Justice of the European Union ruled on the case following a reference for a preliminary ruling. While

eral advocacy recommendations[2] that are shaping the legal and economic landscape in the sector, alongside commitments and merger prohibitions, the examples of the interplay between sports and competition law are abundant in the country.

2. This article focuses on the competition law and policy implications arising from the sale of football media rights. Following a recommendation issued in 2019 by Portugal's Competition Authority (Autoridade da Concorrência or (AdC)), subsequently transposed into law by the Portuguese Government through Decree-Law 22-B/2021, the commercialisation of football broadcasting rights in Portugal is undergoing a structural transformation – from a decentralised model, based on individual bilateral and multilateral agreements between clubs, telecommunications operators and distribution platforms, to a collective or centralised sales system.

3. Decree-Law 22-B/2021 mandates the collective selling of football media rights as from the 2028–2029 season, to be conducted through the competition organisers (Liga Portugal and the Football Federation). The specific terms and conditions of this collective selling, which is expected to take the form of a series of auctions, are to be self-regulated by the competition organisers and the clubs, subject to approval by the AdC. In the absence of agreement between the relevant stakeholders, Decree-Law 22-B/2021 provides that the commercialisation model shall be determined by law, following consultation with the AdC.

4. This is, therefore, a defining moment for Portuguese football. The design and implementation of the forthcoming auction process, together with the criteria for allocating the revenues thus obtained, between the clubs, will be instrumental in shaping the competitive landscape for years to come. The choices made regarding allocation mechanisms, the balance between exclusivity and accessibility, and the conditions governing market participation will have far-reaching consequences – not only for the market for audiovisual sports rights, but also for adjacent markets such as streaming platforms, telecommunications services and digital content distribution, not to mention the quality and sustainability of the Portuguese football league and its clubs. Understanding the regulatory foundations and competitive

confirming the nature of a no-poach agreement as a by-object restriction, the Court held that such an agreement might be justified in light of the relevant legal and economic context, including the specific nature of sport and the circumstances of the Covid-19 pandemic - an assessment ultimately falling within the remit of the national court. Notably, the Court did not address the fact that the agreement had been concluded unilaterally, following unsuccessful negotiations with the players' union, another key aspect of the legal and economic context. (Case C-133/24 *CD Tondela and Others* ECLI:EU:C:2026:361). AdC, Case PRC/2020/1 *Liga No-Poach* (2020) <https://extranet.concorrencia.pt/PesquisAdC/PRC_OR_INC_OR_PCC_Page.aspx?Ref=PRC_2020_1&isEnglish=False> accessed 18 May 2026.

2 In 2020, the Football Federation submitted to public consultation a draft regulation governing the women's football league, which included a salary cap on total wages payable to female athletes, supposedly to encourage new club entries in the wake of the pandemic - a restriction not imposed in any other league. The proposal prompted significant public criticism on grounds of discrimination. The AdC issued a recommendation advising the Federation that such a provision would amount to indirect price-fixing in the labour market, as salary caps constitute an indirect fixing of the purchase price of an input – namely labour – and are therefore incompatible with competition rules. The authority further stressed that sports associations, as associations of undertakings, must refrain from coordinating commercial conditions related to remuneration, given the risk of artificially harmonising costs across clubs and distorting competition. See AdC, "Studies, opinions and recommendations" (2020) <https://extranet.concorrencia.pt/PesquisAdC/EPR.aspx?IsEnglish=False&Ref=EPR_2020_19> accessed 18 May 2026.

dynamics underpinning this transition is essential to assessing the opportunities and risks that lie ahead.[3]

5. This article is structured as follows. First, it examines the role of broadcasting rights in modern sports and their significance for the financial sustainability of professional football. Second, it provides the necessary background by analysing the antitrust and merger control investigations that prompted the AdC's 2019 recommendation, including their underlying theories of harm. Third, it addresses the principal features of that recommendation, before turning to the structural drawbacks of an individualised commercialisation model, including the emerging investment dynamics associated with centralised media rights. Fourth, it assesses the competition risks inherent in a collective sales model and the key safeguards that should inform the competitive design of an auction process, drawing on established EU precedents. Fifth, it offers a comparative analysis of broadcasting rights sales models across major European football leagues, providing a broader perspective on the Portuguese transition. The article concludes with reflections on the way forward and the implications of the forthcoming auction for the competitive landscape.

II. The Role of Broadcasting Rights in Modern Sports

6. The commercialisation of sports broadcasting rights has become a central issue in both sports governance and competition law, particularly in markets where audiovisual rights represent the primary source of revenue for professional football competitions. The model through which these rights are marketed and distributed can significantly influence competitive dynamics between clubs, broadcasters and telecommunication operators, as well as the access to sports content by consumers.

7. In contemporary football, audiovisual rights represent a substantial share of clubs' revenues[4] and play a decisive role in shaping the financial sustainability of sports competitions, the competitive balance between teams, and the accessibility of sports content for fans. As a result, the legal and economic framework governing the sale and distribution of these rights has attracted increasing attention from regulators and competition authorities.

---

3 Paul Smith, Tom Evens and Petros Iosifidis, "The Next Big Match: Convergence, Competition and Sports Media Rights" (2016) 31(5) European Journal of Communication 536–550, 6: "in an increasingly converged media environment, premium sports rights remain as important, if not more important, than ever. In fact, the commercial strategies adopted by some of Europe's major telecommunications companies suggest that control of, or at the very least, guaranteed access to premium sports content has also become a key source of market power in the wider communications market beyond pay-TV", <https://openaccess.city.ac.uk/id/eprint/14867/3/EJC%20article%20-%202016.pdf > accessed 18 May 2026.

4 Quansah et al., "The Importance of Club Revenues for Player Salaries and Transfer Expenses – How Does the Coronavirus Outbreak (COVID-19) Impact the English Premier League?" (2021) 13(9) Sustainability 5154 <https://doi.org/10.3390/su13095154> accessed 18 May 2026. According to Urdaneta-Camacho et al., broadcasting revenue accounted for nearly 59% of total income for EPL clubs by 2019, Rudemarlyn Urdaneta-Camacho et al., "The Other Side of the "League of Stars': Analysis of the Financial Situation of Spanish Football" (2023) 11(1) IJFS 4 <https://www.mdpi.com/2227-7072/11/1/3> accessed 18 May 2026.

8. In Portugal, a decentralised marketing model has been established over the last two decades through direct agreements between clubs and telecoms operators or sports channels. One of the most significant examples occurred in 2015, when the telecommunications operator NOS signed long-term contracts with clubs such as Benfica and Sporting, in a comprehensive package valued at over €400 million, which included broadcasting rights and the exploitation of content associated with the clubs' channels.[5] At the same time, Altice secured significant rights with FC Porto, in a competitive move among operators that contributed to the fragmentation of the Portuguese football audiovisual market.[6] Both moves prompted antitrust investigations by the AdC, which are examined in more detail in the subsequent sections.

III. From Competition Enforcement to Ex-Ante Regulation of Football Media Rights

9. The structural limitations inherent in the decentralised sales model have given rise to an increasingly prominent debate regarding the need to reform the framework for the commercialisation of audiovisual rights in Portuguese professional football. This debate culminated in the adoption of Decree-Law 22-B/2021, which mandates the centralisation of the marketing of television and multimedia broadcasting rights for professional football competitions as from the 2028–2029 season. Under this legislative framework, the Portuguese Professional Football League and the Portuguese Football Federation are required to submit a centralised or collective sales model for prior approval by the AdC,[7] with the overarching objectives of maximising the commercial value of audiovisual rights and ensuring a more equitable distribution of revenue among participating clubs.

10. Critically, the legislative intervention embodied in Decree-Law 22-B/2021 did not emerge in a regulatory vacuum. Rather, it was the culmination of a series of antitrust enforcement actions and merger control proceedings conducted by the AdC over the preceding decade, which progressively revealed the structural and behavioural market challenges inherent in the decentralised model. These investigations – spanning abuse of dominance cases, assessments of long-term exclusivity arrangements, reciprocal rights-sharing agreements and common ownerships by vertically integrated players – exposed the extent to which the existing framework facilitated market foreclosure, entrenched incumbent positions and undermined the conditions for effective competition in the markets for premium sports content and downstream pay-for-TV services. Understanding the substance and rationale of these proceedings is essential to appreciating the foundations upon which the AdC's 2019 recommendations were built, as well as the competitive safeguards that must inform the design and implementation of the forthcoming centralised

---

5 "Benfica Sells Game Rights to NOS for 400 Million Euros" (*TSF*, 2 December 2015) <https://www.tsf.pt/desporto/artigo/benfica-vende-direitos-dos-jogos-a-nos-por-400-milhoes-de-euros/4912748> accessed 18 May 2026.

6 "FC Porto announces multi-million dollar deal" (*Renascenca*, 27 December 2015) <https://rr.pt/noticia/porto/2015/12/27/fc-porto-anuncia-acordo-milionario/42773/> accessed 18 May 2026.

7 Decree-Law No. 22-B/2021, art 5(1).

sales model. The following sections examine these investigations in greater detail, before turning to the content and implications of the 2019 recommendation itself.

1. Abuse of Dominance by the Leading Premium Sports Content Distribution Platform

11. In 2013, the AdC found that the leading distribution platform of premium sports content in Portugal, Sport TV, had abused its dominant position between 2005 and 2011 by imposing discriminatory and unfair contractual conditions on pay-for-TV operators. The authority imposed a fine of €3.7 million, subsequently reduced to €2.7 million on appeal.[8]

12. The case also reflected broader structural concerns regarding the competitive dynamics of the Portuguese pay-for-TV market, particularly the interplay between premium sports content and vertically integrated telecommunications operators.

2. Merger Prohibition of the "Triangle Operation"

13. In 2014, the AdC blocked a merger by which Sport TV's share capital would be divided between rival telecom operators NOS and PT, together with Sport TV's original shareholder, Controlinveste. The AdC concluded that the transaction would create significant impediments to effective competition in the markets for premium sports broadcasting rights, premium sports pay-for-TV channels, and downstream-related markets,[9] identifying concerns related to customer foreclosure, input foreclosure and coordinated effects.

3. Commitments Offered by Controlinveste in Relation to Exclusive Arrangements with Football Clubs

14. In 2015, following the opening of an antitrust investigation,[10] the AdC accepted commitments proposed by Controlinveste, Sport TV's main shareholder, to address the risks of market foreclosure arising from the excessive duration of exclusivity agreements between football clubs and the company. These commitments[11] included, in particular, the removal of preferential rights and the limitation of exclusivity clauses. Specifically, Controlinveste undertook not to include, in new agreements concerning the rights, any clauses granting a right of first refusal for subsequent sporting seasons, and not to enter into contracts establishing exclusivity periods exceeding three consecutive sporting seasons, including any renewals, amendments, or suspensions of their duration, thereby ensuring greater contractual flexibility and reducing barriers to market entry.

---

8 AdC, Case PRC/2010/2 *Sport TV Portugal SA* (2010) <https://extranet.concorrencia.pt/pesquisAdC/Page.aspx-?isEnglish=False&Ref=PRC_2010_2> accessed 18 May 2026.

9 See Adc, *Ccent. 4/2013 Controlinveste*ZON Optimus*PT /Sport TV*Sportinveste*PPTV* (2014) (in Portuguese) <https://www.concorrencia.pt/sites/default/files/processos/ccent/AdC-CCENT_2013_04-Decisao-VNC-final-net.pdf> accessed 18 May 2026.

10 AdC, Case PRC/2013/02 *Controlinveste Media* (2013) <https://www.concorrencia.pt/sites/default/files/processos_e_decisoes/prc/decisoes/AdC-PRC_2013_02-Decisao-VNC-final-net.pdf> accessed 18 May 2026.

11 Controlinveste Commitment Letter to the AdC (2015) <https://www.concorrencia.pt/sites/default/files/imported-media/ConsultaPublica_PRC201302_Anexo1.pdf > accessed 18 May 2026.

4. Antitrust Investigations into Exclusive Agreements and Minority Stakes in Leading Sports Media Platforms

15. The concerns surrounding the commercialisation of football broadcasting rights in Portugal were also notably addressed in the investigations conducted by the AdC into the duration and scope of the exclusive agreements concluded between clubs from the first and second professional leagues and the telecommunications operators Altice[12] and NOS,[13] respectively.

16. These arrangements were found to significantly foreclose the market for premium sports content, as they effectively rendered a substantial share of broadcasting rights unavailable for extended periods of time, thereby limiting access for potential new entrants.

17. In particular, NOS had acquired, on an exclusive basis, audiovisual and multimedia broadcasting rights for matches of at least 10 out of the 18 clubs competing in the 2018–2019 edition of the Primeira Liga, with most of these agreements taking effect in the 2019–2020 sporting season, as well as rights relating to certain clubs in the Segunda Liga. By contrast, the Altice group secured exclusive rights for at least five clubs in the Primeira Liga, with most of its agreements commencing earlier, in the 2018–2019 season. As a result, NOS was estimated to hold a market share of between 45% and 55% in the relevant market for the period 2019–2026, whereas Altice/PT was expected to hold a comparatively lower share, of between 25% and 35%, over the period 2018–2028.

18. There were notable parallels between these cases and the principles established in the *Coditel II* judgment, in which the Court of Justice of the European Union held that an exclusive right does not, in and of itself, constitute a restriction of competition. Rather, the Court emphasised that the compatibility of such exclusivity with EU competition law must be assessed by reference to its actual effects on the market, having regard to the relevant legal and economic context and the specific characteristics of the sector in question. In particular, the Court identified that restrictive effects may arise where exclusivity gives rise to artificial and unjustified barriers that are not required by the legitimate needs of the industry, or where it enables the possibility of charging financial consideration exceeding a fair return on the investment made. These considerations proved directly relevant to the assessment of the exclusive agreements concluded with Altice and NOS,[14] in which analogous concerns were identified.

19. However, additional concerns arose from the role of Sport TV, the leading premium sports content distribution platform, in which the key telecom market players – namely Altice, NOS and Vodafone – had in the meantime collectively acquired equal non-controlling stakes.

---

12 AdC, Case PRC/2016/3 *Altice Picture SARL* (2016) <https://extranet.concorrencia.pt/PesquisAdC/Page.aspx?IsEnglish=False&Ref=PRC_2016_3> accessed 18 May 2026.

13 AdC, Case PRC/2016/2 *NOS SGPS SA* (2016) <https://www.concorrencia.pt/sites/default/files/processos_e_decisoes/prc/decisoes/AdC-PRC_2016_02-Decisao-VNC-final-net.pdf> accessed 18 May 2026.

14 Case 262/81 *Coditel SA v Cine Vog Films SA (Coditel II)* ECLI:EU:C:1982:334 <https://eur-lex.europa.eu/legal-content/EN/TXT/PDF/?uri=CELEX:61981CJ0262> accessed 18 May 2026.

20. Given that Sport TV shareholders' agreement had been designed so as not to confer exclusive or joint control to any or all of the respective shareholders, the AdC assessed the arrangement not under merger control rules but under Article 101 of the Treaty on the Functioning of the European Union (TFEU) and the equivalent national provisions. The AdC found that this ownership structure not only reduced incentives for the telecom operators to compete directly in the acquisition of sports rights but also facilitated a degree of coordination across the value chain – from acquisition to distribution – ultimately weakening competitive pressure and softening price competition.

21. Since these same operators also held significant positions in downstream markets such as pay-for-TV and bundled telecommunications services, their ability and incentive to restrict or disadvantage new entrants became a central concern. The alignment of interests within the existing market structure contributed to preserving the status quo, limiting both entry and innovation.

5. Antitrust Investigation into the Reciprocal Rights-Sharing Agreement among Telecommunications Operators

22. A further relevant development was investigated by the AdC – the reciprocal rights-sharing agreement entered on 26 July 2016 between all telecommunications operators, namely Altice, MEO, NOS, Vodafone and NOWO.[15] The agreement provided for the reciprocal supply of premium sports content, notably broadcasting rights for matches of the Primeira Liga and Segunda Liga, following the prior acquisition of such rights by these operators from professional football clubs.

23. The case is particularly significant insofar as its scope extended beyond the upstream market for the acquisition of sports rights to encompass downstream retail markets, namely pay-for-TV services and bundled electronic communications offerings, in which the parties accounted for substantially the entirety of the market. The AdC found that the agreement could facilitate coordination between the parties, both by reducing incentives to compete for the acquisition of premium sports rights – given the cost-sharing mechanism and guaranteed access – and by potentially excluding third-party entrants, as well as softening competition in retail markets. As such, the arrangement was considered liable to weaken competitive dynamics across multiple levels of the value chain.

24. Despite the above competition concerns, the AdC concluded that said reciprocal rights-sharing agreement had been substantially emptied of its practical effect by the transfer to Sport TV of the majority of the broadcasting rights relating to the Primeira Liga and the Segunda Liga. This significantly limited the scope of the cost-sharing arrangements embodied in the agreement and, consequently, the potential anticompetitive effects arising therefrom. Nevertheless, subsequent changes in Sport TV's shareholder structure, mentioned above – namely the entry

---

15 AdC, Case PRC/2016/9 *Reciprocal Football Media Rights-Sharing Agreement* (2016) <https://www.concorrencia.pt/sites/default/files/processos_e_decisoes/prc/decisoes/AdC-PRC_2016_09-Decisao-VNC-final-net.pdf> accessed 18 May 2026.

of Vodafone in 2016 and Altice in 2017 – gave rise to additional competition concerns regarding the potential for coordination in the acquisition, exploitation, and distribution of broadcasting rights.

6. Conclusion

25. The AdC concluded that the competition concerns identified in the abovementioned investigations could not be effectively addressed through isolated antitrust interventions, such as reducing the duration of exclusivity clauses, and that a broader and more structural approach was required – an assessment that would later underpin its 2019 recommendation advocating for the collective sale of media rights as a means to enhance transparency, foster competition, and rebalance the market.

IV. Portugal's Competition Authority Recommendation on the Collective Selling of Football Broadcasting Rights

26. Against this background, in 2019 the AdC addressed a recommendation to the Portuguese Government advocating for legislative intervention[16] to regulate the commercialisation model for television and multimedia broadcasting rights relating to football matches of the Primeira Liga and Segunda Liga. The recommendation envisaged the collective selling of these rights through triennial auctions organised and administered by Portugal's Professional Football League (Liga Portugal) and the Football Federation.[17]

27. In support of its recommendation and building on the experience gathered in previous antitrust and merger investigations, the AdC identified structural and behavioural risks inherent to the decentralised model prevailing in Portugal. On the one hand, the long-term exclusive agreements concluded between clubs and major telecommunications groups, notably NOS and Altice, were found to create significant barriers to entry for potential competitors seeking to acquire premium sports content. The staggered expiration dates of these agreements compounded the difficulty of market entry, as prospective new entrants were unable to assemble a sufficiently broad portfolio of rights to develop a competitive sports channel capable of meeting consumer demand. On the other hand, coordination risks were identified as arising from the reciprocal rights-sharing arrangement between telecommunications operators and from a common ownership structure in the key content distribution platform, discussed above.

28. The AdC's recommendation placed particular emphasis on the inclusion of competition safeguards in the design of future auctions, notably the requirement

---

16 AdC "Recommendations on the Organisation and Sale of Football Broadcasting Rights" (2019) <https://www.concorrencia.pt/sites/default/files/processos/epr/Recomenda%C3%A7%C3%A3o%20relativa%20a%20altera%C3%A7%C3%B5es%20na%20comercializa%C3%A7%C3%A3o%20dos%20direitos%20de%20transmiss%C3%A3o%20televisiva%20e%20multim%C3%A9dia.pdf> accessed 18 May 2026.

17 See AdC, "AdC recomenda venda em leilão de direitos de transmissão televisiva dos jogos de futebol" (2019) <https://www.concorrencia.pt/sites/default/files/processos_e_decisoes/epr/2018/2019%2520-%2520Nota%2520explicativa%2520-%2520Recomendação%2520comercialização%2520dos%2520direitos%2520de%2520transmissão%2520televisiva%2520e%2520multimédia.pdf> accessed 18 May 2026.

to ensure the presence of at least two *independent* buyers and the prohibition of joint participation by vertically integrated operators active in both the commercialisation and distribution of broadcasting rights.

29. Considering the reluctance of the clubs to accept a collective selling model in Portugal to date, the AdC further found that a legislative intervention would be the most appropriate means to overcome this problem. More importantly, the envisaged regulatory framework should also determine the criteria underlying the distribution among the clubs of the revenue obtained from the collective auction of media rights.

V. The Drawbacks of an Individualised Commercialisation Model

30. The drawbacks of an individualised commercialisation model to the league competitiveness also underpinned the AdC's rationale. The AdC concluded that individual sales systems tend to generate greater financial disparities among clubs, as they channel a disproportionate share of revenues toward those with greater market power, thereby undermining competitive balance within the league.

31. From a competitive and economic perspective, individual negotiations tend to favour clubs with a larger fan base and greater media appeal, enabling them to secure significantly more lucrative contracts than other participants in the competition[18] and thereby contributing to a marked concentration of television revenue at the top of the competitive pyramid. Portugal is said to have one of the most polarised distributions of television revenue in Europe, with the top clubs capturing a disproportionately large share of income. In 2021, the ratio between the highest-earning and median club widened from 9x to 12x.[19]

32. Such concentration of revenue can produce significant structural effects on competitive balance. The economic literature on sport has consistently shown that uncertainty regarding the outcome of competitions is a central element of the economic value of professional leagues. When the distribution of revenue becomes excessively unequal, financially weaker clubs face greater difficulties in competing on the pitch, which in turn diminishes the overall appeal of the competition – a phenomenon often cited as one of the structural weaknesses of Portuguese football, particularly when compared with leagues that have adopted collective sales models and more balanced redistribution mechanisms.

33. Uncertainty as to the championship winner is crucial to the financial viability of a league, as greater unpredictability increases the perceived value of sporting competitions and strengthens fan engagement. In this regard, the relative

---

18 By way of example, in Spain, prior to the introduction of a centralised collective selling system in 2015, broadcasting rights were negotiated individually by clubs, resulting in a significant concentration of revenues, with Real Madrid and FC Barcelona earning substantially more than the remaining club. Urdaneta-Camacho et al (n 4).

19 UEFA, *The European Club Footballing Landscape 2022* (2022) 100 <https://editorial.uefa.com/resources/027e-1747424ecde1-af32c4128081-1000/ecfl_bm_report_2022_low_resolution_.pdf> accessed 18 May 2026.

strengthening of smaller clubs can be beneficial for overall competitive balance: it reduces dominance by a limited number of teams, introduces greater variability in results and enhances the unpredictability of the league. This, in turn, tends to increase audience interest, media value and commercial revenues, creating a virtuous cycle in which improved competitiveness generates higher financial returns for the league as a whole.[20]

34. Maintaining a sufficiently high degree of competitive balance is therefore not only desirable from a sporting perspective but also essential from an economic standpoint. Leagues characterised by the persistent dominance of a small number of clubs tend to experience declining outcome uncertainty and, consequently, diminishing consumer interest over time. By contrast, more balanced competitions – in which smaller clubs are able to challenge established teams on a more regular basis – tend to generate broader and more sustained audiences, increase the overall attractiveness of the league for broadcasters and sponsors, and enhance its long-term commercial viability. Redistributive mechanisms and structural reforms aimed at reducing financial disparities can thus play a central role in maximising both sporting integrity and economic performance.

35. Furthermore, the contractual fragmentation inherent in the decentralised model may reduce efficiency in the commercial exploitation of football broadcasting rights. Individual negotiation makes it difficult to assemble comprehensive and coherent broadcasting packages, thereby limiting collective bargaining power vis-a-vis television broadcasters and digital platforms. As a result, the commercial value of broadcasts may fall short of the potential that a centralised and structured offering would achieve.[21]

1. Investment Dynamics in Centralised Media Rights

36. The move toward centralisation also aimed to consolidate broadcasting rights under a single entity, thereby strengthening collective bargaining power and promoting a more balanced financial ecosystem across the league.[22]

37. Recent developments suggest that Liga Portugal is considering going a step further by selling a stake in the business unit responsible for managing and commercialising

---

20 Pedro Garcia-del-Barrio and James J Reade, "Does Certainty on the Winner Diminish the Interest in Sport Competitions? The Case of Formula One" (2022) 63 Empirical Economics 1059–1079 <https://link.springer.com/article/10.1007/s00181-021-02147-8> accessed 18 May 2026: "Uncertainty of outcome is a major factor explaining the interest in sporting competitions and their financial success."

21 According to key stakeholders, under an individual marketing model, annual broadcasting revenues in Portugal would tend to remain between €150 and €170 million, figures significantly lower than those estimated under a joint (centralised) sales scenario, where revenues could range between €275 and €325 million annually (see interview by Rui Caeiro, the executive director of Liga Portugal, in Pedro Castro Alves and Eduardo Soares da Silva, "How Will the Money from the Centralization Be Divided? Half Is "Distributed Equally"" (*Renascenca*, 11 January 2024) <https://rr.pt/bola-branca/especial/futebol-nacional/2024/01/11/como-sera-dividido-o-dinheiro-da-centralizacao-metade-e-distribuido-de-forma-igualitaria/362183/> accessed 18 May 2026).

22 "Liga Portugal Prepares to Sell Part of the Company Holding Television Rights" (*SAPO*, 9 March 2026) <https://eco.sapo.pt/2026/03/09/liga-portugal-prepara-venda-de-parte-da-empresa-dos-direitos-televisivos/> accessed 18 May 2026.

these centralised media rights.[23] Such a move would effectively open the door to external investors – including private equity firms, media conglomerates and global streaming platforms – that are increasingly seeking access to premium live sports content. The reported interest from seven potential buyers underscores the growing attractiveness of Portuguese football as a scalable and monetisable media product in an increasingly competitive global market.

38. The entry of external investors could have several important implications. First, it may provide an immediate injection of capital, enabling the league to modernise its commercial operations, invest in digital infrastructure, and enhance the overall quality of its broadcasting product. Second, it could accelerate international expansion efforts, helping Portuguese football to reach new audiences and strengthen its global footprint.

39. At the same time, this strategy raises important questions regarding governance, long-term control and revenue distribution. The involvement of private investors typically brings a strong focus on profitability and return on investment, which may influence strategic decisions in ways that do not always align with sporting priorities. Ensuring that clubs retain sufficient influence over key decisions may therefore be crucial to maintaining the integrity and competitive balance of the league.

VI. Joint Sales of Sports Broadcasting Rights: Competition Risks and Safeguards under EU law

40. From a policy perspective, the joint commercialisation of broadcasting rights presents significant advantages but also gives rise to material competition risks that must be carefully managed.

41. As discussed above, collective selling enhances the bargaining power of clubs by enabling the aggregation of rights into commercially attractive packages, thereby increasing their overall market value. It also facilitates the redistribution of revenues among participating clubs according to predefined criteria, contributing to greater competitive balance within the league and improving the overall quality and unpredictability of sporting competitions.

42. Moreover, centralised sales may lower barriers to entry for broadcasters by enabling them to compete for clearly defined bundles of rights at regular intervals. This structure can foster innovation in distribution methods – including digital streaming services – while providing consumers with more comprehensive access to sports content through fewer subscriptions.

43. However, the centralisation of rights may also diminish competitive pressure in the upstream market for broadcasting rights if not accompanied by appropriate structural and procedural safeguards.

---

23 A comparable model can be found in Spain, where La Liga entered into a landmark agreement in 2021 with the private equity firm CVC Capital Partners. Under the deal, CVC invested approximately €2.7 billion in exchange for a stake of around 8% in a newly created commercial entity responsible for managing La Liga's media rights and related business activities. Jasper Jolly, "Spain's La Liga Agrees €2.7bn Deal with Private Equity Firm CVC" *The Guardian* (4 August 2021) <https://www.theguardian.com/football/2021/aug/04/spains-la-liga-agrees-27bn-deal-with-private-equity-firm-cvc> accessed 18 May 2026.

44. In this respect, the 2003 decision of the European Commission concerning the UEFA Champions League[24] established a set of foundational principles for the regulation of sports broadcasting rights markets, which were subsequently reflected in the AdC's 2019 recommendations.

45. In that case, the Commission examined UEFA's centralised marketing of media rights for the Champions League. While acknowledging that such an arrangement, in principle, restricts competition under Article 101(1) TFEU – by replacing individual club sales with a single selling entity – the Commission ultimately accepted this under Article 101(3) TFEU. The exemption was granted on the basis that the arrangement generates significant efficiencies, including the creation of a more attractive and coherent media product and a reduction in transaction costs.

46. Crucially, the decision was subject to conditions designed to limit potential anti-competitive effects. These included, inter alia, the requirement for transparent and non-discriminatory allocation procedures, the division of rights into several distinct packages and the imposition of limits on the duration of exclusive contracts – typically restricted to three-year cycles – thereby enhancing market contestability and facilitating periodic re-entry by competing operators. The decision further emphasised the need to ensure effective competition through the presence of multiple buyers and the prevention of excessive concentration, notably through the application of a "no single buyer" principle. It also encouraged the efficient exploitation of rights, including the possibility of reallocating unused rights to prevent output restrictions.

47. The principal remedies underpinning the clearance of the collective sale of television broadcasting rights for football matches, as established by this decision, may be summarised as follows:

- *Partial unbundling*: television broadcasting rights must be divided into at least two balanced and commercially meaningful packages;
- *No single buyer*: the packages must be awarded to different broadcasters so as to prevent monopolistic concentration and promote competition among distributors;
- *Competitive tendering*: the bidding process must be non-discriminatory and transparent, affording all potential buyers an equal opportunity to compete for each package;
- *Sunsetting*: contract duration must be limited and may not be extended automatically. Current European Commission practice in football requires that contract duration should not exceed three years;
- *Use it or lose it*: a fallback mechanism to remedy potential output restrictions, whereby unused rights revert to the individual clubs for parallel, competitive exploitation;
- *Trustee supervision*: an independent trustee must oversee the tender procedure to ensure compliance with the applicable conditions.[25]

---

24 Case AT.37398 European Commission Decision *UEFA Champions League – Joint selling of the commercial rights* (23 July 2003) <https://eur-lex.europa.eu/legal-content/EN/TXT/?uri=CELEX%3A32003D0778>accessed 18 May 2026.

25 Budzinski et al., as cited in David Henriques, "A Combinatorial Auction to Sell TV Broadcasting Rights in League Sports" (2023) 47(6) Telecommunications Policy 102539 <https://www.sciencedirect.com/science/article/abs/pii/S0308596123000502> accessed 18 May 2026.

48. The significance of this decision extends well beyond UEFA competitions, as it effectively established the analytical framework subsequently applied to domestic leagues across Europe. It confirmed that collective selling is not inherently incompatible with EU competition law, provided that it is proportionate and accompanied by mechanisms that preserve a sufficient degree of market openness and ensure fair revenue distribution.

49. The decision has been repeatedly invoked to justify national reforms introducing centralised rights commercialisation. More broadly, it underpins the regulatory balance between competition law and the specificities of sport, legitimising collective arrangements where they contribute to competitive balance, solidarity and the overall sustainability of professional football.

50. In sum, the regulation of sports broadcasting rights demands a careful equilibrium between promoting efficiency and safeguarding competition. While centralised commercialisation models can yield significant economic and sporting benefits, their implementation must be accompanied by robust competition law oversight and carefully calibrated auction design to prevent market foreclosure and ensure that broadcasters, clubs and consumers alike benefit from a competitive and transparent marketplace.

VII. A Comparative Analysis of Sales Models across European Football Leagues

51. Most major European football leagues market their broadcasting rights collectively through the competition organiser. In Germany, for example, the rights to the Bundesliga are sold centrally by the Deutsche Fußball Liga through periodic auctions supervised by the Bundeskartellamt.[26] Historically, these auctions incorporated a "no single buyer" rule designed to prevent any one broadcaster from acquiring all live broadcasting packages, thereby preserving competition among distributors. The inclusion of such mechanisms in sports media rights markets has also been examined in the competition policy literature, with the OECD noting that certain regulatory conditions have been applied within the European Union to mitigate potential anticompetitive risks associated with the collective sale of football broadcasting rights.[27]

---

26 Bundeskartellamt, Press Release, "Conclusion of Proceeding on DFL's Joint Selling of Media Rights: Bundeskartellamt Tolerates DFL's Marketing Model" (26 February 2024) <https://www.bundeskartellamt.de/SharedDocs/Meldung/EN/Pressemitteilungen/2024/26_02_2024_DFL_Medienrechte.html> accessed 18 May 2026.

27 In the European Union, the collective selling of sports broadcasting rights (particularly regarding football) has also been permitted if a set of conditions are fulfilled: (i) limited duration of exclusive contracts (typically three seasons); (ii) partial unbundling and no-single-buyer rule (division of broadcasting rights into a number of separate packages to be sold to different broadcasters, including as regards traditional broadcasting and online streaming); (iii) transparent and non-discriminatory competitive bidding process to sell the rights, with trustee supervision; (iv) fall-back clause (unused rights must fall back to the individual clubs for parallel, competitive exploitation; if the club's home match is not covered by a live package, the club must have the right to individually sell the corresponding broadcasting right). These remedies were first designed in three leading cases in the 2000s and since then have been followed by national competition authorities in local cases, albeit not always in a systematic way." OECD, "Competition and Professional Sports" (4 December 2023) Roundtable on Competition Policy Papers, No 2 (Background Note) <https://one.oecd.org/document/DAF/COMP/WP2(2019)3/en/pdf#:~:text=Independent%20sector%20regulators%20and%20competition,direct%20co-operation%20a%20challenge> accessed 18 May 2026.

52. More recently, however, regulatory authorities have introduced greater flexibility by permitting the possibility, depending on the auction outcome, that a single operator may acquire multiple packages. In Germany, for instance, the Bundeskartellamt accepted that the media rights tender organised by the Deutsche Fußball Liga for the Bundesliga may proceed without a mandatory "no single buyer" rule, meaning that a single broadcaster could potentially acquire all live packages depending on the bids submitted. From a competition law perspective, this flexibility reflects the assessment that the audiovisual market has become sufficiently competitive – owing to the emergence of new distribution platforms – to reduce the risk that the acquisition of multiple packages by a single broadcaster would lead to durable foreclosure of rival operators.[28]

53. In contrast to the German model, the English framework – centred on the Premier League – is widely regarded as one of the most commercially successful examples of centralised broadcasting rights commercialisation. In this regard, the *Murphy* judgment[29] played a key role in shaping the legal boundaries within which collective selling arrangements may operate under EU law, by clarifying the extent to which exclusivity clauses must remain compatible with internal market principles. Specifically, the Court of Justice held that, while the collective selling of sports broadcasting rights is in principle compatible with EU law, it cannot rely on absolute territorial exclusivity that partitions the internal market and prevents cross-border competition. Contractual mechanisms designed to ensure national exclusivity cannot go so far as to eliminate the possibility of cross-border access to services within the EU, thereby reinforcing the principle that the commercial organisation of broadcasting rights must remain consistent with fundamental internal market freedoms, even in the context of centralised rights sales.

54. The English distribution mechanism combines equal shares – constituting a significant portion of total revenue – with merit-based payments linked to league position and facility fees determined by the number of televised matches. This structure enables even lower-ranked clubs to secure substantial revenues, thereby enhancing overall league competitiveness. The audiovisual rights to the Premier League are sold collectively through auctions held every three years, with the current 2025–2029 cycle divided into several packages and subject to limits on the number that a single operator may acquire – a mechanism designed to maintain competition while ensuring that multiple broadcasters can participate in the market.[30] Nevertheless, the financial gap between the Premier League and lower divisions remains pronounced, and ongoing regulatory scrutiny continues to shape how collective selling practices align with competition law.

---

28 Bundeskartellamt, Press Release (n 26).

29 *Football Association Premier League v Murphy* concerned the use of foreign decoder cards to access Premier League broadcasts and led the Court of Justice of the European Union to rule that absolute territorial exclusivity in broadcasting agreements infringes EU law, particularly the principle of the free movement of services. See Joined Cases C-403/08 and C-429/08 *Football Association Premier League Ltd v QC Leisure* ECLI:EU:C:2011:631 <https://eur-lex.europa.eu/legal-content/EN/TXT/PDF/?uri=CELEX:62008CJ0403> accessed 18 May 2026.

30 "Premier League Issues Invitations to Tender for UK Audio-Visual Rights" (*Premier League*, 18 October 2023) <https://www.premierleague.com/en/news/3741409> accessed 18 May 2026.

55. In Spain, the shift toward centralised audiovisual rights commercialisation was formalised through Royal Decree-Law 5/2015,[31] which fundamentally restructured a market that had previously been dominated by individual club negotiations. Under this regime, La Liga sells broadcasting rights collectively, with revenues distributed according to a hybrid model that combines equal sharing, sporting performance and social impact criteria such as audience reach. This approach has significantly reduced the financial gap between clubs compared to the earlier system, although notable disparities persist, particularly with respect to top clubs such as Real Madrid and FC Barcelona.

VIII. Conclusion: How Today's Auction Will Shape Tomorrow's Competitive Landscape

56. The centralisation of media rights in Portuguese football, prompted by the AdC's 2019 recommendation and mandated by Decree-Law 22-B/2021 as from the 2028–2029 season, marks a structural shift from a fragmented, club-driven model to a coordinated and redistributive framework. Far more than a technical reorganisation, this transition will reshape competitive dynamics across the markets for audiovisual sports rights, streaming platforms, telecommunications services and digital content distribution.

57. At this critical juncture, the design of the forthcoming auction process will play a decisive role in shaping the future landscape. The choices made regarding allocation mechanisms, exclusivity, accessibility and conditions of market participation will determine whether centralisation delivers on its promise of enhanced competition and more equitable revenue distribution – or merely replicates existing imbalances under a new institutional arrangement.[32]

58. The stakes extend well beyond revenue maximisation. The chosen model will directly affect competitive balance within Portuguese football, with lasting implications for sporting integrity and the league's – and clubs' – financial sustainability. Liga Portugal has already submitted the proposed regulatory framework governing the auction process and revenue distribution for the AdC's approval, and the review is currently ongoing.

59. This is a defining moment. Portugal currently exhibits one of the most unequal distributions of audiovisual revenues in European football.[33] The forthcoming

---

[31] The sale of television rights is the main source of revenue in Spanish football, representing on average 63% of the total revenue of the teams in the sample for the 2016–2017 season and an item that has been gradually increasing in both amount and relative importance. This is largely due to the implementation of Real Decreto-ley 5 (2015) that centralised the sale of television rights. This allowed revenues to rise from €826 million in the 2013–2014 season to more than €1.4 billion in the 2016–2017 season (CSD 2020). Again, it is worth noting, the great heterogeneity in the situation of the clubs regards the percentage that this item represents, ranging from less than 38% of the revenues of Real Madrid, F.C. Barcelona and Atlético de Madrid, to more than 80% in the case of Osasuna, Huesca, Leganés and Eibar. The median is 69%, indicating that most clubs are concentrated in an above-average situation. Urdaneta-Camacho et al (n 4), 8.

[32] Smith, Evens and Iosifidis (n 3), 6

[33] Nuno Travassos, "TV Rights: Portugal Has the "Most Polarized" Distribution in Europe" (*A BOLA*, 26 February 2026) <https://www.abola.pt/noticias/direitos-tv-portugal-tem-a-distribuicao-mais-polarizada-da-europa-2026022618121575619?srsltid=AfmBOoqxd_svd_ShP8BeZm2RNuYHqXuY4FOr3wcT9TlMsh-CXsfZK8yp> accessed 18 May 2026.

centralised model has already attracted multiple bidders and will be executed through a series of auctions whose outcome will be decisive. The regulatory and market choices made now will set the trajectory for years to come – determining whether centralisation becomes a catalyst for a more competitive and equitable ecosystem, or a missed opportunity with lasting structural consequences.

Sports and U.S. Antitrust Law

Ryan Lipes[*]
Global Sports Advocates – Washington, D.C., USA

I. Introduction

1. Antitrust law has long played a central but uneasy role in shaping organized sports in the United States. From the earliest days of professional leagues to the modern era of global media rights and athlete mobility, courts have been asked to reconcile the cooperative features inherent in sports with the competitive principles that animate federal antitrust law. Unlike most industries, sports require a degree of coordination among competitors to produce the product. Yet that necessity has repeatedly tested the boundary between permissible collaboration and unlawful restraint of trade.

2. This tension has produced a distinctive body of antitrust doctrine. Professional sports leagues have sought protection through claims of single-entity status, judicially created exemptions, statutory carveouts, and labor law immunities. Athletes, rival leagues, team owners, promoters, and consumers, in turn, have invoked antitrust law to challenge restraints on wages, mobility, market entry, and competition. The resulting case law reflects neither wholesale deference to sports leagues nor full assimilation into ordinary antitrust analysis.

3. This chapter traces how antitrust law continues to reshape American sports. Section II outlines the basic antitrust framework in the United States, focusing on Sections 1 and 2 of the Sherman Act and the private-enforcement regime created by the Clayton Act. Section III examines the major exemptions and immunities that

---

[*] Ryan Lipes is Counsel at Global Sports Advocates, headquartered in Portland, Maine, USA, where he represents athletes and sports bodies in sporting disputes and litigation. Previously, he worked for the U.S. Department of Justice and the Manhattan District Attorney's Office. Ryan resides in the Washington, D.C. area.

distinguish sports from other industries, including baseball's anomalous antitrust exemption, as well as the Sports Broadcasting Act, implied immunity for Olympic organizations, and the non-statutory labor exemption. Section IV turns to the courts' role in applying antitrust law to league governance, labor markets, rival leagues, and international sports federations.

4. The chapter concludes by focusing on the most consequential antitrust battleground today: collegiate athletics. A series of lawsuits against the National Collegiate Athletic Association (NCAA) has dismantled long-standing assumptions about amateurism and accelerated a transition toward direct athlete compensation. These cases do not merely refine existing doctrine; they challenge the economic foundations of college sports and raise fundamental questions about the future regulation of athlete labor markets.

5. Taken together, the evolution of sports antitrust law in the United States reveals a broader trend: as sports become more commercialized and centralized, courts are increasingly unwilling to exempt them from the ordinary demands of antitrust law.

II. The Antitrust Framework in the United States

6. Antitrust law in the United States is primarily governed by two statutes: the Sherman Antitrust Act of 1890 and the Clayton Act of 1914. These laws apply broadly to commercial activity in the United States, including to sports.

1. The Sherman Antitrust Act

7. The Sherman Antitrust Act of 1890 is the foundation of U.S. competition law. The first two sections of the Sherman Act govern most antitrust litigation. Broadly speaking, Section 1 prohibits agreements to restrain trade, while Section 2 prohibits monopolization.[2] Over 130 years later, the Sherman Act continues to play a leading role in American sports litigation.

A. *Section 1*

8. Section 1 of the Sherman Act prohibits contracts, combinations, and conspiracies that restrain trade.[3] But not every "restraint on trade" is illegal. Rather, only unreasonable restraints on trade violate the Sherman Act. Some types of conduct, which courts have determined "always or almost always" restrict competition, are *per se* violations.[4] *Per se* violations, including price fixing, geographical allocation by direct competitors, and group boycotts, are unlawful and do not require proof of actual competitive harm beyond the existence of the violation. For that reason, antitrust plaintiffs prefer pursuing *per se* violations when possible. Yet courts have largely avoided finding *per se* violations in major sports-related antitrust litigation.[5]

---

2. *See* 15 U.S.C. §§ 1–2.
3. *Id.* at § 1.
4. *See* Broadcast Music v. CBS, 441 U.S. 1, 19–20 (1979).
5. For example, in National Collegiate Athletic Association (NCAA) v. Board of Regents, 468 U.S. 85 (1984), the Supreme Court found it inappropriate to apply *per se* rules to the NCAA's television broadcast agreement, despite recognizing that it was a horizontal price-fixing agreement that is "ordinarily condemned as a matter of law under an "illegal *per se*" approach[.]"

9. Outside of *per se* violations, however, courts apply the "rule of reason" to determine whether a challenged restraint, on balance, harms competition, weighing anticompetitive effects against legitimate pro-competitive justifications.[6] How the rule of reason applies to sports leagues – which necessarily require some amount of collusion amongst teams to promote a sport – has been a source of consistent litigation (discussed in Section IV).

10. Whether Section 1 of the Sherman Act even applies to sports leagues has not always been a clear question. Because Section 1 applies to contracts, combinations, and conspiracies, it necessarily takes at least two actors to violate Section 1, as a single entity cannot conspire with itself or a wholly controlled subsidiary.[7] This so-called "single entity" defense, if successful, thus eliminates one of the largest classes of antitrust litigation.

11. How sports leagues fit into this paradigm has been a puzzle (and source of litigation) for decades. In some cases, the "single entity" defense carries intuitive appeal, as sports leagues often function as unified enterprises that collectively establish rules and promote their sport. On the other hand, individual teams and clubs often have separate ownership and economic incentives from the league, that can undercut the "single entity" argument.

12. Starting in the 1990s, professional sports leagues and antitrust plaintiffs argued extensively about whether a league can be a "single entity." Due to complex league and team ownership structures, courts struggled to determine when a league acts as a single entity for antitrust purposes. In a long-running lawsuit between the Chicago Bulls and the National Basketball Association (NBA) over the NBA's broadcasting rules, the U.S. Court of Appeals for the Seventh Circuit held that the NBA was "closer to a single firm" when "acting in the broadcast market."[8]

13. Six years later, another federal circuit confronted whether Major League Soccer (MLS) constitutes a "single entity." Shortly after its formation, MLS became embroiled in a class-action lawsuit with the U.S. Soccer Federation. A group of players brought claims under both the Sherman Act and Clayton Act relating to MLS's control over players and salaries.[9] MLS's structure differed from the NBA,

---

[6] The rule of reason first came about in Standard Oil Co. of New Jersey v. United States, 221 U.S. 1 (1911). Since then, the rule of reason has developed into a specific burden-shifting framework that has guided many recent sports antitrust cases. The analysis proceeds in three steps. The plaintiff bears the initial burden of showing that the challenged restraint has a substantial anticompetitive effect in a relevant market. If that burden is met, the burden shifts to the defendant to demonstrate procompetitive justifications. If the defendant makes that showing, the plaintiff must demonstrate that the restraint is not reasonably necessary to achieve those procompetitive benefits; in other words, that the same objectives could be achieved through less restrictive means. *See* Ohio v. Am. Express Co., 585 U.S. 529, 540–41 (2018); NCAA v. Alston, 594 U.S. 69, 97–98 (2021).

[7] In Copperweld Corp. v. Independence Tube Corp., 467 U.S. 752 (1984), the U.S. Supreme Court held that a corporation and its wholly owned subsidiary are a "single entity," and a single entity cannot conspire with itself.

[8] *See* Chicago Prof'l Sports Ltd. P'ship v. Nat'l Basketball Ass'n, 95 F.3d 593, 600 (7th Cir. 1996).

[9] *See* Fraser v. Major League Soccer, 284 F.3d 47 (1st Cir. 2002). The players agreed to dismiss U.S. Soccer from this case after U.S. Soccer agreed not to "impose, implement or enforce" FIFA's regulations "relating to payment of transfer fees or training and development fees." For that reason, U.S. Soccer operated outside FIFA's training compensation and solidarity fees payment system for decades. That came to an end after several youth soccer clubs filed a lawsuit challenging this decision and sought payment under FIFA's rules. *See* Dallas Texans Soccer Club v. Major League Soccer Players Union, 247 F. Supp. 3d 784 (E.D. Tex. 2017). The lawsuit was dismissed for jurisdictional reasons, *see id.*, but it led to MLS announcing that it was joining the global training compensation and transfer fee system.

as the league retained centralized control and ownership over both the league and its teams. All players even signed contracts with the league and not the individual teams. Investors both had a controlling stake in the league and shared league profits, while individual investors had some control over teams. The District Court found that, for antitrust purposes, MLS operated as a "single entity" and dismissed the Section 1 count under the Sherman Act. A jury later ruled for MLS on the Section 2 monopolization claim. The Court of Appeals affirmed the result, but not before casting doubt on whether MLS was actually a single entity, calling it a "hybrid arrangement somewhere between a single company … and a cooperative arrangement between existing competitors."[10]

14. The Supreme Court finally addressed the "single entity" question in *American Needle v. National Football League (NFL).*[11] The case arose after the NFL granted Reebok, rather than American Needle, an exclusive license to produce NFL-branded headwear. The NFL argued that it fell outside Section 1's scope because its teams collectively owned brand licensing rights, which constituted conduct by a single entity. The Supreme Court rejected the argument, holding that Section 1 applies whenever separate economic actors, pursuing distinct economic interests, coordinate in ways that restrain trade. The NFL teams, the Court reasoned, were independent firms that competed against each other for players, coaches, merchandise sales, and fan loyalty. Those separate economic interests did not vanish simply because teams had acted collectively through the league. Although the Court recognized that some degree of cooperation is necessary to produce the league's product, that necessity did not immunize all league decisions from antitrust scrutiny. Instead, it requires that such restraints be evaluated for reasonableness.

15. The holding of *American Needle* means most sports leagues are not categorically "single entities" that fall outside Section 1's scope. While sports leagues have continued to argue the "single entity" defense post-*American Needle*, the decision made clear that the test is not organizational form but economic reality: do the actors retain independent economic interests that the challenged conduct suppresses? Where they do, Section 1 applies.

B. *Section 2*

16. Section 2 of the Sherman Act prohibits monopolization, attempted monopolization, and conspiracy to monopolize.[12] Simply being a big business, even one with monopoly power, is not enough to show monopolization. To prevail on a Section 2 monopolization claim, the plaintiff must prove both monopoly power in a relevant market and exclusionary conduct. In other words, gaining monopoly power from a "superior product, business acumen, or historic accident" is not enough.[13]

---

[10] *See Fraser* 284 F.3d 47, at 58. At the time of *Fraser*, MLS players were not unionized and had no collective bargaining agreement in place. The MLS quickly recognized the MLS Players Union (now the MLS Players Association), so the issues in *Fraser* would today likely be protected by the non-statutory labor exemption discussed in Section III.D.

[11] Am. Needle v. Nat'l Football League, 560 U.S. 183 (2010).

[12] 15 U.S.C. § 2.

[13] *See* United States v. Grinnell Corp., 384 U.S. 563 (1966).

The "single entity" defense discussed in relation to Section 1 of the Act does not apply to Section 2 claims, as Section 2 claims involve unilateral business conduct. For that reason (as discussed in Section IV below) Section 2 claims have been the focus of much recent sports litigation by professional athletes in individual sports (including golf, tennis, and mixed martial arts) against league governing bodies.

2. The Clayton Act of 1914

17. The Clayton Act of 1914 expanded U.S. antitrust law in two important ways. First, it restricted mergers and acquisitions that "substantially ... lessen competition" or tended "to create a monopoly."[14] While mergers and acquisitions are not the focus of this chapter, some sports-related mergers have been the focus of antitrust scrutiny.[15] Second, it empowered and incentivized private parties to pursue antitrust litigation by authorizing private plaintiffs to sue for treble damages (three times the actual loss) plus attorney's fees.[16] The Clayton Act thus provides powerful financial incentives for both plaintiffs and their lawyers to pursue antitrust claims. While the U.S. government retains its own antitrust enforcement power,[17] this private right of action drives U.S. antitrust litigation in sports.

III. The Major Sports Exemptions

18. Although the Sherman Act and Clayton Act apply broadly to commercial activity in the United States, sports are subject to several distinctive statutory and judicially created antitrust exemptions. Four major exemptions govern the sports industry today. The first is a judicially created exemption for Major League Baseball (MLB). The second, the Sports Broadcasting Act of 1961, exempts from antitrust scrutiny a professional league's collective negotiation of TV broadcast rights. The third is an implied immunity for the U.S. Olympic and Paralympic Committee (USOPC) and the sport National Governing Bodies (NGBs) under the USOPC's authority.

19. The final exemption, the non-statutory labor exemption, is a judicially created compromise between antitrust and labor law that exempts most collectively bargained employment terms from antitrust scrutiny. Given collective bargaining's prevalence in American professional sports, the labor exemption serves as a massive protection for professional sports leagues from antitrust scrutiny.

---

14 15 U.S.C. § 18.

15 For example, antitrust scrutiny has surrounded the proposed merger between PGA and LIV Golf. Likewise, in 2017, the Federal Trade Commission moved to block the merger of sports betting platforms FanDuel and DraftKings, a merger which the companies ultimately abandoned. *See In the Matter of DraftKings, Inc./FanDuel Limited*, FTC Dkt. No. 9375, https://www.ftc.gov/legal-library/browse/cases-proceedings/161-0174-draftkings-inc-fanduel-limited-matter.

16 15 U.S.C. § 15.

17 In the United States, the Federal Trade Commission and the Antitrust Division of the U.S. Department of Justice split enforcement power over civil antitrust enforcement. The U.S. Department of Justice has exclusive power over criminal antitrust enforcement. In addition to the federal government, many states have their own antitrust and competition laws.

1. The Baseball Exemption

20. Since 1922, professional baseball in the United States has enjoyed a special status under antitrust laws. In *Federal Baseball Club of Baltimore v. National League*, the U.S. Supreme Court held unanimously that the Sherman Act did not apply to what is now Major League Baseball.[18]

21. The case arose when the Federal Baseball Club of Baltimore, Maryland, filed an antitrust lawsuit under the Sherman Act against the two then-existing national baseball leagues. At trial, the Federal Baseball Club prevailed, obtaining an $80,000 judgment which was trebled under the Clayton Act to $240,000.[19] The Supreme Court, however, rejected application of the Sherman Act to baseball. Even though baseball teams traveled frequently across state lines for competition (even in 1922), the Supreme Court held that the "business is giving exhibits of baseball, which are purely state affairs."[20] By judicial decree, professional baseball did not involve the interstate commerce necessary to trigger the Sherman Act.

22. *Federal Baseball* is an anomalous exception, both for sports leagues under U.S. antitrust law and for how the Supreme Court analyzes interstate commerce.[21] The decision has been routinely criticized by courts and commentators alike. Today, *Federal Baseball*'s logic is incomprehensible: baseball "exhibitions" are a multibillion-dollar industry, and games are broadcast across the United States (and the world). But even in 1922, the *Federal Baseball* decision appeared to give a special carveout to baseball from the Sherman Act.[22] As one commentator put it, the Court "exempted baseball from the antitrust laws because it was the national pastime."[23]

23. Despite its questionable logic, the U.S. Supreme Court has twice foregone the opportunity to overrule *Federal Baseball*, leaving MLB's special antitrust exemption in place.

---

18 Federal Baseball Club of Baltimore v. National League, 259 U.S. 200 (1922).

19 In 2026 terms, the treble damages awarded amount to approximately $4.6 million USD.

20 *Id.* at 208.

21 Twenty years later, the Supreme Court would hold that a farmer growing wheat on his own farm for his own use affected interstate commerce. *See* Wickard v. Filburn, 317 U.S. 111 (1942). But the unanimous 1922 decision likely reflected a fundamentally different understanding of interstate commerce in the 1920s than the understanding that would come to dominate U.S. jurisprudence. *See* Marc Edelman & John Holden, *Baseball's Anticompetitive Antitrust Exemption*, 65 B.C. L. Rev. 1695, 1718 (2024) (describing how the "consensus view as to the scope of the Commerce Clause in 1922 was significantly different from today" and that "perhaps the Court's conclusion in 1922 made some sense for its time.").

22 Certainly, baseball was a quite popular (and growing) sport by the 1920s in the United States. By this point, former U.S. President William Howard Taft – an avid baseball fan – had become Chief Justice of the U.S. Supreme Court. President/Chief Justice Taft had been offered the job of league commissioner after serving as president, *id.* at 1708 and was the first president to throw a ceremonial first pitch on opening day of the baseball season in 1910, beginning a tradition that has resulted in every U.S. president since him throwing at least one ceremonial pitch on the opening day of baseball during their term as president. *See* Samuel A. Alito Jr., *The Origin of the Baseball Antitrust Exemption: Federal Baseball Club of Baltimore, Inc. v. National League of Professional Baseball Clubs*, 34 J. Sup. Ct. Hist. 183, 186 (2009). Additionally, the opinion's author, Justice Oliver Wendell Holmes, generally disliked federal antitrust laws and had referred to the Sherman Act as a "humbug based on economic ignorance and incompetence." *Id.* at 185.

23 Roger Abrams, *Blackmun's List*, 6 Va. Sports & Ent. L.J. 181, 183 (2007).

24. The first opportunity came in a 1953 decision in *Toolson v. New York Yankees.*[24] In a one-paragraph decision, the Supreme Court refused to overrule *Federal Baseball*, "so far as that decision determines that Congress had no intention of including the business of baseball within the scope of the federal antitrust laws."[25] Without engaging on the substantive merits of the interstate commerce question, the Supreme Court pushed the question from the courts to Congress to decide. Two justices dissented, writing that it was a "contradiction in terms" to say that baseball was not engaging in interstate commerce as contemplated by the Sherman Act.[26] Still, baseball's antitrust exemption survived.

25. The next opportunity came twenty years later in *Flood v. Kuhn.*[27] The case arose after the St. Louis Cardinals traded star player Curt Flood to the Philadelphia Phillies without consulting him, as permitted under the reserve clause in Flood's contract. Flood learned of the trade when a sportswriter called him to ask about it.[28] Because of baseball's antitrust exemption, the reserve clause – which would otherwise present significant antitrust challenges – was ever-present in professional baseball player contracts. It allowed teams to reassign, trade, or release players at the team's sole discretion. The reserve clause even prevented players from entering into contracts with another team after their contracts had expired. Flood, who was near the end of his career, decided to sue, opening the door again to overruling *Federal Baseball.*

26. By the 1970s, the Supreme Court could no longer deny that baseball was big business that plainly affected interstate commerce. Yet the Supreme Court still declined to overrule *Federal Baseball.* Instead, it admitted that "baseball is, in a very distinct sense, an exception and an anomaly" in U.S. antitrust law.[29] Although the Court gutted the reasoning behind *Federal Baseball*, it left in place the antitrust exemption: the "aberration," the Court said, "is an established one."[30] In recognizing this historical anomaly, the Court fully closed the door to other sports receiving the same favorable antitrust treatment: "Other professional sports operating interstate – football, boxing, basketball, and presumably, hockey and golf – are not so exempt."[31]

27. The result is a doctrinal anomaly with significant practical consequences. Unlike every other major professional sport in the United States, MLB has historically been able to maintain practices that would have been struck down as violations of the Sherman Act in any other sport. Baseball's minor league system, ownership structures – and even the Chicago Cub's deals with rooftops overlooking Wrigley Field[32] – have operated largely outside antitrust scrutiny as a result.

---

24 Toolson v. New York Yankees, 346 U.S. 356 (1953).

25 *Id.* at 357.

26 *Id.* at 358.

27 Flood v. Kuhn, 407 U.S. 258 (1972).

28 Edelman & Holden, *supra* note 20, at 1725.

29 *Flood*, 407 U.S. at 282.

30 *Id.*

31 *Id.* at 282–83. Despite losing before the Supreme Court, Flood's lawsuit ultimately led to the demise of the reserve clause in baseball. A few years later, in the "Seitz decision," an arbitrator declared that players became free agents after one year of playing without a contract. Edelman & Holden, *supra* note 20, at 1728.

32 *See* Right Field Rooftops v. Chicago Cubs Baseball Club, 870 F.3d 682, 689 (7th Cir. 2017).

28. Congress partially addressed this anomaly through the Curt Flood Act of 1998, which lifted baseball's antitrust exemption in the limited context of major league player employment, allowing major league players to bring antitrust claims arising from labor disputes.[33] The Flood Act represents the only congressional modification to the baseball exemption to date. The rest of the exemption, untouched by the Flood Act, remains alive and the source of continuing litigation.[34] Notably, the Flood Act does not extend to minor league players, who would have benefited from its provisions. Without congressional action, the anomalous "baseball exemption" continues to apply over MLB's control over the minor league system.[35]

2. Sports Broadcasters Act of 1961

29. The Sports Broadcasting Act of 1961 marks one of the few Congressional actions relating to sports antitrust law beyond baseball.[36] The law followed a series of lawsuits against the NFL. The law grants professional sports leagues a limited antitrust exception for the joint sale and licensing of TV network broadcast rights. The law has been critical in allowing professional leagues to pool and license league members' broadcast rights.

30. Yet new challenges have arisen as TV network broadcasting is displaced by other streaming options. Currently, one of the biggest challenges is the NFL "Sunday Ticket" Antitrust litigation, in which a class of consumers challenged the NFL's "Sunday Ticket" deal with satellite and internet streaming operator DirecTV.[37] The deal allowed viewers to buy a bundled package of out-of-market Sunday football games exclusively from DirecTV. Despite a jury awarding $4.7 billion in damages (which would be trebled to over $14 billion), the District Court vacated the verdict.[38] An appeal on the case is currently pending. Given the money at stake for both consumers and sports leagues, antitrust challenges to sports broadcasting agreements are likely to continue for the foreseeable future.

3. Implied Antitrust Immunity for Olympic Organizations

31. Several courts have found that the United States Olympic and Paralympic Committee (USOPC) and the National Governing Bodies (NGBs) for sport in the United States enjoy implied antitrust immunity. Although these organizations are private nonprofits, their operations are governed by a federal statute, the Ted Stevens Olympic and Amateur Sports Act (Amateur Sports Act).[39] While the Act does not explicitly grant antitrust immunity, courts have found it implied immunity

---

33 Curt Flood Act of 1998, Pub. L. No. 105–297, 15 U.S.C. § 26b.

34 As recently as March 2026, the Supreme Court denied certiorari in a case asking to overturn the baseball exemption. *See* Cangrejeros de Santurce Baseball Club v. Liga de Béisbol Prof'l de P.R., 146 F.4th 1 (1st Cir. 2025), cert denied, No. 25-416, 2026 WL 568339 (Mar. 2, 2026).

35 *See* Nostalgic Partners, LLC v. Off. Of Comm'r of Baseball, No. 22-2859, 2023 WL 4072836 (2d Cir. June 20, 2023).

36 Sports Broadcasting Act of 1961, Pub. L. No. 87-331, 15 U.S.C. §§ 1291–1295.

37 *See* In re NFL "Sunday Ticket" Antitrust Litig., No. ML 15-02668-PSG (SKX), 2024 WL 3628118, at *1–2 (C.D. Cal. Aug. 1, 2024).

38 *Id.*

39 Ted Stevens Olympic and Amateur Sports Act, 36 U.S.C. § 220501 *et seq.*

when the organization's "actions were necessary to implement the clear intent of Congress," thereby exempting them from the federal antitrust laws.[40]

32. *Behagen v. Amateur Basketball Association* was the first federal Court of Appeals decision to address implied antitrust immunity for NGBs.[41] The dispute centered on a Fédération Internationale de Basketball Amateur (FIBA) amateurism rule known as the "no-second-reinstatement rule."[42] Ronald Behagen had alternated between playing professionally in the NBA and for an amateur league in Italy, until the rule barred him from returning to Italy a second time after a stint in the NBA. After failing to convince FIBA to reconsider the rule, Behagen sued both FIBA and the Amateur Basketball Association for violating Section 1 of the Sherman Act.[43] A jury initially ruled in his favor, awarding nearly one million dollars in damages, attorney's fees, court costs, and interest. But the U.S. Court of Appeals for the Tenth Circuit reversed, holding that the Amateur Basketball Association was entitled to implied antitrust immunity because, as an NGB, it was exercising the "monolithic control" over basketball that the Amateur Sports Act required.[44]

33. More than 15 years later, *JES Properties v. U.S. Equestrian Federation* established the same antitrust immunity for the U.S. Equestrian Federation.[45] The case involved an antitrust challenge to the U.S. Equestrian Federation's "mileage rule," which required that the highest-rated equestrian competitions scheduled for the same day be held between 125 and 250 miles apart, depending on location.[46] JES Properties challenged the rule as a violation of Section 1 of the Sherman Act.[47] The U.S. Court of Appeals for the Eleventh Circuit found that the U.S. Equestrian Federation had implied antitrust immunity because the Amateur Sports Act required it to minimize scheduling conflicts and develop an interest in the sport of equestrian in the U.S.[48]

34. In 2018, *Gold Medal LLC v. USA Track & Field* extended implied antitrust immunity beyond sporting rules to reach advertising restrictions.[49] Run Gum, a company making chewing gum infused with caffeine and vitamins, was restricted from advertising at the U.S. Olympic Trials based on USOPC rules. Run Gum sued the USOPC[50] and USA Track & Field, the national governing body for athletics in the United States, under Section 1 of the Sherman Act.[51] The U.S. Court of Appeals for the Ninth Circuit held that both entities had implied antitrust immunity over Olympic advertising and logo restrictions.[52]

---

40 *See* Behagen v. Amateur Basketball Ass'n, 884 F.2d 524, 530 (10th Cir. 1989).

41 *Id.*

42 In 1989, the same year *Behagen* was decided, FIBA ended the distinction between amateur and professional basketball players. Despite the "A" originally standing for "amateur," as captioned in Behagen's lawsuit, the renamed International Basketball Association kept the acronym FIBA.

43 *Behagen*, 884 F.2d at 525–27.

44 *Id.* at 529.

45 JES Properties v. U.S. Equestrian Federation, 458 F.3d 1224 (11th Cir. 2006).

46 *Id.* at 1226-27.

47 *Id.*

48 *Id.* at 1231.

49 Gold Medal LLC v. USA Track & Field, 899 F.3d 712 (9th Cir. 2018).

50 At the time, the USOPC was named the United States Olympic Committee.

51 *Gold Medal LLC*, 899 F.3d at 713–14.

52 *Id.* at 718.

35. The scope and limits of implied antitrust immunity for Olympic organizations remains unsettled. At this time, three federal circuits have recognized implied antitrust immunity under the Amateur Sports Act, and a fourth has indicated agreement with *Behagen.*[53] The U.S. Supreme Court, however, has never addressed the question. Nor is the immunity without limits. Courts have rejected attempts to stretch its intended scope to affiliates of an NGB for rules that the affiliate imposes.[54] And a U.S. District Court has declined to extend the implied antitrust immunity beyond amateur sports, rejecting antitrust immunity for U.S. Soccer's oversight of professional soccer in a case alleging an antitrust conspiracy between U.S. Soccer and Major League Soccer.[55] Although its scope remains unsettled, the immunity remains a powerful defense for Olympic sport organizations operating under the Amateur Sports Act.

4. Collective Bargaining and the Non-Statutory Labor Exemption

36. Although professional sports outside of baseball have no formal antitrust exemption, labor law – through the judicially created non-statutory labor exemption – has functionally insulated many core league practices from antitrust scrutiny. Despite a significant decline in labor unions and collective bargaining overall in the United States, collective bargaining has remained central to the professional athlete labor market. The non-statutory labor exemption shields collectively bargained terms and conditions of employment from antitrust challenges. The logic of the exemption is that players cannot collectively bargain with the league concerning salaries and working conditions and then challenge that agreement on antitrust grounds. The effect of the exemption is enormous: salary caps, player drafts, rookie salary schedules, and restrictions on player movement, all of which could face extensive antitrust scrutiny in other industries, are off-limits from antitrust enforcement in almost all the major professional leagues in the United States.[56]

37. The Supreme Court articulated the foundation for this exemption in a series of decisions culminating in *Brown v. Pro Football. Brown* held that the non-statutory labor exemption protects conduct when it is reached through bona fide collective bargaining between a league and a players' association, grows out of the labor relationship, and primarily affects parties to that relationship.[57] Under *Brown*, the NFL's imposition of a wage scale for developmental squad players, even after negotiations broke down and the players' association claimed impasse, was protected from antitrust challenge because it emerged from the collective bargaining process.

---

53 *See* Eleven Line v. N. Tex. State Soccer Ass'n, 213 F.3d 198, 204 (5th Cir. 2000).

54 *Id.* at 204–05 (finding no antitrust immunity for regional soccer affiliate when U.S. Soccer, the national governing body, did not promulgate or approve the sport rule at issue); *see also* Minn. Made Hockey v. Minn. Hockey, 789 F. Supp. 2d 1133, 1142 (D. Minn. 2011) (finding no implied antitrust immunity for rule promulgated by local district of a state hockey affiliate).

55 *See* Championsworld LLC v. U.S. Soccer Fed., 726 F. Supp. 2d 961, at *970 (N.D. Ill. 2010).

56 *See* Michael C. Harper, *Multiemployer Bargaining, Antitrust Law, and Team Sports: The Contingent Choice of a Broad Exemption*, 38 Wm. & Mary L. Rev. 1663, 1664 (1997) (noting that the exemption "effectively enables leagues in every sport to be as free of antitrust constraints in order to control player mobility and salaries as Major League Baseball has been under its special, long standing antitrust exemption").

57 *See* Brown v. Pro Football, 518 U.S. 231, 250 (1996).

38. The full scope of the non-statutory labor exemption has been the subject of much litigation, with conflicting results. In a pre-*Brown* decision, the NFL's "Rozelle Rule," which required compensation to a free agent's former club, was found to constitute an illegal restraint on trade outside the scope of the labor exemption because the union's "acceptance of the status quo" did not constitute bona fide bargaining on the issue.[58] Yet the exemption did exempt from antitrust scrutiny the NFL's eligibility rule requiring a three-year period after high school before joining the NFL, even though the eligibility rules did not appear in the text of the collective bargaining agreement.[59] But the National Women's Soccer League's age eligibility rule, adopted before the league recognized a union, fell outside the exemption's scope even after the union signed a voluntary recognition agreement.[60]

39. While the non-statutory labor exemption removes most antitrust scrutiny through the collective bargaining process, it leaves players with one major negotiating leverage: dissolving the union. By doing so, players can then bring antitrust claims, as both NBA and NFL players did during 2011 contract negotiations.[61] The non-statutory labor exemption diverges from most competition law outside the U.S. In doing so, the exemption allows for employment practices that would face serious antitrust scrutiny in any other context, while also giving players significant bargaining leverage in contract negotiations with league owners.

IV. The Courts' Role in Shaping Sports Antitrust Law

40. Outside of these exemptions, Congress has left it to the courts to delineate how the antitrust laws apply to sports. Through a series of cases, the U.S. Supreme Court made clear that professional leagues outside baseball were not entitled to sport-based exemptions.[62] But that did not mean that sports received the same scrutiny as other industries. Over time, however, the trend has been for the courts to apply more serious antitrust scrutiny to sports leagues. Both non-unionized professional athletes and rival leagues have aggressively used antitrust claims to force change. Today, longstanding sports institutions like the NCAA face severe antitrust scrutiny, with court decisions upending decades of reverence for "amateurism" and fundamentally reshaping college sports in the United States.

1. Antitrust Challenges to Labor Market Restrictions

41. Through the non-statutory labor exemption (plus baseball's special carveout), professional sports leagues have largely shielded their labor market restrictions from antitrust scrutiny. For professional athletes in individual sports, however, restrictions on their labor remain open to antitrust challenges. The past decade has seen numerous antitrust challenges on this front, particularly arguments that a sport

---

58 *See* Mackey v. Nat'l Football League, 543 F.2d 606, 615–23 (8th Cir. 1976).

59 *See* Clarett v. Nat'l Football League, 369 F.3d 124, 127–143 (2d Cir. 2004).

60 *See* O.M. v. Nat'l Women's Soccer League, 541 F. Supp. 3d 1171, 1182–83 (D. Or. 2021).

61 *See* Nathaniel Grow, *Decertifying Players Unions: Lessons from the NFL and NBA Lockouts of 2011*, 15 Vand. J. Ent. & Tech. L. 473 (2020).

62 *See, e.g.*, Haywood v. Nat'l Basketball Ass'n, 401 U.S. 1204 (1971); Radovich v. Nat'l Football League, 352 U.S. 445 (1957); United States v. Int'l Boxing Club, 348 U.S. 236 (1955).

governing body is acting as a "monopsony"[63] in the labor market for individual athletes, lowering wages, and restricting professional opportunities. These claims recognize the reality that the market for professional athletes is often limited to one league. A professional athlete, after all, cannot easily switch to another sport.

42. One long-running antitrust lawsuit involved professional Mixed Martial Arts fighters. A group of MMA fighters sued the Ultimate Fighting Championship (UFC) alleging UFC violated Section 2 of the Sherman Act, primarily through UFC's monopolization of elite MMA promotion and its monopsony over the professional MMA fighters labor market.[64] The MMA fighters alleged that UFC's monopsony power led to suppressed professional MMA fighters' income and forced them into unfavorable contract terms. The class action lawsuit settled for $375 million, although long-term questions remain going forward.

43. Likewise, professional golf was subject to antitrust litigation when several professional golfers challenged the PGA Tour's restrictions on golfing in competing tournaments. At issue was LIV Golf, a rival startup tour financed by the Saudi sovereign wealth fund.[65] Under the PGA Tour's rules, golfers faced restrictions, including suspensions and bans, for participating in other tours. Professional golfers sued, arguing that this restriction on labor talent violated Section 2 of the Sherman Act because the PGA Tour had monopolized the market for professional golfers and the promotion of elite golf events. The case eventually settled with the unusual announcement of a merger between the PGA Tour and LIV Golf, a remedy that has itself raised more antitrust questions.[66]

44. A similar lawsuit has now come to professional tennis. The Professional Tennis Players Association (PTPA) has alleged anticompetitive practices by a "cartel" of tennis's professional governing bodies. These governing bodies include the Association of Tennis Professionals (ATP), the Women's Tennis Association (WTA), United States Tennis Association (USTA), the All England Lawn Tennis Club, and the Fédération Française de Tennis.[67] The PTPA has alleged collusion amongst these organizations to suppress tournament competition that, among other things, has had the effect of lowering player salaries and fixing prize money.[68] The lawsuit remains ongoing.

45. For athletes outside collective bargaining agreements, antitrust law has proven to be a highly effective vehicle for change. In the absence of union protection,

---

63 A monopsony is a "buyer's monopoly" and occurs when there is substantial market power on the buyer's side of the market, such as in the market for professional athlete services. *See* Cung Le v. Zuffa, 216 F. Supp. 3d 1154, 1163 (D. Nev. 2016).

64 *Id.*

65 *See* Mickelson v. PGA Tour, No. 22-cv-04486-BLF, 2022 WL 3229341 (N.D. Cal. Aug. 10, 2022). In an interesting early preliminary decision in the case, the U.S. District Court denied a temporary restraining order based on a lack of evidence of irreparable harm, noting that the "evidence shows almost without a doubt that [the golfers] will be earning significantly more money with LIV Golf than they could reasonably have expected to make through [PGA] TOUR play over the same time period." *Id.* at *20.

66 *See, e.g.*, Joe Lipper, *(W)hole in One: Why Both the PGA Tour and LIV Golf Should Wish for a Mulligan*, 62 Hou. L. Rev. 705 (2025).

67 Other organizations have been dismissed or settled as well.

68 *See* Second Amended Complaint, Pospisil v. ATP Tour, ECF 139, No. 1:25-cv-022207 (MMG) (S.D.N.Y. Sept. 26, 2025).

athletes have successfully used antitrust claims to challenge restrictions that suppress wages, limit professional opportunities, and entrench governing bodies' market power. For these athletes, antitrust law often serves the role of collective bargaining, a practical tool allowing athletes to negotiate with often entrenched governing bodies.

2. Antitrust Challenges to League Structure and Competition

46. Beyond labor and employment disputes, antitrust challenges in sports have increasingly arisen in cases involving league governance and competition among rival leagues.

47. Team owners have repeatedly turned to antitrust law to challenge league rules that govern franchise operations and constrain competitive freedom. For example, the then-Oakland Raiders, a professional NFL team, successfully challenged the NFL's league relocation rules, which required a three-fourths supermajority of team owners to approve a franchise relocation.[69] While courts have given wide latitude to sports organizations on market distribution, the Raiders prevailed in showing that the relocation rules unreasonably restrained trade (thus permitting the team's relocation that led to the lawsuit from Oakland to Los Angeles).[70] In another example, the Dallas Cowboys used an antitrust suit to ward off attempts by the NFL to centralize intellectual property licensing.[71] And recently, a major settlement was announced in a case involving NASCAR brought by former basketball star Michael Jordan's racing team, which brought changes to NASCAR's charter system, including more contractual stability.[72] But not every rule that may hurt team profits is an antitrust injury, as the New York Rangers learned in their failed attempt to use antitrust law to stop the NHL's attempt to centralize team website management (which can include a significant source of advertising profit).[73]

48. Another recurring set of antitrust issues arises from the rules of international sports federations that may restrain competition within the United States. Under the rule of reason, courts will generally give latitude to international federations given the "unique antitrust contexts" they present, including a legitimate need to have uniform rules around a given sport.[74] But that does not foreclose antitrust scrutiny, particularly as an international federation's conduct gets closer to a *per se* violation, such as a group boycott, and more attenuated from a legitimate sporting rationale.[75]

---

69 *See* Los Angeles Mem'l Coliseum Comm'n v. Nat'l Football League, 726 F.2d 1381, 1384 (9th Cir. 1984).

70 *Id.* at 1397–98.

71 *See* Alicia Jessop, *Jerry Jones' 1995 Risk Allows the Dallas Cowboys to Become leaders in the Growing Women's Sports Apparel Market*, FORBES (Nov. 29, 2013), https://www.forbes.com/sites/aliciajessop/2013/11/29/jerry-jones-1995-risk-allows-the-dallas-cowboys-to-become-leaders-in-the-growing-womens-sports-apparel-market/.

72 *See* Jordan Bianchi, *What 23XI, Front Row, and NASCAR's Other Teams are Getting in the Settlement*, N.Y. TIMES (Dec. 11, 2025), https://www.nytimes.com/athletic/6882943/2025/12/11/nascar-settlement-23xi-front-row-details/.

73 *See* Madison Square Garden v. Nat'l Hockey League, 270 F. App'x 56 (2d Cir. 2008).

74 *See* Shields v. World Aquatics, No. 23-15092 and 23-15156, 2024 WL 4211477, at *7 (9th Cir. Sept. 17, 2024).

75 *Id.* at *6–7.

49. For example, International Federation rules concerning geographical market divisions can raise antitrust issues, as was the case in *Relevent Sports v. U.S. Soccer Federation.*[76] Relevent, a U.S.-based soccer promoter, sought to host a regular season La Liga match for the first time in the United States (between Barcelona and Girona). But FIFA then announced a policy that barred playing regular season games outside a team's home territory. This led to Barcelona withdrawing from the planned match in the U.S. Relevant tried again to host a foreign regular season game in the U.S., this time announcing a match between two Ecuadorian teams. But this time U.S. Soccer refused to sanction the match due to FIFA's newly adopted policy.[77] Relevant filed suit, alleging an antitrust conspiracy. After a multi-year court battle, a court decided that U.S. Soccer's adherence to FIFA's rule could constitute an agreement for antitrust purposes without proof of an "agreement to agree" between FIFA and U.S. Soccer.[78] After the decision, the parties settled, leading FIFA to withdraw the rule and opening the door to hosting international regular-season matches in the U.S.[79]

50. Finally, antitrust challenges by rival leagues continue to arise, but success has proven elusive for upstart leagues competing against entrenched professional leagues. In the 1980s, the United States Football League successfully proved the NFL had monopolized football, but the jury awarded only $1 in nominal damages.[80] The jury, it appears, believed many of the United States Football League's financial problems were not due to the NFL's actions.[81] More recently, a federal jury found in favor of U.S. Soccer and MLS in an antitrust challenge by the now-defunct North American Soccer League (NASL).[82] NASL had sought to be a Division 1 competitor of MLS, but U.S. Soccer denied the league Division 1 status (and later Division 2 status). The NASL alleged Section 1 and Section 2 claims under the Sherman Act.[83] U.S. Soccer and MLS's defense centered around NASL's poor financial management and the fact that there had been team and league movement within the divisions during the relevant time – including the United Soccer League (USL), which moved from Division 3 to Division 2.[84]

51. Similarly, the International Swimming League won a moral victory, but only $1 in damages, when a jury found that World Aquatics engaged in anticompetitive behavior to block swimmers from participating in the upstart league's events.[85]

---

76 Relevent Sports v. U.S. Soccer Fed'n, 61 F.4th 299 (2nd Cir. 2023).

77 *See* Melanie Anzidei, *Relevent Sports, U.S. Soccer Settle Antitrust Lawsuit, Ending Years-Long Legal Battle*, N.Y. Times (Apr. 10, 2025), https://www.nytimes.com/athletic/6271264/2025/04/10/relevent-sports-us-soccer-lawsuit-settlement/.

78 *See Relevent Sports*, 61 F.4th at 307.

79 *See* Melanie Anzidei, *Relevent Sports, U.S. Soccer Settle Antitrust Lawsuit, Ending Years-Long Legal Battle*, N.Y. Times (Apr. 10, 2025), https://www.nytimes.com/athletic/6271264/2025/04/10/relevent-sports-us-soccer-lawsuit-settlement/.

80 *See* U.S. Football League v. Nat'l Football League, 644 F. Supp. 1040, 1041–42 (S.D.N.Y. 1986).

81 *Id.* at 1054–55.

82 *See* N. Am. Soccer League v. U.S. Soccer Fed'n, No. 17-cv-5495-HG, 2025 WL 1311115 (E.D.N.Y. May 6, 2025).

83 *Id.* at *5–7.

84 *See* Jeff Carlisle, *Jury Sides with MLS, USSF in NASL Anti-trust Suit*, ESPN (Feb. 3, 2025), https://www.espn.com/soccer/story/_/id/43680111/jury-sides-mls-ussf-nasl-suit.

85 A class of athletes that had joined in this suit and ultimately settled with World Aquatics fared better, reaching a $4.6 million settlement with World Aquatics.

And in a slight twist on the concept of a rival league, the Enhanced Games – created to allow athletes to compete while using performance-enhancing drugs – failed in its antitrust case against WADA, World Athletics, and USA Swimming.[86] The lawsuit concerned a World Aquatics' bylaw that effectively banned anyone supporting or participating in the Enhanced Games from participating in World Aquatics events. But the court found that a shared belief in clean sports (and distaste for the Enhanced Games) did not amount to an antitrust violation, since World Aquatics' bylaw applied only to World Aquatics' events.[87]

52. Antitrust law will remain central to disputes within and between sports leagues. Its most transformative impact, however, is now unfolding in collegiate athletics.

3. Antitrust, Collegiate Sports, and the End of Amateurism

53. The most significant antitrust challenges today involve college sports. A series of lawsuits against the NCAA has brought fundamental changes to college sports, including the demise of college amateurism. And all indications are that more antitrust challenges, and more fundamental changes to the NCAA and college sports, are likely to come.

54. In many ways, the fundamental changes are, from an antitrust perspective, unsurprising. The NCAA has long acted like a cartel that would be illegal in almost any other industry.[88] For decades, the NCAA benefited from the perception that its rules served pro-competitive purposes, most notably that preserving amateurism constituted a distinctive and valuable product.[89] Underneath the surface, however, was the reality that college sports were big business, one in which it seemed everyone was profiting but the athletes.[90]

55. The dam began to break in 2009, when a former NCAA college basketball player learned that the NCAA had licensed his likeness to a private company for use in a video game without his authorization.[91] At the time, NCAA rules prevented college athletes from receiving compensation for their name, image, or likeness (NIL). A class of athletes sued the NCAA, arguing that this rule violated

---

86 *See* Enhanced US v. World Aquatics, No. 25-cv-7096-JMF, 2025 WL 3206662 (S.D.N.Y. Nov. 17, 2025).

87 *Id.* at *28–33.

88 *See, e.g.*, James V. Koch, *A Troubled Cartel: The NCAA*, 28 Law & Contemp. Probs. 135 (1973).

89 *See* NCAA v. Board of Regents, 468 U.S. 85, 120 (1984) ("The NCAA plays a critical role in the maintenance of a revered tradition of amateurism in college sports.").

90 For example, in *NCAA v. Board of Regents*, the University of Oklahoma and the University of Georgia sued the NCAA over its college football television rights restrictions. The U.S. Supreme Court held that the NCAA's rules violated the Sherman Act, a major win for member institutions to profit from college football. But the U.S. Supreme Court made clear at the time that it's holding was about output, not input (student-athlete labor): "the role of the NCAA must be to *preserve* a tradition that might otherwise die; rules that restrict output are hardly consistent with this role." *Id.*

91 The video game was part of Electronic Arts NCAA games series. The series allowed gamers to play teams and players from specific years. Although computer graphics were not what they are today, it took little effort to identify specific players in the game. Discovery confirmed what was obvious; an Electronic Arts internal spreadsheet showed how each avatar in the video game was matched to dozens of specific characteristics of real athletes, including 26 dimensions of physical characteristics, 22 dimensions of athletic ability, and 28 dimensions of how they dressed for the game. *See* Tom Farrey, *Players, Game Makers Settle for $40M*, ESPN (May 30, 2014), https://www.espn.com/espn/otl/story/_/id/11010455/college-athletes-reach-40-million-settlement-ea-sports-ncaa-licensing-arm.

Section 1 of the Sherman Act. The NCAA argued that the rule was a necessary pro-competitive restriction needed to preserve amateurism and competitive balance. The District Court rejected those rationales and ordered the NCAA to allow full cost-of-attendance scholarships and permit small cash payments (up to $5,000 per year of eligibility) to athletes that could be placed in trust. The Court of Appeals approved the remedies except for cash payments.[92] Perhaps presciently, the Court of Appeals warned that allowing cash payments untethered to education would spell the end of NCAA amateurism: "Once that line is crossed, we see no basis for returning to a rule of amateurism and no defined stopping point; it is a quantum leap."[93] What the court did not foresee, however, was how quickly amateurism would cease to function as a coherent product at all. The reality was that college sports in the United States had become an unmistakably commercial enterprise.

56. The Supreme Court's unanimous 2021 decision in *NCAA v. Alston* ushered in the next wave of changes.[94] The Supreme Court found under the rule of reason that the NCAA's limitation on education-related benefits for student athletes violated Section 1. On its face, the ruling was limited to education-related benefits, like computers, academic stipends, study abroad programs, and postgraduate internships.[95] More fundamentally, *Alston* marked a sea-change. The U.S. Supreme Court was no longer willing to accept amateurism as a shield against antitrust laws. As Justice Brett Kavanaugh wrote in his concurrence to *Alston*, "nowhere else in America can businesses get away with agreeing not to pay their workers a fair market rate on the theory that their product is defined by not paying their workers a fair market rate. And under ordinary principles of antitrust law, it is not evident why college sports should be any different."[96]

57. Almost immediately, the NCAA's entire amateurism model was in doubt. By 2024, the *House v. NCAA* settlement cemented the move to direct college athlete compensation.[97] In that case, class members–student-athletes seeking compensation for use of their names, images, and likeness – entered into a far-reaching settlement with the NCAA that resulted in profound institutional changes, most critically allowing for direct revenue sharing for athletes. The settlement also made changes to NIL regulations, setting up a separate College Sports Commission to regulate college revenue sharing deals and certain NIL deals, and replacing scholarship limits with roster limits. And the NCAA agreed to pay $2.8 billion for back payments to class members.[98]

58. The settlement ended NCAA amateurism, but it left more questions than answers. One significant question concerns the intersection between the *House* settlement and Title IX, a federal civil rights law that prohibits sex-based discrimination

92 *See* O'Bannon v. NCAA, 802 F.3d 1049, 1079 (9th Cir. 2015).

93 *Id.* at 1078.

94 NCAA v. Alston, 594 U.S. 69 (2021).

95 *Id.* at 103–107.

96 *Id.* at 112 (Kavanaugh, J., concurring).

97 *See* Opinion Regarding Order Granting Motion for Final Approval of Settlement Agreement, ECF 978, In Re College Athlete NIL Litigation, No. 20-cv-03919-CW (N.D. Cal. June 6, 2025). Although it has been referred to as the *House* settlement, the settlement resolved three combined class-action lawsuits against the NCAA.

98 *Id.*

in education. Since the 1970s, Title IX has played a leading role in equalizing the availability of women's collegiate sports. The *House* settlement has threatened to upend that progress, as the settlement's terms give most of the benefits to two men's sports: American football and basketball. In approving the *House* settlement, the court explicitly ruled that the case was not a Title IX case and left that question for another day.[99]

59. The *House* settlement will not be the last word. Both members of Congress and the President have weighed in, although it remains unclear whether Congress can pass any legislative changes. In July 2025, President Trump issued an executive order on "Saving College Sports."[100] The executive order proclaimed that college sports are "under unprecedented threat," which has "created an out-of-control, rudderless system in which competing university donors engage in bidding wars for the best players[.]"[101] While the executive order had highly favorable language for the NCAA, the President lacked the authority to give the NCAA the relief it needed without Congressional action.[102] Some current bills floating around Congress (including the SCORE Act) would legislate certain NIL and revenue sharing deals while giving the NCAA limited antitrust immunity.[103]

60. Despite all the changes, one thing is clear: the NCAA has an antitrust problem. As part of a settlement with the U.S. Department of Justice, the NCAA agreed to stop enforcing its transfer eligibility rule, which required transferring athletes to sit out one year before playing at a new school.[104] And numerous athletes have now brought antitrust challenges to the NCAA's five-year eligibility clock.[105] Barring a legislative solution, what is left of the NCAA's restraints on the student-athlete labor market are in peril.

V. Conclusion

61. Sports antitrust law has come a long way since *Federal Baseball*. Since 1922, courts have steadily narrowed the gap between the antitrust treatment of sports and that of commercial industries. That change has been driven not by any change

---

99 *Id.* at 63–64.

100 *Saving College Sports*, Exec. Order 14322 (2025).

101 *Id.*

102 In March 2026, the White House hosted a "Saving College Sports" roundtable. While the NCAA president was there, no college athletes were invited to attend. Among other things at the roundtable was a call for giving the NCAA antitrust immunity. *See* Justin Williams & Nicki Jhabvala, *Trump's College Sports Roundtable: Two Hours of Talk, with Few Solutions*, N.Y. Times (Mar. 7, 2026), https://www.nytimes.com/athletic/7095330/2026/03/06/trump-saving-college-sports-roundtable-executive-order-score-act/.

103 *See* The Student Compensation and Opportunity through Rights and Endorsements Act (SCORE Act), H.R. 4312, 119th Congress (2025).

104 *See* Final Judgment and Permanent Injunction, ECF 146, Ohio v. NCAA, No. 1:23-cv-100-JPB (N.D.W. Va. Aug. 30, 2024).

105 *See, e.g.*, Pavia v. NCAA, 154 F.4th 407 (6th Cir. 2025) (finding the NCAA's appeal of a preliminary injunction against its rule counting junior college playing time toward NCAA eligibility moot because the NCAA had granted a waiver); Blythe v. NCAA, No. 3:26-cv-100-ART, 2026 WL 483345 (D. Nev. Feb. 20, 2026) (granting a temporary restraining order and preliminary injunction against the NCAA's "Five-Year Rule"); Ortega v. NCAA, No. 4:25-cv-00496 (S.D. Iowa) (challenging the NCAA's eligibility rules); *but see* Coley v. NCAA, 792 F. Supp. 3d 634 (E.D.N.C. 2025) (finding the Sherman Act does not apply to the eligibility rules).

in U.S. law, but by a change in how courts perceive sports. The judicial deference once extended to amateurism, league self-governance, and the social value of sport has eroded as the commercial stakes involved have exploded.

62. The NCAA's experience is the clearest illustration of this shift. An institution whose amateurism rules were once treated as axiomatic now finds itself under sustained and existential antitrust scrutiny for those same rules. *Alston* did more than merely resolve a dispute about education-related benefits; it signaled that the U.S. Supreme Court is no longer willing to treat sports leagues as presumptively entitled to an antitrust shelter that no other industry enjoys. The *House* settlement resolved one set of claims while leaving many others unresolved. Future challenges to the NCAA's remaining restraints on athlete labor are sure to follow. But the NCAA will not be the last institution reshaped by antitrust law. And the trend is clear: more litigation, more scrutiny, and less deference to the argument that sports deserve special treatment.

63. The baseline principle has not changed since the Sherman Act was passed in 1890: agreements that unreasonably restrain competition are unlawful. What has changed is the willingness to apply that principle to sports with the same degree of rigor as courts do to other industries.

Sports and Competition Law in Brazil

Alexandre Cordeiro Macedo, Ricardo Medeiros de Castro and Maria Luiza Bittar Khouri*
Administrative Council for Economic Defense (CADE), Brazil

I. Introduction

1. The UNESCO International Charter of Physical Education and Sport, promulgated on 21 November 1978, asserts that the practice of physical education and sport is a fundamental right for all. The Brazilian Federal Constitution, in its Article 217, stipulates that it is the "duty of the State to foster formal and informal sports practices", while preserving the autonomy of sports governing bodies and associations in terms of their organisation and functioning.[1]
2. Recently, in Brazil, the General Sports Law (Law 14.597/2023) consolidated various sports legislations. These include the Supporter Statute (Law 10.671 2003), the Law on Labor Relations of Professional Football Coaches (Law 8.650 1993), and the Athlete Scholarship Law (Law 10.891 2004). These laws, along with the Pelé Law (Law 9.615 1998), the Sports Incentive Law (Law 11.438 2006), the Program for Modernization of Management and Fiscal Responsibility of Brazilian Football (PROFUT) (Law 13.155 2015), and the Football Corporation Law (Law 14.193 2021), form a strong set of rules for the national sports sector.[2]

---

* Alexandre Cordeiro Macedo, Former President of CADE; Ricardo Medeiros de Castro, Former Head of Technical Advisory Unit of CADE's Presidency; Maria Luiza Bittar Khouri, Former Chief of Staff of the Presidency of Cade.

1 Paulo Sérgio Feuz and Filipe Orsolini Pinto de Souza, "Sports and Human Dignity" (2023) 10(10) DIGE 149–166. <https://revistas.pucsp.br/index.php/DIGE/article/view/60699> accessed 24 August 2025.

2 In 2018, Brazil legalized sports betting with the enactment of Law 13.756/2018 (later amended by Provisional Measure No 1.182/2023).

3. There is also the potential for state legislation to incorporate international sports law norms into domestic legislation. This was exemplified during the Rio 2016 Olympic Games, when Law 13.284/2016 was integrated into Brazilian law norms originally part of the *lex olympica*.[3]

4. In addition to state regulation, there are sports confederations and federations, which are private organisations operating at both national and state levels tasked with the organisation of various aspects of sports disciplines. These entities are responsible for conducting championships and regulating sports activities. For example, the Brazilian Football Confederation (CBF) oversees the rules of football and the organisation of national championships, whereas state federations, such as the Football Federation of the State of Rio de Janeiro (FERJ) and the Football Federation of the State of São Paulo (FPF), are responsible for the administration of state-level championships.

5. Similarly, when sports disciplines are practiced within team sports, it is common for them to be conducted through clubs. These clubs are private organisations, traditionally structured as non-profit entities, that participate in specific championships.

6. There are numerous other markets and economic agents that are integral to the sports sector core activities. These include media conglomerates, investment funds, advertising agencies, advertisers and various other stakeholders in this dynamic sector.

7. Another aspect is that the concept of what constitutes a sport is also a contested terrain. The Olympic Games frequently incorporate and recognise new sports disciplines, such as skateboarding, surfing and breakdancing. Currently, there are authors who also advocate for the recognition of electronic sports (or e-sports) as an activity distinct from pure physical games.[4]

8. Regardless of such a precise definition, the Brazilian competition law (Law 12.529/2011), applies to various economic sectors, with no antitrust immunity whatsoever provided in this legislation, including any sports activity.

9. Given this scenario, the purpose of this chapter is to evaluate, through an exploratory analysis, how Brazilian competition law has analysed the sports sector. Thus, this contribution aims to provide a non-exhaustive overview of CADE's current jurisprudence on the subject, as well as a discussion on some ongoing cases. Furthermore, it intends to briefly describe a recent judicial debate about football agents, in which CADE acts as *amicus curiae*.

---

[3] Cristiane Cardoso Avolio Gomes, "Regulação Estatal de Esporte de Rendimento" (DPhil thesis, FGV 2024), 97 <https://repositorio.fgv.br/server/api/core/bitstreams/12d110e8-627d-452b-9911-4f5da0f0fc4e/content> accessed 24 August 2025, legal rules the International Olympic Committee created to govern the Olympic and Paralympic movement. Jean Eduardo Nicolau, *Private International Sports Law* (Quartier Latin 2018).

[4] Ricardo Georges Affonso Miguel, "The Social Function of Electronic Sports (Esports)" (DPhil thesis, BDTD 2023) <https://bdtd.ibict.br/vufind/Record/PUC_SP-1_db87a73b8d4c0652fe5f77d508e919ec> accessed 24 August 2025.

II. Analysis of CADE's Jurisprudence

10. To accurately assess CADE's understanding of this issue, in this chapter, it will be used a "term counting" methodology in official documents to evaluate the intensity of discourse and arguments. This methodology has been used in other scientific works.[5]

11. The following table presents a short and non-exhaustive list of terms containing various sports disciplines. Subsequently, the CADE Electronic Information System was checked to determine how many documents referenced each of these disciplines, both in general and in decisions rendered by Tribunal members. This analysis is summarised in the table below:

Sport	Term in Portuguese	Total documents referring to the specific term	Tribunal´s Decisions referring to the specific term
Football (Soccer)	Futebol	3020	83
Gymnastics	Ginástica	1339	15
Tennis	Tênis	1245	12
Basketball	Basquete	296	8
Volleyball	Vôlei	263	6
Surfing	Surf	125	6
Swimming	Natação	517	3
Boxing	Boxe	339	2
Judo	Judô	1286	0
Karate	Karatê	312	0
Auto Racing	Automobilismo	166	0
Athletics (Track and Field)	Atletismo	164	0
Futsal	Futsal	116	0
Cycling	Ciclismo	80	0
Fencing	Esgrima	26	0
Canoeing	Canoagem	18	0
Bodybuilding	Fisiculturismo	10	0
Baseball	Basebol	3	0

Table 1: Word count of frequency the term in Portuguese, referring to the specific sports activity, appeared in documents stored in CADE's Electronic Information System.

---

5 Blaise Cronin, *The Citation Process: Role and Significance of Citation in Scientific Communication* (Taylor Graham 1984). Gregory J Feist, "Quantity, Quality and Depth of Research as Influences on Scientific Eminence: Is Quantity Most Important?" (1997) 10 CRJ 325–335. Richard A Posner, "An Economic Analysis of the Use of Citations in the Law" (2000) 2 ALER 381–406.

12. Soccer/football, according to the specified list, was the most frequently referenced to and discussed sport in documents submitted to CADE, as well as in decisions rendered by CADE's Tribunal.

13. Many of the aforementioned documents, however, contain only indirect references to sports activities. For example, among the 83 documents categorised as votes, 57 were drafted by two former CADE commissioners, João Paulo Resende and Cristiane Alkmin Junqueira Schmidt, in cases where they were in the minority. These commissioners aimed to discuss the appropriateness of the calculation basis for certain Consent Decrees, in cases involving cartels related to the construction of football stadiums. However, the majority of CADE found it appropriate to sign the referred Consent Decrees, wherein the calculation basis for fines would not be in the general market of "construction of buildings and housing", but rather, by a criterion of proportionality, should be restricted to the national market of civil construction works, modernisation, and/or renovation of sports facilities (football stadiums) intended for the FIFA 2014 World Cup in Brazil.

14. In any event, it was determined within the context of Request No 08700.007078/2016-45 (Ref restricted section No 08700.006737/2016-26) that the sub-sector of football stadium construction revenue could serve as the basis for calculating fines and contributions in specific Consent Decrees addressing anticompetitive conduct. Commissioner Gustavo Augusto Freitas de Lima made further references within the context of Voluntary Appeal No 08700.005936/2022-62. Although this case did not pertain to sports, but rather to the exclusivity of sales points in the beer market, he highlighted that beer consumption increases during football matches, indicating strategic business considerations during these periods of sporting championships. According to Commissioner Gustavo, given the proximity of events of such magnitude, there was an urgency for CADE to examine the legality of exclusive beer sales at specific points. However, in this case, as in many others in CADE's Electronic Information System, the reference to soccer/football is incidental and only indirectly addresses the topic.[6]

1. Some Cases About Broadcasting Rights

15. A recurring theme in CADE's jurisprudence has been the understanding of broadcasting rights for sports in general and football in particular.

16. In merger agreement (case No 08700.009574/2022-81), Commissioner Victor Fernandes,[7] recognised that channels specialising in sports (notably those broadcasting national tournaments, such as the Brazilian football championship aired by SporTV) possess characteristics that render them essential for the success of a

---

6 Another indirect reference was made in the vote of former Commissioner Eduardo Pontual Ribeiro in Case No 08012.010215/2007-96, where members of a liquid fuel resale cartel in Caxias do Sul, Rio Grande do Sul, were allegedly organising a football game among themselves. Further instances of indirect and incidental references to football can be found in the votes of former Commissioners Carlos Emmanuel Joppert Ragazzo (DocSEI 907793 in Case No 08700.006317/2020-26) and Mauricio Oscar Bandeira Maia (DocSEI 846569 in Case No 08700.006317/2020-26).

7 Commissioner Victor Fernandes, citing Commissioner Carlos Ragazzo's vote in Merger Act No 08012.002417/2010-60 (HBO/Sony).

pay-tv operator, which is why they have been considered unique relevant markets in certain CADE's precedents.

17. On this topic, Cade analysed and approved merger (case No 08012.003675/2001-72), through which Groupe Canal+ and RTL acquired joint control of Groupe Jean-Claude Darmon SA (GJCD). GJCD operated as a joint venture with the objective of consolidating the activities of Sport+ and UFA Sports for the commercialisation of sports broadcasting rights and the exploitation of advertising and marketing rights for sporting events.

18. In this case, CADE analysed the commercialisation of broadcasting rights segmented according to the sport broadcast, distinguishing it from other television programming based on the following:

    1. The appeal of sporting events, particularly live broadcasts, generally surpasses the value of the other rights exercised in the advertising market and for subscribers.
    2. The sponsorship value of sporting events varies particularly for popular sports and major international events like the Olympic Games or World Cups.
    3. The ephemeral nature of a sporting event, where the public primarily values its live presentation, significantly diminishes after the event.

19. In this specific decision rendered on January 23, 2001 – and in several subsequent cases – the issue of the proper definition of the relevant market was raised: whether it should be defined broadly to encompass the sale of broadcasting rights in general, or narrowly to include only the sale of football broadcasting rights. Although the Secretariat for Economic Affairs of the Ministry of Finance (SEAE) at the time recommended the broad definition, the Reporting Commissioner chose to analyse both possible approaches, given that football rarely finds substitutes in the broadcasting of other sports.

20. During the in-depth investigation of the Clube dos 13 (13´s Club), case No 08012.006504/1997-11,[8] the Reporting Commissioner comprehended that football sets itself apart from other sports, particularly due to the recurrence of various championships broadcast throughout the year and the revenue these events generate on television. The Commissioner also highlighted that football championships do not have the same relevance for the Brazilian audience. The Brazilian Championship is the competition that brings together the best and most traditional teams in the country, especially those with the largest fan bases. In this sense, it can provide more interesting matches from a television broadcasting perspective when compared to other national tournaments (State Championships and the Copa do Brasil) or international ones, where the participation of Brazilian clubs is limited (Libertadores and Sulamericana).

---

[8] The 13's Club case (Administrative Procedure No. 08012.006504/1997-11) marked a pivotal moment in Brazilian competition law, as it involved allegations of cartelization through the collective negotiation of broadcasting rights by major football clubs and the exclusive contracts with Rede Globo. The settlement in 2010 reshaped the market by ending the collective negotiations, requiring auctions with separate contracts for different media platforms, and allowing sublicensing of rights, ultimately leading clubs to negotiate individually with broadcasters.

21. In the ESPN/Globosat operation merger (case No 08012.005864/2000-07), SEAE debated whether the market for acquiring broadcasting rights for sports events could be segmented by sports, such as football, motorsport, basketball and tennis, among others, and even more specific segmentations, such as regular football events (national championships, for example) and occasional events (such as the World Cup). However, since both Globosat and ESPN Brasil acquired broadcasting rights for various sports, SEAE understood that there was no need to define multiple relevant markets segmented by sport. The understanding was that the broader definition of the relevant market would not compromise the analysis of the merger's impact on this specific market. However, there was no final understanding on this issue due to the specificities of the case.

22. In the DirecTV/NewsCorp operation merger (case N°s 53500.002423/2003 and 53500.029160/2004), the Reporting Commissioner understood that programmers could acquire football broadcasting rights from third parties and that exclusivity rights in the football segment could have detrimental effects on competition among programmers, given that football is essential content for a Brazilian programmer. Consequently, in order to approve the merger, CADE imposed some obligations to NewsCorp, demanding that this company refrain from exercising exclusivity rights over the broadcast of the five most important professional football championships in Brazil.

23. Moreover, in the context of the AT&T/Time Warner operation merger (case 08700.001390/2017-14), the Brazilian Film Agency (ANCINE) responded to a CADE inquiry, stating that audiences could not easily replace football with other sports, especially given that football is the most popular sport in Brazil. Live broadcasts of football matches are also essential for attracting an audience, obtaining advertising investments, building an image, and establishing the programmer's brand.

24. Although CADE considered the possibility of broadening the segment to include the sale of broadcasting rights for sports events in general, the Perform Group and WME Entertainment Parent merger (case No 08700.006955/2017-41), left a precise definition of the market for the sale of broadcasting rights open.

25. Although there is no definitive conclusion on the subject, these cases demonstrate the complexity of the debate.

2. Case of 13's Club

26. The Administrative Procedure No 08012.006504/1997-11, (13's Club case) represents a significant case in the competition domain in Brazil. This club, officially known as the Union of the Major Football Clubs of Brazil, was a Brazilian organisation established on 11 July 1987, to advocate for the political and commercial interests of 13 prominent football clubs in Brazil. At the time of its founding, the member clubs were the top thirteen in the Brazilian Football Confederation (CBF) ranking: Atlético-MG, Bahia, Botafogo, Corinthians, Cruzeiro, Flamengo, Fluminense, Grêmio, Internacional, Palmeiras, Santos, São Paulo and Vasco da Gama. Years later, the organisation expanded its membership to 20 associated clubs, while retaining its original name. This club negotiated broadcasting rights

for championships such as the Brazilian Championship with radio and television networks. It also engaged with the Brazilian Football Confederation (CBF) regarding the formats of national championships. Rede Globo, as a television network, negotiated with this club for exclusive broadcasting rights to the Brazilian Championship games, covering the five relevant media platforms: open tv, cable tv, pay-per-view, internet and mobile phones.

27. In 1997, a complaint was filed with the Secretariat of Economic Law (SDE) regarding the exclusive broadcasting rights acquired by Globo for the Brazilian Football League (BFL), the joint sale of these rights by the "13's Club" (that according to the complaint, could constitute a cartel) and the bundling of rights across multiple media platforms. After an investigation, SDE recommended market intervention to limit exclusivity and proposed unbundling the media platforms. In 2010, CADE settled the case, leading to Rede Globo waiving its renewal preference clause, and the 13's club agreeing to auction broadcasting rights with clear rules, awarding separate contracts for different media platforms and allowing sublicensing of broadcasting rights.[9].

28. In the end, the 13's Club stopped negotiating collectively, and several clubs began to negotiate directly with television broadcasters, such as Rede Globo network.

3. Merger – Galo Holding/Atlético SAF

29. Another interesting case refers to the first merger involving a Football Joint Stock Company, *Sociedade Anônima do Futebol* – (SAF), notified on 5 September 2023. In merger case No 08700.006273/2023-87, Galo Holding SA (Galo Holding) acquired control of Atlético Mineiro SAF (Atlético SAF), previously held by Club Atlético Mineiro (CAM). The controllers of Galo Holding also hold stakes in Banco BMG, MRV Engenharia, LOG, and Banco Inter. CADE approved this transaction on 20 September 2023.

30. The transaction concerns the investment agreement between CAM, Galo Holding and Atlético SAF, through which CAM and Galo Holding will contribute capital and rights to exploit Arena MRV to Atlético SAF.

31. The rights transferred by CAM to Atlético SAF include sponsorship contracts, production and commercialisation of team products, operation rights of Arena MRV, men's and women's football teams, youth categories, as well as broadcasting rights and intellectual property exploitation of the team.

32. According to Opinion No 379/2023/CGAA5/SGA1/SG issued by the CADE General-Superintendence, the operation pertains to the professional football market and resulted in a vertical integration between professional football activities and the national market for advertising, sponsorship and marketing rights of sports events.

33. Regarding the first relevant market, the General-Superintendence stated that there was no settled definition of the relevant market for professional football activities by CADE. This market has only been mentioned in the context of Gun Jumping

---

9 César Mattos, "Broadcasting Football Rights in Brazil" (2012) 42(2) EE 337–362 <www.scielo.br/j/ee/a/QPgTLWRrBZXH47sp5GTRFVm/?lang=en> accessed 24 August 2025.

Analysis No 08700.003312/2022-11 (involving Cruzeiro Esporte Clube – Sociedade Anônima de Futebol and Tara Sports) and No 08700.003313/2022-58 (involving SAF Botafogo and Eagle Holding). However, the CADE General-Superintendence considered a discussion initiated by the French Competition Authority (Autorité de la Concurrence) in the context of the acquisition of control of SASP Olympique Gymnaste Club de Nice by the Ineos Group, the *Ineos/Gymnaste Club de Nice* merger case.[10] In its analysis, the French authority considered the existence of a market where professional football clubs buy and sell player contracts. To estimate the total market, the Autorité de la Concurrence used FIFA's global transfer report.[11] In other words, the market was analysed from an international perspective.

34. Nevertheless, after acknowledging this comparative reference, the General-Superintendence proceeded to assess the relevant markets specifically in the context of the Galo Holding/Atlético SAF transaction.

35. Despite this definition, CADE's General-Superintendence also evaluated this market, both at the national level (analysing the revenue of Brazilian football clubs according to the 2022 Ernst & Young Report) and at the state level. In all these scenarios, the market share of the involved parties was low. It was understood that due to the vertical relationship (and given that in all possible scenarios the market share was minimal), a precise definition of the product and geographic dimensions was not necessary in this case. The data gathered in this matter were deemed sufficient to dismiss any hypothesis of competitive harm.

36. Regarding the second affected market, the General-Superintendence similarly clarified that the market for advertising, sponsorship and marketing of sports events includes the sale of these rights and consists of public relations services, consumer relations management and the sale of advertising space, both in stadiums and on athletes' clothing. These activities are closely related to broadcasting rights and the prize money guaranteed to football clubs, from ancillary markets to the exploitation of sports rights.[12]

37. Regarding the geographic scope of the market for the sale of advertising, sponsorship and marketing rights, although there are no physical restrictions or limits on the activities related to the advertising and marketing rights of football games, it was understood that this tends to be national, in line with the interests of advertisers.

38. Once again, CADE left the relevant market definition open, analysing all possible scenarios. The General-Superintendence concluded that the *Galo Holding/ Atlético SAF*merger should be unconditionally approved in all cases due to the low market shares.

---

10 Case 19-DCC-160 Autorité de la concurrence Decision *Ineos/Gymnaste Club de Nice* (21 August 2019)

11 FIFA, *Global Transfer Report* (2022) <https://digitalhub.fifa.com/m/2ee0b8943684e25b/original/FIFA-Global-Transfer-Report-2022.pdf> accessed 24 August 2025.

12 CADE's General-Superintendence noted that, in 2020, CADE, within the context of merger Case No 08700.000439/2020-17 (Grupo Endeavor and FC10), understood that the services provided were ancillary to the exploitation of other rights acquired through the operation (broadcasting and sponsorship rights).

4. Gyms

39. In Administrative Proceeding No 08700.001312/2021-98, CADE analysed the acquisition by Smartfit Escola de Ginástica e Dança SA (Smartfit) of 100% of the shares representing the total and voting capital stock of Just Fit Participações em Empreendimentos SA (Just Fit). In Opinion No 156/2021/CGAA5/SGA1/SG, CADE's General-Superintendence clarified that, in previous precedents,[13] the gym market was analysed in an aggregated manner, without specific segmentations, although it was not necessary to adopt a precise definition of the relevant market.

40. Therefore, regarding the product dimension of the relevant market, the applicants of the Smartfit/Just Fit concentration initially defined "gyms" as all types of establishments aimed at physical activities, encompassing cardiovascular activities, weight training, functional activities, Pilates, dance, "Crossfit" and swimming, excluding team sports and tennis, as well as recreational activities in clubs.

41. Despite this aspect, CADE has already assessed more segmented dimensions of the product market. In fact, in Administrative Proceeding No 08700.006225/2023-99, involving MC Brazil Fitness Holding SA and Bluefit Academias de Ginástica e Participações SA, the applicants asked for a narrower definition that focused on product aspects and included only cardiovascular activities, weight training and functional activities. This case referred to the acquisition of control by MC Brazil Fitness Holding SA (Buyer) of Bluefit Academias de Ginástica e Participações SA (Bluefit or the Target Company and, together with the Buyer, Parties) (Transaction), through the subscription of new shares and acquisition of existing shares corresponding jointly to 51% of Bluefit's capital stock. On the geographic aspect, CADE considered that, as in previous cases, gyms typically compete in a local market, but in the present case a precise definition was not necessary.

42. In the analysis of Administrative Process No 08012.005524/2010-40, a complaint was filed by Smart Rio Academia de Ginástica Ltd against the Gym Academies Union of the State of Rio de Janeiro (SINDACAD/RJ) and its President Ricardo Marques de Abreu. In this case, CADE found that SINDACAD had acted in a way that hindered the development of the low-cost gym model, seeking to prevent Smart Rio's low prices, restricting the number of students per teacher, and actively campaigning against the low-price model. After examining the evidence, CADE decided to punish the defendants for creating unfair campaigns and difficulties for competitors. CADE's analysis, in this case, was limited to gyms, studios and fitness schools, weight training and other physical activities (product dimension), in the Municipality of Rio de Janeiro (geographic dimension).

43. There is also Administrative Proceeding No 08700.005683/2019-24, which is still ongoing before CADE's Administrative Tribunal. In this case, the complainants are Smartfit Escola de Ginástica e Dança SA (Smart Fit) and Self It Academias

---

13 The following cases were mentioned: Administrative Proceeding Case No 08700.008463/2016-18 (acquisition by Stratus SCP Brasil Fundo de Investimento em Participações of a stake in the capital stock of Just Fit Participações em Empreendimentos SA); and Administrative Proceeding Case No 08012.005872/2012-89 (acquisition by BPMB Lambda Participações SA, through the subscription of convertible debentures into shares, of a stake in the capital stock of A! Bodytech Participações SA).

Holdings SA (Self It), and the defendants are the Gym Academies Union of Rio de Janeiro (SINDACAD/RJ), Maria José Montenegro Marques Dale, the Union of Physical Education Professionals of Rio de Janeiro (SINPEF/RJ) and Diego Gonçalves Marques. The case debates whether a new clause was inserted in the 2019–2020 Collective Labor Agreement, limiting the minimum number of Physical Education Professionals in gyms, and whether this limitation could constitute an influence of uniform anticompetitive conduct, typified in Article 36, caput, items I and IV, in conjunction with Section 3, items II and IV, Law No. 12.529/2011. Thus, CAED's General-Superintendence, the Specialized Federal Prosecutor's Office, and the CADE's Public Prosecutor's Office have all suggested condemning the aforementioned conduct. The case is currently being analysed before CADE's Tribunal.

5. *Gympass* Case (Digital Platforms)

44. An interesting case involving a wide range of sports disciplines pertains to Administrative Inquiry No 08700.004136/2020-65. In this precedent, CADE analysed the sector of digital platforms aggregating gyms in Brazil.

45. Founded in 2012, Gympass provides employees of registered companies access to various gyms located in Brazil and other countries with a single subscription. Through the Gympass platform, employees can choose plans that involve unlimited daily passes or individual daily passes at the registered gyms.

46. The investigations aimed to assess whether Gympass was abusing its dominant market position, particularly through the imposition of exclusivity clauses with gyms on the platform, as well as other preferential clauses that would allow Gympass to control the minimum price set by the registered platforms, thereby influencing the prices practiced in the segment nationwide.

47. CADE entered into an agreement with the Gympass, which restricted exclusivity clauses to 20% of its gym base in municipalities or municipal zones.[14] However, in 2025 CADE found non-compliance with the Cease-and-Desist Agreement (TCC) and decided to prohibit all exclusivity contracts between Wellhub and gyms, as well as to declare invalid the contracts executed since September 27, 2022. The administrative inquiry was reopened to assess compliance and to impose sanctions, if necessary.

6. The *Fox and Disney* Merger

48. The merger case No 08700.004494/2018-53 pertains to the Walt Disney Company's (TWDC) proposed acquisition of Twenty-First Century Fox.

49. CADE analysed the effect of the transaction in different relevant markets. However, the market for basic sports channel programming for pay-tv was the most debated within the council. According to the vote of former Commissioner Paulo Burnier, considering this market definition, the transaction would practically result in the formation of a duopoly in the basic sports channel market, as, in the

---

14 It was understood in this case that a gym would be any commercial establishment with which Gympass has a contract for the practice of physical activities, including but not limited to establishments offering cardiovascular activities (on treadmills, bicycles, ellipticals or without equipment), weight training, functional activities, crossfit, pilates, dance, swimming, among other sports.

post-merger scenario, Globosat (Sport TV) and the applicants, together, would control more than 90% of the audience.

50. It was argued that the reduction from three to two players in the market had the potential to directly affect the well-being of consumers, either through a loss of quality in the content broadcast on sports channels (with fewer commentators, for example), a decrease in content diversity (less demanded sports, apart from football), or an increase in prices to access these contents.

51. The applicants argued that the transaction would enable the formation of a player better positioned to compete with the Globosat group. However, according to the General-Superintendence and former Commissioner Paulo Burnier, the Globosat Group had a distinct profile from the applicants. While Globosat, through the SporTV and Première channels, essentially broadcast national championships, such as the A and B Series of the Brazilian Championship, the Brazil Cup and the main state football championships, the applicants controlled the broadcasting rights of the main international championships. Indeed, the Fox Group (through Fox Sports) was responsible for broadcasting the South American Cups and the Copa Libertadores, while the TWDC Group, through ESPN channels, broadcast various European championships and leagues of great appeal to Brazilian consumers, such as the English Premier League, the Italian Cup, the Spanish Super Cup, the Spanish Championship (La Liga), in addition to games from important sports leagues, such as the NBA (basketball) and NFL (American football).

52. In this case, former CADE Commissioner João Paulo Resende mentioned in his vote that there was no guarantee that the transaction would intensify competition between the applicants and the Globosat group. On the contrary, there might be greater incentive for tacit coordination, where the applicants could specialise in broadcasting foreign sports, especially from the United States (such as NBA, NFL, US Open and MLB) and some international football championships, while Globosat would broadcast football and volleyball with a national scope.

53. Considering these arguments, CADE drafted a Consent Decree in which the parties agreed to divest a set of assets necessary for the operation of Fox Sports in Brazil in the market of producing and licensing basic sports linear channels for pay-tv in Brazil. Considering the specific difficulties of the Covid-19 pandemic, among other issues, the initially proposed structural remedy proved unfeasible. In this regard, CADE changed the structural obligations to behavioural ones, and in August 2023, through Presidential Dispatch 74/2023, compliance with these obligations was fully certified.

7. Ongoing Investigation Regarding Cartel for Construction of Football Stadiums

54. A case still under review by CADE concerns Administrative Proceeding No 08700.006630/2016-88. This case, described in Technical Note No 22/2024/CGAA8/SGA2/SG/CADE, involves an Administrative Proceeding initiated on 17 July 2019, through Technical Note No 68/2019 (SEI 0633553; 0634265) and its annex, approved by Dispatch SG No 19/2019 (SEI 0634338), published in the

Official Gazette[15], to investigate an alleged cartel in the national market for civil construction works, modernisation and/or renovation of Football Stadiums for the 2014 FIFA World Cup in Brazil. This conduct could potentially be classified under Articles 20, I to IV, and 21, I, III, IV, and VIII, Law No 8.884/1994, as well as Article 36, I–IV in conjunction with its Section 3, I, items (a), (c), and (d), and III, Law No 12.529/2011, in accordance with Article 69 and following Law No 12.529/2011.

55. According to the accusation, the economic order violations consisted of agreements for, (i) price fixing, conditions, advantages and abstentions among competitors; (ii) market division and project allocation; and (iii) the exchange of competitively sensitive information. These agreements allegedly involved the exchange of information on strategic interests in the stadiums, the formation of consortia, the suppression of bids, the submission of cover bids and the promise of future subcontracting.

56. The accusation claims that contacts between competitors preliminarily began with the designation of Brazil as the host of the 2014 World Cup by FIFA in October 2007, intensifying in the second half of 2008, and lasting until at least mid-2011, when the contracts for the public works of the World Cup stadiums were signed. The case is still under review by CADE's Tribunal.

8. Ongoing Investigation Regarding Unfair Treatment Related to Broadcasting Rights of Football Games

57. Another case under review by CADE concerns Administrative Inquiry No 08700.004453/2019-48, initiated on 25 September 2020 through Dispatch SG No 28/2020, to investigate economic order violations of a public nature by Globo Comunicações e Participações SA (GCP) in the market for broadcasting football games, under Articles 13, III, and 66, Section 1, Law No 12.529/2011. The decision to initiate this inquiry was motivated by the analysis expressed in Technical Note No 1/2020/GAB-SG/SG/CADE, drafted within the context of the Preparatory Procedure for Administrative Inquiry related to the market for broadcasting rights of football games, initiated *ex officio* by Dispatch No 27/2019, where it was concluded that there were indications of alleged conduct by GCP in the investigated market, which, if proven, could constitute economic order violations. It is noted that after the investigation began, a complaint of anticompetitive conduct filed by a representative of Fortaleza Esporte Clube was attached. In the complaint, the club alleged that it was disadvantaged in its contract with Turner International Inc, as other clubs contracted by the broadcaster received more favourable remuneration conditions. In this scenario, the club pointed to a violation of Article 36, Section 3, IV, VIII, and X Law No 12.529/2011. Subsequently, on 20 August 2020, the club requested the withdrawal of the complaint and the filing of the case. However, the General-Superintendence continues to investigate the case.

---

15 Government of Brazil. Despacho No. 19, 16 July 2019. Diário Oficial da União, Brasília. Retrieved from https://www.in.gov.br/web/dou/-/despacho-n-19-de-16-de-julho-de-2019-196325079 (accessed on September 11, 2025).

III. Judicial Debate on Football Agent Regulations

58. An intriguing case of competition advocacy emerged in a recent judicial discussion about football agents.

59. A football agent acts as a representative and intermediary for football players, managing various aspects of their careers. These professionals negotiate contracts with clubs and sponsors, handle public relations and identify opportunities to advance their clients' careers. Consequently, agents need an in-depth understanding of the football market and sports industry, along with expertise in management and legal matters. Sports agencies, law firms or freelancers can employ football agents. Additionally, some football clubs hire agents to recruit players.[16]

60. The Brazilian Association of Football Agents (ABAF or the Plaintiff) filed a collective action against FIFA and the CBFregistered under No. 0837583-33.2023.8.19.0209, due to the following facts.

61. On 1 December 2023, dozens of football agents, mostly from other states and not affiliated with ABAF, filed a lawsuit against the CBF. This action was registered under case No 0837583-33.2023.8.19.0209 and assigned to the Honourable Court of the Seventh Civil Court of the Regional Forum of Barra da Tijuca in the Capital District, where it is currently proceeding.

62. Both actions seek to immediately cease the application of provisions from the new 2023 CBF National Football Agent Regulations. However, ABAF claims that its case has a broader cause of action and request, as it also targets the new FIFA Football Agent Regulations (FFAR), which were not challenged in the initial demand.

63. ABAF explained that Article 95, Section 2 of the new General Sports Law (Law No 14.957/2023) delegated the issuance of regulatory acts governing its activity to FIFA and CBF. It was clarified that, after a transition period beginning on 9 January 2023, the FFAR came fully into effect on 1 October 2023. Furthermore, on 4 October 2023, CBF issued the new 2023 National Football Agent Regulations (RNAF), replacing the Working with Intermediaries Regulations model that was in effect from 2015–2023. ABAF challenges specific provisions of these two regulations, arguing they impose severe restrictions on professional practice. ABAF argues, for example, that the maximum service fees fixed as percentages in Article 15, No 2 represent restrictions on competition. ABAF claims that these fees constitute a uniform behaviour prescribed for all potential clients of football agent services, amounting to anticompetitive behaviour.

64. ABAF's concerns, as outlined in the text, revolve around various provisions in the FFAR that they see as intentional restrictions on competition. ABAF points out that these rules could influence remuneration by delaying payments, thus restricting financial flow to agents. The regulations also standardise market activity and eliminate competitive terms and conditions, further constraining the freedom

---

16 See indeed.com <https://uk.indeed.com/career-advice/finding-a-job/how-to-become-a-football-agen>t accessed 24 August 2025.

of agents and their clients. Furthermore, the requirement for agent payments to be processed through FIFA's Clearing House is considered a control mechanism that tracks and restricts market activities. The prohibition on agents representing multiple parties in a transaction is also viewed as a limitation on choice and competition. The mandatory licensing and compliance with FIFA's statutes, according to ABAF, create barriers to market entry, effectively excluding agents who do not comply. Therefore, ABAF claims that these rules collectively limit the economic autonomy of market participants and have a significant impact on the Brazilian market due to the international nature of football.

65. When asked to comment, CADE's Presidency, in an official letter, stated that CADE did not have full access to the judicial records and there was insufficient time to hear the involved parties. On the other hand, the international debate on the issue was mentioned. Information was provided to the Brazilian Judiciary about the arbitral decision that analysed Swiss legislation and ruled in favour of FIFA, understanding that the issue did not affect competition.[17]

66. It was also clarified that, in early 2023, the Court of Justice of the European Union (CJEU) received a request for a preliminary ruling in *RRC Sports Gmb v FIFA*, concerning the compatibility of the FFAR with EU competition law, the free movement of services and EU data protection rules. This request was submitted by the Ninth Civil Chamber of the Regional Court of Mainz (Landgericht Mainz, Germany) in a case brought by an agent (FT) and RRC Sports GmbH against FIFA.[18]

67. Thus, a European court sought clarification from the Court of Justice on whether these regulations could represent a form of anticompetitive conduct. As of now, there has been no ruling on the case's merits, highlighting the complexity of the issue.

68. The European Commission recently submitted its observations on the matter to the CJEU. Although CADE did not have access to the full position of the Commission, Ali Walker indicated that the European Commission is backing FIFA's attempt to regulate the world's top football agents, suggesting that the restriction on competition caused by the FFAR could be justified by legitimate objectives pursued by FIFA. The Commission emphasised the importance of protecting contractual stability, limiting conflicts of interest and safeguarding players who lack experience or information about the transfer system.

69. Regarding the cap on agent fees, the Commission's legal service stated that

> the defendant has plausibly pointed out that very high agency commissions, which are completely decoupled from the cost of the consideration, create

---

[17] Case 2023/O/9370 CAS Decision *PROFAA v FIFA* (2023); Erkut Sogut and Jamie Khan, "Why did the Court of Arbitration for Sport Find in Favour of the FIFA Football Agent Regulations?" (*The Football Week*, 2024) <https://thefootballweek.org/2024/01/14/why-did-the-court-of-arbitration-for-sports-find-in-favour-of-the-fifa-football-agent-regulations/>; FIFA, Press Release, "FIFA welcomes CAS Decision on FIFA Football Agent Regulations" (24 July 2023) <https://inside.fifa.com/transfer-system/agents/media-releases/fifa-welcomes-cas-decision-on-fifa-football-agent-regulations> accessed 24 August 2025.

[18] Case C-209/23 *RRC Sports Gmb v FIFA* (pending)

a strong incentive to exert massive influence on players in particular in order to force an early transfer.[19]

70. On the prohibition of agents representing the player, the buying club, and the selling club in the same deal, the Commission stated that the regulation also "appears suitable" to combat this potential conflict of interest:

> Insofar as a player agent is mandated simultaneously by the releasing club, the player and the receiving club, it is not evident how the player agent can act simultaneously in the best interests of all three principals.[20]

71. On the other hand, there are debates on these topics in various countries, including the UK, Germany, Spain and Belgium.

72. As referenced in the initial petition, in Spain, the Asociación Española de Agentes de Futbolistas and others filed an action against FIFA and the Real Federación Española de Fútbol (RFEF). In this case, according to the Madrid Commercial Court No 3, a decision rendered on 2 November 2023 by Judge Jorge Montull Urquijo, prohibited FIFA and RFEF from applying parts of their new regulations to football agents in that country, specifically regarding the limitation on commissions.

73. Similarly, as mentioned in the initial petition, in the case involving football agents against FIFA and the Deutscher Fußball-Bund eV (DFB – German Football Association), the Eigth Civil Chamber of the Regional Court of Dortmund (Landgericht Dortmund), a decision rendered on 24 May 2023, prohibited FIFA and DFB from applying certain FFAR provisions that violate competition law in Germany, under penalty of fines of up to €250,000 per violation.[21]

74. In the UK, there are also decisions challenging FIFA's rules.[22] Given this context, it is reasonable to state that there is no consensus on the effect of this type of conduct, even among the different agencies responsible for understanding and interpreting competition laws worldwide. There are arbitral decisions and positions from the European Commission that support the effects of the analysed regulations, while some countries have issued decisions to oppose them.

75. In any case, considering that it is the responsibility of CADE's General-Superintendence to initiate investigations regarding anticompetitive conduct, these facts have been reported to the competent authority, as well as to CADE's Federal Specialized Attorney's Office, which represents CADE in the Judiciary.

---

19 Ali Walker, "EU Commission Supports FIFA in Row with Football Agents" (*Politico*, 31 October 2023) <www.politico.eu/article/european-commission-support-fifa-row-football-agents-court/> accessed 24 August 2025.

20 Ibid.

21 Tim Lichtenberg, "FIFA's Football Agents Regulation Violates Competition Law" (*Kluwer Competition Law Blog*, 20 July 2023) <https://legalblogs.wolterskluwer.com/competition-blog/fifas-football-agents-regulation-violates-competition-law/> accessed 24 August 2025.

22 Chiranjit Ojha and Mitch Phillips, "FIFA's Agent Fee Cap Breaches British Competition Law: FA Tribunal" (*Reuters*, 1 December 2023) <www.reuters.com/sports/soccer/fifas-agent-fee-cap-breaches-british-competition-law-fa-tribunal-2023-12-01/#:~:text=FIFA's%20agent%20fee%20cap%20breaches%20British%20competition%20law%3A%20FA%20Tribunal,-Reuters&text=Dec%201%20(Reuters)%20%2D%20Pro> accessed 24 August 2025.

IV. Final Remarks

76. The purpose of this chapter was to provide an overview of CADE's jurisprudence and recent debates on the intersection between sports and antitrust law in Brazil.

77. After analysing all the above cases and discussions, it is possible to conclude that the intricate landscape of sports regulation and competition law in Brazil highlights the critical role of CADE. The Brazilian Federal Constitution and the General Sports Law establish a robust framework for sports regulation. Ongoing investigations and analyses of anticompetitive practices underscore CADE's vigilance in this market. By monitoring and addressing these issues, CADE ensures a fair and dynamic sports market, protects the interests of all stakeholders and maintains the integrity of sports in Brazil. This proactive approach is crucial in navigating the global complexity of sports regulation and fostering a competitive environment.

The Egyptian Competition Authority's Enforcement Policy in Sports

Mohamed El Far[*] and Mahmoud A Momtaz[**]
German University in Cairo

I. Introduction

1. The Egyptian Competition Authority (ECA) has developed throughout the years its policy when it comes to the sports industry in Egypt.

2. Most importantly, as will be shown, the ECA has developed its own policy when it comes to market definition in this sector: definition of persons, dominance and anticompetitive restraints. This chapter is intended to explore the main themes that the ECA has adopted in those matters when it comes to the sports industry along with the development of the ECA's enforcement policy in this sector. It is important to note that the ECA has mainly explored sports tournaments related to football as it is the most important national sport in Egypt from a consumer/ fan's perspective.[1] Yet, the ECA has also considered other sports where concerns came to its attention.[2]

---

* Lecturer at the German University in Cairo (GUC). Email: moh.elfar@gmail.com.

** Dr iur Lecturer of Competition Law and Economics at the German University in Cairo (GUC) and, University of Hamburg and Cairo University. Email: momtazmahmoud@gmail.com.

The personal views in this chapter are those of the author and do not reflect the opinion of the Egyptian Competition Authority or any of its officials.

1 ECA, *BeIN Sports Report* I (2017) 10.

2 ECA, *Marathon Report* (2014).

II. Market Definition

3. In a series of cases, the ECA has started developing its market definition approach when it comes to different sports tournaments. For example, in 2010, the ECA conducted a study in the exclusive agreement entered into by the Confederation of African Football (CAF) and AlJazeera Sports (known since 2014 as BeIN Sports). The main concern in this case, was that the six-year exclusive agreement is likely to infringe the Egyptian Competition Law (ECL).[3]

4. In this case, the ECA decided that the market definition, as far as CAF is concerned, is "CAF football tournaments",[4] which meant that all of the CAF football tournaments were grouped together in one relevant market. However, in the same report, the ECA noted that "each sports tournament is a separate relevant market".[5] In this respect, the ECA highlighted a number of factors that it had considered in its assessment to reach this conclusion which were as follows:

   1. Viewership of sports tournaments as compared to other non-sports-related tournaments.
   2. Number of advertisements that is associated with sports events as compared to other non-sports-related tournaments.
   3. The popularity of football/soccer in Egypt which distinguishes it from other sports tournaments.
   4. The special nature of each football tournament, and the fact that the Egyptian national team is playing in a tournament might even consider that those specifics are a separate product market.
   5. The temporal nature of these football tournaments and the importance of live coverage.

5. As noted above, the ECA had then concluded that CAF football tournaments for the purposes of this case were the relevant product market. While this conclusion might seem inconsistent given the narrow approach adopted in the analysis as compared to the wider product market concluded in this case, this might be a justified position. This is because, the ECA noted that BeIN Sports has acquired the exclusive rights for all CAF tournaments for a period of six years.[6] As a result, BeIN Sports was deemed dominant in this case for being in control of all CAF tournaments for the set period of time (ie 100% market share). According to the ECA, this practice could have restricted competition.[7]

6. In 2014, the ECA initiated another case against BeIN Sports. However, this time, the case related to the broadcasting of the FIFA World Cup. In the assessment of the market definition, the ECA noted again that from a consumer perspective "each and every tournament is a separate relevant market". Yet, the ECA later noted in the assessment, that given the resemblance in quality and popularity of different tournaments that run simultaneously, it might be harder to consider them

---

3 Law No 3 of 2005 on the Protection of Competition and the Prohibition of Monopolistic Practices (ECL).

4 ECA, *CAF Report* (2010) 8.

5 Ibid.

6 Ibid 6.

7 Ibid 10.

as separate markets from an Egyptian consumer's perspective (English Premier League, Spanish La Liga and Italian Legal Series A).[8]

7. However, the ECA did not need to address the question on whether each tournament was an independent relevant market. This is because, the primary focus was on the World Cup. As a result, the ECA conducted its assessment and decided that the FIFA World Cup 2014 was a separate relevant market.[9]

8. Building upon the ECA report of 2010, the ECA has mainly taken the following factors into its assessment:

   1. The timing of the World Cup.
   2. The popularity of the World Cup.
   3. The importance of the live broadcasting nature of the said tournaments.

9. Based on the above, the ECA concluded that the relevant market in this case was the World Cup 2014. The ECA used the available evidence and the uniqueness of this tournament to implement the standards it had identified for market definition in this sector. It can be argued that the World Cup is generally easier to establish as a separate relevant market.

10. In 2017, the ECA brought three separate cases against CAF and BeIN Sports.[10] In the CAF case, the ECA in a more detailed analysis concluded that each CAF tournament was a separate product market. Similarly,, the ECA established the various factors previously considered and reached a more definitive conclusion on market definition as noted above.

11. It is worth mentioning that a criminal action was triggered in this case and the court of appeal in Egypt upheld the infringement finding of CAF, including the narrow market definition established in this case. It is important to note that while considering the African Cup of Nations, the CAF Champions League and CAF Confederation Cup as separate product markets is sensible, arguing that CAF Beach Soccer Championship and CAF Under 17 Championship are stand-alone relevant markets each, is a lot more challenging. However, the ECA did not differentiate and decided, as upheld by the court, that each CAF tournament was a separate product market.[11]

12. In another important case, the ECA issued an infringement decision against BeIN Sports for engaging in tying while being in a dominant position. In the market definition assessment, the ECA built upon prior experience in cases and provided the same justifications as stated in the CAF case. However, in this case, the ECA not only concluded that each football tournament was a separate relevant market on its own but rather clearly listed more than 15 regional, global and local tournaments around the world and stated that each tournament was a separate product market.[12]

13. Similarly to the CAF case, the Egyptian courts have upheld the infringement decision of the ECA on appeal including the market definitions identified

---

8 ECA, *BeIN Sports Report* 5 (2014).

9 Ibid 6.

10 ECA, CAF Report (2017), ECA, BeIN Sports I Report (2017) and ECA, BeIN Sports II Report (2017)

11 Case 397 *Cairo Economic Misdemeanors* 14 (2017).

12 *BeIN Sports Report* (n 1), 7–12.

in the ECA report. One of the notable points in this regard is that the ECA, as upheld by the courts, ruled that local EU-based leagues are separate product markets from the perspective of the Egyptian consumer.

14. In a different case, in 2014[13], the ECA issued an infringement decision against a marathon race organiser for abusing its dominant position in the market of organising recognised marathons in Egypt. In the market definition assessment, the ECA noted a number of factors to establish the market definition in that case including the following:

   1. The infringing company is the only company that is licensed by the international organising body of marathons (ie The Association of International Marathons and Distance Races) to organise such events in Egypt.
   2. The organiser provides a number to each athlete, on road services and healthcare.
   3. These marathons are of an international nature. In other words, non-Egyptian contestants are entitled to join.
   4. These marathons are located in prime tourist spots.
   5. The length of the marathon is around 42 kms on average.

15. As a result, this marathon was distinguished from other local unrecognised marathons and other sports events in Egypt more broadly. The ECA noted that the market definition was the "organisation of the service of marathons in Luxor" which was also a narrow market definition in light of the above justifications.

16. It can be noted that there are a number of themes that the ECA focuses on when assessing market definitions in the sports sector and the ECA jurisdiction more broadly, which are as follows:

   1. The licenses required to conduct a business and provide a service.
   2. The IP rights held by the licensing/organising body in that sport whether it is regional or local.
   3. International recognition and popularity are also determinative factors that the ECA has taken into consideration when assessing market definition.

III. Means of Establishment

17. Under the ECL, a person subject to the law is defined as any:

> Natural and juristic persons, economic entities, unions, financial associations and groupings, groups of persons, whatever their means of incorporation, and other related parties as set forth in the Executive Regulations concurrently with the objectives and provisions of this Law.[14]

18. The Executive Regulations of the ECL add:

> Persons mean natural or juristic persons, economic entities, unions, federations, associations and financial grouping, whatever the method of their

---

13 *ECA, Marathon, ECA Report, (2014).*

14 ECL, art 2.

establishment, mechanisms of their financing, their nationalities, headquarters or main centres of activities...[15]

19. This means that regardless of the method of establishment or means of finance, an entity might be defined as a "person" under the ECL. In the sports-related cases in Egypt, these notions were tested where they were put into effect. A number of outcomes emerged from the ECA's practice including the following:

    1. *Location of the organising body*: it was determined by the ECA that the location of the organising body of this sport does not need to be in Egypt in order for the ECA to have jurisdiction. In other words, whether the organising body is located in Egypt or not was not a determinative factor to the ECA.
    2. For example, in the *BeIN Sports* case, the ECA brought the case against the CEO of BeIN Sports even though the entity was established under the laws of Qatar and was not located in Egypt and the CEO was a foreign national who did not reside in Egypt.[16] However, the ECA still assumed jurisdiction which was upheld by Egyptian courts.[17]
    3. *Means of establishment*: The ECA also expanded the scope of "persons" to include sports organisations regardless of their means of establishment.
    4. For example, in the *CAF* case, CAF was established by virtue of a regional treaty between the African countries. Among the arguments raised by the defendants was that the ECA did not have jurisdiction over an international organisation that was established by a treaty. However, the courts in Egypt confirmed that the ECA had jurisdiction to assess and decide on this case.[18]
    5. *Group of persons*: as noted, CAF was established by virtue of a regional treaty between the federations of 54 countries.[19] Yet, the ECA and Egyptian courts applied and enforced the ECL on this regional body which is composed of a "group of persons" as defined under the ECL.[20]
    6. *A person does not need to generate profit*: According to the ECA enforcement practice, it was established that in order to engage in an economic activity, that entity (person) did not necessarily need to generate profit.
    7. For example, the Fédération Internationale de Football Association (FIFA) "is a non-profit international organisation".[21] However, as shown, given that was is engaged in an economic activity which offers of services and licenses to market players, it was still subject to the jurisdiction of the ECA where the ECA was able to impose an interim measure in relation to the World Cup 2018.[22]

---

15 ECL Executive Regulations No 1316 of 2005, art 5.

16 *BeIN Sports Report* (n 1), 6.

17 Case 2721 Judicial Year 1989 Egyptian Court of Cassation.

18 ECA, *CAF Report* (2017) 15; *Cairo Economic Misdemeanors* (n 10).

19 CAF, "About us, CAF History" <https://www.cafonline.com/inside-caf/about-us/caf-history/> accessed 6 August 2025.

20 Case 327 *Cairo Economic Misdemeanours* (2017).

21 FIFA, *Annual Report 2021 – General Information and Statement of Compliance* (2021) <https://publications.fifa.com/en/annual-report-2021/2021-financials-and-2023-budget/2021-financial-statements/significant-accounting-policies/>accessed 6 August 2025.

22 ECA, Decision 1 of 2018 regarding FIFA 2023 Regulations on the Status and Transfer of Players (RSTP).

8. **Any person whatever their means of incorporation:** Indeed, in the *Marathon* case report, the ECA did not discuss the legal framework governing the incorporation of the entity subject to the investigation which was called "Event Sports". In this respect, as part of the initial jurisdiction assessment, the ECA stated that: "Event Sports is engaged in an economic activity as it provides the service of organising marathons, hence, it would qualify as a juristic person that is subject to the ECL…".[23]

   The above indicates that once the ECA was able to establish that there was an economic activity, it also established the satisfaction of the jurisdiction requirement, regardless of the means of incorporation of the investigated entity.

20. The above examples indicate that the ECA is willing to implement the concept of "person" to its maximum limits. To date, the ECA has been successful in all its attempts in this regard. In particular, the ECA has indeed applied many of the "person" concepts to sports-related organisations.

21. In addition, it seems that the ECA is adopting an approach in this regard which is somehow similar to that of the EU concept of "undertaking" under the EU competition law. Indeed, the EU Commission and national EU competition authorities have, in numerous cases, applied the concept of "undertaking" to sports bodies including FIFA and UEFA,[24] and an association of undertakings as in the *Wouters* case.[25]

22. What remains to be seen is how the ECA will implement the notion of "person" on players in different sports. It will be interesting to see whether the ECA will also follow the footsteps of the EU Competition Commission and the European Court of Justice or whether it will take a different turn. In the EU, it is settled legally that players are generally subject to competition law.

23. Under EU Competition Law, the European Court of Justice has clearly confirmed that,

> …the rules adopted by FIFA and UEFA to establish a framework for participation by professional football clubs and players in international inter-club football competitions also come within the scope of those provisions. Although they do not formally govern the players' conditions of work or of performance of services or the conditions of performance of services or, more broadly, of the exercise of their economic activity by professional football clubs, those rules must be regarded as having a direct impact, as the case may be, on that work, that performance of services or the exercise of that economic activity, since they necessarily affect whether the players and clubs may participate in the competitions in question…[26]

24. From the above, it can be noted that players are subject to competition rules. In Egypt, many disputes have been reported in relation to players in different types

---

23 *Marathon Report* (n 2), 2.

24 Case C-333/21 *European Super League (ESL)* ECLI:EU:C:2023:1011.

25 Case C-309/99 *Wouters* ECLI:EU:C:2002:98.

26 *ESL* (n 22), para 91.

of sports with their respective clubs and federations. This is also very common for many artists who sign "monopoly contracts" with producers or venues or otherwise, that are in many cases very restrictive.

IV. Dominance

25. Based on all the cases brought by the ECA so far, it seems that the ECA has defined markets narrowly to the extent that the market share of the defendants were 100% of the relevant market.

26. For example, in CAF cases, the ECA has defined the market in two different ways, but both resulted in the same outcome. On one hand, in the CAF case of 2014, the ECA defined the market as "African football tournaments". In that case, CAF was found to have 100% of that market share.[27] However, more accurately, in the CAF case of 2017, the ECA defined the market more narrowly by specifying that each tournament was a separate relevant market on it its own.[28] It can be noted that in both cases the ECA findings were that the market share of CAF was 100% of the market share.[29]

27. Similarly, in the *Marathon* case and *BeIN* cases, the ECA reached the same conclusion, that the defendants had a 100% market share in the relevant market. This was a direct result of the fact that relevant markets were defined narrowly. As a result, the ECA was able to establish such a high market share and also establish market power.

28. This enforcement approach does not seem unusual given that most federations have commonly some sort of monopoly of official tournaments in the region. This monopoly status of the organisation, regulation and management of the tournaments was also raised and disputed in the EU.[30] The European Court of Justice has also noted that,

> …such rules [of FIFA and UEFA] are liable to enable both entities on which they confer a monopoly in this area, consisting in total control over supply, to charge excessive, and therefore abusive, prices …, faced with which actual or potential buyers of rights prima facie have only limited negotiating power, given the fundamental and inescapable place held by professional interclub football competitions and matches… Moreover, by obliging all actual or potential buyers of rights to purchase from two vendors… thereby leading to a narrowing of choice and less innovation, to the detriment of consumers and television viewers.[31]

29. From the above, it seems that a common theme going forward would be to expect that regional and national federations will likely be found to be in a super

---

27 *CAF Report* (n 4), 8.

28 *CAF Report* (n 16), 15.

29 Case 372 *Cairo Economic Misdemeanours* 15 (2017).

30 Case CAS 2014/A/3776 *Gibraltar Football Association (GFA) v Fédération Internationale de Football Association (FIFA)*, award (27 April 2016), para181.

31 Case C-333/21 *European Super League (ESL)* ECLI:EU:C:2023:1011, para 228.

dominant position in the relevant product (ie 100% of the market share) by the ECA. This adds a special responsibility on the respective regional and national sports federations not to hamper effective competition. In other words, it was clearly stated that[32],

> In the Panel's view, special responsibilities accompany the special power held by FIFA as the supreme regulatory authority within its sport, and as the organiser of the most important worldwide competition between national football associations (ie the FIFA World Cup). The Panel is persuaded that FIFA, albeit a private body, must respect general principles that also constrain legislators and governmental administrations...

30. The ECA is more likely to adopt a similar approach to that of the EU on this front in the future. As a matter of fact, in the *CAF* case, the ECA has already recognised the concept of special responsibility where it stated that,

> ...according to the ECL, a person that holds a dominant position in the Egyptian market has a special responsibility not to obstruct or limit the freedom of competition in any way in the relevant market or other related markets to it with the object of weakening competition by virtue of measures that fall outside the scope of normal competition that would take place between market players [ie competition on the merits]...[33]

31. Considering the above statement, it is clear that the ECA has not only followed the EU approach in market definition and in establishing dominance in the sports sector but has also recognised the "special responsibility" of those dominant players.

V. Tying Practices in the Sports Sector

32. The predominant theme in the infringements brought by the ECA in the sports sector, is that of tying. In almost all the ECA cases, the main infringement identified was that of tying unrelated products into one bundle. This has resulted in an abundance of guidance and case law on how the ECA implements the tying prohibition. It is worth noting that all the ECA's cases that were brought to court were upheld.

33. For a tying prohibition to be established, the ECA and courts have had to establish the following conditions:[34]

    1. Presence of a dominant position (as noted above).
    2. Two or more distinct products.

34. It is noteworthy, that tying under the ECL is prohibited *per se*. This means that once the ECA establishes that there is a dominant person that is engaged in a tying arrangement, this conduct will automatically be deemed anticompetitive. Courts in Egypt that have upheld the ECA's interpretation did not require any effects-based analysis or require the ECA to establish any foreclosure effects

---

32 ECA, Decision 1 of 2018 regarding FIFA 2023 Regulations on the Status and Transfer of Players (RSTP).

33 *CAF Report* (n 16), 17.

34 Case 1507 *Cairo Economic Misdemeanours* 15 (2017).

that could potentially arise from this arrangement.[35] In one of the *BeIN* cases, the court rejected an expert's opinion submitted by the defendant arguing that the tying arrangement even if it existed did not have any effect on competition.[36] This means that the court in this case actively considered this argument and rejected it.

35. In those cases, the ECA has indeed considered both contractual and technical tying arrangements. Both were equally sanctioned by the courts. For example, in one *BeIN* case, the ECA accused BeIN of abusing its dominance for requiring consumers/subscribers to user a satellite (Sohail Sat) instead of Nile Sat which was the satellite previously used by consumers and BeIN. Among the arguments raised by the defendant was that technically BeIN could only be broadcast via Sohail Sat and not via Nile Sat. The court ruled that this was unfounded, upheld the ECA decision and imposed a fine on the defendant.[37]

36. As for contractual tying, for example, in the other BeIN case,[38] the ECA established that BeIN Sports had engaged in contractual tying by engaging in the following conduct:

    1. Required consumers who wanted to watch Euro CUP 2016 to also subscribe to another package that had other tournaments even though each tournament was a separate relevant market.
    2. Required consumers who wanted to watch a tournament to subscribe to a package that included other tournaments that they did not want to watch even though each tournament was a separate relevant market.

37. Based on the above points, the various courts upheld the ECA's findings and imposed a fine on the defendant.

VI. Conclusion

38. In conclusion, the ECA has tackled the sports sector on a number of occasions. It is important to note that the ECA did not shy away from bigger international or regional institutions but was rather proactive in addressing the anticompetitive concerns that were raised in this sector.

39. It is also notable that as far as market definition, definition of a person and dominance, there seems to be resemblance between ECA standards and EU competition case law and jurisprudence. There is quite a difference when it comes to tying arrangement. From the ECA and Egyptian courts' perspective, they seem to be less willing to entertain any arguments that would justify a tying arrangement, and it could be argued that this is due to the objectives of ECL and the concentrated nature of Egyptian markets.

40. As also indicated above, it remains to be seen how the ECA will consider and assess player contracts and more generally those of artists where what is known as "monopoly contracts' are common and in some cases result in disputes between the parties.

---

[35] Ibid; Case 1171 *Cairo Economic Misdeamours* (2017).

[36] Case 1507 *Cairo Economic Misdemeanours* 19 (2017).

[37] Ibid 16.

[38] ECA, BeIN Sports I Report (2017).

41. Given the developing nature of the federations and sports in general in Egypt and how this is structured financially and aided by regional bodies and the Egyptian Government, it is not expected that other independent leagues would feasibly emerge in the near future. In other words, it is unlikely that similar independent leagues as that of the European Super League would be organized in any time soon.

Sport and Competition Law in Australia: A Fertile Environment for Players and Lawyers?

Deborah Healey*
University of New South Wales

I. Introduction

1. Competition law has routinely been applied to sport in Australia and there are a number of leading cases about sport which are influential in a general Australian competition law context. However, the Competition and Consumer Act 2010 (CCA) (renamed from the Trade Practices Act 1974 (TPA) in 2010) has been amended on multiple occasions, meaning that some were cases decided under earlier provisions, and uncertainties about the application of the current CCA to sport remain. The complexity of CCA drafting and its very technical application by courts, along with competition law dependence on changing economic theories, add to this uncertainty. Finally, competition law is intensely fact specific. These factors, coupled with a unique sporting landscape, mean that one cannot assume conduct which breaches competition law overseas will be prohibited in Australia. This chapter focuses on recent scenarios in the European Union and United States involving rival competitions in established areas of professional sport and explores how the Australian competition law might respond. The exploration shows that competition law has been applied in Australian sport in similar situations, and that it will continue to be relevant going forward.

---

* Professor Deborah Healey, University of New South Wales Faculty of Law and Justice

II. Competition Law and Sport: The Australian Context

2. The universal goal of competition law is to create a level playing field for competition to enhance efficiency and benefit the economy and consumers, although this is reflected globally in different legislative provisions and enforcement schemes. The central feature of a competition law is its prohibition of anticompetitive conduct: conduct that is exclusionary, foreclosing existing competitors in the market and/or which raises barriers to entry. While most nations have competition laws which target anticompetitive conduct such as cartels, abuse of dominance and consider mergers for their impact on competition, wordings and court systems vary considerably between jurisdictions.[1]

3. At its most basic, the Australian competition law, the Competition and Consumer Act 2010, has the express goals of enhancing the welfare of Australians by promoting competition and fair trading and protecting consumers, and it is interpreted accordingly.[2]

4. Recent overseas events indicate that competition law must be a significant strategic legal consideration for sporting organisations, teams and individuals. Examination of specific examples shows that not only could Australian competition law apply in similar circumstances, but in some cases, it already has. As part of this current examination, cases such as the seminal (*Australian Super League*) case of 1996, which involved litigation between an incumbent competition organiser and a newcomer, will be examined,[3] but particularly in the context of amendments to the Australian competition law since that time.

III. The Landscape of Australian Sport

5. The landscape of Australian sport is important to this chapter because analysis of markets is an essential part of applying competition law. Sport in Australia shares global growth in commercialisation, but national sporting tastes, issues arising from the population size and shape, and the relative isolation of the country, dictate that the landscape of Australian sport differs significantly from that in the US and EU. It is unique. Australia, for example, has four main professional football sports: Australian Rules Football, Rugby League, Rugby Union and Football, all with significant popularity in some or all of the country, and some embraced by most of the sporting public. Swimming is particularly important with most children learning from a very early age and surfing is incredibly popular given our extensive coastline. There are many other popular and influential sports.

6. A larger sponsorship pool, with more viewing options for fans with streaming and other options, gaming, gambling and consistent government funding has contributed to a growing sporting economy. More athletes are better compensated

---

1 See generally, Deborah Healey, "The Ambit of Competition Law: Comments on Its Goals" in Deborah Healey, Michael Jacobs and Rhonda Smith (eds), *Research Handbook on Methods and Models of Competition Law* (Edward Elgar 2020) 12–37.

2 Competition and Consumer Act 2010 (CCA), s 1.

3 *News Ltd v Australian Rugby Football League (Australian Super League)* [1996] FCA 1256. Leave to appeal to the High Court was refused.

and have greater expectations of fair and transparent treatment because of the significant commercial impact of decisions on them, and improved standards of professionalism and governance in the running of sporting organisations.

7. But the pool of funds is not consistent among the sports. The landscape is fragmented, with Australia's Federal system of states and territories dictating that sport is traditionally played at local, state and national levels, with separate organisations managing each level, usually affiliated to an organisation further up the hierarchy. National-level athletes represent internationally. To some extent it is similar to the traditional EU pyramid structure. There is a large gap between the resources of wealthy top-tier high-profile professional sports such as the football codes, cricket, golf, tennis and horse racing, other sports, and the community or "grass roots" levels of most sports. The popular top-tier professional sports are often integrated with their non-professional community cohort. Professional teams may be privately or community owned, as are some sports theselves. The top-tier sports have substantial funds to develop and organise all levels, and, in addition, some still receive government funding for athlete development and to support community-level participation. Other sports have lesser funds, and some are viewed only by those who attend. These sports are likely to be dependent on government funding at federal and state level to support athlete development and participation goals, using many volunteer coaches and officials. In most sports substantial efforts are committed to ensure the integrity of competitions. Many sports viewed as commercial but which are not wellfunded grapple with funding, governance and other strategic challenges.

8. Competition law has been the subject of a number of highly significant sports cases in Australia.[4] The *C7* case, for example, involving the collapse of a pay TV sports channel and involving claims against other broadcasters and a large number of sports, was among the largest pieces of Australian litigation at the time, and was the largest broadcasting and competition law litigation ever conducted in the country.[5]

1. Relationships between Sports, Their Teams and Players

9. Organisation of sport is unlike most other areas of commerce in that it is a mix of commercial and non-commercial objectives and outcomes and cooperative relationships. There is a dichotomy between the nature and aims of professional sport and its grass roots levels. In jurisdictions like the US, the two are completely separate, while in the European Union and Australia many are part of a pyramid structure moving up from grassroots to the pinnacle of professional competition.

10. Sport also has elements which do not sit well with traditional competition law norms. First, competition law generally prohibits arrangements between competitors

---

4 Ibid; *News Ltd v South Sydney District Rugby League Football Club Ltd* [2003] HCA 45.

5 *Seven Network Ltd v News Ltd* [2007] FCA 1062; Ibid [2009] FCAFC 166 (appeal 2 December 2009). Channel 7 claimed some $1.1 billion in damages. Costs of Channel 7 were reportedly in excess of $200 million. The proceedings were dismissed. See Deborah Healey, "Seven Loses the Football: Why all the Fuss?" in *Essays in Sport and Law* (ASSH 2008).

on the grounds that they reduce competition and damage the market. But it is clear that in many cases, sporting teams and other organisations within their particular sports league or competition are co-dependent on their internal rivals for their survival. Sports leagues and competitions require competitors. The more evenly matched the competitors, the better and more saleable the contest. Relationships of this kind commercially have been termed "co-opetition".[6] By way of contrast, competition laws aim to create a level playing field for competition in markets – but despite the sporting analogy, this is a different type of competition from that of sport.[7] It aims to foster efficiency which will provide the best goods and services to consumers at the lowest prices, with the benefits flowing to them and to the economy as a whole.

11. As noted above, globally there are many questions about what the aims/objectives of competition law should be, but most competition laws are based to some extent on this premise that a level playing field will deliver the best competitive outcomes for the economy and consumers.[8] But "co-opetition" can be recognised in competition law analysis of sporting arrangements and competitions by examining the purpose of particular rules and arrangements. Co-ordination of rules by collaboration is essential to the participation rules of the sport or event, and issues around organisation of competitions, eligibility and discipline. Arrangements between competitors are the focus of competition laws on anticompetitive arrangements and cartels.

12. Second, other essential features of sport are the focus of other areas of competition law. Many overarching sporting organisations are "monopolistic and pyramidal" which arguably makes competition law oversight of them more important.[9] Sporting organisations often act as the de facto market regulator for their sport or their competition, and in so doing may exercise both horizontal and vertical power. In these contexts, behaviour such as exclusion, which exhibits and uses unilateral market power, is subject to competition rules on abuse of dominance (EU)[10] or monopolisation (US).[11] In Australia, this is termed "misuse of market power".[12] There is also significant scope for conflicts of interest, increasing the chance of challenges to rules and authority of organisers.

13. For all these reasons, the organisation of sport is inherently risky in terms of the focus and application of competition law. But the idea of co-opetition is a concept which needs to be factored into competition law analysis.

---

6 See generally, Adam M Brandenberger and Barry J Nalebuff, *Co-opetition* (Doubleday 1998).

7 See *Adamson v West Perth Football Club Inc* [1979] FCA 122, per Northrop J at 64, where the judge noted this distinction.

8 "Even If it is accepted that welfare and efficiency should be the sole or main goal of competition law, there are questions as to whether the welfare standard should be total/ social welfare or consumer welfare, how markets work and when, and on what basis, competition authorities should intervene." Alison Jones and Brenda Sufrin, *EU Competition Law Text Case and Materials* (6th edn, Oxford University Press 2016) 1. See also Healey (n 1), 12.

9 See Rupprecht Podszun and Alexander Kirk, "FIFA's Football Agent Regulations and European Competition Law" (2024) 5 <https://ssrn.com/abstract=4741763> accessed 28 May 2026.

10 Treaty on the Functioning of the European Union (TFEU) [2008] OJ C115/120, art 102.

11 Sherman Act 1890, s 2.

12 CCA, s 46.

14. It is in this context that the following two recurring issues will be examined under the lens of Australian competition law:

- Can an incumbent sport or competition organiser stop its members or participants (individuals, teams or clubs) from participating in a rival or unaffiliated competition, or make participation subject to approval? If approval is not obtained and they compete in the rival competition, can the incumbent sport discipline them or stop them coming back?
- What happens if the two rival competitions settle their differences and wish to merge or set up a joint venture to continue to run the sport or competition?

2. Approach of US and EU law

15. This section notes very briefly some fundamental legal distinctions between the relevant EU, US and Australian competition laws and their sporting environments which may result in different decisions. These are in addition to the very different wording of individual provisions aimed at similar conduct. The legal systems of the three jurisdictions overall are dissimilar in many respects. Of note, EU decisions are administrative in character, while US decisions are mainly court based.

16. A major distinction between EU and other competition laws is the EU single market imperative, which is a significant objective of the Treaty on the Functioning of the European Union (TFEU), and is a relevant factor in the application of the competition law provisions.[13] The TFEU contains provisions ensuring free movement of goods, services, persons and capital.[14] The TFEU has also "fairness" as a stated object and the TFEU provisions seek efficiency through competitive markets, but also seek to ensure that a fair distribution of wealth occurs.[15] In addition to the competition provisions, these additional TFEU provisions affect the ability of sporting organisations to make rules.[16]

17. TFEU competition law provisions apply to undertakings engaged in economic activity, and the application to sport has shifted over the last 30 years from a traditional position, recognising the special place of sport, and a reluctance to apply competition law to it.[17] Growing commercialisation has increased the potential for sporting activities to be subject to the TFEU, and while there is still some recognition that sport is "special" and should be exempt to some extent, there is an increasing recourse to competition law in seeking to resolve sporting issues

---

13 The TFEU promotes the European Union internal market, with aims of fostering economic, social and territorial cohesion, and solidarity among Member States within Europe.

14 TFEU, art 26.

15 TFEU, arts 101 and 102. See generally, Rhonda L Smith and Deborah Healey, "Unilateral conduct analysis: focus on harm in multiple guises" in *Research Handbook on Methods and Models of Competition Law* (2020) 204–227.

16 The overarching European Convention on Human Rights (ECHR) is relevant. Free movement of persons has affected the outcome in a number of cases.

17 The position of sport has been reviewed a number of times: European Commission, *Helsinki Report on Sport* COM (1999) 644; European Council, Nice Declaration (2000), and the European Commission, *White Paper on Sport* COM (2007) 391 final; more recently, European Parliament resolution of 23 November 2021 on EU sports policy: assessment and possible ways forward [2022] OJ C224/2 <https://eur-lex.europa.eu/legal-content/EN/TXT/?uri=CELEX%3A52021IP0463> accessed 28 May 2026.

involving commercial behaviour and commercial rules which apply to sporting organisations and their competitions.[18] The competition provisions which potentially apply to sport are contained in Articles 101 and 102 TFEU. While they will not be discussed here in very broad terms they are the equivalent to the CCA provisions on cartels, anticompetitive agreements and misuse of market power. Mergers are reviewed for their impact on competition under the EC Merger Regulation.[19]

18. In the United States, traditionally, amateur and professional sports were quite separate. College sport is currently in disarray and its traditional amateur status and organisation under the National Collegiate Athletic Association (NCAA) and other supervisory organisations is likely to change.[20] Two proposed US Federal laws will, if passed, revolutionise the system. Very briefly, they will set national standards for payments to students, give antitrust immunity to student sport, among other things, codify athletes' rights and protections and attempt to bring stability to the college sports system. One will give name, image and likeness rights to students.[21] As to competition law, the Sherman Act 1890 applies to conduct in "trade and commerce" and it, and other US antitrust laws, apply to many areas of professional sport. There are quite specific exemptions to US antitrust law,[22] and some apply to sport. Antitrust law applies to all sports except baseball after a US Supreme Court decision exempting it almost 100 years ago, so Major League Baseball is not subject to antitrust law despite the extent of its commercial activities.[23] While sporting joint ventures potentially attract competition law sanctions for collusive activity, some professional sports leagues have been successful in arguing that they constitute a single entity which is not therefore capable of colluding, while

---

18 Cases such as Case C-415/93 *Union Royale Belge Sociale de Football Association, RCL and UEFA v JM Bosman* ECLI:EU:C:1995:463; Case C-519/04 P *David Meca-Medina and Igor Majcen v Commission of the European Communities* ECLI:EU:C:2006:492 and the recent cases of Case C-333/21 *European Super League (ESL)* ECLI:EU:C:2023:1011 and the Case C-124/21 P *International Skating Union (ISU)* ECLI:EU:C:2023:1012 case illustrate the growing trend to apply the competition laws to sport. In the *ESL* case it was stated that: "Only certain specific rules which were adopted solely on non-economic grounds and which relate to questions of interest solely to sport per se must be regarded as being extraneous to any economic activity.'

19 Council Regulation (EC) 139/2004 of 20 January 2004 on the control of concentrations between undertakings (the EC Merger Regulation) [2004] OJ L24/1. Transactions which are internal to a jurisdiction are generally subject to the merger control laws of the individual Member State.

20 See J Nafziger, "A Comparison on the European and North American Models of Sports Organisation" (2008) ISLJ 100, 102.

21 Proposed SCORE Act (Student Compensation and Opportunity through Rights and Endorsements) (*CBS Sports*, 22 October 2025) <https://www.cbssports.com/college-football/news/college-sports-federal-legislation-update-score-act-safe-act/> and the SAFE Act (Student Athlete Fairness and Enforcement) <https://www.commerce.senate.gov/2025/9/senators-cantwell-booker-blumenthal-introduce-student-athlete-fairness-enforcement-safe-act> both accessed 28 May 2026. More recently, the Protect College Sports Act was introduced into the Senate in May 2026, and reportedly provides the NCAA with an antitrust exemption to enforce several rules which have been challenged in recent years. The Bill states that it is to protect the name image and likeness rights of student athletes and to promote fair competition among intercollegiate athletics. .Bill available at https://www.commerce.senate.gov/wp-content/uploads/2026/05/Protect-College-Sports-Act-Bill-Text.pdf.. See also Ralph D. Russo, "Nick Saban lends support to Senate college sports bill amid SEC, Big Ten opposition, available at https://www.nytimes.com/athletic/7329848/2026/06/03/senate-protect-college-sports-act-nick-saban/

22 Sherman Act 1890 and a variety of other laws.

23 Federal Baseball Club of Baltimore Inc v National League of Professional Baseball Clubs, 259 US 200 (1922). For a complete list of exemptions from US antitrust law see Antitrust Modernization Commission, *Report and Recommendations* (2007) ch IV A.

antitrust law has been applied to others.[24] The collective sale of sports broadcast rights to broadcast major professional leagues is exempt from antitrust laws by the Sports Broadcast Act 1961.[25] The provisions which are likely to apply to this discussion are Sections 1 and 2 of the Sherman Act and Section 7 of the Clayton Act. Again, they are broadly aimed at cartels, monopolisation which is the equivalent of misuse of market power and anticompetitive mergers.

3. The Nature of the CCA, the Australian Competition Law

19. As noted at the outset, Australian competition law broadly reflects the standard prohibitions in competition laws globally. It contains provisions which prohibit cartels and other anticompetitive agreements, misuse of market power and mergers which have the purpose, effect or likely effect of substantially lessening competition. The current Australian competition law, the CCA, is the amended and renamed Trade Practices Act 1974, under which a number of cases which will be noted or discussed where relevant. The regulator is the Australian Competition and Consumer Commission (ACCC).[26] It should be noted that the ACCC and its predecessor Trade Practices Commission (TPC) have taken very few cases in relation to sport. While it may be thought that this is due to some reluctance to deal with sport, it is more likely to be due to the inability of the regulator to prosecute all conduct which might be anticompetitive in the marketplace, and its enforcement priorities which are set annually. There have been many situations where the regulator has become involved in sport over the years, although it is true to say that all the important competition law cases mentioned in this contribution have been taken as private actions.[27]

---

24 *Copperweld v Independence TubeCorp*, 104 S Ct 2731 (1984); see more recently, *American Needle, Inc v National Football League, et al* 500 US (2010).

25 See A Kaburakis, "The US and EU Systems of Sport Governance: Commercialise v Socio Cultural Model-Competition and Labour Law" (2008) ISLJ 108. As of 22 August 2025, this law was under reconsideration by the US House Judiciary Committee. See, for example, "Old Laws, New Games: The House Judiciary Committee Re-examines the 1961 Sports Broadcasting Act" (*Linklaters*, 21 August 2025) <https://www.linklaters.com/en/insights/blogs/sportinglinks/2025/august/old-laws-new-games-the-house-judiciary-committee-re-examines-the-1961-sports-broadcasting-act> accessed 28 May 2026.

26 The ACCC was the successor to the Trade Practices Commission in 1995 following a major review of Australian competition law and policy, and significant amendments to the TPS, see the Independent Committee of Inquiry, *National Competition Policy Report (Hilmer Review)* (1993) <htpp://ncp.ncc.gov/docs/National%Competition%20Policy%20report,%20Hilmer%20Report,20August%20201993.pdf> accessed 28 May 2026.

27 See, for example, *ACCC v Fila Sport Oceania Pty Ltd (Administrators Appointed)* [2004] FCA 376 for exclusive dealing and misuse of market power in licensed AFL sporting merchandise; ACCC, Tenpin Bowling Australia Ltd & Ors –Authorisation A91531 (9 June 2016) where authorisation was granted for seven years for a requirement that bowlers be a member of the organisation in order to participate in competitions at bowling centres registered with Ten Pin Bowling; Australian Swimmers Association Incorporated – Authorisation A40106 (22 March 2006) and Australian Swimmers Association Incorporated – Revocation & Substitution A91260 (6 April 2011). In both cases the authorisation was for current and future members to collectively bargain with Swimming Australia Ltd in relation to issues such as its use of athlete images, code of conduct for swimmer behaviour and disciplinary proceedings. The authorisation lasted until 30 August 2021. Authorisation is a well-established administrative approval by ACCC in respect of particular named conduct and parties following a detailed review which weighs anticompetitive detriment and public benefit. See CCA, Part VII. See also revocation of notification for apparel licensing schemes under previous third line forcing per se provisions in The Australian Baseball Federation Inc – Notification N90853 (revoked

20. Amendments over the 50 years of competition law have been many and varied, with the wording of existing provisions amended and refined on multiple occasions and other areas of regulation added to the CCA over time.[28]

21. When discussing the relevant provisions below, a brief history of the amendments and their relationship to decided cases assists in defining the current scope and approach. This is essential in considering how the CCA applies to the questions raised previously. Where the provisions are the same under both the TPA and CCA, we refer to "the competition law". The areas of cartels and other anticompetitive arrangements, misuse of market power and mergers and joint ventures are discussed briefly below.

IV. Scope of the TPA/CCA

22. At the outset, there are important points to make about the application of the competition law in Australia which affect its application to sport. The first is that, as noted above, there are no special competition law rules regarding the application of competition law to sport. The application of the competition law depends on the conduct occurring in a commercial context, as opposed to a non-commercial scenario, although not-for-profits may carry on a business in respect of some of their activities.[29] Many Australian sports are incorporated as not- for- profit organisations, which means that they are incorporated as companies limited by guarantee and not shares, and do not pay tax on their income. But they may have some commercial activities which fall within the scope of the competition law. Others are limited by shares and are solely profit-making. The CCA applies to constitutional corporations and also to other bodies which are acting in trade or commerce.[30] There has been no difficulty finding that major sports are trading corporations subject to the competition law. Seminal competition law (not just sport law) cases such as *World Series Cricket* in 1977,[31] *Hughes v West Australian*

---

4 September 2006); Football Queensland Ltd – Notification N93402 (revoked 15 December 2011); New South Wales Rugby League Ltd – Notification N98569 (allowed to stand 8 September 2015); South Sydney District Rugby League Football Club Ltd – Notification N98426 (allowed to stand 7 August 2015); other notification of collective bargaining (still relevant) Coalition of Major Professional and Participation Sports Association Inc (COMPPS) (allowed to stand 26 November 2021). The ACCC forced changes to the refund policies for tickets to games following a review of various professional sporting clubs Australia wide following an industry wide check for compliance with the Australian Consumer Law (part of the CCA): ACCC, Press Release, "AFL and NRL Clubs Fix Refunds and Returns Policies" (16 August 2018) <https://www.accc.gov.au/media-release/afl-and-nrl-clubs-fix-refunds-and-returns-policies> accessed 28 May 2026. There are also a number of collective bargaining notifications in relation to wagering.

28 Major reviews of the competition law include Trade Practices Act review Committee (Swanson Committee) 1976; House of Representatives Standing Committee on Legal and Constitutional Affairs (Griffiths Committee) 1989; Senate Standing Committee on Legal and Constitutional Affairs (Cooney Committee); Committee of Inquiry into National Competition Policy (Hilmer Review) 1993; Review of the Competition Provisions of the Trade Practices Act (Dawson Review) 2003; Competition Policy Review (Harper Review) 2015; Competition Review 2023–2025 <https://treasury.gov.au/review/competition-review-2023> accessed 28 May 2026.

29 See for example, *Re, E v Australian Red Cross Society* (1991) 31 FCR 299.

30 CCA, s 4. A corporation for the purposes of the CCA is a body corporate that is: (a) a foreign corporation; (b) a trading corporation formed within the limits of Australia or is a financial corporation so formed; (c) is incorporated in a Territory; or (d) is the holding company of a body corporate of a kind referred to paragraph (a), (b) or (c). There are provisions extending the application to persons in some cases: CCA, s 6. See definition of "trade or commerce" CCA, s 4.

31 *World Series Cricket Pty Ltd v Parish* [1977] FCA 77.

Cricket Association,[32] the *Rugby League Draft* case,[33] the *Australian Super League* case,[34] the *Souths* case,[35] *Hospitality Group Pty Ltd v Australian Rugby Union*,[36] *McHugh v Australian Jockey Club Ltd*[37] were all conducted on the basis that the sports were trading corporations and the competition law applied.[38] Competition law has even been applied to a country rodeo association in NSW that sought to claim exclusivity of participation, in a very small picture version of the conduct we are currently reviewing, on the basis that it sold tickets to its events and catered for them.[39] So, unlike the EU there has never been any special treatment for sport. And unlike the US, Australia has no specific exemption for particular sports or sporting conduct.[40]

23. The second issue of application, which has been very significant to the way sporting cases are argued and decided in Australia, is that the competition law does not apply to conduct involving employment contracts.[41] These are traditional contracts of service: contracts where the players or participants can be categorised as "employees", with all that implies. In contrast, the competition law does apply to players or participants engaged under a contract for services ie those contracts entered into by players or participants as independent contractors. The competition law expressly exempts arrangements relating to the remuneration, conditions of employment, hours of work or other terms of employment from the prohibitions against anticompetitive conduct.[42] In addition, most CCA provisions depend on the supply or acquisition of goods or services. The definition of "services" in Section 4 of the CCA is broad and inclusive, and while it includes services provided under a contract for work, the definition expressly excludes "the performance of work under a contract of service".[43] Put simply, this means that it clearly distinguishes between the position of an employee and that of an independent contractor. Employees do not supply services to their employer. Taking this exemption further in a practical sense, as a matter of judicial interpretation, any arrangement which centres around the provision of services supplied under

---

32 *Hughes v West Australian Cricket Association Inc* [1986] FCA 465.

33 *Adamson v New South Wales Rugby League Ltd* [1991] FCA 550.

34 *Australian Super League* (n 3).

35 *South Sydney District Rugby League Football Club Ltd v News Ltd (Souths)* [2000] FCA 1541.

36 *Hospitality Group Pty Ltd v Australian Rugby Union Ltd* (2001) 110 FCA 1040.

37 *McHugh v Australian Jockey Club Ltd* (2012) 13 FCA 1441.

38 In 1995 the operation of the competition law was broadened to cover circumstances outside the Commonwealth Constitutional power by agreement between the Commonwealth, the States and Territories under the Conduct Code Agreement following the Hilmer Review (n 26). The States and Territories agreed to enact Schedule Versions of Part IV which would have broader application.

39 In *McCarthy & Ors v. Australian Rough Riders Association & Anor* [1988] ATPR 40-836, where a rodeo association sought to exclude members who competed in the events of another rodeo association. Its primary function was "the provision of entertainment to the public in return for entrance fees as well as the provision of bar facilities and food. The prize money for the contestants is funded by the nomination fees of the contestants and prize money secured from sponsors." Per Spender J, at 49-028.

40 *Federal Baseball Club of Baltimore Inc* (n 23).

41 There are some employment related exemptions in other jurisdictions, but they will not be discussed here.

42 TPA/CCA, s 51(2). This was done on the basis that these contracts were covered by the heavily regulated area of employment law in Australia. Although the areas covered by regulation under the employment laws has significantly decreased, the TPA/CCA provisions have not changed at this point. As to this, see further below.

43 CCA, s 4(1).

an employment contract, arrangement or understanding, is outside the scope of the CCA, even if the arrangement itself is not made between the employer and the employee.[44] So, the competition law does not apply to third party arrangements regarding athletes/players who are employees.

24. This exemption is well illustrated by the case of *Adamson v New South Wales Rugby League Ltd*,[45] an important sporting case which involved a player draft in professional rugby league. The conduct in question was a set of rules (a potential cartel arrangement under Section 45 TPA, anti-competitive arrangements) known as the "Draft Rules". It was made between the sport governing body, the NSW Rugby League Ltd (NSWRL), and its member clubs, regarding the way their employee players would be engaged. As a matter of course, players were contracted with the clubs, and the contracts were registered with the NSWRL. The Draft Rules were agreed to by the NSWRL and employer clubs, to be imposed upon their employee players and enforced by NSWRL. The Draft Rules covered issues such as the club a player could play for, when a player could contract and what would happen at the end of the contract ie how a player could transfer to another club. The Court found that the Draft Rules did not fall within the narrow exemption in Section 51(2)(a), because they did not concern the elements listed there, so the Draft Rules were not exempt in principle.[46] However, the Draft Rules did fall outside the CCA definition of "services", as the services to be supplied were services of professional football players supplied to their clubs under a contract of employment. So, the complaints by the players about the Draft Rules could not be attacked under the then TPA. Ultimately, these were resolved in the same case under common law restraint of trade and were found to be a restraint of trade which was unreasonable and was therefore void. So, in this case, the services exemption applied because the conduct was about employees, even though the arrangement in question was between their employers and another party. To reiterate, the exemption does not apply to independent contractors or to other arrangements that involve the supply of labour, such as franchisees. In practical terms, this means that conduct involving the engagement of players such as professional rugby league, rugby, Australian football, football players, cricketers, basketball and netball players, who are likely to be employees will be outside the scope of the competition law.[47] By way of contrast, conduct/rules around the engagement of professional tennis players, golfers and others who are routinely engaged as independent contractors for a particular event, may be subject to the competition law.

25. This position may change. Currently, overseas and in Australia, the place of competition law in labour markets is subject to re-examination. The reviews focus

---

44 *Ausfield Pty Ltd v Leyland Motor Corporation of Australia* [1977] ATPR 40-025.

45 *Adamson* (n 7).

46 As noted above, remuneration, conditions of employment, hours of work or other terms of employment.

47 This means that threatened sanctions against rugby league players who go to play in the proposed R360 Rugby competition would likely not be judged under the CCA but under restraint of trade law, unless the Super Rugby competition contracted with them as independent contractors and not employees. See "NRL confident there is "no loophole" in 10-year R360 sanctions" (*ESPN*, 18 November 2025) <https://www.espn.com.au/nrl/story/_/id/47002415/r360-10-year-ban-nrl-confident-no-loophole-avoid-sanctions> accessed 28 May 2026.

on behaviour such as no-poach agreements by employers, other third party arrangements which affect employment contracts and restraint of trade clauses, because these are said to inhibit employee movement and market competition. In Australia, the re-examination is ongoing with the express aim of increasing flexibility, competition and productivity in the workplace. The Treasury has announced changes to the application of the CCA to employment markets but the specific wording has not been released at this point.[48] But the amendments will likely apply the CCA to employment contracts, and if so will bring significant change to the way competition law applies to sports participants who are employees, and to how sports markets are viewed for the purposes of competition law cases.

V. Market Definition in Australia

26. Market definition is foundational to the application of competition law in Australia, as elsewhere. So, how will markets be defined in Australia? Provisions other than per se prohibitions[49] depend upon an assessment of the effect or likely effect of the conduct in a market with consideration of product, geographic, functional and time elements. Principles of market definition depend upon fairly standard tests such as substitutability.[50] It is a purposive exercise to determine the degree of market power and must be done in the context of the conduct in question.[51] Market power is assessed using the usual factors such as concentration market share and barriers to entry, but market features such as the sporting landscape, consumer choices and the degree of isolation from other markets, etc., significantly affect market definition. A few cases will be outlined below to indicate sport markets which have been defined.

27. In the *Australian Super League* case, News Ltd approached the Australian Rugby League (ARL) to run the existing professional rugby league competition for them so that News Ltd could be the pay tv broadcaster. The ARL declined. News Ltd then started to set up its own competition, targeting clubs which were already in the ARL competition and signing players and coaches despite existing contractual relationships. The ARL requested its member clubs to sign "commitment and loyalty agreements" under which they and their players would stay in the ARL competition for a number of years and not play in other competitions. News Ltd argued that this was a breach of the misuse of market provisions (Section 46 CCA) and also constituted breach of the prohibition on exclusionary provisions (Section 4D CCA). The trial judge found almost exclusively for the sport. He focused on

---

48 See statement of relevant ministers outlining the proposed amendments: Australian Treasury, Press Release, "Cracking Down on Non-Compete Clauses to Boost Wages and Productivity" (25 March 2025) <https://ministers.treasury.gov.au/ministers/jim-chalmers-2022/media-releases/cracking-down-non-compete-clauses-boost-wages-and> accessed 28 May 2026.

49 Those applied without specific consideration of their impact on competition in a market.

50 *Re Queensland Co-operative Milling Society and Defiance Holdings* [1976] ATPR 40-012 generally. This old case is routinely cited for its seminal and important comments on the nature of competition, markets and market power, as recently as 2025.

51 See, for example, *Queensland Wire Industries Pty Ltd v The Broken Hill Proprietary Co* [1989] ATPR 40-932, at 50-104 (Full Federal Court); Sackville J in *Seven Network Ltd v News Ltd* [2007] FCA 1062, at 1763; Allsop J in *ACCC v Liquorland (Australia) Pty Ltd* [2006] FCA 826, 429.

the markets in which the organisers of the two sports competitions would be selling services to sponsors, broadcasters and spectators, determining that other sports such as rugby union, basketball, Australian rules football and soccer were competitors, rather than just a rugby league market which was argued. Although it has been suggested that this was incorrect and that the market was one for the acquisition of player services, because of the employment exemption, this was not an argument that could really be made.[52] The question of market was not considered on appeal, where the appeal succeeded and the sport lost on a number of points;. Without the employee exemption, the player acquisition market would have been an obvious choice. In contrast, in *McCarthy v Australian Rough Riders Association* where members were prohibited from competing in an unaffiliated rodeo, the participants were not employees but independent contractors and so the markets were found to be the market for rodeo rider services and the market for affiliated rodeos.[53] These two cases indicate the significant impact that the exemption can have on the operation of the CCA.[54]

1. Cartels and Arrangements between Competitors and Others Which May Lessen Competition

28. Arrangements between members of a sport, either teams, clubs or players, which impact competition may breach the competition law. The risk is heightened as they are naturally competing commercially for sponsors, players, broadcast and streaming deals, etc, and they may be in close contact as sporting competitors in one organisation or competition. Conduct potentially caught by these provisions includes arrangements to exclude clubs or some participants who are players, from competition for disciplinary or other reasons, or to fix prices of tickets or player payments. However, the exemption for employment contracts and its scope should be noted.

29. The Trade Practices Act 1974 contained provisions which prohibited contracts, arrangements or understandings (arrangements) which had the purpose, effect or likely effect of substantially lessening competition.[55] All of the current Australian cases on anticompetitive arrangements were decided under these, mainly horizontal, conduct provisions. Arrangements in this context may range from formal contracts such as the rules of sporting organisations depending upon how they are made or promulgated, to more informal "understandings" satisfying judicial criteria which might not be legally enforceable in themselves.[56] The former TPA also provided that within anticompetitive arrangements, price fixing and exclusionary provisions were per se provisions- i.e.,considered so anticompetitive that they were presumed to have an anticompetitive purpose or effect. So, plaintiffs did not need

52 See *Australian Super League* (n 3), at 500. The case went on appeal to the Full Federal Court and leave to appeal was sought but refused by the High Court. But the market definition was not the subject of either appeal.

53 *McCarthy & Ors* (n 39).

54 In *Hospitality Group Pty Ltd* (n 36), the court found that the market was limited to the supply of hospitality services for rugby union games, which was a very narrow market.

55 Trade Practices Act 1974, s 45.

56 Of course, there is much case law on the ambit of these terms from the time of the TPA which is still relevant today.

to show likely effect on competition in a market, which made it easier to prove a case, although some, or all of the participants in the arrangement needed to be competitors, but this required only a truncated consideration of market.

30. Price fixing[57] involved an arrangement which had the purpose of fixing, controlling or maintaining price.[58] So arrangements, for example, for fixing ticket prices among competitors or groupings which include competitors, such as clubs in a competition, could breach this provision without proof of anticompetitive effect or likely effect.

31. "Exclusionary provisions'[59] prohibited arrangements which had the purpose of refusal to deal with a supplier or acquirer where two or more of the parties to the arrangement were in competition with one another. This meant that if a group including competitors agreed not to deal with someone supplying or acquiring goods or services to or from them, it was prohibited absolutely. There were several important cases under the now amended provisions Section 4D TPA in relation to sport exclusions, some of which are discussed below.

32. Since those cases, there has been a complete overhaul of the cartel provisions. Criminal cartel provisions (Part IV Division 1 CCA) were included alongside amended parallel civil prohibitions (Part IV Division 2 CCA) in 2009 and amended in 2017. The new dual track provisions are based on the traditional contract, arrangement or understanding wording mentioned above but are more complex. Cartel behaviour, both civil and criminal, involves "cartel provisions" which are per se provisions (prohibited regardless of effect) involving price fixing, bid rigging, market sharing and output/input restriction.[60] They wording includes the concepts of "fixing, controlling or maintaining" price for price fixing, and "restricting, limiting or preventing" supply or acquisition of goods or services in relation to market sharing, which were in the repealed provisions. Where proceedings are taken under the criminal provisions, the basic elements are the same as the civil provisions, but additional proof of physical elements and fault elements, and proof beyond reasonable doubt, are required. Both civil and criminal provisions require the making of, or giving effect to, a contract arrangement or understanding containing a cartel provision, so the old case law on contracts, arrangements or understandings still applies.

33. Finally, the traditional general Section 45 CCA civil provisions aimed at arrangements which have the purpose/effect or likely effect of substantially lessening competition remain. And, in addition, there are new provisions prohibiting concerted practices, which are aimed at price signalling, which would not ordinarily constitute an "understanding" for Section 45 purposes.[61]

34. So, against the background of the old law and cases, and these new provisions, we will reconsider some of the existing important cases. Recent examples of disputes

---

57 TPA, s 45A.

58 Price is a cost or charge of any description. TPA, s 4.

59 TPA, s 4D.

60 OECD, *Hard Core Cartels: Recent Progress and Challenges Ahead* (OECD Publishing 2003). These are accepted worldwide as the hardcore cartel provisions: see <https://www.oecd.org/en/publications/hard-core-cartels_9789264101258-en.html> accessed 28 May 2026.

61 CCA, s45(1)(c).

and cases from overseas involving sports such as football, rugby and golf focus on the setting up of new professional sporting competitions, resultant threats, exclusions and disciplinary actions.

35. There have been a number of Australian sporting cases under the TPA which dealt with the exclusion of new competitors and of players and clubs, from competitions, or with access to competitions for individuals, and these will be discussed in more detail now.

36. In the *Australian Super League* case mentioned above, News Ltd started a parallel rugby league competition to provide vision for its new pay TV channel and began to poach clubs and players contracted to the existing competition. The traditional competition organiser, the Australian Rugby League, retaliated by seeking to sign up their existing clubs to their competition for five years under individual agreements between the League and each club (loyalty agreements). The case was conducted, among other claims, as one under the Section 4D exclusionary provisions of the former TPA. The trial judge found that there was no agreement between the clubs to activate the provision, as the agreement was between each club and the ARL, and thus there was no exclusionary provision between the competitor clubs.[62] The judge stated that Section 4D required that one or more of the parties be competitive in relation to the goods or services, the subject of the restriction. In this case, he found that the clubs did not compete to supply their teams or acquire a competition organiser: rather, they gave the League the power to decide these issues. There was also no competition between the clubs for the acquisition of News Ltd's services. In addition, the purpose requirement of Section 4D was not present. So, there was no breach of the provision.[63]

37. On appeal, the Full Court of the Federal Court of Australia (Full Court) took a different view of the circumstances on the exclusionary provisions claim, the subject of the appeal. The Full Court found that the agreements between the ARL and the clubs, on the facts, were examples of a "hub and spoke agreement" which was relevant for the application of Sections 45 and 4D. Each club knew that the other clubs were signing and that the signing was facilitated by the ARL. The Full Court found that there was no need for the parties to the loyalty agreements to be in competition at the time of making them the trial judge had not focused on "likely to be" in competition in his analysis, and "likely" was a lesser threshold than "more probable than not". As the clubs were required to apply to play in the competition each year, they were in competition for the services of a competition organiser. They were also in competition with one another for the services of premier players, who did not necessarily need to be engaged as employees, which meant that the employee exemption did not apply.[64] With respect, this seems unrealistic given

62 See *Australian Super League* (n 3). An exclusionary provision required an agreement between parties two or more of whom were competitors to refuse to deal with a party, ie here the rival competition organiser News Ltd.

63 Claims against the sport on other grounds were also dismissed.

64 With respect this seems unrealistic given the degree of control exercised over players by their coaches and clubs, which quite clearly have the characteristics of a traditional employment relationship. For this to be realistic, the nature of engagement of athletes in professional sports like rugby league would really need to change. But, of course, this is only relevant to these types of professional relationship, as discussed earlier.

the continuous degree of control exercised over players by their coaches and clubs, which under employment law quite clearly gives the relationship the characteristics of a traditional employment relationship. The relevant purpose for Section 4D was present, since the purpose of the commitment and loyalty agreements was to prevent, for five years, the supply by the clubs of teams to another organiser, and the acquisition of services of an alternative competition organiser.

38. So, under the earlier provision Section 4D, this exclusionary agreement was in breach. In similar circumstance under the current cartel provisions, it seems that conduct of this kind would also be likely to breach the CCA. In addition, under the current general Section 45 provision, it may well offend as having the purpose, effect or likely effect of substantially lessening competition.

39. Of course, these conclusions would clearly depend on the way the arguments were structured, and the nature of the arrangements between the parties involved.

40. In a second case, *Souths*, the exclusionary provision was considered in the context of the competition organiser seeking to reduce the number of teams competing in its competition.

41. After the *Australian Super League* case, the two competition organiser parties, the ARL and News Ltd came together to form a joint-venture running one competition and agreed that the number of teams should be reduced. Teams were assessed under objective criteria. Some were incentivised to merge to reduce numbers by large cash payments. Ultimately, the criteria were applied, and the South Sydney team was excluded from the competition. Souths took action under Section 4D TPA exclusionary provisions for the refusal to allow them to compete. The High Court confirmed the decision of the trial judge, which had been overturned by the Full Court.[65] The High Court found that there was no specific subjective purpose to exclude Souths from the competition. The criteria for reducing the number of teams had been applied and Souths was ranked lowest. Following the National Rugby League (NRL)'s loss in the Full Court and a groundswell of public support for Souths, they were returned to the competition prior to the High Court outcome. However, the High Court decision confirmed that the NRL had the right to terminate Souths' membership of the competition in circumstances where there were clear criteria and no predetermined outcome. A similar exclusion would now be tested under the new CCA provisions which do not have an equivalent provision. Ability to exclude would depend on a purpose, effect or likely effect on competition test. The actual circumstances would determine the outcome.

2. Misuse of Market Power

42. Misuse of market power in Section 46 TPA/CCA is the broad equivalent of abuse of dominance in the EU and many other jurisdictions, and monopolisation in the US. It expressly sets a slightly lower threshold than dominance, given that Australia is a jurisdiction with an economy containing few dominant companies and many oligopolies, making it difficult to apply the dominance threshold which

---

65 *South Sydney District Rugby League Football Club Ltd v News Ltd* [2000] FCA 1541 (Trial judge); Ibid [2001] FCA 862 (Full Court); Ibid [2003] HCA 45.

was previously in the TPA. Section 46 until recently was based on a substantial degree of market power, taking advantage of that power and an anticompetitive purpose of exclusion, but did not look at the effect of the conduct. The provision has been problematic over the years and has been modified on a number of occasions.

43. The provision was also the subject of a claim in the *Australian Super League* case, previously discussed. There News Ltd argued that the agreements between the ARL and clubs were a misuse of ARL's substantial market power, within the market for the professional sport of rugby league. As discussed above, the trial judge found that the market was wider than simply rugby league, based mainly on the evidence of the industry's perception of the market. Evidence also showed that a significant body of supporters outside the core rugby league supporters would switch to other sports should admission prices rise. This has significant implications for sports, as it is unusual for there to be a single product market in Australia.[66] The question of market was not considered on appeal.

44. Section 46 CCA was simplified in 2017 to remove previous difficulties of proof, and the focus solely on purpose. It now provides that a corporation with a substantial degree of market power must not engage in conduct which has the purpose, effect or likely effect of substantially lessening competition. The test is similar to other provisions of the CCA. The first cases under the new provision suggest that causation is not an essential part of the claim unless it is based on the likely effect limb of the provision, but the caselaw is in early stages of development.[67]

3. Mergers and Joint Ventures

45. Section 50 CCA currently provides that mergers will be in breach of the CCA if they have the effect or likely effect of substantially lessening competition in the market.[68] This is tested by comparing the position going forward with and without the merger under a test known as the "future with or without" test, or counterfactual test. It is not a snapshot of competition at those times but an examination of the position in a dynamic market environment. Joint ventures under competition law are basically collaborations between parties that have complementary skills to deliver a business project. The co-opetition idea raised earlier is relevant to this. Joint ventures set up under a company structure are subject to the merger provisions. Joint ventures constituted by an agreement are tested under the cartel provisions or under the general provisions on anticompetitive arrangements,

---

66 Yane Svetiev, *Corones' Competition Law in Australia* (8th edn, Thomson Reuters Australia 2023) 78.

67 *Epic Games Inc v Apple Inc* [2025] FCA 900, para 300ff.

68 For example, in 2023 it was reported on 6 June 2023 that the LIV Golf/PGA Tour dispute which involved antitrust law claim and counterclaim would be settled between the parties on the basis of a merger under a negotiated Framework Agreement to be finalised by a later "Definitive Agreement". It is unclear that this was ever done. It was reported that the US Federal Trade Commission was investigating the proposal, and that there were Senate and Congressional investigations into it. A global merger would likely have had competition law implications in the US, EU, Saudi Arabia and other jurisdictions. For a brief summary of the history of the dispute and the competition law implications see Louise Radnofsky and Andrw Beaton, "Inside the Battle for Golf's Future" (*The Wall Street Journal*, 19 July 2022) <https://www.wsj.com/articles/pga-tour-department-of-justice-liv-golf-saudi-arabia-lawsuit-11658232518 2/5> accessed 28 May 2026.

discussed below. "Purpose" is particularly important if a joint venture seeks to apply the exemption from, per se, cartel provisions.[69]

46. While Australia has traditionally had a voluntary system of informal merger review by the ACCC with court action following, in January 2026 mandatory notification over a set turnover threshold commenced. Under the new system the ACCC issues a formal written determination under set timelines, appealable to the Australian Competition Tribunal, and to the Federal Court only on questions of law.[70] The test has not changed. The system will be similar to that of most other jurisdictions globally.

47. As to Australian merger examples, no formal information is available regarding competition law consideration of the formation of the News Ltd and ARL joint-venture partnership which resolved the *Australian Super League* war in 1998, the classic example of a joint venture in Australian sport. The all-out war between the two parties led to substantial increases in player payments following the bidding war for their services. The overall costs of running each of the competitions were significant. The Super League competition ran only for one year.[71] At that time, the ACCC conducted merger review under a very informal merger clearance process as Australia had no mandatory merger notification scheme[72] There is no concrete evidence of competition law consideration of the joint venture issue, but recollections from around that time by those involved generally suggest that the ACCC was approached under the informal scheme and found that there was no competition issue. News Ltd ultimately exited the joint venture in 2013 when a new company was formed with shareholders who are the state rugby league bodies, the NRL clubs and others. It is controlled by an independent board.[73]

48. It is difficult to consider in a vacuum any future merger or joint venture between two rival competitions to resolve a two-stream sport. However, given the nature of the competition law merger provisions, which require assessment of the purpose, effect or likely effect of the merger, the issue would be resolved having regard to consideration of competition in the future with and without the merger. The outcome of this analysis would depend on the market definition selected. The broader the market, the less the impact of the conduct. So, if the market

---

69 CCA, s 45AO(1) and s 45AP.

70 Both of these approaches are adopted in most other jurisdictions.

71 It was reported in 2005 that New Corporation had lost between $560 million and $700 million during *Australia Super League* war. See Neil Chenowith, "Lachlan's Legacy: $560m Lost on Super League" (5 August 2005) <https://www.afr.com/companies/lachlans-legacy-560m-lost-on-super-league-20050805-jkhav> accessed 28 May 2026. At the heart, it was a battle between the Rupert Murdoch and Kerry Packer broadcast empires over content for their free to air and pay-for-TV channels. Ultimately after the two competitions came together, the broadcasters began to recoup their losses. The NRL which ran the major professional competition was originally a joint venture between the Australian Rugby League and News Ltd. News Ltd exited in 2013 and the NRL is now controlled by a reconstituted Australian Rugby League Commission with an independent board.

72 The CCA was amended in 2024 to adopt a formal notification process for mergers over a set turnover similar to those of other jurisdictions, operative from 1 January 2026. Previously this had been done on a voluntary basis.

73 For the history of the *Australian Super League* case and the formation of the joint venture, see David Trodden, *The Commission We Had To Have: Rugby League as a Sport and Business, From Dally M to the NRL* (Stoke Hill Press 2019).

were confined to a single sport, it is more likely that an anticompetitive impact could be shown. The future with the merger is known as the factual; the future without the merger, which is generally more tentative, is the counterfactual. But in considering the uncertainty of the future, and depending upon the circumstances, one might find that in a future without the merger, one of the competitions would not survive. One might find that in future without the merger, neither competition would flourish. One might find that the popularity of the sport itself plummeted because fragmentation meant that the quality of competition (in the sporting sense) in the multiple competitions declined. In this particular situation, it might also be argued that the ability of the sport to compete with other sports for participants and viewers would decline. For these reasons, the future with the merger might be no more anticompetitive than the future without the merger. But again, it would all depend upon the facts.

49. Joint ventures can be constructed by way of a new corporate body or by agreement between the two joint venturers. So, in some cases the transaction may need to be considered under the merger provisions, and in others under the cartel provisions as an agreement between competitors. There are specific exception provisions relating to joint ventures in the cartel provisions of the CCA. Their application depends on the specific conduct being contained in a written contract and the joint venture involving joint production or supply. In short, where the provisions are essential for the conduct of the joint venture and there is no purpose of substantially lessening competition, the conduct may be allowed.[74]

VI. Conclusions

50. So where does this all leave Australian sport in terms of the application of competition law? Not surprisingly, there is clear scope for some of the conduct under consideration to fall within the CCA provisions. A number of conclusions can be drawn: Where a sport is not involved in business it is unlikely that the competition law will apply.

51. Sports may make rules and decisions to facilitate the organisation of the sport, including participation and individual competitions, as long as they do not have an anticompetitive purpose or likely effect, factoring in "co-opetition".

52. Competition law analysis in Australia does not at this stage appear to place the same emphasis on a monopoly sport as a "regulatory body", as does the EU.

53. As to new competitions, sports can't completely stop new market entrants establishing new competitions but may be able to modify the behaviour of the newcomer, particularly if they are acting for legitimate purposes (see *Souths* case),[75] where purpose of exclusion was not anticompetitive and there was no complaint about the criteria for exclusion or its application to Souths.

54. Given that a new competition organiser may have a claim against an incumbent under the CCA depending on how a case is put together, an outstanding issue

---

74 See CCA, ss 45AO and 45AP.

75 *Souths* (n 35).

for administrators is who will provide the players for a commercially focused competition if new and more commercial entities enter their markets. What if there is no overarching sporting organisation which has funds to do so, and the newer commercial entity prioritises shareholder returns and has no interest? In this context, Australia has a longstanding and well-developed system of authorisation by the ACCC for conduct which would otherwise breach the CCA based on overriding public benefit.[76] It is available for all Part IV CCA conduct. It may be that issues such as rules which would otherwise breach the CCA could be authorised in some cases to protect the development of athletes. To be successful, applications for authorisation must relate to very specific conduct and named parties, and make a strong case for public benefit not otherwiseavailable. . They can be revoked on change of circumstances under a process which allows for procedural fairness.[77] Authorisations are always time limited, but can be the subject of a new application when they expire

55. Finally, mergers and joint ventures established to resolve a conflict between two sporting bodies or competitions, depending on their construction, would now need formal approval by the ACCC and this approval would be granted if the conduct was not likely to substantially lessen competition..[78] As to contract joint ventures, they would need to pass the substantial lessening of competition test if a merger or fall within the joint-venture exceptions to the cartel provisions. More generally, resolution by merger/joint venture may have significant implications in Australia and for global sports and markets if the particular transaction needs to be cleared in multiple jurisdictions. Authorisation may be available for joint-venture conduct, and where the joint venture is considered under the merger law, there is a similar process relying on public benefit under the new compulsory notification procedure which can be launched if the ACCC has refused permission for the merger based on the basis of likely anticompetitive outcome.[79].

56. In conclusion, it can be seen that there has been and still is fertile scope for the application of competition law to sport in Australia, and it seems that it is only a matter of time before cases will be taken to court on these complex areas of dispute.

---

76 This is well illustrated by the examples listed at (n 27) above. CCA Part VII.

77 See CCA, s91B.

78 See CCA s51AZBE.

79 See CCA s51ABZW.

Sports and the Japanese Antimonopoly Act

Reiko Aoki*
Japan Fair Trade Commission, Tokyo

I. Introduction

1. Nippon Professional Baseball (NPB) is an organisation of professional baseball teams with the status of a trade association under the Japanese Antimonopoly Act (AMA).[1] While any special dispensation offered to trade associations under the AMA applies to NPB, no unique exemptions exist for any sports teams. The Japan Fair Trade Commission (JFTC) has looked into professional sports recently as part of a study into competition issues concerning human resources and the market. The findings were published in the Report of the Study Group on Human Resources and Competition Policy.[2]

2. Although people sell their human resources services on the market, the human resources required for professional sports are very specialised, often requiring substantial investment in addition to talent. Thus, the report is very relevant to creative industries and professional sports. Professional sports include either solo sports, such as golf and tennis, or team sports, such as baseball and rugby. Golf and tennis players are self-employed, while baseball players have employment

---

* Commissioner, Japan Fair Trade Commission (JFTC). Views expressed are those of the author and do not necessarily reflect those of JFTC.

1 Act on Prohibition of Private Monopolization and Maintenance of Fair Trade (Act No 54 of 14 April 1947) <www.jftc.go.jp/en/legislation_gls/AMA.pdf> accessed 1 August 2025.

2 JFTC, *Report of the Study Group on Human Resources and Competition Policy* (2018) <www.jftc.go.jp/en/pressreleases/yearly-2018/February/180215_files/180215_3.pdf> accessed 1 August 2025.

contracts with a team. In this chapter, I review the "Guidelines concerning transfer restriction rules in the sports business fields under the Antimonopoly Ac" (2019 (the Guidelines)[3]. This concerns voluntary actions by sports associations in response to the Guidelines and a consultation with the JFTC by a sports organisation regarding transfer restrictions. Much of this chapter is based on a submission by the JFTC to the Organisation for Economic Co-operation and Development Working Party on 2 December 2023.[4]

3. The Guidelines concerning transfer restriction rules in the sports business fields under the Antimonopoly Act[5] were published to clarify the concerns of the JFTC regarding competition in sports, particularly regarding restrictions on transfers between teams. When publishing the Guidelines, the JFTC also called on relevant entities, including sports governing bodies, to review their transfer restriction rules voluntarily. The Guidelines were based on the Report of the Study Group on Human Resources and Competition Policy[6] published in February 2018 by the JFTC Competition Policy Research Center..

II. Report of the Study Group on Human Resources and Competition Policy

4. The report was the result of a study conducted by a group of the same name, headed by Professor Fumio Sensui, now JFTC Commissioner, who was then a professor of law. The study group consisted of academics and legal practitioners. The economic environment of human resources is changing in Japan as the size of the working-age population declines, and more female and senior citizens offer their services in response. The types of services people offer and the ways in which they work have become more heterogeneous. Many people work outside the traditional framework of the labour market, including athletes. They are therefore not protected by labour laws and are vulnerable to individual contractual relationships with firms. The study group was convened to address new competition concerns arising as a result. Issues of competition for human resources are no longer limited to employers jointly restricting competition, as was the case in the past.

1. Concerted Actions

5. Terms of trade with individual service providers should be determined by the human resources market. In principle, if multiple enterprises decide jointly to set the terms of trade, it violates the AMA because this can severely affect and restrict competition.

6. However, concerted action may have other effects than restricting competition, depending on how it is conducted. The legality of such actions is determined

---

3 *https://www.jftc.go.jp/dk/guideline/unyoukijun/sports_files/sports.pdf.* Accessed 14 August 2025.

4 OECD, "Competition in Professional Sports" (13 November 2023) Note by Japan <https://one.oecd.org/document/DAF/COMP/WP2/WD(2023)29/en/pdf> accessed 1 August 2025.

5 JFTC, Press Release, "Guidance Concerning Regulations on Player Transfers in Sports Business Sectors" (2019) <www.jftc.go.jp/houdou/pressrelease/2019/jun/190617_files/190617.pdf> (in Japanese) accessed 1 August 2025.

6 *JFTC Report* (n 2).

by consideration of multiple factors, including whether concerted action has a pro-competitive effect or a social or public purpose or whether the action and its implementation are reasonable and proportionate in achieving its purposes. A pro-competitive effect alone is insufficient for the action to be deemed a non-violation. The factors determining legality or illegality include the action's pro-competitive effects and whether these outweigh the anticompetitive effects in each relevant market for human resources, goods or services.

7. The specific findings of the report include the following regarding concerted actions:

- In principle, jointly fixing the price paid to an individual violates the AMA.
- Jointly agreeing to restricting an individual from transferring between or switching jobs may violate the AMA.
- Restrictions on transferring or switching jobs to recover the necessary costs of training the individual may be a violation because there are usually other alternatives.
- If agreements to restrict player transfers aim to maintain and improve the quality of consumer services, such as by making the professional league more appealing, decisions on illegality must consider the pro-competitive effects of such agreements.

2. Unilateral Actions

8. The specific findings of the report include the following regarding unilateral action:

- Imposing an obligation that an individual must deal only with one enterprise (exclusive obligation) may have pro-competitive effects if it is to commit the individual exclusively to the deal or to recover the individual's training costs. Such a condition would not directly pose a problem under the AMA when imposed to the extent reasonably necessary to achieve the purpose. However, an exclusive obligation may be problematic under the AMA, for example, in cases where it exceeds the scope necessary for the purpose and may impede or prevent other enterprises from dealing with individual providers to supply goods or services to their respective markets.
- An enterprise requiring an individual to license the exclusive use of their image (portrait) without reasonable grounds may violate the AMA if it is likely to prevent other enterprises from providing goods and services.
- An individual assuming obligations or restrictions after an enterprise has provided a false explanation for or insufficient information on the content of the obligations or restrictions may violate the AMA.
- The AMA may be violated if an enterprise uses its superior bargaining position to impose obligations or restrictions that unjustly disadvantage an individual.

III. Guidelines Concerning Transfer Restriction Rules in the Sports Business Fields under the AMA[7]

9. After the report was published, the JFTC advocated for applying the AMA to competition for human resources and ascertained the state of the market, in areas such as trade practices. In the course of these activities, the JFTC found that sports governing bodies had rules restricting the transfer of players in sports business fields. Based on this finding, the JFTC conducted interviews with individuals in sports governing bodies to assess the transfer restriction rules and published the findings with comments regarding the applicability of the AMA as per the Guidelines in June 2018.

10. First, the Guidelines state that the goal of the AMA is to secure consumer interests and revitalise the economy by maintaining and promoting free and fair competition. This is also true regarding the sports business industry, and the Guidelines stipulate that ensuring a free and fair environment for player acquisition by sports teams is in the interests of sports fans and consumers in general.

11. The Guidelines note that transfer restrictions will either prevent or hinder competition among sports teams for players. This will, in turn, hinder competition in the sports business industry. It will also make it difficult for new entries into the field because new teams would be unable to acquire players.

12. By contrast, the Guidelines also indicate that transfer restriction rules may have pro-competitive effects. Restrictions increase incentives to train players by securing the opportunity to recoup training costs. They also maintain and improve the sport's appeal by balancing or levelling the capability and strength of teams.

13. Given these factors, the Guidelines state that the necessity for and the reasonableness of transfer restriction rules are decided based on whether their intended purpose is reasonable from the viewpoint of promoting competition and whether the rules are proportionate in achieving that purpose. There is a wide variety of transfer restriction rules in sports businesses, and whether they are problematic under the AMA is determined on a case-by-case basis.

14. However, the Guidelines also state that it is hard to justify rules that indefinitely limit or restrict transfers (eg rules that prohibit transfers without exception, that do not permit a transfer unless the player's current team allows it, and that allow transfers but prohibit participation in any other sports leagues or competitions held by the sports governing bodies) as reasonable and necessary.

15. In conjunction with the publication of the Guidelines, the JFTC recommended that each sports governing body voluntarily review its transfer restrictions. According to news reports, several sports governing bodies eliminated or eased their transfer restrictions after the recommendations were made.[8]

---

7 JFTC Press Release (n 4).

8 For example, see "Rugby Top League to Revise Transfer Rrules" Nihonkeisai Newspaper February 19, 2018 < https://www.nikkei.com/article/DGXLSSXK11006_Z10C18A2000000/4> (in Japanese) for rugby, "Japan Induustrial Field and Track Association Revises Regulation to respect "Freedom to Transfer"", Nihonnkeizai Newspaper, February 8, 2020"https://www.nikkei.com/article/DGXLSSXK60621_Y0A200C2000000/ for athletics, and < https://www.nikkei.com/article/DGXMZO51886060X01C19A1US0000/ > (in Japanese) for boxing.

IV. Individual Cases Concerning the Antimonopoly Act and Sports

1. Transfer Restrictions

16. The JFTC, which has been committed to ascertaining the state of trade since the publication of the Report of the Study Group on Human Resource and Competition Policy (Section 2), investigated suspected conduct by the NPB organisation whereby its member teams refused to sign a contract with a certain baseball player. The JFTC announced the results of its investigation in November 2020.[9]

17. There are 12 professional baseball teams in Japan, all of which are members of the NPB, a trade association. The NPB deliberates on matters related to the operation of official professional baseball games.

18. The 12 teams hold an annual meeting (the Draft Conference), where each team nominates players it wishes to contract with and obtains the right to negotiate with these players. However, in 2008, a prominent player requested that the 12 teams should not nominate him in the Draft Conference because he wanted to contract directly with a team in the United States. The NPB recognised that if such incidents became regular occurrences in the future, they may lessen the appeal of Japanese professional baseball. This concern led the NPB to reach an agreement among its members in 2008. Under this agreement, a player refusing nomination by the 12 teams before the Draft Conference or refusing to join a team with the right of negotiation at the Draft Conference and contracting with a foreign team, would not be nominated by the 12 teams in the Draft Conference for three years after the foreign contract expires, if the player is a high school graduate, and for two years if the player is a college graduate or belongs to a company team. This agreement has been maintained by the NPB ever since and remains in force. However, there have been no cases where the agreement was applied, or where the 12 teams have refused to contract with a player.

19. The AMA prohibits concerted refusal to deal as an unfair trade practice and prohibits trade associations with member enterprises engaging in such practices. In general, when members of a trade association jointly refuse to receive services from a service provider, making it difficult for the service provider to find an equivalent business partner, such conduct may exclude the service provider from the market for such services, thereby that trade association is likely to be impeding fair competition.

20. In view of such concerns, the JFTC initiated an investigation of the 2008 agreement. The NPB then voluntarily abolished the arrangement, publicised the abolition and informed related organisations. The NPB then reported the measures it had taken to the JFTC. After reviewing the NPB's actions, the JFTC decided that these measures dispelled the suspicion of a violation of the AMA and closed the investigation.

---

9 JFTC, Press Release, "Regarding the Handling of the Case of Alleged Violation of the Antimonopoly Act against Nippon Professional Baseball Organization" (5 November 2020) <*www.jftc.go.jp/houdou/pressrelease/2020/nov/201105.html*> (in Japanese) accessed 1 August 2025.

2. Interference with a Competitor's Transaction

21. The JFTC has long consulted with enterprises and trade associations concerning whether specific actions they plan to take are problematic in light of the provisions of the AMA and relevant rules. One such consultation in 2011 was with a sports enterprise regarding player participation. In this case, the JFTC responded that the restriction of professional players by an enterprise that organises athletic events may violate the AMA.[10]

22. A consultation was held with Company X, an enterprise that organises competitions, such as tournaments, in which professional players of Sport A participated. At the time of the consultation, only three companies, including Company X, held such competitions. The three companies held competitions for participants who had passed a test and had been registered as professional players of Sport A (registered professional players). Company X had more registered professional players than the other two companies, and many players were very competent and popular. Company X did not train its registered professional players and had no employment relationship with them.

23. Company X considered imposing restrictions on its registered professional players to forbid participation in any competition held by other companies because it had learned that new entrants, other than the three companies holding such competitions, would hold new professional competitions for players of Sport A.

24. Company X stated that the purpose of the above restrictions was to avoid a situation in which the company's registered professional players participated in rival companies' competitions, and the spectators at Company X's competitions would be disappointed when they were unable to watch their favourite professional players.

25. The JFTC responded that Company X's restrictions forbidding its registered professional players to participate in competitors' competitions may violate the AMA by interfering with a competitor's transaction, which is an unfair trade practice as stipulated in the Designation of Unfair Trade Practices legislation,[11] for the following reasons:

    1. Company X's justifications are unreasonable, and the suspicion that the restrictions have an unfair purpose, such as the exclusion of new entrants, cannot be dispelled.
    2. Unlike restrictions on the entry into competitors' competitions of professional players trained by the company, the restriction in this case appears unreasonable.

---

[10] JFTC, "Trade Interference by Businesses that Hold Tournaments and Other Competitions in which Professional Athletes Participate" (2012) <www.jftc.go.jp/dk/soudanjirei/h24/h23nendomokuji/h23nendo03.html> (in Japanese) accessed 1 August 2025. The JFTC also provides for individual prior consultations for specific actions by enterprises and trade associations. It compiles a summary of major consultations that may assist non-consultants and publishes these annually as the *Consultation Casebook*. In principle, the names of those involved are kept confidential in the *Consultation Casebook*, see <www.jftc.go.jp/dk/soudanjirei/> (in Japanese) accessed 1 August 2025.

[11] JFTC, Designation of Unfair Trade Practices (Fair Trade Commission Public Notice No 15 of 18 June 1982) <www.jftc.go.jp/en/legislation_gls/unfairtradepractices.html> accessed 1 August 2025.

3. For new entrants to have successful competitions, it is considered essential for popular and competent professional players to participate, so such restrictions by Company X may impede the ability of new entrants to conduct business activities.

3. Unjust Restriction

26. On September 19, 2024, JFTC issued a warning to Nippon Professional Baseball for restricting player's ability to contract with player agents.[12]s

27. Nippon Professional Baseball (NPB) is an organization consisting of the Pacific League, the Central League and the 12 professional baseball teams in Japan. The organization mandated the players regarding player agent contract that 1) the player agent must be a qualified lawyer (according to Attorneys Act (Act No. 205 of 1949), and 2) players agent does not hold contract with any other player that plays for NPB.

28. There is no rational reason that an agent has only one baseball client. An agent is able to work on behalf of multiple players, as is often the case in sports, such as soccer, in Japan and in baseball abroad. If conflict of interest is an issue, player can always choose not to have common agent with another player. On the other hand, such restriction will keep players from accessing talented agents which can lead to economic loss.

29. JFTC concluded that this rule was violation of violation of the provision of Article 8 (falling under item (iv) unjustly restricting the functions or activities of the constituent enterprise) of the AMA. It issued a warning to NPB to cease the practice and not to engage such behaviour in the future. NPB withdrew the rule on September 2, 2024. Although actions of the NPB is not mentioned in the I. Report of the Study Group on Human Resources and Competition Policy, JFTC's response is in the sprit of the Report. It protects the condition of self-employed professionals from large organization.

4. Interfering with Rival's Business

30. On June 11, 2025, JFTC issues a waring to Nippon Professional Baseball for interfering with rival's ability to conduct business.[13]

31. Television station A had contracted with NPB to broadcast Nippon Series (game between winners of Pacific League and Central league, to determine Japan champion team) game three. Station A aired (recorded) Major League Baseball (MLB) game at the same time as another Nippon Series game aired by a television station under contract with NPB.

32. NPB took following actions against station A: 1) collected all press passes that had been issued to station A for Nippon Series games and other NPB games, prohibiting station A from reporting on Nipon Series and other NPB games from October 26 to November 10, and 2) started negotiation with another station to switch broadcasting rights of Nippon Series game three.

---

12 *https://www.jftc.go.jp/file/240919.pdf*

13 *https://www.jftc.go.jp/houdou/pressrelease/2025/jun/250611_4jyou.html*

33. JFTC found that this actions may interfere with MLB business, violation of AMA Article 19 (interfering in rival's business). NPB reissued passes to station A and agreed to continue to honor contract for Nippon Series game three with station A.

CHAPTER VI

Transnational Football Law Issues

Bosman, Thirty Years Later

Ian S. Forrester KC*
University of Glasgow, Competition Appeals Tribunal, London

34. Litigators, at the time of the oral argument, are usually fluent in the merits of their case. Usually, they are able to see the merits of both sides' arguments, and sometimes, if they are on the losing side, they can see that the slope of history favoured the victor; sometimes they remain persuaded that they had the better side of the dispute. With that in mind, I offer a recollection of the *Bosman* 1993 case.[1].

35. The backgrounds to the controversy, both legal and sportive, are highly relevant. The early judgements of the ECJ (the Court) which touched sport were notably abstentionist as in the case of *Walrave and Koch*,[2] when the Court took the view that it would not interfere with a "purely sporting" controversy (concerning a rule governing the nationality of cyclists in certain races, the effect of which was to prohibit professional cyclists from having a pacemaker from another Member State). However, there was no shortage of sporting questions which called for a community response. In the absence of court guidance, football's administrators dealt with the European Commission. The relation between the authorities of football and the European Commission were political and transactional, rather than legalistic. There were several points of potential tension. Broadcasting rights were national, not European, with some spillover reception in neighbouring territories. The sport was highly structured and administered nationally. FIFA was the world governing body, with continental federations beneath it, such as UEFA.

---

* Honorary Professor, University of Glasgow, KC, LLD, Counsel for UEFA, Judge of EU General Court 2015–2020.

1 Case C-415/93 *Union Royale Belge Sociale de Football Association, RCL & UEFA v JM Bosman* ECLI:EU:C:1995:463.

2 Case 36/74 *Walrave and Koch v Association Union Cycliste Internationale and others* ECLI:EU:C:1974:140.

The national football association was at the apex of several leagues, amateur and professional, which organised competitions between teams from schools, universities, the military and many amateur enthusiasts for the game. At the highest level were the professional leagues with full-time players, some few of whom were celebrities in famous teams, earning fabulous salaries. Many lesser teams employed part-time players for lack of money. At the other end of the bell-curve were the schoolboy teams, coached by parents and teachers, moved not by money but by love of the game. Football was said to be the most important single pursuit outside the home. But the vast majority of players were unpaid, and most clubs existed for sporting pleasure and covered their expenses by raffles, donations, fund-raising parties and – if they were lucky – sponsorship by local businesses. In the professional leagues in England, surveys confirmed that the great majority of clubs in the lower leagues did not operate at a profit, at least on the basis of orthodox accounting. Player transfers were a significant source of revenue. A few of the elite clubs in the top divisions made substantial sums through broadcasting rights, sales of tickets, sponsorships and other promotional techniques. But the majority of clubs in even the top division, did not make a profit. One technique for generating revenue was the sale of players. To state the obvious, talent makes a team successful. The better the players, the better the chance of team victory, firmer support from fans, and the higher the income from the sale of team merchandise like shirts. The *Bosman* case involved a player at the start of his adult career.

36. Young players were a powerful means of advancing the fortunes of the club which recruited them. Many elite clubs had youth teams which helped to recruit young players, give them training, and exposure to high standards of sporting performance and then offer to a very few teenagers the chance of a professional career. Some grass roots clubs were particularly successful in finding, developing and launching talent.

37. Now, it was – and is – the case that player transfers between professional clubs are a crucial element in delivering "uncertainty of outcome" which is an economist's definition of what spectators would call an exciting match. Although football engenders fierce passions, physical conflicts between rival fans, betting of large and small amounts (and the socially important phenomenon of football pools and lotteries), and countless manifestations of zealous support or hostility, a game which is a foregone conclusion is not much fun to watch. To maintain balance between clubs in a league, success is crowned by promotion to a division with tougher competition, and failure punished by demotion. The hiring of players is controlled in various ways: transfers in most leagues may occur during specific "windows" to limit the significance of money when the season is well advanced. In the United States for certain sports, the least successful professional clubs were offered the chance of hiring the most promising players leaving college. So, control of player transfers is a normal element in the governance of a professional team sports league. All players are registered with the national football governing bodies.

38. Young players presented a special category: the lucky few who do so well in the youth leagues that a professional career beckons, enjoyed contractual benefits in terms of conditions and remuneration. I observe that some parents have told me that they were surprised by the extent of the contractual constraints placed

upon their young sons (female football scarcely existed 30 years ago in reflection of the game leaders' opposition to female players from about 1922 to 1970), who joined the youth teams of professional clubs. Today's marketplace is more respectful of the social, human and contractual standards appropriate to the hiring of a young player.

39. In any event, when a promising young player was ready to move from the youth team to the professional game, if he were hired by a professional club, the new club was obliged to pay the former club a "training indemnity" or "*indemnité de formation*". It was not an open-ended haggle: the amount was calculated by reference to objective criteria, such as goals scored, games for the national youth team, and the like. The principle was to reward the former club for its investment in finding the player, training him for several years and dealing with the human and managerial problems that a teenage sports start can present. The purpose of the payment was to encourage all clubs, but especially small clubs, to invest effort in the development of the skills of young players, not only because the young start might play locally but also because he might be good enough to be hired by a famous professional club. So, there was a sporting incentive and a (possible) financial incentive.

40. The rule was clear that if there was a controversy between the new club and the former club, that must not hinder the player's capacity to take to the field for his new club. In the event that the hire involved two clubs from the same country, the supervision of player transfers was done within one country's national football association. If the hiring club was in another country, the two national football associations would cooperate in case of a problem. Again, the rule was explicit: a disagreement about the sum to be paid as *indemnité de formation* should not delay the player's right to play. The "respectability" of the scheme was confirmed for me at least by the fact that in Scotland a dispute about the amount of the indemnity was to be resolved by the arbitration of a football-loving judge of the Court of Session, Scotland's highest court.

41. So, it was said, there was a regime which corresponded to the needs of the sport, which applied indistinctly to national and international transfers, and which had existed for decades. It is easy to see the for and the against. This system had existed for decades. There were very few problems. The goal was the laudable one of an encouraging investment in the search for youthful talent. Jean Marc Bosman should be compensated for the deplorable way he had been treated. But why should the system be dismantled if it was operating smoothly as to the other transfers?

42. Bosman's team replied that the system was archaic and prone to being abused. Some commentators referred to professional footballers as modern slaves and saw the *indemnité de formation* as one of a suite of repressive measures intended to maintain footballers in an economically inferior position. Analogies were drawn with horse racing which used to treat jockeys as inferior beings who should know their place: again, an element of exaggeration could be noted.

43. Indeed, from the employment point of view it would seem surprising that an employee could not freely seek a new job even after his contract had expired. There was discussion of whether the regime might work for a young well trained

pâtissier who is hired by a famous restaurant: pay something to the corner shop where she or he learned their trade? So, there were arguments on both sides. The case developed into a battleground for wider governance issues.

44. There was a problem: which part of the EC Treaty should be relevant; competition or freedom of movement of workers? The Court opted for Article 48 and freedom of movement. That Article had been drafted to apply to governmental discrimination against foreigners. It had, as best I can remember, never been applied to private regulation of an employment market. The Court concluded that the *indemnité* regime was liable to constitute an obstacle to a player's free movement, if he were to seek a transfer to another country. The system could only be justified by pressing reasons of "public interest" and only if the measures were proportionate. While the preservation of equality and uncertainty as to results was a legitimate goal, the indemnity did not prevent the richest clubs from winning. Certainly, that was true, but the system did help the small clubs earn money. As the fees are uncertain, said the Court, they could not be a decisive factor in recruiting young players. The Court did not invite the Belgian judge to consider the facts but rather made the factual determination.

45. Relations between the respective leaders of football and the European Commission were for many years political rather than legalistic. The responsible Commissioner would negotiate with the leaders of the UEFA whether national leagues could require that teams field national players, and how many. This regime lasted for years. But in a further blow to the traditions of the beautiful game, the Court condemned the rule whereby the Commission and football authorities had agreed that in the first division of each national league, there could be a ceiling on the number of foreign players who could play. Bosman was a second division player so the rule did not affect him directly, but the Liege judge wanted to know the answer and so the Court, having found the question *not* hypothetical, found against the long-standing purely political practice of agreeing on how many "foreign" and how many "assimilated" foreign players could be fielded in a first division match.

46. The argument was in French, the language of the case, before a crowded courtroom. Each year, the Court invites national supreme courts for a journée des magistrats, and chooses an interesting matter case for the visitors to attend. Hence it was an eminent crowd…

47. It is the only time that I was quoted on page three of *l'Equipe* because I started with a joke about my accent. Judgement followed within a few weeks.

48. I fear that Jean Marc Bosman derived little benefit of a professional or financial kind from his victory, but for sure the hiring and transferring of professional players was transformed, liberated and made more money driven. Whether that is a *good thing* or a *bad thing*, I leave to others to decide.

The FIFA Regulations on the Status and Transfer of Players in Light of European Union Competition Law

Fabrice Rizzo*
Centre de Droit Économique, Aix-Marseille University

I. Introduction

1. Description of The Player Transfer Mechanism

1. A transfer, peculiar to team sports and especially to football, may be presented as a triangular contractual technique by which a club agrees to terminate, before its stipulated term, the employment contract of a player so as to enable him to commit to another club, in return for the latter's payment of a financial fee. In a judgment of 16 September 2010, the Douai Court of Appeal described it as

> a complex operation which affects the legal relationships of three persons bound by bipartite contractual links: the two football clubs, each on its own account, and the player himself; one of the two clubs is bound to the player by a contract of employment, and that link is intended to be brought to an end by the operation; the second of those clubs, on

* Professor at Aix-Marseille University, Co-Director of the Professional Master's in Sports Law.

the contrary, has the vocation of concluding a contract of employment with the player and thus forging a new link with him; finally, the two clubs must agree between themselves on the financial terms of the transfer.[1]

2. It is this commercial agreement between the two clubs that must be characterised as the transfer (or move) contract. It principally determines the amount and the modalities of payment of the transfer fee, that is to say, the economic consideration for the consent given by the "selling" club to release its player.[2]

2. The Normative Framework Governing Player Transfers

3. Such an operation raises, from a legal standpoint, several questions, since it gives rise to often considerable financial flows founded on agreements whose object lies in the professional qualities of an employee. The lawyer cannot but be wary when confronted with contractual instruments that serve as vehicles for speculation on the market value of employees' labour and that appear to turn the very person of the worker into a marketable object.[3] To address these questions, certain kinds of national legislation frame transfer operations with varying degrees of intensity.[4] In France, the Code du Sport remains almost silent.[5] The actors concerned must turn to labour and contract law to identify the various acts that make up transfer operations and to translate into legal terms the practices implemented on the professional sports labour market. For their part, national and international federal regulations give no precise indication on the definition and characterisation of the operation of moving a player. They focus essentially on its legal regime. By way of illustration, in most team sports, national and international federations restrict the movement of players by establishing one or two transfer windows outside which clubs may not recruit a player. On a reference for a preliminary ruling concerning the regulations of the international basketball federation, the Court of Justice of the European Communities (CJEU) accepted the lawfulness of such windows.[6] But it found that transfer deadlines constitute obstacles to the free movement of workers, in that, by prohibiting the moves of athletes after a given date, they prevent the latter from joining the club of their choice, which

---

1 Case 09/05120 *SASP Société Stade Malherbe de Caen Calvados Basse Normandie v SASP LOSC Lille Métropole* (16 September 2010) Douai Court of Appeal.

2 Frédéric Buy et al., *Droit du sport* (7th edn, LGDJ 2023) 1503.

3 Fabrice Rizzo, "A propos de la réification de la personne du sportif professionnel salarié" (2005) 1 Les Cahiers de droit du sport 42.

4 KEA–CDES, *Report to the European Commission – Study on the Economic and Legal Aspects of Transfers of Players* (2013) 2 <https://ec.europa.eu/assets/eac/sport/library/documents/cons-study-transfers-final-rpt.pdf> accessed 25 May 2026.

5 Only Article L.222-7 of the French Sports Code refers to it implicitly, stating that the activity of a sports agent may consist in bringing together the parties interested in "the conclusion of a contract providing for the conclusion of a contract of employment having as its object the paid exercise of a sporting activity".

6 Case C-176/96 *Lehtonen v FRBSB* ECLI:EU:C:2000:201. Marc Thill, "La reconnaissance de la spécificité du sport en droit communautaire" (2000) 6 Europe 4. Fabrice Rizzo, *Libre circulation des sportifs: Les études thématiques – Etude no 236* (2024) 155. Fabrice Rizzo, "Les opérations de transfert de joueurs confrontées au droit de l'Union européenne" (2013) 31 Les Cahiers de droit du sport 160. Treaty on the Functioning of the European Union (TFEU) [2008] OJ C115/120, arts 101 and 102.

may be in another Member State of the European Union.[7] However, it accepted that transfer windows could be justified in the name of the requirement of the regularity of sporting competitions. Late moves of players in the course of a championship undermine the equality of opportunity between teams, in so far as they allow certain clubs to reinforce their squad in view of fixtures decisive for the award of the titles at stake.[8] The Court thus conferred upon the objective of the integrity of sporting competitions the nature of an overriding reason in the public interest capable of justifying a restriction on the free movement of workers. Asked also about a possible infringement of competition law, the Court did not consider itself sufficiently informed by the order for reference to rule on the basis of Articles 85 and 86 of the EC Treaty (Articles 101 and 102 TFEU).[9] Advocate General Alber likewise pointed out the insufficiency of the information communicated by the national court, but he recognised the compliance of transfer windows with Article 85(1) at the end of a line of reasoning similar to that developed in respect of free movement of persons. He took the view that, even if transfer windows have effects restrictive of competition, they may be justified because they are necessary for the establishment and maintenance of fair competition between clubs.[10]

4. Beyond that judgment, which concerns all team disciplines, it is essentially the FIFA Regulations[11] on the Status and Transfer of Players (RSTP) that hold the attention of European regulatory authorities and courts, on account of the magnitude of the economic stakes attached to international transfers of footballers and the litigation generated by their implementation before state courts and arbitral tribunals.[12]

3. Litigation Relating to the FIFA RSTP before the Commission and the EU Courts

5. The FIFA RSTP was adopted in 1991 and has regularly been subject to revision procedures. It deals with every legal and regulatory aspect of international transfers of senior and minor players between clubs affiliated to different national federations. It also addresses other matters, such as the release of players for national team duty. However, those FIFA Regulations remain relatively fragile from a legal

---

7 *Lehtonen* (n 6), para 49.

8 Ibid paras 53 and 54.

9 Ibid paras 28 and 29.

10 Case C-176/96 *Lehtonen v FRBSB* ECLI:EU:C:1999:321, Opinion of AG Alber, paras 101 et seq. Advocate General Alber did not consider the application of Article 85(3) of the EC Treaty (Article 101(3) TFEU) since no exemption application had been filed (para 109).

11 Samba Thiam, "Règlement FIFA sur les transferts de mineurs versus droit européen de la concurrence" (2019) 52 Les Cahiers de droit du sport 163; Grégory Singer, "Les indemnités de formation et de solidarité de la FIFA" (2019) 199 Jurisport 29; D. Jacotot, "La notion de juste cause. Réflexions sur une règle matérielle de droit du travail d'essence privée" in *Mélanges E. Loquin* (LexisNexis 2018) 829; Juan de Dios Crespo Perez, "Les transferts internationaux de joueurs mineurs" (2020) 207 Jurisport 30; Jean Nicolleau, "Les indemnités de transfert dans les règlements et la jurisprudence de la FIFA" in *Les transferts de sportifs dans un monde globalisé* (LexisNexis 2021) 179.

12 FIFA 2001 Regulations on the Status and Transfer of Players (RSTP). On the litigation brought before the Court of Arbitration for Sport, see Buy et al (n 2), 1505.

standpoint, in so far as their validity may be called into question principally in the light of Articles 45 and 101 TFEU. Several cases bear witness to this legal fragility and to the risk of the Court of Justice (ECJ) delivering a fatal blow to the system of football transfers organised under FIFA's aegis.[13]

6. The first gave rise to the *Bosman* judgment.[14] At the end of his employment contract, Mr Bosman had refused its renewal on the ground that the Liège club wished to reduce his salary substantially. He was then placed on the transfer list by his employer. Faced with the refusal of clubs interested in his services (in particular Dunkerque) to pay a financial sum to the Liège club, Mr Bosman was suspended by the latter and was unable to practise his profession during the 1990–1991 season. He decided to take the case before the Belgian courts, which led the Liège Court of Appeal to refer two questions to the ECJ for a preliminary ruling.[15] The ECJ was asked, in particular, whether Articles 48, 85 and 86 of the Treaty of Rome (Articles 45, 101 and 102 TFEU) had to be interpreted as prohibiting a football club from demanding and receiving the payment of a sum of money (transfer fee) upon the engagement, by a new employing club, of one of its players who had reached the end of his employment contract.[16] The European judge replied by unambiguously affirming the incompatibility, with the principle of free movement of workers, of transfer fees for players at the end of their employment contract.[17] Consequently, contrary to the Advocate General's Opinion, the Court did not consider it necessary to rule on the legality of those regulations in the light of European competition law.

7. The second case did not give rise to a judgment of the Court of Justice, because the parties brought their dispute to an end just before the hearing was held;

---

13 Melchior Wathelet, "Il y a bien eu du sport à la CJUE…et il y en aura encore" (2024) <https://www.stradalex.com/fr/sl_rev_utu/toc/jt_2024_13-fr/doc/jt2024_13p213> accessed 25 May 2026.

14 Case C-415/93 *Union Royale Belge Sociale de Football Association, RCL and UEFA v JM Bosman* ECLI:EU:C:1995:463; Mathieu Maisonneuve and Gaylor Rabu (eds), *Les grandes décisions du droit du sport* (Dalloz 2024) 145, obs. Fabrice Rizzo.

15 Gilbert Parléani, "Transferts internationaux de footballeurs professionnels et droit communautaire" (1994) 107 LPA 11.

16 The other question referred for a preliminary ruling concerned the power of national and international sports federations to include in their regulations, provisions limiting the access of foreign players who are EU nationals (nationality clauses) to the competitions they organise. The Court likewise answered that question in the negative, holding that federation nationality clauses are incompatible with the principle of free movement of workers.

17 The Court of Justice has also ruled on the recruitment of young players in training (Case C-325/08 *Olympique Lyonnais SASP v Olivier Bernard and Newcastle UFC* ECLI:EU:C:2010:143). In the *Olympique Lyonnais* judgment, the Court held that a sporting rule providing for a financial penalty where a young player decides not to conclude a professional employment contract with his training club and signs with a club from another Member State is incompatible with Article 45 TFEU in so far as it is liable to deter the player from exercising his right to free movement. The aim of "encouraging the recruitment and training of young players" may indeed justify the restriction but, in accordance with the principle of proportionality, the scheme must still be apt to achieve that objective and must not go beyond what is necessary to attain it. The Court therefore considered that the validity of the system requires that the compensation for the harm suffered by the club take the form of an indemnity whose amount corresponds to the actual cost of the training given to the sportsman, or even to the cost incurred for the training of the whole intake to which he belongs. Unlike the transfer fee condemned by the *Bosman* judgment, training compensation is therefore a lawful restriction on free movement, provided that its amount is not dissuasive for the young player's future employers.

the Advocate General had, however, delivered his Opinion.[18] In that case, a Hungarian footballer, Tibor Balog, whose employment contract with the Royal Charleroi Sporting Club had expired on 30 June 1997, had refused the extension offered by the Belgian club. Since the latter required a transfer fee to release the player, no club wished to engage him, which led Mr Balog to bring summary proceedings before the Court of First Instance of Charleroi. By an order of 2 July 1998, the court asked the Court of Justice, by way of a reference for a preliminary ruling, to rule on the compatibility with Article 85 of the Treaty of Rome (Article 101 TFEU), of the Charleroi club's claim – based on the rules of the national and international federations (URBSFA, UEFA, FIFA) – to obtain payment of a transfer fee upon the engagement of its Hungarian player, at the end of his contract, by a new club established in a Member State of the European Union or in a third state. The situation was similar to that of the *Bosman* judgment. But the significance of this litigation lies in the fact that, the Court being asked to take a position exclusively on the ground of competition law, the Advocate General concluded – at the end of a particularly interesting line of reasoning – that the FIFA Regulations infringed the provisions of Article 85 of the EC Treaty.

8. In parallel with the *Balog* litigation, the European Commission had opened in 1998 infringement proceedings against the FIFA transfer system. A statement of objections had been issued challenging principally the incompatibility, with Article 81 of the EC Treaty (Article 101 TFEU), of the provisions of the RSTP and of FIFA Circular no 616 of 4 June 1997 which prohibited players from unilaterally terminating their employment contract, even where they complied with the requirements of the applicable national law.[19] Moreover, even though the Commission had no means of coercion against the federations on the basis of Article 39 EC (Article 45 TFEU), it nonetheless noted the contradiction between the contested rules and the principle of free movement of workers.[20]

9. The third case led the ECJ to deliver the *Diarra* judgment on 4 October 2024.[21] In August 2013, the footballer Lassana Diarra had committed himself for four years to FC Lokomotiv Moscow. One year later, following various contractual breaches by the player, the club terminated the employment contract early. Considering that termination to have been imputable to the footballer and without just cause, the Russian club brought the matter before FIFA's Dispute Resolution Chamber (DRC) in order to obtain an order requiring the player to pay a substantial indemnity. Released from any commitment to his employing club, Lassana Diarra entered into negotiations with the Charleroi club, which made him a recruitment offer conditional, in particular, on a guarantee from FIFA and the Belgian federation that it would not be held jointly and severally liable with the player for any termination indemnity that the latter might owe to Lokomotiv Moscow, pursuant to Article 17.2 of the RSTP. Having obtained no such assurance, the Charleroi

---

18 Case C-264/98 *Tibor Balog v Royal Charleroi Sporting Club*, Opinion of AG Stix-Hackl.

19 Case AT.IV36.583 European Commission Decision *SETCA/FGTB v FIFA* (28 May 2002) <https://ec.europa.eu/competition/antitrust/cases/dec_docs/36583/36583_54_3.pdf> accessed 24 May 2026.

20 Ibid paras 15 and 29.

21 Case C-650/22 *Lassana Diarra and FIFPRO v FIFA and URBSFA* ECLI:EU:C:2024:824.

club decided to suspend its recruitment of the French player. On 18 May 2015, the DRC eventually ordered the player to pay €10.5 million to his former employer, pursuant to Article 17.1 of the RSTP. Given the time elapsed between the date of termination of the contract and the delivery of its decision, the DRC nevertheless considered that the principle of joint and several liability under Article 17.2 was not intended to apply in the event that Lassana Diarra found a new club. The Court of Arbitration for Sport (CAS) upheld that decision.[22] Despite that heavy condemnation, the player did not give up asserting his rights. He brought proceedings against FIFA and the Belgian federation before the Hainaut Commercial Court in order to obtain reparation for the loss resulting from his being unable to exercise his professional activity for a year.[23] According to the applicant, faced with the risk of being penalised on the basis of Articles 17.2 and 17.4 of the FIFA Regulations, the clubs interested in his services had given up engaging him, thereby forcing him to remain without professional activity for one year. Ordered to pay €60,001 to the player by the first-instance court, FIFA appealed. By its judgment delivered on 19 September 2022, the Mons Court of Appeal referred a question to the CJEU for a preliminary ruling, contrary to the lower court which had set aside that option.[24] For the first time, the Court was called upon to rule on the lawfulness, in the light of Articles 45 and 101 TFEU, of several provisions of the FIFA Regulations imposing financial and sporting sanctions on players who unilaterally terminate their employment contract and on clubs that engage them following such early termination: Article 17.1 imposes a financial sanction and the criteria for its assessment where a party to the employment contract decides to terminate it unilaterally without just cause. Article 17.2 provides, as a matter of principle, for the joint and several liability of the new club for payment of the indemnity owed by the player to his former club in the event of unilateral termination of the contract without just cause. Under Article 17.4, in addition to joint and several liability for payment of the unilateral-termination indemnity, the new club is presumed, subject to proof to the contrary, to have induced the player to break the contract without just cause and, where that player's engagement takes place during the protected period of his contract with the former club, the new club incurs as a result a sporting sanction consisting in a general prohibition on registering new players during two consecutive registration periods. Article 9.1 of the Regulations and Article 8.2.7 of Annex 3 prohibit the federation of the club left, in a general and automatic manner – subject to exceptional circumstances – from issuing an international transfer certificate (ITC) where the former club and the player are involved in a contractual dispute relating to a lack of mutual agreement on early termination of the employment contract. More precisely, the Court of Justice was asked to indicate whether Articles 45 and 101 TFEU must be interpreted as precluding:

- The principle of joint and several liability of the player and of the club wishing to engage him for payment of the indemnity owed to the club with which

22 Case 2015/A/4094 CAS Decision *Lassana Diarra v FC Lokomotiv Moscow* (27 May 2016).

23 Case A/16/00141 *Lassana Diarra* (19 January 2017) Hainaut Commercial Court.

24 Case 236 *Lassana Diarra* (19 September 2022) Mons Court of Appeal 8.

the contract was broken without just cause, as laid down in Article 17.2 of the FIFA RSTP, combined with the sporting sanctions provided for in Article 17.4 of that same regulation and with the financial sanctions laid down in Article 17.1;

- The possibility, for the federation on which the player's former club depends, of not issuing the ITC needed for the player's engagement by a new club, where there is a dispute between that former club and the player (Article 9.1 of the FIFA RSTP and Article 8.2.7 of Annex 3 thereof)?

10. In line with the Opinion of AG Szpunar,[25] the Court concluded that the contested regulatory provisions were manifestly unlawful and could hardly be justified in the light of European cartel law and of the principle of free movement of workers.[26] Admittedly, it will be for the referring court, in the final analysis, to rule on the legality of the RSTP, but in light of the guidelines for interpretation of Articles 45 and 101 TFEU sent by the Court of Justice to the Belgian court, it seems that FIFA will, in due course, have no choice but to undertake a further revision of its Regulations.[27]

11. Thus, in its various successive versions, the RSTP has laid down a series of rules, applicable upon expiry or in the course of performance of the player's employment contract, intended to prevent or strictly limit the possibilities of changing club where there is no agreement between all the parties to the transfer. In those conditions, the European Commission and the Court of Justice were logically called upon to assess the lawfulness of the contested provisions of the FIFA Regulations in the light of the requirements of Articles 45 and 101 TFEU.[28] They did not prohibit the actors in professional football from concluding agreements organising the for-value transfer of players between two clubs. However, the confrontation of the RSTP with the principle of free movement of workers and with competition law led the EU judge to condemn, in particular, the rule requiring clubs wishing to recruit a player whose employment contract had expired to pay the former employing club a transfer fee, and the main provisions sanctioning players who unilaterally terminate their employment contract before its term and clubs which seize the opportunity of their release to engage them. For the purposes of this work on *Sport and Competition Law*, it seems logical to limit our discussion to the examination of the compatibility of the sporting rules concerned with European Union competition law. The *Bosman*, *Lehtonen* and *Olympique Lyonnais* judgments had founded their solution essentially on the impairment of the freedom of movement of players. The *Diarra* judgment confirmed and even

---

25 Case C-650/22 *Lassana Diarra and FIFPRO v FIFA and URBSFA* ECLI:EU:C:2024:375, Opinion of AG Szpunar; Robby Hauben, Oliver Budzinsky and Melchior Wathelet, "The Transfer System in Football: Diarra and What's Next" (2024) <https://papers.ssrn.com/sol3/papers.cfm?abstract_id=4871477> accessed 25 May 2026; Xavier Aumeran, "Affaire Diarra et liberté de circulation des footballeurs: avis de tempête pour le système des transferts" (2024) 140 RLDC 31.

26 *Diarra* (n 21).

27 It should also be noted that on 25 November 2024, FIFA suspended all proceedings pending before its Disciplinary Committee concerning Article 17 of the RSTP.

28 In his Opinion in *Diarra* (n 25), AG Szpunar also raised the question of the compatibility of the contested provisions with Article 15 of the Charter of Fundamental Rights of the European Union.

refined that case law on the ground of Article 45 TFEU, but it also developed a competition law line of reasoning whose pertinence and didactic dimension – which appreciably reinforces its reach – must both be underscored. In the line of the reflections of AGs Lenz and Stix-Hackl, respectively in the *Bosman* and *Balog* cases, of the European Commission decision of 28 May 2002 and of its decisions delivered in sporting matters on 21 December 2023,[29] the Court tested the contested provisions of the RSTP against competition law in order to conclude that there exists a restrictive arrangement within the meaning of Article 101(1) TFEU for which an exemption on the basis of Article 101(3) TFEU appears to it to be impossible.

II. Characterising the Restrictive Arrangement

1. The Relevant Market

12. In the *Bosman*, *Balog* and *Diarra* cases, the players were perceived as the principal factor of production for the various sporting competitions in which they take part.[30] They constitute a fundamental source of supply for their clubs. The clubs operate both as demanders and as suppliers of footballers on the market for sources of supply, which constitutes the relevant market for player transfers. That market lies upstream of the market for the production of football competitions, and on it the players do not act as demanders or suppliers of services but as factors of production of competitions for whose acquisition the clubs compete. On that market, the Commission, the Advocates General and the Court identified a restriction of competition flowing from the contested provisions of the RSTP and characterised it, most often, as a restriction of competition by object.

2. A Restriction of Competition

13. Whatever the version of the RSTP brought before the European Commission or referred for a preliminary ruling, the various contested provisions have always been recognised as restrictive of competition within the meaning of Article 101(1) TFEU. In the *Bosman* case, the position of AG Lenz regarding the transfer fees required at the end of the employment contract was unambiguous:

> In our view, it is also perfectly clear that the rules we have to examine here have the effect of restricting competition within the meaning of Article 85(1). The nationality clauses curtail the possibilities for the various clubs to compete with each other through the players they field. (…) The Commission has rightly indicated that those clauses amount to a sharing of the sources of supply within the meaning of Article 85(1)(c). The same applies to the transfer rules. As the Commission has explained, those

---

29 Case C-680/21 *Royal Antwerp FC* ECLI:EU:C:2023:1010; Case C-124/21 P *International Skating Union (ISU)* ECLI:EU:C:2023:1012; Case C-333/21 *European Super League* ECLI:EU:C:2023:1011.

30 *Diarra* (n 25), Opinion of AG Szpunar, para 54. *Balog* (n 18), Opinion of AG Stix-Hackl, paras 86 to 93. Case C-415/93 *Union Royale Belge Sociale de Football Association, RCL and UEFA v JM Bosman* ECLI:EU:C:1995:293, Opinion of AG Lenz, paras 262–267; *SETCA/FGTB v FIFA* (n 19).

rules substitute, for the normal interplay of supply and demand, a uniform mechanism which results in preserving the existing competitive situation and depriving clubs of the possibility of exploiting the opportunities to engage players that would be available to them under normal conditions of competition. If transfer sums did not have to be paid, a player could freely change club at the end of his contract and look for the club offering the best conditions. In those circumstances, the club could then demand a transfer sum only where that had been stipulated in advance in the contract concluded with the player. By contrast, the current transfer regime mainly results in keeping the player bound to his former club even after his contract has expired. As a transfer can take place only against payment of a transfer sum, that regime tends to preserve the existing competitive situation. (...) Thus the transfer rules themselves restrict competition.[31]

14. This position rests on the principle that players constitute a factor of competition between clubs. Practices aimed at restricting the freedom of movement of athletes necessarily harm competition. In the same way that two manufacturers may not collude to share the market or to oppose the entry of other operators, agreements concluded between clubs which seek to allocate certain players between them and/or to prevent their recruitment by other competing clubs are liable to infringe the rules on restrictive agreements. In the *Balog* case, AG Stix-Hackl likewise condemned the obligation on the club to pay transfer fees in order to recruit a player at the end of his contract, on the ground that they limited clubs' access to their sources of supply and replaced the free play of supply and demand on the relevant market with a sharing of players contrary to Article 81(1) of the EC Treaty (Article 101(1) TFEU).[32]

15. For its part, the European Commission considered in 2002 that the FIFA rules constituted decisions of an association of undertakings whose object or effect was to limit the sources of supply of clubs as regards players, within the meaning of Article 81(1)(c) of the EC Treaty (Article 101 TFEU).[33] Competition between clubs was hampered on the relevant market as well as on the downstream markets relating to the production and marketing of competitions. The FIFA rules substituted for the normal regime of labour supply and demand, a uniform and rigid mechanism of player moves which prevented sporting bodies from optimising their recruitment, in so far as they could not engage players released from any contractual obligation following the unilateral termination of their employment contract. As regards international transfers of players under contract, FIFA Circular no 616 accepted only those operating on the basis of a mutual agreement between the three interested parties (club of departure, player and host club), and most often giving rise to the payment of an indemnity defined arbitrarily. The obstacles thus created to club opportunities to build their teams limited their chances of achieving sporting and economic success. They affected the movement of players and the development

---

31 *Bosman* (n 30), Opinion of AG Lenz, para 262.

32 *Balog* (n 18), Opinion of AG Stix-Hackl, paras 98 to 100.

33 *SETCA/FGTB v FIFA* (n 19), paras 31 to 35.

of the economic activities generated by football competition. They were liable appreciably to restrict trade between Member States and therefore constituted, in the Commission's view, an unlawful restrictive arrangement. Taking note of the criticisms addressed by the Commission, FIFA finally amended its RSTP on 5 July 2001, leading the Commission to reject the application for a finding of infringement and to close the procedure.[34]

16. In the *Diarra* case, AG Szpunar and the Court likewise took the view that the contested rules of the RSTP constitute restrictions of competition within the meaning of Article 101(1) TFEU.[35] According to the former, "(...) the consequences of a termination without just cause by a player are so draconian that it is very unlikely that a player would make that choice. The contested provisions are designed in such a way as to produce a deterrent effect and to discourage every player. The same is true of clubs that might be interested in the possibility of attracting players towards new opportunities while those players are bound by a contract still in force. The "price to be paid" for such an operation would be extremely high". He thus denounced rules which limit, where the player has terminated his employment contract without just cause, the ability of athletes and clubs to enter into new employment relationships. In line with the Advocate General's Opinion, the Court recognised that the recruitment of talented players is one of the essential parameters of the competition in which professional clubs engage, which gives players the character of "factors of production" essential for clubs in the quest for sporting and economic success. The Court accordingly inferred that the contested rules, by limiting the capacity to recruit players, necessarily affect competition between clubs on the market for the acquisition of professional footballers, that is to say the market for sources of supply.

17. In short, the contested provisions of the RSTP have always been regarded as restrictive of competition. But it remains necessary to specify their degree of harmfulness with regard to free competition. On that point, the Court of Justice did not hesitate to characterise them as restrictive by their very object.

3. A Restriction of Competition by Object

18. Restrictions by object are more toxic to free competition than those which merely produce a restrictive effect. The Commission, in its decision of 28 May 2002, and AG Stix-Hackl, in the *Balog* case, did not rule expressly on this point, but they observed a high level of impairment of competition. The latter indicated, at point 124 of her Opinion, that: "Having regard to all those considerations, it must be found that the contested transfer rules have the effect of restricting competition on the relevant market". That said, it is not certain that she intended to exclude the qualification of a restriction by object, in so far as the question had not been addressed under the alternative of object or effect. Moreover, she had earlier emphasised the appreciable nature of the restriction of competition (paragraph 121).

---

[34] Ibid.

[35] *Diarra* (n 25), Opinion of AG Szpunar, paras 51 to 56.

19. According to AG Lenz, in the *Bosman* case: "The constitutive elements of Article 85(1) are present where the cartel has the object or effect of restricting competition. In the present case, it is plain that that restriction of competition is not merely an effect of the rules in question, but that the clubs and associations have willed it".[36] By emphasising the parties' manifest intention to harm competition, AG Lenz appeared to opt for the characterisation of a restriction by object seriously distorting competition between clubs.

20. On the occasion of the *Diarra* litigation, the Commission expressed a dissenting opinion in favour of a restriction of competition by effect. It argued that the contested provisions could not be considered as having the object of restricting competition, in so far as they applied only in the event of termination of the contract without just cause and therefore had no bearing on the possibility for clubs freely to compete by recruiting players upon expiry of their employment contract or during its performance, where the player and the two clubs gave their agreement to the transfer.[37] On the contrary, AG Szpunar identified serious indicia of the existence of a restriction of competition by object. Even though he acknowledged that not all transfer operations are made impossible, he considered that, in the event of unilateral termination of the employment contract without just cause, the contested provisions – whose consequence is to cause every form of competition to disappear – necessarily fall within the category of restrictions of competition by object.[38] The Court likewise adopted that characterisation at the end of a precise, rigorous and exhaustive analysis of the content of the rules at issue, of the economic and legal context in which they are inserted and of their purpose.[39]

21. As regards the content of the rules, the Court examined them as an indissociable whole. It first engaged in a trenchant critique of Article 17.1 of the RSTP, which sets out the criteria for assessing the indemnity owed by the player in the event of unilateral termination without just cause.[40] It deplored the failure to give effect to the criterion concerning the "law of the country concerned" as well as the abstract and imprecise character of the criterion relating to the "specificities of sport", which facilitate its discretionary – and therefore unpredictable and uncontrollable – implementation. As to the other criteria, it regretted that they allow excessive and deterrent indemnities to be set, contrary to those resulting from national laws,

---

36 *Bosman* (n 30), Opinion of AG Lenz, para 262.

37 *Diarra* (n 25), Opinion of AG Szpunar, para 50.

38 Ibid para 56. In support of his position, AG Szpunar further noted, in fn 34 of his Opinion, the European Commission's statement in Commission Communication – Guidelines on the application of Union competition law to collective agreements regarding the working conditions of solo self-employed persons [2022] OJ C374/2. According to that Communication, where the professional sports clubs of a Member State agree not to poach athletes from each other's clubs during the term of the athletes' contracts, such an arrangement is liable to infringe Article 101 TFEU by reason of its object, in so far as it restricts competition between sports clubs to sign the best athletes on the market. In other words, the Commission considered that the system requiring an agreement between the two clubs in order to permit the player's transfer constitutes a restriction by object. Provided that the two analyses bore on the same provisions of the RSTP, this position is at odds with the one it adopted in the *Diarra* case.

39 *Diarra* (n 21), paras 124 to 148.

40 Ibid para 135.

taking as an example Belgian law.[41] The Court then noted the anticompetitive aspects of the measures laid down in Articles 17.2 and 17.4 of the RSTP and in Article 8.2.7 of Annex 3 to the FIFA Regulations. Finally, the Court considered that it follows from the combination of the RSTP rules that clubs are able to retain their players for as long as they do not decide to part with them by mutual agreement or by a negotiated transfer to another club, against payment of a transfer fee. It accordingly inferred the existence of a generalised and drastic restriction of cross-border competition between clubs, in so far as the possibility of recruiting players free from any commitment following the unilateral termination of their employment contract constitutes an essential parameter of competition in the professional football sector.[42]

22. As regards the economic and legal context, the Court recognised FIFA's legitimacy in adopting regulatory measures intended to guarantee the integrity of its competitions, whose principal corollaries are the equality of opportunity of clubs and the principle of sporting merit. More precisely, it accepted that the latter principle requires that, for one season, the stability of club squads be preserved, by prohibiting – as Article 16 of the RSTP does – the unilateral termination of players' employment contracts during a competition. The stability of the composition of teams throughout a championship is indispensable to preserving its regularity. That said, taking into account the specific features of the football ecosystem consists, for the Court, in simply accepting the need to ensure the stability of club squads for a maximum of one season. The Court took the view that respect for the principle of sporting merit does not justify going beyond that by providing for a generalised, drastic and permanent prohibition or restriction of the right of clubs to recruit players who have unilaterally terminated their employment contract, or to induce them to do so in order to be able to engage them.[43] The contested rules constitute unlawful no-poach agreements between clubs[44] that artificially partition national transfer markets and crystallise the distribution of players among clubs. The Court was careful to note that such no-poach agreements are, moreover, unnecessary, in so far as the general law of contracts offers efficient means of guaranteeing the stability of squads as well as free competition between clubs on the market for football transfers. Indeed, the general theory of obligations provides that the player must compensate his employer if he decides to terminate his employment contract unilaterally before its term. The purpose is to make good the contractual loss suffered by the club. Furthermore, contractual freedom enables clubs to recruit players whose employment contract has expired, or to negotiate a financial agreement with a club so that it consents to release its player before the end of the employment contract.[45]

---

41 In France, Article L.1243-3 of the Labour Code provides that "early termination of a fixed-term employment contract at the employee's initiative outside the cases provided for in Articles L.1243-1 and L.1243-2 gives the employer the right to damages corresponding to the loss suffered". It should be noted that some judgments have taken into account the market value of the player ((21 May 2008) Lyon Court of Appeal (2009) 15 Les Cahiers de droit du sport 65; (27 June 2008) Toulouse Court of Appeal (2008) 15 Les Cahiers de droit du sport 69).

42 *Diarra* (n 21), paras 138 to 141.

43 Ibid paras 145 and 146.

44 AG Szpunar had already emphasised this in his Opinion (*Diarra* (n 25), Opinion of AG Szpunar, para 56).

45 *Diarra* (n 21), para 145.

23. The Court concluded its reasoning by noting that the aim of the contested rules lies in the will to prevent or to restrict the competition between clubs for access to the essential resources constituted by the players. Having regard to the legal, financial and sporting risks weighing on clubs, it is not possible for them to poach a player whose employment contract is being performed, nor to take advantage of a unilateral termination without just cause that he has already carried out. The only way to recruit a player consists in the ability to employ him when his employment contract has expired, or by means of a negotiated transfer based on a tripartite agreement between the clubs and the player.[46]

24. All in all, there can be no doubt, for the EU judge, that the degree of harmfulness of the rules at issue with regard to competition between clubs on the transfer market confers on them the character of rules whose very object is to restrict, or even to preclude, that competition in the territory of the European Union. The seriousness of the impairment of free competition is such that the Court ruled out the possibility for FIFA of obtaining an exemption of the restrictive arrangement on the basis of Article 101(3) TFEU.

III. The Exemption of Anti-competitive Agreements

1. The Exclusion of the *Wouters* Doctrine

25. Since the RSTP rules constitute a restriction of competition by object, it is not possible to apply the theory of regulatory ancillary restraints (or the *Wouters* doctrine), according to which certain specific agreements or conduct pursuing one or more objectives of general interest may escape the prohibition laid down in Article 101(1) TFEU[47] In its *Super League* judgment, the ECJ affirmed that a restriction by object affects free competition too seriously for it to be conceivable that it could be justified and proportionate to the legitimate objectives it pursues.[48] The only way to justify this form of restrictive arrangement consists in obtaining from the judge an exemption under Article 101(3) TFEU when all the conditions laid down by that provision are satisfied. First, it must be established, with a sufficient degree of probability, that the provisions of the RSTP concerned must make it possible to achieve efficiency gains, by contributing to improving the production or distribution of the spectacle of professional football. Second, it must be established, to the same extent, that a fair share of the profit resulting from those efficiency gains is reserved to users. Third, the rules of the RSTP at issue must not impose restrictions on clubs which are not indispensable for achieving such efficiency gains. Fourth, the contested provisions must not give clubs the possibility of eliminating all effective competition on the relevant markets. The Commission had considered, in its decision of 20 May 2002, that the conditions for exemption were satisfied,

---

46 Ibid para 147.

47 Case C-309/99 *Wouters* ECLI:EU:C:2002:98, para 97; Case C-519/04 P *David Meca-Medina and Igor Majcen v Commission of the European Communities* ECLI:EU:C:2006:492, paras 42 to 48.

48 *Super* League (n 29), para 183.

but the Court of Justice, in its judgment of 4 October 2024, opted for the opposite solution.

2. The Commission Decision of 20 May 2002

26. The reform of the RSTP adopted by FIFA on 5 March 2001 had, in particular, substituted measures of limitation for the absolute prohibition of unilateral termination of employment contracts. The European Commission considered, in its decision of 28 May 2002, that the rules framing unilateral termination did not constitute restrictions of competition within the meaning of Article 81(1) of the EC Treaty (Article 101(1) TFEU) and, at the very least, satisfied the requirements of Article 81(3) (Article 101(3) TFEU).[49] In effect, it found, first, that the new rules contributed to improving the production and distribution of the football spectacle, on account of the preservation of the integrity of competitions and the stability of the composition of teams throughout each sporting season. The possibility, for players as for clubs, of unilaterally breaking their contract during the championship would have the effect of changing the sporting value of teams while the competition was being played, and thus of calling into question, by distorting competition between clubs, the sincerity of the resolution of the contests. Likewise, the periods of contractual stability imposed during the first two or three years of the employment contract contributed to the achievement of the legitimate objective of squad stability and championship integrity. Second, the Commission recognised that consumers – that is, spectators, television viewers and supporters of football competitions – derived a fair share of the benefit from those restrictions, because the preservation of the integrity of competitions made the spectacle more balanced and interesting. Safeguarding the fairness of contests between clubs gives competitions the sporting balance that is indispensable to optimising their interest. Third, the Commission considered that protecting contracts during a limited period was indispensable to guaranteeing the construction of a competitive team. If a player could break his contract unilaterally as early as the first year and be transferred at the end of the season, to another club, with no sanction other than a financial compensation, his club would meet real difficulties in assembling a high-performing squad. The sporting sanctions applicable to players therefore aimed at preventing them from breaking their contracts unilaterally during the first two or three years, so as to allow the existence of stable teams. By reason of the specific features of the sector at issue, the duration of the protected period and the content of the sanctions seemed proportionate to the legitimate objectives they sought to attain. Finally, the Commission considered that the limitation of the unilateral termination of employment contracts did not give clubs the possibility of eliminating competition on the market for the production and sale of football competitions, since they retained the freedom to recruit, during transfer windows and on the basis of negotiated transfers, players bound to other clubs. The Commission therefore concluded that the application for a finding of infringement against the FIFA RSTP resulting from the reform of 5 July 2001 should be rejected.

---

[49] *SETCA/FGTB v FIFA* (n 19), paras 55 to 59.

3. The Position of the Court of Justice of the European Union

27. In the *Bosman* and *Balog* cases, the rules of European Union law gave the Commission alone the power to grant an exemption under Article 85(3) (Article 101(3) TFEU). As no such application had been made, neither the Commission nor the Advocates General considered the question.[50] Advocate General Lenz added that the infringement of Article 48 of the EC Treaty (Article 45 TFEU) by the RSTP should in any event have the consequence of excluding the exemption under Article 85(3), in the name of consistency of reasoning.

28. Advocate General Szpunar considered in his Opinion in the *Diarra* case, that since the conditions for a possible exemption under Article 101(3) TFEU were manifestly not satisfied, it was unnecessary to examine them. We regret the Advocate General's silence on this point, since it does not allow the merits of his position to be assessed. The stakes attaching to the question of the durability of the transfer system imposed on the Court the duty not to bypass the analysis of the conditions for exemption under Article 101(3) TFEU. That was all the more important since it had the opportunity to respond to the argument developed by the Commission in its decision of 28 May 2002. Accordingly, the analysis adopted in the judgment of 4 October 2024 is not satisfactory, in that it focused exclusively on the indispensable or necessary character of the rules at issue.[51] The Court specified that it is for the referring court to compare the respective effects of those rules and of alternative measures, in order to determine whether the hoped-for efficiency gains may be obtained by less restrictive means. However, the Court of Justice invited the Belgian court not to lose sight of the fact that, on the one hand, the combination of those rules constitutes an unlawful obstacle to the free movement of players, since they provide for disproportionate sanctions and/or sanctions imposed in a discretionary manner and, on the other hand, the framing of the unilateral termination of the employment contract by the player has as its object a generalised, drastic and permanent restriction of competition between clubs on the transfer market. For the Court of Justice, there is therefore no doubt that the referring court must refuse to consider the contested rules to be indispensable or necessary to the achievement of the efficiency gains, assuming the latter to be established. The particularly high degree of harmfulness of the contested rules with regard to competition on the market for the transfer of footballers, leaves FIFA with virtually no hope of benefiting from the exemption under Article 101(3) TFEU.

29. Thus, the Court did not call into question the whole of the normative framework relating to the transfer of footballers, but it held that several of its emblematic provisions were incompatible with Articles 45 and 101 TFEU. It insisted on the seriousness of the obstacle to the free movement of footballers and of the impairment of free competition between clubs on the transfer market. It relied on numerous occasions on its judgments of 21 December 2023 to underline its determination to compel FIFA and UEFA scrupulously to comply with the

---

50 *Bosman* (n 30), Opinion of AG Lenz, paras 277 and 278; *Balog* (n 18), Opinion of AG Stix-Hackl, para 123.

51 *Diarra* (n 21), paras 153 to 157.

requirements of European Union law, without being able to benefit from, or even to claim, any immunity based on the specificities of the ecosystem of international football. It also recalled the guidelines of the judgments of 21 December 2023 concerning standards of evidence: the parties must base their claims on truly convincing arguments. FIFA cannot justify the encroachments on European Union law brought about by certain provisions of the RSTP by referring only, in a general and abstract manner, to principles of sports law such as the preservation of the integrity of competitions, the equality of opportunity of competitors, or the contractual stability of club squads. It must be in a position to provide concrete, precise and consistent evidence of the effectiveness and proportionality of the contested measures of its regulations and of their capacity to satisfy all the conditions of Article 101(3) TFEU. FIFA must therefore manifest its political will to comply with European Union law and, in legal terms, demonstrate conscientiously and meticulously the merits of its claims by means of empirical evidence (where applicable of an accounting and financial nature).

4. The Reform of the Footballers' Transfer System

30. In the author's view, it will fall to FIFA to amend its regulatory framework by purging it of the rules that are manifestly irreconcilable with the free movement of workers and the law of restrictive arrangements. FIFA and the representative organisations of clubs and players will have to agree on a lighter regulation of unilateral terminations of employment contracts, by principally determining a new point of equilibrium between the preservation of the contractual stability of squads and the players' freedom to change employer, to guarantee effective competition between clubs on the labour market.[52] It will certainly be necessary to amend the modalities of assessing the financial indemnity payable by the player in the event of unilateral termination of his employment contract without just cause, so that it is reasonable, proportionate and predictable. More generally, all sanctions provided for in the event of unilateral termination of an employment contract without just cause will have to be removed or else imposed on the basis of criteria that are transparent, objective, non-discriminatory, proportionate and capable of being subject to effective review. It will likewise be difficult to avoid reflection on the reduction of the duration of the protected periods. Other rules of the RSTP will, in all likelihood also have to be revised. But, in any event, the principle of squad stability cannot purely and simply be set aside, since, by fostering the unpredictability of results, it contributes to the balance, fairness and integrity of competitions. That is why, in order to exclude the possibility for players to change club at any time during the sporting season, the RSTP has set up transfer windows whose principle, validated by the CJEU,[53] must be preserved. That said, even though we consider that the principle of squad stability is legitimate, it would be most useful for FIFA to demonstrate by means of precise, concrete, relevant and consistent evidence, that the contractual stability of squads effectively contributes to the balance and integrity of competitions.

---

52 Hauben, Budzinsky and Wathelet (n 25).

53 *Lehtonen* (n 6).

31. Following the *Diarra* judgment, on 25 November 2024 FIFA suspended all proceedings then pending before its Disciplinary Committee concerning the provisions of Article 17 of the RSTP. It then slightly modified its normative framework on 22 December 2024 so that a temporary regulation would enter into force on 1 January 2025. In parallel, within the framework of the EU Sectoral Social Dialogue Committee for professional football (EU SSDC), the European social partners adopted, on 26 November 2025, a resolution setting out the fundamental principles on which a future reform of the footballers' transfer system must be based.[54] It should also be underlined that the French professional footballers' union (UNFP) announced, in a press release published on 16 October 2025, that it had joined the class action brought by the Dutch foundation Justice for Players. Its objective is to obtain a lasting reform of transfers and a fair compensation for the players harmed.[55] In the short or medium term, it therefore appears inevitable that the RSTP will be genuinely revised (far more deeply than the so-called reform of 22 December 2024) or abandoned in favour of an agreement collectively negotiated by all the interested actors of international professional football.

---

54 If the parties enact the RSTP within the framework of a collective agreement, it should be immune from competition law in application of the *Albany* case law (Case C-67/96 *Albany International BV v Stichting Bedrijfspensioenfonds Textielindustrie* ECLI:EU:C:1999:430; Hauben, Budzinsky and Wathelet (n 25); Aumeran (n 25), 31).

55 In any event, since the dispute between Mr Diarra and FIFA has not been settled amicably, the player has brought proceedings against FIFA and the URBSFA before the Belgian courts, claiming €65 million in damages.

The Home-Grown Player Rules

Vanja Smokvina*
University of Rijeka, Croatia

I. Introduction

1. In modern sport, especially in professional football, there are clubs that spend huge sums on signing new players in order to become ever more competitive, as in Europe or as in Saudi Arabia and the US with stars like Ronaldo or Messi, trying to bring their competition into the focus of spectators, fans and the media.
2. According to FIFA in 2023 USD 9.63 billion were spent on international transfer fees, which is an increase of 48.1% compared to 2022. A total of 1,024 clubs spent money on international transfers in 2023, the first-ever time that more than 1,000 clubs invested in transfer fees for new players from abroad. The number of clubs that received transfer fees, 1,241, was also another new high.[1]
3. In order to protect the pool of players for the national teams, protect the competitive balance between the clubs, promote the work of the football clubs' academies and generally promoting the training and development of youth, the sport governing bodies, like UEFA or the national football federations try to regulate their competition with specific rules. The home-grown players (HGP) rule is one of them.

---

* Associate Professor at the University of Rijeka, Faculty of Law – Croatia; Sports Law, Sports Policies & Sports Diplomacy Centre & EU Sports Law, Policy & Diplomacy Jean Monnet Chair Holder; CAS Arbitrator. Edge Hill University (UK), Centre for Sports Law Research Academic Member; Universidad Carlos III de Madrid (Spain) UNESCO ELIS Chair (Educational Linkage through International Sports) Member & Aspira University of Applied Sciences (Croatia) Visiting Professor. The research for this paper was financed within the EU Erasmus+ Project – Erasmus 2027 Programme: Jean Monnet Chair in EU Sports Law, Policy & Diplomacy (Project ID 101085643).

1 FIFA, *Global Transfer Report 2023* (January 2024) <https://digitalhub.fifa.com/m/114622e4e17cf6a8/original/FIFA-Global-Transfer-Report-2023.pdf> accessed 2 September 2025.

4. Recently, the HGP rule and its compatibility with the EU Law was analysed by the Court of Justice of the EU (CJEU).[1] This chapter will only analyse the rules *per se*, without entering the reasoning and legal argumentation of the compatibility of the rules with the EU law.

II. The HGP Rule

5. In this part of the chapter, we will explain the HGP rule, first as the rule applied by UEFA for its competitions and then as the rule applied at national level by the national football associations. We will also provide some data showing the number of HGP used at both competition levels.

1. The UEFA HGP Rule

6. The UEFA HGP rule was endorsed on 21 April 2005 during its congress in Tallinn, Estonia, when presented to UEFA's, at the time, 52 national member associations.[2]

7. The initial proposal was made after UEFA identified a number of perceived negative trends in European football, including: a lack of incentive in training players, lack of identity in local/regional teams, "hoarding" of players, and related problems for national teams. UEFA intention with the implementation of the HGP rule was to fight less competitive balance in UEFA club competitions and domestic leagues, an increased link between money and sporting success, and fewer opportunities for locally trained players to play. As a result, it was claimed that clubs were re-evaluating whether it was worthwhile developing young talent when the best young players would gravitate to the richest clubs without necessarily providing a good return on the training club's investment. We may conclude that such trends are present even after almost 20 years. The question is also, do those clubs' talents, when minors, have the opportunity to play at the highest level? The International Centre for Sports Studies (CIES) data shows that in matches of the five major European leagues[3] played over the 15-year-period between the 1 January 2009 until the 31 December 2023, no less than 402 footballers played before turning 18 in Big 5 league matches. With 119 underage players fielded, the French Ligue 1 is the leader in this domain, which reflects both its status as a stepping stone for the other Big 5 championships and the excellence of the French training system. From a historical point of view, no noticeable change in the use of minors by Big 5 league clubs was observed over the first ten years studied, with annual values situated around 30. A first increase was recorded between 2019 and 2021, with an average of 36.7 minors fielded, as opposed to 30.1 during the previous decade. An even more important increase was recorded over the past two years, with no less than 61 minors fielded in 2022 and 49 in 2023.[4]

8. Of course, investing in the clubs' academia and the training of young players is important since it could also be a profitable way of running a club. The ten most profitable

---

1 Case C-680/21 *Royal Antwerp FC* ECLI:EU:C:2023:1010.

2 UEFA, "Declaration of the UEFA Congress on the Subject of Local Training of Players" (2005) <www.uefa.com/MultimediaFiles/Download/uefa/UEFAMedia/297202_DOWNLOAD.pdf>> accessed 2 September 2025.

3 Ligue 1 (FRA), Serie A (ITA), Premier league (ENG), Bundesliga (GER) and La Liga (SPA).

4 CIES Football Observatory, *Monthly Report No 91: Younger Than Ever? The Use of Minors in the European Big-5 (2009–2023)* (January 2024) <https://football-observatory.com/MonthlyReport91> accessed 2 September 2025.

football club academies worldwide in terms of revenue generated over the last ten years by the transfer of players who spent at least three seasons there between the ages of 15 and 21 are all European football clubs, with the Portuguese side SL Benfica clearly in the lead with 516 million euros, two thirds of which has been collected in the last five years. The other clubs in the top ten are (in euros) AFC Ajax (376 million), Olympique Lyonnais (370 million), Real Madrid (364 million), Chelsea FC (347 million), AS Monaco (325 million), Portuguese Sporting CP (306 million), Tottenham Hotspur (256 million), Manchester City (254 million) and Italian side Atalanta BC (250 million). Outside Europe, the clubs with the most profitable academies are Brazil's CR Flamengo (thirteenth with 228 million) and Argentina's River Plate (fourteenth with 223 million).[5]

9. The basis of the solution to the problems of investing in the training and developing of youth players instead of just signing players for a transfer fee or as free agents was to introduce rules which encouraged clubs participating in UEFA club competitions to include a minimum number of locally trained players (LTP) in their squad (commonly referred to as HGP). The implementation of the rules was staggered to afford clubs a transition period with minimum numbers of HGP to be implemented gradually as follows: season 2006–2007: 4 HGP in 25-man squad; season 2007–08: 6 HGP in 25-man squad, and season 2008–2009 onwards: 8 HGP in 25-man squad.[6] In the end, clubs have no obligation to put a certain number of HGP on the field of play, or on the match sheet. They are entirely free in their team and matchday squad selection.

10. To give a picture how the rule looks like, we will take the UEFA Champions league regulations.[7] The same rules apply also in other two UEFA competitions, the Europa League,[8] the Conference League[9] and additionally to the Super Cup Competition. Clubs must submit an "A" List of players (List A) and a "B" List of players (List B) duly signed by the club and verified, validated and additionally signed by its association. No club may have more than 25 players on List A during the season. As a minimum, eight places are reserved exclusively for "locally trained players", what UEFA is calling the "home-grown players" and no club may have more than four "association-trained players" listed in these eight places on List A. List A must specify the players who qualify as being "locally trained", as well as whether they are "club-trained" or "association-trained".[10]

11. A "club-trained player" is a player who, between the age of 15 (or the start of the season during which he turns 15) and 21 (or the end of the season during which he turns 21), and irrespective of nationality and age, has been registered with their current club for a period, continuous or not, of three entire seasons (ie a period starting with

---

[5] CIES Football Observatory, "Weekly Post No 446: Most Profitable Club Academies Worldwide" (10 January 2024) <https://football-observatory.com/WeeklyPost446> accessed 2 September 2025.

[6] Dalziel Murray and others, *Study on the Assessment of UEFA's "Home Grown Player Rule* (2013) 9–10 <https://ec.europa.eu/assets/eac/sport/library/studies/final-rpt-april2013-homegrownplayer.pdf> accessed 2 September 2025.

[7] UEFA Champions League Regulations (2022–2024) <https://documents.uefa.com/r/Regulations-of-the-UEFA-European-Football-Championship-2022-24-Online> accessed 2 September 2025.

[8] UEFA Europa League Regulations (2022–2024), art 45 and Annex H <https://documents.uefa.com/r/Regulations-of-the-UEFA-European-Football-Championship-2022-24/Article-4-Admission-criteria-and-procedure-Online> accessed 2 September 2025. see footnote 9.

[9] Ibid.

[10] Ibid art 45.02.

the first official match of the relevant national championship and ending with the last official match of that relevant national championship) or of 36 months. In the context of this paragraph, the season immediately preceding a player's 15th birthday may be counted if their birthday is after the last match of the relevant national championship but on or before 30 June (winter championships) or 31 December (summer championships), and the season immediately following their 21st birthday may be counted if their birthday is on or after 1 July (winter championships) or 1 January (summer championships) but before the first match of the relevant national championship.[11]

12. An "association-trained player" is a player who, fulfilled all the conditions to be defined a "club-trained player" with an exception that has been registered with a club or with other clubs affiliated to the same association as that of their current club.[12]

13. It is important to highlight that, if a club has fewer than eight locally trained players in its squad, then the maximum number of players on List A is reduced accordingly.[13]

14. Table 1 below, illustrates how the List A of a team competing in UEFA Champions League Competition 2023–2024 could look with the implementation of the HGP rule.[14]

	Potential List A	'Free' players	Club-trained	Association-trained	Actual List A
1	25	17	8	0	25
2	25	17	7	1	25
3	25	17	7	0	24
4	25	17	6	2	25
5	25	17	6	1	24
6	25	17	6	0	23
7	25	17	5	3	25
8	25	17	5	2	24
9	25	17	5	1	23
10	25	17	5	0	22
11	25	17	4	4	25
12	25	17	4	3	24
13	25	17	4	2	23
14	25	17	4	1	22
15	25	17	4	0	21
16	25	17	3	4	24
17	25	17	3	3	23
18	25	17	3	2	22
19	25	17	3	1	21
20	25	17	3	0	20
21	25	17	2	4	23
22	25	17	2	3	22
23	25	17	2	2	21
24	25	17	2	1	20
25	25	17	2	0	19
26	25	17	1	4	22
27	25	17	1	3	21
28	25	17	1	2	20
29	25	17	1	1	19
30	25	17	1	0	18
31	25	17	0	4	21
32	25	17	0	3	20
33	25	17	0	2	19
34	25	17	0	1	18
35	25	17	0	0	17

Table 1: UEFA Champions League Regulations 2023/2024

---

11 Ibid art 45.04.

12 Ibid art 45.05.

13 Ibid art 45.06.

14 Ibid Annex H – Locally Trained Players.

15. It is important to note that before enacting the HGP rule, UEFA organised a two-year consultation with fans, national associations, national leagues, clubs, players' unions and all the institutions of the EU, meaning that the stakeholders were consulted in drafting the rule. In parallel, UEFA spent two years providing detailed research to the European Commission DGs that were most interested in the rule (education and culture, employment and social affairs, competition, and the legal service).[15] It is not only a highly appreciated sign of good governance, but also an important sign of real stakeholder involvement in the creation of a rule and a real sign of the social dialogue in professional football.

16. Now the question is, how is the rule implemented in reality and what are the data? Has the rule achieved its aims? According to UEFA reports it could be concluded that there is an insufficient number of locally trained players in UEFA competitions group stage squads.

17. As shown in Figure 1, in the 2020–2021 season, half (16 out of 32) of the clubs in the UEFA Champions League group stage and almost two-thirds (31 out of 48) of the clubs in the UEFA Europa League group stage, failed to include the full contingent of eight locally trained players in their squads. The number of A-list players they could register was reduced accordingly.[16]

18. In 2021–2022, more than half (17 out of 32) of the clubs in the group stage of the UEFA Champions League, almost two-thirds (20 out of 32) of the clubs in the group stage of the UEFA Europa League and more than half (17 out of 32) of the clubs in the group stage of the UEFA Europa Conference League, failed to include the full contingent of eight locally trained players in their squads. While there is some fluctuation from year to year, the number of clubs that are unable to register enough locally trained players at the group stage does appear to be increasing, with an average of 56% of clubs being in that situation in the period between 2015–2016 and 2020–2021, up from 47% in the period between 2009–2010 and 2014–2015, with a figure of 56% being seen in 2021–2022 also. Players who are still young are placed on List B, so do not count towards the List A quota. The analysis suggests that the 2022–2023 group stages followed the same pattern, with 56% of clubs registering reduced squads.[17]

---

15 UEFA, "Protection of Young Players" (*EUFA.com*, 2025) <www.uefa.com/development/youth-players/promoting-young-talent/> accessed 2 September 2025.

16 UEFA, *The European Club Footballing Landscap*e (13th edn, 2022) 46 <https://editorial.uefa.com/resources/0272-145b03c04a9e-26dc16d0c545-1000/master_bm_high_res_20220203104923.pdf> accessed 2 September 2025.

17 Ibid (14th edn, 2023) 29 <https://editorial.uefa.com/resources/027e-174740f39cc6-d205dd2e86bf-1000/ecfl_bm_report_2022_high_resolution_.pdf> accessed 2 September 2025.

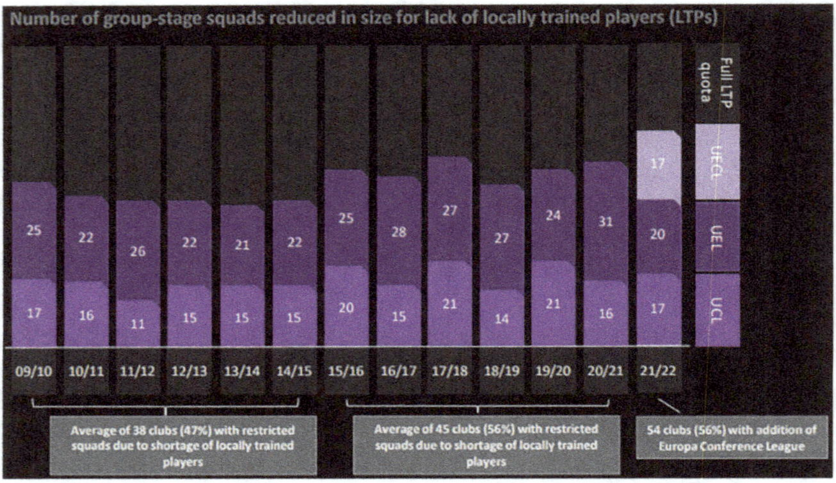

Source: UEFA, *The European Club Footballing Landscape (2023), p. 29*

Figure 1: Number of group-stage squads reduced in size for lack of locally trained players (LTPs)

19. To be listed on List A of 25 players does not mean that the HGP will actually take part in the game. There were even four UEFA Champions League, four UEFA Europa League and five UEFA Europa Conference League clubs that did not give a single group-stage start to a club-trained player in 2021–2022.[18] Locally trained players accounted for only 37% of total minutes played in the group stage of the 2021–2022 UEFA Champions League (including young club-trained List B players, who accounted for 5%), compared with 41% for the UEFA Europa League (4% for List B players) and 46% for the UEFA Europa Conference League (4% for List B players). While this is clearly influenced by the clubs that qualify in any given season, the chart below indicates a downward trend in minutes for locally trained players. Preliminary analysis of the 2022–2023 group stages shows an increase in minutes played by LTP+ players: 39% of total minutes in the UEFA Champions League; 44% in the UEFA Europa League; 45% in the UEFA Europa Conference League. In 2021–2022, club-trained players on Lists A and B (CTP+) accounted for just 17% of total minutes in the UEFA Champions League group stage, 16% in the UEFA Europa League and UEFA 15% in the Europa Conference League, with significant variation from club to club. Only four UEFA Champions League clubs (FC Dynamo Kyiv, BSC Young Boys, Manchester United FC and AFC Ajax) recorded figures of more than 30%, while FC Sheriff Tiraspol, Atalanta BC and LOSC Lille relied entirely on bought-in talent, with no CTP+ featuring in the group stage. Although the marked differences between clubs creates a lot of fluctuation, CTP+ have never accounted for more than 19% of total minutes in the group stage of a UEFA competition.[19]

18 Ibid.

19 Ibid 30.

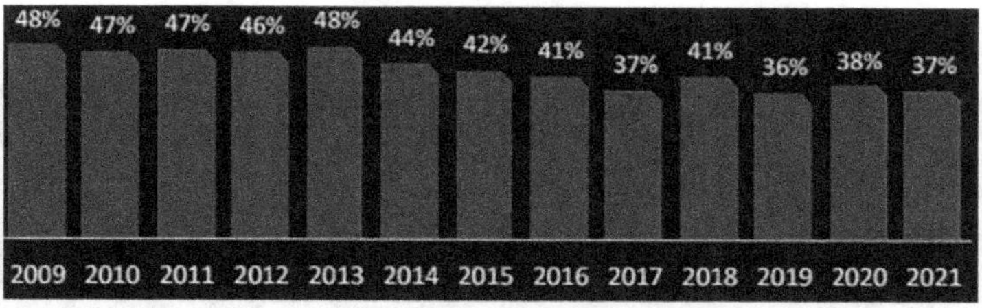

Source: UEFA, *The European Club Footballing Landscape* (2023), p. 30

Figure 2: Minutes played in the UEFA Champions League by locally trained players + players[20]

2. UEFA Members HGP Rule

20. The UEFA HGP rule applies to UEFA competitions. On the other hand, national Football Associations (FA), as members of UEFA, may also implement exactly the same rule in their competitions or they could modify it.[21] Of 55 UEFA member FAs, in 2022–2023 there were 29 FAs with association-trained player requirements and 11 FAs with club-trained player requirements in their national regulations. Eight FAs apply the same HGP rule as UEFA (4+4 or 4+2), 21 FAs have some regulation on HGP, while 25 FAs do not have any kind of regulation at all.[22]

21. According to the UEFA report, domestically, locally trained footballers played an estimated 52% of total minutes in the 2022–2023 season in the 20 leagues analysed: 13% for club-trained players and 39% for association-trained players. These are the same percentages as observed in the 2021 season. Denmark recorded the highest figure for club-trained players (24%), followed by Switzerland and Norway (19%), while association-trained footballers in Ukraine spent 76% of the total minutes on the pitch, pushing Ukrainian clubs' combined average for club and association-trained players to 91%. Four countries (Scotland, Italy, Türkiye and Greece) recorded figures of less than 8% for club-trained players, which is less than one in eleven. Turkish clubs had the lowest average for club-trained players (5%) while Greek clubs had the lowest average for association-trained players (23%). Looking at the Big 5, Spanish clubs had locally

---

20 Locally trained players (LTP) + players are defined as locally trained players plus any B-list players. Similarly, CTP+ players are defined as club-trained players on list A plus all players on list B. Although the requirements for list B are separate from the locally trained player rules, the combination of the two provides a better overview of clubs' use of academy players past and present. The main differences in terms of eligibility relate to the minimum period of time with the club (two years for list B; three seasons to be regarded as locally trained), the continuity of the player's time with the club (uninterrupted for list B; between the ages of 15 and 21 for locally trained players) and current age (under 21 for list B; any age for locally trained players).

21 UEFA, *The European Club Footballing Landscape* (14 September 2023) 44 <https://editorial.uefa.com/resources/0272-145b03c04a9e-26dc16d0c545-1000/master_bm_high_res_20220203104923.pdf> accessed 2 September 2025.

22 UEFA, *The European Club Talent and Competition Landscape* (2023) 30 <https://editorial.uefa.com/resources/0285-18fa5d2b2412-a34231ef95e1-1000/uefa_bm_report_2023_digital_hires.pdf> accessed 2 September 2025.

trained players on the pitch for 62% of the total minutes, compared with 57% in France, 50% in Germany, 42% in England and 39% in Italy.[23]

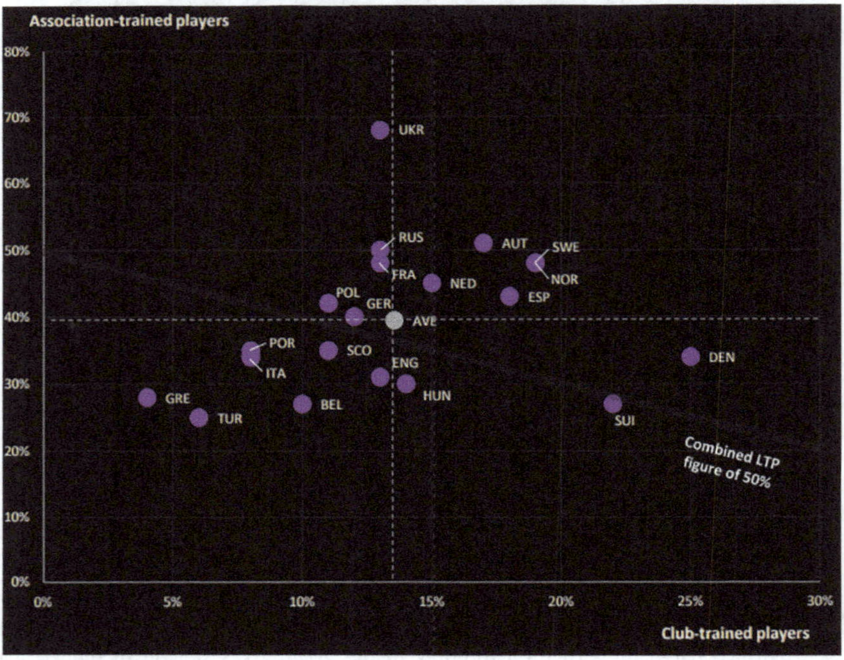

Source: UEFA, *The European Club Footballing Landscape* (2023), p. 31

Figure 3: Percentage of total domestic league minutes accounted for by locally trained players

22. According to the CIES Football Observatory data, the employment rate of club-trained footballers (ie those having been for at least three seasons between the ages of 15 and 21 in their employer club) in 2021 in teams from 27 top divisions of UEFA member associations shows that the highest percentage of minutes by club-trained players overall was recorded for the Slovakian side MŠK Žilina (61.5%), while Athletic Club (50.9%) has the greatest figure for Big 5 league teams. Home-grown footballers played a majority of domestic league minutes also at Dynamo Kyiv (60.2%), Sigma Olomouc (52.0%) and FC Slovácko (51.1%). At the level of the five major European championships, the highest employment rates after Athletic Club were observed in two Spanish sides: Celta Vigo (49.0%) and Real Sociedad (48.5%). AS St-Étienne (35.0%), Brighton & Hove Albion FC (30.1%), FSV Mainz (25.0%) and Genoa CFC (21.0%) top the table in the remaining Big 5 leagues. Per championship, the values stretch from 27.1% in Israel to 5.0% in Italy. Among the Big 5 leagues, only the Spanish Liga (16.3%) is above the European average (13.2%), with a minimum of 5.0% in the Italian Serie A. English teams (12.8%) relied more on club-trained footballers than French (12.4%) and

[23] UEFA, *The European Club Footballing Landscape* (14 September 2023) 31.

German (11.7%) ones.[24] For 2023, the data slightly changed. For 60 leagues around the world according to the percentage of domestic league minutes played by club-trained footballers during the 2023 season, the Basques of Athletic Club (68.9%) tops the Europe's Big 5 leagues table again, while the Ukrainians of Dynamo Kiev (82.9%) have the highest proportion in absolute terms and the Colombians of Envigado (67.8%) among non-European clubs. Olympique Lyonnais (45.6%) and Real Sociedad (45.4%) complete the podium in the Big 5. The highest values in the English Premier League were measured for Arsenal (22.1%), Manchester United (20.4%) and Chelsea (19.8%), while the teams with the most confidence in youth academy graduates in the Italian Serie A and the German Bundesliga are, respectively, Atalanta BC (18.7%) and SC Freiburg (34.5%). Outside Europe, Envigado is ahead of Argentina's Gimnasia La Plata (60.1%) and Vélez Sarsfield (52.1%), followed by Shanghai Port (51.4%) and two Mexican clubs: Pachuca (51.3%) and Chivas (48.8%). The CIES post also shows the number of club-trained players fielded, with a maximum of 30 for Gimnasia, as well as their average age, with a minimum of 18.56 years for the Venezuelan side UCV FC among teams having used at least ten club-trained players.[25]

23. Let's give an overview of the HGP rule in England and in one of the (if not), the top Big 5 leagues. In the Premier League the HGP rule was introduced for the start of the 2010–2011 season and it does not distinguish between association and club-trained players.[26] "Home-grown player" means a player who, irrespective of nationality or age, has been registered with any Club (or club) affiliated to the UK Football Association or the Football Association of Wales for a period, continuous or not, of three seasons or 36 months prior to their 21st birthday (or the end of the season during which they turn 21) and, for the purposes of this definition of "home-grown player", a season will be deemed to commence on the date on which the relevant summer transfer window closes and to expire on the date of the final league match of the season.[27] Each Premier League club submits a squad list after each transfer window closes and it can contain no more than 17 players who do not fulfil "HGP" criteria.[28] The remainder of the squad, up to a total of 25 players, must be HGP.[29] Here, it is important to stress that for the 2023–2024 season any player born on 1 January 2002 or later qualifies as under 21. There is no limit on how many such players can be included in a club's top-flight squad, so even if they're not English, they aren't classed towards the non-home-grown quota.

---

24 CIES Football Observatory, "Weekly Post No 337: Club-trained Players' Employment across Europe" (10 May 2021) <https://football-observatory.com/IMG/sites/b5wp/2020/wp337/en/> accessed 2 September 2025.

25 CIES Football Observatory, "Weekly Post No 440: Global Rankings of Club-Trained Players' Employment" (22 November 2023) <https://football-observatory.com/WeeklyPost440> accessed 2 September 2025.

26 Nick De Marco, *Football and the Law* (2nd edn, Bloomsbury Professional 2022) para 4.139.

27 Premier League, *Handbook: Premier League Rules* (2023–2024) A.1.124 <https://resources.premierleague.com/premierleague/document/2024/03/04/0910e1b3-f94a-41a5-9818-6e1b5c961a9a/PL_Handbook_2023-24_DIGITAL_26.02.24-v3.pdf> accessed 2 September 2025.

28 Premier League, "Squad List" (2023–2024) <https://resources.premierleague.com/premierleague/document/2023/09/13/089c9257-538d-45d2-a00e-3952ffd648d7/PLSquadLists2023-24.pdf> accessed 2 September 2025.

29 Premier League (n 28), A.1.228.

24. In November 2022 the Premier League has published a report marking ten years of the Elite Player Performance Plan (EPPP),[30] highlighting the significant progress that has been made in the development of young, homegrown players throughout the football pyramid. The EPPP is the result of consultation between the Premier League and its clubs, representatives of the Football League, the Football Association and other key football stakeholders. The mission is producing more and better home-grown players, the plan promotes the empowerment of each individual player through a player-led approach. After ten years, the result is that there were 566 home-grown premier league debutants since the launch of the EPPP and out of 1,866 players that have featured in the Premier League since season 2012–2013 47% were HGP.[31]

25. Finally, it is important to analyse how the rule is applied in Belgium, where the Royal Belgian Football Association (RBFA) rules have been challenged before the CJEU in the *Royal Antwerp FC* case.[32]

26. In the present case RBFA rules have been challenged as incompatible with EU Law. The relevant rules of the RBFA federal regulations provide for football clubs participating in the professional football divisions 1A and 1B to submit *lists* containing a maximum list of 25 players, which must include at least eight trained by Belgian clubs (meaning players who have been affiliated to a Belgian club for at least three full seasons before their 23rd birthday). Furthermore, at least three of those eight players must have been affiliated to a Belgian club for at least three seasons before their 21st birthday. Moreover, as regards *match sheets*, clubs must resort to players on the abovementioned lists and must include at least six players who have been affiliated for at least three full seasons before their 23rd birthday, two of which before their 21st birthday. In both instances, if the minimum thresholds are not met, such players cannot be replaced by players who do not satisfy the relevant conditions.[33]

27. The CJEU deliberated in December 2023, deciding on the compatibility of the HGP rule in respect of EU competition law and EU free-movement rights. The CJEU decided that:[34]

> Article 101(1) TFEU must be interpreted as precluding rules that have been adopted by an association responsible for organising football competitions at European level and implemented both by that association and by its member national football associations, and which require each club participating in those competitions to enter in the list of its players and to include on the match sheet a minimum number of players trained either by that club itself or within the territory of the national association to which that club is affiliated, and rules that have been adopted by an association responsible for organising football competitions at national level, and which require each

---

30 Premier League, *Elite Player Performance Plan* (2022) <https://resources.premierleague.com/premierleague/document/2022/11/17/5c3d5e72-567e-4886-80ab-9a2e68857b8b/Premier-League-Elite-Player-Performance-Plan-Report-2022.pdf> accessed 2 September 2025.

31 Ibid 11.

32 *Royal Antwerp* (n 2).

33 Case C-680/21 *Royal Antwerp FC* ECLI:EU:C:2023:188, Opinion of AG Szpunar, paras 8–10.

34 *Royal Antwerp* (n 2), paras 135, 150.

club participating in those competitions to enter in the list of its players and to include on the match sheet a minimum number of players trained in the territory of that association, if it is established, first, that those decisions by associations of undertakings are liable to affect trade between Member States and, second, that they have either as their object or their effect the restriction of competition between professional football clubs, unless, in the second of those scenarios, it is demonstrated, through convincing arguments and evidence, that they are both justified by the pursuit of one or more objectives that are legitimate and strictly necessary for that purpose.

28. Furthermore, Article 101(3) TFEU

> must be interpreted as meaning that it allows such decisions by associations of undertakings, if they prove to be contrary to paragraph 1 of that article, to benefit from an exemption to the application of that paragraph only if it is demonstrated, through convincing arguments and evidence, that all of the conditions required for that purpose are satisfied.

29. And finally, Article 45 TFEU

> must be interpreted as precluding rules which have been adopted by an association responsible for organising football competitions at national level, and which require each club participating in those competitions to enter in the list of its players and to include on the match sheet a minimum number of players trained in the territorial jurisdiction of that association, unless it is established that those rules are suitable for ensuring, in a consistent and systematic manner, the attainment of the objective of encouraging, at local level, the recruitment and training of young professional football players, and that they do not go beyond what is necessary to achieve that objective.

30. To conclude, the CJEU has not made the final decision regarding the incompatibility of the HGP rules of UEFA and RBFA. It will therefore be for the referring court (the Tribunal de Première Instance Francophone de Bruxelles – Brussels Court of First Instance (French-speaking)) to rule on whether the UEFA and RBFA rules at issue in the main proceedings satisfy those conditions, in light of the arguments and evidence produced by the parties.

3. Major League Soccer HGP Rule

31. North American football or soccer also faces the use of the HGP rule. To have a good comparison to the European HGP rule in this section we will give a short review of the Major League Soccer (MLS) rule. It must be stressed that the MLS rules and regulations are quite complex and importantly different in comparison to the European rules.

32. According to the MLS roster rules and regulations,[35] an MLS club players list, named the "active roster" comprises up to 30 players. All 30 players are eligible

---

[35] MLS Roster Rules and Regulations (2025) <www.mlssoccer.com/about/roster-rules-and-regulations> accessed 2 September 2025.

for selection to the game-day squad during the regular season and playoffs. Up to 20 players, occupying roster slots 1–20, count against the club's 2024 salary budget of5,470,000 USD and are referred to collectively as the club's senior roster. Clubs are not required to fill roster slots 19 and 20, and clubs may spread their entire salary budget across 18 senior roster players. A minimum salary budget charge will be imputed against a club's salary budget for each unfilled senior roster slot below 18. Slots 21–24 may be filled with, (i) Senior Minimum Salary Players (89,716) USD, which may include home-grown players; (ii) generation adidas players; (iii) any specifically designated players eligible for the MLS SuperDraft; or (iv) home-grown players earning more than the senior minimum salary subject to the home-grown player subsidy. Slots 25–30 may be filled with, (i) players earning the reserve minimum salary (71,401) USD, which may include home-grown players; (ii) home-grown players earning more than the reserve minimum salary subject to the home-grown player subsidy; or (iii) generation adidas players (earning the reserve minimum salary).

33. Home-grown player(s) in supplemental roster slots 21–30 may earn in aggregate each year up to 125,000 USD above the reserve minimum salary (if occupying slots 25–30) or senior minimum salary (if occupying slots 21–24). Clubs may use up to 200,000 USD of their currently available targeted allocation money or general allocation money to sign new home-grown players to their first MLS contract, subject to league review and approval. Targeted allocation money cannot be used on a home-grown player previously signed to MLS.

34. There is a specific HGP rule called "home-grown international rule" defining that any player who, at the time of their initial signing with MLS, meets the requirements to qualify as a home-grown player as a member of an MLS club academy, either in the US or Canada, or has met similar requirements as a member of a Canadian Approved Youth Club, will count as a domestic player (ie they will not occupy an international roster slot) on either US or Canadian club rosters provided that, (i) the player became a member of an MLS club academy, either in the US or Canada, or a Canadian Approved Youth Club no later than the year in which he turned 15 years old; and (ii) The player signs his first professional contract with MLS or an MLS club's affiliate (MLS NEXT Pro).

35. Players signed through the home-grown player mechanism meaning that a club may sign a player to a contract without subjecting him to the MLS SuperDraft if the player has been a member of that club's youth academy for at least one year and has met the necessary requirements. Players joining MLS through this mechanism are known as home-grown players and will receive the designation of "home-grown player" on a club's roster. There is no limit on the number of home-grown players a club may sign in any given year. Home-grown players may occupy a slot on the senior or supplemental roster.

III. Conclusion

36. This chapter has shown that, despite the HGP rule as it is currently in force, the number of locally trained players in the group stage squads of UEFA competitions is insufficient. Being on List A-list with 25 players does not mean that the HGP

actually play in a game, and we have seen that there have been clubs that have not used a single HGP in all their matches. On the other hand, it is obvious that clubs are constantly (re)evaluating whether it has been worthwhile to develop young talent when the best young players are leaving for the richest clubs without necessarily seeing a return on the investment from the training club. Working hard to develop football academies will certainly make a difference. The English model has shown that it is possible to have one of the richest competitions in the world – the Premier League, perhaps even the richest national competition – and over the last ten plus years achieve quite good results in developing youth football academies and getting more HGP playing in that competition.

37. Although the *Royal Antwerp FC* case has not generated much media or public interest, like the *European Super League (ESL)* case for instance, it is an important case legally, as the CJEU's decision will certainly have regulatory implications. Those regulatory implications will certainly also demand a further development of good governance with participation of representative stakeholders in drafting the rule at European level. Since the clubs' representatives[36] already have their important voice in drafting the UEFA regulations, especially those for competitions, probably in the near future FIFPro and Football Supporters Europe will also attain a stronger, much deserved position "at the table". This kind of a social dialogue and good governance is always welcome at the European level. In addition, the CJEU decision and consequently the Belgium Court decision is likely to affect how clubs organise their squad lists and, more importantly, how clubs will promote the education and training of young players, which is highly recognised also by Article 165 TFEU and the CJEU case law.

38. It should be recalled, first, that, bearing in mind both the social and educational function of sport recognised in Article 165 TFEU, and more broadly, the considerable importance of sport in the EU, repeatedly highlighted by the CJEU, the aim of encouraging the recruitment and training of young professional football players constitutes a legitimate objective in the public interest. Second, as regards the suitability of rules such as those at issue in the main proceedings for attaining the objective in question, it should be noted, that that objective may, in certain cases and under certain conditions, justify measures which, without being designed in such a way as to ensure in a certain and quantifiable manner in advance, an increase or intensification of the recruitment and training of young players, may nonetheless create real and significant incentives in that direction.[37,38]

39. The author is of the opinion that a so-called "club-trained player" rule is highly important in existing in line with the promotion and the training of young players and has much more relevance than the "association-trained player" rule, which

---

36 Currently, with the European Clubs Association (ECA) as the only representative stakeholder representing the clubs with European Leagues (EL), representing a higher-level association of clubs (ie leagues) there is a tendency of having a new important stakeholder as an association of clubs: Union of European Clubs, which would represent other medium or small size clubs that are not members of ECA.

37 Case C-415/93 *Union Royale Belge Sociale de Football Association, RCL and UEFA v JM Bosman* ECLI:EU:C:1995:463, paras 106, 108–109; Case C-325/08 *Olympique Lyonnais SASP v Olivier Bernard and Newcastle UFC* ECLI:EU:C:2010:143, paras 39, 41–45.

38 *Royal Antwerp* (n 2), para 144–145.

is in force in England and Belgium, for instance. The richest clubs can easily attract "nationally trained players" but on the other hand such a rule is in line with the FIFA Regulation on Status and Transfer of Players (RSTP)[39] rules on protection of minors and prevention of transfer of minors from one country to the other. One possible solution which would be in line with EU law would be to determine a squad of, for example, 20 players for all clubs with additional right of clubs to fill up to five or even ten more club trained players, meaning that the squad for UEFA competitions could be composed of 20 players but if a club have a minimum of eight or even ten club-trained players the squad could have 28 players, or like in the MLS a 30-player squad list. In such a way additionally, we would promote the training and growth of young athletes not taking the place of EU citizens enjoying free movement rights as workers, which is what professional players deserve.

---

39 FIFA Regulations on the Status and Transfers of Players RSTP (2024) arts 6, 19, 19bis <https://digitalhub.fifa.com/m/6a0797ec77cbc02c/original/Regulations-on-the-Status-and-Transfer-of-Players-February-2024-edition.pdf> accessed 2 September 2025.

Legitimate Objectives in Antitrust Analysis: FIFA Regulation of Agents and the Right to Regulate Football in Europe

Petros C. Mavroidis* and Damien Neven**
Columbia University, New York
Graduate Institute for International and Development Studies, Geneva

I. Introduction

1. Fédération Internationale de Football Association (FIFA) has adopted a new regulation of the market for the agents of players, the FIFA Football Agent Regulation (FFAR), in December 2022.[1] Agents provide services to players as well as clubs primarily in the case of transfers. They thus operate in a market for the provision of services to stakeholders involved in the market for one type

---

* Edwin B. Parker Professor of Foreign & Comparative Law, Columbia University, New York.

** Professor, International Economics, Graduate Institute for International and Development Studies, Geneva. We would like to thank Jean-François Bellis, Daniele Boccucci, Fabien Cagneux, Giovanni Maria Fares, Pablo Ibañez Colomo, Miguel Poiares Maduro, Mislav Mataija, Kirtikumar Mehta, Alex Phillips, Georges I. Siotis, and Stephen Weatherill for discussions and comments on earlier versions of this chapter. All remaining errors are our own. There is no conflict to report.

[1] FIFA Football Agent Regulation (FFAR) (2022) <https://digitalhub.fifa.com/m/1e7b741fa0fae779/original/FIFA-Football-Agent-Regulations.pdf> accessed 2 September 2025.

of labour (players) used as an important input in clubs' activities. The FIFA regulation essentially involves:

1. A restriction on entry into the market for agents through a licensing procedure;
2. A restriction on the conduct of agents regarding the provision of services to different stakeholders involved in a transaction; and
3. A restriction regarding the prices that agents can charge for their services through the imposition of a cap.

2. Thus, the regulation does not relate to the organisation of football competitions as such but to a market for inputs used by clubs. Accordingly, the question of the appropriate scope of FIFA's regulation naturally arises. At the moment of writing, a challenge against the consistency of FFAR with EU law has been submitted for consideration before the Court of Justice of the European Union (CJEU). In his opinion (C-209/23 RRC Sports, and C-408/23 ROGON and others) Advocate General decided that the FFAR might involve a restriction by effect and an abuse of dominance and the Court will soon decide the issue in definitive manner.

3. In this chapter, it will be argued that the CJEU will be led to confront the issue of the scope of activities that FIFA can legitimately regulate through the assessment of the legitimate objectives that FIFA can invoke to ensure that the restrictions of competitions caused by FFAR fall outside the scope of Article 101 Treaty on the Functioning of the European Union (TFEU). The framework in which the CJEU will need to assess the legality of the FFAR regulation has been significantly affected by its three judgments in the *ISU*,[2] the *ESL*,[3] and the *Royal Antwerp FC*[4] cases.

4. The main consequences of these judgments for the assessment of the FFAR[5] are that:

- When a measure involves a restriction by object, no legitimate objective can be invoked to ensure that it would fall outside the scope of Article 101 TFEU; in this instance, FIFA/UEFA can only invoke Article 101(3) TFEU and carry the associated burden of production to demonstrate the existence of efficiency gains that compensate for the anticompetitive effect.
- If the challenged measure involves a restriction by effect, FIFA/UEFA can invoke a legitimate objective to ensure that it falls outside the discipline of Article 101 TFEU, but they cannot invoke Article 165 TFEU to this effect, as this provision is addressed to the EU institutions only.
- By contrast, FIFA/UEFA can always invoke a legitimate objective to justify violations of Article 49 TFEU (free movement).
- The question regarding the consistency of challenged measures with EU law can obtain an authoritative answer only if it is submitted to courts of the EU Member States (and ultimately the CJEU).

---

[2] Case C-124/21 P *International Skating Union (ISU)* ECLI:EU:C:2023:1012.

[3] Case C-333/21 *European Super League (ESL)* ECLI:EU:C:2023:1011.

[4] Case C-680/21 *Royal Antwerp FC* ECLI:EU:C:2023:1010.

[5] As discussed below, these judgments have also introduced a discipline of private undertaking that exercise special and exclusive rights, inspired by TFEU, art 106. But this additional discipline is not directly relevant for the FFAR. On this issue, see Colomo (2022).

5. Two key consequences flow from this development as far as the treatment of FFAR under EU law is concerned. First, if the FFAR involves restrictions by object, FIFA's regulation will fall within the scope of Article 101 TFEU and would violate its provision. Second, if it involves restrictions by effect, the CJEU will be led to consider the legitimate objective eventually invoked to ensure that the challenged measure falls outside the scope of Article 101 TFEU. We review the case law in this respect and find that, even if it has not pronounced itself clearly on the matter, the CJEU has only accepted public policy objectives that the undertakings under consideration had been entrusted to pursue either in the context of an explicit regulatory framework or by delegation. We will argue that this approach should be confirmed and become the dominant approach of the CJEU when dealing with instances where a legitimate objective has been invoked. It has the merit of imposing a discipline on the objectives that can be offered to escape from the provision and hence reduces the risk that the scope of Article 101 TFEU is restricted without organising principle. In the context of the FFAR, it implies that the CJEU will be led to consider whether the objectives that the FFAR may pursue in the agent's market are related to the regulatory task entrusted to FIFA.

6. The chapter is structured as follows. First, some background is provided on FIFA's regulation of agents. Second, FFAR is assessed under the prism of competition law; the consequences of the December judgments are evaluated; case law on the legitimate objectives that have been put forward to ensure that measures that restrict competition fall outside the scope of Article 101 TFEU are reviewed; and the question is explored on whether the objectives put forward by FIFA in regulating the market for agents would be adequate to ensure that the restriction by effect that they might involve could still fall outside the scope of Article 101 TFEU. Finally, a conclusion is drawn..

II. Background on the FFAR and Predecessors

7. FFAR is not the first attempt by FIFA to regulate the agents' market. Earlier in 1994, FIFA had issued a statute to this effect. It imposed entry restrictions to the profession in the form of a down payment that agents had to pay to FIFA and the submission of candidates to an examination evaluating their qualifications. The statute was challenged and the question of FIFA's legitimacy to regulate the market was raised before the CJEU in the *Laurent Piau* judgment.

1. Prior Dispute on the Regulation of Agent's Market – the *Laurent Piau* Case

8. Laurent Piau, a French football agent, challenged the consistency of the 1994 regulation before the CJEU.[6] He first complained before the EU Commission, but the EU Commission rejected his complaint for lack of Community interest. Piau appealed the Commission decision before the Court of First Instance in

6 There is a long history of regulating the agents' market comprehensively discussed in Richard Parrish and others, *Promoting and Supporting Good Governance in the European Football Agents Industry* (European Commission 2019).

March 1998. He alleged that the FIFA statute contravened the provisions on free movement because of its restrictions on access to the profession, which could give rise to discrimination between citizens of the various EU Member States. This complaint led to a remarkable *obiter dictum* by the Court of First Instance.[7] The court found that the regulation was "adopted by FIFA of its own authority and not on the basis of rule-making powers conferred on it by public authorities in connection with a recognised task in the general interest concerning sporting activity". Therefore, it constituted a decision by an association of undertakings. The court then observed that the legitimacy of FIFA to enact such rules was open to question[8] as the market for agents was peripheral to sporting activity. The Court also observed that the regulation of an economic activity without delegation from a public authority could not be regarded at the outset as compatible with EU law.[9] Finally, the Court also found that in the context of the dispute, FIFA's regulation could only be examined in relation to EU competition rules.[10] Hence, even though the Court raised the issue of the legitimacy of FIFA in regulating the market for agents, it did not have the opportunity to analyse it in detail.[11] Undeniably, though, the Court cast doubt on FIFA's right to regulate this market.

2. Current Challenges to the FFAR

9. Football agents have challenged the regulation of FFAR in front of courts of Member States of the EU, and more specifically, German courts. The Dortmund court ruled that the FFAR was in violation of EU competition law and more specifically Article 101 TFEU,[12] as it involved restrictions by object. It then issued a preliminary injunction prohibiting the application or enforcement of the FFAR in Germany.[13] FIFA has lodged an appeal against this decision before

---

7 Case T-193/02 *Laurent Piau v Commission of the European Communities* ECLI:EU:T:2005:22, paras 74–75.

8 Ibid para 76 reads: "With regard to FIFA's legitimacy, contested by the applicant, to enact such rules, which do not have a sport-related object, but regulate an economic activity that is peripheral to the sporting activity in question and touch on fundamental freedoms, the rule-making power claimed by a private organisation like FIFA, whose main statutory purpose is to promote football (see above), is indeed open to question, in the light of the principles common to the Member States on which the European Union is founded".

9 Ibid para 77: "The very principle of regulation of an economic activity concerning neither the specific nature of sport nor the freedom of internal organisation of sports associations by a private-law body, like FIFA, which has not been delegated any such power by a public authority, cannot from the outset be regarded as compatible with Community law, in particular with regard to respect for civil and economic liberties".

10 Ibid para 78: "In principle, such regulation, which constitutes policing of an economic activity and touches on fundamental freedoms, falls within the competence of the public authorities. Nevertheless, in the present dispute, the rule-making power exercised by FIFA, in the almost complete absence of national rules, can be examined only in so far as it affects the rules on competition, in the light of which the lawfulness of the contested decision must be assessed, while considerations relating to the legal basis that allows FIFA to carry on regulatory activity, however important they may be, are not the subject ...".

11 The CJEU rejected Piau's claim since it adhered to the Commission's view that there was no Community interest to act; See Stephen Weatherill, "The EU as Sports Regulator" in James AR Nafziger and Ryan Gauthier (eds), *Handbook on International Sports Law* (2nd edn, *Edward Elgar Publishing* 2022) 112–140.

12 The Court of Arbitration of Sport (CAS) decision found the opposite in Case 2023/O/9370 CAS Decision *Professional Football Agents Association (PROFAA) v FIFA* (24 July 2023). The award is available at <www.tas-cas.org/fileadmin/user_upload/CAS_Award_9370.pdf> accessed 2 September 2025.

13 Ibid District Court of Dortmund; See Tom Lichtenberg, "FIFA's Football Agents Regulation Violates Competition Law' (*Kluwer Competition Law Blog*, 20 July 2023) <https://legalblogs.wolterskluwer.com/competition-blog/fifas-football-agents-regulation-violates-competition-law/> accessed 1 September 2025.

Dortmund's Higher Court, and its decision is expected in the next months. Note that the questions before the Dortmund court strictly concerned the consistency of FFAR with competition law.

10. Football agents also filed a complaint in front of the Mainz Regional Court. The Mainz court submitted a request for a preliminary ruling to the CJEU regarding the question of whether the FFAR violates competition law, and the case RRC Sports is now pending.[14] Another request for a preliminary ruling was submitted by the German Federal Court in the context of a proceeding initiated in front of the Frankfurt Regional Court, and this case ROGON and others is also pending in front of the CJEU, as already noted above.[15] This latter proceeding relates to the previous version of the regulation of the market for agents (adopted in 2015) and focuses on whether the restriction imposed by the regulation could fall outside the scope of Article 101 TFEU because of its pursuit of a legitimate objective. None of these proceedings directly challenge head-on the legitimacy of FIFA to regulate the agents' market. Yet, will be argued in this contribution, this is likely to be one of the key issues that the CJEU will have to confront in evaluating the merits of the challenge.

3. FFAR in Limbo

11. There is considerable uncertainty at this stage regarding the implementation of the FFAR. The procedures have effectively frozen the implementation of FFAR in Germany. Initially, neither FIFA nor the Deutscher Fußball-Verband, the German Football Association (DFB) complied with the Dortmund court order. They were sanctioned and a fine was imposed on them for behaviour akin to contempt of court at the level of 150,000 euros. FIFA and DFB then informed German clubs that only conduct occurring in Germany would be exempted from the FFAR. The Dortmund court found that this was an illegitimate interpretation of its judgment, as the suspension should and would apply to any case in which the court had jurisdiction (implying that through the "effects" doctrine, it might have decided that it was competent to adjudicate cases occurring beyond Germany but which had a sufficiently strong jurisdictional link with Germany). Following this order, FIFA exempted all cases with a jurisdictional "link" to Germany from the obligation to observe FFAR. Players moving in and out of German clubs and all German players could, in principle at least, come under this exemption.

12. The Italian Football Federation (FIGC) communicated its decision not to implement FFAR.[16] So did the Danish Federation (DBU).[17] Anecdotal evidence suggests that Dutch clubs have been putting pressure on their national football association to delay implementation of FFAR because of the concern that, if it were implemented, they may find themselves at a disadvantage in a market in which clubs from other countries would not face the hurdles deriving from the FFAR.

---

14 Case C-209/23 *RRC Sports* (pending).

15 Case C-428/23 *ROGON and others*(pending).

16 FIGC Decision (in Italian) <www.figc.it/media/218405/comunicato-stampa-consiglio.pdf> accessed 2 September 2025.

17 DBU Decision *www.instagram.com/the_football_forum/* accessed 2 September 2025.

13. In Spain, the picture is clearer. Following a request by the Spanish Association of Football Agents and 18 individual agents, a Spanish court issued a decision on 6 November 2023,[18] finding that the FFAR was a restriction by object because it imposed a maximum/fixed price for services. The judge also indicated that the fact that there had been allegedly widespread consultation between FIFA and stakeholders did not affect the question whether the regulation was ultimately anticompetitive.

14. No action, at least until 30 November 2023, had been undertaken in England either. The English FA Football Association (FA) participated in an arbitration proceeding brought by football agencies CAA Base, Wasserman, Stellar and ARETÉ. The proceedings have now concluded, and the Tribunal has now confirmed that the new FIFA regulation is in breach of UK competition law.[19] Consequently, it will not apply in England either. Finally, the US National Football Association has informed clubs that only some provisions of the FFAR may be applied (eg licensing), but some other provisions, like the cap on agent fees, would not be applicable because they are in breach of the CBA (collective bargaining agreement between players and owners) and US antitrust law. The Brazilian authorities also decided to defer the implementation of FFAR.[20]

15. Following all these reactions, FIFA has decided to suspend the application of the price cap provision in FFAR worldwide.[21]

16. The preliminary rulings of the CJEU will thus have an important effect on the actual implementation of the FFAR in Germany but also in Europe and the rest of the world, given that a partial implementation would raise concerns about the heterogeneity of the conditions under which clubs in different countries would operate.

III. Assessment of FFAR under EU Competition Law

17. The CJEU has long recognised that the activities of FIFA and UEFA are subject to competition law to the extent that they involve economic activities[22] and that FIFA and UEFA (and more generally sports governance bodies (SGBs)) can be seen as

---

18 AEAF Injunction (6 November 2023) Juzgado de lo Mercantil No 3 de Madrid, paras 15–19.

19 Chiranjit Ojha and Mitch Phillips, "FIFA's Agent Fee Cap Breaches British Competition Law: FA Tribunal" (*Reuters*, 1 December 2023) <www.reuters.com/sports/soccer/fifas-agent-fee-cap-breaches-british-competition-law-fa- tribunal-2023-12-01/> accessed 2 September 2025.

20 Case 0838927-49.2023.8.19.0209 (18 December 2023) Poder Judiciário do Estado do Rio de Janeiro.

21 David Ornstein, "FIFA Suspends Introduction of New Agent Regulations" (*The Athletic*, 30 December 2023) <www.nytimes.com/athletic/5169636/2023/12/30/fifa-agent-regulations-suspend/> accessed 2 September 2025.

22 According to the Court in *ISU* (n 2), para 92, some specific rules that are adopted solely on non- economic grounds can be seen as extraneous to any economic activity and hence might fall outside the scope of competition rules altogether. This is sometimes presented as a distinction between "rule of the game" and "rules about the game". The General Court has relied on such distinction in its ruling in *Meca-Medina* (Case T-313/02 *David Meca-Medina and Igor Majcen v Commission of the European Communities* ECLI:EU:T:2004:282). However, the distinction was not validated by the CJEU in its own judgment on appeal in that case (Case C-519/04 P *David Meca-Medina and Igor Majcen v Commission of the European Communities* ECLI:EU:C:2006:492). It is indeed difficult to identify rules that would not, in one way or another, affect the economic activity of a stakeholder in professional sports. See also Stephen Weatherill, "The Rulings of 21 December 2023: Their Impact on the Structure of EU Sport Law" (2023) 23 ISLJ 409–415.

associations of undertakings.[23] Hence, agreements involving SGBs (or unilateral conduct by SGBs) should be assessed in terms of whether they involve restrictions of competition by object or by effect (or an abuse of a dominant position) like those of any other undertaking involved in an economic activity. Assuming that a challenged measure involves a restriction of competition, the activities of SGBs can in principle be assessed in terms of whether they are necessary and proportionate for the achievement of a legitimate objective. The *Wouters* Court judgment established this approach: if the restriction is inherent in the achievement of the objective pursued, and the means proportional to ends, then restrictions will be found to fall outside the scope of Article 101 TFEU altogether.[24] In the area of sports, the most prominent case in which this approach was adopted is *Meca-Medina.* In this case, the CJEU found that the anti-doping rules adopted by the International Olympic Committee (IOC) did not come within the scope of Article 101 TFEU, even though they had the inherent effect of reducing competition among athletes, as they contributed to the "fairness, integrity and objectivity of the conduct of competitive sport".[25] This case will be discussed in more detail shortly.

18. The December 2023 (*ESL, ISU* and *Royal Antwerp*) judgments have clarified the analysis in three important respects:

- They drew a parallel between the exercise of powers by SGBs and instances where EU Member States have granted entities special and/or exclusive rights and imposed on SGBs a discipline similar to that of Article 106 TFEU;
- They endorsed Advocate General (AG) Szpunar's analysis in *Royal Antwerp* (and thus rejected AG Rantos' views expressed in *ESL*)[26] to the effect that only the EU institutions (and not UEFA/FIFA) can invoke Article 165 TFEU to justify a restriction of competition;
- They held that legitimate objectives cannot be invoked in relation to restrictions by object. These points are taken in turn.

1. Obligations for Entities Bestowed with Special and Exclusive Rights

19. Arguably the most significant innovation in the *ESL* judgment relates to its assessment of whether the UEFA is abusing its dominant position when acting as regulator and commercial operator with respect to the competitions it organises. Under Articles 51 and 52 of the UEFA statutes,[27] European national football associations have bestowed UEFA with the exclusive right to organise pan-European (cross-national) competitions. To assess the claim against UEFA, the CJEU drew

---

23 Case 36/74 *Walrave and Koch v Association Union Cycliste Internationale and others* ECLI:EU:C:1974:140; Stephen Weatherill, *Principles and Practice in EU Sports Law* (OUP 2017), for an extensive discussion.

24 Case C-309/99 *Wouters* ECLI:EU:C:2002:98.

25 *Meca-Medina* C-519/04 P (n 22). 2004 CASE 2006 DECISION

26 *ESL* (n 3); See Petros C Mavroidis and Damien J Neven, "The EU Court of Justice AG Rantos argues that a football federation's exclusion of a rival football competition is not a restriction by object and is necessary to protect the European Sport Model (ESLC / UEFA / FIFA)" (2022) *e-Competitions art. No. 112799.*

27 UEFA Statutes (2025) <https://documents.uefa.com/r/Regulations-of-the-UEFA-Champions-League-2025/26-Online> accessed 2 September 2025.

a parallel with the situation in which Member States regulate markets by granting special and exclusive rights. The CJEU acknowledges that Member States are not prohibited from granting such rights.[28] Nevertheless, they cannot place undertakings in a position to abuse their dominant position, for instance, by restricting entry through regulatory measures that they eventually adopt.

20. In circumstances in which an undertaking enjoying special and exclusive rights can affect entry, its power must be subjected to conditions that eliminate the risk of abuse of its dominant position.[29] When Member States grant special and exclusive rights, the combination of Articles 106 and 102 guarantees that competition in the relevant market will not be negatively affected. The CJEU disaggregated this obligation: it held that when an undertaking has the power to affect entry through a decision of prior authorisation (as in the *ESL* or *ISU* cases), that power must be placed "within a framework of substantive criteria which are transparent, clear and precise (…) so that it may not be used in an arbitrary manner".[30]

21. The CJEU clarified that while FIFA/UEFA are not companies with special and exclusive rights, the above- mentioned reasoning applies by analogy:

> Requirements identical to those recalled in the three preceding paragraphs of the present judgment are all the more necessary when an undertaking in a dominant position, through its own conduct and not by virtue of being granted exclusive or special rights by a Member State, places itself in a situation where it is able to deny potentially competing undertakings access to a given market (see, to that effect, judgment of 13 December 1991, GB-Inno-BM, C-18/88, EU:C:1991:474, paragraph 20). That may be the case when that undertaking has regulatory and review powers and the power to impose sanctions enabling it to authorise or control that access, and thus a means which is different to those normally available to undertakings and which govern competition on the merits as between them.[31]

22. By drawing this analogy,[32] the CJEU effectively imposed on SGBs the obligation to regulate their own conduct with respect to the authorisation of entry in such a way as to eliminate the risk of abuse.[33] The imposition of self-discipline on (quasi-)regulators with respect to requirements regarding the authorisation of entry has important implications for antitrust enforcement toward SGBs and beyond.

23. First, it implies that the question of whether restrictions on entry can be justified through the invocation of legitimate objectives has become irrelevant.

---

[28] *ESL* (n 3), para 132.

[29] Ibid para 134.

[30] Ibid para 135.

[31] Ibid para 137.

[32] See Pablo Ibañez Colomo and Alfonso Lamadrid de Pablo, "On Superleague and ISU: The Expectation was Justified (and EU Competition Law May Be Changing before Our Eyes)" (*Chillin'Competition*, 2023) <*https://chillingcompetition.com/2023/12/21/on-superleague-and-isu-the-expectation-was-justified-and-eu-competition-law-may-be-changing-before-our-eyes/*> accessed 1 September 2025, who, to our knowledge, were the first to underscore this point.

[33] The same constraint was imposed under TFEU, art 101 with respect to agreements affecting entry (para 179).

The approach of the CJEU implies that the system of prior authorisation needs to eliminate the risk of abuse (or that of restriction by object). There is, by construction, no scope for keeping the restriction outside the scope of Article 101 TFEU or conduct outside the scope of Article 102 TFEU (because of the pursuit of a legitimate objective) simply because the *ex ante* system of authorisation should have eliminated the occurrence of such events in the first place.

24. One can, of course, legitimately wonder whether the imposition of this self-discipline on quasi-regulators is credible. Unlike Member States, which are meant to pursue public policy objectives in the design of regulation, private undertakings with quasi-regulatory roles presumably pursue their own interest. Accordingly, one can expect Member States to have incentives broadly in line with the enforcement of Articles 106/102 (or 106/101) TFEU. This is not the case with respect to private undertakings with a quasi-regulatory role.[34] Whether enforcement of the discipline imposed on the SGB through *ex post* enforcement will suffice is debatable. Some *ex ante* review of the framework that SGBs put in place to constrain their own conduct might be warranted.

25. This aspect of the *ESL* ruling is possibly the most significant. Still, it has no immediate bearing on the FFAR. In the case of the regulation of the market for agents, FIFA is not regulating entry into the market in which it is itself active.

2. FIFA Cannot Invoke Article 165 TFEU

26. According to AG Rantos in *ESL*, the protection of the European Sport Model embedded in Article 165 TFEU[35] could serve as a legitimate objective to ensure that a restriction of competition falls outside the scope of Article 101 TFEU. The Union, as per this provision, has support competence[36] to "carry out actions to support, coordinate or supplement the actions of the Member States" in the area of sports. AG Szpunar, in *Royal Antwerp*, took the view that it is the EU institutions that are targeted by Article 165 TFEU and that SGBs cannot invoke it as the source of legitimate objectives.[37]

27. The CJEU in *ESL* adopted AG Szpunar's view, that the Union institutions must take into account the elements of Article 165 TFEU whenever they adopt measures or recommendations in the area of sport. The CJEU left no one in doubt that Article 165 TFEU cannot be regarded as "a special rule exempting sport from (…) other provisions of primary EU law". That is not to say, however, that the special characteristics of sports cannot be taken into account in

---

[34] Case C-680/21 *Royal Antwerp FC* ECLI:EU:C:2023:188, Opinion of AG Szpunar.

[35] This provision reads: "The Union shall contribute to the development of quality education by encouraging cooperation between Member States and, if necessary, by supporting and supplementing their action, while fully respecting the responsibility of the Member States for the content of teaching and the organisation of education systems and their cultural and linguistic diversity. The Union shall contribute to the promotion of European sporting issues, while taking account of the specific nature of sport, its structures based on voluntary activity and its social and educational function".

[36] The term "support" competence denotes that, while the competence remains with the Member States, the EU can support the exercise of national discretion, whenever it finds it appropriate to do so. Sport (football) is a national competence.

[37] Opinion of AG Szpunar (n 34), para 54. Compare Maduro (2023).

the enforcement of Articles 101 and 102 TFEU (as well as the internal market rules). The CJEU also held that sports specificity may be taken into account only "in compliance with the conditions and criteria of application provided for in [these] articles".[38]

3. If FFAR Were to be Judged a Restriction by Object

28. In the *ESL* judgment, the Court indicated that the Wouters approach "does not apply (...) in situations involving conduct which, far from merely having the inherent "effect" of restricting competition, at least potentially, by limiting the freedom of action of certain undertakings, reveals a degree of harm in relation to that competition that justifies a finding that it has as its very "object" the prevention, restriction or distortion of competition."[39]

29. The same approach has been adopted by the Court with respect to unilateral conduct, which "by its very nature" infringes Article 102 TFEU.[40]

30. Alas, the CJEU did not provide a detailed reasoning to support this important finding. It refers in *ESL* to its *MOTOE* judgment[41] where, ostensibly, this approach was "already implicitly but necessarily apparent". *MOTOE* concerned the organisation of motorcycle races and involved a potential conflict of interest: MOTOE was both authorising the organisation of motorcycling events and organising them itself. The conditions for authorising events organised by other entities had not been clearly spelled out. In its conclusion, the Court affirmed positively that Article 102 TFEU applied, so it implicitly ruled out the possibility of appealing to legitimate objectives. It is, of course, a stretch to extend this approach beyond the specific circumstances of the case. This case involved a blatant incentive to restrict entry.

31. I n *ESL*, the CJEU affirmed that this approach applied to all cases invoking a restriction by object, thereby reinforcing the argument that restrictions by object can be identified by looking into formal criteria only. There is arguably still some ambiguity about the concept or restrictions by object.[42] On the one hand, according to *Cartes bancaires*,[43] the essential legal criterion for ascertaining whether there is a restriction of competition by object is the response to the question whether the challenged measure "reveals in itself a sufficient degree of harm to competition for it to be considered that it is not necessary to assess its effects". This formulation suggests that assessing whether a restriction is by object still requires an understanding of how the challenged measure operates in its "legal and economic context", and hence the formulation of a theory of

38 *ESL* (n 3), paras 101, 104; See Weatherill (n 22) and Miguel Delgado, "The European Game: The ECJ and its Sports Model after "European Super League" (*Verfassungsblog*, 2024) <https://verfassungsblog.de/the-european-game/> accessed 1 September 2025.

39 *ESL* (n 3), para 186.

40 Ibid para 185.

41 Case C-49/07 *MOTOE* ECLI:EU:C:2008:376, para 53.

42 For a discussion, Mavroidis and Neven (n 26).

43 Case C-67/13 P *Groupement des cartes bancaires (CB) v European Commission* ECLI:EU:C:2014:2204, and ibid Opinion AG Wahl. See also Case C-228/18 *Gazdasági Versenyhivatal v Budapest Bank Nyrt. and Others* ECLI:EU:C:2020:265, para 37.

effects. The assessment thus requires the formulation of a counterfactual as acknowledged by the Court in *MasterCard*.[44] In this context, it would seem feasible from a methodological perspective to assess whether – relative to the appropriate counterfactual – the measure is both very likely to entail a sufficient degree of harm and whether the legitimate objectives pursued by the agreements are likely to be better fulfilled. The assessment of the magnitude and likelihood of harm and the assessment of the extent to which legitimate objectives are fulfilled are two different perspectives of the discrepancy between the factual and the counterfactual.[45] On the other hand, if one emphasises the purpose of an agreement as the decisive feature of whether it restricts competition by object, there may indeed be little room to advance legitimate objectives: an agreement that strives to restrict competition might not be compatible with the pursuit of a legitimate objective. This is, for instance, the perspective taken by Colomo and Lamadrid.[46]

32. We find that the former approach has clear advantages. Comparing with a counterfactual has the merit of providing an appropriate comparator to decide whether a detailed examination of effects is necessary. By contrast, inquiring into the purpose sought is a delicate operation given persistent asymmetric information between the adjudicator, the plaintiff, and the respondent. Only future practice will determine where the CJEU stands on this issue.

4. If FFAR Were to be Judged a Restriction by Effect

33. If FFAR were to be judged as a restriction by effect, FIFA could thus invoke a legitimate objective to ensure that it is beyond the scope of the prohibition. We have already referred to the *Wouters* jurisprudence, which established the two conditions for successful invocation of a legitimate objective: the pursuit of the objective must be inherent in the restriction, and the means employed to achieve it must further be proportional to the ends sought. That much is clear. But can a dominant private entity or association of undertakings invoke, say, freedom of expression to ensure that its conduct/agreements fall outside the scope of Articles 101 and 102 TFEU? Can they do that even in the absence of mandate to do so?

34. To shed light on this question, which, we should add, has yet to be addressed head-on by the CJEU, we propose to first look into prior relevant case law by the CJEU, then examine to what extent the December 2023 decisions follow the same approach, and finally apply our key conclusions to FFAR.

---

44 Case C-382/12 P *MasterCard Inc and Others v European Commission* ECLI:EU:C:2014:2201, para 164: "By contrast, the Court should, to that end, assess the impact of the setting of the MIF on the parameters of competition, such as the price, the quantity and quality of the goods or services. Accordingly, it is necessary, in accordance with the settled case-law referred to in paragraph 161 of the present judgment, to assess the competition in question within the actual context in which it would occur in the absence of those fees".

45 This approach would come very close to what is known in US law as a "truncated rule of reason". See David Eisenstadt and James Langenfeld, "The Role of Economics in Truncated Rule of Reason Analysis" (2013) 28 *Antitrust* 52–61.

46 Colomo and de Pablo (n 32).

5. The Invocation of Legitimate Objectives in Prior Case Law

35. In what follows, we will refer to the key, mostly CJEU, decisions only, and not exhaustively to all case law.

A. *Wouters*

36. *Wouters* is the leading case in this context.[47] The Court was facing an appeal by a Dutch attorney-at-law who had entered into a business arrangement with Arthur Andersen, an accounting firm, contravening the statutes adopted by the Bar of Netherlands which prohibited similar arrangements. The justification offered by the Bar was that, through the ban, it was serving legitimate objectives – namely, the independence of attorneys and their loyalty to their customers.

37. The delegation of authority from the Dutch state to the Dutch Bar was clear, and the CJEU built on this feature to find that the restriction was inherent in pursuance of an objective that was legitimate. It further found that the means employed were proportional to the objective sought. The Court underscored the importance of the context when evaluating the proportionality of means to ends.[48]

B. *OTOC*

38. In its decision of 28 February 2013, *Ordem dos Técnicos Oficiais de Contas (OTOC)*, the Court confirmed the *Wouters* approach. OTOC is a public legal entity representing the interests of chartered accountants in Portugal. It was subjecting all chartered accountants to periodic compulsory training of sixteen hours. Accountants would have to submit a request to be admitted to this training. OTOC would sometimes reject requests and sometimes would delay its response. These practices were challenged before the NCA (national competition authority). Eventually, the dispute was submitted before the CJEU.[49]

39. The Court first held that acts connected with the exercise of public authority escape the purview of Articles 101/102 TFEU. Cases where an entity recommends but the state retains the power to decide by rejecting the recommendation would thus escape antitrust scrutiny. This was not the case here.[50] The Court accepted that the objective pursued (guaranteeing the quality of services provided) was legitimate but found that the means were disproportional to the end, as OTOC could have attained its stated objective by monitoring the behaviour of Portuguese accountants or through courses of less than sixteen hours.[51]

---

47 *Wouters* (n 24).

48 Ibid para 3, esp 23 and paras 53–73, 97.

49 Case C-1/12 *Ordem dos Técnicos Oficiais de Contas (OTOC)* ECLI:EU:C:2013:127, para 3, 18ff.

50 Ibid paras 40, 54–55. But this had been the case in the Court's 2002 decision in Case C-35/99 *Criminal proceedings against Manuele Arduino*ECLI:EU:C:2002:97, para 6. A public body operating under the auspices of the Ministry of Justice had been setting the remuneration levels for the Bar members. As this was but a recommendation that did not bind the Minister, who could disregard it with no further ado, the Court held that no delegation of public authority had ever taken place, and hence no violation of Article 85 (now TFEU, art 101) could have been established (paras 41 etc). We observe a very similar outcome in the *Cipolla* (2006) judgment by the Court (Joined Case C-94/04 *Federico Cipolla v Rosaria Fazari* and Case C-202/04 *Macrino and Capodarte* ECLI:EU:C:2006:758).

51 Ibid paras 94–95.

C. *Consiglio Nazionale dei Geologi – (CNG)*

40. In its decision of 18 July 2013, the Court faced a decision by the Autorità Garante della Concorrenza e del Mercato (Italian Competition Authority) regarding the Consiglio Nazionale dei Geologi (CNG).[52] CNG was given by law the task of protecting the qualification and the profession of geologists. It consequently imposed enrolment in a registry to gain access to the Italian geologist market. CNG could also impose disciplinary measures against members who would fail to act in a manner consistent with the integrity or dignity of the profession. It adopted a code of conduct involving a scale of fees and geologists had to ensure that the fees that they charged were commensurate with the difficulty of the task and the dignity of the profession. The Autorità challenged this provision, claiming that it amounted to a restriction of competition in so far as the reference to the dignity of the profession lent to the presumption that the scale had to be regarded as compulsory.

41. The Court found that CNG, which had been given the right to regulate the profession of geologists by law, was not exercising state authority. It also found that the fee scale, even if it was considered a mere recommendation, was liable to restrict competition. It did not, however, explicitly conclude that it restricted competition by object. The Court acknowledged, on the other hand, that CNG was arguably pursuing the legitimate objective of ensuring that the ultimate consumers of the services of geologists are provided with the necessary guarantees. The Court did not exclude the possibility that criteria relating to the dignity of the profession may be considered necessary for the achievement of the legitimate objective. In the absence of adequate information to this effect, the Court remanded the case back to the Italian court, asking it to assess if this had indeed been the case in light of its observations. Importantly for our argument, this is again a case in which regulatory powers had been delegated to the undertaking and in which the legitimate objective accepted by the Court was derived from the regulatory role with which the CNG had been entrusted.[53]

D. *Meca-Medina*

42. In this case (decision of 18 July 2006), two swimmers had complained against a decision by FINA, the World Swimming Federation, which had banned them because they had been found in contravention of the doping rules. The Court did not have to decide on the existence of a restriction of competition. It held that, even if this had been the case, the anti-doping rule was a limitation inherent in the organisation and proper conduct of competitive sport as its very purpose was to ensure healthy rivalry between athletes.[54] The Court also found that the appellants did not establish the requisite threshold for finding that the anti-doping rule was excessively strict in relation to the objective pursued.

---

52 Case C-136/12 *Consiglio nazionale dei geologi v Autorità garante della concorrenza e del mercato* ECLI:EU:C:2013:489, paras 3–10.

53 Ibid paras 44–46, 50.

54 *Meca-Medina* C-519/04 P (n 22), para 40.

43. The Court thus recognised the objective of ensuring healthy rivalry among athletes as legitimate, and it further acknowledged the role that anti-doping rules could play in achieving this objective. Importantly, the FINA statute that had incorporated the anti- doping rule had been signed by all the national swimming federations members of FINA. FINA had thus been entrusted with the authority to implement these rules. FINA had not enacted and/or implemented the anti-doping rule without the explicit consent of its members.

44. There is still a difference between *Meca-Medina* and the other decisions, as in the context of *Wouters*, *OTOC*, and *CNG*, the Court was facing actions by an entity entrusted with public authority. That is not the case with FINA. Still, in *Meca-Medina*, assuming that the competent authorities (the national swimming federations) were granted regulatory power by their respective governments, FINA had explicitly adhered to the (legitimate) objective pursued through the enactment of its anti-doping statute, namely, the protection of fair competition. We will return to this issue later below.

E. *Ordre National des Pharmaciens – (ONP)*

45. In its 2014 judgment on the *Ordre national des pharmaciens (ONP)*,[55] the Court was facing a Commission decision finding that the French Association of Pharmacists had violated Article 101 TFEU by imposing (*inter alia*) minimum prices for lab tests, banning discounts beyond 10%. The association argued that the restriction escaped Article 101 TFEU as it pursued the legitimate objective of protecting public health as well as the independence of pharmacists. The French State had delegated four main functions to the association, namely:

1. To ensure compliance with professional duties;
2. To ensure the defence of the honour and independence of the profession;
3. To supervise the competence of pharmacists; and
4. To contribute to promoting public health and the quality of healthcare, and in particular the reliability and safety of professional procedures.

46. The Court noted, however, that "unlike the professional body concerned in the judgment in Wouters …, the association does not have regulatory powers". The Commission had considered whether the restriction of competition associated with the imposition of minimum prices could be justified by a legitimate objective but had rejected that argument. Upon appeal, the Court found that:

> Admittedly, the Association must ensure compliance with the ethical rules in the context of its legal remit, including the defence of the independence of pharmacist-biologists and the promotion of public health. However, its action must remain within the legal framework set up by the legislature and the administrative authorities, as the Association itself has no regulatory power. Accordingly, when it acts on the basis of an interpretation that is contrary to the literal meaning of the relevant provisions, and indeed adopts

---

55 Case T-90/11 *Ordre national des pharmaciens (ONP) and Others v European Commission* ECLI:EU:T:2014:1049, para 347.

> the most restrictive interpretation in the context of a particular strategy, its conduct cannot fall outside the scope of Article 101(1) TFEU on the basis of the argument that it is inherent in the pursuit of a legitimate objective. The Commission rightly finds in that regard that it is not for a body representing private persons to extend the scope of protection of the law with the desire of protecting the interest of a group when the legislature had defined the limits of the protection offered and left the possibility for a certain amount of competition.

47. Hence, the Court found in this case that the power to pursue a legitimate objective vested in an undertaking is not sufficient. It is also necessary for the undertaking to explicitly have the power to adopt the measures that might be found to fall outside the scope of Article 101 TFEU in order to pursue a legitimate objective. This is an innovation.

F. *International Skating Union – (ISU)*

48. The most comprehensive treatment of the question of legitimate objective is in the Commission's decision on *ISU*.[56] There, the Commission had the opportunity to present its understanding of all its prior practice as informed by the case law evolution of the CJEU. The relevant passages regarding the factual claims that ISU submitted to justify its restrictions are quoted below:

> First, in line with the case law (see recital (212)), the Commission considers that the protection of the integrity of the sport, the protection of health and safety and the organisation and proper conduct of competitive sport may constitute legitimate objectives that justify a restriction of competition. …
>
> Second, the protection of economic and/or financial interests does not, however, constitute a legitimate objective that can justify a restriction of competition. …
>
> Third, as to the protection of the ISU's jurisdiction, the Commission notes that, without prejudice to the question whether the principle of having one regulator per sport can be considered as legitimate objective capable of justifying restrictions of competition law, the measures established by the ISU (that is, the pre-authorisation system embodied by the ISU's Eligibility rules and by Communication No 1974 on Open International Competitions) are neither inherent in the pursuit of those objectives nor proportionate to them for the reasons set out in Section 8.5.2.
>
> Fourth, with regard to the claimed protection of the solidarity model in skating, the Commission recognises that some forms of horizontal solidarity (for instance, equal distribution of revenues to all the clubs participating in the same competition) or vertical solidarity (for instance, redistribution of

---

56 Case AT.40208 European Commission Decision *International Skating Union's Eligibility* (*ISU* Decision) (8 December 2017).

> revenues from the elite/professional level of a sport to the low/grassroots level) may justify limited restrictions to the economic freedom of undertakings involved in sport, in particular within a sport pyramid
>
> Fifth, the Commission does not exclude that the protection of the volunteer model of sport, as mentioned in Article 165 of the Treaty, may be considered as a legitimate objective of general interest.
>
> Sixth, as regards the arguments that third [-]party organisers of speed skating events would free-ride on the ISU's costs incurred for the administration of the sport, the prevention of free-riding cannot be considered as a legitimate objective but rather as a claim related to the economic efficiencies generated by the ISU rules.

49. It becomes obvious that, while the Commission uses the term "legitimate objective" that the Court had used in its *Wouters* jurisprudence, it does so in a contextual manner. It does not recognise to ISU, a sports federation, the right to advance and promote society-wide preferences (social objectives). ISU can strictly pursue objectives that it can in light of its mandate. Indeed, there is no better confirmation of this than the explicit wording of the Commission decision: "Legitimate objectives of sporting rules will normally relate to the "organisation and proper conduct of competitive sport" and may include, for instance, ensuring fair competitions with equal chances for all athletes as well as the protection of athletes' health, the integrity and objectivity of competitive sport and ethical values in sport".[57]

50. In line with the case law of the Court of Justice, the Commission considers that the protection of the integrity of sport, the protection of the health and safety of skaters and the organisation and proper conduct of competitive sport can be regarded as legitimate objectives in the general interest.

51. The Commission leaves no doubt that this is the correct reading when a few lines later, it states: "Even if one were to assume that this case-law applies to the ISU, which is not a Member State, it is not to the ISU's avail because the ISU does not apply its ethical principles concerning the risks of betting in a consistent and systematic manner".[58]

52. Thus, the Commission (and the CJEU, for that matter) has never adhered to the idea that football associations can invoke legitimate objectives that lie above and beyond their mandate. And, of course, to justifiably invoke a similar objective, they must observe the Commission's standard embedded in the same judgment: "To fall outside the scope of Article 101(1) of the Treaty, the restrictions caused by the Eligibility rules need to be inherent in the pursuit of legitimate objectives and proportionate to them."

53. Overall, thus, it appears that the Court has only acknowledged as legitimate objectives that are related to the public policy objectives that the undertakings

---

57 Ibid paras 211–212.

58 Ibid para 232.

under consideration were entrusted to pursue within a specific regulatory framework (either directly or by delegation).[59]

54. In four paragraphs that because of their interest we reproduce in their entirety, the *ESL* jurisprudence confirmed ISU's insistence on a contextual understanding of what constitutes a "legitimate objective":

> In the present case, in view of the aspects discussed in paragraphs 142 to 144 and 196 of the present judgment, the Court finds that the adoption of rules on prior approval of interclub football competitions and on the participation of professional football clubs and players in those competitions may be justified, in terms of its very principle, by public interest objectives consisting in ensuring, prior to the organisation of such competitions, that they will be organised in observance of the principles, values and rules of the game underpinning professional football, in particular the values of openness, merit and solidarity, but also that those competitions will, in a substantively homogeneous and temporally coordinated manner, integrate into the "organised system" of national, European and international competitions characterising that sport.
> Nevertheless, those objectives are not capable of justifying the adoption of such rules where they do not include substantive criteria and detailed procedural rules suitable for ensuring that they are transparent, objective, precise and non-discriminatory, as follows from paragraphs 147, 175, 176 and 199 of the present judgment.
> Indeed, in order for a prior approval scheme like the one introduced by those rules to be held to be justified, it must, in any event, be based on objective, non-discriminatory criteria which are known in advance, in such a way as to circumscribe the exercise of the discretion conferred thereby on the body empowered to grant or refuse that prior approval, so that that power is not used arbitrarily (see, to that effect, judgments of 22 January 2002, Canal Satélite Digital, C-390/99, EU:C:2002:34, paragraph 35, and of 13 June 2019, TopFit and Biffi, C-22/18, EU:C:2019:497, paragraph 65).
> In the present case, in the light of the statements of the referring court referred to in paragraph 248 of the present judgment, the rules at issue in the main proceedings do not appear to be capable of being justified by a legitimate objective in the public interest.[60]

55. Hence, the Court has held that the UEFA could only involve a legitimate objective in relation to the organisation of pan-European competitions, which falls squarely within the mission that it has been entrusted with by the member federations (Articles 51 and 52 UEFA Statutes)[61]. In this regard, it is consistent with prior

---

59 Ibid para 225. Whether an undertaking can invoke a legitimate objective could also be informed by its practice. In this respect, a convincing track record in the pursuit of an objective that is claimed as legitimate in the context of TFEU, art 101 as part of the institution's general conduct, would reinforce the credibility of the claim.

60 *ESL* (n 3), paras 253–256.

61 The AG Emiliou, who refers to the current paper, takes a similar position. In § 42 of the Case C-428/23, he takes the view "that "although it is not strictly necessary for the competent authority (be it EU and/or national) to have formally assigned the body in question the responsibility to pursue, with the ambit of its

cases and in particular with the Commission decision in *ISU*. It is also noteworthy that unlike what happens in earlier cases, there is no explicit regulatory framework approved by a public authority from which the public policy objectives can be derived.

6. Application to FFAR

56. Where does this all lead? And how does it affect the evaluation of FFAR? Article 1 of FFAR mentions the objectives sought through its enactment, namely, to:

- Raise ethical standards;
- Ensure quality of services;
- Limit conflicts of interest;
- Serve transparency;
- Address asymmetric information;
- Enhance contractual stability; and
- Prevent abusive practices.

57. The level of aggregation of these objectives varies, but the least one can say is that none of them is functionally informative. Nevertheless, in accompanying documentation, FIFA has clarified that FFAR addresses three well-known distortions, namely, moral hazard, adverse selection and the hold-up problem. How the restrictions of competition address these issues is unclear, but a full discussion is beyond the scope of this chapter.

58. First, it is necessary to underscore a discrepancy in EU practice between *Meca-Medina* and *ONP*. In *Meca-Medina*, the CJEU probably assumed (without verifying that this was indeed the case) that national associations had the power to commit their states to the FINA anti-doping rules. In *ONP*, the Court held that the power to pursue a legitimate objective by an undertaking is not sufficient. It is also necessary for the undertaking to explicitly have the power to adopt the measures that might be found to fall outside the scope of Article 101 TFEU in order to pursue a legitimate objective. The Court did not explicitly repeat this statement in *ESL*. We probably read too much into the omission, but it would have helped a great deal if the Court had been more precise in this context. Requesting this extra layer of demonstration of competence is all the more necessary when dealing with SGBs. While there is a legitimate presumption that an entity like the ONP is vested with public authority, there is no such presumption for SGBs. Some of their members are purely private associations. The Royal Belgian Football Association (RBFA), a member of both FIFA and UEFA, is a private entity. It has no right to regulate the agent's market in Belgium. How can it then transfer to FIFA a competence that it does not possess?

59. Second, in its *ESL* and *Royal Antwerp* judgments, the Court resuscitated its "purely sporting rule" jurisprudence that many had legitimately considered obsolete

---

statutory activities, a legitimate objective in the public interest, those authorities must have, at the very least, acknowledged and accepted the body's activities of self regulation".

following the *Meca-Medina* judgment.[62] The "incompleteness" of this term could be a tool to exonerate FFAR from the scope of Article 101 TFEU. To do this, the Court would have to be persuaded that FFAR is a purely sporting rule. Is it?

60. The Court has claimed in (*ESL*, *Royal Antwerp* and *ISU*) that "certain specific rules which were adopted solely on non-economic grounds and which relate to questions of interest solely to sport per se must be regarded as being extraneous to any economic activity." The example mentioned in the three decisions concerns the rules on the exclusion of foreign players from the composition of teams participating in competitions between teams representing their country.[63]

61. Weatherill has argued that the Court's claim is "demonstrably false" as even the rules mentioned in the judgments are clearly not extraneous to economic activity.[64] Eligibility to play for a country has an impact on an athlete's earning capacity, and the same goes for qualification for international competition. Even more so the FFAR, we would add, which is a regulation that has clear economic objectives and uses economic instruments (price caps, limitation in the scope of activities, and entry restrictions)[65]. FIFA thus cannot appeal to hide behind the "purely sporting rule" to avoid the discipline of Article 101 TFEU as a result.

7. Efficiency Gains

62. The CJEU underscored its consistent case law that any violation of Article 101(1) TFEU can be justified through recourse to Article 101(3). Irrespective of whether FFAR involves a restriction by object or by effect, FIFA could point to efficiency gains to justify its restriction of competition. To succeed, FIFA would have to meet four conditions cumulatively:[66]

> … First, it must be demonstrated with a sufficient degree of probability (…), that the agreement, decision by an association of undertakings or concerted practice in question makes it possible to achieve efficiency gains, by contributing either to improving the production or distribution of the products or services concerned, or to promoting technical or economic progress.

63. In other words, the restrictions must be necessary to achieve the efficiency gains.

> … Second, it must be demonstrated, to the same degree of probability, that an equitable part of the profit resulting from those efficiency gains is reserved for the users.
>
> As regards the second condition referred to in paragraph 190 of the present judgment, it involves establishing that the efficiency gains made possible by the agreement, decision by an association of undertakings or concerted

---

62 See Stephen Weatherill, "Football Revolution: How Do the Court's Rulings of 21 December 2023 affect UEFA's Role as a *Gatekeeper*?" (*EU Law Analysis*, 4 January 2024) <https://eulawanalysis.blogspot.com/2024/01/football-revolution-how-do-courts.html> accessed 2 September 2025.

63 *ESL* (n 3), para 84; *Royal Antwerp* (n 4), para 54; *ISU* (n 2), para 92.

64 Weatherill (n 61).

65 In Tondela (C-133/24), AG Emiliou confirms that the sporting exception does not apply when the rules affect economic activities.

66 *ESL* (n 3), paras 189, 190, 193.

> practice in question have a positive impact on all users, be they traders, intermediate consumers or end consumers, in the different sectors or markets concerned…

64. The formulation, however, leaves some issues unanswered. The Commission has clarified that the scope of the efficiency gains can exceed the relevant market,

> [a]lthough the weighing of the positive and negative effects of the restrictive agreements is normally done within the relevant market to which the agreement relates, where two markets are related, efficiencies generated on separate markets can be taken into account, provided that the group of consumers that is affected by the restriction and that benefits from the efficiencies is substantially the same.[67]

65. Nevertheless, whether the requirement of a positive balance applies to each individual group of users or all users taken together is not entirely clear.[68] In addition, the requirement of a positive balance might also apply within a substantial part of the common market (which could be a subset of the former). *ESL* "… Third, the agreement, decision or practice in question must not impose on the participating undertakings restrictions which are not indispensable for achieving such efficiency gains".

66. This condition clarifies that not only the restrictive agreement as such must be reasonably necessary in order to achieve the efficiencies but also that "individual restrictions of competition that flow from the agreement must also be reasonably necessary for the attainment of the efficiencies".[69] *ESL* "… Fourth, that agreement, decision or practice must not give the participating undertakings the opportunity to eliminate all effective competition for a substantial part of the products or services concerned". According to the 2023 Guidelines on Article 101 TFEU,

> [t]his last condition may be satisfied even if the agreement restricting competition covers the entire industry, as long as the parties to the agreement continue to compete vigorously on at least one important parameter of competition. For instance, if the agreement eliminates competition on quality or variety, but price is also an important parameter of competition in the industry concerned, and prices are not restricted, this condition may still be fulfilled.[70]

67. Whether these conditions can realistically be met in the case of a restriction by object is unclear as, in the instance, in the absence of an assessment of the magnitude of the anticompetitive effects, there may not be a clear metric along which anticompetitive effects can be balanced against efficiency gains. This may be particularly relevant in the case of FFAR, which, as mentioned above, has been assessed as involving a restriction by object in a couple of proceedings.

---

67 European Commission, Guidelines on the applicability of Article 101 of the Treaty on the Functioning of the European Union to Horizontal Co-Operation Agreements [2023] OJ C259/1, para 583 (2023 Guidelines).

68 European Commission, Guidelines on the Application of Article 81(3) of the Treaty [2004] OJ C101/97 (2004 Guidelines).

69 Ibid para 73.

70 2023 Guidelines on TFEU, art 101, para 593.

IV. Conclusion

68. As discussed in this chapter, in assessing whether FFAR pursues a legitimate objective, the CJEU must first ensure that FIFA is entitled to pursue it. It must, in other words, ask whether FIFA is entitled to legislate in this realm and has the power to adopt the necessary means to this end. This is arguably an appropriate constraint as otherwise, there is a risk that the pursuit of legitimate objectives might undo the distribution of competences decided between Member States and the EU institutions or possibly conflict with national regulations.[71] It is striking in this respect that while the FFAR regulation is comprehensive, the FIFA Statutes[72] are almost totally silent as to the precise ambit of its competences.[73]

69. The dichotomy that case law draws between antitrust and free movement of factors regarding the possibility to invoke a legitimate objective is also a source of concern. In *ESL*, the Court held that

> once the existence of an obstacle to the free movement of workers is established, the association which adopted the rule in question may yet demonstrate that it is justified, necessary and proportionate in view of certain objectives which may be regarded as legitimate (see, to that effect, judgment of 15 December 1995, Bosman, C-415/93, EU:C:1995:463, paragraph 104), which themselves are contingent on the specific characteristics of the sport concerned.[74]

70. In *Bosman*,[75] the Court had acknowledged the possibility for SGBs like FIFA/UEFA to invoke a legitimate objective without reference to a specific regulatory framework: It could only be otherwise if those rules pursued a legitimate aim compatible with the Treaty and were justified by pressing reasons of public interest. But even if that were so, application of those rules would still have to be such as to ensure achievement of the aim in question and not go beyond what is necessary for that purpose (see, *inter alia*, the judgment in *Kraus*, cited above).[76]

71. In *Kraus*,[77] the case mentioned in this passage, a German citizen had challenged the consistency of Baden-Württemberg, a German Land vested, of course, with public authority to reject the recognition of a graduate title that Kraus had obtained in the United Kingdom. The Court stated that the German Land could lawfully refuse recognition if it were pursuing a legitimate objective: "The situation would be different only if such a measure pursued a legitimate objective compatible

---

71 For instance, the FFAR could be in conflict with the labour market regulations or contravene public order in some Member States.

72 By contrast, UEFA Statutes, arts 49 and 51 state clearly that UEFA (and no one else) has the right to organise pan-European competitions: its signatories (national football associations), by signing on the UEFA Statutes, agreed to delegate to UEFA the right to organise pan-European competitions <https://digitalhub.fifa.com/m/7e791c0890282277/original/FIFA-Statutes-2021.pdf> accessed 2 September 2025.

73 UEFA (n 25).

74 *ESL* (n 3), para 106.

75 Case C-415/93 *Union Royale Belge Sociale de Football Association, RCL and UEFA v JM Bosman* ECLI:EU:C:1995:463, para 104.

76 Case C-19/92 *Dieter Kraus v Land Baden-Württemberg* ECLI:EU:C:1993:125, para 32.

77 Ibid.

with the Treaty and was justified by pressing reasons of public interest (see to that effect, judgment in Case 71/76 Thieffry v Conseil de l'Ordre des Avocats à la Cour de Pans [1977] ECR 765, paragraphs 12 and 15)".

72. The Court, however, did not explain why the *Kraus* approach, which involves a state entity vested with public authority, should find application when an SGB is involved. Besides, an association of undertakings can invoke a legitimate objective to justify discriminatory behaviour (a fundamental principle of EU law), but it cannot do so when engaging in practices that qualify as restrictions by object (definitely not a fundamental principle of EU law).[78]

73. We believe it is high time for the Court to revisit its case law. What matters is whether the party invoking a legitimate objective is legitimised to do so. The question to ask then should be whether it has been endowed with the requisite public authority. Association of undertakings are not by themselves vested with similar authority. The Court should state as much in a clear-cut manner, and then the distinction between restriction by object or by effect could become immaterial as far as the invocation of legitimate interest is concerned. Moreover, this construction will guarantee coherence in EU case law across competition law and the four freedoms. It will also enhance democratic legitimacy, as societal choices in the realm of Member States' competence will be part of the democratic dialogue therein and not usurped by associations of undertakings through acrobatic constructions of open-ended language.

74. There is one additional issue that deserves our attention. In *ISU*, the Court adopted stronger language towards the Court of Arbitration for Sport (CAS), and the possibility of submitting to CAS disputes that come under the purview of EU law.[79] The Commission had instigated this turn as the Court itself acknowledged:

> [T]he Commission found that that judicial review was entrusted to a court established in a third country, thus outside the European Union and its legal order, and that, according to the case-law of that court, such awards could not be reviewed in the light of the EU competition rules. In so doing, the Commission, ultimately, complained not of the existence, organisation or operation of the CAS as an arbitration body, but rather of the legal immunity enjoyed by the ISU, in its view, in the light of EU competition law, in the exercise of its decision-making and sanctioning powers, to the detriment of persons who may be affected by the lack of a framework for those powers and the discretionary nature which derives therefrom.

75. The Court explained under what conditions submissions of disputes to CAS concerning the interpretation of EU law would be consistent with the EU legal order:

---

78 Besides, the fact that legitimate objectives can be invoked with respect to internal market rules and not with respect to restrictions by object will affect incentives in terms of the scope of legal challenges.

79 *ISU* (n 2), para 184. (Note that the CJEU has had the opportunity to pronounce on the relevance of CAS awards a few times. In *Meca-Medina* C-519/04 P (n 22) and *Meca-Medina* (n 22), as well as in *Piau* (n 7) and in Case C-269/12 P *Guillermo Cañas v European Commission* ECLI:EU:C:2013:415, the Court referred to CAS awards in a matter-of-factual way without engaging in the question regarding their legal significance.

> [I]n so far as they confer on the CAS mandatory and exclusive jurisdiction to review decisions that the ISU may adopt by virtue of its powers in respect of prior authorisation and sanctions, disregards, as the cross-appellants and the Commission essentially argue, the requirements that must be satisfied for an arbitration mechanism such as that at issue in the present case to be capable of being regarded, on the one hand, as allowing effective compliance with the public policy provisions that EU law contains to be ensured and, on the other hand, as being compatible with the principles underlying the judicial architecture of the European Union.[80]

76. CAS, in other words, is deficient to the extent that it does not include a mechanism to submit its decisions concerning interpretation of EU law to the CJEU,[81] which retains the exclusive right to interpret EU law:

> In the absence of such judicial review, the use of an arbitration mechanism is such as to undermine the protection of rights that subjects of the law derive from the direct effect of EU law and the effective compliance with Articles 101 and 102 TFEU, which must be ensured – and would therefore be ensured in the absence of such a mechanism – by the national rules relating to remedies. Compliance with that requirement for effective judicial review applies in particular to arbitration rules such as those imposed by the ISU.[82]

77. Of course, there is no mechanism available to CAS to submit disputes to the CJEU. Unsurprisingly thus, and consistently with its prior case law that preserved its exclusive right to interpret EU law, the Court found that CAS judgment could not be relied on for the interpretation of EU law; what is striking is that the Court annulled the General Court assessment of the suitability of CAS in such strong terms:

> Thus, the General Court erred in law by merely finding, in an undifferentiated and abstract manner, that the arbitration rules "may be justified by legitimate interests linked to the specific nature of the sport", in so far as they confer on "a specialised court" the power to review disputes relating to the prior authorisation and eligibility rules, without seeking to ensure that those arbitration rules complied with all the requirements referred to in the preceding paragraphs of the present judgment and thus allowed for an effective review of compliance with the EU competition rules, even though the Commission correctly relied on those requirements in recitals 270 to 277, 282 and 283 of the decision at issue in concluding that those rules reinforced the infringement identified in Article 1 of that decision.[83]

78. The fact that CAS is not suitable in the eye of the CJEU to adjudicate matters of EU law is of particular practical importance as the Court has over the years

---

80 *ISU* (n 2), para 188.

81 On this issue, see Nils Wahl and Luca Prete, "The Gatekeepers of Article 267 TFEU: On Jurisdiction and Admissibility of References for Preliminary Rulings" (2018) 55 CMLR 511–548.

82 *ISU* (n 2), 194–195.

83 Ibid para 199.

understood in an increasingly "liberal" manner the scope of its jurisdiction. To the extent that an activity "affects" economic agents in the EU, the Court is quite likely to assert jurisdiction. How much scope is then left for CAS disputes under the circumstance? More recently, in Seraing (C-600/23) the Court went one step further and pronounced that CAS awards have no res judicata effect in the EU legal order to the extent that they deal with matters of EU public policy (the four freedoms and competition) Mataija and Mavroidis (2025)[84] have claimed that this is the bulk of case law before CAS. One could thus expect that losing parties will be incentivized to re-litigate their CAS disputes before an EU civil court. Of course, practice has often defied predictions. Future experience will be telling in this respect.

79. Ibañez Colomo, Pablo, 2022, Competition Law and Sports Governance: Disentangling a Complex Relationship, *World Competition*, Vol. 45, Issue 3, pp. 323–350

80. Maduro, Miguel, 2023, A New Season: Will it Also Be a New Beginning for Sports and EU Law? *Weekend EU Law Live Edition*, No. 157, pp. 2–14

[84] Mataija, Mislav, and Petros C. Mavroidis. 2025. The Court of Arbitration for Sport (CAS) and EU Law: Never the Twain Shall Meet? EU Law Live Weekend Edition, no 235, June 2025: 1-17.

Multi-Club Ownership – Multi-Club Investment

Romain Soiron, Olivier Cavezian and Antoine Burgensis
Joffe & Associés, Paris, France

1. The increasing financialisation of football and the resulting inflation in player transfer fees are leading to budgetary constraints and financial difficulties for football clubs. To stay the course or continue to evolve in this situation, clubs are seeking to increase their economic power by opening up their capital to new investors, whether majority or minority shareholders.

2. In this respect, in the football sector, the only sport analysed in this contribution, the trend of multi-club ownership, defined as "a situation where a party exerts control and/or decisive influence over more than one club", and multi-club investment, which refers to "a situation where a party has investment interests in more than one club (without exercising control or influence)",[1] have grown significantly in recent years. These majority or minority shareholdings in football clubs are acquired by investment funds, private companies or individuals, but can also be made by clubs themselves becoming owners of or acquiring a stake in another club.

3. Following the example of Manchester City, owned by City Football Group, which holds stakes in twelve other clubs around the world,[2] or Olympique Lyonnais whose control was recently acquired by the Eagle Football investment fund,[3] also holding majority or minority stakes in Brazilian, Belgian, English and

---

1 UEFA, *The European Club Footballing Landscape* 206 <https://editorial.uefa.com/resources/027e-174740f39cc6-d205dd2e86bf-1000/ecfl_bm_report_2022_high_resolution_.pdf> accessed 30 August 2025.

2 Manchester City website <www.cityfootballgroup.com/club> accessed 30 August 2025.s

3 Eagle Football website <www.eaglefootball.com/club> accessed 30 August 2025s

American clubs, no fewer than 230 clubs were part of a multi-club ownership or multi-investment structure in 2023, compared with less than 100 clubs in 2018 and less than 40 in 2012.[4]

Years	2014	2015	2016	2017	2018	2019	2020	2021	2022	2023
Acquisition of a minority stake	2	6	5	8	3	13	12	20	15	7
Acquisition of a majority stake	9	8	14	8	18	17	24	19	31	31
TOTAL	**11**	**14**	**19**	**16**	**21**	**30**	**36**	**39**	**46**	**38**

Source: UEFA, *The European Club Finance and Investment Landscape* (2024) 79.

4. The development of multi-club ownership and investment can be explained in particular by FIFA's recent ban on "third party ownership",[5] which enabled clubs to finance the acquisition of players with the help of third parties who were then part owners of the economic rights of the player acquired. Faced with this ban, and in order to bear the growing costs associated with their management and transfer fees, clubs are now turning to other methods of financing, including opening up their capital to new investors.

5. Investors, for their part, are attracted to acquiring multiple stakes in clubs, with the prospect of substantial returns and profits. In this context, multi-club ownership and investment allow investors, as with any other business model for corporate portfolio management, to diversify their assets and reduce the risks inherent in these investments, while maximising returns.

6. Multi-club ownership and investment also enable synergies to be created between the various clubs, in particular by pooling costs and optimising detection and training networks and the development of players in order to reduce the financial risks associated with sporting uncertainty. These multiple investments help to improve the overall performance of clubs as a sporting and economic entity.

7. In addition, when these investments are made indirectly by states,[6] they can also be implemented as part of a soft power strategy, for diplomatic, communication and image improvement purposes.

8. Whatever the objective pursued, multiple ownership and multi-club investment nevertheless present risks with regard to the independence and autonomy of clubs and their sporting strategies and, consequently, risks of conflicts of interest likely to undermine the integrity and fairness of sporting competitions. The concentration of economic forces could also lead to a concentration of sporting talent within

---

4 UEFA, *The European Club Finance and Investment Landscape* (2024) 79 <https://editorial.uefa.com/resources/028c-1aa8afe670df-ba6bbce7e604-1000/20240415_circular_2024_16_en.pdf> accessed 30 August 2025.

5 FIFA, Regulations on the Status and Transfer of Players (RSTP) (2022) adopted in 2015, art 18bis (Third-party influence on clubs) and art 18ter (Third-party ownership of players' economic rights).

6 For example, Paris Saint-Germain is indirectly owned by Qatar through the sovereign wealth fund Qatar Investment Authority, while Manchester City is indirectly owned by Abu Dhabi United Group, a company owned by a member of the Abu Dhabi royal family and ruler of the United Arab Emirates.

certain groups of clubs, with UEFA noting in particular that "The growth in multi-club investment has the potential to distort transfer activity, with an increasing percentage of transfers being executed within multi-club investment groups at prices that suit investors, rather than at fair values, to the detriment of trainer clubs (which receive less compensation in the form of solidarity payments)".[7]

9. Eventually, these abuses could have a negative impact on football itself, with the public losing confidence in the fairness and integrity of competitions and the honesty of their results and ultimately losing interest in the game.

10. In response to these growing risks, FIFA and UEFA have specifically regulated these types of investment and ownership structures, although they have not completely banned them. In addition, many European countries, such as France, have introduced rules to regulate such investments and structures, which are subject to the general rules of competition law (Section I).

11. However, while these specific sports regulations seem necessary to avoid the excesses associated with multiple investments, it also creates constraints for clubs and investors and may harm investment and the development of football, generating new sporting and economic risks. In this context, although the strict regulation of multi-club ownership and investment can be explained by the specific nature of sport, this regulation may, in some respects, appear disproportionate and unjustified, particularly with regard to the imperatives of competition law, which fully apply to the sporting sector as soon as it is part of an economic activity (Section II).

I. The Legal Framework for Multi-Club Ownership and Investment

12. Competition between football clubs is a key factor in the success of the competitions in which they participate and in the success of the sport in general. However, as detailed above, multi-club ownership and investment can undermine the independence of clubs and therefore reduce competition between them.

13. In order to maintain rivalry between competing clubs and a competitive balance in football, FIFA and UEFA, as well as certain countries such as France, have introduced specific rules aimed at regulating multi-club ownership and investment. In addition, these types of investment in clubs and their consequences are also governed by the general rules of competition law.

1. Specific Sporting Rules Governing Multi-Club Ownership and Investment

14. UEFA took up the issue of multi-club ownership and investment, and their abuses, very early, on regulating these types of investment as early as the 1990s.[8] In order

[7] UEFA (n 1), 211.

[8] UEFA, Multi-Club Ownership Regulations (2025) adopted in May 1998 <https://documents.uefa.com/r/Regulations-of-the-UEFA-Women-s-Champions-League-2025/26/Article-5-Integrity-of-the-competition/multi-club-ownership-Online> accessed 30 August 2025.

to prevent certain individuals from controlling several sports clubs in the same discipline and thus being in a position to distort the course of a competition, restrictions were introduced at European and world level, as well as in France, significantly reducing the investment capacity of sports companies.

A. *The European and Global Multi-Club Ownership and Investment Framework*

15. FIFA recognises the crucial importance of club independence in its statutes, in order to guarantee fairness and sporting integrity. Article 20 of its statutes stipulates that,

> the member association shall ensure that neither a natural nor a legal person (including holding companies and subsidiaries) exercises control in any manner whatsoever (in particular through a majority shareholding, a majority of voting rights, a majority of seats on the board of directors or any other form of economic dependence or control, etc.) over more than one club whenever the integrity of any match or competition could be jeopardised.[9]

16. In other words, FIFA requires its member associations to ensure that no one exercises control over more than one club that could jeopardise the integrity of the competition.

17. As for UEFA, whose purpose is to "organise and conduct international football competitions and tournaments at European level", its mission is to "promotes and protects ethical standards and good governance in European football" and "ensures that sporting values always prevail over commercial interests".[10]

18. With this objective in mind, UEFA has incorporated provisions relating to the integrity of competitions in the regulations governing the organisation of European club football competitions,[11] particularly with regard to multi-club ownership:

    a. No club participating in a UEFA club competition may, either directly or indirectly:

        i. hold or deal in the securities or shares of any other club participating in a UEFA club competition;

        ii. be a member of any other club participating in a UEFA club competition;

        iii. be involved in any capacity whatsoever in the management, administration and/or sporting performance of any other club participating in a UEFA club competition; or

---

9 FIFA Statutes (2022), art 20 <https://digitalhub.fifa.com/m/3815fa68bd9f4ad8/original/FIFA_Statutes_2022-EN.pdf> accessed 30 August 2025.

10 UEFA Statutes (2024), art 2<https://documents.uefa.com/v/u/07zyuoc_69TV_sHbFYvA2w> accessed 30 August 2025.

11 UEFA Champions League Regulations (2025); UEFA Europa League Regulations (2025); UEFA Europa Conference League Regulations (2025); UEFA Women's Champions League Regulations; UEFA Youth League Regulations (2023–2024).

iv. have any power whatsoever in the management, administration and/or sporting performance of any other club participating in a UEFA club competition.

b. No one may simultaneously be involved, either directly or indirectly, in any capacity whatsoever in the management, administration and/or sporting performance of more than one club participating in a UEFA club competition.

c. No individual or legal entity may have control or influence over more than one club participating in a UEFA club competition, such control or influence being defined in this context as:

i. holding a majority of the shareholders' voting rights;

ii. having the right to appoint or remove a majority of the members of the administrative, management or supervisory body of the club;

iii. being a shareholder and alone controlling a majority of the shareholders' voting rights pursuant to an agreement entered into with other shareholders of the club; or

iv. being able to exercise by any means a decisive influence in the decision-making of the club.[12]

19. Under the terms of these regulations, UEFA covers and regulates situations of multiple ownerships by investors in the broadest sense of the term, since it covers cases of multiple ownerships of clubs by legal entities (including the clubs themselves) as well as natural persons, whether through the ownership of shares in several clubs, memberships of other clubs or a role in the management, administration or sporting performance of several clubs.

20. UEFA regulations stipulate that, in such cases of multi-club ownership, only one of the clubs held may be admitted to a UEFA club competition.[13]

21. In this respect, the rule gives priority to the club in the multi-club ownership structure that qualifies for the most prestigious UEFA club competition (ie in descending order, the UEFA Champions League, the UEFA Europa League or the UEFA Europa Conference League) and, subsidiarily, to the highest-ranked club in the domestic championship giving access to the relevant UEFA club competition. As a last resort, access is granted to the club whose national association has the highest ranking in the access list corresponding to the UEFA ranking of the countries to which the clubs belong.[14]

22. Therefore, although UEFA regulations provide a framework for multi-club ownership, they do not prohibit it. On the contrary, on several occasions, certain clubs with a single owner have adapted their governance structure in response to these regulations in order to be able to take part in UEFA club competitions despite a situation of multi-club ownership. These adaptations show that these regulations do not seem to be hindering the development and the increase of multi-club

---

12 UEFA Champions League Regulations (2023–2024), art 5.

13 Ibid art 5.02.

14 Ibid.

ownership, a trend which even seems to be indirectly encouraged by recent UEFA decisions (see below).

23. In 2023, the First Chamber of the UEFA Club Financial Control Body (CFCB First Chamber) opened proceedings against clubs owned by the same owner, which had qualified for UEFA club competitions (in particular AC Milan and Toulouse FC, which were both owned by the American investment fund RedBird Capital Partners) and were therefore in potential breach of Article 5 of the regulations relating to these competitions.

24. The participation of these clubs in UEFA club competitions was, however, allowed by the CFCB First Chamber following significant changes put in place by these clubs and their investors regarding their ownership, governance and financing structure, significantly limiting the influence and decision-making power of investors over several clubs and ensuring compliance with the rule on multiple club ownership. The changes included:

    1. A significant reduction of the investors' shareholding in one of the clubs, or transfer of the effective control and decision making of one of the clubs to an independent party;
    2. Significant restrictions in the ability to provide financing to more than one club;
    3. The lack of representation on the board of directors and the lack of capacity to directly appoint new directors on the board of more than one club;
    4. The lack of ability to participate in the general assembly or ability to participate in key decisions (such as the approval of the budgets of more than one club); and
    5. The lack of ability to exercise control over more than one club at the level of the board of directors or their general assemblies through veto rights or contractual arrangements entered into with other shareholders.

25. In addition, these clubs have agreed to a number of conditions imposed by UEFA as further evidence of their independence, namely:

    1. Not to transfer any players to each other, whether permanently or on loan, directly or indirectly, until September 2024;
    2. Not to enter into any kind of cooperation, joint technical or commercial agreements; and
    3. Not to use any joint scouting or player database.[15]

26. Previously, UEFA had also agreed that FC Salzburg and RB Leipzig, both owned by the Red Bull Group, could participate in the UEFA Champions League for the 2017–2018 season, after noting changes to their ownership, governance and financing structure.[16]

---

15 UEFA, Press Release, "The CFCB Renders Decisions on Multi-Club Ownership Cases for the 2023/24 UEFA Club Competitions" (*EUFA.com*, 7 July 2023) <www.uefa.com/news-media/news/0283-186f6a2609f6-77d919fb7eff-1000--the-cfcb-renders-decisions-on-multi-club-ownership-cases-for/ accessed 30 August 2025.

16 UEFA, Press Release, "Salzburg and Leipzig admitted into UEFA Champions League" (*EUFA.com*, 20 June 2017) <www.uefa.com/insideuefa/news/023a-0f8e547c3c4e-b72e21e04486-1000--salzburg-and-leipzig-admitted-into-uefa-champions-league/> accessed 30 August 2025.

27. The changes made by the Red Bull Group included giving up all managerial functions at FC Salzburg and retaining only a sponsorship contract, as well as removing Red Bull's participation from the General Assembly of the FC Salzburg.[17] At UEFA's request, Red Bull Salzburg was also forced to change its logo so that it no longer featured the group's eponymous brand.

B. *National Multi-Club Ownership and Investment Framework – the French Regulations*

28. In Europe, approximately two-thirds of all national football associations have rules directly limiting or restricting multi-club ownership or investment at domestic level, whether through a cap on the share held in several clubs or a total ban on holding shares in more than one club within the country concerned.[18]

29. In this respect, France specifically regulates capital and financial links in the field of sport. The French Sports Code states that:

The same private individual is prohibited from:

1. To exclusively or jointly control several sports companies whose corporate purpose relates to the same discipline or to exercise significant influence over them, within the meaning of Article L. 233-17-2 of the French Commercial Code;
2. Be a director of more than one sports company whose corporate object is the same sporting discipline;
3. Solely or jointly controlling a sports company or exercising significant influence over it, within the meaning of Article L. 233-17-2 of the French Commercial Code, and being a director of another sports company whose corporate purpose relates to the same sport.[19]

30. French regulations are therefore more restrictive than those of UEFA and FIFA, insofar as they simply prohibit multiple ownerships of clubs operating in the same sport in France.

31. However, the geographical scope of this prohibition is limited to the national territory and does not apply if only one of the clubs owned is located in France. Therefore, while a French or foreign investor is not authorised to own several French football clubs, it is legally possible to own a foreign club and a French club within the meaning of the French Sports Code.[20]

32. The French legislation also offers some flexibility, since the same person may hold both control of a sports company and a stake in another company in the same sport, provided that this stake does not enable him to control or have a "significant

---

17 Case AC-01/2017 UEFA Decision *RasenBallsport Leipzig v Red Bull Salzburg* (16 June 2017) para 50 <https://editorial.uefa.com/resources/0258-0e2dece33fb8-5cc21edafedf-1000/rb_leipzig_fc_salzburg_-_cfcb_adjudicatory_chamber_decision_-_june_2017.pdf> accessed 30 August 2025.

18 In 2023, 39 top divisions in UEFA member countries had rules restricting multiple ownership of clubs at national level; UEFA (n 4), 81.

19 French Sports Code, art L 122-7.

20 For example, the BlueCo consortium, which owns Racing Club de Strasbourg Alsace in France, also owns Chelsea FC in England.

influence" over this other company.[21] Furthermore, the text also authorises the control of sports companies operating in different sports, following the example of the control exercised by the investment fund Qatar Sports Investments over the Paris Saint-Germain football and handball clubs.[22]

33. In addition, since 2017, the ban on private individuals controlling sports companies in the same sport has been amended to allow them to control or exercise significant influence over two sports companies operating in the same sport, provided that the companies in question operate in men's and women's sport respectively.[23]

34. This exception is designed to catalyse the structuring and professionalisation of women's sport by removing the obstacles to its development and enabling women's club sections to benefit from the financing provided by men's sections, in particular through the creation of groups of companies where the men's club and the women's club can be sister companies. This exception therefore does not affect the primary principle of these provisions governing multi-club ownership, which is to preserve the integrity of inter-club competitions insofar as, by definition, men's and women's club teams cannot compete against each other in the same competition.

35. Despite its restrictive nature, French regulations define multi-club ownership by reference to the concepts of control and significant influence set out in the French Commercial Code (applicable to accounting consolidation). However, it does not cover all situations of multi-club ownership, which may involve minority investors who have "decisive influence" over the club within the meaning of merger control rules.

36. These situations are governed by the general rules of competition law.[24]

2. Competition Law Rules Governing Multi-Club Ownership and Investment

37. While the specific sporting rules of FIFA, UEFA or the various European nations such as France aim to maintain healthy sporting competition between the clubs and to guarantee the fairness and integrity of competitions, the general competition law rules aim to ensure healthy economic competition, by regulating the balance of power between economic players and preventing anticompetitive behaviour and the creation of monopolies.

38. These competition law rules relating to merger control and cartels and abuses of dominant position are fully applicable to the sports sector and by themselves regulate multi-club ownership and investment.

---

21 Significant influence over the management and financial policy of a company is presumed when a company holds, directly or indirectly, at least one-fifth of the voting rights of that company.

22 France Info, "Le Qatar officialise la reprise du Paris Handball" (*Franceinfo.fr*, 4 June 2012) <www.franceinfo.fr/monde/proche-orient/le-qatar-officialise-la-reprise-du-paris-handball_102671.html> accessed 30 August 2025.

23 French Sports Code, art L 122-7 was amended by Law 2017-261 of 1 March 2017 aimed at preserving the ethics of sport, strengthening the regulation and transparency of professional sport and improving the competitiveness of clubs.

24 Ibid art L 233-16; French Commercial Code, art L 233-16.

A. *The Application of Merger Control Rules to Multi-Club Ownership and Investment Situations*

39. Merger control monitors transactions before they are carried out, to ensure that they do not result in a significant reduction in competition and may make authorisation conditional on the implementation of appropriate solutions if there is a risk of harm to competition.

40. Merger control rules therefore offer several advantages when it comes to controlling investment in football clubs. First of all, they make it possible to prevent and regulate any "monopoly" situation or any situation that would give rise to competition problems, unlike the FIFA and UEFA rules specific to multi-club ownership, which simply aim to regulate the sporting aspect of multi-club ownership and investment, without regulating any possible economic abuses. Merger control in this type of situation is even more relevant in that it is an *ex ante* control, applied before the investment is made.

41. They then cover situations of control in the broadest sense, encompassing not only the acquisition of "control" over a company within the meaning of Article 5 of the UEFA regulations or the French regulations (see Section I. above) but also the acquisition of "decisive influence" over a company.[25]

42. Such decisive influence can result from the simple acquisition of a minority share of a company's capital and voting rights, coupled with specific rights enabling to take or block strategic decisions on its own, such as the appointment or dismissal of the senior management, decisions relating to the budget, the *business plan* or certain investments.[26]

43. As a result, merger control can be used to apprehend minority investments that do not fall within the scope of sports regulations specific to multi-club ownership.

44. However, the merger control procedure only applies if a given transaction meets the control thresholds. Whether at European level or at the level of most national competition authorities, these thresholds, which are generally expressed in terms of annual sales, are very high and therefore only cover investments involving companies with particularly high turnovers.

45. For instance, an acquisition of a club will not have to be notified to the European Commission if the target club's turnover is less than 250 million euros within the Community or, alternatively, if it has a turnover of more than 100 million euros within the Community but less than 25 million euros in at least three Member States of the European Union, which, by nature, is rarely the case.[27]

46. At national level, the thresholds are generally lower. For example, in France, a club acquisition will have to be notified to the French Competition Authority (FCA) if the target club and the acquirer individually have a turnover in France

---

25 UEFA Champions League Regulations (n 11).

26 Consolidated Commission Notice on the competence of the Commission under Council Regulation (EC) No 139/2004 on the control of concentrations between undertakings [2008] OJ C95/1.

27 Council Regulation (EC) No 139/2004 of 20 January 2004 on the control of concentrations between undertakings [2004] OJ L24/1, arts 1.2 and 1.3.

of more than 50 million euros and together have a combined turnover worldwide of more than 150 million euros.[28] This was the case for the acquisition of the Olympique Gymnaste Club (OGC Nice) (see below).

47. There have been few cases to date where the merger control procedure has been applied to club acquisitions. For example, to the best of our knowledge, the European Commission has not controlled any acquisition of football clubs, mainly because of its particularly high control thresholds.

48. At national level, the acquisition of Manchester United by Red Football Ltd was authorised in 2005 by the UK's Competition Authority (the Office of Fair Trading, the predecessor of the CMA).[29]

49. More recently, in 2019, the French competition authority cleared the acquisition of OGC Nice by the INEOS group,[30] which since 2017 has already owned FC Lausanne-Sport in the Swiss top division and has a number of other sports facilities in cycling and Formula 1.

50. This is the first time, to the best of our knowledge, that the FCA has examined a transaction in the football club sector. The decision regarding the Ineos group's acquisition of sole control of the OGC Nice football club defined the relevant markets, setting the framework applicable to the analysis of future mergers involving football clubs.

51. The FCA found that there was, (i) a market for the transfer of professional players, on which professional football clubs compete to attract the best players, which is at least European in scope insofar as transfers are most often made between clubs belonging to the same confederation; and (ii) a market for marketing communication and sponsorship services, which is at least national in scope.

52. Under the terms of this decision, the FCA unconditionally cleared the acquisition of OGC Nice by the Ineos group on the basis that the market share of the new entity would remain below 1% on the various markets analysed, regardless of the geographical delimitation adopted, so that the new entity would remain subject to competition from all French and European professional football clubs.[31]

B. *Anticompetitive Practices Law as a Framework for Multi-Club Ownership and Investment*

53. The aim of competition law and the regulation of anticompetitive practices is to guarantee the conditions for free competition and to maintain rivalry between companies, ensuring that they retain their independence and act autonomously in the markets in which they operate.

54. However, as explained above, multi-club ownership and investment present risks for the independence and autonomy of these clubs and their sporting strategies and could give rise to anticompetitive situations.

---

28 French Commercial Code (n 24), art L430-2.

29 Case ME/1783/05 UK Competition Authority Decision *Red Football Ltd / Manchester United plc* (12 August 2005) <www.gov.uk/cma-cases/red-football-ltd-manchester-united-plc> accessed 30 August 2025.

30 Case 19-DCC-160 FCA Decision *Ineos/Gymnaste Club de Nice* (21 August 2019).

31 Ibid.

55. First, clubs which are, in principle, autonomous and competitors, must not exchange sensitive information which could relate to their development strategy, particularly commercial, the acquisition of assets or players, prices and offers on the transfer market or with sponsors, or sales and marketing plans. Although two or more clubs owned by the same owner belong to the same group as a single economic entity and therefore may in some cases exchange this type of information without incurring penalties for anticompetitive practices,[32] investors in several clubs who do not control them remain subject to the competition law rules.

56. Thus, a non-controlling minority investor must not use their position to obtain sensitive information about a club and then disseminate it to another club in which they are also a shareholder. If such exchanges had the object and/or effect to distort or restrict competition, such access to this information by a club via its common shareholder and the use made of it to adjust its strategy could constitute a cartel. Exchanges of information relating to competitors' sensitive commercial information, for example on costs, sales data, market shares, customers or on competitors' current and future commercial and pricing strategies, and in particular on prices and price parameters, are regularly sanctioned by the competition authorities.[33]

57. Furthermore, the increase of multi-club investment groups is also likely to distort the transfer market, with an increasing proportion of transfers being made between these clubs owned by the same owner, at prices that suit the investors.[34] In the same way as for exchanges of sensitive information, a non-controlling shareholder of several clubs must not use their position within these clubs to facilitate transfers whose price is not set autonomously by the selling club. Otherwise, the agreement on prices between the various clubs can be regarded, by their very nature, as being harmful to the proper functioning of normal competition and thus be considered as a restriction of competition by object.

58. Moreover, a shareholder who owns several clubs could theoretically find themselves in a dominant position in the market in which they are active. In such a case, its behaviour would be regulated by competition law, preventing it from abusing this position by foreclosing its competitors, for example by charging abusive prices for transfers of players to competing clubs, by refusing to sell players to certain clubs or by bundling the sale of several players.[35]

59. Each of these types of anticompetitive behaviour likely to result from multi-club ownership and investment is governed by the competition law rules.

---

32 Under point 11 of the Guidelines on the applicability of TFEU, art 101 to horizontal cooperation agreements, the European Commission states that: "When a company exercises decisive influence over another company, they form a single economic entity and, hence, are part of the same undertaking. Companies that form part of the same undertaking are not considered to be competitors for the purposes of these Guidelines, even if they are both active on the same relevant product and geographic market(s)".

33 See for example the European Commission decisions in Case AT.40522 European Commission Decision *Metal Packaging* (12 July 2022); Case AT.40135 European Commission Decision *Forex-Three Way Banana Split* (16 May 2019); Case C-8/08 *T-Mobile Netherlands* ECLI:EU:C:2009:343; Case 23-D-06 FCA Decision *Restauration Hauts-de-France* (14 June 2023).

34 UEFA (n 4), 84.

35 TFEU, art 102; French Commercial Code (n 24), art L 420-2.

60. This body of rules is further strengthened by the rules on the control of foreign subsidies, which govern investments by third countries in clubs. In this respect, any acquisition of a club must be notified to the European Commission, which will analyse the effects of the transaction on the internal market, if the acquisition involves financial contributions of more than 50 million euros from public authorities in non-EU countries. However, as in the case of merger control, the transaction will not have to be notified if the target club has a turnover of less than 500 million euros in the European Union, which limits the number of clubs concerned by this regulation.[36]

61. Competition law therefore allows the regulation of investment in clubs and maintains free competition between them as economic players. While these rules do not guarantee sporting fairness in the competitions in which clubs take part, they may, in some respects, appear to be adequate and sufficient to control the economic abuses of multi-club ownership and investment.

62. This raises the question of whether the sporting rules laid down by FIFA, UEFA or individual countries are really necessary to provide a framework for investment in football. Does the specificity of sport justify the implementation of these rules, which may hinder competition law?

II. Compatibility of Multi-Club Ownership and Investment Rules with Competition Law

63. Sport and the competition it creates between its players is different from the competition that exists between economic players active in other sectors. For competition authorities and courts, this specificity of sport, recognised by the Article 165 TFEU, justifies the application of rules which, if implemented on another market, could constitute restrictions of competition or be incompatible with EU law.[37]

64. However, this specificity of sport cannot be interpreted in such a way as to justify a general exemption from the application of EU law, which applies to sport.[38] Although rules which relate of "sporting interest only" may initially have appeared to fall outside the scope of competition law because they did not concern economic activity,[39] the European Court of Justice (ECJ) ruled in the *Meca-Medina* judgment of 2006 that "the mere fact that a rule is purely sporting in nature does not have the effect of removing from the scope of the Treaty the person engaging in the activity governed by that rule or the body which has laid it down".[40]

---

36 Council Regulation (EU) No 2022/2560 of the European Parliament and of the Council of 14 December 2022 on foreign subsidies distorting the internal market [2022] OJ L330/1.

37 TFEU, art 165. For example, sports federations or associations, such as UEFA, can set the maximum number of players who can take part in a competition over a given period, thus preventing any new players from entering the competition during that period.

38 European Commission, *White Paper on Sport* (11 July 2007).

39 Case 36/74 *Walrave and Koch v Association Union Cycliste Internationale and others* ECLI:EU:C:1974:140, point 8; Case 13/76 *Gaetano Donà v Mario Mantero* ECLI:EU:C:1976:115, point 14.

40 Case C-519/04 P *David Meca-Medina and Igor Majcen v Commission of the European Communities* ECLI:EU:C:2006:492, point 27.

65. Consequently, sporting activities, insofar as they constitute an economic activity, are subject to all the obligations arising from the various European provisions and, in particular, the competition rules set out in Articles 101 and 102 of the TFEU.[41]

66. When assessing whether sports rules comply with competition law, the European Commission and the Court of Justice apply the analytical framework adopted by the *Wouters* judgment, verifying, on a case-by-case basis, whether the rule in question pursues legitimate objectives and whether their anticompetitive effects, if any, are inherent and proportionate to the objectives pursued.[42]

67. In these circumstances, in order to analyse the compatibility of the multi-club ownership and investment sports rules with competition law, it is necessary to verify whether they may constitute restrictions of competition and whether, in the overall context in which they are applied, they appear justified and proportionate with regard to the objective they pursue.

1. Restrictions on Competition Potentially in Sporting Rules for Multi-Club Ownership and Investment

68. As detailed in Section I, FIFA and UEFA, which are not only undertakings but also associations of undertakings within the meaning of the French and European competition rules,[43] have enacted sporting rules relating to multi-club ownership and investment. These rules therefore constitute a decision by an association of undertakings which must be compatible with Article 101 TFEU and Article L 420-1 of the French Commercial Code and a decision by an undertaking which must be compatible with Article 102 TFEU and L 420-2 of the French Commercial Code.[44]

A. *The Compatibility of Multi-Club Ownership and Investment Sports Rules with Article 101 TFEU and Article L 420-1 French Commercial Code*

69. According to the terms of Articles 101 TFEU and L 420-1 of the French Commercial Code, as well as the decision-making practice of competition authorities, decisions by associations which have as their object or effect of controlling or limiting investment, freezing the structure of a market or creating barriers to market entry are anticompetitive.

70. In light of these observations, UEFA's rules may be anticompetitive in several respects.

---

41 TFEU, arts 101 and 102; *Walrave and Koch* (n 39), point 4; *Donà* (n 39), point 12; Case C-415/93 *Union Royale Belge Sociale de Football Association, RCL and UEFA v JM Bosman* ECLI:EU:C:1995:463, point 73; Joined Case C-51/96 *Christelle Deliège v Ligue francophone de judo et disciplines associées ASBL* and Case C-191/97 *Christelle Deliège v ASBL and François Pacquée* ECLI:EU:C:2000:199, point 41; Case C-176/96 *Lehtonen v FRBSB* ECLI:EU:C:2000:201, point 32; *Meca-Medina* (n 40), point 22.

42 Case C-309/99 *Wouters* ECLI:EU:C:2002:98, point 97; *Meca-Medina* (n 40), point 42; Case AT.37806 UEFA Decision *ENIC* (25 June 2002), points 30, 40–42.

43 Case C-333/21 *European Super League (ESL)* ECLI:EU:C:2023:1011, para 115.

44 TFEU, art 101; French Commercial Code (n 24), art L 420-1.

71. First of all, the rules on multi-club ownership and investment can have the effect of freezing the market positions of players insofar as they prevent clubs owned by the same owner from taking part in the same UEFA club competition.

72. These regulations can encourage owners to create a hierarchy between the various clubs they own. Thus, the owner determines a main club and "satellite" clubs, the main club being destined to take part in the most prestigious UEFA club competitions, while the satellite clubs are owned solely for economic reasons, to create synergies, pool costs, optimise detection networks, training and the development of players in order to improve the performance of the main club. For example, players can be trained or loaned to satellite clubs with the sole aim of being transferred to the main club at a favourable price. This scheme promotes the improvement of the main club's sporting performance, to the detriment of that of the satellite clubs, which are merely "player development platforms with no clear ambition to improv sporting results in the long term",[45] used as a subsidiary of a football multinational and which, in any case, will not be able to take part in the same competition as the main club.

73. Eventually, this could have the effect of freezing the positions of these clubs in the various European championships and competitions in which they participate and, as a result, harm sporting fairness within these same championships and competitions.

74. Moreover, UEFA's rules may have the effect of limiting investment in the football market. Indeed, investors may be discouraged from investing in several clubs at the same time, as these clubs will not be able to participate simultaneously in the most prestigious European competitions, harming the attractiveness of the clubs and the interest of these investments. Investors could also be dissuaded from acquiring stakes in several clubs to avoid ending up in a situation of non-compliance with UEFA rules, which would force them to adapt the structure of the clubs they have invested in or to disinvest, thereby jeopardising all the efforts made.

75. For example, French multi-club ownership regulations have recently changed to allow clubs practicing the same sport in France to be owned by a common owner if they play in a men's or women's league respectively.[46] Recognising the potentially negative impact that multi-club ownership regulations could have on investment, the French public authorities introduced this change to encourage investment in women's clubs and enable them to benefit from the advantages of multi-club ownership.

76. Furthermore, by limiting investment, multi-club ownership rules could also create barriers to entry for new clubs, but also a barrier to expansion for existing clubs that are not owned by an investor having shares in other clubs. These clubs, which would not be able to benefit from investments by multi-club shareholders who would be dissuaded from investing in several clubs due to regulations, would also be unable to take advantage of the economic and sporting benefits and synergies of multi-club ownership to improve their performance and market entry and/or expansion.

77. All things considered, the multi-club ownership rules could be seen as restrictive of competition in breach of Article 101 of the TFEU and Article L 420-1 of the French Commercial Code.

---

45 UEFA (n 4), 84.

46 French Sports Code (n 19).

B. *The Compatibility of Multi-Club Ownership and Investment Sports Rules with Article 102 TFEU and Article L 420-2 French Commercial Code*

78. The ECJ has recently pointed out that FIFA and UEFA hold a dominant position on the market for the organisation and marketing of interclub football competitions on European Union territory.[47] Consequently, the imposition of multi-club ownership and investment rules must not lead to an abuse of this dominant position by FIFA or UEFA.

79. However, by imposing these rules, which may have the effect of limiting investment and freezing the position of players on the market (see above), FIFA and UEFA are behaving in a way that can influence the structure of the market where the degree of competition is already weakened by the special and dominant position of these two associations.

80. These rules could also constitute a disproportionate means of achieving the objective of protecting the integrity of UEFA club competitions insofar as they discriminate between clubs by creating a competitive disadvantage for clubs that have common owners and are therefore unable to participate freely in UEFA club competitions, despite their sporting achievements.

81. In these circumstances, it might be argued that UEFA and FIFA are abusing their dominant position by enacting discriminatory rules that have the effect of foreclosing investors from the acquisition and management of clubs and limiting the development of clubs which cannot benefit from such investment.

82. This risk seems even more serious given that the ECJ recently ruled that FIFA and UEFA had abused their dominant position by enacting rules relating to the organisation of a competition,[48] paving the way for actions for anticompetitive practices by clubs or their investors.

83. As a result, multi-club ownership and investment sports rules might contain restrictions of competition and might be challenged on that basis, unless it can be proved that they are justified by the pursuit of legitimate and proportionate objectives or, more generally, justified by the specificity of sport as recognised by Article 165 TFEU.[49]

2. Justification and Proportionality of Multi-Club Ownership and Investment Sporting Rules in Relation to the Objective

84. For the reasons set out above, the sporting rules governing multi-club ownership and investment could, in some respects, constitute a restriction of competition.

85. The ECJ has consistently held that rules which have the effect of restricting competition, and which are inherent in the organisation and proper conduct of a

---

[47] *ESL* (n 43), points 117, 207.

[48] Ibid.

[49] TFEU, art 165.

sport, do not constitute an infringement of Community competition law where those effects are proportionate to the genuine legitimate sporting interest pursued.[50]

86. Accordingly, as is clear from the analytical grid laid down by the ECJ in the *Wouters* judgment of 19 February 2002,[51] it is necessary to examine, taking into account the overall context in which the rules were adopted or produce their effects, whether those rules pursue legitimate objectives and whether the consequential effects restrictive of competition are inherent in the pursuit of those objectives and proportionate to them.

87. With regard to the overall context in which the multi-club ownership rules were adopted, it should be noted that their general objective, as stated in the first paragraph of Article 5 of the UEFA regulations in question, is to "ensure the integrity of UEFA club competitions".[52] These rules were enacted with the aim of ensuring healthy competition in UEFA club competitions and combating the abuses arising from multi-club ownership and investment.

88. In these circumstances, as these measures are necessary to ensure the fairness and integrity of competitions, their effects, in particular on, (i) clubs whose participation in competitions may be limited if their shareholders are also shareholders in other clubs; and (ii) investors whose investments are limited, may be considered to be inherent to the proper functioning of competitions.

89. Therefore, even if the multi-club ownership and investment rules were to be regarded as restrictive of competition, they would nevertheless appear to be inherent and proportionate in relation to the objectives pursued and would not appear to constitute an infringement of competition law.

90. On the contrary, under the conditions set out above (Section II.), it might be argued that, while the objective pursued seems legitimate, the restrictions on competition resulting from the multi-club ownership and investment rules are neither necessary nor proportionate to that objective. Indeed, these rules might seem inadequate to ensure fairness between clubs and the integrity of competitions insofar as they freeze the positions of players on the market and limit investment and the attractiveness of the market.

91. In addition, the sanction of a ban on taking part in a competition for breaching these rules therefore appears particularly severe, as it prevents certain clubs from taking part in those competitions necessary to their visibility and development.

92. In some respects, these rules would not appear to be the least restrictive means of achieving the objective pursued, since general competition rules could provide a fairer framework for multi-club ownership and investment.

93. However, on various occasions and under certain conditions, multi-club ownership rules have been considered compatible with competition law.

94. For example, the European Commission has already held that UEFA's multi-club ownership rules were not intended to distort competition, but to guarantee

---

50 *Meca-Medina* (n 40).

51 *Wouters* (n 42), points 97, 110; *Meca-Medina* (n 40), point 42.

52 See, for example, UEFA Champions League Regulations (n 11), art 5.

the integrity of the competitions organised by UEFA and the uncertainty of their results. In particular, the Commission found that the rule was intended to ensure that the public, as consumers, retained the feeling that sporting competition was taking place between autonomous participants, without any conflict of interest, despite situations of multiple ownership of clubs which could, in the consumer's mind, reduce competition between those clubs.[53]

95. The Commission therefore held that the restriction on freedom of action resulting from the multi-club ownership rule was necessary and proportionate to the need to maintain public confidence in the integrity and authenticity of competitions, the objective pursued by that rule.

96. Consequently, the Commission indicated that, given the particular context in which the rule was applied, the restriction on freedom of action that it entailed was justified and could not be considered a restriction of competition.

97. More specifically, in this case, the Commission held that without this rule, the proper functioning of the market where the clubs develop their economic activities would be under threat, since the public's perception that the underlying sporting competition is fair and honest is an essential precondition to keep its interest and marketability. If UEFA's competitions were not credible and if consumers did not have the perception that the matches played represented an honest sporting competition between the participants, those competitions would be devalued, with the inevitable consequence, over time, of a decline in consumer confidence, interest and marketability.

98. In addition, the Commission found that the rule did not prevent capital investment in football clubs but merely prohibited several clubs with the same owner from participating in the same UEFA club competition. The Commission concludes that "investors or managers remain free to take control of or manage whatever number of clubs they want if they accept the risk that should more than one of these clubs qualify for the same UEFA competition, only one would play".[54]

99. All things considered, although this decision is old, it appears that its conclusions concerning the justification and proportionality of the regulations on multi-club ownership and investment could quite easily be applied today for the same reasons, and all the more so as these regulations appear to be more important than ever in controlling fast-growing multi-club ownership and investment in recent years.

100. In the same way as for the fair play regulations,[55] the regulations on multi-club ownership and investment could continue to apply in the long term by adapting to changes in the markets where football clubs operate.

---

53 *ENIC* (n 42).

54 Ibid.

55 In 2013, the European Commission rejected a complaint lodged by players' agent Daniel Striani against UEFA's financial fair play rules, which he considered incompatible with European competition rules. Although reformed, the financial fair play rules continue to apply today.

Multi-Club Ownership (MCO) and Multi-Club Investment (MCI) in South America: Corporate Structures, Regulatory Fragmentation and Competition Law across CONMEBOL

Vitor Butruce*
University of the State of Rio de Janeiro

1. Consider the following scenario. Club A and Club B, from different countries, but under the common ownership of Group C, qualify simultaneously for the CONMEBOL Libertadores. The Group is presented with an unenviable choice: either withdraw one of the clubs from the tournament or transfer control of one entity to a third party, thereby relinquishing the ability to direct its sporting and financial decisions. Group C chooses then to transfer the controlling shares and remove all directors from Club B to avoid any influence over the club while both clubs play the same competition. How to implement such a structure?

2. Now imagine a second situation, months later: the star player of Club B suffers a serious injury that may jeopardise his career. Group C also controls a top-flight

* CAS Arbitrator. Former President of the National Dispute Resolution Chamber of the Brazilian Football Confederation (2016–2022). Professor of Commercial Law at the University of the State of Rio de Janeiro (UERJ). Doctor of Commercial Law from the University of São Paulo (USP). Partner at BMA Advogados. Attorney in Rio de Janeiro and São Paulo, Brazil.

European club with one of the most advanced training centres in the world. The player wishes to undergo rehabilitation at that facility. Would it be reasonable to deny him access on the grounds that Club B must remain outside the scope of Group C's influence?

3. These are but two of the challenges brought about by multi-club ownership (MCO) and multi-club investment (MCI) structures, a phenomenon that is here to stay and whose new problems the football industry is currently trying to understand, while discussing potential responses.

4. A coherent regulatory roadmap on the matter is particularly pressing in South America, the world's principal exporter of football talent. The flow of players from the continent is one of the structural pillars of the global football economy, and any regulatory framework that fails to account for this reality risks either stifling legitimate investment or allowing the continent's clubs to be reduced to satellite operations within globally integrated ownership networks – which is incompatible with the status of those clubs as iconic institutions embedded in the social fabric of their communities, carrying deep historical legacies.

5. It is in this context that this contribution examines the MCO/MCI phenomenon from a South American perspective, adopting a transnational comparative methodology across the ten, South American Football Confederation (CONMEBOL), member associations. Where relevant, comparisons with European structures are drawn as a reference point. The contribution does not take a position for or against MCO as a corporate phenomenon but seeks to map the legal terrain and to offer constructive reflections on the regulatory framework that may best accommodate it.

I. The Phenomenon of MCO/MCI Groups

6. The expression "multi-club ownership" – or, in a broader formulation that has gained increasing currency, "multi-club investment" – refers to the situation in which the same natural or legal person acquires or exercises control, influence or economic interests over more than one football club, whether directly or through intermediaries. MCO typically refers to situations involving the exercise of control through majority shareholdings, board representation or contractual arrangements, whereas MCI captures a wider spectrum of relationships, including minority investments, indirect holdings and de facto influence exercised without formal equity participation. This chapter uses both concepts interchangeably where the context does not require differentiation.

7. The scale of the phenomenon is considerable. According to a CIES Sports Intelligence report on the matter, considering figures from 2023, more than 60% of the 128 overseas investments in football identified across the top two divisions of ten European countries constituted a case of MCO at the time the deal was concluded. As of December 2023, nearly 40% of the 341 clubs analysed were part of an MCO structure, with the majority-owner link accounting for 80% of these cases.[1]

---

[1] CIES, Club *Ownership* in *European Football: Foreign Investments, Private Capital & Multi-Club Ownership* (2024) 12 <https://www.cies.ch/fileadmin/OLD-SITE/documents/Research/20240306_ClubOwnership.pdf> accessed 27 May 2026.

8. Yet the phenomenon is far from monolithic in its effects.

9. MCO networks have produced remarkable sporting results: the legendary Brazilian club Botafogo, controlled by the Eagle Football group, won the 2024 CONMEBOL Libertadores and the national Campeonato Brasileiro after years of financial struggle; Manchester City, flagship of the City Football Group (CFG), has dominated the Premier League in the past decade and won the 2023 UEFA Champions League.

10. At the same time, these very same structures have generated significant distortions. The Botafogo case itself became emblematic of the risks: several key players were transferred to the French club within the same network and the USD 24 million prize money from the Libertadores victory was reportedly channelled to the group's European operations.[2] Concerns have also multiplied regarding opaque intra-group transfers that undermine the solidarity mechanism and sell-on clauses[3] – a particularly sensitive issue for South American clubs, whose economic model depends substantially on training and exporting talent.

11. This portrait allows us to identify at least four spheres in which MCO raises fundamental concerns: (a) the *integrity of competitions* – the credibility of the sporting contest when commonly owned clubs face each other or compete for the same title; (b) *financial and market integrity* – intra-group transfers at artificial values and circumvention of the solidarity mechanism and sell-on clauses; (c) *labour integrity* – players trapped in contractual arrangements that force circulation within the ownership network; and (d) the *sustainability of clubs* – the risk that South American institutions are instrumentalised as feeder operations within a global financial engineering structure.

II. The Current Regulatory Landscape

12. The regulatory treatment of MCO in South America can be described as fragmented at the transnational level, disparate within the federations, and potentially dispersed across domestic jurisdictions.

13. Unlike the European experience, where UEFA has developed a relatively cohesive regulatory framework since 1998, progressively refined through CAS jurisprudence, European Commission scrutiny and the practical demands of an expanding continental competition calendar, South America lacks an integrated normative structure on the subject. There is no harmonised set of rules and no unified enforcement mechanism. What exists is a patchwork of provisions at different levels

---

2 Case FC2413FE CFCB Decision *Olympique Lyonnais* (17 December 2024), noting Olympique Lyonnais's representation that anticipated cash inflows could include "prize money from Conmebol related to Botafogo after its Copa Libertadores victory". UEFA, Press Release, "2024/25 Club Monitoring: CFCB Takes Decision in Respect of Olympique Lyonnais" (3 February 2025) <https://fr.uefa.com/news-media/news/0296-1cf88fd4dcb7-b4c67990563e-1000--2024-25-club-monitoring-cfcb-takes-decision-in-respect-o/> accessed 27 May 2026.

3 Luiz Fernando Pimenta Ribeiro and Bernardo Fruchtengarten, "How Associated Party Transactions and Fair Market Value Assessment Are Redefining Multi-Club Ownership" (*Football Legal*, November 2025) 17 <https://www.football-legal.com/content/how-associated-party-transactions-and-fair-market-value-assessment-are-redefining-multi-club-ownership-by-luiz-fernando-pimenta-ribeiro-bernardo-fruchtengarten> accessed 27 May 2026.

of governance, each responding to different logics, adopted at different moments and operating with varying degrees of effectiveness.

14. That said, this landscape is not entirely devoid of reference points. Certain normative instruments offer relevant guidance and may constitute the regulatory lighthouses by which practitioners and regulators may orient themselves. Taken individually, none of them provides a comprehensive response to the challenges posed by MCO. But examined together, they reveal an emerging consciousness that the phenomenon demands attention and that the integrity of South American football competitions cannot be left entirely to the market. What follows is a survey of these instruments, beginning at the supranational level and descending to the domestic sphere.

1. FIFA

15. At the global level, FIFA's regulatory treatment of MCO has historically been characterised by a delegative approach.

16. Article 20, point 2, of the FIFA Statutes provides that member associations shall ensure that no natural or legal person "exercises control in any manner whatsoever" over more than one club "whenever the integrity of any match or competition could be jeopardised".[4] The provision does not define the concept of control, does not prescribe specific thresholds, and does not create a centralised enforcement mechanism. It establishes a general principle of prohibition, but delegates implementation to member associations.

17. A significant regulatory development occurred with the Regulations for the 2025 FIFA Club World Cup (FCWC).[5] Its Article 10, point1 introduced a detailed and directly enforceable MCO prohibition, establishing that no club may, directly or indirectly: (a) hold securities or shares of another participating club; or (b) be a member of another club; and that (c) no one may be involved or have any power in the management or sporting performance of more than one participating club. The provision goes beyond formal control: no individual or legal entity may have "control or influence" over more than one participating club, with this concept defined to include not only majority shareholdings, board appointment rights or other rights derived from shareholders' agreements, but also the ability "to exercise by any means a decisive influence in the decision-making of the club".

18. A third element of FIFA's framework concerns player loans. The current edition of the FIFA Regulations on the Status and Transfer of Players (RSTP) contains quantitative limitations on international loans (Article 10) and a prohibition on bridge transfers (Article 5bis). While not designed exclusively to address MCO, these provisions bear directly on the phenomenon: intra-group loan arrangements have been one of the principal mechanisms through which MCO networks circulate players across jurisdictions without triggering transfer fees.

---

4 FIFA Statutes (2021) <https://digitalhub.fifa.com/m/7e791c0890282277/original/FIFA-Statutes-2021.pdf accessed> 27 May 2026.

5 FIFA Regulations for the World Cup (2025) <https://digitalhub.fifa.com/m/18848e4224efbd91/original/FCWC25_Regulations_EN.pdf> accessed 27 May 2026.

19. Finally, a further layer of FIFA regulations that bears on MCO dynamics is Article 18bis of the RSTP – the rule known as the ban on third-party influence (TPI), – which provides that no club can enter into a contract which enables third parties to acquire "the ability to influence in employment and transfer-related matters its independence, its policies or the performance of its teams". Although the provision was not designed with MCO structures specifically in mind, its operative language is broad enough to serve as a normative reference point for the assessment of player movements within multi-club groups.

20. Taken together, these instruments reveal that FIFA has progressively expanded its regulatory footprint on MCO. Its current stance – articulated by its Chief Legal and Compliance Officer Emilio García Silvero at the 2025 AIAF Congress, held in Miami – favours progressive regulation over prohibition, emphasising transparency through potential enhanced disclosure obligations in the Transfer Matching System (TMS).

2. UEFA: The Comparative Benchmark

21. UEFA has developed a comprehensive regulatory framework, which operates at multiple levels and is the most developed reference point available. It comprises the specific regulations of each major European competition (the UEFA Champions League, the UEFA Europa League and the UEFA Conference League) and the UEFA Club Licensing and Financial Sustainability Regulations.[6]

22. Article 5.01 of the Regulations of each competition contains the substantive rules on MCO, structured around three pillars: (a) restrictions on clubs holding securities or shares in other participating clubs; (b) restrictions on clubs or individuals being simultaneously involved in the management of more than one club; and (c) prohibition on any individual or legal entity exercising "control or influence" over more than one club in the same competition.

23. The third pillar is the most significant. Under Article 5.01(c)(iv), "control or influence" is defined to include not only majority voting rights, board appointment powers, and shareholders" agreements, but also the ability "to exercise by any means a decisive influence in the decision-making of the club". This formulation – which was subsequently adopted by FIFA in Article 10.1 of the FCWC Regulations – extends the regulatory reach beyond formal equity ownership to capture de facto influence exercised through economic dependence, contractual arrangements or other non-equity mechanisms.

24. The interpretive framework regarding the matter was set out in a Circular Letter issued by the UEFA Club Financial Control Body (CFCB) First Chamber on 14 May 2024. The Circular provided a set of indicators used by the CFCB to assess whether a party has the capacity to exercise "decisive influence" over a club. These indicators are organised across four categories: (a) *shareholders' or members' rights* – triggered if a party holds 30% or more of a club's total

---

6 UEFA Regulations (2026) <https://documents.uefa.com/search/all?value-filters=FT_Competition_custom~%2522Clubs%2522*FT_ContentType_custom~%2522Competition+Regulations%2522*FullSeasonYears~%25222026%252F27%2522&content-lang=en-GB> accessed 27 May 2026.

shares, voting or economic rights or holds 10% or more while being the largest shareholder; (b) *financial support* – triggered if a party accounts for 30% or more of operating revenue, related-party borrowings, or share premium reserves, or provides financial security over the club's borrowings or secured financing through share pledges or asset charges; (c) *governance* – triggered if a party holds any position in the club's governing bodies or key executive roles, or has the ability to appoint or remove 30% or more of governing body members, or can influence key executive decisions through veto or other privileged rights; and (d) *player transfers* – triggered if three or more players have been transferred between the clubs during a season, or where a party enters into contracts that confer the ability to influence player-related decision-making (such as scouting or database arrangements).

25. Two features of the Circular merit particular attention. First, the CFCB clarified that these indicators are not exhaustive: even where none is formally triggered, a "detailed multi-criteria assessment" will still be performed, "taking into account the substance and not merely the form". Second, recognising that the short interval between the approval of the Competition Regulations (20 March 2024) and the compliance deadline (3 June 2024) could render divestiture unfeasible, the CFCB offered a temporary alternative: the transfer of all shares to an independent third party, such as a blind trust, under which the trustee would hold sole decision-making authority and be bound by a fiduciary duty to act exclusively in the club's best interest.

26. Under this approach, the CFCB permitted blind trust arrangements as a temporary solution for clubs within MCO structures that qualified for the same competition, notably Manchester City and Girona FC (both owned by the CFG) and Manchester United and Olympique Gymnaste Club (OGC) Nice (linked through INEOS). According to the Circular Letter, this alternative was limited to the 2024–2025 season and was subject to CFCB oversight of the independent structure.

27. In addition to the competition-specific eligibility rules, the UEFA Club Licensing and Financial Sustainability Regulations contain provisions that bear directly on MCO structures through the discipline of related-party transactions. Licence applicants must disclose their full legal group structure, including any football club in respect of which any identified party or its key management personnel holds any ownership interest, voting rights or "any other involvement or influence whatsoever" in its management, administration or sporting performance. All related-party transactions must be disclosed in the financial statements, broken down by category of related party, with details of amounts, terms, guarantees and outstanding balances, and arm's-length equivalence may only be asserted if it can be substantiated.

28. The regulations further prescribe specific accounting adjustments for intra-group player transfers, and, for the calculation of football earnings under the stability requirements, all income transactions – whether or not with a related party – must be reflected at fair value, with any excess above fair value excluded from relevant income; expense transactions below fair value must be adjusted upwards. Where the declared fair value of a transaction is contested, the CFCB may require an independent assessment by a UEFA-approved third-party assessor, free from conflicts of interest with the licensee or its related parties.

3. CONMEBOL: Club Licensing as an Indirect Regulatory Tool

29. CONMEBOL's treatment of MCO consists of an indirect approach, which operates through the mechanisms of club licensing rather than through a standalone, directly enforceable prohibition.[7]

30. The foundational statutory provision is Article 7 of the CONMEBOL Statutes, which requires member associations to include in their own statute's provisions ensuring that no natural or legal person can control more than one club. The formulation mirrors Article 20, point 2 of the FIFA Statutes – a delegative norm that transfers the responsibility for implementation to the domestic level without defining control, prescribing thresholds or creating a transnational enforcement mechanism.

31. The more consequential instrument is the CONMEBOL Club Licensing Regulations – the Reglamento de Licencia de Clubes.[8] Article 100 establishes that FIFA and CONMEBOL reserve the right to intervene where the same natural or legal person can influence the management, administration, or sporting performance of more than one club in the same competition. The specific legal criteria for club licensing relevant to MCO are set out in Table IV, Criterion J.03, which requires each licence applicant to submit a declaration confirming that no person involved in its management or sporting performance: (a) owns or trades securities of another club in the same competition; (b) holds majority voting rights in another participating club; (c) has the right to appoint or dismiss a majority of the board of another club; (d) controls majority voting rights of another participating club through a shareholders' agreement; or (e) is involved in any capacity in the management, administration, or sporting performance of another participating club.

32. A comparison between the CONMEBOL framework and the UEFA model analysed above reveals two points of attention. First, the enforcement mechanism: CONMEBOL operates through a self-declaration model that relies on the veracity of clubs' own declarations, without an independent investigatory capacity comparable to UEFA's CFCB or a specialised adjudicatory body to resolve contested cases. Second, the CONMEBOL framework does not employ the concept of "decisive influence" as a trigger for non-compliance with MCO regulations. The criteria in Criterion J.03 do not contain a catch-all provision designed to reach situations of indirect or de facto control exercised through economic dependence, contractual arrangements, or other non-equity mechanisms, but only an item forbidding involvement in the administration or sporting performance of another club.

33. In short, CONMEBOL's regulatory framework on MCO can be described as a first-generation instrument: it establishes a principle of disclosure and enumerates formal criteria, but it lacks the depth and the enforcement infrastructure that would be necessary to address the phenomenon in its current complexity.

---

7 On the matter, see Júlia Pons Huguet and Alejandro Naranjo Acosta, "Multi-Club Ownership: A Challenge for Sport Governance Institutions" (*Football Legal*, November 2025) 19.

8 CONMEBOL Club Licensing Regulations (2018) <https://cdn.conmebol.com/wp-content/uploads/documents/reglamento-de-licencia-de-clubes-espanol.pdf> accessed 27 May 2026.

4. Brazil: A Multi-Layered Regulatory Approach

34. Brazil has been the primary gateway for the arrival of MCO in South America, catalysed by the enactment of Law No. 14.193/2021, which created the sociedade anônima do futebol (SAF) – a corporate vehicle designed for football clubs. The SAF legislation enabled traditional clubs to attract investors by transforming their football operations into companies. In rapid succession, the Eagle Football group acquired Botafogo SAF, 777 Partners acquired Vasco da Gama SAF and the City Football Group gained control of Bahia SAF.

35. Among the ten CONMEBOL member countries, Brazil has the most developed normative framework on MCO, distributed across three layers. The first is federal legislation. The General Sports Law (Lei Geral do Esporte, Law No. 14.597/2023) establishes, in Article 62, a broad prohibition on simultaneous participation in capital or management of two clubs competing in the same professional competition. The prohibition extends to situations of indirect control through contractual relationships and to spouses and relatives up to the second degree, as well as to controlling companies, subsidiaries and affiliated entities (Article 62, Sections 1–2). It addresses the scenario in which commonly controlled clubs compete in the same domestic championship, without reaching cross-border ownership structures.

36. The second layer is the SAF Law itself (Law No. 14.193/2021). Article 4 establishes that: (a) the controlling shareholder of a SAF may not hold participation in another SAF, directly or indirectly; and (b) a shareholder holding 10% or more of the voting or total share capital, without controlling it, may neither vote nor participate in the management of that or another SAF if it also participates in the capital of another SAF. Article 6 requires any legal entity holding 5% or more of the share capital to disclose to the club and to the Brazilian Football Confederation (Confederação Brasileira de Futebol – CBF) the identity of its ultimate beneficial owner, failing which its shareholder rights may be suspended.[9]

37. The third layer, which is the most recent addition to the Brazilian regulatory framework, is the CBF's own regulatory instrument: the Financial Sustainability Regulation (Regulamento de Sustentabilidade Financeira), approved in December 2025.

38. Articles 85 to 88 of this Regulation address MCO directly and constitute the most detailed set of MCO rules adopted by a South American national football association to date. The framework is structured around four pillars: prohibition, remediation, transactional controls and disclosure.

39. The core prohibition is set out in Article 86: no natural or legal person may hold, directly or indirectly, control or "significant influence" (influência significativa) over more than one club if both clubs, in the same season, are eligible to participate in

[9] The disclosure obligation under Article 6 of the SAF Law became particularly significant in the dispute involving CR Vasco da Gama and the 777 Partners group, where an alleged undisclosed change of control in the ownership chain formed part of the argument that led a Brazilian court to remove representatives linked to that MCO group from Vasco's management: Court of Justice of the State of Rio de Janeiro, Case 0858899-13.2024.8.19.0001 (15 March 2024) 4th Business Court.

the same CBF professional competition, or compete in divisions of the Campeonato Brasileiro with a direct promotion-and-relegation relationship (first and second divisions, for example). The concept of "significant influence" is defined in Article 86, Section 1, as the capacity to direct financial or operational policies, exercise material veto rights, appoint key executives, or hold individually or jointly more than 10% of voting rights coupled with voting agreements, veto powers, or financing covenants conferring decision-making authority. The calculation aggregates the participations of the person (or ultimate controllers, in the case of legal entities) with those of their spouse or partner and relatives up to the second degree (Section 2).

40. The remediation mechanism is particularly noteworthy. Article 86, Section 3, provides that, if a prohibited situation is identified – the CBF's National Authority for Regulation and Financial Sustainability (Autoridade Nacional de Regulação e Sustentabilidade Financeira (ANRESF)) – must set a remediation deadline for the divestiture of participations, the constitution of a blind trust previously approved and supervised by the ANRESF or other measures of effective separation. Remediation must be completed at least 30 days before the start of the competition in which the conflict arises. Article 86, Section 4 imposes a comprehensive standstill on inter-club operations within the same ownership ecosystem until remediation is achieved: player transfers and loans, sponsorship arrangements, service-sharing, exchange of sensitive or strategic information and secondment of technical staff or executives are all prohibited, unless the ANRESF grants prior authorisation on the basis of an independent valuation confirming market-rate terms.

41. Two additional features complete the framework.

42. Article 86, Section 6, prohibits the simultaneous participation of key executives in clubs within the same ownership structure, extending this prohibition to their spouses and relatives up to the second degree (Section 7). In addition, Article 87, subjects player transfers between related clubs to the specific associated-party transaction rules, establishing a framework for fair market value assessment that echoes the Premier League's Associated Party Transaction regime.

43. Finally, Article 88 imposes a mandatory disclosure obligation: clubs and their ultimate controllers must declare to the ANRESF, at the beginning of each season and whenever changes occur, the existence of any participation or interest that may constitute control or significant influence over another club – with the omission or falsification of such declaration constituting an autonomous serious infraction triggering automatic disciplinary proceedings. Non-compliance with the MCO rules may result in sanctions ranging from licence refusal or revocation, as well as transfer ban and point deductions, regulatory fines, and relegation or exclusion from the competition, in cases of gravity or recidivism (Article 86, Section 5).

5. Argentina: The Structural Resistance Model

44. Argentina occupies a singular position in the South American regulatory landscape, since its legal framework for football clubs is designed in such a way that makes MCO structurally very difficult.

45. Under Argentine law, football clubs are required to be constituted as non-profit civil associations (asociaciones civiles sin fines de lucro), pursuant to Law No. 20.655 (Ley del Deporte, 1974), and the Asociación del Fútbol Argentino (AFA) Statutes entrench this requirement as a mandatory condition for membership: Article 10(2) provides that only civil associations without profit motive may be affiliated to the AFA. Article 18(5) adds a further layer, prohibiting the president, vice-president or any other member of the executive board of a club from holding executive functions in another AFA member club if this would endanger fair play or football integrity. The result is a regulatory structure in which the question of MCO does not arise in its conventional form: if clubs cannot have shareholders, they cannot have common shareholders.[10]

46. The Argentine experience, however, is not entirely free from MCO dynamics. Grupo Pachuca, which controls Club de Fútbol Pachuca and Club León in Mexico and Everton de Viña del Mar in Chile, was involved between 2014 and 2016 with Club Atlético Talleres through advisory and commercial arrangements that did not require a formal equity stake.[11] This illustrates a broader dynamic: even in a jurisdiction where the civil association model formally precludes direct equity ownership, the influence channels associated with MCO can operate through contractual and relational mechanisms that do not require a formal shareholding.

47. From a comparative regulatory perspective, the Argentine case offers an important counterpoint to the Brazilian model. While Brazil has embraced private investment through the SAF structure and is now constructing a multi-layered regulatory framework to manage its MCO consequences, Argentina has maintained a structural prohibition rooted in associative law and social policy.

6. The Remaining CONMEBOL Members: A Panoramic Survey

48. While the limits of this contribution do not allow a detailed analysis of each of the ten CONMEBOL member associations, an overview of the remaining eight jurisdictions may help the reader to have a broader view of the status of the subject in the region.

49. Uruguay presents perhaps the most developed regulatory framework outside Brazil. Law No. 17.292/2001 established a specific corporate form for clubs in official competitions, the sociedades anónimas deportivas (SADs). Crucially for the MCO analysis, Article 73 (as amended by Article 89 of Law No. 20.212) provides that no natural or legal person may simultaneously hold shares exceeding 1% of the capital in two or more SADs that participate in the same competition. The calculation

---

10 This resistance, however, has been the subject of a remarkable political and judicial confrontation between President Javier Milei, the AFA and the football community in Argentina. For more detail on the matter, see Pablo Barbieri, *Football Law* (DyD 2024) 45–57; and Ariel Reck, "The Dispute between the Government and the Argentine Football Federation over the Civil or Corporate Structure for Football Clubs" (*Football Legal*, May 2024) 250–251.

11 ESPN Digital, "Grupo Pachuca's Agreement with Talleres has Ended" (22 December 2016) <https://espndeportes.espn.com/futbol/mexico/nota/_/id/2901822/finalizo-acuerdo-de-grupo-pachuca-con-talleres> accessed 27 May 2026.

aggregates shares held by the holder and by any person or entity constituting with them a "decision-making unit" (unidad de decisión). Infringements trigger a mandatory divestiture obligation within 30 days, enforced through public auction without reserve, if necessary.

50. Uruguay's framework is notable for two reasons: it is the only jurisdiction in CONMEBOL that prescribes a quantitative threshold (1%) for cross-ownership, rather than relying on the qualitative concept of "control" or "decisive influence"; and the concept of "decision-making unit" introduces a form of consolidated beneficial ownership assessment absent from the CONMEBOL licensing regulations. The practical relevance of this framework is illustrated by the CFG's acquisition of Club Atlético Torque (now Montevideo City Torque) in 2017, which transformed a small Uruguayan club into a node of the CFG global network.[12]

51. Chile occupies a distinctive position as well. Chilean law permits clubs to adopt corporate structures, and the country has been receptive to foreign investment in football – Grupo Pachuca currently controls Everton de Viña del Mar as part of a wider network. However, at the time of writing, Chile did not have a statutory provision specifically prohibiting or regulating MCO. This gap is set to be addressed by a comprehensive reform of Law No. 20.019, approved by Congress on 6 April 2026, which amends the regime governing professional sports organisations. The new Article 21 establishes a prohibition on multi-club integration: ultimate beneficial owners and their related persons who hold 3% or more of the voting shares in one professional sports base organisation (organización deportiva profesional de base) may not hold shares in another base organisation within the same league. In the specific case of football, the prohibition is absolute: no person may be a shareholder of more than one entity regulated by the law, or a member of more than one corporación or fundación with a professional sports fund, within the same league. Non-compliance triggers a mandatory three-month divestiture period, followed by suspension of political and economic rights attached to the shares, escalating fines and a prohibition on participating in the ownership of any professional sports entity while the infringement persists. The law also introduces a broad definition of "beneficial owner" (beneficiario final), drawing on the criteria of the Securities Market Law (Law No. 18.045), and requires leagues to publish annual lists of beneficial owners, subject to semi-annual review by the supervisory authorities. If enacted in its current form, the Chilean reform would place the country alongside Brazil and Uruguay as the third CONMEBOL jurisdiction with a dedicated statutory MCO framework.[13]

52. Bolivia offers a particularly instructive case of MCO dynamics operating outside formal regulatory frameworks. Marcelo Claure, a Bolivian-born entrepreneur, controls Club Bolívar – Bolivia's most successful club. In January 2021, Club

12 City Football Group, "Montevideo City Torque Launches Brand-New Identity to Kick-Off Season" (22 January 2020) <https://espndeportes.espn.com/futbol/mexico/nota/_/id/2901822/finalizo-acuerdo-de-grupo-pachuca-con-talleres> accessed 27 May 2026.

13 At the time this chapter was finalised, the reform of Law No. 20.019 had been approved by both chambers of the Chilean Congress (Oficio No. 21.134, 6 April 2026) and transmitted to the Constitutional Court for mandatory constitutional review but had not yet been promulgated.

Bolívar became the CFG's first "partner club", entailing a long-term collaboration granting access to scouting methodologies, proprietary data platforms and youth development resources, without CFG acquiring an equity stake.[14] The case is significant because it demonstrates that MCO influence can operate through contractual and advisory arrangements that fall outside the formal criteria of the CONMEBOL licensing regulations. Claure is also indirectly connected with the City Football Group through his investment of 35% of the shares of Girona FC in Spain – creating a web of indirect links spanning three confederations (CONMEBOL, CONCACAF and UEFA) that illustrates the type of indirect MCO the current regulatory framework is least equipped to address.[15]

53. Peru has enacted specific sports corporate legislation: Law No. 29.504/2010 promotes the transformation of professional football clubs into sociedades anónimas abiertas (open stock corporations), establishing governance requirements including mandatory ethics and audit committees, annual audited financial reporting and disclosure obligations to the Instituto Peruano del Deporte. While the legislation does not contain a specific MCO provision, the disclosure infrastructure it creates provides a foundation upon which MCO monitoring could, in principle, be constructed.

54. Colombia, Ecuador, Paraguay and Venezuela complete the CONMEBOL panorama. The author's research has not identified specific statutory provisions on MCO in any of these jurisdictions, nor dedicated MCO rules in their federation statutes beyond the general obligation delegated by Article 7 of the CONMEBOL Statutes. These jurisdictions are not, however, entirely untouched by MCO dynamics: the CFG has maintained partnerships with Atlético Venezuela,[16] and the growing presence of cross-border investment networks means that MCO influence can reach these markets through contractual and advisory channels even in the absence of formal equity ownership.

55. A synthesis of the panoramic survey suggests a taxonomy of three regulatory models across the CONMEBOL region: (a) jurisdictions with specific corporate legislation for football and domestic MCO provisions (Brazil, Uruguay and upon promulgation, Chile); (b) jurisdictions with specific corporate legislation but without domestic MCO provisions (Peru); and (c) jurisdictions without either specific corporate legislation for football or domestic MCO provisions (Argentina, Colombia, Paraguay, Bolivia, Ecuador and Venezuela).

56. The regulatory asymmetry across the region creates the conditions for what practitioners refer to as *regulatory arbitrage*: the ability of sophisticated investors to structure their operations through the jurisdiction that offers the least resistance, while accessing the talent and commercial markets of the most attractive ones.

---

14 City Football Group, "Club Bolívar Joins City Football Group as first Partner Club" (11 January 2021) <https://www.cityfootballgroup.com/post/club-bolivar-joins-city-football-group-as-first-partner-club> accessed 27 May 2026.

15 Girona FC, "Marcelo Claure Strengthens the Girona FC Project" (28 August 2020) <https://www.gironafc.cat/en/news/marcelo-claure-strengthen-the-girona-fc-project> accessed 27 May 2026.

16 Manchester City FC, "CFG Extends South American Footprint" (5 April 2017) <https://www.mancity.com/news/club-news/club-news/2017/april/city-football-group-extends-south-american-footprint-club-atletico-torque-atletico-venezuela> accessed 27 May 2026.

III. The Key Precedents Shaping the Understanding of MCO

57. The regulatory framework examined in the preceding sections has been shaped, tested and in several cases validated by a body of case law that spans more than 25 years.

1. The ENIC Case

58. It was the rise of ENIC plc, an English company listed on the London Stock Exchange, that brought the issue of cross-border MCO to the centre of international attention. ENIC had acquired controlling interests in AEK Athens (Greece), SK Slavia Prague (Czech Republic), Vicenza Calcio (Italy) and FC Basel (Switzerland), while holding a minority stake in Glasgow Rangers FC (Scotland). The critical moment arrived during the 1997–1998 season, when AEK, Slavia and Vicenza qualified simultaneously for the quarterfinals of the UEFA Cup Winners' Cup. Although the draw avoided pitting them against one another, the scenario was sufficiently alarming to prompt UEFA into action.

59. On 19 May 1998, the UEFA Executive Committee adopted the rule: Integrity of the UEFA Club Competitions: Independence of the Clubs, prohibiting any individual or legal entity from being able to influence the management, administration or sporting performance of more than one club in the same UEFA competition. This regulatory response precipitated the foundational legal dispute in the history of MCO: the arbitration brought by AEK Athens and SK Slavia Prague against UEFA before the CAS.

60. The CAS Panel delivered its award on 20 August 1999, which became a relevant guide on MCO regulation in football.[17]

61. The Panel began by clarifying the concept of "integrity of the game" – a notion that had occupied the centre of the parties' arguments. Integrity, the Panel held, encompasses not only honesty and uprightness, but also the "authenticity of results": the requirement that matches and competitions be publicly perceived as "a true test of the best possible athletic, technical, coaching and management skills of the opposing sides". As the Panel observed, drawing upon the language used by EC Commissioner for Competition Policy Karel Van Miert, "if clubs with the same owner can take part in the same competitions, whether national or international, doubts may arise as to whether the outcome is really undecided in advance".

62. The Panel also identified three specific dimensions in which MCO creates conflicts of interest – dimensions that arise even on the assumption that multi-club owners act in compliance with the law and do not try to directly fix any match. The first concerns the *allocation of resources* by the common owner among its clubs: the Panel reasoned that a rational common owner would tend to concentrate the best players and resources on a "first team" – typically the club situated in the more lucrative market, – while relegating the other to a secondary role, useful for,

---

17 Case 98/200 CAS Decision *AEK Athens and SK Slavia Praha* (20 August 1999). For an authoritative first-hand account of the CAS proceedings, by the President of the CAS Panel that decided the case, see Massimo Coccia, "The Multi-Club Ownership Issue: When and How It All Started" (*Football Legal*, November 2025) 72–75.

inter alia, "allowing younger players to gain experience and to be tested with a view to a possible transfer to the first team". The second dimension relates to the *administration of commonly owned clubs* before a match between them: even without direct match-fixing, a common owner has means of conditioning competitive outcomes – through bonus structures, player transfers, insider information and the day-to-day logistics of team management. The third concerns the *interest of third clubs*: in round-robin group stages, a third club placed alongside two commonly owned clubs may be structurally disadvantaged, as the common owner can facilitate an "entente cordiale" between its clubs.

63. On the question of proportionality, the Panel held that the UEFA rule was "objectively necessary in order to provide the consumers with a credible sporting contest" and that it was "not more extensive than necessary to serve the fundamental goal of preventing conflicts of interest which would be publicly perceived as affecting the authenticity, and then the uncertainty, of results in UEFA competitions". The Panel also observed that the rule did not prohibit MCO as such: it merely prevented commonly controlled clubs from participating in the same UEFA competition, leaving investors free to acquire shareholdings in multiple clubs across different competitions. Having examined the various less restrictive alternatives proposed by the claimants – including codes of ethics, ad hoc case-by-case examinations, independent trusts and restrictions on bonuses and transfers, – the Panel found none to be a viable substitute: control of more than one club in the same competition was, in the Panel's assessment, "so inherently conducive to a conflict of interest, and to the related public suspicions, that there is no scope for the examination of individual cases".

2. Subsequent CAS Proceedings

64. From 1999 until 2025, several proceedings have tested the boundaries and confirmed the direction established by the *ENIC* award, albeit in distinct factual and regulatory settings.

65. In, the Panel addressed multiple ownership in Mexican football. Club de Fútbol Atlante appealed against a decision of the *Federación Mexicana de Fútbol* (FMF) which, in essence, allowed TV Azteca to acquire control of Club Atlas despite already controlling Club Monarcas Morelia.[18] The Panel dismissed the appeal, finding that the FIFA rules on multiple ownership were not directly applicable, since the absence of domestic MCO regulation in the FMF framework reflected a "conscious decision" rather than an inadvertent gap. The Panel also held that the FIFA rule on multiple ownership "is not absolute but is based on a case-by-case assessment of the jeopardy caused to the integrity of football matches or competitions", affording the competent sporting bodies "a certain degree of discretion" – a standard of review under which Atlante failed to substantiate that the common ownership of Atlas and Monarcas had in fact jeopardised the integrity of the Liga MX.

---

[18] Case 2014/A/3523 CAS Decision *Club de Fútbol Atlante v Federación Mexicana de Fútbol (FMF)* (31 October 2014).

66. More recently, the 2024–2025 season produced three CAS awards: *Drogheda United FC v UEFA*, *FK DAC 1904 v UEFA*, and *Crystal Palace FC v UEFA*, all of which signalled that the compliance deadline set in the Regulations would be strictly enforced, that blind trust arrangements were acceptable only when they genuinely severed control and influence, and that "decisive influence" would be applied functionally rather than formally.[19]

3. The Pachuca/León Case

67. The most significant recent addition to the MCO jurisprudence is the consolidated proceeding, in which the CAS addressed a paradigmatic MCO situation in Mexican football.[20]

68. The case arose from the qualification of both Club Pachuca and Club León, two Mexican clubs controlled by the same family through Grupo Pachuca, for the inaugural FIFA Club World Cup 2025. The patriarch of the controlling family held 87% of the shares in Club Pachuca and approximately 66% of the shares in Club León, with the boards of both clubs composed almost entirely of family members. Liga MX itself had imposed restrictions on the clubs and required divestiture by 2027.

69. Following a preliminary investigation into the clubs' ownership structure, the FIFA Disciplinary Committee opened proceedings against the clubs for an alleged breach of Article 10.1 of the FCWC Regulations, which were then referred directly to the FIFA Appeal Committee. On 20 March 2025, the Chairperson of the FIFA Appeal Committee found that both clubs failed to meet the eligibility criteria under Article 10.1 – the first appealed decision. On the following day, the FIFA Secretary General exercised his discretion under Article 10.4 to admit Club Pachuca and exclude Club León from the competition – the second appealed decision. Both clubs appealed to the CAS.

70. The clubs' main attempt to resolve the MCO situation was the establishment of the León Trust, settled on 1 March 2025 under Texas law. However, the trust agreement granted the settlors an unrestricted right to reacquire trust assets by substituting other property of equivalent value, exercisable "without the consent of any other person (including the Trustee)". The Panel found that this right constituted a fundamental deficiency, since the trust "could easily cease to perform its function during the Competition". Multiple channels of continuing influence were identified: the absence of meaningful restrictions on communication between trustees and settlors; the trustees' lack of experience in football management; and the continuing role of the patriarch's son as president of Club León, a position from which the trustees could not remove him. The principle of substance over form pervaded the analysis, with the Panel stating: "while a trust, in principle, might have allowed the Clubs to comply with the CWC Regulations (depending

[19] Case 2025/A/11495 CAS Decision *Drogheda United FC v UEFA* (16 June 2025); Case 2025/A/11566 CAS Decision *FK DAC 1904 v UEFA* (14 July 2025); Case 2025/A/11604 CAS Decision *Crystal Palace FC v UEFA* (11 August 2025).

[20] Cases 2025/A/11314; 11315 and 11316 CAS Decisions *Pachuca/León* (6 May 2025).

on its concrete features), the mere settlement of any trust whatsoever cannot lead to a presumption of compliance". The Panel dismissed all three appeals and upheld both appealed decisions, albeit for partially different reasons than those stated by the FIFA Appeal Committee.

71. On the broader question of the proportionality of Article 10 of the FCWC Regulations, the Panel confirmed the analysis established in *AEK Athens*. Noting that "MCO poses a threat to the integrity of sporting competition, both in practical terms (eg inter-team transfers, unequal resource allocation and potentially match fixing, to name a few) and in the public's perception", the Panel held that FIFA had a "prima facie legitimate aim in tackling these issues through regulatory means, particularly when it comes to its own competitions". The criteria of Article 10.1 were found to be "necessary" and "not so onerous as to deprive owners from having two clubs participate, as long as they can demonstrate that only one participating club is under their direct control and influence".

72. Finally, the Panel acknowledged that a trust could, in principle, constitute a valid compliance mechanism "when constructed correctly", thereby leaving the door open for future structures while setting a demanding standard of genuine operational independence.

IV. The Competition Law Dimension: Limits and Possibilities of Sports Regulation at the Frontier of Antitrust

73. The regulatory analysis of MCO cannot be confined to the instruments of sports governance. The subject engages the frontier of Competition Law – a discipline that has emerged as a decisive arbiter of the limits of sports governing bodies' regulatory autonomy, particularly due to the European Court of Justice (ECJ) activity over major football cases.

74. In the European context, the ECJ's judgments in *European Super League*[21] and *Royal Antwerp FC*[22] establish that FIFA and UEFA hold a dominant position on the market for the organisation and marketing of interclub football competitions, and that their regulatory activity is subject to the discipline of EU antitrust law. For South America, one must wonder whether an analogous framework of external constraint exists or might be constructed.

75. For present purposes, it is sufficient to establish two foundational premises for the ECJ analysis.[23] First, regulations adopted by sports governing bodies are viewed by the ECJ as "decisions by associations of undertakings" within the meaning of Article 101(1) of the Treaty on the Functioning of the European Union (TFEU), which

---

21 Case C-333/21 *European Super League (ESL)* ECLI:EU:C:2023:1011.

22 Case C-680/21 *Royal Antwerp FC* ECLI:EU:C:2023:1010.

23 For a detailed analysis on the application of antitrust law to sports governing bodies, see Peter W Heermann, "How Does Antitrust Law Apply to Sports Governing Bodies? Which Sporting Rules Fall Under the Scope of EU Antitrust Law?" (*Football Legal*, May 2024) 52–61 <https://www.football-legal.com/content/how-does-antitrust-law-apply-to-sports-governing-bodies-which-sporting-rules-fall-under-the-scope-of-eu-antitrust-law-by-peter-w-heermann> accessed 27 May 2026.

means that they are prohibited if they "affect trade between Member States" and "have as their object or effect, the prevention, restriction or distortion of competition within the internal market". Second, the analytical tool for assessing whether such regulations are compatible with competition law is the *Meca-Medina* test:[24] a sporting rule that restricts competition does not infringe Article 101 TFEU if: (a) it pursues a legitimate objective; (b) its restrictive effects are inherent in the pursuit of that objective; and (c) the restriction is proportionate to the objective pursued.

76. That the existence of MCO rules satisfies this test has been confirmed by both the CAS and the European Commission. In the *ENIC* case, the CAS Panel held that the UEFA rule did not have the object or effect of restricting competition: by preventing a concentration of club ownership into fewer hands, the rule preserved economic competition between club owners and sporting competition between clubs. The European Commission endorsed these findings, confirming that without the rule "the proper functioning of the market where the clubs develop their economic activities would be under threat".[25] The *Pachuca/León* CAS Panel reaffirmed this reasoning, holding that "MCO poses a threat to the integrity of sporting competition" and that FIFA had a "prima facie legitimate aim in tackling these issues through regulatory means".

77. Beyond the compatibility of sports regulations with competition law, MCO structures may themselves be subject to scrutiny by domestic antitrust authorities through merger control. The paradigmatic case is the decision of the French Competition Authority (Autorité de la concurrence) in the acquisition of OGC Nice by the INEOS Group[26] – reported as the first known case in which a competition authority defined a market for the transfer of professional football players as a relevant market, with at least European dimensions.[27]

78. In Brazil, the Administrative Council for Economic Defense (Conselho Administrativo de Defesa Econômica (CADE) also operates a mature merger control system, and the acquisition of SAF structures by MCO groups constitutes, in principle, a notifiable act, provided that the statutory criteria regarding the turnover of the parties involved in the transaction are met.[28]

79. There is, moreover, an emerging dynamic that warrants attention: CADE has signalled an increasing willingness to intervene in the football sector. The authority proactively notified the clubs involved in the first transactions carried out under the

---

24 Case C-519/04 P *David Meca-Medina and Igor Majcen v Commission of the European Communities* ECLI:EU:C:2006:492.

25 Case AT.37806 UEFA Decision *ENIC* (25 June 2002).

26 Case 19-DCC-160 Autorité de la concurrence Decision *Ineos/Gymnaste Club de Nice* (21 August 2019).

27 On the matter, see "Takeover of OGC Nice by INEOS Group: An Analysis by the French Competition Authority" (*Football Legal*, January 2021) 90–91 <https://www.football-legal.com/content/takeover-of-ogc-nice-by-ineos-group-an-analysis-by-the-french-competition-authority> accessed 27 May 2026.

28 This was the case, for example, in the transaction involving the transfer of control of the shares of the SAF constituted to conduct the activities of Clube Atlético Mineiro (CADE Case No 08700.006273/2023-87 September 2023) and in the sale of the shares comprising the controlling block of the holding company that controlled Cruzeiro SAF, by Ronaldo Nazário to the current controlling shareholder (CADE Case No 08700.003369/2024-74 June 2024). In the *Atlético Mineiro* case, it is also worth noting that one of the shareholders had to divest its interest in Coimbra Esporte Clube SAF, a club whose main activity is the training of young talents, which was required in light of the restrictions on the simultaneous participation of a controlling shareholder in more than one SAF.

new law, with the purpose of investigating whether they had failed to notify them – which turned out not to be the case, as neither transaction reached the thresholds set out in the law for mandatory notification to the antitrust authority.[29] This signalling also stems from CADE's ruling on an alleged gun jumping practice concerning the commercialisation of broadcasting rights for the Brazilian Football Championship[30] and in the recent announcement of a cooperation agreement between CADE and the Ministry of Sport aimed at strengthening integrity and competition in the industry.[31]

80. Since the French precedent demonstrates that the analysis of a football club acquisition may involve the delineation of football-specific markets, this methodological step, if applied by South American authorities, could produce consequences far beyond the immediate transaction. This reminds the industry of a broader regulatory lesson: the inertia of sports governing bodies in addressing structural problems tends to open space for state intervention.

81. It is at this point that the sharpest contrast with the European experience becomes apparent. FIFA and UEFA, while headquartered in Switzerland, operate a system that extends its effects across EU territory and encounters the external constraints of EU law, including the adjudicatory function of the ECJ. The South American market has neither of these features.

82. At the regional level, Mercosur, the Southern Common Market established by the Treaty of Asunción, operates as an intergovernmental arrangement, not a supranational legal order: its normative instruments lack direct applicability, it does not possess a supranational court, and its competition law instruments have progressively retreated from harmonisation towards mere cooperation between national authorities.

83. The trajectory of Mercosur's competition instruments confirms this assessment. The 1996 Fortaleza Protocol – the first regional instrument with harmonising ambition – was ratified only by Brazil and Paraguay and was subsequently revoked by the 2010 Competition Defence Agreement,[32] which abandoned normative harmonisation in favour of cooperation between national authorities. The EU–Mercosur Provisional Agreement on Trade[33] includes a chapter on competition that mirrors, to some extent, the language of Articles 101 and 102 TFEU, but operates through cooperation and does not create a supranational enforcement mechanism.

84. Separately, the Andean Community comprises Bolivia, Colombia, Ecuador and Peru, and Decision 608/2005 establishes a competition framework of a more supranational character.[34] To date, however, no application of that regime to the

---

[29] This was the case in the transactions involving the constitution and sale of the controlling block of shares of the SAFs relating to Botafogo (CADE Case No 08700.003313/2022-58) and Cruzeiro (CADE Case No 08700.003312/2022-11), both decided in October 2022.

[30] CADE Cases No 08700.007461/2023-22 and No 08700.005511/2023-37 February 2026.

[31] CADE, "CADE Signs Technical Cooperation Agreement with the Ministry of Sport" (9 April 2026) <https://www.gov.br/cade/pt-br/assuntos/noticias/cade-firma-acordo-de-cooperacao-tecnica-com-ministerio-do-esporte-1> accessed 27 May 2026.

[32] Decision of the Common Market Council No 43/10 (16 December 2010).

[33] EU–Mercosur Partnership Agreement (Trade Pillar) COM (2025) 357 final.

[34] Andean Community of Nations Antitrust Law Decision 608/2005.

sporting sector appears to have been reported in the Andean Community's official competition practice.

85. In sum, unlike FIFA or UEFA, whose regulatory output is currently being tested against Articles 101 and 102 TFEU before the ECJ, CONMEBOL operates in a space where external competition law constraints remain comparatively less developed. Any such challenge would likely have to proceed either before a national authority applying domestic competition law, or under the Andean Community regime, which – although supranational in structure and capable of reaching cross-border effects – has no recorded history of application in sports-related matters and, in this field, does not play a role comparable to that of the ECJ in the European Union.

86. This observation cuts in two directions. On one hand, it suggests in theory that CONMEBOL may enjoy a wider margin of regulatory discretion than UEFA. On the other hand, it means that the proportionality of CONMEBOL's regulatory choices would potentially be taken to the CAS – which, as the *Pachuca/León* award demonstrates, applies the *ratio decidendi* established in the *ENIC* case and, by extension, the principles of the *Meca-Medina* test. In other words, the CAS precedents, while not strictly binding, function as a de facto quality and legitimacy benchmark for CONMEBOL's future regulation on the matter.

V. The CONMEBOL Challenge: Regulatory Design for a Fragmented Continent

87. The preceding topics have mapped a regulatory landscape in South America that is, by any measure, fragmented – three normative layers (domestic, regional, supranational), ten jurisdictions with heterogeneous legal rules, the absence of a direct external enforcement authority over continental regulation and an emerging body of CAS jurisprudence that provides analytical orientation. It is in this context that CONMEBOL now faces the challenge of designing a regulatory framework for one of the most consequential movements in the industry in decades.

88. The issue has already arrived: as Monserrat Jiménez, CONMEBOL's Deputy General Secretary and Legal Director, acknowledged, the Confederation has encountered its first concrete MCO conflict – two clubs within the same ownership group qualifying simultaneously for a continental competition in 2026. The case was apparently resolved, on an ad hoc basis, through a "Chinese wall" arrangement implemented with UEFA's technical assistance.[35] But Jiménez's own assessment captures the structural nature of the problem: "Unlike UEFA, where the cases mostly won't repeat in history, in South America, this will be a problem every year".[36] In other words, what was once a matter of hypothetical concern for European investors participating in South American clubs has become an operational reality with annual recurrence, demanding a systematic regulatory solution.

---

35 Intervention by Monserrat Jiménez in a panel on the second day of the FIFA Football Law Annual Review 2026, (Budapest, February 2026).

36 Intervention by Monserrat Jiménez in a panel on the first day of the 12th AIAF Congress, (Miami, 6 November 2025).

89. The responsibility is immense. A framework that is too restrictive could deter investment and generate transnational litigation comparable to that provoked by FIFA's Football Agent Regulation; a framework that is too permissive risks allowing the consolidation of ownership structures whose competitive distortions become progressively more difficult to unwind.

90. The challenge is rendered especially complex by three structural features that distinguish the South American context.

91. First, *scale and asymmetry*: Brazil accounts for approximately 50% of the continent's territory and is unquestionably the strongest economy in the region. Since 2019, every Copa Libertadores champion has been a Brazilian club; the 2024 final between Botafogo and Atlético Mineiro was a contest between two SAF-constituted clubs, one of which was part of an MCO network. An overly restrictive CONMEBOL regulation risks further concentrating investment in Brazil at the expense of other jurisdictions that might benefit from MCO capital.

92. Second, *scarcity of alternative competitions*: CONMEBOL operates with ten associations and two principal continental competitions – the Copa Libertadores and the Copa Sudamericana. Unlike UEFA, where 55 associations and three competitions dilute MCO conflicts, the probability of two commonly owned clubs qualifying for the same CONMEBOL competition is structurally higher. The regulatory design must therefore account for a higher frequency of integrity conflicts.

93. Third, the *absence of an external normative parameter*: as demonstrated above, CONMEBOL does not operate under the discipline of a supranational competition law authority. The CAS jurisprudence from *ENIC* to *Pachuca/León* provides a valuable quality benchmark, but it operates as persuasive authority, not binding constraint. CONMEBOL must therefore construct its regulatory legitimacy through institutional quality: the robustness of its rules, the transparency of its procedures and the coherence of its enforcement mechanisms.

94. Against this backdrop, it seems appropriate to identify a few propositions that are progressively consolidating in the international debate and that may serve as building blocks for a continental regulatory framework.

95. Three features of the UEFA model are relevant as a comparative reference on the *structure of the regulatory model*: (a) the progressive layering of the regulatory framework over more than two decades; (b) the institutional presence of the CFCB as a specialised body with investigatory and adjudicatory chambers; and (c) the external validation of the framework by both the CAS and the European Commission. This last element creates the sharpest contrast with South America: the CONMEBOL regulatory space operates without an equivalent external discipline. The FCWC Regulations' convergence with the UEFA model suggests that FIFA regards the UEFA framework as the benchmark; the challenge for CONMEBOL is to adapt its principles to a markedly different institutional environment.

96. On the *protection of competition integrity*: the proposition that control or decisive influence over two clubs in the same competition is incompatible with sporting integrity appears to be settled. The challenge lies in operationalisation: defining what constitutes an acceptable mechanism for separating ownership structures. The *Pachuca/León* award demonstrated that blind trusts are not inherently invalid, but

that they must be "constructed correctly" – a formulation that invites regulatory specification. In the South American context, where MCO conflicts may recur annually, the need for durable and legally enforceable separation mechanisms is particularly acute.

97. On the *integrity of the transfer market*: intra-group player transfers cannot be treated as ordinary arm's-length transactions when both clubs answer to the same parent entity. In a continent whose football economy is structurally dependent on the export of players, the circumvention of the solidarity mechanism and sell-on clauses through below-market-value intra-group transfers directly undermines the financial sustainability of training clubs. CONMEBOL has a particularly important role to play in its dialogue with FIFA: when a player is transferred within an MCO group for a nominal fee, the solidarity contribution that would ordinarily flow to the clubs that trained that player is effectively eliminated. The introduction of mandatory fair market value assessment mechanisms for intra-group transfers would constitute a proportionate measure that CONMEBOL could advocate for implementation in the FIFA RSTP.[37] The transparency mechanisms that FIFA is considering – mandatory disclosure of MCO affiliations in the TMS – are a positive first step, but insufficient without substantive rules ensuring that the financial flows of the transfer system are not short-circuited by intra-group arrangements.

98. On *players' rights*: within MCO structures, the position is more nuanced. FIFA RSTP already establishes quantitative limits on loans and prohibits bridge transfers and TPI; it would seem premature to introduce additional MCO-specific restrictions before the existing framework has been properly evaluated. Any future development should ensure that protective measures do not inadvertently restrict the opportunities – international exposure, access to superior training infrastructure, career development – that MCO structures can legitimately provide.

99. On *financial sustainability*: the implementation of a continental financial fair play framework would be salutary, though the brutal disparity of revenues across the continent means that any viable framework will require a tiered approach, considering the economic realities of different segments of the market.

100. On the broader question of whether CONMEBOL should create *restrictions designed to discourage MCO investment* – whether by entities holding interests in clubs in other countries or by specific categories of investors such as private equity funds, – the balance of considerations suggests that outright prohibitions tend to deter responsible, long-term investors while encouraging speculative operators willing to assume the regulatory risk.

VI. Conclusion: Charting the Regulatory Course

101. Multi-club ownership has arrived in South America as an operational reality – one that has already generated its first cases, its first ad hoc solutions and its first institutional anxieties.

---

37 On the matter, see Ribeiro and Fruchtengarten (n 3), 18–23.

102. The analysis conducted in this contribution reveals a regulatory landscape that is uneven in density, inconsistent in methodology and largely reactive in its genesis. FIFA has adopted a posture of cautious incrementalism; CONMEBOL's club licensing framework remains an instrument lacking the enforcement infrastructure that characterises the UEFA model; and the ten member associations present a spectrum ranging from Brazil's multi-layered architecture – now including the CBF's dedicated MCO provisions – to the structural resistance of the Argentine civil association model. This fragmentation invites regulatory arbitrage.

103. At the same time, the jurisprudential foundations are quite consistent: from *ENIC* to *Pachuca/León*, the CAS has confirmed that the protection of competitive integrity is a legitimate objective capable of justifying restrictions on ownership, provided those restrictions satisfy the requirements of necessity and proportionality. What has changed in the 25 years that separate both rulings is not the basic legal principles, but the complexity of the corporate arrangements subjected to them.

104. The competition law dimension adds an important nuance. CONMEBOL may enjoy a wider margin of regulatory autonomy than UEFA, since no supranational competition authority exists in South America with the same history of application of its rules in sports-related matters to play a role comparable to that of the ECJ in the European Union. But this autonomy carries a corresponding burden of self-legitimation – and the CAS, applying the *Meca-Medina* proportionality framework, functions as the de facto quality benchmark against which any future CONMEBOL regulation will be assessed.

105. It seems to us, therefore, that the challenge facing CONMEBOL is all about finding the right balance that attracts investment while preventing South American clubs from being instrumentalised as mere components of global financial engineering. The building blocks identified in the current debate on the matter – competitive integrity as a settled principle, transfer market safeguards anchored in fair market value, beneficial ownership transparency, financial sustainability as institutional infrastructure and regulatory direction rather than prohibition – suggest that a graduated regulatory approach is feasible. Such an approach could begin with transparency and disclosure, progress to financial sustainability requirements and culminate in substantive MCO-specific rules, advancing at a pace commensurate with the continent's institutional capacity.

106. The European experience demonstrates that effective regulation of MCO is a generational project. South America enters this process at a different stage of institutional development, with different market structures, and with a talent-exporting model that creates vulnerabilities without parallel in European football. The clubs that develop the world's finest talent deserve a regulatory environment that protects their developmental investment, ensures the integrity of the competitions in which they participate, allows the injection of capital and preserves the cultural significance of the *pasión* that makes South American football irreducible to a business proposition.

The Organisation of Football Competitions and Calendar Management – A European Competition Law Perspective

Sven Demeulemeester[*] and Quentin van Outryve d'Ydewalle[**]
ATFIELD, Brussels, Belgium

1. Given the pyramid structure of professional football, the international match calendar is currently primarily set by international sports governing bodies (SGBs), notably the Fédération Internationale de Football Association (FIFA) and – to a lesser extent[1] – the Union of European Football Associations (UEFA), with Europe's national football associations and leagues organising domestic league and cup matches on the remaining dates.
2. The professional football calendar, with its tight schedule of ever more intense matches and tournaments, shows a number of alarming trends. More and more matches are being crammed into one single season, much to the detriment of players' physical and mental health. So, players, (some) clubs[2] and leagues are increasingly taking issue with the way the professional football calendar is currently organised. The fact that clubs must release the players, on their

* Partner, Sports and Employment Law, ATFIELD, Brussels, Belgium
** Associate, Sports Law, ATFIELD, Brussels, Belgium.
1 The FIFA Council makes the final decision on the international match calendar.
2 The European Club Association (ECA) endorses the international match calendar until 2030, as approved by the FIFA Council on 14 March 2023, and supports the new FIFA Club World Cup from 2025.

payroll, for national team competitions organised by FIFA and UEFA without full compensation is seen as an aggravating factor.

3. This trend of calendar congestion seems a direct result of initiatives undertaken by FIFA and UEFA, although the role of certain top clubs cannot be underestimated.[3] Moreover, it is important to stress that FIFA and UEFA have commercial functions in addition to their regulatory functions, which cause an inherent conflict of interest. The increase in international games can be seen as a move to monetise further their own international competitions or, for UEFA, to protect their position as leading European competition organiser against breakaway competitions. This is why a primary competency of FIFA and UEFA to organise and coordinate football competitions, and to impose an international match calendar, should be analysed from a European competition law perspective. An analysis of this issue through the prism of Articles 101 and 102 of the Treaty on the Functioning of the European Union (TFEU) is required to assess whether the regulatory powers that lie in the hands of FIFA and UEFA are exercised correctly by these SGBs.

4. By dissecting key legal principles, landmark judgments, and emerging case law, this contribution aims to provide a nuanced understanding of the legality, legitimacy and potential challenges surrounding the professional football calendar in a European context.

I. Setting the Scene: Issues in Terms of the Organisation of Football Competitions

1. Calendar Congestion and Increased Player Workload

5. The congestion of calendars and increased player workload is becoming a growing concern in professional football, and with player unions in particular.

6. In 2023, the Fédération Internationale des Associations de Footballeurs Professionnels (FIFPRO), which aims to promote and protect players rights, has produced a report analysing players' annual workloads and the detrimental effects of this workload on their health.[4] The report aimed to establish a clear link between the footballing calendar's congestion and its negative impact on players' health and wellbeing. To achieve a scientifically significant correlation, FIFPRO analysed the workload of approximately 1,500 male professional footballers, primarily from Europe's top five leagues (England, France, Germany, Italy, and Spain) during the 2022–2023 season, which allowed for trends to be identified. To facilitate comparison of data across various players, FIFPRO introduced a new tool called the Player Workload Index (PWI) composed of four main components, namely: (i) on-field workload;

---

[3] The request for having additional lucrative international games, for example, in the framework of the revamped FIFA World Cup, is endorsed by a number of top clubs. Also, reforms of UEFA competitions are often clearly a result of top clubs threatening to start break away competitions (cf Tsjalle van der Burg, "How Can UEFA React to the Super League Ruling" (2023) 3 ISLJ 447–452).

[4] FIFPRO "*Report: Extreme Calendar Congestion: The Adverse Effects on Player Health & Wellbeing* (2023) <https://fifpro.org/en/supporting-players/health-and-performance/player-workload/congested-professional-football-calendar-raises-mental-health-concerns-for-players> accessed 2 September 2025.

(ii) rest time between matches; (iii) breaks during and between seasons; and (iv) long-distance travel.

7. In each of these four components, according to FIFPro, certain trends have emerged over the past few years.

8. First, regarding *on-field workload*, the implementation of new stoppage time rules during the 2022 FIFA World Cup in Qatar resulted in a 60% increase in added time compared to the 2018 World Cup in Russia. Additionally, there has been a notable increase in the number of matches played, particularly among younger players, along with a tendency to overburden key players within teams.

9. Second, regarding the *rest time between matches*, structural changes overburden the already congested calendar with additional matches. For instance, starting from the 2024–2025 season, the UEFA Champions League will expand from 32 to 36 participating clubs, resulting in more matches. Additionally, FIFA intends to augment the number of matches per season by introducing a new format known as the "Mundial de Clubes FIFA".[5] This quadrennial tournament will feature 32 clubs from around the globe competing for the title of world's best football club. It is clear that the increased number of matches, predominantly involving elite players, will further reduce the potential rest time between matches.

10. Third, the *breaks that players should have during and between seasons* are also significantly threatened by the congested calendar. A prime example of this is the recent FIFA World Cup in Qatar. Due to the extreme temperatures, it was medically unjustifiable to hold it during the summer, resulting in the cancellation of the anticipated winter break for many international players. FIFA has once again chosen to host a World Cup in a country (Saudi Arabia in 2034) where temperatures reach levels that make playing close to summer almost physically impossible.

11. Lastly, *long-distance travel and time-zone shifts* further aggravate the accumulation of fatigue and sleep deficits. It is becoming increasingly common for players based in Europe to participate in international matches with their national teams in for example South America, and they then participate in a Club World Cup in the Middle East.

12. Medical studies seem to reveal that sustaining such an overload in the long term is unsustainable for players, with significant impact on their physical and mental health.[6] For FIFPro, the detrimental consequences of this overload are evident: between July 2022 and April 2023, there were 3,000 reported injuries in the top five European leagues, averaging over 30 injuries per club in a span of ten months. Additionally, teams also suffer from a player's injury both in sporting terms, with a decline in performance due to the player's absence, and financially,

---

[5] FIFA, "Mundial de Clubes FIFA 25: Dates, Format and Qualifiers" (*FIFA*, 17 December 2023) <www.fifa.com/en/articles/fifa-club-world-cup-2025-dates-format-and-qualifiers> accessed 2 September 2025.

[6] Gregory Dupont and others, "Effect of 2 Soccer Matches in a Week on Physical Performance and Injury Rate" (2010) 38 AJSM 1752–758; Magni Mohr and others, "Muscle Damage, Inflammatory, Immune and Performance Responses to Three Football Games in 1 Week in Competitive Male Players" (2016) 116 EJAP 179–193; Mathieu Nédélec and others, "Recovery in Soccer: Part I – Post-Match Fatigue and Time Course of Recovery" (2012) 42 SM 997–1015.

as revenues decrease from ticket sales, sponsors and media rights.[7] Therefore, according to FIFPro, it is crucial for all stakeholders, including clubs, fans and leagues, to ensure that players are available to play and maintain the sport's allure and competitiveness.[8]

13. In its player workload monitoring report looking into the 2024-25 season, FIFPRO argued rising health and performance risks due to calendar congestion, especially for players who took part in the Club World Cup.[9]

14. Some question the effective increase in games and hence player workload "across the board". As per the CIES 2024 Summer Series on Player Workload[10], the number of games and minutes played per player have not significantly increased over the last decade and are not projected to increase significantly over the next couple of years. This seems predominantly due to the five substitutions rule and the increase in squad sizes. Some therefore argue that, instead of an increase in workload, there rather seems to be a shift in player workload. The quantity of football has not changed, but its physical intensity has, especially at certain (top) clubs. Play has become more intense, with both the number of passes per game and sprints per game increasing.[11] But whether it is the quantity of games or the intensity of games, the increased player workload is real and requires attention.

15. From their end, most clubs are likewise unhappy about the current calendar and the related impact in terms of player injuries and fatigue and their sporting results and revenues. It should however be stressed that not all clubs are opposed. A number of top clubs, ie those likely to participate in the lucrative FIFA World Cup and the UEFA Champions League, are happy with some of the additional games. What's more, it can be argued that professional football's absolute top clubs are the ones that have pushed for more lucrative games on the international calendar. This has made these clubs stronger, also on the pitch, and led to a decrease in competitive balance.[12] This fault line between elite clubs and other clubs is also reflected in the current rift between clubs' representative bodies.[13] This being said, even if those clubs are in favour of the newly added (more lucrative) games, they would probably still prefer less (domestic league) games.

---

7 Ronan David, "FIFPRO Report – Extreme Congestion of Calendars: Detrimental Effects on Health and Well-Being of Players" (*Football Legal*, 2023) <www.football-legal.com/content/fifpro-report-extreme-congestion-of-calendars-detrimental-effects-on-health-and-well-being-of-players> accessed 2 September 2025.

8 *FIFPRO Report* (n 4), 43. The English Professional Footballers' Association (PFA) is likewise vocal on the issue and considers that the packed schedule not only jeopardises players' health but diminishes the quality of the sport and, ultimately, the fan experience (Andrew Warshaw, "PFA Boss Says Over-Used Players is 'Killing the Product'" (*Inside World Football*, 2 September 2025) <www.insideworldfootball.com/2024/02/29/pfa-boss-says-used-players-killing-product> accessed 2 September 2025).

9 https://fifpro.org/media/1cbjrm0y/english_pwm_men-s-annual-report_digital.pdf.

10 https://football-observatory.com/-Serie-.

11 Simon Kuper, "Injury time – the hidden shift in player workload", *Financial Times*, 15 May 2025 *https://www.ft.com/content/36ebc96e-18d7-4601-9826-d799d73f38b8* accessed 2 September 2025..

12 van der Burg (n 3).

13 In particular, ECA's representativeness is currently being challenged by other clubs and other club federations, such as the Union of European Clubs (see UEC, Press Release, "UEC Letter to Clubs and Stakeholders – Whose Interests Does ECA Really Represent?" (22 September 2023) <www.ueceurope.org/post/uec-letter-whose-interests-does-eca-really-represent> accessed 2 September 2025).

16. National leagues in turn argue that FIFA and UEFA not only increase the number of matches but also prioritise their own competitions to the detriment of domestic leagues.[14]

2. The Dual Role of FIFA and UEFA: Regulatory v Commercial Role

17. Originally, SGBs like UEFA and FIFA served primarily as regulatory entities, tasked with establishing standardised rules, organising and overseeing events, and promoting the sport across all levels.[15] SGBs typically have had exclusive competence on the organisational level, as is the case with FIFA[16] and UEFA.[17] It is acknowledged that FIFA and UEFA play essential roles in regulating football, setting rules, managing calendars, and ensuring player and fan welfare.

18. Yet, it is also recognised that regulatory decisions directly impact commercial outcomes, blurring the lines between regulatory and commercial motivations in sports governance. Moreover, modern SGBs have transformed into commercial entities with clear economic interests in the sports they oversee. They exploit sports' commercial potential and are now significant financial beneficiaries of lucrative sporting events. As competition organisers, they engage in various business agreements to market all kinds of commercial rights associated with sporting events. This shift largely stems from changes in the regulatory and technological landscape of the audiovisual media sector, where sports have become increasingly commercially viable. SGBs have consequently expanded their traditional regulatory roles to include these commercially sensitive functions through a gradual process of accumulation.[18] Notably, FIFA and UEFA have explicitly reserved media rights for the competitions they organise within their statutes.[19]

19. The market for the supply of football competitions, in Europe in particular, is moreover immensely lucrative. Fans, sponsors, consumers and broadcasters around the world clearly covet European football. But with only a finite amount of broadcasting cash available to spend, an expansion of FIFA and UEFA competitions risks depreciating the value of national broadcasting rights, which are already under pressure.[20] The friction between domestic leagues and football's governing bodies regarding who's going to cash in on European football is therefore obvious.

---

14 World Leagues Forum, "World Leagues Forum's statement on the European Super League Ruling" (*World Leagues Forum*, 22 December 2023) <www.worldleaguesforum.com/en/media/world-leagues-forums-statement-on-the-european-super-league-ruling> accessed 2 September 2025.

15 Andrea Cattaneo and Richard Parrish, *Sports Law in the European Union* (Wolters Kluwer 2020) 58.

16 FIFA Statutes (2022), arts 69, 70.

17 UEFA Statutes (2020), art 49.1.

18 Stephen Weatherill, "Never Let a Good Fiasco go to Waste: Why and How the Governance of European Football Should Be Reformed after the Demise of the 'Super League'" (*Asser International Sports Law Blog*, 23 April 2021) <www.asser.nl/SportsLaw/Blog/post/never-let-a-good-fiasco-go-to-waste-why-and-how-the-governance-of-european-football-should-be-reformed-after-the-demise-of-the-superleague-by-stephen-weatherill> accessed 2 September 2025.

19 FIFA Statutes (n 16), art 66; UEFA Statutes (n 17), art 47.1.

20 Matt Slater, "Ligue 1 Broadcast Rights Auction Scrapped as Minimum Valuation Not Met" (*The Athletic*, 8 November 2023) <www.nytimes.com/athletic/4971534/2023/10/17/ligue-1-broadcast-deal-auction/> accessed 2 September 2025.

20. The convergence of regulatory and commercial roles within a single body inherently leads to conflicts of interest as organisations seek to maintain control over their traditional functions, potentially disadvantaging competitors in the market. For instance, SGBs may be tempted to uphold their monopoly by imposing market restrictions in their statutes and rulebooks, hindering the emergence of rival leagues or organisations in the market for their events and risking antitrust violations under Articles 101 and 102 TFEU.[21] While the hierarchical structure of SGBs is defended for reasons of efficiency in establishing standardised rules, addressing integrity issues, coordinating international calendars and safeguarding athlete welfare, it also discourages alternative, competitive structures.[22] Also, there are still major concerns regarding good governance. Criticisms include claims of lack of transparency, lack of democratic controls, and limited stakeholder involvement in decision-making, particularly as commercial interests drive stakeholders to seek greater revenue generation from sports. Hence, the allegations that SGBs develop their regulatory powers to advance commercial agendas, constraining the economic activities of key stakeholders.[23] As Szymanski observes, "governing bodies have become internal monoliths, claiming to regulate every aspect of their particular sport".[24]

3. Mandatory Player Release

21. Clubs are required to release their players for participation with their national teams.[25] Players are, in general, obliged to respond affirmatively when called by their national association.[26]

22. Such release is of course necessary to organise national team matches and tournaments, such as the FIFA World Cup and the UEFA European Football Championship and the UEFA Nations League. Clubs and players refusing a call-up may be sanctioned, including the player being ineligible to play for the club during the envisaged period of the release, plus an additional period of five days.[27]

23. The release of players moreover does not entitle clubs to financial compensation as such.[28] Clubs must rely on specific programmes, such as the Club Benefits Programme (CBP) and the Club Protection Programme (CPP), agreed in the framework of specific memoranda of understanding between the ECA and SGBs.

---

21 Cattaneo and Parrish (n 15); Katarina Pijetlovic, "European Model of Sport: Alternative Structures" in Jack Anderson and others (eds), *Research Handbook on EU Sports Law and Policy* (Edward Elgar 2018) 326–330.

22 Stephen Weatherill, *European Sports Law Collected Papers* (2nd edn, Asser Press 2014) 302–303.

23 Cattaneo and Parrish (n 15), 19–20.

24 Stefan Szymanski, *The Comparative Economics of Sport* (Palgrave Macmillan 2010) 83.

25 FIFA Regulations on the Status and Transfers of Players RSTP (2024) art 1 Annex 1: "Clubs are obliged to release their registered players to the representative teams of the country for which the player is eligible to play on the basis of his nationality if they are called up by the association concerned. Any agreement between a player and a club to the contrary is prohibited".

26 Ibid art 3 Annex 1: "As a general rule, every player registered with a club is obliged to respond affirmatively when called up by the association he is eligible to represent on the basis of his nationality to play for one of its representative teams".

27 Ibid art 5 Annex 1.

28 Ibid art 2(1) Annex 1: "Clubs releasing a player in accordance with the provisions of this annexe are not entitled to financial compensation".

The CBP provides for a limited amount of financial compensation on the basis of a predetermined formula to the clubs that release players to final tournaments. The CPP, on the other hand, provides for a compensation mechanism in the event of an injury sustained by a player whilst on national team duty.

24. Both programmes are a direct result of a legal challenge mounted by clubs[29] in the *Charleroi* case.[30] At the time of the *Charleroi* case, there was no compensation or protection whatsoever in place for clubs. Advantages to clubs were received indirectly, via proceeds transferred to the national association of which they were a member, and a hard-to-quantify increase of a player's value following an international tournament. Such a system was unjustifiably unbalanced in favour of SGBs and national associations. Clubs paying the player's salaries for them to perform in international tournaments generating revenue for SGBs, was paramount to clubs effectively subsidising national associations and UEFA/FIFA and contrary to EU competition law.[31]

25. The current mandatory player release rules certainly offer better protection to clubs but have not yet been challenged from an EU competition law perspective and it remains to be seen whether the current mandatory player release rule would survive such a legal challenge. The gradual current shift to more international games organised by governing bodies, arguably at the expense of national competitions, and the detrimental impact this has on (a majority of) clubs and their players, may revamp club's arguments that they are being treated unfairly by SGBs through the mandatory player release rule.

* * *

26. Given the abovementioned issues, it is no surprise that player unions and leagues, in 2024, filed an anti-trust complaint to the European Commission over FIFA's imposition of international match calendar.[32] This complaint is still pending.

II. EU Competition Law and Sports

1. The Rise and Death (and Resurrection?) of the Sporting Exemption

27. The CJEU's judgment in *Walrave and Koch* established the fundamental principle that the practice of sport is subject to EU law only in so far as it constitutes an economic activity[33], with the CJEU making a distinction between rules of "purely

---

29 The case was mounted by the G-14, the predecessor of the ECA.

30 Case C-243/06 *SA Sporting du Pays de Charleroi and Groupement des clubs de football européens v FIFA* ECLI:EU:C:2008:649. Following a settlement between the parties, the case was struck from the dockets by the CJEU's president on 25 November 2008.

31 Stephen Weatherill, *Principles and Practice in EU Sports Law* (OUP 2017) 267.

32 *https://fifpro.org/en/who-we-are/fifpro-members/fifpro-europe/player-unions-and-leagues-file-complaint-to-european-commission-over-fifa-s-imposition-of-international-match-calendar*. This complaint followed up on a claim on behalf of English and French player unions before the Brussels' Commercial Court based, predominantly, on the EU Charter of Fundamental Rights.

33 Case 36/74 *Walrave and Koch v Association Union Cycliste Internationale and others* ECLI:EU:C:1974:140, para 2.

sporting interest" and those with economic implications. The scope of the Treaty was confined to its proper objective,[34] which led to the establishment of the sporting exception in EU sports law. This line of reasoning was reaffirmed in subsequent rulings involving the EU free movement rights like *Donà*,[35] *Bosman*,[36] *Deliège*[37] and *Lehtonen.*[38]

28. The question subsequently was whether this sporting exception extended to the application of EU competition law.

29. In this respect, *Meca-Medina*[39] rejects the dichotomy between "purely sporting" and economic rules and recognises that the two spheres necessarily overlap, in which decisions or regulations of a primary sporting nature can still exert economic effects that have to be analysed under EU law.[40] In that case, involving swimmers claiming that the doping rules of the Fédération Internationale de Natation (FINA) violated European competition rules, the CJEU reaffirmed that sport falls under EU law "in so far as it constitutes an economic activity",[41] excluding rules solely of sporting interest.[42] By referring to the "difficulty of severing the economic aspects of a sporting activity from the sporting aspects of a sport", the CJEU distinguished between, on the one hand, a purely sporting rule and, on the other hand, the person carrying out the activity governed by the rule or the body that issued it.[43] The CJEU added that even where one finds a rule of a purely sporting nature, this "does not have the effect of removing from the scope of the Treaty the person engaging in the activity governed by that rule or the body which has laid it down".[44] Furthermore, the CJEU emphasised the need for a contextual analysis, considering objectives and proportionality in assessing compliance with competition law by stating that "account must first of all be taken of the overall context in which the decision of the association of undertakings was taken or produces its effects and, more specifically, of its objectives" and it "has then to be considered whether the consequential effects restrictive of competition are inherent in the pursuit of those objectives…and are proportionate to them".[45] The *Meca-Medina* approach, borrowed from *Wouters,*[46] has the advantage of not a priori excluding a sports case from the application of European law, but at the same time leaving sufficient scope to consider the specificities of sport. *Meca-Medina* in a way abandons the search for purely sporting rules, recognising that most practices – such as anti-doping

---

34 Ibid para 9.

35 Case 13/76 *Gaetano Donà v Mario Mantero* ECLI:EU:C:1976:115, paras 14–15.

36 Case C-415/93 *Union Royale Belge Sociale de Football Association, RCL and UEFA v JM Bosman* ECLI:EU:C:1995:463, para 76.

37 Joined Case C-51/96 *Christelle Deliège v Ligue francophone de judo et disciplines associées ASBL* and Case C-191/97 *Christelle Deliège v ASBL and François Pacquée* ECLI:EU:C:2000:199, para 43.

38 Case C-176/96 *Lehtonen v FRBSB* ECLI:EU:C:2000:201, para 34.

39 Case C-519/04 P *David Meca-Medina and Igor Majcen v Commission of the European Communities* ECLI:EU:C:2006:492.

40 Cattaneo and Parrish (n 15), 40–41.

41 *Meca-Medina* (n 40), paras 22, 31.

42 Ibid para 25.

43 Ibid para 26.

44 Ibid para 27.

45 Ibid para 42.

46 Case C-309/99 *Wouters* ECLI:EU:C:2002:98.

rules – may be of a sporting nature and perhaps even "purely sporting" in *intent*, but nevertheless must be tested against the demands of EU law where it exerts its economic *effects*. This requires a case-by-case examination, with rules justified by legitimate objectives escaping the label of forbidden restrictions of competition.[47] *Meca-Medina* established a nuanced approach to analysing the economic and sporting aspects of sports regulations, ensuring compliance with EU competition law while respecting the specificities of sport with the compatibility of allegedly "sporting rules" in the context of one Treaty proposition not necessarily leading to a similar conclusion in respect of others.[48]

30. The CJEU seemingly revisited the purely sporting exemption, which was considered all but dead after *Meca-Medina*, in its recent *ESL*,[49] *ISU*[50] and *Royal Antwerp FC*[51] decisions, by again emphasising that "questions of interest solely to sport" are considered to be extraneous to economic activity and, thus, not subject to EU scrutiny. Although this "resurrection" of the sporting exemption seems to have limited value in practice given the tighter grip of EU competition law on SGBs and their rules and decisions as a result of those very same recent decisions[52], SGBs may pursue this line of reasoning further to shield their actions from judicial review.[53] As argued by AG Emiliou, in his opinion on the ROGON v DFB-case, SGBs may have a *"somewhat wider* room for manoeuvre than what other undertakings and associations of undertakings may enjoy when pursuing purely commercial objectives".[54]

2. Increased Scrutiny of Sports Governing Bodies' Dual Role

31. In football in particular, UEFA and FIFA exert a huge economic power. Reliant on commercial sponsorships and broadcasting rights, they operate with considerable financial autonomy, making decisions that can profoundly affect the internal market and trade between EU Member States.[55]

32. In *MOTOE*,[56] the CJEU made it clear that the (monopolistic) regulatory role of a sports governing body did not offer immunity from EU competition law insofar as it engaged in economic activities as well. The case originated from a preliminary ruling by the Court of First Instance in Greece, focusing

---

47 Weatherill (n 33), 12–16.

48 Richard Parrish and Samuli Miettinen, *The Sporting Exception in European Union Law* (Asser Press 2018) 99.

49 Case C-333/21 *European Super League (ESL)* ECLI:EU:C:2023:1011, para 84.

50 Case C-124/21 P *International Skating Union (ISU)* ECLI:EU:C:2023:1012, para 92.

51 Case C-680/21 *Royal Antwerp FC* ECLI:EU:C:2023:1010, para 54.

52 SGBs seem at risk nowadays of seeing their decisions or rules being labelled as a restriction by object more quickly than before, with hence even less room to manoeuvre (cf. CJEU, 4 October 2024, Diarra, ECLI:EU:C:2024:824, paras 149 and following). In the present of a restriction by object, the Meca-Medina test cannot be applied, the stricter exception of Article 101(3) TFEU would have to be relied on. Suffice to conclude that the alleged resurrection of the sporting exemption may have been greatly exaggerated.

53 Jan Zglinski, "Can EU Competition Law Save Sports Governance?" (2024) 23 ISLJ 475–481. The tighter grip will ultimately depend on how narrow courts and competition authorities will, in the future, interpret a particular rule or decision as being a "question of interest solely to sport".

54 Case C-428/23 *ROGON v DFB*, ECLI:EU:C:2025:363, Opinion of AG Emiliou, para 41.

55 Katarina Pijetlovic, *EU Sports Law and Breakaway Leagues in Football* (Asser Press 2015) 9.

56 Case C-49/07 *MOTOE* ECLI:EU:C:2008:376.

on MOTOE, a Greek non-profit motorcycling federation governed by private law. MOTOE contested the Greek State's refusal to authorise its competitions and sought compensation for the financial losses it claimed to have incurred as a result. ELPA, being the National Motorcycling Federation in Greece, held a monopoly position granted by Greek law, which MOTOE alleged it had exploited. Article 102 TFEU, prohibiting the abuse of dominant positions, prompted the CJEU to examine ELPA's dual role in regulating and commercially exploiting motorcycling events.[57] The referring Greek court highlighted that while ELPA was designated under Greek law as the sole entity authorised to approve applications for motorcycling events, it also directly organised events and engaged in associated economic activities like sponsorship and advertising itself.[58] This conflict of interest was at the heart of the CJEU's judgment in *MOTOE*. The CJEU thus identified a conflict of interest inherent in ELPA's position, where its regulatory powers intertwined with its commercial activities potentially hindered fair competition. Even without evidence of actual abuse, the CJEU emphasised the need to prevent situations conducive to abuse. A Member State violates the Treaty, specifically Articles 102 and 106 TFEU, where the undertaking exercises the special or exclusive rights conferred upon it and so is led to abuse its dominant position. A violation occurs where such rights are liable to create a situation in which that undertaking is led to commit such abuses; or where they give rise to a risk of an abuse of a dominant position. In this respect, it is thus not necessary that any abuse should actually occur.[59] The CJEU went on to insist that a "system of undistorted competition, such as that provided for by the Treaty, can be guaranteed only if equality of opportunity is secured as between the various economic operators". ELPA itself organised and commercially exploited motorcycling events and also decided whether to give consent to applications to organise competing events, while itself needing no consent from any other body, it therefore has "an obvious advantage over its competitors" and its right could have lead it "to deny other operators access to the relevant market".[60] In *MOTOE*, the Court of Justice signalled a shift towards requiring strict separation between regulatory and commercial functions to avoid potential abuses of dominant positions. The ruling highlights the necessity for transparent, non-discriminatory procedures in sports governance, by stating that a combination of Articles 106(1) and 102 TFEU precludes "a national rule which confers on a legal person which organises motorcycling events and enters, in that connection, into sponsorship, advertising and insurance contracts, the power to give consent to applications for authorisation to organise such competitions, without that power being made subject to restrictions, obligations and review".[61] While recognising the expertise of sports regulators, the ruling emphasises the importance of

57 Weatherill (n 22), 473.

58 Case C-49/07 *MOTOE* ECLI:EU:C:2008:142, Opinion of AG Kokott, paras 2 and 11.

59 Case C-41/90 *Klaus Höfner and Fritz Elser v Macrotron GmbH* ECLI:EU:C:1991:161, cited in *MOTOE* (n 56), paras 49–50.

60 *MOTOE* (n 56), para 51.

61 Ibid para 53; Pijetlovic (n 21), 341.

accountability and impartiality in decision-making to prevent the exploitation of regulatory power for commercial gain.[62]

33. In its *ISU* and *ESL* decisions, the CJEU built further on this principle. The *ISU* case was initiated by a complaint filed by Dutch speed skaters Mark Tuitert and Niels Kerstholt to the European Commission against the International Skating Union's (ISU) regulations. These regulations prohibited skaters from participating in skating competitions not organised by the ISU and imposed severe penalties, including lifelong exclusion, for violations of those regulations.[63] The *ESL* case comprised 12 highly successful football clubs from England, Spain, and Italy wishing to create a transcontinental club tournament, ensuring themselves permanent positions called the European Super League (ESL).[64] However, FIFA and UEFA regulations stipulated that any new competition must secure prior approval from the governing bodies. At the time of the *ESL* announcement, UEFA had not yet established the criteria for such authorisation. Nevertheless, UEFA swiftly responded by threatening to eject the participating clubs from their national leagues and to disqualify their players from representing their countries in international matches.[65] The CJEU's rulings of 21 December 2023 in both cases found practices associated with prior approval of new sporting competitions organised by third parties and the sanctions related to those to be incompatible with EU law. The most prominent reason for this finding was the absence of a transparent, non-discriminatory, clear and precise substantive framework of criteria and procedures as the proceedings reveal that the rules at issue, by their very nature, do a sufficient degree of harm to competition and thus have as their object the prevention thereof.[66] The absence of such a framework thus enables the SGBs to exclude from the market any competing undertaking or to at least restrict the creation and marketing of alternative or new competitions in terms of their format or content.[67]

34. In summary, the CJEU transposes the principles developed under Article 106 TFEU to Articles 101 and 102 TFEU. A sports governing body – arguably functionally comparable to a Member State[68] – becomes therefore subject to the sort of obligations that apply to Member States pursuant to Article 106 TFEU. Where an organisation is, *de jure* or *de facto*, in a position that is comparable to that of an undertaking enjoying exclusive rights, it must ensure that equality

---

62 Weatherill (n 22), 482.

63 An Vermeersch, "The impact of the *ISU* Case" (2021) Voetbal & Sportjuridische Zaken <www.boomportaal.nl/tijdschrift/VSZ/VSZ_2772-6738_2021_001_001_002> accessed 2 September 2025.

64 Ed Aarons and Sean Ingle, "European Super League: Premier League "*Big Six*" Sign up to Competition" *The Guardian* (London, 19 April 2021) <www.theguardian.com/football/2021/apr/18/five-english-clubs-sign-up-to-european-super-league-report-says> accessed 2 September 2025.

65 UEFA, "President Čeferin: Footballing World and Society Stand United against Closed Super League" (*UEFA*, 20 April 2021) <www.uefa.com/news-media/news/0268-1215571df751-a59f73c3216f-1000--president-ceferin-footballing-world-and-society-stand-unit>/ accessed 2 September 2025.

66 *ESL* (n 50), para 178; *ISU* (n 51), para 108.

67 Ibid para 176; Ibid para 146; Stephen Weatherill, "Football Revolution: How Do the Court's Rulings of 21 December 2023 affect UEFA's Role as a *Gatekeeper*?" (*EU Law Analysis*, 4 January 2024) <https://eulawanalysis.blogspot.com/2024/01/football-revolution-how-do-courts.html> accessed 2 September 2025.

68 Opinion of AG Spunzar (n 54), 75.

of opportunity between all economic operators is guaranteed.[69] This means *in concreto* that there must be a substantive and procedural framework detailing how its regulatory powers are to be exercised. As a result, a distinct and stricter tier of EU competition law now governs the activities of SGBs.[70]

3. The European Sports Model

35. In the European Union, sport is structured in a pyramid model. At the base of this pyramid are the players and clubs, spanning across various levels of professionalism, from amateur to semi-professional and professional. These players and clubs are affiliated with national federations, which serve as their governing bodies and representatives, forming the second tier of the pyramid. The primary responsibilities of these national federations include organising competitions and establishing a national regulatory framework.[71] At the pinnacle of the pyramid are continental and global organisations comprised of national federations. The structure characterised by the "one federation per sport" principle, highlights the evident monopolistic stance of SGBs, which oversee professional, amateur and youth sports alike. As such, they possess the authority to establish rules and regulations that influence clubs across various levels, encompassing matters ranging from clubs' commercial rights to disciplinary measures that subsequently impact their profits.[72] In football, the global federation (FIFA) consists of multiple international federations organised geographically by continent (including for Europe, UEFA). The continental organisation UEFA adheres to the principle of one federation per country for their composition. Therefore, it can be deduced that the apex of the pyramid, and FIFA and UEFA in particular, wield significant influence over the entities below.

36. The EU's sports policy, overseen by the European Commission, European Council, and the European Parliament, endorses the preservation of traditional organisational structures and acknowledges the considerable social and cultural importance of European sports. Certain specificities of the European Sports Model, such as the pyramid structure, the openness of competitions (promotion and relegation) and meritocracy, are generally accepted.

37. Although *Meca-Medina* made it clear that any sporting rule could fall under EU law scrutiny if it had economic implications, *Bosman*, *Deliège*, *Lehtonen*, and *Meca-Medina* also underscored the unique characteristics of sport, particularly regarding the application of free movement and competition rules, by emphasising the importance of maintaining competitive balance, fostering the development of young players, preserving the integrity of sport, and safeguarding national teams as legitimate objectives.[73] The 2011 Commission Communication on Developing the

---

69 *ESL* (n 50), para 133; *Royal Antwerp* (n 52), para 125.

70 See Pablo Ibañez Colomo and Alfonso Lamadrid de Pablo, "On Superleague and ISU: The Expectation was Justified (and EU Competition Law May Be Changing before Our Eyes)" (*Chillin'Competition*, 2023) <*https://chillingcompetition.com/2023/12/21/on-superleague-and-isu-the-expectation-was-justified-and-eu-competition-law-may-be-changing-before-our-eyes/*> accessed 1 September 2025.

71 Parrish and Miettinen (n 49), 18.

72 Pijetlovic (n 55) 37.

73 Parrish and Miettinen (n 49), 50.

European Dimension in Sport defines the "specificity of sport" as "encompassing all the characteristics that make sport special, such as for instance the inter-dependence between competing adversaries or the pyramid structure of open competitions" and added that "the concept of the specific nature of sport is taken into account when assessing whether sporting rules comply with the requirements of EU law".[74] A key characteristic of the European Sports Model is the focus on win maximisation rather than profit maximisation – as opposed to the US sports model – and the greater amount of welfare and, hence, social effect this entails.[75]

38. Since the Lisbon Treaty, which entered into force on 1 December 2009, sport is moreover explicitly included in the EU's founding Treaties, granting it formal recognition. Article 165(1) TFEU states that "The Union shall contribute to the promotion of European sporting issues, while taking account of the specific nature of sport, its structures based on voluntary activity and its social and educational function".

39. In the *ESL* and *Royal Antwerp* cases, the CJEU did consider the relevance of Article 165 TFEU, taking into account the (diverging) opinions of respectively AG Rantos and AG Szpunar. In his (non-binding) opinion, AG Rantos had argued that Article 165 TFEU should be used as a standard in the interpretation and the application of the provisions of competition law,[76] and as a *constitutional* recognition of the "European Sports Model".[77]

40. However, in its decisions, the CJEU deemed Article 165 TFEU as not "being a special rule exempting sport from all or some of the other provisions of primary EU law liable to be applied to it or requiring special treatment for sport in the context of that application".[78] The CJEU underlines the limited character of the norm, which only gives the EU a supporting competence but does not allow it to pursue a sports "policy", just an "action".[79]

41. This being said, the CJEU acknowledged the fact that the specific characteristics of sporting activities may need to be "taken into account".[80] The CJEU acknowledges that sporting activities have specific characteristics that need to be considered when applying provisions of EU law. In this respect, it is of particular importance that the CJEU seems willing to even give constitutional protection to an essential feature of European sports (as opposed to, for instance, US sports), namely the need for open competitions, based on sporting merit.[81] However, it should be stressed that any consideration for the specific characteristics of sport can only happen in compliance with the conditions set out in those rules. By doing so, the CJEU seeks to avoid conceding too much power to SGBs that had, it is worth

---

74 European Commission, "Developing the European Dimension in Sport" COM(2011) 12 final; Pijetlovic (n 21), 330–331.

75 van der Burg (n 3).

76 Case C-333/21 *European Super League (ESL)* ECLI:EU:C:2022:993, Opinion of AG Rantos, para 35.

77 Ibid para 30.

78 *ESL* (n 50), para 101.

79 Ibid para 99; *Royal Antwerp* (n 52), para 67.

80 Ibid para 104.

81 Weatherill (n 67).

remembering, lobbied for inserting the article into the Treaties precisely as a safeguard against perceived interferences into their autonomy.[82]

III. EU Competition Law and the Calendar of Competitions

42. As explained above, the CJEU has, in its *ISU* and *ESL* decisions, clearly set the boundaries for FIFA and UEFA on how to exercise their gatekeeping powers, ie how they can regulate access to the market for the organisation and marketing of interclub football competitions on European Union territory and the exploitation of the various rights related to that. The regulatory power of FIFA and UEFA to organise the market for competitions logically includes a power to set the calendar of competitions. The regulatory power to arrange and authorise or control the access to the calendar should however be exercised in accordance with the guiding principles laid down in established case law and thus be subject to restrictions, obligations and controls[83]. If FIFA and UEFA fail to exercise their regulatory power correctly, then decisions by FIFA and UEFA on the calendar could be challenged on the basis of EU competition law by national leagues, clubs, players and any other stakeholder concerned by those decisions.

1. EU Competition Law Requirements and their Application to the Calendar

43. There is no doubt that both FIFA and UEFA can be categorised as being *undertakings* in the sense of Articles 101 and 102 TFEU. The European Commission has for a long time indicated that international sports associations – FIFA and UEFA explicitly being mentioned as examples –, "are undertakings to the extent they themselves carry out activities of economic nature such as the conclusion of advertising contracts, the commercial exploitation of sport events or the conclusion of contracts relating to broadcasting rights".[84] The CJEU repeated in *ESL* that "associations which, according to their statutes, have as their purpose the organisation and control of a given sport, in so far as those entities exercise an economic activity in relation to that sport, by offering products or services, and where they must, in that capacity, be categorised as undertakings".[85]

44. It is likewise clear that *trade between Member States is affected.* Such effect is clear in the event of an overburdened and (at least partly) unilaterally imposed calendar, limiting clubs and players in their choice of the matches they participate in, with access to the relevant market heavily regulated by UEFA and FIFA.

45. Under Article 101 TFEU, it will have to be proven that there exists an *agreement or a decision by an association.* The CJEU found in that regard that: "a decision of an association consisting in adopting or implementing rules having a direct impact on the conditions in which the economic activity is exercised by undertakings

---

82 Zglinski (n 53).

83 *ESL* (n 50), para 138.

84 European Commission, "The EU and Sport: Background and Context – Accompanying document to the White Paper on Sport" COM(2007) 391 final, Annex I, para 2.1.3.

85 *ESL* (n 50), para 113.

which are directly or indirectly members thereof may constitute such a [decision by an association] of undertakings".[86] The "imposition" – due to the lack of any meaningful consultation of national federations, clubs and players – of a match calendar by means of Article 62 of the FIFA Statutes[87], combined with a mandatory release of players and the non-compliance by FIFA with its own calendar[88], therefore clearly falls within the scope of Article 101 TFEU.

46. Whether the decision has the *object* or *effect* to prevent, restrict or distort competition is another question. A restriction of competition by object concerns anticompetitive behaviour that is, by its very nature, harmful to the proper functioning of a competitive market. In order to determine whether an agreement, a decision by an association of undertakings or a concerted practice reveals, by its very nature, a sufficient degree of harm to competition that it may be considered as having as its object the prevention, restriction or distortion thereof, it is necessary to examine,[89] first, the content of the agreement, decision or practice in question; second, the economic and legal context of which it forms a part; and, third, its objectives. The concept is meant to be interpreted strictly and requires a sufficient degree of harm to competition, with the content, context and objectives of practice mattering. As a rule, regulatory practices of governing bodies are unlikely to be treated as restrictions of competition by object, unless the regulatory practice is influenced by a conflict of interest.[90] However, in *ISU* and *ESL*, the CJEU made it clear that certain rules set by an organisation with a regulatory function must respect the principles of transparency, objectivity, non-discrimination and reviewability if they are to comply with Article 101 TFEU.[91] Where they do not, they may amount to a restriction of competition by object. Although *ISU* and *ESL* concerned cases where access to competitions and thus the relevant market was blocked, and the process of managing a match calendar is *prima facie* a less far-reaching regulatory power, it cannot be contested that FIFA and UEFA have a conflict of interest when deciding on the calendar. UEFA and FIFA may want to heed the abovementioned principles when organising (additional) football competitions (of their own), reforming their own competitions (and, by doing so, creating an impact on existing competitions) and deciding on an (ever more expanding) international match calendar. At present, a due process seems deficient. In the absence of objective criteria and clear and transparent procedural rules, the presence of an (unjustifiable) restriction *by object* can certainly not be excluded. It is therefore recommended that FIFA and UEFA build a case to meet the (high) threshold of Article 101(3) TFEU. If the coordination of different

---

86 *ESL* (n 50), para 118.

87 FIFA Statutes (2024), art 62: "The Council shall compile an international match calendar that shall be binding upon the confederations, member associations and leagues, after conferring with the confederations.

88 Reference is made to the FIFA Club World Cup organized by FIFA and wherefor FIFA disregarded its own sporting rules regarding transfer periods for its own economic purposes and to the detriment of national competition.

89 This is a question of fact, to be assessed by the national courts.

90 Stephen Weatherill, "Is Sport *Special*" (*EULAW Live*, 2024) <https://eulawlive.com/competition-corner/op-ed-is-sport-special-by-stephen-weatherill/> accessed 2 September 2025.

91 *ISU* and *ESL* specifically dealt with rules regarding third-party organisers. Not all SGB rules may fall under this prism.

competitions and the adoption of an overall match calendar would be considered a mere restriction *by effect*, then UEFA and FIFA could try to demonstrate that their decisions constitute an appropriate and necessary response to their legitimate regulatory objectives (the "lighter" *Meca-Medina* test, now limited in scope).

47. Under Article 102 TFEU, it is required that the undertaking holds a *dominant position* on the relevant market and that this dominant position is *abused.* Given the pyramid structure of sports – a club or player becomes a member of a national association, a single national sports association per sport, which operates under the umbrella of a single European confederation and a single worldwide association (*Ein-Platz-Prinzip*) – SGBs are in a (collective) dominant position in their respective sporting market. In *ESL*, the CJEU expressly held that both FIFA and UEFA hold a dominant position "on the market for the organisation and marketing of interclub football competitions on European Union territory and also the exploitation of the various rights related to those competitions".[92] FIFA does however also have a dominant position on the market for player services because, although it does not directly demand or offer such services, it coordinates the behavior of clubs through binding regulations like the International Match Calendar. These rules align the conduct of clubs, restrict the autonomy of players, and ensure uniform compliance under threat of sanctions, thereby fulfilling the conditions for collective dominance as recognized by the CJEU.[93] As FIFA is dominant in several markets it can be considered as having "superdominance" and as such having a special responsibility to ensure non-discrimination and thus not to favor its own competitions[94]. Although a dominant position is as such not prohibited by Article 102 TFEU,[95] holding a dominant position does confer a special responsibility not to abuse market power and therefore does not allow a SGB's conduct to impair genuine undistorted competition in the internal market.[96] The concept of abuse is an objective concept relating to the behaviour of an undertaking in a dominant position that is such as to influence the structure of a market where, as a result of the very presence of the undertaking in question, the degree of competition is weakened and that, through recourse to methods different from those which unable normal competition in products or services on the basis of the transactions of commercial operators, has the effect of hindering the maintenance of the degree of competition still existing in the market or the growth of that competition.[97] As far as the calendar of competitions is concerned, FIFA and UEFA have a special responsibility not to abuse their market power and can only use their discretion to organise competitions through appropriate substantive and procedural criteria.

---

92 *ESL* (n 50), para 117.

93 Case T-193/02 *Laurent Piau* ECLI:EU:T:2005:22, para 111.

94 Case C-48/22 *Google Shopping* ECLI:EU:C:2024:726, paras 175-200.

95 It is not the purpose of TFEU, art 102 to prevent an undertaking from acquiring, on its own merits, a dominant position on a market. Nor does that provision seek to ensure that competitors less efficient than the undertaking with the dominant position should remain on the market (Case C-413/14 P *Intel Corporation Inc v European Commission* ECLI:EU:C:2017:632, para 33).

96 Case 322/81 *NV Nederlandsche Banden Industrie Michelin v Commission of the European Communities* ECLI:EU:C:1983:313, para 57.

97 Case 85/76 *Hoffmann-La Roche & Co. AG v Commission of the European Communities* ECLI:EU:C:1979:36, para 91.

48. Specifically regarding the organisation of the latest FIFA Club World Cup, FIFA seems to have abused its (super)dominance and saw its regulatory role tainted by a conflict of interest as a result of which it gave priority to its commercial interest as a competition organiser. This can be demonstrated by the fact that FIFA, according to its own statutes[98], was itself not bound by the international match calendar and used its regulatory power to create and impose an extra competition. Also, reference can be made to the fact that the 2025 FIFA Club World Cup overlapped with other competitions organised by confederations, whereby FIFA made an exception to the existing obligation imposed by FIFA itself on national teams to release players in view of facilitating those players participating in the FIFA Club World Cup.[99] Finally, the FIFA 2025 Club World Club Regulations provided that FIFA would itself determine the slot of the host club at a time the other competing teams had already had to qualify.[100] Apart from belonging to the confederation of the host country, the regulations do not provide objective criteria, let alone sporting criteria, for selection, a principle itself imposed by FIFA upon other competition organisers.

2. A Glimpse at Future Calendar Management

49. How do the abovementioned rules now apply *in concreto* to calendar management?

50. The arrangement of the calendar and the ordering of events and/or tournaments is a primary competency of FIFA and UEFA as regulators of football. FIFA and UEFA enjoy a sporting autonomy. Such sporting rules are needed for the "organisation and proper conduct of competitive sport".[101] Neither the Commission, the General Court nor the CJEU object to the notion that SGBs are able *in principle* to arrange the calendar and to decide how many events should be permitted.

51. The *ESL* ruling stipulates as follows:

> Those various specific characteristics support a finding that it is legitimate to subject the organisation and conduct of international professional football competitions to common rules intended to guarantee the homogeneity and coordination of those competitions within an overall match calendar as well as, more broadly, to promote, in a suitable and effective manner, the holding of sporting competitions based on equal opportunities and merit. It is also legitimate to ensure compliance with those common rules through rules such as those put in place by FIFA and UEFA on prior approval of those competitions and the participation of clubs and players therein.[102]

52. The *Royal Antwerp* ruling further highlights as follows:

> As regards the economic and legal context of the rules in respect of which the national court is referring questions to the Court, it is apparent, first

98 Article 62 of the FIFA Statutes reads "The Council shall compile an international match calendar that shall be binding upon the confederations, member associations and leagues, after conferring with the confederations." The international match calendar seems not to be binding upon FIFA itself.

99 Article 22.5 FIFA Club World Cup Statutes (Appendix 4)

100 Article 11 FIFA 2025 Club World Cup Regulations.

101 European Commission (n 84), para 2.1.5; Pijetlovic (n 21), 337.

102 *ESL* (n 50), para 118.

> of all, from the case law of the Court that, bearing in mind the specific nature of the products, which sporting competitions are from an economic point of view, it is generally open to associations that are responsible for sporting discipline, such as UEFA and the URBSFA, to adopt rules relating, inter alia, to the organisation of competitions in that discipline, their proper functioning and the participation of athletes in those competitions, provided that, in so doing, those associations do not limit the exercise of the rights and freedoms that EU law confers on individuals.[103]

53. There is hence little doubt that UEFA and FIFA are allowed to regulate football, under CJEU case law, to ensure the homogeneity and coordination of competitions. FIFA and UEFA can refer to the need to protect the health of players (by limiting the overall amount of competition matches and by overseeing that matches are being played in the best possible conditions) and the need to ensure that matches take place under similar conditions to allow fairness, equal opportunities for clubs and players and, especially, to ensure a competition that is based on merits (as per the European Sports Model). FIFA and UEFA may argue that any restrictions that they impose are necessary to obtain these legitimate objectives.[104] Hence, they should be able to arrange the calendar and to decide how many events should be permitted. In short, they can impose order on the calendar.

54. However, the sporting autonomy of UEFA and FIFA remains very much conditional.

55. As set out above, given the dominant position of both UEFA and FIFA on the market, they will have to adopt, within a competition model based on merits as endorsed by the CJEU, appropriate *procedural* and *substantive* criteria for arranging a calendar.

56. UEFA and FIFA ought to adopt a neutral, transparent and non-discriminatory *procedure* for decisions on match calendars, in view of offering clubs, domestic leagues and, for that matter, other competition organisers equal opportunities.

57. At present, the FIFA statutes remain all too vague.[105]

> The Council shall be responsible for issuing transparent, objective, non-discriminatory and proportionate regulations for organising international matches and competitions between representative teams and between leagues, club and/or scratch teams. No such match or competition shall take place without the prior permission of FIFA, the relevant confederations and/or the relevant member associations in accordance with the Regulations Governing International Matches. The Council may issue further provisions for such matches and competitions.

58. There is still no approval procedure in place, let alone an approval procedure that meets the requirements established by the CJEU in *ESL*. It should be noted that agreements in place with ECA cannot replace said approval procedure.

---

103 *Royal Antwerp* (n 52), para 103.

104 FIFA and UEFA may however not invoke the protection of employees to regulate the workload and the calendar, as the protection of workers is not among the objectives of FIFA. (Case C-650/22 *Lassana Diarra and FIFPRO v FIFA and URBSFA* ECLI:EU:C:2024:824, para 99).

105 Article 63 FIFA Statutes.

59. The lack of concrete match calendar regulations is in stark contrast with the very concrete prohibition for clubs and players from participating in competitions that have not been approved by FIFA itself.[106]

> Players and teams affiliated to member associations or provisional members of the confederations may not play matches or make sporting contacts with players or teams that are not affiliated to member associations or provisional members of the confederations without the approval of FIFA.

60. As a result of the above, to this day, games or competitions outside FIFA or its confederations are practically inconceivable. This shall have to be addressed.

61. Going forward, FIFA, UEFA and some (top) clubs may try and prioritize international and European games and competitions. Given the importance awarded by the CJEU to the European Sports Model, the trend of prioritising the development of international and European games and competitions over domestic games and competitions may be questioned. A calendar aimed at maintaining a balance between clubs, by preserving a certain degree of equality and uncertainty as to the results and securing a (better) distribution of revenue down the football pyramid, is better defendable than a calendar aiming at concentrating power and revenue in the hands of a limited number of elite clubs, playing each other ever more frequently. In taking decisions, proper consultation with all relevant stakeholders – or rather, each stakeholder's representative organisation(s) – will be key. Much of the criticism now directed mainly at FIFA is precisely the lack of stakeholder involvement when deciding on its international match calendar. Consultation that is, at least to some extent, present in other regulatory fields – such as changes to the regulations on the status and transfer of players – is practically non-existent when it comes to decisions on the calendar. At present, the pyramid structure of professional football operates on the basis of decision-making through a consultation process, but this is frequently limited to higher-ranking actors within the hierarchy.[107] Also, the consultation mechanism is far from flawless.[108] FIFA's Football Stakeholders Committee, for instance, convenes very irregularly and has little power in reality. At present, important decisions predominantly emanate from the apex of the pyramid and cascade down from continental to national associations, ultimately influencing clubs' participation in a range of domestic and international competitions.[109] Players and their unions especially have made it clear that the current unilateral imposition of additional games has become untenable.

62. Given the impact of the calendar planning on players, it could be envisaged for stakeholders to have recourse to collective bargaining between employer and employee representative organisations, to protect the players in terms of on-field workload, rest times, breaks and travel. If FIFA and UEFA are serious about striking the right balance for players in the execution of their regulatory

---

106 Article 64.1 FIFA Statutes.

107 Clubs and leagues convey their perspectives through their national associations or representative organisations, which, in turn, relay these views to international bodies.

108 Robby Houben "Sports Governance (in Football) under Attack" (2023) 23 ISLJ 271–292.

109 Weatherill (n 22), 302–303.

powers, they have an interest in integrating such collective bargaining in their decision-making process. Moreover, collective bargaining would have the benefit of potentially falling outside the scope of the *Albany* exception.[110]

63. More generally, good governance in terms of the ultimate decision-making process will be crucial. Good governance will have to go beyond a general and vague self-serving exercise merely to "protect and preserve the autonomy of sport".[111] Avoiding conflicts of interest will be essential.[112] For one, SGBs will themselves have to abide by the international match calendar, which is not the case now. It will likewise be important to assess whether all of the representative organisations are truly representative[113] and whether those representative organisations have proper corporate governance in place themselves. If the level of governance standards is deficient, then the mechanism in place for deciding on the organisation of the competition and the adoption of match calendars becomes vulnerable.[114]

64. In terms of *substantive* criteria, UEFA and FIFA will have to devise a set of criteria built around the proclaimed legitimate objectives. A limitation of the overall number of games for individual players seems a logical criterion, as is the requirement to include open competitions in the calendar only. Even though UEFA and FIFA have the "first mover" advantage on the present-day international competition market, they will have to adhere to their own rules and may not discriminate. They will have to be careful not to design the competition calendar in a way that would favour themselves as dominant undertakings.[115] Given the scarcity of remaining capacity on the match calendar, football's governing bodies will have to deal with their own tournaments at arm's length. They shall not be able to invoke the *status quo* – "the calendar is already full" – to avoid a reshuffling of the calendar. As a rule, UEFA and FIFA may not reserve a disproportionate

---

110 This exception refers to three judgments of the Court, handed down on 21 September 1999, relating to compulsory affiliation to sectoral pension schemes. In *Albany*, a Dutch company challenged the compulsory affiliation of all workers in a given sector to a supplementary pension scheme, arguing that such a requirement restricted competition and infringed what is now TFEU, art 101 because companies could not offer alternative pensions to attract employees. In its judgment of 21 September 1999 (Case C-67/96, *Albany International BV v Stichting Bedrijfspensioenfonds Textielindustrie* EU:C:1999:430, para 59), the Court held that while it was "beyond question that certain restrictions of competition are inherent in collective agreements between organisations representing employers and workers", such agreements "must, by virtue of their nature and purpose, be regarded as falling outside the scope of Article [101(1) TFEU]".

111 Roger Pielke Jr and others, "An Evaluation of Good Governance in US Olympic Sport National Governing Bodies" (2020) 20 ESMQ 496.

112 See the criticism voiced by Union of European Clubs: "ECA is led by unelected Chairman who has major conflict of interest being a Chairman of the Qatari sports channel beIN Sports that buys TV rights from UEFA, while sitting on UEFA Executive Committee".

113 See the current challenge concerning the ECA's representativeness brought by UEC.

114 This being said, good governance is not sufficient reason to avoid EU competition law scrutiny. Mataija even argues that a less demanding standard of review over SGB's measures as long as a certain level of good governance is ensured, entails risks (Mislav Mataija, "False Friends: Proportionality and Good Governance in Sports Regulation" in Antoine Duval, Alexander Krüger and Johan Lindholm (eds), *The European Roots of the Lex Sportiva: How Europe Rules Global Sports*, (Bloomsbury Collections 2024).

115 *ESL* (n 50), para 151; Migual Poiares Madura, "Sports governance after the Superleague judgment: going into extra time?" (2024) 23 ISLJ 482–490.

portion of the calendar to their own tournaments,[116] unless perhaps they are able to demonstrate efficiency gains (cf below). This may entail reducing existing competition formats rather than expanding them, as seems to be the practice now.[117] Also, they will have to make sure that the compensation mechanism in place for the mandatory release of players for international competitions does not offer them an unfair advantage. In particular, the benefits enjoyed by clubs under the existing CBP and CPP mechanism need further review and adjustment to ensure full compensation for clubs in return for the release of players. FIFA and UEFA might actually start to understand the legal threats coming their way as can be evidenced by the implementation of a tool for standardized handover of medical data between national teams and clubs, aiming at increasing trust and cooperation between them with regard to the release of players.

65. Finally, insofar as their regulatory power regarding the calendar is clearly tainted by a conflict of interest, UEFA and FIFA will have to rely, rather than on the *Meca-Medina* test – which may be ruled out by the non-consistent application of the rules on the international calendar by itself - to a greater extent on Article 101(3) TFEU or, in the case of Article 102 TFEU, the objective necessity and efficiency defences, to justify their actions.[118] FIFA and UEFA will have to demonstrate that the exclusionary effects of their restrictive behaviour are outweighed by efficiency,[119] taking into account the impact on the entire ecosystem in and around football.[120] However, efficiency gains will have to correspond not to any advantage enjoyed by FIFA or UEFA – or, for that matter, a selection of elite clubs – but only to "the appreciable objective advantages" that practice makes it possible to attain in the market concerned.[121] Those efficiency gains must have a positive impact on all users, be they traders, intermediate consumers or end consumers, which in football means, amongst others, national football associations, professional or amateur clubs, professional or amateur players, young players and, more broadly, consumers, be they spectators, television viewers or others.[122] In particular, UEFA and FIFA may wish to keep an eye an improvement on professional football's contribution to aggregate welfare,[123] a laudable social goal in line with the European sports model, and increase their focus on maintaining (or rather, restoring[124]) competitive balance and promoting solidarity in professional

---

116 Case law requiring a dominant undertaking to leave at least 20% of the available capacity to smaller rivals seems difficult to invoke in the case of UEFA and FIFA (Moritz Lorenz, "UEFA as a neutral regulator of football tournaments? What is to come from the CJEU's Super League judgment?" (*Lawinsport*, 2024) <www.lawinsport.com/topics/item/uefa-as-a-neutral-regulator-of-football-tournaments-what-is-to-come-from-the-cjeus-superleague-judgment> accessed 2 September 2025.

117 UEFA added the UEFA Nations League to the international calendar and increased the number of participants in the UEFA Champions League from 32 to 36. FIFA replaced its FIFA Confederations Cup (last organised in 2017) with a FIFA World Cup, which will be further expanded from 2025 onwards.

118 Zglinski (n 53).

119 Case C-209/10 *Post Danmark A/S v Konkurrencerådet* ECLI:EU:C:2012:172, paras 40–41.

120 Migual Poiares Madura, "Sports governance after the Superleague judgment: going into extra time?" (2024) 23 ISLJ 482–490.

121 *ESL* (n 50), para 152; *Royal Antwerp* (n 52), para 121.

122 Weatherill (n 67), 7.

123 The sum total of the welfare of all individuals in the EU.

124 van der Burg (n 3).

football[125] through adequate distribution of revenue to all clubs, as opposed to the "happy few". Moreover, a justification requires the demonstration of convincing arguments[126] and evidence, involving establishing the actual existence and extent of those efficiency gains.[127] This is a serious inquiry, which has to be undertaken by the national courts. Making the ultimate decision process more robust against competition law challenges would require FIFA and UEFA substantiating the perceived benefits of their approach on aggregate welfare.

IV. Conclusion

66. After scrutinising the imposition of the football calendar in Europe through the lens of European competition law, it appears that UEFA and FIFA may invoke their sporting autonomy to justify their monopoly on arranging one international match calendar.

67. There is room for one homogenous competition organisation with clubs doing well in domestic competitions qualifying for European competitions and even worldwide competitions. Open competitions – as opposed to closed competitions such as in the US – even seem a must. Certain specificities of the European Sports Model have clearly been recognised and embraced in the *ESL* ruling, including the principle of openness of the competitions and meritocracy. This leaves room for UEFA and FIFA to maintain a competition model building from domestic leagues to continental championships to global championships, without however having a monopoly on organising either type of competition.

68. With great power comes however great responsibility. According to AG Szpunar, the power of SGBs is "functionally comparable to the power of Member States",[128] as a result of which SGBs must act accordingly. The regulatory power to arrange the calendar should hence be exercised in accordance with the guiding principles laid down in established case law of the CJEU. The most recent CJEU decisions, and especially the 2023 December trilogy (*ISU, ESL* and *Royal Antwerp*), clearly set the bar at a high level and will likely trigger an overhaul of the way the calendar of competitions is to be set going forward. The inclusion of the recent 2025 FIFA Club World Cup on the International Match Calendar likely serves as an example for FIFA on how not to proceed.

69. To successfully fend-off EU competition law challenges going forward, UEFA and FIFA will in our view have to redesign their consultation and decision process in terms of the calendar of competitions. All relevant stakeholders will have to be included in the process, information and consultation will need to be exhaustive and effective, and a mere lip service will no longer suffice. The SGBs will have to

---

125 For instance, reinforcing the trickle-down effect from top competitions to smaller professional football clubs and amateur football clubs which, whilst not participating therein, invest at local level in the recruitment and training of young, talented players, some of whom will turn professional and aspire to join a participating club. The solidarity role of football, as long as it is genuine, serves to bolster the educational and social function with the EU (*ESL* (n 50), para 236).

126 *ESL* (n 50), para 120.

127 *Royal Antwerp* (n 52), para 121; *ESL* (n 50), para 204.

128 Opinion of AG Spunzar (n 54), para 75.

make sure that they adhere to good governance standards at all times throughout the process (transparency, non-discrimination, etc). They will have to ensure that their role as neutral regulator does not go beyond what is necessary to ensure a proper functioning of the specific market that is the organisation of professional football. A substantive and procedural framework detailing how they will use their regulatory powers in terms of organising competitions *in general*, and arranging an overall calendar *in particular*, will be needed. UEFA and FIFA may not prioritise their own competitions in arranging a match calendar and will have to make sure that the compensation mechanism in place for the mandatory release of players for international competitions does not offer them an unfair advantage.

70. UEFA and FIFA will have to make sure – and, more importantly, be able to demonstrate – that the exclusionary effects of any restrictive behaviour are outweighed by efficiency gains. Given the prevalence of the European Sports Model, the best possible route to follow for UEFA and FIFA would in our view be to devise the competition calendar in such a way that it improves professional football's contribution to aggregate welfare, maintains or restores competitive balance and promotes solidarity in professional football with due respect for smaller clubs and smaller competitions and an adequate distribution of revenue. These will have to be the drivers, for UEFA and FIFA, in determining the way competitions are organised going forward, and how that will ultimately be reflected in one calendar.

The Court of Justice, UEFA and the Super League: The European Sports Model Put to the Test

Stéphane Gervasoni*

Court of Justice of the European Union, Luxembourg

1. For anyone who has seen Jean-Claude Bonichot, a skilled fencer in every sense of the word, "fencing" in the courtyard of his Burgundy home, it was obvious that the friendly tribute paid to him in this book should have a sporting slant. In the year that Paris is hosting the Olympic Games, it would have been ideal for the supreme discipline of fencing to be illustrated in the pages that follow. Unfortunately, sporting events in recent months have led lawyers to take a greater interest in the charms of football, which is nevertheless very popular on the banks of the Yonne River in Auxerre, where the dedicatee of these writings also has some ties. As luck would have it, two landmark rulings, handed down respectively by the two courts to which Jean-Claude has dedicated his talents, the Council of State and the Court of Justice of the European Union (CJEU), relate to football, from two different perspectives but revealing certain developments, particularly regarding the place of the individual in his or her social group: respect for religious beliefs and the free exercise of economic activity.

2. Pierre de Coubertin believed he could say that "only one sport has known neither stops nor setbacks: football. What else could this be due to but the intrinsic value

* State Councillor, Judge at the Court of Justice of the European Union April 2024. This article was first published in French in *La ligne claire. Mélanges en l'honneur de Jean-Claude Bonichot* (Lefebvre-Dalloz 2025). The original publication appears in a collective scholarly volume dedicated to the work and career of Jean-Claude Bonichot, former Judge at the Court of Justice of the European Union. This version is reproduced with the author's permission. The views expressed are solely those of the author.

of the game itself, the emotions it provokes, and the interest it presents?" He has once again been proven wrong by these two rulings, as was already spectacularly demonstrated by the *Bosman* case law of the Court of Justice (ECJ).[1]

3. In the first ruling, the judges at the Palais Royal, departing from the conclusions of the public prosecutor, ruled that the smooth running of matches justified the French Federation's rules prohibiting the wearing of signs or clothing that ostensibly demonstrate religious, political or union affiliation.[2] The specific conditions under which football competitions take place meant that, to avoid any source of tension or confrontation inside or outside the stadiums, the participants, in this case the players whom the media had dubbed the "Hijabeuses" because they wanted to wear the hijab, had to remain strictly neutral and not wear any distinctive signs. Considering existing case law, this solution was not obvious, as the activities in question took place in the private sphere and, except for players on national teams representing their country, had no connection with public service. This new case law, the result of a delicate balance between the rights of the players concerned and social harmony, can however be explained if we consider the specific nature of the sport in question, its place in French society and the enthusiasm and passion it arouses.[3] The individual who claimed the right to respect for his beliefs had to comply with the common rule.

4. In the second ruling, the Grand Chamber of the CJEU, also departing from its Advocate General and, like the Council of State, evolving its case law, found that the statutory rules of the governing bodies of world and European football, FIFA and UEFA, allowing them to prevent the organisation of a "Super League," a new European competition competing with the UEFA Champions League, were in breach of EU competition law.[4] In this context, unlike the solution adopted by the French administrative court, it was the rights of the individual vis-à-vis the group that seemed to have prevailed: the most renowned football clubs, which wanted to break free from UEFA's control[5] and "secede" by creating their own competition outside of the one organised by the confederation, appear to have obtained their exit pass, at least in principle. The specific nature of sport, which was invoked by the federations and the many member state governments arguing the same case before the Court, did not allow the competition rules to be bent.

5. Such a solution deserves attention, particularly because of the contrast that a practitioner of French administrative law can see with the case concerning the wearing of the veil and because of the surprise effect of the outcome of this case, which was not anticipated in the Advocate General's conclusions. Identifying the

---

1 Case C-415/93 *Union Royale Belge Sociale de Football Association, RCL and UEFA v JM Bosman* ECLI:EU:C:1995:463.

2 Case 458088 Conseil d'État Decision *Association Alliance citoyenne et autres* (29 June 2023) <https://www.conseil-etat.fr/arianewebtraduite/#/view-document/> accessed 22 May 2026

3 Alexis Goin, "La Main de Dieu" (The Hand of God) (2023) 31 AJDA 1646.

4 Case C-333/21 *European Super League* ECLI:EU:C:2023:1011, known as the "*Super League*" judgment.

5 The Court's judgment rules on the statutory rules of FIFA and UEFA, but this contribution, which focuses on the organisation of European competitions, will concentrate on those of UEFA.

basis for the Court's analysis in such an emblematic case is also instructive in terms of the Court's conception of its mission.

6. This is not the place for an in-depth exegesis of the judgment, as the format of the analysis does not lend itself to this. At most, we will find a few personal reflections, which are solely those of the author, providing a broad understanding of what the Court ruled and its possible consequences. The lessons learned from another case brought before the Court and decided on the same day, concerning a breach of competition law by the International Skating Union (ISU), will be included. The terrain is therefore undoubtedly slippery. We hope you will forgive us for any legal shortcuts or linguistic approximations.

7. The analysis will begin with sport. It is important to know where we stand, and no fencer would disagree with that. It is also important to understand the market in question to grasp what competition law infringements were involved.

I. Some "Cooperative" Characteristics of Sports Federations

8. International sports federations do not have a good reputation. Without even mentioning the cases that may have tarnished certain personal reputations or revealed breaches of integrity, objective factors do not contribute to a climate of spontaneous trust in them. Their financial clout in an era of mass enthusiasm for the most popular sports, the influence they can exert on political leaders, their Swiss roots and their "associative" autonomy, which seem to place them outside the jurisdiction of Member States, their lack of transparency in governance, the importance of the decisions they make regarding the allocation of major competitions, and the disinterest cultivated in certain circles at with regard to sports are among the considerations that may come to mind, giving rise to an unfavourable presumption of exclusivity.

9. A quick look back at the history of the creation of federations shows that there was no alternative to setting up, within an associative framework, at national and then international level, entities independent of public authorities, bringing together clubs and participants. At a time when sports disciplines were still in their infancy and practiced by mere amateurs, tournaments and competitions had to be organised by a few willing individuals. Aristocrats, who had the time, the means, and a taste for travel in the era of "yesterday's Europe" dear to Stefan Zweig, were often involved. The International Olympic Committee was established in Lausanne in 1913 in search of a permanently peaceful headquarters in a neutral country, sheltered from the turmoil of the First World War. During this founding period at the beginning of the 20th century, the need to harmonise practices, adopt common rules and provide the means to punish violations became apparent. The structuring of national federations, accompanying the professionalisation of high-level sport, then international federations, the gradual recognition of the social, health and cultural role of sport, and its increasingly significant economic and even political importance, justified, especially since World War II, the establishment of state intervention. Control mechanisms, which were quite extensive in France, maintained, for the most part, the freedom of association that had presided over the development of the sports movement since its inception.

10. FIFA, founded in 1904 in Paris by the football committee of the Union of French Athletic Sports Societies (*Union des sociétés françaises de sports athlétiques*), and to which many federations gradually joined, was for a long time the only federation bringing together national football federations. For a national team to take part in its competitions, notably the first World Cup in 1930 in Uruguay, FIFA required, quite legitimately, that the national federation concerned be recognised. With the principle of recognition of one federation per country prevailing, except for the influential British Football Association, which was adopted in relation to the football "nations" of the United Kingdom, participation in international matches was a powerful factor in uniting clubs within a single national federation.

11. It was only after the death of Jules Rimet, FIFA president from 1920 until his death in 1954, that the world federation accepted the possibility of creating continental confederations, an idea that the deceased had always fought against. Thus, in 1954, UEFA was born and quickly implemented the project that was the raison d'être of its existence: the organisation of European football competitions, between national teams of course, but also between the best clubs, champions in their own countries.[6] The project, initiated by members of the editorial staff of the newspaper *L'Équipe* in 1955, was quickly placed under the auspices of UEFA. The first season of the European Cup in 1956 was a great success, which would continue to grow after the creation in 1992 of its successors, the Champions League; two other competitions were also created, the Cup Winners' Cup and the UEFA Cup, also organised by UEFA.

12. It is worth noting that 1956 was the year of the Spaak Report, which was so influential in the negotiations that led to the signing of the Treaty of Rome in 1957. European football was born at the same time as political Europe. As the European Community was being built, the most prestigious football competition took root, bringing together all the best teams from an even larger Europe, from Lisbon to Prague via Edinburgh and Copenhagen, and allowing the best of them to be crowned at the end of each season. The ambition, the dream of every club, for reasons of both sporting prestige and profitability, is to participate and, for this reason, to finish at the top of their national league, in first place or, for the major footballing nations, in the top four places of that league, which qualify for the competition. The very meaning of this tournament, which pits dozens of teams against each other from August to the following May, is therefore to bring together clubs based on sporting merit.

13. This dynamic was amplified by the ECJ in its *Bosman* ruling, cited above, which revolutionised both the career paths of players, by liberalising the conditions for their transfers between clubs, and the composition of teams, by removing the previous limit on the number of foreign players. Since this landmark ruling, teams with the highest revenues have been able to maximise their income and add to their trophy cabinets by recruiting the stars of the game, who perform best on the pitch and/or enhance the club's reputation. One fundamental point can be

---

[6] Laurent Barcelo, "L'« europe des 52 »…: L'Union Européenne de Football Association (UEFA)" (Europe of 52, UEFA) (2007) 228(4) *Guerres mondiales et conflits contemporains* 119–133.

highlighted: by giving more advantages to the richest teams, the *Bosman* ruling has certainly altered the chances of success for "average" teams, which now only rarely appear at the top of national rankings and have disappeared from European rankings.[7] However, this case law has not called into question the cardinal principle of competitions organised since the creation of UEFA, namely that European tournaments, particularly the Champions League, bring together teams based on sporting merit. There is no question of buying participation in such a competition or of ensuring a sustainable level of income that is disconnected from sporting results. At the national championship level, the same rule applies: only the clubs with the best results are included in the first division, whose top place(s) open access to the European leagues, with the clubs at the bottom of the table being relegated at the end of the season in favour of clubs promoted from the lower divisions, the same mechanism applies to all lower levels, down to amateur clubs.

14. In the market for these competitions, to comply with the competition law analysis framework that structures this discussion, competition is based on merit, whether this is achieved through tangible results in the rankings, through playing an attractive game that draws large crowds and television audiences, or through a history steeped in legends of yesteryear. The combination of these elements is, of course, the hallmark of the big clubs, which only maintain their status over time if these elements remain present. There are indeed big clubs whose history is mainly in the past, Reims and Saint-Étienne being among them in France. Just as a company whose products are no longer sold loses its commercial base, a club without sporting results achieved in adversity, without the threat of relegation under pressure from lower division clubs, runs the risk of ultimately being abandoned by the public, both in stadiums and in front of television screens. It is the participation of all clubs in this football community that ensures the widest and most intense competition possible: everyone can try their luck, and any club can one day hope to reach the top, as AJ Auxerre, a club from a medium-sized city with a limited budget, demonstrated in the 1990s. Another specific feature of competition between teams is that, for the competition to be successful, it is often necessary for the outcome to be open and for several teams of comparable strength to compete against each other: if one club consistently outclasses its rivals, it may satisfy its supporters, but the disappearance of the "glorious uncertainty of sport" may ultimately affect the public's interest in the tournament. This results in an interdependence between competitors that is not found in a traditional market, where a company has every interest in seeing its rivals disappear or in outperforming them in the long term. Such interdependence is one of the key factors in the cooperative dynamic between clubs and national federations.[8]

15. Even though UEFA is a non-profit organisation, organising a competition such as the Champions League generates substantial revenue for its organiser and participants, particularly through television broadcasting rights for matches,

---

7 On the economic consequences of the Bosman ruling, see, among many other works, Jean-Jacques Gouguet, "*Le sport professionnel après l'arrêt Bosman*" (*Professional sport after the Bosman ruling*) (PU 2004).

8 See in particular Pablo Ibañez Colomo, "Competition Law and Sports Governance: Disentangling a Complex Relationship" (2022) 45(30) World Competition 45 323–350.

such that it constitutes an economic activity.[9] It is also undeniable that, since its creation, UEFA has, by the will of the national federations of which it is composed, had exclusive control over the organisation of that competition. Under its statutes, it even has sole discretion to decide on the organisation and abolition of international competitions in Europe in which its members, the national federations and their member clubs, participate. Matches that are not organised by UEFA but take place on its territory must be authorised in advance, where they involve its members, either by UEFA itself or by the competent national federation that is a member of UEFA.

16. But can we deduce from these rules that UEFA is in a "monopoly" situation, as usually understood in competition law? A monopolistic company is one that is the sole supplier in the market to buyers. It is therefore the only one to receive revenue from its activity. However, in the European football competition market, UEFA is not a separate entity from the federations and clubs, external to them, which develops an activity in this market from which it alone receives the revenue, and which has arrogated economic exclusivity to itself by its own will. UEFA operates on a cooperative basis: the federations are its members, just as the clubs are members of the federations. The association of members within UEFA is not justified by the pursuit of an agreement that would be detrimental to other market players, since all players in sports competition, ie clubs wishing to organise European matches, are part of UEFA. No club is excluded from the market in this cooperative perspective. Revenues from European competitions are distributed to participating clubs.[10] Solidarity mechanisms are also in place, for example to finance clubs in difficulty or to contribute to the development of football, including amateur football, outside the professional leagues. UEFA's annual accounts clearly show that most of the revenue generated by the Champions League is shared among all participating clubs and feeds into the organisation's budget, which is partly dedicated to funding football in general.[11] It is because of these redistribution flows that regular discussions are held between UEFA and its members on changes to the format of the Champions League or other European competitions it organises, some want to lighten the competition schedule to relieve the players while others want to add matches to increase club revenues, etc.

17. Of course, not all clubs or federations may benefit from this cooperation or may feel that they are not being listened to or taken into consideration sufficiently. Some clubs or economic operators may also view this cooperation as a constraint, since it is the legacy of decisions made by previous generations. As in any collective entity, membership of the group may be or appear to be of greater interest to some than to others. The governing bodies of UEFA, the Congress and the

---

9 Established case law since Case 36/74 *Walrave and Koch v Association Union Cycliste Internationale and others* ECLI:EU:C:1974:140, point 4.

10 UEFA Letter No 35/2023 to EUFA Association Members (7 July 2023), concerning the distribution of revenue from the three European competitions to clubs, <https://editorial.uefa.com/resources/0283-1874e21d8957-30a439a30e08-1000/20230707_circular_2023_35_en.pdf> accessed 22 May 2026.

11 Ibid, and the UEFA, *Annual Report 2022–2023* (2024), and the accompanying financial report, <https://editorial.uefa.com/resources/0288-199d4c62d529-a4b86a243d5b-1000/uefa_annual_report_2022-23.pdf> accessed 22 May 2026.

Executive Committee, are supposed to represent the interests of all members of the organisation. However, it cannot be ruled out that national affiliations, friendships or other considerations may interfere with collective decision-making. The same tension can also arise between the continental confederations and FIFA: when FIFA appeared to be considering the possibility of organising the World Cup every two years rather than every four years, UEFA was the first to protest against this schedule, which would have disrupted the organisation of the Euro football championship, bringing together the national teams of European countries every four years, alternating with the World Cup. In addition, UEFA may be led to sanction clubs for violating certain rules, such as those of financial fair play, imposing limits on their budgets. This has resulted in several disputes that have fuelled criticism of the federation.[12]

18. For the same reasons that lead us to consider, in our analysis of UEFA's monopoly on licensing, the economic context under consideration here, which is that of a cooperative environment in which all clubs participate, the concept of abuse of a dominant position appears to require special consideration. Can a member of the organisation consider that the organisation is abusing its dominant position in relation to it? A company that abuses its dominant position is one which, in each market, drives out competitors or prevents competitors, even potential ones, from remaining in or entering a market, by means of abnormal behaviour that is unrelated to competition on merit. A large club that participates in the Champions League, which generates substantial revenue for it as part of a cooperative structure to which it belongs, along with its national federation, which at the same time generates revenue from its participation in the national championship thanks to the federal structure in which it operates, may be justified in complaining that it does not receive enough revenue from UEFA and in calling for a change in the format of the competition or the rules for the redistribution of revenue, in particular broadcasting rights. But can it claim to be "excluded from the market" if it does not have the opportunity to organise, with others, a competition that competes with that of UEFA? It is not certain that it is the club itself that is excluded from the market, but rather economic actors outside the federal structure who are devising competition projects that are, in essence, foreign to the cooperative dimension of football. In such a cooperative model, is it conceivable that clubs could continue to participate in all national competitions organised by their federation and initiate the creation of another competition that would be more interesting for them than the one organised at the European level by UEFA, without undermining the foundations of the model? It was this "à-la-carte" reasoning that the Court was confronted with for the first time in the *Super League* case.[13]

---

12 See, for example, "Football: Tense Relations between Manchester City and UEFA" *Le Monde* (26 February 2020) <https://www.lemonde.fr/sport/article/2020/07/13/football-manchester-city-echappe-a-une-exclusion-des-coupes-d-europe_6046057_3242.html> accessed 22 May 2026.

13 For an overview of the debate from a competition law perspective, see in particular Oliver Budzinski et al., "The Future of Sport Governance in Europe" (13 January 2023) 1 Concurrences Art. No. 111158. www.concurrences.com/111158.

II. The Super League Project and the Speed Skating Case: Sports Federations "Seized" by Competition Law

19. On 18 April 2021, with the Covid-19 pandemic still posing a serious threat, the football season having been played in empty stadiums, club finances under severe strain and clubs, like all businesses, having survived thanks to public funds mobilised in these exceptional circumstances, a bombshell hit the football community. The *New York Times* announced the imminent launch of a new European league, the "Super League." Twelve of Europe's most renowned and influential clubs (six English, three Italian and three Spanish) were presented as the promoters of this project, which would be financed by a major American investment bank and would compete with the Champions League. Real Madrid, the most iconic club in this competition by far, holding the record for the number of trophies won, was one of these clubs. The project has not been officially notified to UEFA. No request for authorisation to create this competition has been submitted to it.

20. On the same day, UEFA, along with the national federations of the clubs concerned, responded with a press release threatening that should the project go ahead, the clubs involved would be banned from participating in any other national, European or global competitions. It added that their players could be denied the opportunity to represent their national teams. It is worth noting the difference between the ban on clubs participating, which was presented as certain, and the more hypothetical announcement that players would be excluded from their national teams. The project was described as "cynical, based on the self- interest of a few at a time when society is more than ever in need of solidarity." That same evening, an official statement announced the launch of the Super League. It specified that this competition would bring together 15 permanent clubs, with three clubs ready to join the 12 founders and five clubs invited, without specifying the criteria for this invitation. This competition would therefore be a closed competition, bringing together permanent members, without a promotion and relegation mechanism. Admittedly, these clubs had earned their reputation and prestige on the pitch, through their matches, but they intended, thanks to guaranteed participation in a competition that is presumed to be much more lucrative than the Champions League,[14] to secure their revenues and investments by bringing together teams of stars for exclusively high-level matches. Significantly, the announcement was made on the eve of a UEFA executive committee meeting to approve the new format of the Champions League after 2024, so it can be assumed that it was a means of putting pressure on UEFA to take greater account of the interests of the big clubs. It should be remembered that in 1998, an initial version of a "breakaway league" was considered but quickly abandoned.

21. To say that the announcement of the project caused an outcry in Europe would be an understatement. The front pages of the newspapers in the days that followed

---

14 The participating clubs seemed to be expecting a sum of around €300 million each. To give an idea of the scale, Manchester City, winner of the Champions League in 2023, has a turnover of around €800 million, with around €150 million coming from UEFA for this tournament.

are proof of this.[15] National federations and many fans, particularly in the United Kingdom, see the project as an attack on the cooperative model, a challenge to sporting merit and a selfish move by the clubs with the highest revenues. Leading politicians voiced their opposition.[16] Faced with widespread opposition and the threat of exclusion from competitions, most of the clubs involved, particularly the English clubs, quickly abandoned the project.[17]

22. Two of the Spanish clubs, the most determined to implement the project, continued to promote it and while the press echoed all the criticism, the company behind the project, ESLC, brought the case before the Madrid Commercial Court, which, on 19–20 April 2021, issued an interim order requiring UEFA, FIFA and the federations to refrain from obstructing the project and sanctioning participating clubs and players, until a judgment on the merits was made. In May 2021, the Spanish court referred the matter to the CJEU for a preliminary ruling, asking it, in essence, to rule on whether Articles 101 and 102 TFEU, which prohibit cartels and abuse of a dominant position,[18] prohibit UEFA and FIFA from stipulating in their statutes that the creation of a competition such as the Super League must be subject to prior authorisation, from threatening to sanction its participants and from providing that the rights to competitions organised by UEFA and FIFA are reserved for them. The referring court also asked the Court to clarify whether the rule requiring prior authorisation for competitions is compatible with the freedoms of movement, in particular the freedom to provide services.

23. During the same period, another case concerning the organisation of sports federations was pending before the European Commission. Two Dutch professional speed skaters, winners of international competitions organised by the ISU, had requested permission from the ISU to participate in a competition that a Korean company was planning to organise in Dubai. Rules similar to those of FIFA and UEFA are included in the statutes of this federation, providing for its power to give prior authorisation for competitions and to impose sanctions in the event of a breach of the statutes. The ISU considered that this competition violated the federation's principle of prohibiting sports betting, threatened the skaters with lifetime bans from all competitions if they participated. The skaters gave in to this threat but lodged a complaint with the European Commission, which in 2017 resulted in a decision in which it was found for the first time in relation to a sports federation, that the rules in question had the object and effect of restricting competition within the meaning of Article 101 TFEU.[19] In view of the unprecedented nature of the grounds for its decision, the Commission did not impose a fine on the ISU. The latter brought an action for annulment against the infringement finding before the General Court of the European Union.

---

15 The documentaries broadcast in 2022 on Sky TV, *Super Greed: The Fight for Football* and in 2023 on Apple TV, *Super League, The War for Football*, recount this turbulent episode, focusing mainly on the point of view of the project's detractors.

16 Danny Boyle, "PM Takes on Football Giants over New Super League Plan" *Daily Telegraph* (19 April 2021) <https://www.telegraph.co.uk/news/2021/04/19/monday-morning-uk-news-briefing-todays-top-headlines-telegraph/> accessed 22 May 2026.

17 "Fans Celebrate as Super League Plan Stands on Brink of Collapse" *The Guardian* (21 April 2021).

18 Treaty on the Functioning of the European Union (TFEU) [2008] OJ C115/120, arts 101 and 102.

19 Case AT.40208 European Commission Decision *International Skating Union's Eligibility* (8 December 2017).

III. The Legal Framework Prior to the Court of Justice Ruling: The *Wouters/Meca-Medina* "Test" and Article 165 TFEU

24. The conditions for applying competition law to sports competitions have been the subject of several landmark judgments by the Court since the 1970s. The landscape was therefore not entirely blank before the *Super League* case. The General Court of the European Union had also ruled in the first instance on the appeal lodged by the ISU, rejecting it for the most part. The Commission's decision in the *ISU* case and the judgment handed down by the General Court had already led UEFA to amend its statutes in 2022. This judgment was appealed to the Court by the ISU. It was therefore for the Court to rule on the Spanish preliminary ruling and on the merits of the appeal in the skating case.

25. The Court's case law provided clear guidance on the application of competition law to the prerogatives of sports federations, on which the General Court relied in the *ISU* case. The Court had long considered that certain rules of an exclusively sporting nature, "relating solely to sport" were "unrelated to economic activity" and thus fell outside the scope of European competition law.[20] In the landmark *Bosman* case, the ECJ preferred to stick to a conventional analysis of the reconciliation between the rules on player transfers and team composition and the free movement of workers, carefully avoiding ruling on the questions posed by the referring court in relation to competition law.

26. This "sports exception"[21] appeared to still apply in a case in the mid-2000s concerning anti-doping rules enacted by the International Olympic Committee (IOC). Two long-distance swimmers who tested positive for nandrolone, Mr Meca-Medina and Mr Majcen, suspended from competition for two years, asked the European Commission to rule that these anti-doping measures violated EU competition law. While the Commission, the Court of First Instance hearing the case and AG Léger before the Court at the appeal stage had all considered that the doping provisions were exempt from competition law constraints, the ECJ ruled in 2006 that this was not the case. It considered that these provisions, insofar as they allowed professional athletes to be excluded from competitions, were of an economic nature. In a statement of principle, the Court ruled that "the mere fact that a rule is of a purely sporting nature does not mean that the person carrying out the activity governed by that rule or the body which laid down that rule falls outside the scope of the Treaty".[22] In other words, there

---

20 *Walrave and Koch* (n 9), point 8, on the formation of national teams; Case 13/76 *Gaetano Donà v Mario Mantero* ECLI:EU:C:1976:115, point 14, on the exclusion of foreign players on non-economic grounds

21 Already partially challenged by Joined Cases C-51/96 and C-191/97 *Deliege v Ligue Francophone de Judo et Disciplines Associees ASBL* ECLI:EU:C:2000:199, point 64, in which the Court did not apply the criterion of "purely sporting" rules but allowed a restriction on the freedom to provide services inherent in the conduct of an international competition.

22 Case C-519/04 P *David Meca-Medina and Igor Majcen v Commission of the European Communities* ECLI:EU:C:2006:492, point 27.

is no longer any sports exception that would grant competitive immunity to the organisations responsible for organising sports.

27. However, while it signalled the end of the sports exception, the Court did not consider that anti-doping rules fell within the scope of the prohibition of agreements provided for in Article 81 EC (now Article 101 TFEU). To determine whether these rules had the "object" of restricting competition and thus seriously undermined market law, it applied the analytical framework it had developed in a 2002 judgment in *Wouters*, concerning the professional conduct of lawyers in the Netherlands.[23] The Bar Association of that state had prohibited integrated collaborations between lawyers and accountants, to guarantee the independence of lawyers and compliance with their own professional ethics, distinguishing them from accountants. The Court found that a professional association adopting such rules, which had an impact on the functioning of the market concerned, was acting as an association of undertakings within the meaning of Article 81 EC. However, after examining the overall context, the objectives pursued by the contested rules, their suitability for those purposes and their proportionality, it found that those rules, although restrictive of competition, did not go beyond what was necessary to ensure the proper exercise of the profession of lawyer. It concluded that the prohibition in question did not infringe Article 81 EC. In other words, the Court reconciled competition law with the legitimate interests pursued by the contested regulations.

28. Applying the same test in the *Meca-Medina* case, the Court ruled that the IOC's anti-doping rules, including the sanctions attached to them, although restrictive, were inherent in the objective of combating doping and necessary for the fair conduct of sporting competitions, equal opportunities for athletes, their health, integrity and ethical values in sport. The same test was subsequently used by the Court in 2013 to rule that the regulations of the Portuguese Association of Chartered Accountants requiring mandatory training credits to be obtained exclusively through training provided by the Association itself constituted a restriction of competition that went beyond what was necessary to ensure the quality of the services provided by chartered accountants.[24] The EU General Court followed the same reasoning in 2014 in a case concerning restrictive measures on competition in terms of pricing and the development of analysis laboratories adopted by the French Order of Pharmacists. In concluding that there had been a violation of Article 81 EC, the Court found that the measures in question went beyond the tasks entrusted to the Order by law and could not therefore be justified by the public interest objectives pursued by the public authorities.[25] In these last two cases, both the Court and the General Court took into consideration the findings of a 2008 judgment in *MOTOE*, concerning the organisation of motorcycle competitions in Greece. In that judgment, the Court warned sports federations against the risk of abusing their dominant position in the market for the organisation of competitions: a federation which

---

23 Case C-309/99 *Wouters* ECLI:EU:C:2002:98.

24 Case C-1/12 *Ordem dos Técnicos Oficiais de Contas (OTOC)* ECLI:EU:C:2013:127.

25 Case T-90/11 *Ordre national des pharmaciens (ONP) and Others v European Commission* ECLI:EU:T:2014:1049.

organises its own competitions and has the power to grant prior authorisation for competitions by third parties is in a position to potentially favour its own competitions on the relevant market, so that in order to prevent the risk of abuse of its dominant position, its power of authorisation must be subject to limits, obligations and controls.[26] This ruling does not condemn the combination of regulatory and economic activities by the same federation but requires it to use its powers in such a way that third parties are not unduly deprived of access to the market.

29. During the 2000s, as the *Wouters/Meca-Medina* case law developed, the economic and social importance of sport and the corresponding need to clarify the legal framework for its development justified the implementation of a European sports policy by the European Commission and the Member States. The report by the European Commission's High-Level Group on Sport prepared for the Helsinki European Council in 1999 emphasised that sport must "sport must be able to assimilate the new commercial framework in which it must develop, without at the same time losing its identity and autonomy, which underpin the functions it performs in the social, cultural, health and educational areas." The document proposed promoting sporting merit based on the promotion-relegation mechanism, regulating the conditions for the acquisition of clubs by commercial entities, combating doping and protecting young athletes. In December 2000, the Nice European Council issued a declaration on the specific characteristics of sport, reiterating the Member States' commitment to solidarity between all levels of sporting activity, the autonomy of sports federations, fair competition, the involvement of volunteers and the protection of athletes' physical integrity. In its 2007 White Paper on Sport, the European Commission recognised the specific nature of sport in terms of its practices and organisational structures and acknowledged that restrictive competition rules laid down by federations may not constitute infringements of competition law or freedom of movement, if they are proportionate and justified by the pursuit of a genuine legitimate sporting interest. In Annex I to its White Paper, the Commission set out its methodological approach to reconciling the economic dimension of sport with the objectives pursued by the regulations of the bodies in charge of competitions, following the *Wouters/Meca-Medina* test in every respect.

30. These developments have been given political and legal recognition in the treaties, with the inclusion in the Treaty of Lisbon of Article 165 TFEU on education, vocational training, youth and sport. This article states, in its seventh indent, that the Union's action shall aim "to develop the European dimension in sport, by promoting fairness and openness in sporting competitions and cooperation between bodies responsible for sport, and by protecting the physical and moral integrity of sportsmen and sportswomen, especially the youngest sportsmen and sportswomen."[27] This text does not refer to the "specific nature of sport" or the "pyramidal structure" of federation activities, nor even to

---

26 Case C-49/07 *MOTOE* ECLI:EU:C:2008:376.

27 TFEU, art 165(2).

a principle of solidarity. Nevertheless, it explicitly recognises as legitimate, insofar as the Union's action must support these objectives, on the one hand, the principle of open competitions that respect sporting fairness, ie merit and the condemnation of doping, the protection of the physical and moral integrity of athletes, and on the other hand, the promotion of cooperation between the bodies responsible for sport. It is reasonable to assume that this wording supports the cooperative model described above. In any case, this is how the Member States interpret it, as confirmed by the resolution of the Council of the Union and the representatives of the governments of the Member States, adopted unanimously on 30 November 2021, on the main characteristics of a European model for sport.[28] According to this resolution, these characteristics include a pyramid structure, management by a single federation per discipline, an open promotion and relegation system, solidarity, the social function of sport and the integrity of sport. Point 28 of the document draws attention to "the consequences that closed sports competitions could have on organised sport in Europe, such as a fundamental change in the sports qualification processes that are generally based on sporting merit."

31. In the *ISU* case, the EU General Court had to draw on all of these sources to separate the wheat from the chaff in terms of competition law. While recalling the important lessons of the *MOTOE* judgment, it stuck to the *Wouters/Medina* compass, citing Article 165 TFEU from the outset of its analysis of the objectives alleged by the applicant federation.[29] Having pointed out the obvious, namely that the ISU was an association of undertakings within the meaning of Article 101 TFEU, active in the speed skating competition market, it examined the overall context, the objectives allegedly pursued by the ISU through the disputed rules, the adequacy of those rules in relation to the objectives put forward and their proportionality. It noted that the alleged objective of protecting the integrity of competitions by prohibiting sports betting did not appear in the federation's statutes, unlike the reference to preserving its economic interests. It found that the procedure for prior authorisation of competitions did not include clearly defined, transparent, non-discriminatory, verifiable authorisation criteria capable of guaranteeing competition organisers effective access to the relevant market. It noted that the penalties imposed on athletes participating in competitions not authorised by the federation were particularly severe and dissuasive. While it agreed with the Commission that a federation, when acting as a business, is perfectly entitled like any business, to protect its economic interests, it concluded after weighing up all the factors, that the rules in question, in view of their content, their objectives and the context in which they operate, were sufficiently harmful to be considered as restricting competition by object within the meaning of Article 101 TFEU, so that there was no need to examine their effects on competition. It is clear from the judgment that if legitimate sporting objectives, such as the integrity of competitions, the protection of athletes' health, and respect

---

28 European Council, "European Sports Model" No 13711/21 (30 November 2021) <https://data.consilium.europa.eu/doc/document/ST-14430-2021-INIT/en/pdf> accessed 21 May 2026.

29 Case T-93/18 *International Skating Union* ECLI:EU:T:2020:610.

for competitions organised by the federation, had been pursued in an appropriate manner by proportionate means, the finding of an infringement could have been ruled out. Such a positive outcome for the ISU was all the more unlikely given that the complainant skaters, unlike the clubs promoting the Super League, which benefited from the substantial revenues generated by the Champions League, were excluded from the few competitions that could have enabled them to monetise their sporting talents, without undermining the competitions organised by the federation, sporting fairness or the physical integrity of the skaters.

IV. The Court's Super League and ISU rulings: Competition Law Takes Precedence over the Specific Nature of Sport

32. For sports law practitioners, Member States, and the European Commission, the Court was expected to apply the *Wouters/Meca-Medina* test, as did the EU General Court. In line with this approach, the Commission and the many Member States (more than 20) that submitted observations to the Court in the *Super League* case, except for the Czech Republic and the Grand Duchy of Luxembourg in their written observations, essentially supported the views of FIFA and UEFA, with some variations in their arguments. Many of them referred to Article 165 TFEU and proposed that the Court rule that making the organisation of a competition such as the Super League subject to prior authorisation by UEFA and threatening sanctions for those who disregarded a refusal of authorisation did not constitute a violation of Articles 101 and 102 TFEU, since these rules pursued legitimate objectives relating to the preservation of the European sports model and did not go beyond what was necessary to achieve them. The Commission was certainly more nuanced in suggesting that it should be left to the referring court to assess the proportionality of the rules and sanctions at issue. However, it did not immediately see these measures, regardless of their context, as seriously undermining competition and acknowledged that the objectives pursued by UEFA were legitimate.

33. It appeared to many of those involved in the Court proceedings that the format of the new competition, which was essentially closed, based on considerations other than sporting merit and contrary to the principle of cooperation, could justify UEFA's restrictive approach, reminding the project's promoters that if they went ahead with it, they would be excluded from the federative structure at both European and national level. Advocate General Rantos for his part, believed the contested rules did not in any way prevent the clubs promoting the Super League project from creating this competition outside the framework of UEFA, the only consequence for them being to agree to see through this secessionist ambition, ie to leave UEFA. He therefore did not see this as anticompetitive, but simply as the consequence of a refusal to adhere to the cooperative functioning of the football community. However, the Advocate General went a step further than some of those involved in the "UEFA side": he considered that the Court should take the opportunity of this case to recognise the constitutional existence, under Article 165 TFEU, of the European sports model, based on its "pyramidal structure" and its solidarity mechanisms. In the same vein, he considered in his

conclusions on the ISU's appeal against the General Court's judgment, that the latter had vitiated its analysis with an error of law by failing to take due account of the legitimate sporting objectives pursued by the federation, which should have justified a finding that there was no infringement of Article 101 TFEU.[30]

34. The Court's judgment in the *Super League* case wrong-footed, if we may use that metaphor, the international federations, the Member States, the European Commission and the Advocate General. The Court could have limited the scope of its response to the specific context of the creation of the Super League, as the parties to the preliminary ruling proceedings believed it should. No doubt in search of a more general response to the issues raised by the referring court and in line with the case law policy it has been pursuing for several years, the Court preferred an approach that seems more abstract, to the point of being decontextualised here. The Court thus indicated that it was not for it to rule on the compatibility of the Super League project with competition law, as "the characteristics of that project are not particularly relevant to the answers to the questions raised".[31] In an unprecedented analysis, focused on the rules themselves, detached from their context, their objectives and the controversial project, the Court ruled that these rules constituted an abuse of a dominant position by object and a cartel between undertakings with the object of restricting competition, falling respectively under Articles 102 and 101 TFEU, without examining the effect of these rules on competition.

35. It is significant to note that this judgment – as in its judgment concerning the ISU, handed down on the same day[32] – repeatedly affirms a kind of competition law primacy, with competition law rules appearing to be given a higher ranking among the provisions of the Treaty. It is likely that competition law practitioners, confident in their expertise and the influence of their discipline, will be satisfied with this. Proponents of an approach that synthesises fundamental rights and reconciles their purposes may have more questions. Indeed, the Court's assertion of the primacy of competition regulation over the specific characteristics of sport is supported by a series of converging grounds underlined in the judgment.

36. First, the Court gives only marginal significance to Article 165 TFEU and does not set out in its judgment the arguments of the Member States based on that provision.[33] It notes that this article is included in Part Three of the TFEU,

---

30 For comments on the Advocate General's conclusions: see, in support of his position, Johan Karlsson, "Sport and Competition Law: Opinion of Advocate General Ranto in Case C-333/21 European Superleague" (2023) 1 ELJ 83–100, or Pablo Ibañez Colomo, "AG Rantos in Super League and ISU: Towards Continuity and Consistency in the Case Law" (*Chillin'Competition*, 15 December 2022) <https://chillingcompetition.com/2022/12/15/ag-rantos-in-super-league-and-isu-towards-continuity-and-consistency-in-the-case-law/> accessed 22 May 2026; and against, Stephen Weatherill, "A Judicial Coronation of the European Model of Sport? The Conclusions of AG Rantos in the Superleague Case" (13 January 2023) 1 Concurrences 2–7, and, in the same issue, Oliver Budzinski, "Economics Upside Down? A Comment on the AG Opinion in Superleague" (13 January 2023) 1 Concurrences.

31 *Super League* (n 4), para 81.

32 Case C-124/21 P *International Skating Union* ECLI:EU:C:2023:1012.

33 Following the amendment of Article 23 of the Statute of the Court of Justice in 2024, the observations of the parties to the preliminary ruling proceedings will in principle be published on the Court's website after the proceedings have been closed.

relating to "internal policies and actions of the Union", and not in Part One, which contains provisions of principle, and that it is therefore not a provision of general application with a cross-cutting nature. It follows that, while Article 165 TFEU recognises the specific characteristics of sport, these may "possibly" be taken into account, provided, according to the Court, that "such consideration may only be given within the framework and in compliance with the conditions and criteria for application laid down in Articles 101 and 102 TFEU." It should be noted in passing, that Articles 101 and 102 TFEU are not provisions of general application with a cross-cutting nature either, since they appear, like Article 165 TFEU, in the third part of the Treaty on the Union's internal policies and actions. The General Court had ruled in the *ISU* case that Article 165 TFEU had to be taken into account in the application of Article 101 TFEU.

37. Second, the Court appears, at least in the circumstances of the *Super League* case, to have abandoned the *Wouters/Meca-Medina* test, which made it possible to reconcile the competition law approach with the pursuit of legitimate objectives. In reaching the conclusion that the UEFA rules constitute an abuse of a dominant position and a cartel, it merely notes that those rules are not accompanied by substantive criteria or procedural arrangements to ensure that they are transparent, objective, non-discriminatory and proportionate. However, the Court's case law, particularly since the 2014 *Cartes bancaires* judgment, had emphasised that the classification of an agreement as constituting a "by object" restriction, apart from "hardcore" restrictions such as price agreements, must be based on an analysis of the functioning of the market concerned, the context and the finding that the restriction in question is sufficiently harmful.[34] In the *Wouters/Meca-Medina* test, such a classification could only be concluded in light of the objectives pursued by the regulations in question and the appropriateness or otherwise of the rules at issue. The Court appears to have departed from this method in the *Super League* case: even if the UEFA rules had pursued a legitimate objective, in particular in that they would have made it possible to prevent the implementation of a project that undermined the cooperative model, or even the implementation of an agreement contrary to competition on the merits, they were so deficient that they had to be regarded as seriously harmful because they were restrictive by object.

38. It could have been conceivable that the substantive criteria whose deficiency was highlighted by the Court were constituted, at least in part, by the objectives pursued by UEFA. Indeed, an authorisation procedure aims to ensure compliance not with criteria as such, but with the purposes that they seek to protect. It is clear that if the Super League project had been submitted to UEFA for authorisation – which was not the case and which may not even have been required, according to AG Rantos' approach – the likely refusal would have been based on the violation of the principles of the cooperative model promoted by the federation. Would a refusal on such grounds have been considered arbitrary and discriminatory? In any

---

34 Case C-67/13 P *Groupement des cartes bancaires (CB) v European Commission* ECLI:EU:C:2014:2204, paras 49, 50, and 58; see also, for the requirement to take into account the context and objectives of the relevant decision on the association of undertakings: Case C-172/14 *ING Pensii* ECLI:EU:C:2015:484, para 33 and case law cited.

event, in the parallel *ISU* case, the Court, following its reasoning in the *Super League* case, dismissed the ISU's appeal against the General Court's judgment. The same legal analysis in both cases therefore enabled it to validate the outcome of the dispute brought before the General Court, even though the General Court's examination grid, based on the *Wouters/Meca-Medina* test, was very different.

39. In the same vein, the Court seized the opportunity given to it by the referring court to innovate in competition law in two respects. On the one hand, it removed doubt for the first time about the possibility that the same conduct could be classified as an infringement under both Articles 101 TFEU and 102 TFEU.[35] Second, and perhaps more spectacularly, the Court recognised the existence of an abuse of a dominant position by object, a new concept, thereby aligning the conditions for application, at least in the *Super League* case, of the two key provisions of EU competition law even though their wording differs significantly. This new concept could have the advantage for the Commission of considerably simplifying, in certain cases, the demonstration of an abuse of a dominant position. In this scenario, it is no longer necessary to define the relevant market, and it seems that the Commission – or the competent competition authority – is no longer required to identify the restrictive effects on competition in that market. According to the Court, once the rules in question have an anticompetitive purpose, it is not necessary to examine their restrictive effects. Admittedly, it has never been necessary to demonstrate the actual effects of a practice on a market in order to find abuse on the part of the dominant operator. However, to date it has always been considered necessary to identify at least potential effects on the relevant market.[36] The Court therefore surprised competition law experts, who in recent years had become accustomed to more demanding methodologies for competition authorities. In the cases between the Commission and Google, to stick with this illustration, the difficulties thus focused on the definition of the relevant markets and the ability of the alleged conduct to restrict competition in those markets. In the *Google Shopping* case, the issue at stake was Google's self-favouritism, which is not so far removed from the Court's criticism of UEFA's rules, suspected of favouring competitions organised by UEFA to the detriment of those organised by third parties.[37] In this case, the Commission sought to define the relevant market and establish Google's ability to restrict competition.

---

35 The Commission had already acknowledged this in Cases IV/34.073, IV/34.395 and IV/35.436 European Commission Decision *Van den Bergh Foods* Ltd (11 March 1998) and in Case AT.39612 European Commission Decision *Perindopril – Servier* (9 July 2014).

36 See, in particular, Case C-280/08 *Deutsche Telekom AG v European Commission* ECLI:EU:C:2010:603, paras 250 to 25; Case C-52/09 *Konkurrensverket v TeliaSonera Sverige AB* ECLI:EU:C:2011:83, paras 61 to 66. Even for conduct that is in principle anticompetitive, by means of exclusive loyalty discounts (Case 85/76 *F Hoffmann La Roche & Co AG v Commission of the European* Communities ECLI:EU:C:1979:36, para 89), if the dominant company disputes, with supporting evidence, that its conduct had the capacity to restrict competition, the competition authority must analyse all the relevant circumstances (*TeliaSonera Sverige AB*, para 68; Case C-23/14 *Post Danmark A/S v Konkurrenceradet* ECLI:EU:C:2015:651, para 68, and Case C-413/14 P *Intel Corp Inc v European Commission* ECLI:EU:C:2017:632, paras 138 and 139).

37 Case C-48/22 P *Google LLC v European Commission (Google Shopping)* ECLI:EU:C:2024:726, appeal against the judgment of the General Court in Case T-612/17 *Google LLC v European Commission* ECLI:EU:T:2021:763.

40. In short, in its *Super League* ruling, the Court opens the door wide to effective regulation of the sports sector through competition law. One might wonder whether this shift in case law calls into question the 2017 *Intel* case law,[38] which, by departing from previous case law on exclusive loyalty rebates,[39] seemed to bring back a more economic and less "automatic" approach to the analysis of abusive behaviour by dominant operators. Perhaps the Court was influenced by the contributions of the Digital Markets Act (DMA[40]), which in its new approach to ex-ante regulation, determines a priori which practices are prohibited for companies designated as "gatekeepers". However, the analogy between these gatekeepers and international sports federations seems difficult to draw. These federations do not exclude any clubs from sporting competition: as holders of control and authorisation powers delegated by their members, they allow sporting competition to take place as widely as possible among all clubs at both European and national levels.

41. Another very clear element in favour of the primacy of competition rules is that the Court appears to intend to apply them differently from the freedom of movement. While the assessment of the compliance of UEFA rules with freedom of movement, in particular the freedom to provide services, continues to follow the traditional paths of reconciliation between these economic freedoms and the objectives of general or sporting interest that these rules aim to achieve in the *Super League* judgment, when it comes to competition rules, the Court appears to apply them according to their own logic, without taking into account objectives of this nature. Restrictive conduct by UEFA or FIFA on the basis of the competition authorisation rules they have adopted can therefore, according to the Court, only benefit from an exemption on the basis of Article 101(3) TFEU. However, that paragraph only takes into account economic objectives aimed at improving the production or distribution of products or promoting technical or economic progress, while reserving a fair share of the resulting profit for users. It is difficult to find any trace in these provisions of social, ethical, health or sporting objectives, which the Court duly takes into account when it is alleged that sports regulations infringe these freedoms. It is this approach of conciliation and synthesis that the Court followed in another ruling on the same day as those relating to the Super League and the ISU, in a case involving Royal Antwerp Football Club, concerning the obligation for football clubs to have a certain number of "locally trained" players in their squads, in the part of this judgment relating to the free movement of workers.[41] This difference in treatment between the provisions of the Treaty relating to freedom of movement and the rules on competition seems to result in a form of hierarchy between them, or at least, the impression of greater flexibility in the application of freedom of movement, allowing for better recognition of legitimate sporting interests than when competition rules are at stake. However, all these provisions

---

38 *Intel Corp* Inc (n 36).

39 *Hoffmann La* Roche (n 36), para 89.

40 Regulation (EU) 2022/1925 of the European Parliament and of the Council of 14 September 2022 on contestable and fair markets in the digital sector and amending Directives (EU) 2019/1937 and (EU) 2020/1828 (Digital Markets Act (DMA)) [2022] OJ L265/1.

41 Case C-680/21 *Royal Antwerp FC* ECLI:EU:C:2023:1010.

are intended to contribute to the establishment of the internal market, in the same way as the rules on state aid, for which case law has long recognised that they must be implemented in accordance with the objectives of other Union policies,[42] as required by Article 7 TFEU. It cannot be ruled out that this "disconnection" between competition and freedom of movement may lead to the conclusion that a rule that is compatible with the free movement of workers, for example, is restrictive of competition by object.[43] It seems that the *Wouters/Meca-Medina* test, by incorporating the examination of objectives into the analysis of the existence of a restriction by object, made it easier to resolve such tensions.

42. More specifically, with regard to UEFA's exclusive power to market the rights relating to the competitions it organises (audiovisual broadcasting, multimedia, marketing etc.), the Court is also more demanding in verifying the conditions for exemption under Article 101(3) TFEU than the Commission has been since an important decision in 2003.[44] Since that decision, relating to the Champions League, the Commission has taken the view that the centralised sale of audio-visual rights to sporting events constitutes a restriction of competition contrary to Article 101(1) TFEU. However, it considers that, subject to certain commitments by UEFA (limited duration of exclusive rights, transparent tendering procedure etc.), these centralised selling arrangements may benefit from the exemption provided for in Article 101(3) TFEU because they contribute to improving production and distribution by creating a clearly identified "Champions League" product with a strong brand image, which is marketed through a single point of sale, reducing costs for audiovisual operators and clubs while benefiting consumers. The Court could have followed the same line of reasoning, but it appears to have taken a more severe view of this practice, particularly because of its link with the prior authorisation rules, which it has also condemned. It left it to the referring court, as is customary in preliminary rulings, to examine whether these centralised sales agreements could be exempted under Article 101(3) TFEU, with the burden on UEFA to convince it of the possibility of an exemption with strong evidence.

43. Finally, the Court ruled on an important issue for the world of sport that arose only in the cross-appeal brought by the Commission in the *ISU* case, concerning the jurisdiction of the Court of Arbitration for Sport (CAS). Here again, the Court gave precedence to EU competition law over the specific nature of sport, this time departing from the EU General Court. The Court ruled that the obligation on complainants, as laid down in the ISU statutes, to challenge sanctions before the CAS alone reinforced the infringements of competition already found in the Commission's decision.

---

42 Case C-390/06 *Nuova Agricast Srl v Ministero delle Attività Produttive*, paras 50 and 51; Case C-594/18 *Republic of Austria v European Commission* ECLI:EU:C:2020:742, paras 44 and 45.

43 Case C-650/22 *Lassana Diarra and FIFPRO v FIFA and URBSFA (Diarra)* ECLI:EU:C:2024:375, Opinion of AG Szpunar, the Advocate General considers that FIFA's rules governing the termination "without just cause" of football players' contracts may be compatible with the free movement of persons but are nevertheless restrictive of competition by object.

44 Case AT.37398 European Commission Decision *UEFA Champions League – Joint selling of the commercial rights* (23 July 2003).

44. Although the General Court upheld the Commission's classification of the restriction by object, it departed from that institution in the final part of its judgment, which dealt with the issue of the CAS. It had considered that the arbitration jurisdiction conferred on the CAS did not make the infringement more serious and was justified by legitimate interests linked to the specific nature of sport, relying on a judgment of the European Court of Human Rights.[45] It agreed with the Commission that this jurisdiction precluded the complainant skaters from challenging the sanction before a national court on the basis of Article 101 TFEU. However, it considered that the other legal remedies available to them, in particular the one that led to their case being brought before the EU courts, were sufficient to ensure compliance with EU competition law.

45. Although invited by AG Rantos to follow the General Court's position, the ECJ censured this part of the judgment, which had been criticised by the Commission before it. It emphasised that the mandatory jurisdiction of the CAS did not allow for effective judicial review by a court capable of ensuring the full application of Articles 101 and 102 TFEU. The Court did not repeat the terms of the Commission's contested decision, which saw this mandatory arbitration mechanism as "reinforcing" the restriction of competition. The General Court was sceptical that the rules governing the arbitration of a dispute could be economic in nature and reinforce a restriction of competition. However, the Court empowers the competent competition authority to take into account, when examining anticompetitive behaviour, the fact that legal remedies are insufficient to ensure compliance with EU competition rules. This approach is not unprecedented, as the Court recently accepted that a competition authority may take into account in its analysis a violation by the undertaking concerned of rules outside the field of competition law, in this case the provisions of the regulation on the protection of personal data.[46]

V. What are the Consequences of the *Super League* Ruling for the European Sports Model?

46. This is the question being asked by many sports law practitioners. As the author of these lines is not a fortune teller, basic caution suggests a nuanced response. The consequences of the ruling are uncertain, to the extent that on the day it was handed down, both UEFA and the Super League promoter claimed victory.

47. One assumption is clear from the outset. If authorisation rules are not sufficient to rule out arbitrariness and self-favouritism, they must be amended. As mentioned above, UEFA complied with this requirement in advance in 2022 by amending its statutes, without any guarantee that the EU judge would consider them to be in line with the standards it has set. However, the reason for requiring a review of the authorisation procedure to prevent discrimination in access to the market for the organisation of European football competitions is not for the sake of appearances or to cloak oneself in theory, but rather to ensure that, in the event of a request

---

45 Case *Mutu and Pechstein v Switzerland* App nos 40575/10 and 67474/10 (ECtHR 4 February 2019), para 98.

46 Case C-252/21 *Meta Platforms Inc v Bundeskartellamt.*

from a third party, certain authorisations are granted and that competitors have tangible access to the market. This raises the central question: which competitions should UEFA authorise, or legitimately refuse? And a second question arises: is the organisation of European competitions by an entity other than UEFA likely to disrupt the European cooperative model?

48. In response to the first question, it appears from the judgment, and this is the opinion of informed commentators, that the initial format of the Super League which had provoked so much opposition when it was announced in April 2021, is unlikely to see the light of day and would be likely to encounter certain legal obstacles highlighted by the Court.[47] In several points of its ruling the Court effectively gave a "thumbs up" to the sporting objectives justifying the exercise of regulatory power by federations, in particular UEFA and FIFA. It thus recognised the legitimacy in principle of this power, including the prerogative of prior authorisation, for the purposes of ensuring the organisation and conduct of international competitions and the participation of clubs and players in them. It emphasised that participation in competitions, at both European and national level, was reserved for teams that had achieved certain sporting results and that the conduct of competitions was based essentially on sporting merit, ensuring equal opportunities. It noted that these various specific features made it legitimate to subject the organisation and conduct of international football competitions to common rules, in particular concerning the prior authorisation of such events and the participation of clubs in them, designed to ensure the consistency and coordination of these competitions within an overall calendar and to promote equal opportunities and merit.[48] In light of this explanation, it seems likely that UEFA would have been justified in refusing to authorise the organisation of the Super League as initially envisaged, if the project had been submitted for its prior authorisation, since this competition was closed, was not based primarily on sporting merit and did not fit into an overall competition calendar organised by the continental federation. This raises the question: if this tournament could have given rise to legitimate objections on the part of UEFA, would an infringement by object have been established in such a context, solely based on deficiencies in the authorisation procedure?

49. In any event, the two Spanish clubs and the company promoting the project, which still support the Super League project, announced a new version on the day the Court handed down its ruling, seemingly admitting that the 2021 format was no longer feasible. At first glance, it appears that this new format would allow its promoters to avoid several criticisms of the initial model: it would bring together 64 non-permanent clubs, divided into three divisions, Star, Gold and Blue. The competition would therefore not be closed and would be based more on sporting merit, with qualification for the Blue division via national championships. It has

---

47 Philippe Bonneville and Anne Iljic, "Chronicle of CJEU Case Law" (2024) 7 AJDA 378–386; Stephen Weatherill, "Football Revolution: How Do the Court's Rulings of 21 December 2023 Affect UEFA's Role as Gatekeeper?" (*EU Law Analysis*, 4 January 2024) <https://eulawanalysis.blogspot.com/2024/01/football-revolution-how-do-courts.html> accessed 23 May 2026.

48 *Super League* (n 4), paras 142, 143 and 147.

been presented as something that could fit into the existing competition calendar. However, this last statement raises doubts that warrant clarification: the number of matches involved at the European level may be compatible with the national championship schedule, but it remains to be demonstrated whether it would disrupt the schedule of European competitions organised by UEFA, particularly the most important of these, the Champions League.

50. This is the crux of the problem, to which the Court's ruling does not provide a clear answer. Would it be possible for UEFA, without infringing EU competition law, to refuse to allow the organisation of a competition in a format that is in fact similar to that of the Champions League and in direct competition with it? The General Court's ruling in the *ISU* case provides a clue that the answer may be yes, albeit in a very different context, which calls for the scope of the ruling to be put into perspective. The General Court noted that a federation, as an undertaking, was entitled to defend its economic interests and its own competitions, the organisation of which was its raison d'être. However, in the *ISU* case, the competitions organised by the ISU did not constitute the market to which the skaters wanted to gain access. The participation of skaters in other competitions did not affect the economic interests of the federation to the same extent as the Super League project would affect the organisation of the Champions League, which has been part of the European federation's DNA since its creation in 1956. Can UEFA be required, in the name of the principle of free competition and third-party access to the European football competition market, to undermine a competition that is its raison d'être? In cases of abuse involving self-preferencing by the dominant operator, it may be required to abandon practices of exclusion or refusal of access to the market, but it is not required to call into question its own economic activity. However, this appears to be at stake with the Super League: if some of the major European clubs took part in a competing competition, even if this were authorised without the clubs being excluded from their national championships, these clubs would probably no longer be able to participate in the Champions League at the same time. The latter competition would lose its unity and would no longer designate the best team in Europe at the end of the season. Nor is it certain that all football fans would benefit from this, or that Member States would recognise the values of cooperation that they prioritise.[49]

51. One could argue that another European football competition could coexist with the Champions League. Are there not already several competitions at European level, all under the "jurisdiction" of UEFA, such as the Europa League, the Europa Conference League, women's competitions and youth competitions? It could be conceivable that part of this market could be occupied by an operator other than UEFA. The Court itself opened up this possibility in its judgment by noting that the disputed rules in UEFA's statutes were

> such as to allow, if not to exclude from that market any competing undertaking, even one that is equally efficient, at least to limit the design and

---

[49] On 8 February 2024, the sports ministers of 26 Member States reaffirmed their support for the European sports model, based in particular on the pyramid structure, sporting merit, and solidarity.

marketing of alternative or new competitions in terms of their format or content. In so doing, they are also such as to deprive professional football clubs and players of any possibility of participating in those competitions, even though they could, for example, offer an innovative format, while respecting all the principles, values, and rules of the game that underpin that sport. Ultimately, they are likely to deprive spectators and television viewers of any opportunity to attend or watch broadcasts of such competitions.

52. Could the innovative format envisaged by the Court be integrated into the championship calendar? Could it coexist with a Champions League that remains true to its essence, that of a competition designed to identify the best team on the continent? It is clear that the organiser of such a competition would have to, in order to be as "effective" as UEFA, bring together a sufficient number of European-level clubs, all of which are stakeholders in national championships and members of national federations. The same clubs would undoubtedly have to give up the current competitions organised by UEFA.

53. The competitive standard that requires several competitors to compete for the benefit of consumers in a given market could lead to a division of the market into several competitions, one under the banner of UEFA and another under that of an operator that has convinced clubs to join and has obtained the federations' agreement to maintain their participation in their national championships, assuming that the latter condition is feasible within the cooperative framework of football. It remains to be seen whether this new, more diverse landscape, separating audiences geographically and no longer allowing the selection of the best European club team, would be more attractive to consumers/football fans.[50]

54. In any case, we should be wary of extrapolating the effects of this competitive compass on the overall organisation of world sport. It is hard to believe that the principles affirmed by the Court could be transposed to the Olympic Games. Admittedly, the IOC has a monopoly on the organisation of the Games and this activity, which generates considerable revenue, is economic in nature. But if new players were to consider organising a global inter-sport competition, with prize money for participants, to challenge the IOC's dominant position and offer an innovative format, the balance between competition rules and the specificity of sport might not be the same as in the *Super League* case.

55. At the end of this brief overview, it is easy to understand that the competition law momentum that has driven the Court should not remain without impact.[51] It is beneficial that it has led UEFA to improve its procedures. More generally, it could contribute to a better-regulated exercise of the prerogatives of international

---

50 The company promoting the "new look" Super League has given assurances that matches will be broadcast free of charge. This is likely to make it attractive, as recent polls seem to confirm. However, this economic gamble can only succeed if many clubs sign up to the project and if significant advertising revenue is generated by large audiences.

51 Rafael Amaro and Jean-Christophe Roda, "Arrêt European Superleague: une révolution ?" (European Super League Ruling: A Revolution?) (*Dalloz Actualité*, 12 February 2024) <https://www.dalloz-actualite.fr/flash/l--arret-european-superleague-company-une-revolution-apports-regulation-du-sport-et-theorie-gen> accessed 23 May 2026; M Gros, Sports Law Column (February 2024) No 5 Semaine Juridique Édition Générale 20.

federations and perhaps, to a better promotion by them of the legitimate objectives they claim to pursue. It remains for the promoters of competitions competing with those of UEFA to convince clubs that the game is worth the candle, which is not a foregone conclusion given the broad support shown during the hearing of the Court for respect for the European sports model and the interdependence of clubs and federations in this football community. If the threat of competing competitions improved the governance of federations and the values of solidarity between the professional and amateur worlds, the dispute would not have produced only losers. In our view, the Court's ruling should not be interpreted as an attack on the European sports model, but as a reminder that sport does not enjoy any more immunity from competition law than any other economic activity. Sport, particularly football, nevertheless deserves to be recognised for what it is: a passion that unites Europeans and brings them together in major peaceful competitions,[52] contributing to social cohesion, education, health and team spirit. Is all this not precious in these troubled times for our Old Continent? It has been said that the English invented football, the French organised it and the Italians put it on stage. Let us hope that the European Union and its Court of Justice have not set out to deconstruct its foundations. Such a conclusion would unnecessarily sadden the dedicatee of this article, to whom this contribution is offered as a token of esteem and friendship, particularly in the sporting arena!

52 If we disregard the violent and even racist behaviour of certain "supporters."

TABLE OF CONTENTS

Contributors VII

Summary of contents IX

Foreword XIII

Introduction XV

CHAPTER I
SPORTS UNDER COMPETITION LAW

Competition Law and Sports Governance: Is the *ESL* Judgment a Real "Game Changer"? 3
Romain Ferla
- I. "Into the Game": When the ECJ Steps into the Debate on Sports Governance 4
- II. "After the Game": What Will Come Next? 7
- III. The "Object of the Game': Is FIFA's Way of Setting the International Match Calendar Anticompetitive "*Per Se*"? 11
- IV. Towards a "Fair Game"?: Can We Expect Fair Sports Governance in the Near Future? 13

How Does Antitrust Law Apply to Sports Governing Bodies? Which Sporting Rules Fall Under the Scope of EU Antitrust Law? 15
Peter W. Heermann
- I. Introduction 15
- II. Judgments of the ECJ 16
  1. *Walrave and Koch* and *Doná* 16
  2. *Bosman* 17
  3. *Deliège* 18
  4. *Meca-Medina* 19
  5. *MOTOE* 20
  6. *European Super League (ESL) International Skating Union (ISU)* and *Royal Antwerp FC* 21
- III. Position of the EU Commission and Opinion in the Academic Discourse 23
- IV. Critical Review 24
  1. Approaches of the ECJ and the EU Commission in General 24
  2. Certain Specific Rules Being Extraneous to Any Economic Activity 24
  3. Some Criticism of the ECJ's Approach 25

V. Alternative Approach ... 27
VI. Conclusion ... 28

EU Competition Law Scope vs National Competition Law ... 31
Jacques Steenbergen
I. Sports ... 31
II. Governance and Governance Bodies ... 33
III. Other Issues ... 35
IV. Type of Decision ... 35
V. Assessment ... 36
1. EU and National Competition Law ... 36
2. EU and National Institutions ... 36
VI. Conclusion ... 37

CHAPTER II
RESTRICTIONS ON COMPETITION IN SPORTS MARKETS

***ESL* and *ISU* Cases: What Consequences for Sports Federations?** ... 41
Mathieu Le Bescond de Coatpont
I. Recognition of the Regulatory Power of Sports Federations ... 44
1. Acceptance of a Regulatory Power Justified by the Specific Characteristics of Sport ... 44
A. Validation of the Principle of Regulation of a Sport by a Federation ... 45
B. The Specific Nature of Sport as a Legal Basis ... 48
2. No Justification for Unrestricted Regulatory Power ... 51
A. Serious Restrictions on Economic Freedoms ... 51
B. The Illusory Justification for Restrictions on Economic Freedoms ... 53
II. A Framework for the Sports Federations' Regulatory Powers ... 54
1. The Substantive and Procedural Limits of the Power ... 55
A. The Substantive Limits on Power ... 55
B. The Procedural Framework of the Power ... 58
2. Judicial Review of the Power ... 58
A. The Possible Review by an Arbitral Tribunal ... 59
B. The Need for a Review by a European Union Member State Court ... 60

Exclusivity in Sports – Beneficial or Harmful to Competition? ... 65
Benoît Durand and George Tucker
I. Introduction ... 65
II. The Multiple Layers of Exclusivity in Sports ... 66
III. Challenging the Incumbent: The Growing Antitrust Assault on Sports League Exclusivity ... 68

IV. The Economic Framework: Balancing Efficiency and Harm 71
V. Strategic Foreclosure in Action 74
1. The "Tax" and the Entry Barrier (Aghion and Bolton) 75
2. Coordination Failure: The "Divide and Conquer" Strategy (Segal and Whinston) 76
3. The Dimensions of Consumer Harm 76
4. Closeness of Competition and Consumer Harm 77
VI. Pro-Competitive Justifications for Exclusivity 78
1. The Necessity of Coordination in Joint Production 79
A. Sports Competitions as Jointly Produced Products 79
B. Internalising Externalities and the Management of Spill-Over Effects 80
C. Protecting Competitive Balance and Uncertainty of Outcome 80
2. Preserving Prestige and Avoiding Product Dilution 82
A. Talent Concentration and Contest Quality 82
B. Title Integrity and the Uniqueness of the Champion 82
C. Preserving Long-Term Prestige and Continuity 83
D. The Single-Tournament Problem: When Exclusivity Reflects Market Reality Rather Than Strategic Foreclosure 84
3. Protecting the "European Sports Model" and the Solidarity Pyramid 85
A. Preserving the Hierarchical Structure and Sporting Merit 85
B. Protecting Financial Solidarity 85
C. The Systemic Risk: A Prisoner's Dilemma at the Pyramid Level 86
VII. Conclusion 87

What is a Public Interest in Sport? What Are the Legitimate Sporting Objectives? 89
Benoît Keane
I. Pure Sporting Rules: Rules of the Game and Organisational Rules 93
II. Recruitment and Development of Young Players and Athletes 95
III. Competitive Balance, Sporting Merit and Regularity of Sporting Competitions 97
IV. Health and Safety of Athletes and Spectators 99
V. Integrity of Sporting Competitions 100
VI. Financial Sustainability 100
VII. Good Functioning of the International Calendar 102
VIII. Uniform Interpretation of Rules 103
IX. Ethical Values 104
X. Future Problems, Future Justifications 104

Specific Characteristics of Sport and EU Law 107
Pieter Paepe
I. Specific Characteristics of Sport in the Context of EU Primary Law 108
II. Dual Role of the Specific Characteristics of Sport 109
1. Common Rules for the Organisation of Sporting Competitions 109
2. EU Law Limits to the Exercise of the Powers to Adopt Common Rules 111
III. An Obstacle to the Internal Market Freedoms and a Restriction of Competition 112
1. Identification of an Anticompetitive "Object" 113
A. Rules on Prior Approval of Interclub Football Competition (ESL) 114
B. Homegrown Player Rules (Royal Antwerp) 114
C. Certain FIFA Rules on Contractual Stability (Diarra) 116
D. Exclusive Exploitation of Rights Related to Sporting Competitions (ESL) 118
2. Identification of an "Abuse of a Dominant Position" 118
3. Identification of an Obstacle to an Internal Market Freedom 119
IV. Justification of an Obstacle or Restriction of Competition 120
1. Application of Article 101(3) TFEU 120
A. Efficiency Gains – Objective Advantages (First Condition) 120
B. Reservation of Efficiency Gains for All Users – Favourable Effect for All Users (Second Condition) 121
C. Indispensable for Achieving the Efficiency Gains (Third Condition) 122
D. No Elimination of Competition (Fourth Condition) 123
2. Legitimate Objective in the General Interest 123
A. Rules on Prior Approval of Interclub Football Competitions (ESL) and Homegrown Player Rules (Royal Antwerp) 123
B. FIFA Rules on Contractual Stability (Diarra) 124
V. Conclusion 126

CHAPTER III
PROCEEDINGS

Is the CAS Arbitration System Anticompetitive? 129
Jean-Michel Marmayou
I. *ISU* Ruling 131
II. *RFC Seraing* Ruling 135

CHAPTER IV
STATE AID AND FOREIGN SUBSIDIES DISTORTING THE MARKET

European State Aid Law Applied to Professional Sport 143
Colin Miege
I. Introduction 143
II. The Framework for National Public Aid Granted to Sports Clubs 143
III. Implementation of Checks on the Legality of Aid Granted to Professional Clubs 145
1. A Gradual Start 145
2. In-Depth Scrutiny of Aid Granted to Certain Spanish Football Clubs 146
3. The Dispute Over State Aid to Spanish Clubs 147
A. Rejection of Athletic Club de Bilbao's Application 147
B. Annulment and Subsequent Validation of the Commission's Decision Against FC Barcelona 148
C. Annulment of the Commission's Decision Against Real Madrid 149
D. Annulment of the Commission's Decision Concerning Valencia CF 150
IV. The Framework for Public Aid for the Construction or Renovation of Sports Facilities 152
1. European Commission Decisions 152
2. Introduction of a Blanket Exemption for Certain Sports Facilities 153

CHAPTER V
NATIONAL COMPETITION LAW ISSUES

National Competition Law Issues Europe: Belgium Recent Belgian Decisions Delivered in the Sports Markets 161
Carmen Verdonck and Nina Methens
I. Introduction 161
II. Restrictive Measures and Abuses through Sports Associations' Regulatory Powers 162
1. Introduction 162
2. Barriers to Entry for Third Party Organisers 163
A. International Skating Union (ISU) 163
B. Belgium's Fédération Equestre Internationale (FEI) Saga 166
3. Barriers to Entry and Unfair Conditions of Participation for Athletes and Other Stakeholders 168
A. Football – Seraing and Doyen Sports 168
B. Football – Waasland-Beveren 170
C. Football – CVBA Kortrijk 171
D. Bumper Pool 172

E. Football – RE Virton ... 174
F. Football – Lommel SK ... 175
G. The Pigeon Racing Sector ... 177
H. Football – U23 quota ... 177
I. Inline hockey ... 179
III. Sports and Media Rights ... 180
1. Introduction ... 180
2. Redistribution of Media Rights between Individual Football Clubs ... 181
A. BACS: Virton v Pro League ... 182
B. BCA proceedings: RFC Liège, Francs Borains and Patro Eisden ... 183
IV. Conclusion and Outlook ... 184

Competition Law and Sport: An Overview of the French Competition Authority's Decision-Making Practice ... 185
Mathias Pigeat
I. The Application of the Law on Anticompetitive Practices to the Sports Sector: An Unconditional Application ... 188
1. Sanctioning Concerted Practices in the Organisation of Sporting Professions and the Distribution of Sports Equipment ... 188
2. Abuses of Dominant Position: Controlling the Economic Power of Organisers and Major Equipment Manufacturers ... 190
II. The French Competition Authority as Actor in the Economic Structuring of Sport: Opinions, Regulation, and Merger Control ... 193
1. Building a Competitive Framework for Audiovisual Rights: From Sanctioning Abuses to Structuring a Key Market in the Sports-Entertainment Sector ... 193
2. Merger Control: A Limited but Strategic Field ... 198

Panorama of the French Competition Authority Decision-Making Practice in the Field of Sport ... 201
Romain Soiron, Olivier Cavezian and Arthur Roquebert
I. FCA Decision Regarding the Dispute Between Mediapro and GCP ... 201
1. Background ... 202
2. The French Audiovisual Sector and the Relevant Markets, as Analysed in the FCA Decision-Making Practice ... 203
A. Organisation of the Audiovisual Sector ... 203
B. Definition of Relevant Markets in the Pay-tv Sector ... 205
3. Mediapro and GCP Proceedings before the Economic Activity Court Paris ... 205
4. The FCA Decision ... 207

II. Opinion on the Duration of Contracts Concluded for the Marketing of Audiovisual Exploitation Rights ... 209
1. Background and Content of the 2023 Decree ... 209
2. FCA Opinion ... 211

Sport and Competition Law in Italy: Overview of Decisional Practice ... 215
Andrea Bozza and Emilio Cucchiara
I. Introduction ... 215
II. Sports Regulatory Framework in Italy ... 216
III. Sporting Activities and Notion of Undertaking ... 216
IV. Sports and Antitrust Scrutiny ... 219
V. Proceedings for Abuse of Dominant Position ... 221
VI. Anticompetitive Agreements in the Sports Sector ... 224

Germany: National Competition Law Issues ... 229
Lukas Kretschmann
I. Introduction ... 229
II. Regulations Regarding Access to Sports Competitions ... 230
1. Nomination, Admission and Exclusion ... 230
2. DFL's 50+1-Rule ... 232
A. Relevant Markets and Restrictions of Competition ... 233
B. Restriction by Object or by Effect? ... 234
C. Meca-Medina Doctrine ... 235
a) Legitimate Objective ... 235
b) Genuinely Necessary ... 236
c) The Restriction Does Not Go Beyond What Is Necessary ... 237
D. Outlook ... 237
III. Regulations Regarding the Marketing of Sports Competitions ... 238
1. Advertising during the Olympic Games ... 238
2. FIS's Centralisation of Media and Broadcast Rights ... 239
3. DFL's Centralised Selling of TV Broadcasting Rights ... 240
A. Relevant Markets ... 240
a) Upstream Market ... 241
b) Downstream Market ... 241
B. Restriction of Competition ... 242
a) Centralised Selling ... 242
b) Exclusivity ... 243
c) Restriction by Object ... 243
C. Exemption under Article 101(3) TFEU ... 244
IV. Conclusion ... 246

Collective Sale of Football Media Rights in Portugal: Competition Law, Market Transformation and Investment Dynamics 247
Fernando Veiga Gomes and Maria João Melícias
I. Introduction and Scope 247
II. The Role of Broadcasting Rights in Modern Sports 249
III. From Competition Enforcement to Ex-Ante Regulation of Football Media Rights 250
1. Abuse of Dominance by the Leading Premium Sports Content Distribution Platform 251
2. Merger Prohibition of the "Triangle Operation" 251
3. Commitments Offered by Controlinveste in Relation to Exclusive Arrangements with Football Clubs 251
4. Antitrust Investigations into Exclusive Agreements and Minority Stakes in Leading Sports Media Platforms 252
5. Antitrust Investigation into the Reciprocal Rights-Sharing Agreement among Telecommunications Operators 253
6. Conclusion 254
IV. Portugal's Competition Authority Recommendation on the Collective Selling of Football Broadcasting Rights 254
V. The Drawbacks of an Individualised Commercialisation Model 255
1. Investment Dynamics in Centralised Media Rights 256
VI. Joint Sales of Sports Broadcasting Rights: Competition Risks and Safeguards under EU law 257
VII. A Comparative Analysis of Sales Models across European Football Leagues 259
VIII. Conclusion: How Today's Auction Will Shape Tomorrow's Competitive Landscape 261

Sports and U.S. Antitrust Law 263
Ryan Lipes
I. Introduction 263
II. The Antitrust Framework in the United States 264
1. The Sherman Antitrust Act 264
A. Section 1 264
B. Section 2 266
2. The Clayton Act of 1914 267
III. The Major Sports Exemptions 267
1. The Baseball Exemption 268
2. Sports Broadcasters Act of 1961 270
3. Implied Antitrust Immunity for Olympic Organizations 270
4. Collective Bargaining and the Non-Statutory Labor Exemption 272
IV. The Courts' Role in Shaping Sports Antitrust Law 273
1. Antitrust Challenges to Labor Market Restrictions 273
2. Antitrust Challenges to League Structure and Competition 275
3. Antitrust, Collegiate Sports, and the End of Amateurism 277
V. Conclusion 279

Sports and Competition Law in Brazil ... 281
Alexandre Cordeiro Macedo, Ricardo Medeiros de Castro and Maria Luiza Bittar Khouri
I. Introduction ... 281
II. Analysis of CADE's Jurisprudence ... 283
1. Some Cases About Broadcasting Rights ... 284
2. Case of 13's Club ... 286
3. Merger – Galo Holding/Atlético SAF ... 287
4. Gyms ... 289
5. *Gympass* Case (Digital Platforms) ... 290
6. The *Fox and Disney* Merger ... 290
7. Ongoing Investigation Regarding Cartel for Construction of Football Stadiums ... 291
8. Ongoing Investigation Regarding Unfair Treatment Related to Broadcasting Rights of Football Games ... 292
III. Judicial Debate on Football Agent Regulations ... 293
IV. Final Remarks ... 296

The Egyptian Competition Authority's Enforcement Policy in Sports ... 297
Mohamed El Far and Mahmoud A Momtaz
I. Introduction ... 297
II. Market Definition ... 298
III. Means of Establishment ... 300
IV. Dominance ... 303
V. Tying Practices in the Sports Sector ... 304
VI. Conclusion ... 305

Sport and Competition Law in Australia: A Fertile Environment for Players and Lawyers? ... 307
Deborah Healey
I. Introduction ... 307
II. Competition Law and Sport: The Australian Context ... 308
III. The Landscape of Australian Sport ... 308
1. Relationships between Sports, Their Teams and Players ... 309
2. Approach of US and EU law ... 311
3. The Nature of the CCA, the Australian Competition Law ... 313
IV. Scope of the TPA/CCA ... 314
V. Market Definition in Australia ... 317
1. Cartels and Arrangements between Competitors and Others Which May Lessen Competition ... 318
2. Misuse of Market Power ... 321
3. Mergers and Joint Ventures ... 322
VI. Conclusions ... 324

Sports and the Japanese Antimonopoly Act 327
Reiko Aoki
I. Introduction 327
II. Report of the Study Group on Human Resources and Competition Policy 328
1. Concerted Actions 328
2. Unilateral Actions 329
III. Guidelines Concerning Transfer Restriction Rules in the Sports Business Fields under the AMA 330
IV. Individual Cases Concerning the Antimonopoly Act and Sports 331
1. Transfer Restrictions 331
2. Interference with a Competitor's Transaction 332
3. Unjust Restriction 333
4. Interfering with Rival's Business 333

CHAPTER VI
TRANSNATIONAL FOOTBALL LAW ISSUES

***Bosman*, Thirty Years Later** 337
Ian S. Forrester KC

The FIFA Regulations on the Status and Transfer of Players in Light of European Union Competition Law 341
Fabrice Rizzo
I. Introduction 341
1. Description of The Player Transfer Mechanism. 341
2. The Normative Framework Governing Player Transfers. 342
3. Litigation Relating to the FIFA RSTP before the Commission and the EU Courts. 343
VI. Characterising the Restrictive Arrangement 348
1. The Relevant Market. 348
2. A Restriction of Competition. 348
3. A Restriction of Competition by Object 350
VII. The Exemption of Anti-competitive Agreements 353
1. The Exclusion of the *Wouters* Doctrine. 353
2. The Commission Decision of 20 May 2002. 354
3. The Position of the Court of Justice of the European Union. 355
4. The Reform of the Footballers' Transfer System. 356

The Home-Grown Player Rules 359
Vanja Smokvina
I. Introduction 359
II. The HGP Rule 360
1. The UEFA HGP Rule 360

2. UEFA Members HGP Rule ... 365
3. Major League Soccer HGP Rule ... 369
III. Conclusion ... 370

Legitimate Objectives in Antitrust Analysis: FIFA Regulation of Agents and the Right to Regulate Football in Europe ... 373
Petros C. Mavroidis and Damien Neven
I. Introduction ... 373
II. Background on the FFAR and Predecessors ... 375
1. Prior Dispute on the Regulation of Agent's Market – the *Laurent Piau* Case ... 375
2. Current Challenges to the FFAR ... 376
3. FFAR in Limbo ... 377
III. Assessment of FFAR under EU Competition Law ... 378
1. Obligations for Entities Bestowed with Special and Exclusive Rights ... 379
2. FIFA Cannot Invoke Article 165 TFEU ... 381
3. If FFAR Were to be Judged a Restriction by Object ... 382
4. If FFAR Were to be Judged a Restriction by Effect ... 383
5. The Invocation of Legitimate Objectives in Prior Case Law ... 384
A. Wouters ... 384
B. OTOC ... 384
C. Consiglio Nazionale dei Geologi – (CNG) ... 385
D. Meca-Medina ... 385
E. Ordre National des Pharmaciens – (ONP) ... 386
F. International Skating Union – (ISU) ... 387
6. Application to FFAR ... 390
7. Efficiency Gains ... 391
IV. Conclusion ... 393

Multi-Club Ownership – Multi-Club Investment ... 397
Romain Soiron, Olivier Cavezian and Antoine Burgensis
I. The Legal Framework for Multi-Club Ownership and Investment ... 399
1. Specific Sporting Rules Governing Multi-Club Ownership and Investment ... 399
A. The European and Global Multi-Club Ownership and Investment Framework ... 400
B. National Multi-Club Ownership and Investment Framework – the French Regulations ... 403
2. Competition Law Rules Governing Multi-Club Ownership and Investment ... 404
A. The Application of Merger Control Rules to Multi-Club Ownership and Investment Situations ... 405

B. Anticompetitive Practices Law as a Framework for Multi-Club Ownership and Investment ... 406
II. Compatibility of Multi-Club Ownership and Investment Rules with Competition Law ... 408
1. Restrictions on Competition Potentially in Sporting Rules for Multi-Club Ownership and Investment ... 409
A. The Compatibility of Multi-Club Ownership and Investment Sports Rules with Article 101 TFEU and Article L 420-1 French Commercial Code ... 409
B. The Compatibility of Multi-Club Ownership and Investment Sports Rules with Article 102 TFEU and Article L 420-2 French Commercial Code ... 411
2. Justification and Proportionality of Multi-Club Ownership and Investment Sporting Rules in Relation to the Objective ... 411

Multi-Club Ownership (MCO) and Multi-Club Investment (MCI) in South America: Corporate Structures, Regulatory Fragmentation and Competition Law across CONMEBOL ... 415
Vitor Butruce
I. The Phenomenon of MCO/MCI Groups ... 416
II. The Current Regulatory Landscape ... 417
1. FIFA ... 418
2. UEFA: The Comparative Benchmark ... 419
3. CONMEBOL: Club Licensing as an Indirect Regulatory Tool ... 421
4. Brazil: A Multi-Layered Regulatory Approach ... 422
5. Argentina: The Structural Resistance Model ... 423
6. The Remaining CONMEBOL Members: A Panoramic Survey ... 424
III. The Key Precedents Shaping the Understanding of MCO ... 427
1. The ENIC Case ... 427
2. Subsequent CAS Proceedings ... 428
3. The Pachuca/León Case ... 429
IV. The Competition Law Dimension: Limits and Possibilities of Sports Regulation at the Frontier of Antitrust ... 430
V. The CONMEBOL Challenge: Regulatory Design for a Fragmented Continent ... 433
VI. Conclusion: Charting the Regulatory Course ... 435

The Organisation of Football Competitions and Calendar Management – A European Competition Law Perspective ... 437
Sven Demeulemeester and Quentin van Outryve d'Ydewalle
I. Setting the Scene: Issues in Terms of the Organisation of Football Competitions ... 438
1. Calendar Congestion and Increased Player Workload ... 438

2. The Dual Role of FIFA and UEFA: Regulatory v Commercial Role 441
3. Mandatory Player Release 442
II. EU Competition Law and Sports 443
1. The Rise and Death (and Resurrection?) of the Sporting Exemption 443
2. Increased Scrutiny of Sports Governing Bodies' Dual Role 445
3. The European Sports Model 448
III. EU Competition Law and the Calendar of Competitions 450
1. EU Competition Law Requirements and their Application to the Calendar 450
2. A Glimpse at Future Calendar Management 453
IV. Conclusion 458

The Court of Justice, UEFA and the Super League: The European Sports Model Put to the Test 461
Stéphane Gervasoni
I. Some "Cooperative" Characteristics of Sports Federations 463
II. The Super League Project and the Speed Skating Case: Sports Federations "Seized" by Competition Law 468
III. The Legal Framework Prior to the Court of Justice Ruling: The *Wouters/Meca-Medina* "Test" and Article 165 TFEU 470
IV. The Court's Super League and ISU rulings: Competition Law Takes Precedence over the Specific Nature of Sport 474
V. What are the Consequences of the *Super League* Ruling for the European Sports Model? 480

Table of contents XVII

Concurrences Review

Concurrences is a print and online quarterly peer reviewed journal dedicated to EU and national competitions laws. It has been launched in 2004 as the flagship of the Institute of Competition Law in order to provide a forum for academics, practitioners and enforcers. Concurrences' influence and expertise has garnered contributions or interviews with such figures as Christine Lagarde, Bill Kovacic, Emmanuel Macron, Antonin Scalia and Magrethe Vestager.

Contents

More than 15,000 articles, print and/or online. Quarterly issues provide current coverage with contributions from the EU or national or foreign countries thanks to more than 2,500 authors in Europe and abroad.

Format

In order to balance academic contributions with opinions or legal practice notes, Concurrences provides its insight and analysis in a number of formats:

- Forewords: Opinions by leading academics or enforcers
- Interviews: Interviews of antitrust experts
- On-Topics: 4 to 6 short papers on hot issues
- Law & Economics: Short papers written by economists for a legal audience
- Articles: Long academic papers
- Case Summaries: Case commentary on EU and French case law
- Legal Practice: Short papers for in-house counsels
- International: Medium size papers on international policies
- Books Review: Summaries of recent antitrust books
- Articles Review: Summaries of leading articles published in 45 antitrust journals

Boards

The Scientific Committee is headed by Laurence Idot, Professor at Panthéon Assas University. The International Committee is headed by Frederic Jenny, OECD Competition Comitteee Chairman. Boards members include Douglas Ginsburg, Benoît Cœuré, Howard Shelanski, Richard Whish, Wouter Wils, etc.

Online version

Concurrences website provides all articles published since its inception, in addition to selected articles published online only in the electronic supplement.

Write for Concurrences

Concurrences welcome spontaneous contributions. Except in rare circumstances, the journal accepts only unpublished articles, whatever the form and nature of the contribution. The Editorial Board checks the form of the proposals, and then submits these to the Scientific Committee. Selection of the papers is conditional to a peer review by at least two members of the Committee. Within a month, the Committee assesses whether the draft article can be published and notifies the author.

www.ingramcontent.com/pod-product-compliance
Lightning Source LLC
LaVergne TN
LVHW011101300926
849160LV00008B/251
* 9 7 8 1 9 5 4 7 5 0 1 7 3 *